Business Data Networks and Telecommunications

Raymond R. Panko
Ray@Panko.com

University of Hawai`i

PEARSON

Prentice
Hall

**Upper Saddle River,
New Jersey 07458**

Library of Congress Cataloging-in-Publication Data

Panko, R. R.
  Business data networks and telecommunications / Raymond R. Panko.—6th ed.
    p. cm.
  Various multi-media instructional resources are available to supplement the text.
  ISBN 0-13-221441-5
    1. Business enterprises—Computer networks—Study guides. 2. Computer networks—Management—Study
  guides. 3. Data transmission systems—Study guides. I. Title.

HD30.37.P36 2007
005.7′1—dc22

2006041616

AVP/Executive Editor: Bob Horan
VP/Editorial Director: Jeff Shelstad
Manager, Product Development: Pamela Hersperger
Editorial Assistant: Ana Cordero
Product Development Manager, Media: Nancy Welcher
AVP/Executive Marketing Manager: Debbie Clare
Associate Director, Production Editorial: Judy Leale
Managing Editor: Cynthia Regan
Production Editor: Carol Samet
Permissions Coordinator: Charles Morris
Associate Director, Manufacturing: Vinnie Scelta
Manufacturing Buyer: Michelle Klein
Design/Composition Manager: Christy Mahon
Cover Design: Bruce Kenselaar
Cover Illustration/Photo: Getty Images, Inc.
Composition: GGS Book Services
Full-Service Project Management: GGS Book Services
Printer/Binder: RRDonnelley-Crawfordsville
Typeface: 10/12 NewBaskerville

Pearson Education LTD.
Pearson Education Singapore, Pte. Ltd
Pearson Education, Canada, Ltd
Pearson Education—Japan

Pearson Education Australia PTY, Limited
Pearson Education North Asia Ltd
Pearson Educación de Mexico, S.A. de C.V.
Pearson Education Malaysia, Pte. Ltd.

10 9 8 7 6 5 4 3 2 1
ISBN: 0-13-221441-5

To Jon Fujiwara, who does all this stuff for real.

Brief Contents

Contents

Preface for Teachers

THREE QUESTIONS

Teachers who are considering this book typically have three questions.

- ➤ What are the key reasons to select this book?
    - Job-Relevant Information
    - Great Teacher Support
    - Pedagogy
- ➤ How can I teach with it?
- ➤ What's new since the last edition?

WHY SELECT THIS BOOK?

Job-Relevant Information

The most important reason to select a textbook is the information it covers. This is especially important today because it is much harder for students to get jobs now than it was three or four years ago. Students need to achieve a higher level of content mastery.

In designing this and previous editions, the author talked extensively with working networking professionals and managers. He also got extensive market data on the technologies that corporations actually use. Many textbooks seem to be surprisingly market-blind. They spend time on technologies that were never adopted by the market or on technologies that have not been sold since the previous century—and, as a result, they do not cover important new developments. For example, Ethernet, which is now the only wired LAN technology in almost every firm, is no longer a simple technology. Students need to know about VLANs, STP, 802.1AE MACsec, and other advanced aspects of Ethernet.

Up-to-Date Content

Of course, the content needs to be up to date. The sixth edition has a completely new chapter on wireless LANs, a strong section on wireless metropolitan area networking (MAN), and information on many other important new areas. The sixth edition is not simply a minor update. Most chapters were completely or heavily rewritten to reflect changes since the fifth edition.

Market-Driven Content

Even more important, the book's content is strongly market-driven. Too many textbooks try to cover every technology that ever existed, even when its use today is almost nonexistent. As noted earlier, this leaves far too little time for today's critical technologies and emerging technologies. Students become historians, not market-ready graduates. In fact, some books seem to ignore market data. One recent textbook even called Frame Relay a new technology despite the fact that Frame Relay revenues were almost equal to those of private line revenues in the WAN market in the late 1990s and also despite the fact that Frame Relay is now considered to be a legacy technology in decline. Here are some examples of the book's market-driven content.

> ➤ *Wireless LANs.* The sixth edition chapter on wireless LANs (Chapter 5) looks at WLAN security and at the details of tradeoffs between different WLAN standards. It also looks at WLAN management.

> ➤ *Security.* As you would expect from an author whose security textbook is energizing security teaching in IS, security is pervasive throughout the text. One of the final chapters (Chapter 9) anchors the security information.

> ➤ *TCP/IP.* Above the physical and data link layers used in LANs and WANs, TCP/IP is consolidating its hold on upper-layer technologies. In the sixth edition, TCP/IP is pervasive. Chapter 1 introduces several core concepts; Chapter 2 introduces the basic elements of TCP/IP; and Chapter 8 goes into detail on advanced aspects of TCP/IP standards, including how routers make routing decisions. Chapter 10 discusses key topics in TCP/IP management. Module A covers a number of even more advanced aspects of TCP/IP. Also, the material in the book has been written to allow teachers to cover Chapter 8 after Chapter 3 or even Chapter 2. This allows routers to be handled much earlier.

> ➤ *Ethernet.* As noted earlier, Ethernet has won the LAN wars, but it is no longer a simple install-and-forget technology. The book has a full chapter on Ethernet (Chapter 4).

Job-Ready Detail

In the past, job interviews often asked students to name the OSI layers and stopped at that. Today, however, even job interviews for nonnetworking jobs grill job applicants on the details of networking. The days of feel-good "network appreciation" textbooks with far too little detail for job applicants should be over.

For example, in the Ethernet chapter (Chapter 4), the book goes well beyond basic topology and switch operation to look at VLANs, link aggregation, the Spanning Tree Protocol and the Rapid Spanning Tree Protocol, overprovisioning versus priority, and switch purchasing considerations. Detail has been beefed-up in other areas as well. The TCP/IP chapter (Chapter 8) takes a detailed look at how routers operate, while many other books cover this critical topic poorly or even incorrectly.

Great Teacher Support

Teaching networking is very difficult, so textbooks must provide strong teacher support.

Detailed PowerPoint Lectures

The book has full PowerPoint lectures created by the author—not just "a few selected slides." The PowerPoint lectures include builds for more complex figures. They also include new information since the book went to press. Students can download the lectures in full PowerPoint format. They can also download handouts with six slides per page in PDF format for faster downloading. Teachers can get annotated versions of the PowerPoint presentations to help them prepare and present lectures.

The PowerPoint slides are keyed directly to figures in the book. This is no accident. The book was designed so that almost all key points are covered in figures—including "study figures" that summarize key points in more complex sections. The PowerPoint lectures are created and updated by the author.

Website

The book's website, www.prenhall.com/panko, is rich in teacher resources. This is where teachers can go in order to download answer keys, test item file questions, and the latest versions of the PowerPoint lectures (which are updated once or twice a year). The website also is created and updated by the author.

Flexibility: An Eleven-Chapter Core

The book has eleven core chapters. In a three-credit one-semester course, this leaves one to two weeks for other material. The eleven core chapters—even without advanced information in boxes—form a complete course, so the additional time can be spent in enrichment activities. These may include hands-on activities (discussed later), additional TCP/IP material (or other material in the advanced modules), term projects, or whatever the teacher wishes to cover. In addition, many teachers cover only the eleven core chapters to ease the learning burden on students.

"Letter" Chapters and Advanced Modules

The book has two types of material beyond the eleven core chapters. These should be used judiciously. The book is not intended to be covered front-to-back. Even two or three letter chapters or one advanced module may be pushing it.

Several core chapters are followed by "letter" chapters. For example, after Chapter 1, there are Chapters 1a, 1b, and 1c. Three of these letter chapters are case studies (1a, 1c, and 7a.). Other letter chapters are designed for detailed hands-on learning (1b, 3a, 8a, and 9a).

Although neither 802.5 Token-Ring Networks or FDDI networks are used in corporations today, Chapter 4a gives an overview of ring topologies and token-passing.

There are three advanced modules. For teachers who really want to focus on TCP/IP, Module A has very detailed information about TCP/IP. Module C is designed for courses that focus on telecommunications. Chapter 6 looks at telecommunications from the viewpoint of corporate IS staffs. Module C looks at telecommunications from the carrier's point of view. Module B covers modulation in greater detail for teachers who feel that more information on telephone modems is needed.

Answer Keys and Test Item File

The chapters have test-your-understanding questions roughly once per page so that students can do a brain check on what they have just read. In addition, end-of-chapter thought questions, design questions, and troubleshooting questions help the student attain higher-level mastery of the material. Answer keys for all questions are available to teachers.

Multiple-choice test item file questions are keyed to specific chapter questions. This allows teachers who wish to be selective to specify specific questions that students should master, and it then allows them to develop tests that reflect those selected questions.

Mailing List

There is a low-volume mailing list that is used a few times per year to update adopters on new developments—most commonly new material at the website. The mailing list is also used to solicit adopter feedback on the text.

Pedagogy

Learning networking is difficult. Many students find that networking is the most conceptually difficult course in IS programs. Networking books need to have very strong pedagogy.

Clear Writing

All editions of this book have received accolades for clear writing—especially its ability to teach difficult and complex topics. Every chapter is classroom-tested.

Hands-On Opportunities

Students want opportunities to do things hands-on. With the sixth edition, they can.

- ➤ *OPNET IT Guru and ACE.* OPNET Technologies Inc. has kindly made the student versions of its IT Guru and ACE programs available to adopters—together with a series of lab exercises to reinforce key networking concepts. IT Guru is a powerful network simulation tool, while ACE focuses on application-level performance. (These exercises require 32-bit versions of Windows, so not everyone can run them.)
- ➤ *End-of-Chapter Hands-On Questions.* Chapters 1 and 10 in particular have hands-on questions to reinforce concepts. Chapters 1b, 3a, 8a, and 9a also offer hands-on experiences.
- ➤ *UTP.* Chapter 3a discusses how to cut and connectorize UTP. Teaching this material requires an investment of about $200, but undergraduate students love it.
- ➤ *Windows XP Networking and Security.* Windows XP is rapidly becoming the main client version of Windows, and it is not due to be replaced for some time. Chapter 1a shows students how to set up a Windows XP client for networking. If you have an understanding lab manager, students can go into your lab, set up a connection, set up a workgroup, and then undo what they have done. In turn, Chapter 9a shows students how to set up Windows XP security. Again, the chapter has material that you can have students do in your lab.

Running Case and Case Studies

Students like real-world scenarios because they help make complex concepts more concrete. The book has a running case—the First Bank of Paradise—which is a composite of several actual banks. (Much of the information presented is too sensitive for bank identification.)

Chapter 1 describes how a bank vice president set up a home PC network (a topic that most students will find interesting). In addition, several of the "a" chapters following the main chapters are case studies. Chapter 1a is a case study in the development of a small home network. Chapter 1c, in turn, is a case study in the development of a small SOHO PC network. Chapter 7a is a case study on the First Bank of Paradise's wide area networks (WANs).

Chapter Questions

The book gives the student many opportunities to check his or her knowledge. Approximately once per page, there are Test Your Understanding questions to help the student see if he or she has understood the material that was just read.

End of Chapter questions help the student integrate the material in the chapter. Thought questions help the student think more deeply about the material. Troubleshooting questions and Design questions also help students develop important troubleshooting and design skills, which are critical in networking. Some chapters also have Hands-on questions for your students to do at home.

As noted earlier, test item file questions are keyed to specific Test Your Understanding and End of Chapter questions.

Up Through the Layers/Familiar to the Unfamiliar

Like most books, the sixth edition takes an up-though-the-layers approach. However, this approach is significantly modified because most books that take this approach teach one layer at a time in isolation. Only at the end of the book does the student get the whole picture. During the process, students have only a cursory framework within which to integrate chapter knowledge.

> ➤ The book begins, in Chapters 1 through 3, with a strong framework to help students understand networking broadly so that when new knowledge appears, they understand its place. The difficult concept of layered network architectures is introduced early and is reinforced throughout the book.

> ➤ Chapters 4 through 7 deal with LAN, telecommunications, and WAN technologies. Every LAN and WAN technology is a mixture of Layer 1 (physical) and Layer 2 (data link) technologies. For this reason, this book covers Layer 1 and 2 technologies within the context of specific LAN and WAN technologies rather than individually (although Chapter 3 introduces specific physical layer information).

> ➤ Chapter 8 deals with internetworking, especially TCP/IP internetworking at Layer 3 (internet) and Layer 4 (transport). Once students understand LAN and WAN technologies, they can appreciate the need to interconnect them.

> ➤ Chapters 9 and 10 cover material that cuts throughout the layers—security and network management. These topics are introduced early, but a full discussion has to wait until students have a solid understanding of layer technologies.

> ➤ Chapter 11 covers the application layer (in OSI, application layers). It might seem better to cover this information after Chapter 8, but many schools cover applications in a separate course.

Synopsis Sections

Each chapter ends in a synopsis section that summarizes key points. In classroom testing of the sixth edition chapters, these synopsis sections were very popular with students.

TEACHING WITH THIS BOOK

As noted earlier, this book has eleven core chapters. They form a complete course.

Freshman and Sophomore Courses

For freshman and sophomore courses, it is good practice to stay with the eleven core chapters, going over chapter questions in class. If you want to do hands-on material, it is advisable to cut some material from the core chapters.

Junior and Senior Courses

With courses for juniors and seniors, covering the eleven core chapters (including "a" chapters that are case studies) will probably leave you with one or two semester weeks "free." As noted earlier, this leaves time for hands-on activities (discussed earlier), additional TCP/IP material (or other material in the advanced modules), a term project, or whatever you wish to cover. However, the entire book, including all hands-on material, should not be covered front-to-back in a semester.

Graduate Courses

Graduate courses tend to look a lot like junior- and senior-level courses but with greater depth. More focus can be placed on end-of-chapter questions and novel hands-on exercises, such as OPNET simulations. It is also typical to have a term project.

CHANGES SINCE THE FIFTH EDITION

The sixth edition generally follows the same basic flow as the fifth. The following table lists some specific changes.

Sixth Edition	Remarks Relative to the Fifth Edition (5e)
In General	Several of the chapters have been streamlined to make them easier to cover.
	In every chapter, new developments in the topic area are covered.
Chapter 1. An Introduction to Networking	Similar to Chapter 1 in the fifth edition but streamlined to reduce some concepts. In particular, the Pat Lee case becomes Chapter 1a for separate coverage.
Chapter 1a. Case Study: Pat Lee's Home Network	This case study was in Chapter 1 of the fifth edition.
Chapter 1b. Hands-On: Configuring Windows XP Home for Networking	This chapter complements the Pat Lee case study in Chapter 1a by discussing how to set up Windows XP for home networking and shared Internet access.
Chapter 1c. Case Study: XTR Consulting: A SOHO Network with Dedicated Servers	This chapter is a case study design exercise for how to set up a LAN in a small business with just under twenty workers. It is a good step beyond the Pat Lee home network.
Chapter 2. Network Standards	Similar to Chapter 2 in 5e but has a more streamlined structure. Some specifics, such as TCP session openings and closings, are moved to Chapter 8.
Chapter 3. Physical Layer Propagation: UTP and Optical Fiber	Similar to Chapter 3 in 5e. However, it has a more streamlined treatment of optical fiber, and it does not cover building wiring, which many adopters said was too detailed for an introductory text.

Sixth Edition	Remarks Relative to the Fifth Edition (5e)
Chapter 3a. Hands-On: Cutting and Connectorizing UTP	Unchanged from the fifth edition.
Chapter 4. Ethernet LANs	This chapter covers Ethernet, including the concepts needed for large Ethernet LANs. The switch purchasing information is moved into a box.
Chapter 5. Wireless LANs (WLANs)	Totally rewritten to focus on corporate decisions involving WLANs, especially the selection of standards and options for security. The chapter has a section on deciding where to place access points and on alternative technologies for management. This chapter is a bit longer than other chapters in the book.
Chapter 6. Telecommunications	Similar to Chapter 6 in 5e, but quite heavily rewritten. Focuses on telecommunications from the corporate viewpoint. Carrier information is covered in Module C. Chapter includes Internet access technologies.
Chapter 7. Wide Area Networks (WANs)	With Internet access technologies in Chapter 6, Chapter 7 focuses on corporate WANs using leased lines, public switched data networks, and VPNs for IP networking. Frame Relay is now a legacy technology for corporations.
Chapter 7a. Case Study: First Bank of Paradise's Wide Area Networks	Same as Chapter 7a in 5e.
Chapter 8. TCP/IP Internetworking	Somewhat streamlined, especially in its core treatment of how routers work. Adds ARP and a few other concepts not in the previous edition. The material in the book has been rewritten to allow teachers who wish to do so to teach Chapter 8 after Chapter 3 or even after Chapter 2. This is for teachers who expressed a desire to cover routers early in the course.
Chapter 8a. Hands-On: Packet Capture and Analysis with WINdump and TCPdump	Unchanged from 5e.
Chapter 9. Security	Streamlined from the fifth edition. Firewall section focuses heavily on stateful inspection, which dominates firewall filtering today.
Chapter 9a. Hands-On: Windows XP Home Security	Completely rewritten to deal with SP2 and other new developments.
Chapter 10. Network Management	Based on Chapter 10 in the fifth edition but with some information removed for streamlining.
Chapter 11. Networked Applications	Largely the same as in the fifth edition. Rewritten section on Web services under the name service oriented architecture (SOA).
Module A. More on TCP/IP	Unchanged from 5e.
Module B. More on Modulation	Unchanged from 5e. Now designed to be covered after Chapter 6.
Module C. More on Telecommunications	Covers telecommunications from the carrier's point of view.

Preface for Students

PERSPECTIVE

Initially, information systems (IS) graduates had a single career track: programmer–analyst–database administrator–manager. Today, however, many IS graduates are going into the networking career track—often to their surprise. This course is an introduction to the networking track.

However, even programmers need a strong understanding of networking. In the past, programmers wrote stand-alone programs that ran on a single computer. Today, however, most programmers write networked applications that work cooperatively with other programs on other computers.

LEARNING NETWORKING

Networking Is Difficult

Networking is an exciting topic. It is also a difficult topic. In programming, the focus is on creating running programs. In networking, the critical skills are design, product selection, and troubleshooting. These rather abstract skills require a broad and deep knowledge of many concepts. Many IS students have a difficult time adjusting to these more cerebral skill requirements.

Employers Are Growing More Demanding

In the past, many teachers tried to deal with the complexity of networking by selecting what was in essence a "network appreciation" book—a feel-good book that lacked the detailed knowledge needed for actual networking jobs.

Today, however, employers demand—and get—much strong job readiness from new graduates. If you want to get a job in the IS field, you will need to have a competitive level of knowledge in every IS field you study. Even applicants for database jobs are grilled in networking knowledge (and networking applicants are grilled in database and other areas).

How to Study the Book

There are several keys to studying this book.

> ➤ Reading chapters once will not be enough. You will need to really study the chapters.
> ➤ Slow down for the tough parts. Some sections will be fairly easy; others difficult. Too many students study the harder stuff at the same speed they use to study the easier stuff.
> ➤ When you finish studying a section, do the Test Your Understanding questions immediately. If you don't get one of the questions, go back over the text.

Networking is strongly cumulative, and if you skim over one section, you will have problems with other sections later. Multiple-choice questions in the test item file are taken entirely from the Test Your Understanding questions and the End-of-Chapter questions.

➤ Later, in groups, go over the Test Your Understanding questions to see if you got the correct answers.

➤ Study the figures. Nearly every key point in the chapter is covered in the figures. If there is something in a figure you don't understand, you need to study that section.

➤ If several concepts—for instance, different network technologies—are presented in a section or chapter, do not just study them individually. You need to know which one to use in a particular situation, and that skill requires compare/contrast knowledge. Study figures that compare concepts, and make your own if the book does not have them.

➤ Study the Synopsis at the end of the chapter. The Synopsis summarizes the core concepts in the chapter. Be very sure you know them well. You might even study them before the chapter to get a broad understanding of the material.

Hands-On

One way to make networking less abstract is to do as many hands-on activities as possible.

➤ Be sure to do the hands-on exercises in Chapter 1, 4, and 10.

➤ If you have a Windows XP computer, do the work in Chapters 1b and 9a.

➤ To really understand TCP/IP, download WINdump and play with it. (See Chapter 8a.)

➤ If you can, do the OPNET exercises at the website, www.panko.net.

A NETWORKING CAREER

If you like the networking course and think you want a networking career, there are a number of steps you should take before graduation, even if your school does not have advanced networking courses.

➤ Most important, do a networking internship. Employers really want job experience—often preferring it to an absurd degree over academic preparation.

➤ Learn systems administration (the management of servers). Learn the essentials of Unix and Windows Server. You can download a server version of Linux and install it on your home computer in order to play with Unix commands and network management functions.

➤ Learn about security. Security and networking are now inextricably intertwined.

➤ Think about getting one or more industry certifications. In networking, the low-level CompTIA Network+ certification should be obtainable with just a bit more study after taking your core networking course. Cisco's CCNA (Cisco Certified Network Associate) certification, which focuses on switching and routing, will require substantially more study. Microsoft server certification is also valuable. Employers like applicants who are job-ready.

About the Author

Ray Panko is a professor of IT management at the University of Hawai`i's College of Business Administration. Before coming to the university, he was a research physicist at Boeing, where he flew on an early flight test of the 747 prototype, and was a project manager at Stanford Research Institute (now SRI International), where he worked for Doug Englebart (the inventor of the mouse). He received his B.S. in physics and his MBA from Seattle University. He received his doctorate from Stanford University, where his dissertation was conducted under contract to the Office of the President of the United States. In his spare time, he collects die-cast models and races in six-seat Hawai`ian outrigger canoes.

C h a p t e r   1

An Introduction to Networking

Learning Objectives

By the end of this chapter, you should be able to:

- Define the term *network*. Distinguish between the Internet and the World Wide Web. Distinguish between the Internet and internal corporate networks. Distinguish between data transmission and telecommunications.

- List the nine elements of single networks. Describe packet switching and multiplexing. Describe how to write transmission speeds. Explain the difference between rated speed and throughput.

- Discuss the First Bank of Paradise (FBP), our running case study for this book.

- Distinguish between local area networks (LANs) and Wide Area Networks (WANs), and characterize SOHO LANs.

- Discuss the following concepts and their relationships: internets, the Internet, subnets, intranets, and extranets. Distinguish between frames and packets. Distinguish between switches and routers.

- Discuss IP addresses and Ethernet addresses; discuss IP address management.

- Briefly explain the roles of firewalls, host hardening, and cryptographic protections in security.

WHAT IS NETWORKING?

In a book about networking, it makes sense to begin by defining the term *network*. In general, a **network** is a transmission system that connects two or more applications running on different computers. Notice that transmission between computers is not enough. If the computers cannot work together or if the applications they run cannot work together, you do not have networking.

A network is a transmission system that connects two or more applications running on different computers.

1

What Is a Network?

> A transmission system that connects two or more applications running on different computers

The Internet

> The most famous network
>
> The Internet is a global transmission network
>
> Used by many applications (Figure 1-2)
>
>> The World Wide Web
>>
>> E-mail
>>
>> Etc.
>
> Client/server applications
>
>> PC clients receive service from servers
>>
>> Many applications need special clients
>>
>> Many applications only need a browser

Internal Corporate Network

> For transmission among computers within a corporation
>
> Transaction processing applications
>
>> High-volume clerical applications
>>
>> Accounting, payroll, billing, and others
>
> Voice over IP (VoIP)

Data Communications and Telecommunications

> Data communications: the transmission of data (text, numbers, pictures, and other information)
>
> Telecommunications: the transmission of voice and video, including ordinary telephony and broadcast and cable television
>
> The two are beginning to converge

Digital Transmission

> Information is first converted into a string of ones and zeros
>
> Next, the ones and zeros are converted into signals that propagate over transmission media
>
> More detail in Chapter 3

Figure 1-1   Basic Networking Concepts (Study Figure)

The Internet

When most people hear the word *networking*, they say something like, "Oh, yes, the Internet." This is an understandable reaction. During the past decade, the Internet has revolutionized computing and many aspects of society.

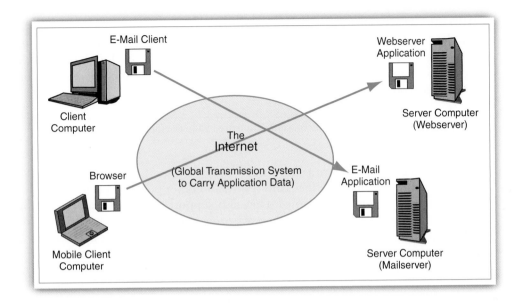

Figure 1-2   The Internet and Applications

The Internet, the World Wide Web, and Other Networked Applications

Although almost everyone is reasonably familiar with the Internet today, there is still widespread confusion about the difference between the Internet and the applications that communicate over the Internet, such as the *World Wide Web*. As Figure 1-2 shows, the **Internet** is a global transmission network. The Web is a **networked application** that runs over the Internet. The figure also indicates that the Internet carries the traffic of other networked applications, such as e-mail.

The Internet is a global transmission network, while the Web is a networked application that runs over the Internet.

Client/Server Applications

Figure 1-2 also shows that most applications on the Internet are **client/server applications**. In these applications, the user works at a **client PC**, which receives services from another computer called a **server**. Thanks to the Internet, your client PC can reach out to literally millions of servers around the world.

In the World Wide Web, the client program is your PC's browser. However, many applications require or allow the use of special clients. For instance, many people use Microsoft Outlook or Outlook Express to handle their e-mail, although others use Web-based e-mail, which only requires a browser.

Internal Corporate Network Applications

Although the Internet is extremely important, this is primarily a book about another type of networking, corporate networking. Organizations use the global Internet extensively, but most of their network traffic flows over internal **corporate networks** that connect computers that are inside the same organization.

Corporate networks connect computers that are inside the same organization.

Transaction Processing Applications

Corporate networks support e-mail, the WWW, and other personal productivity applications that you use on the Internet. They also support organizational applications, including clerically oriented *transaction processing* applications, such as accounting, payroll, billing, inventory, and manufacturing. **Transaction processing** applications are clerical applications characterized by high volumes of traffic. Collectively, transaction processing applications may generate much more traffic in corporate networks than personal applications such as e-mail.

Voice over IP (VoIP)

Another emerging application in corporations is the transmission of telephone calls over networks designed for data. For reasons we will see in Chapter 6, this development is called voice over IP (VoIP). IP is the Internet Protocol, which carries traffic across the Internet. VoIP is an application that transmits voice over the Internet or any other network that uses IP. Many residential users have turned to VoIP, and many organizations are now converting most or all of their telephones to VoIP.

Data Communications and Telecommunications

In addition to being used to describe the Internet and internal corporate networks, the term *networking* is used to describe two separate types of traffic.

> ➤ **Data communications**, as the name suggests, involves the transmission of data (text, numbers, pictures, and other information.)
> ➤ In turn, **telecommunications** is the transmission of voice and video, including ordinary telephony and broadcast and cable television.

As we will see in Chapter 6, telecommunications and data networking have traditionally used different transmission technologies, although, as we will also see in that chapter, the technologies for data communications and telecommunications are beginning to converge. Most corporate networking traffic is data communications traffic, so data communications will be the focus of this book.

TEST YOUR UNDERSTANDING

1. a) Distinguish between the Internet and the World Wide Web. b) Distinguish between the Internet and e-mail. c) Describe client/server applications. d) Distinguish between

the Internet and corporate networks. e) What are the characteristics of transaction processing applications? f) Describe VoIP. g) Distinguish between data communications and telecommunications.

SINGLE NETWORKS

A good place to begin talking about networking is to start with the elements of a single network. Later, we will see how these single networks are connected together to form more complex "internets."

The Nine Elements of a Network

Most networks share nine common elements, as Figure 1-3 illustrates. These elements are applications (application programs), frames (messages), client computers, server computers, switches, routers, access lines, trunk lines, and wireless access points.

TEST YOUR UNDERSTANDING

2. List the nine elements of a network.

Figure 1-3   Elements of a Network

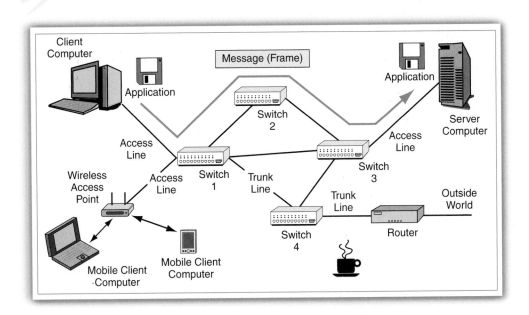

Client Computers, Server Computers, and Applications

Computers

As noted earlier, networked computers usually come in two versions: client computers and server computers. Typically, these two types of computers are referred to simply as **clients** and **servers**. Quite simply, client computers receive services from server computers. For instance, when you use the World Wide Web, your client PC is the client, and the WWW server is the server.

While most clients run client operating systems (Microsoft Windows XP, Macintosh, etc.), most servers run operating systems designed specifically for servers, most commonly Microsoft Windows Server or some version of Unix (including Linux, which is a version of Unix for PCs).

Application Programs

Clients and servers run **application programs**. As we saw earlier, the client in webservice (that is, in World Wide Web service) is a browser, while the WWW server runs a server application program. To users, of course, only the applications are important; everything else is mere details.

TEST YOUR UNDERSTANDING

3. a) Distinguish between client and server computers. (Yes, this repeats an earlier question.)
   b) Which element of single networks do users care about?

Frames and Packet Switching

Frames

When applications need to communicate, computers send messages to one another. In single networks, these messages are called **frames**.

In single networks, messages are called frames.

Packet Switching

In modern networks, transmissions are broken into short messages (typically a few hundred bits long) that are sent individually. As Figure 1-4 shows, breaking transmissions into short messages is known as **packet switching**, even when the message itself is called a frame, as it is in single networks. Transferring a large file will require the sender to transmit hundreds or even thousands of frames. Even sending a relatively short e-mail message is likely to require sending several frames.

The breaking of transmissions into short messages is known as packet switching, even when the message itself is called a frame.

TEST YOUR UNDERSTANDING

4. a) What are messages called in single networks? b) What is packet switching?

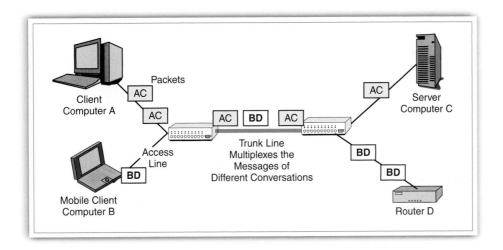

Figure 1-4   Packet Switching and Multiplexing

Switches and Routers

Switches

Frames are forwarded *within* a single network by devices called **switches**. When a computer transmits a frame, the frame goes to the switch to which the computer connects (in Figure 1-3, Switch 1). That switch forwards the frame to a switch closer to the destination computer (Switch 2). This continues at intermediate switches, until the frame is delivered from the final switch (Switch 3) to the destination computer.

Routers

In contrast, **routers** forward messages *outside of* a single network, to another single network. We will look at routers in more detail later, when we discuss internets.

Switches only forward messages within a single network. In contrast, routers forward messages outside of a single network, to another single network.

Ethernet Switch Operation

Figure 1-5 takes a closer look at how packet switches operate. In this case, the switch is an Ethernet switch. Ethernet is the dominant technology for LANs. Each computer has a unique Ethernet address, which looks something like C3-2D-55-3B-A9-4F. (We will look at Ethernet addresses more closely later in this chapter).

The frame contains a destination Ethernet address (C3-2D-55-3B-A9-4F), which is like the address on a postal envelope. When the switch receives a frame, the switch looks at this destination address in the frame. As the figure shows, the switch has a

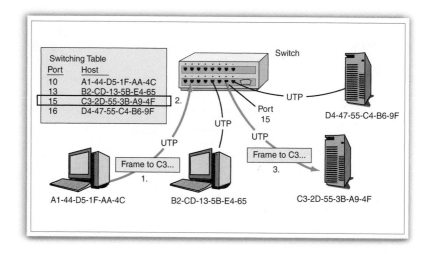

Figure 1-5   Ethernet Switch Operation

switching table that tells the switch what port to use to send the frame back out (Port 15). The switch sends the frame out that port, to the destination computer.

In this example, the network only has a single switch. In a network with multiple switches, each switch along the path from the source computer to the destination computer will receive the frame, read its destination address, and pass it on.

TEST YOUR UNDERSTANDING

5. a) Distinguish between switches and routers. b) On what do Ethernet switches base switching decisions?

Access Lines, Trunk Lines, and Multiplexing
Transmission Lines: Access Lines and Trunk Lines

A **transmission line** connects devices in a network. There are two types of transmission lines.

> ➤ An **access line** connects a computer to the nearest switch. An access line is like your home driveway, which connects you to the road network in your city.

> ➤ A **trunk line**, in contrast, connects a switch to a switch, a router to a router, or a switch to a router. Trunk lines carry the traffic of many computer-to-computer conversations, so they need to have higher speeds than access lines—just as freeways have more lanes than home driveways.

An access line connects a computer to the nearest switch. Trunk lines, in contrast, link switches to each other, routers to each other, and routers to switches.

Multiplexing to Reduce Trunk Line Costs

We saw earlier that most data networks today use packet switching, in which transmission is divided into short messages. Figure 1-4 showed why packet switching is done. Packet switching allows efficient **multiplexing**, in which the messages of many conversations can share a single trunk line, much like cars on a freeway. Short messages fill multiplexed lines more efficiently than longer messages, much as a box can be filled more efficiently with marbles than with footballs.

Multiplexing minimizes trunk line costs. This reduction in the cost of trunk lines is so large that packet switching reduces overall costs, despite the fact that it increases some non–trunk line costs (for instance by making switches more complex and therefore more expensive).

TEST YOUR UNDERSTANDING

6. a) Distinguish between the two types of transmission lines. b) Which type of line has higher speed? Why? c) What type of line is the connection between the server computer and Switch 3 in Figure 1-3? d) What type of line is the connection between Switch 1 and Switch 4 in Figure 1-3? e) What is multiplexing? f) What is the benefit of multiplexing? g) Why is packet switching useful in multiplexing?

Wireless Access Points

The last element found in many networks is the **wireless access point**. Wireless access points connect to switches via access lines. They use radio waves to communicate with wireless mobile clients, linking these mobile clients into the network.[1]

TEST YOUR UNDERSTANDING

7. What is the purpose of wireless access points?

How to Talk About Network Costs

Note that when you discuss network costs, you should mention the specific element or elements of a network involved: computers, switches, routers, access lines, or trunk lines. For instance, packet switching reduces *trunk line* costs, but it does nothing for access line costs, and it actually increases switching costs. However, the cost savings from trunk line multiplexing more than make up for increased switching costs.

Note that when you discuss network costs, you should mention which specific element or elements of a network involved: computers, switches, routers, access lines, or trunk lines.

TEST YOUR UNDERSTANDING

8. When you discuss network costs, what should you mention?

---

[1]It is possible to have entirely wireless networks (for instance, in single homes). In most organizations, however, access points are used to bridge wireless devices to the main wired network.

Figure 1-6   Transmission Speed (Study Figure)

Measuring Transmission Speed

    Transmission speed is measured in bits per second (bps)

    It is measured in increasing factors of 1,000

        Not factors of 1,024

        Kilobits per second (kbps)—note the lowercase *k*

        Megabits per second (Mbps)

        Gigabits per second (Gbps)

        Terabits per second (Tbps)

    What is 15,000,000 bps in metric form?

    It is occasionally measured in bytes per second.

        Written as Bps

Writing Transmission Speeds

    The rule for writing speeds (and metric numbers in general) is that there should be one to three places before the decimal point.

        23.72 Mbps correct (2 places before the decimal point)

        2,300 Mbps: four places before the decimal point, so it should be rewritten as 2.3 Gbps (1 place)

        0.5 Mbps: zero places to the left of the decimal point. It should be written as 500 kbps (3 places)

    Principles

        kbps → Mbps: Move the decimal point left 3 places

            Example: 36,569 kbps → 36.569 Mbps

        Mbps → kbps: Move decimal point right 3 places

            Example: .05679 kbps → 56.79 Mbps

    How should you write the following?

        549.73 kbps

        0.47 Gbps

        1,200 Mbps

Rated Speed Versus Throughput

    Rated speed is the speed a network should provide, based on standards

    Throughput is the speed a network actually provides

    We will use this distinction constantly throughout this book

    When transmission capacity is shared by multiple users,

        The total shared throughput is the aggregate throughput

        Individual throughput is what individuals receive as a fraction of the aggregate throughput

Bits per Second

A key characteristic of any network is transmission speed.[2] **Transmission speed** normally is measured in **bits per second (bps)**. A **bit** is either a one or a zero. Obviously, a single bit cannot convey much information. In increasing factors of 1,000 (not 1,024), we have **kilobits per second (kbps**[3]**)**, **megabits per second (Mbps)**, **gigabits per second (Gbps)**, and **terabits per second (Tbps)**.

Bytes per Second

Occasionally, transmission speed is measured in bytes per second. (A byte is eight bits.) While *bits per second* is written as bps, *bytes per second* usually is written as Bps. However, the use of *bytes per second* is extremely rare. About the only time you see it is when file transfers are being described because file sizes normally are given in bytes.

Writing Speeds

The rule for writing speeds (and metric numbers in general) is that there should be one to three places before the decimal point.

When writing speeds, have one to three places before the decimal point.

➤ Given this rule, 23.72 Mbps is fine (2 places before the decimal point).
➤ However, 2,300 Mbps has four places before the decimal point, so it should be rewritten as 2.3 Gbps (1 place).
➤ Also, 0.5 Mbps has zero places to the left of the decimal point. It should be written as 500 kbps (3 spaces).

Rated Speed Versus Throughput

Note: the distinction between rated speed and throughput is difficult to learn for some students. However, we must use this distinction throughout this book, so be sure to take the time to understand it.

Talking about transmission speed can be tricky. A network's **rated speed** is the speed it *should* achieve based on vendor claims or on the standard that defines it. For a number of reasons, networks often fail to deliver data at their rated speeds. In contrast, a network's **throughput** is the data transmission speed it *actually* provides to users.

Throughput is the data transmission speed a network *actually* provides to users.

---

[2]Some teachers object to referring to bits per second as speed, because speed indicates velocity, and bits per second is a measure of information transmission rate. To give an analogy, transmission speed is not like running faster. It is like talking faster.
[3] A lower-case *k* is always used in *kbps*. (Capital *K* is for "Kelvin"—a unit of temperature.) Networking people generally know the metric system. Some computer science and database people sometimes do not, as evidenced by the fact that they tend to use a capital *K* for *kilo*.

Aggregate and Individual Throughput

When a transmission line on a network is multiplexed, several users will share the line's throughput. Consequently, it is important to distinguish between a line's **aggregate throughput**, which is the total it provides to all users, and the individual throughput that single users receive as their shares of the aggregate throughput.

TEST YOUR UNDERSTANDING

9. a) In what units is transmission speed normally measured? b) Is speed measured as bits per second or bytes per second? c) Give the names and abbreviations for speeds in increasing factors of 1,000. d) What is 55,000,000,000 bits per second in metric notation? e) What is 100 kbps in bits? f) Write the following speeds properly: 0.067 Mbps, 23,000 kbps, and 45.62 Gbps.

10. a) Distinguish between rated speed and throughput. b) Distinguish between individual and aggregate throughput.

LANS AND WANS

Single networks come in two categories: local area networks (LANs) and wide area networks (WANs). Before talking about how LANs and WANs are different, we will introduce this book's running case study, the First Bank of Paradise's (FBP). This running case will help you understand difficult material in more concrete ways.

The First Bank of Paradise

The First Bank of Paradise[4] actually is a composite of several banks in Hawai'i.

FBP is a midsized bank, but it is not a small company. The bank has annual revenues of $4.5 billion. It has 60 branches and 375 ATMs. It has more than 700 switches, 450 routers, 2,300 desktop and notebook PCs, 130 Windows servers, and 60 Unix servers. Its information systems staff has 112 employees. If some of this means little to you now, come back to this paragraph at the end of this chapter. The key point is that FBP is a representative company in terms of networking, and we will use it as our running case study throughout this book.

The Bank's Major Buildings

Figure 1-7 shows the bank's major sites.

Headquarters

The Headquarters building houses FBP's main business offices. About a quarter of the bank's employees work in this building.

---

[4]The First Bank of Paradise case study for this book actually is a composite of several banks in Hawai'i. For security reasons, a single bank cannot divulge identifiable information about itself publicly. However, the banks in this composite were generous with information that could be provided with appropriate disguise.

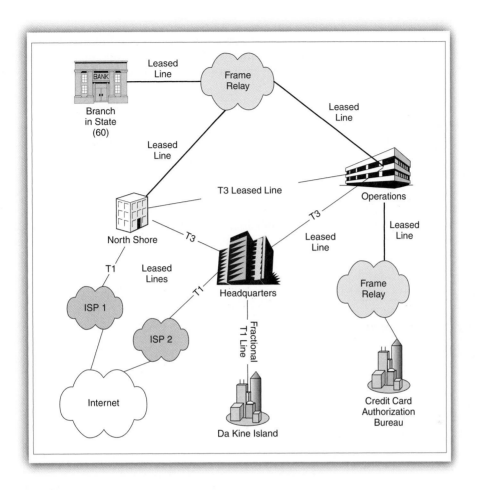

Figure 1-7   The First Bank of Paradise's Wide Area Networks (WANs)

Operations

Another building, called Operations, houses the bank's check-processing computers and other large servers that provide services to many customer and employee computers.

North Shore

The third major building, North Shore, is the bank's application development center. The bank develops all of its new software there. North Shore also has backup facilities for check processing and other major services so that if Operations fails, North Shore can take over the workload in a matter of minutes.

Local Branches and One Distant Affiliate

The bank's branches are scattered across the state. These are the buildings that customers see the most. Many of the ATMs are at these branches, but not all are. The bank also has communication links to a number of other companies, including an FBP affiliate on Da Kine Island and a credit card processing company.

TEST YOUR UNDERSTANDING

11. a) List the First Bank of Paradise's sites. b) Explain the functions of the bank's three main buildings.

Wide Area Networks (WANs)

Networks that link different sites together are called **wide area networks (WANs)**. Figure 1-7 shows that the bank uses a number of wide area networks and that these networks use different technologies. They include a point-to-point private–line leased network, two Frame Relay networks, and several other WANs. We will see these technologies in Chapter 7.

A wide area network (WAN) is a network that links different sites together.

TEST YOUR UNDERSTANDING

12. a) What is a WAN? b) Does FBP use a single WAN or several?

Figure 1-8   LANs Versus WANs (Study Figure)

Characteristics	LANs	WANs
Scope	For transmission within a site. Campus, building, and SOHO (Small Office or Home Office) LANs	For transmission between sites
Cost per bit transmitted	Low	High
Typical speed	100 Mbps to 1 Gbps to each desktop	128 kbps to several megabits per second trunk line speeds
Is this speed shared?	No	Yes
Management	On own premises, so firm builds and manages its own LAN or outsources the work	Must use a carrier with rights of way for transmission in public area
Choices	Can use any product offered by vendors	Only those offered by the carrier

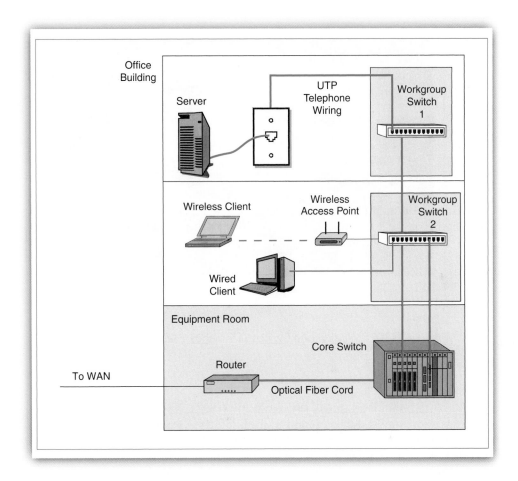

Figure 1-9   Local Area Network (LAN) in a Large Building

Local Area Networks (LANs)

We have seen that WANs carry traffic *between* sites. In turn, networks that operate *within* sites are **local area networks (LANs)**. Note that we define a LAN by where it operates—within a single site—rather than by distance.

Local area networks (LANs) are networks *within* sites.

Building LANs

The bank has a LAN within each of its buildings. Chapter 1a notes that some of the bank's managers also have LANs within their individual homes. Figure 1-9 shows a typical local area network in one of the bank's three main buildings.

Figure 1-10   Workgroup Switch (19 inches / 48 cm Wide)

Workgroup Switches and Core Switches

Switches interconnect the computers in the building. A **workgroup switch** (Figure 1-10) on each floor (except the basement) connects all of the computers on that floor to the network. A central **core switch** in the basement interconnects the workgroup switches. With this hierarchical arrangement, any computer on any floor can talk to any computer on any other floor. The central core switch also connects to a router in the basement, which links the building to the Internet and to other sites within the firm.

As noted earlier, access lines connect computers to switches. The lines on each floor connect computers on the floor to the floor's workgroup switch. Therefore, these are access lines. Similarly, vertical lines that connect the core switch to workgroup switches are trunk lines because they connect a switch to another switch.

SOHO LANs

Not all LANs are as large as the one in Figure 1-9. Many LANs are much smaller. Among these are **small office or home office (SOHO)** LANs. As the name suggests, these are LANs for individual homes (or apartments) or small offices (branch offices, small businesses, and so forth). Chapter 1a can show you how to create a home network. Chapter 1b discusses how to create a small office network.

Campus LANs

There also are LANs that are larger than single buildings. These **campus LANs** occur on university campuses. They also occur in industrial parks, military bases, and other multibuilding facilities.

TEST YOUR UNDERSTANDING

13. a) What are LANs? b) Distinguish between core and workgroup switches. c) In Figure 1-9, how many workgroup switches are there? d) How many core switches? e) Suppose that there is a server connected to Workgroup Switch 2. Through what switches will frames travel when the client connected to Workgroup Switch 1 sends frames to the server?

14. a) For what is SOHO an abbreviation? b) What are campus LANs?

LAN and WAN Transmission Costs and Speeds

So far, we have focused on the technical characteristics of LANs and WANs. However, it is very important to keep in mind their *economic* differences. You know that when you place a long-distance call, the cost per minute will be much higher than the cost per minute for a local call. In transmission, greater distance always means greater costs.

In networking, the issue is the cost per bit transmitted. In LANs, the cost per bit transmitted is very low, while in WANs, the cost per bit is much higher. Although long-distance transmission costs have fallen and will continue to fall, they will continue to remain much higher than local transmission costs.

From your economics course, you know that when the cost of something rises, the quantity demanded will decrease. Quite simply, you usually have to buy less of things if they are more expensive. In networking, this principle is strongly illustrated in the typical speed differences between LANs and WANs.

The typical LAN today brings *unshared* speeds of 100 Mbps or 1 Gbps to each desktop. In contrast, the speeds of WAN transmission links typically range from only 128 kbps to a few megabits per second, and this speed usually is *shared* by many conversations.

The typical LAN today brings unshared speeds of 100 Mbps to a gigabit per second to each desktop.

In contrast, the speeds of WAN transmission links typically range from only 128 kbps to a few megabits per second, and this speed usually is shared by many conversations.

TEST YOUR UNDERSTANDING

15. a) Compare typical LAN and WAN speeds. b) Why are typical LAN speeds faster than typical WAN speeds? Give a complete and logical answer.

WAN Carriers

In addition, LANs are built on the company's **premises**—the land and buildings that the company owns. (For historical reasons, the word *premises* is always written in the plural.) This means that when you build a LAN, it is on your own property, and you can do anything you want. You can select the technology, select the speeds to be provided, and so forth.

Beyond their premises, however, companies do not have "rights of way" to lay wires. (Imagine how your neighbors would react if you started running wires through their back yards.) Instead, they must contract with transmission **carriers**, who do have government **rights of way** (permissions) to install their transmission hardware and transmission lines in public areas. You do this yourself at home; your voice carrier is the telephone company (or telephone companies if you have separate wired and wireless carriers). Telephone carriers also offer data transmission services, but so do other carriers that primarily specialize in data transmission.

TEST YOUR UNDERSTANDING

 16. When are carriers needed?

INTERNETS

In single networks (LANs and WANs), all devices connect to one another by switches. Initially, computers could only communicate within single networks. However, in the 1970s, Vint Cerf and Bob Kahn[5] proved that it was possible to link multiple networks into larger systems called *internets*.

Figure 1-12 shows a simple internet with three networks: Network X, Network Y, and Network Z.

In single networks (LANs and WANs), all devices connect to one another by switches.

These three networks are connected by devices called **routers**. An **internet**, then, is a collection of networks connected by routers so that any application on any host computer on any network in the internet can send messages called **packets** to any other application on any other host computer on any other network in the internet.

An internet is a group of networks connected by routers so that any application on any host computer on any network in the internet can send messages called packets to any other application on any other host computer on any other network in the internet.

TEST YOUR UNDERSTANDING

 17. a) What is an internet? b) What are messages in internets called?

---

[5]Cerf, V. G., and R. E. Kahn, "A Protocol for Packet Network Interconnection," *IEEE Transactions on Communication*, vol. Com-22, no. 5 (May 1974). In this paper, Cerf and Kahn referred to what we now call routers as gateways. Microsoft still tends to call routers "gateways."

Figure 1-11   Internets (Study Figure)

Single LANs Versus Internets

> In single networks (LANs and WANs), all devices connect to one another by switches

> An internet is a group of networks connected by routers so that any application on any host on any single network can communicate with any application on any other host on any other network in the internet

Internet Components

> All computers in an internet are called hosts

>> Servers, clients, PDAs, cellphones, etc.

> Hosts have IP addresses

>> IP addresses are 32-bit strings of ones and zeros

>>> For humans, they are written in dotted decimal notation (such as 10.34.128.17)

>> Hosts also have single-network addresses

>>> Ethernet addresses are 48 bits long

>>> They are usually written in hexadecimal notation (such as A7-91-BF-5H-AG-39)

> Networks are connected by devices called routers

>> Switches provide connections *within* networks, while routers provide connections *between* networks in an internet

> Packets

>> In single networks, messages are called frames

>> In internets, messages are called packets

Packets and Frames

> One packet is transmitted from the source host to the destination host

>> Its IP destination address is that of the destination host

> In each network, the packet is carried in (encapsulated in) a frame (Figure 1-12)

> If there are N networks between the source and destination hosts, there will be one packet and N frames for a transmission

Figure 1-12   Internet with Three Networks

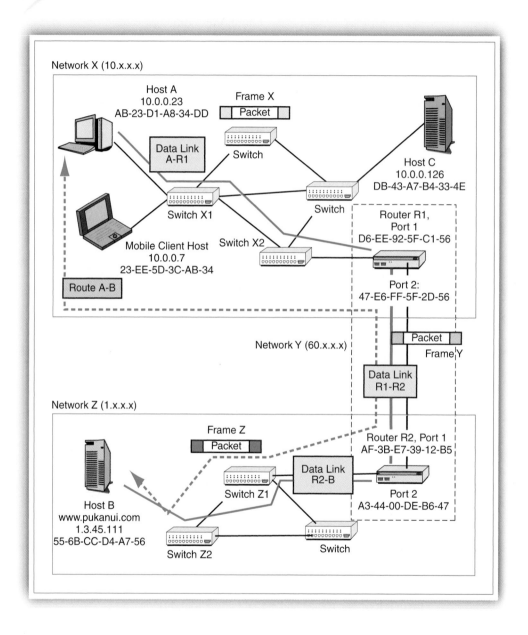

Elements of an Internet

Hosts

In an internet, *all* computers are called **hosts**.[6] Note that home PCs are hosts when attached to internets, including the global Internet. Large server computers are also hosts. We are even beginning to see cellular telephones connect to the Internet; they too are host computers. Soon, even toasters and refrigerators will be Internet hosts.

In an internet, all computers are called hosts, including client PCs.

IP Addresses and Dotted Decimal Notation

In an internet, each host has an Internet Protocol address, or **IP address**. This is the host's address on the internet. IP addresses have to be unique on the internet.

An IP address is a string of 32 bits (ones and zeros). It is usually written in **dotted decimal notation**. Figure 1-13 shows how to convert IP addresses into dotted decimal notation.

➤ First, the 32-bit IP address is broken into four 8-bit segments.

➤ Then, each 8-bit segment is converted into a decimal number. For example, 00000000 is 0 in decimal. At the other extreme, 11111111 is 255 in decimal. All segment values, then, must be between 0 and 255. (In the Hands-on Exercises at the end of this chapter, you can see how to convert between binary and decimal using the Windows Calculator program that comes with your computer.)

Figure 1-13   Converting IP Addresses into Dotted Decimal Notation

IP Address (32 bits long)	10000000101010110001000100001101			
Divided into 4 bytes. These are segments.	1000000	10101011	00010001	00001101
Convert each byte to decimal (result will be between 0 and 255)*	128	171	17	13
Dotted decimal notation (4 segments separated by dots)	128.17.17.13			

*The conversion process is described in the Hands-on section at the end of the chapter.

---

[6] Many students only expect servers to be called hosts. Initially, in fact, the only computers that connected to the Internet (which was the first internet) were large mainframe and minicomputer hosts; users worked at terminals connected to the host (see Chapter 11). Consequently, the Internet was said to connect host computers. When client PCs began to connect to the Internet, the name *host* was kept.

➤ Next, the four segments are written out, separated by dots (periods). This gives something like 10.239.22.112.

Single-Network Addresses (Ethernet Addresses in Hexadecimal Notation)

In addition, each host has a unique address on its single network. Many single networks (but by no means all) follow Ethernet standards. In Ethernet networks, single-network **Ethernet addresses** are 48 bits long. For human comprehension, Ethernet addresses usually are written in **hexadecimal (Base 16) notation**. In "hex" notation,

➤ Ethernet addresses are divided into 6 bytes.

➤ Each byte is then converted into hexadecimal (Base 16) arithmetic. The lowest Base 16 symbol is zero. After *9*, the symbols *A* through *F* are used for *10* to *15*.

➤ This gives an address like A6-B2-EF-89-47-C9.

We will look at hexadecimal addresses again in Chapter 4, which focuses on the Ethernet. (In the Hands-on Exercises at the end of this chapter, you can see how to convert between binary and hex using the Windows Calculator program that comes with your computer.)

Why Two Addresses?

In the telephone network, local and global addresses are coordinated. Your seven-digit telephone number in the United States is unique within your area code. Telephone numbers are then extended to indicate area and even country within the world. However, this type of coordinated addressing was impossible with networks and internets. Several single-network technologies already existed, and as we will see in Chapters 4 and 7, they used different addressing schemes. For internets, the only solution was to create a separate globally unique addressing system, IP addresses.

Switches Versus Routers

If you are confused by the difference between switches and routers, recall from earlier in this chapter that switches provide connections *within* networks, while routers provide connections *between* networks in an internet.

Switches provide connections *within* networks, while routers provide connections *between* networks in an internet.

Switches read the single-network destination address in each frame. They receive the frame in one port, note its single-network destination address, and then send the frame out another port.

Routers, in turn, read IP addresses. They receive the packet in one port, note its destination IP address, and then send the packet out a different port.

TEST YOUR UNDERSTANDING

18. a) In an internet, what are hosts? b) Is a client PC connected to an internet called a host?

19. a) What is a host's official address on the Internet or an internet? b) What is a host's address on an Ethernet network? c) How many bits long is an IP address? d) How many bits long is an Ethernet address? e) How are IP addresses presented for human reading? f) How are Ethernet addresses presented for human reading? g) What kind of address is 10.215.47.88? h) What kind of address is AA-11-BF-47-3C-A9?

20. In an internet, what device connects networks together?

Packets Versus Frames

Caution: The material in this section is dense. Slow down, and go through the example carefully, one step at a time.

As noted earlier, messages in single networks are called frames. Within internets, in turn, messages going from the source host to the destination host are called packets. As Figure 1-12 showed, this is not just a semantic distinction.

Messages in single networks are called frames. Messages in internets are called packets.

The packet goes all the way from the source host to the destination host. However, frames only travel through a single network. More specifically, the packet is carried in (**encapsulated** in, to use a technical term) a frame in each network.

Packets are encapsulated in frames.

➤ Host A creates a packet. It places the IP address of the destination host (Host B) in the packet's address field. This address is 1.3.45.111.

➤ In Network X, the source host places the packet (encapsulates the packet) in Frame X and sends the frame to Router R1. This frame's Ethernet destination address is that of Port 1 in Router R1 (D6-EE-92-5F-C1-56); this port is the final destination of Frame X. (Note that a router has a different Ethernet address for each port. In Router R1, Port 2 has Ethernet address 47-E6-FF-5F-2D-56.) Router R1 receives the frame in one port and sends the packet back out the other port.

➤ Router R1 takes the packet out of Frame X, places it in a new frame, Frame Y, and then sends Frame Y to Router R2 in Network Y. This frame's Ethernet destination address is the Ethernet address of Port 1 in Router R2 (AF-3B-E7-39-12-B5), which is the final destination of Frame Y.

➤ Router R2 takes the packet out of Frame Y, places it in Frame Z, and sends Frame Z to the destination host in Network Z. This frame's Ethernet destination address is the Ethernet address of Host B (55-6B-CC-D4-A7-56), which is the final destination of Frame Z.

➤ The destination host takes the packet out of Frame Z. The packet has now traveled from the source host to the destination host.

Note that the IP address in the packet is never changed because the destination of the packet (Host B) never changes. However, the three frames have different destinations, so each has a different destination address.

TEST YOUR UNDERSTANDING

21. a) Distinguish between frames and packets. b) In a certain internet, the source and destination hosts are separated by five networks (including their own networks). When the source host transmits, how many packets will travel through the internet? c) How many frames?

22. a) For Frame X in Figure 1-12, list the source and destination Ethernet addresses and the source and destination IP addresses of the packet contained in the frame. b) Repeat for Frame Y. c) Repeat for Frame Z.

The Internet

When we spell *internet* with a lowercase *i*, we are using the term generically for any internet, whether it is large or small. However, when we spell Internet with an uppercase *I*, we mean the global **Internet**, which connects hundreds of millions of host computers around the world.

When we spell *internet* with a lowercase *i*, we are using the term generically for any internet, whether it is large or small.

However, when we spell *Internet* with an uppercase *I*, we mean the global Internet, which connects hundreds of millions of host computers around the world.

Figure 1-7 showed that the First Bank of Paradise has two connections to the Internet.

Figure 1-15 shows large routers used to connect FBP to the Internet.

Figure 1-16, in turn, shows a smaller router used to connect a small business or branch office to the Internet. The First Bank of Paradise also uses these small routers to connect their branch office LANs to the corporate WANs.

Host Computers

Figure 1-17 shows the essentials of how the global Internet operates. First, as noted earlier, all computers attached to the Internet (or any individual internet) are called host computers. This includes large servers that provide services to residential and corporate users around the world. WWW servers and mail servers are just two examples of servers.

Internet Service Providers (ISPs)

To connect to the Internet, an organization needs to pay an **Internet service provider (ISP)**, which has three basic functions:

➤ First, the ISP is an organization's on-ramp to the Internet. Companies (and individuals) cannot use the Internet without an ISP.

The Internet
>> Spelled with a lowercase *i, internet* means any internet
>> Spelled with an uppercase *I,* Internet means the global Internet

The Internet (Figure 1-17)
>> Host computers
>> Internet service providers (ISPs)
>>> ISPs make it possible to access the Internet
>>> ISPs carry your packets across the Internet
>>> ISPs collect money to pay for the Internet
>> The Internet backbone consists of many ISPs
>>> ISPs interconnect at network access points (NAPs) to exchange cross-ISP traffic

Subnets
>> Internet professionals call single networks with internets subnets
>> Often just show subnets as lines in internet diagrams (Figure 1-18)
>> Internet specialists and single-network specialists use conflicting terminology (Figure 1-19)

Intranets
>> An intranet is an internal internet for use *within* an organization
>> Intranets use the TCP/IP standards created for the Internet

Extranets
>> Extranets connect multiple firms
>>> Only some computers from each firm are on the extranet
>> Extranets use TCP/IP standards

Intranets, Extranets, and the Internet
>> Confusingly, both intranets and extranets can use the Internet for some of their transmissions

Figure 1-14   The Internet, internets, Intranets, and Extranets (Study Figure)

➤ Second, as we will discuss in the next subsection, ISPs form the Internet backbone that delivers your packets to other hosts on the Internet.

➤ Third, ISPs collect money from residences and organizations to pay for the Internet's operation. The Internet is *not* paid for by the government. The Internet is completely commercial in nearly all countries.

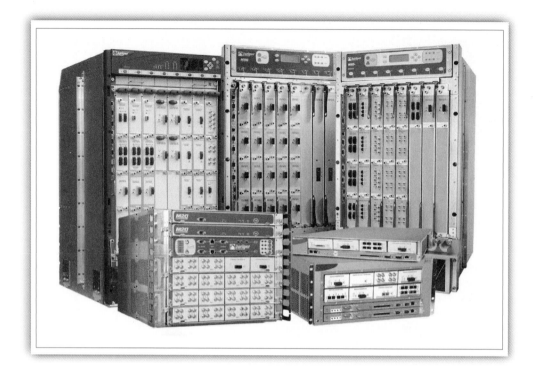

Figure 1-15   Routers (19 inches / 48 cm Wide)

Network Access Points and the Internet Backbone

What if the other host you are trying to reach uses a different ISP? This is quite likely because there are many ISPs. The answer is that ISPs interconnect at sites called **network access points (NAPs)**. ISPs exchange traffic at these NAPs so that any host on any ISP can reach any other host on any other ISP. The collection of all ISPs connected by NAPs is the **Internet backbone**. The Internet, then, is not a single large network. Rather, it is a very large internet composed of thousands of individual networks.

TCP/IP Standards

ISPs can work together because all ISPs (and all hosts) transmit according to the **TCP/IP** standards that we will see throughout the book—especially in Chapters 2 and 8. Hosts also communicate with their ISPs using TCP/IP standards.

An Analogy: The Telephone Network

If creating the Internet out of many independent commercial ISPs may seem odd, this is how the telephone network works. Most countries have multiple competing telephone networks for domestic communication (communication within a country).

Figure 1-16   Small Router for a Branch Office (19 inches / 48 cm Wide)

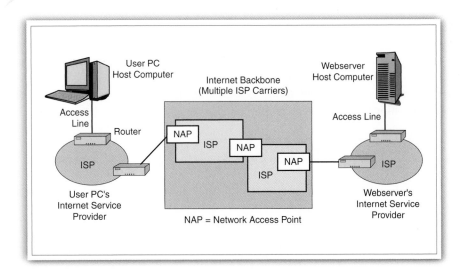

Figure 1-17   The Internet

There also are multiple competing international common carriers that connect telephone systems in different countries. All of these telephone networks are independently and usually commercially owned. However, thanks to connection points and international telephone standards, any telephone in any country can call any other telephone in any other country.

ISPs at the First Bank of Paradise

In Figure 1-7, note that FBP used two ISPs. This provides **redundancy** (duplication of service), so that if one ISP fails, the bank will still be connected to the Internet. Redundancy increases reliability by providing one or more backup systems that take over if one system fails.

Redundancy increases reliability by providing one or more backup systems that take over if one system fails.

TEST YOUR UNDERSTANDING

23. a) Distinguish between internets and the Internet. b) Is a home PC connected to the Internet a host? c) Is the Internet a single network? d) What are the three basic functions of ISPs on the Internet? e) What are NAPs? f) Why are NAPs crucial to universal connectivity on the Internet? g) What standards allow ISPs and hosts to communicate with one another?

24. a) What is redundancy? b) What is the benefit of redundancy? c) Why does FBP use two ISPs?

Subnets

We have noted that an internet is a collection of individual networks. Internet specialists, however, often use different terminologies. They say that routers are connected by communication systems called subnets. A **subnet**, then, is a single network (LAN or WAN) in an internet.

A subnet is a single network (LAN or WAN) in an internet.

Figure 1-18 shows an internet with multiple subnets. Note that a site can have internal routers and that these routers will connect multiple subnets within the site. For reasons we will see in Chapter 8, all hosts on a subnet have IP addresses within a certain range. The x in an IP address range indicates all possible values within the range. Note also that subnets are often drawn as simple lines to which routers connect. In reality, most subnets have many trunk lines and switches.

There also is a difference between how single-network professionals and internet professionals use the term *network* (see Figure 1-19). Single network professionals use the term *network* to mean a single network. In contrast, internet professionals use the term *network* to mean what we call internets.

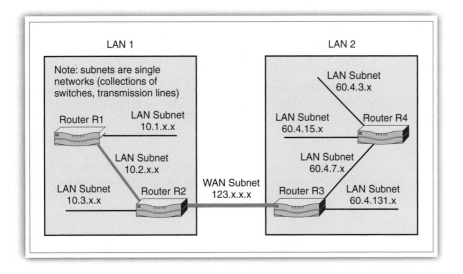

Figure 1-18   Subnets in an Internet

	By Single-Network Professionals	**By Internet Professionals**
Single Networks Are Called	Networks	Subnets
Internets Are Called	Internets	Networks

Figure 1-19   Terminology Differences for Single-Network and Internet Professionals

---

Single-network professionals use the term *network* for single networks and *internet* for internets.

Internet professionals use the term *subnet* for single networks and *network* for internets.

TEST YOUR UNDERSTANDING

25. a) What are subnets? b) What are single networks called by single-network professionals? c) What are single networks called by internet professionals? d) What are internets called by single-network professionals? e) What are internets called by internet professionals? f) How do single-network professionals and internet professionals differ

in their use of the term *network*? (Yes, this question repeats material in some earlier questions.)

Intranets and Extranets

So far, we have looked at differences between internets and the Internet. We need to make two other distinctions relative to internets. We need to distinguish between intranets and extranets.

Intranets

An **intranet** is an internet for *internal transmission within firms*; intranets use the TCP/IP transmission standards that govern transmission over the Internet. The First Bank of Paradise has a widely used intranet for its internal traffic.

An intranet is an internet for internal transmission within firms; intranets use the TCP/IP transmission standards that govern transmission over the Internet.

Extranets

The bank also participates in **extranets**, which use TCP/IP Internet standards to link several firms together but which are not accessible to people outside these firms. Even within the firms of the extranet, only some of each firm's computers are accessible through the extranet.

Extranets use TCP/IP Internet standards to link several firms together but do not allow access by people outside these firms.

Specifically, the bank outsources payroll processing. It communicates with the outsourcing firm via the Internet. The outsourcing firm's extranet consists of its own computers and one host in each client firm, including FBP.

Intranets, Extranets, and the Internet

Confusingly, both intranets and extranets may use the global Internet for some or all of their transmission. The terms *intranet* and *extranet* are service distinctions, not technological distinctions.

TEST YOUR UNDERSTANDING

26. a) What is an intranet? b) What is an extranet? c) Can intranets and extranets use the Internet for transmission? d) What standards do intranets and extranets use?

IP Address Management

IP Addresses Are Official Addresses

We saw earlier that just as you need to have a telephone number for others to be able to call you, your host needs an IP address when it uses the Internet. Otherwise, other hosts on the Internet cannot send you messages. A host's IP address is its official address on the Internet.

Each Host Must Have a Unique IP Address

> Dynamic Host Configuration Protocol (DHCP) (Figure 1-21)
>
> Server hosts are given static IP addresses (unchanging)
>
> Clients get temporary dynamic IP addresses that may be different each time they use an internet
>
> Clients get dynamic IP addresses from DHCP servers (Figure 1-21)

Domain Name System (DNS) (Figure 1-22)

> IP addresses are official addresses
>
> Hosts can also have host names (e.g., cnn.com)
>
> > These names are not "official"; they are like nicknames
> >
> > DNS servers tell your computer the IP address of a target host whose name you know (Figure 1-22)

Figure 1-20   IP Address Management (Study Figure)

A host's IP address is its official address on the Internet.

Static IP Addresses

Server hosts always use the same IP address. Otherwise, client PC users would not know how to reach them. (Imagine what would happen if your favorite store constantly changed its street address!) Hosts that use the same IP address all the time are said to have **static IP addresses**.

Dynamic IP Addresses and the Dynamic Host Configuration Protocol (DHCP)

In contrast, client PCs connected to the Internet usually do not get the same IP address each time they use the Internet. As shown in Figure 1-21, when a client PC wishes to use the Internet, it first contacts a **Dynamic Host Configuration Protocol (DHCP)** server. This server has a pool of IP addresses that it manages.

The DHCP request message asks the DHCP server for an IP address. The server responds by sending back an IP address to the client PC.[7] The client PC will use this IP address until it signs off its ISP or for several hours. This is only a temporary IP address—or to be technical, a **dynamic IP address**.

Although the DHCP server tries to give your PC the same IP address each time you use the Internet, there is no guarantee that it will do so. Consequently, each time you use the Internet, you may get a different IP address.

---

[7]Actually, the process is somewhat more complex. The client PC first broadcasts a message to all nearby DHCP servers. Each server sends back an offer to provide service. These offers include the length of time the client PC may use the IP address and other parameters. The client PC evaluates these offers and then works with the DHCP server that provides the best offer.

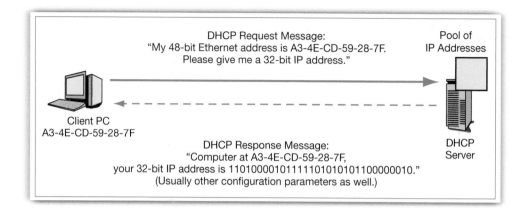

DHCP Request Message:
"My 48-bit Ethernet address is A3-4E-CD-59-28-7F.
Please give me a 32-bit IP address."

Pool of
IP Addresses

Client PC
A3-4E-CD-59-28-7F

DHCP Response Message:
"Computer at A3-4E-CD-59-28-7F,
your 32-bit IP address is 11010000101111101010101100000010."
(Usually other configuration parameters as well.)

DHCP
Server

Figure 1-21   Dynamic Host Configuration Protocol (DHCP)

Host Names and the Domain Name System (DNS)

Even with dotted decimal notation, IP addresses are difficult to memorize. Consequently, many server hosts (but few client hosts) have easier-to-remember host names. **Host names** consist of two or more text labels separated by dots. The name *cnn.com* is a host name, as is *www.hawaii.edu*. You undoubtedly know the host names of many hosts, and you often type host names in uniform resource locators (URLs), such as *http://www.prenhall.com* or *http://panko.info*. In Figure 1-12, Host B had the host name *www.pukanui.com*.

However, recall that IP addresses are the official addresses of hosts on the Internet. Host names are merely easy-to-remember nicknames. To give an analogy, if you want to call someone whose name you know, you must find his or her telephone number before you can place the call.

Fortunately, the Internet provides a way for your computer to look up the IP addresses of hosts if you only know their host names. This is the **Domain Name System (DNS)**. To continue the telephone analogy, the DNS is like a telephone directory for the Internet.

Figure 1-22 shows how the Domain Name System works. When you type a host name in a URL or in some other form of input, a program on your client PC sends a DNS request message to your **DNS server**. This **DNS request message** contains the host name of the *target host*—the host you wish to reach. (In the figure, the target host is *Voyager.cba.hawaii.edu*.)

The DNS server has a table of host names and IP addresses. It looks up the target's host name in the table and notes the target host's IP address. The DNS server sends the IP address of the target host back to the client PC in a **DNS response message**. (In the case of the target host *Voyager.cba.hawaii.edu*, the IP address is 128.171.17.13.) Your PC now has the target host's IP address, and you can now communicate with it.

If you connect from your home to an ISP, your ISP maintains a DNS server for your use. If you connect from a university or a large company, the organization must maintain its own DNS server. There are literally thousands of DNS servers around the world forming a complex system.

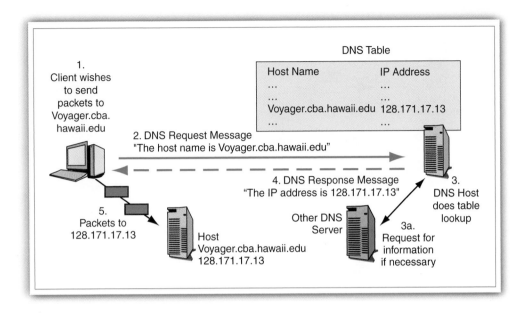

Figure 1-22   The Domain Name System (DNS)

Figure 1-22 shows that if your local DNS server does not know the IP address of the target host, it will pass your request to other DNS servers, which will send back the information. Your own local DNS server always sends you the final DNS response message, however. This contains either the target host's IP address or an error message, typically the dreaded "Error 404" when the host cannot be found.

TEST YOUR UNDERSTANDING

27. a) What is a host's official address on the Internet? b) What kind of IP addresses do server hosts normally receive? c) What kind of IP addresses do client hosts normally receive? d) How does a host get a dynamic IP address?

28. a) You know the host name of a server host you are attempting to reach. What kind of server will you need to use before you can send messages to the server you are attempting to reach? b) If you know the IP address of the host you wish to send packets to, do you need to use a DNS server? c) In DHCP, the IP address the client PC receives is the address of which host? d) In DNS, the IP address the client PC receives is the address of which host?

SECURITY

The First Bank of Paradise has long been a target of hackers attempting to break into the bank's computers. The bank receives approximately one attack packet per second. Most of these packets are simple probes that are looking for vulnerabilities or are part

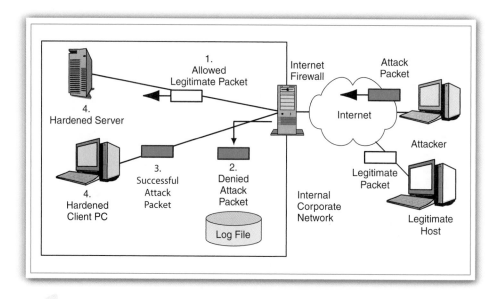

Figure 1-23   Firewall and Hardened Hosts

of unsophisticated attacks. However, a growing number of attack packets are parts of serious break-in attempts.

Disturbingly, organized crime has been developing the ability to hack into banks. Why risk gunfights for a few thousand dollars when hacking thefts can bring vastly more money with little physical risk to the thief? Security will be a major component of the bank's network.

Firewalls

For instance, Yvonne already has a firewall (see Figure 1-23) at every building's connection points to the outside world. A **firewall** examines all incoming and outgoing traffic to look for dangerous content. When it finds provably dangerous packets (as it does thousands of times each day), it drops them and records them in a log file.

> A firewall examines all incoming and outgoing traffic to look for dangerous content. When it finds provably dangerous packets (as it does thousands of times each day), it drops them and records them in a log file.

The firewall shown in the figure is a border firewall. A **border firewall** is one that sits at the border between an internal corporate network or internet and the global Internet. In the future, Yvonne will also use firewalls to divide building LANs into multiple areas that should be separated from one another. For instance, accounting servers should be protected by firewalls that sharply limit access from other departments in the site.

Host Hardening

Although firewalls will stop most incoming attacks, they will not stop them all. Consequently, as Figure 1-23 shows, companies should **harden** their hosts against inevitable attack by keeping all computers backed up, by installing all updates created by operating system and application program vendors, and by taking a number of other actions.

Cryptographic Protections

Another aspect of the network security is the increasing use of cryptographic protections for message dialogues. **Cryptography** is the use of mathematical operations to thwart attacks on message dialogues between pairs of communicating parties (people, programs, or devices). Cryptography provides two forms of protection: initial authentication and message-by-message protections.

Initial Authentication

Initially, the two parties who wish to communicate must conduct **authentication**, in which each determines the other's identity. This is necessary to prevent impostors from claiming to be someone else.

Figure 1-24   Cryptographic Protections (Study Figure)

Cryptography
> Cryptography is the use of mathematical operations to thwart attacks on message dialogues between pairs of communicating parties (people, programs, or devices)

Cryptography is Expensive
> Usually, only sensitive dialogues are cryptographically secured

Initial Authentication
> Initial authentication allows users to determine the other party's identity and thus thwart impostors

Message-by-Message Protections
> Encryption provides confidentiality so that an eavesdropper cannot read intercepted messages

> Electronic signatures provide message-by-message authentication to prevent the insertion of messages by an impostor after initial authentication

> Electronic signatures usually also provide message integrity; this tells the receiver whether anyone has changed the message en route

Message-by-Message Protections

It is also necessary to protect each message transmitted during the dialogue. Cryptography provides three message-by-message protections.

➤ Each message is **encrypted** for **confidentiality** so that an eavesdropper will not be able to read it even if the eavesdropper can intercept it.

➤ Each message is given an **electronic signature** to authenticate the identity of the sender. This keeps impostors from inserting false messages after initial authentication.

➤ In addition to providing authentication, most types of electronic signatures provide **message integrity**, which means that if the message is modified, the receiver will be able to detect this. Receivers will not trust tampered messages and will discard them.

Limited Use of Cryptography

Cryptography requires a good deal of processing power to handle its mathematical operations. Consequently, cryptography is not used for all dialogues in the corporation. However, it is crucial to use cryptography for sensitive dialogues.

TEST YOUR UNDERSTANDING

29. a) Why is the bank especially concerned about security? b) What is the function of a firewall? c) What benefits do cryptographic protections provide?

CONCLUSION

Synopsis

This chapter introduced you to a number of basic networking concepts and issues that we will be seeing throughout this course. Most fundamentally, a network is a transmission system that connects two or more applications running on different computers. When many people hear the term *networking*, they think of the Internet. However, in a book on corporate networking, we will be looking at internal corporate networks, which carry more of a business's traffic than the Internet. We also looked at the difference between data communications and telecommunications (traditional voice and video transmission).

In this chapter, we saw the First Bank of Paradise (FBP), our running case study for this book. FBP is a composite medium-sized firm operating primarily in Hawai'i. Although banks have some industry-specific needs, such as higher-than-average security requirements, the issues and technologies that the bank is facing are similar to those in most firms.

The bank has many single networks (LANs and WANs). Local area networks operate entirely within a company's premises. Wide area networks, in turn, connect different sites together. The typical LAN today brings unshared speeds of 100 Mbps to 1 Gbps to each desktop. In contrast, the speeds of WAN transmission links typically range from only 128 kbps to a few megabits per second, and this speed usually is shared by many conversations. LANs operate on the customer premises, so organizations can build any LAN they wish. In contrast, for WANs, companies must use transmission carriers.

Single networks—both LANs and WANs—have nine general components: applications, client computers, server computers, frames (messages), trunk lines, access lines, switches, routers, and wireless access points. Access lines connect individual computers to the network. Trunk lines connect switches to other switches, routers to other routers, and routers to switches. Switches forward frames within a single network. Routers pass messages into the network and out of the network.

In single networks, computers use packet switching, in which they break their transmissions into small messages. In single networks, these messages are called frames. Packet switching allows messages from multiple sources to be multiplexed (mixed) effectively on trunk lines. This sharing of trunk line capacity reduces the cost of transmission.

Single networks (which are also called subnets) are no longer isolated islands of communication. Routers link them together into internets. Although the worldwide Internet is the dominant internet, most organizations have internal internets (called intranets if they use the TCP/IP standards created for the Internet). In addition, routers can use TCP/IP technology to link groups of companies into closed extranets for buying and selling.

Messages in internets are called packets, and computers in internets are called hosts. As noted earlier, messages in single networks are called frames. A packet will travel through several individual networks. In each network, it is carried in a separate frame. If two hosts are separated by seven networks, a packet between them will be carried by seven different frames—one in each network.

When the word *internet* is spelled with a lowercase *i*, it means any internet. When *Internet* is spelled with an uppercase *I*, this means the global Internet. To use the Internet, you need to connect to an Internet service provider (ISP). ISPs carry traffic across the internet, connecting at network access points (NAPs).

On an internet, all computers are called hosts. This includes client PCs. Every host has a 32-bit IP address that is its official address on the Internet. IP addresses are often written in dotted decimal notation, which looks like 128.171.17.13. Each computer also has an address on its single network. For instance, 48-bit Ethernet addresses in hexadecimal notation look like AF-47-B8-9C-FF-33.

Servers have static IP addresses that do not change. Clients have dynamic IP addresses that may change each time they use the Internet. Client PCs are supplied with dynamic IP addresses by DHCP servers.

Server hosts often have host names, such as Voyager.cba.hawaii.edu. Only IP addresses are official Internet addresses, so if a user types a host name of a host he or she wishes to reach, the PC gets the corresponding IP address by querying a DNS host.

A major concern in all organizations today is security. To reduce the danger of attacks, companies install firewalls, which stop nearly all attack packets. However, hosts still must be "hardened" so that they will survive attack packets that make it through firewalls. In addition, when companies must transmit over the Internet or another untrusted network (such as a wireless LAN), they normally implement cryptographic protections to secure dialogues.

THOUGHT QUESTIONS

1. Is efficiency more important in LANs or WANs? Justify your answer.
2. Your DSL line has a listed speed of 500 kbps. However, when you make downloads, a speed counter tells you that you are only receiving 50 kBps. Can you explain this apparent inconsistency?

TROUBLESHOOTING QUESTIONS

Troubleshooting is identifying and fixing problems. Troubleshooting is an important skill, and we will see troubleshooting questions throughout this textbook. Research has shown that people often make fundamental mistakes when they do troubleshooting. Most fundamentally, they usually only consider one or two possible causes for their problem. Often, the one or two possible causes they consider are incorrect. Consequently, they often waste time trying to solve the wrong problem. Only later do they realize that they need to consider additional possibilities. Premature focusing on one or two possible causes tends to extend downtime needlessly and sometimes leads to "solutions" that fail to fix the real problem.

In troubleshooting questions, you will be expected to create multiple hypotheses, not just one or two. It is almost always best to draw a diagram of all of the components of a system to broaden your perspective. After you develop multiple possible causes for the problem, you can then use logic or experimentation to prioritize them and eliminate false causes.

1. Here is a sample troubleshooting problem for you to solve. You have been using a telephone modem to access the Internet. Its rated download speed is 56 kbps. You switch to a cable modem, which should allow you to receive at 500 kbps. In general, your download speed for webpages is faster than it was with your modem; however, your actual download rates usually vary from only 128 kbps to 256 kbps.

   a) List likely reasons for your not being able to get a full 500 kbps. **Do NOT just come up with one or two possible explanations**. *Hint:* Consider Figure 1-17, which shows the Internet.

   b) Assess the likelihood of each alternative given the facts in the problem description and any other analysis you can consider.

2. In your browser, you enter the URL of a website you use daily. After some delay, you receive a DNS error message that the host does not exist. What may have happened? **Again, do NOT just come up with one or two possible explanations.**

HANDS-ON EXERCISES

Binary and Decimal Conversions

As noted in Chapter 1, it is relatively easy to convert 32-bit IP addresses in dotted decimal notation.

The one thing that is hard to do is converting each group of eight bits into a decimal number. If you have Microsoft Windows, the Calculator accessory shown as Figure 1-25 can convert between binary and dotted decimal notations. Go to the Start button, then to Programs or All Programs, then to Accessories, and then click on *Calculator*. The Windows Calculator will then pop up.

Binary to Decimal

To convert eight binary bits to decimal, first choose *View* and click on *Scientific* to make the Calculator a more advanced scientific calculator. Click on the *Bin* (binary) radio button, and type in the 8-bit binary sequence you wish to convert. Then click on the *Dec* (decimal) radio button. The decimal value for that segment will appear.

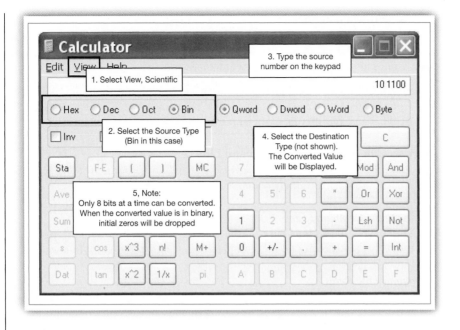

Figure 1-25   Windows Calculator

Decimal to Binary

To convert decimal to binary, go to *View* and choose *Scientific* if you have not already done so. Click on *Dec* to indicate that you are entering a decimal number. Type the number. Now click on *Bin* to convert this number to binary.

One additional subtlety is that Calculator drops initial zeros. So if you convert 17, you get 10001. You must add three initial zeros to make this an 8-bit segment: 00010001.

Another subtlety is that you can only convert one 8-bit segment at a time.

1. a) What is the binary number 11001010 in decimal?
   b) Express the following IP address in binary: 128.171.17.13. *Hint:* The number 128 is 10000000 in binary. Put spaces between each group of eight bits.
   c) Convert the following address in binary to dotted decimal notation: 11110000 10101010 00001111 11100011. (Spaces are added between bytes to make reading easier.) *Hint:* The binary number 11110000 is 240 in decimal.

Binary to Hex

The same process can be used to convert 48-bit Ethernet addresses into hexadecimal notation (hex). First, divide the address into bytes. In the Windows Calculator, click on bin (binary) and enter the byte 10101010. Now click on hex. You will see AA. This is correct.

2. a) What is 11000011 in hexadecimal?
   b) What is 0F in binary? Remember that you will get a one-byte answer.

Test Your Download Speed

How fast is your Internet connection? Test your download speed at *http://www.pcpitstop.com/internet/bandwidth.asp* or *http://webservices.zdnet.com/zdnet/bandwidth*. If you can, test your bandwidth during periods of light and heavy use.

3. a) What kind of connection do you have (telephone modem, cable modem, LAN, etc.)?

   b) What was your download speed during the test?

Working with the Windows Command Line

Windows offers a number of tools from its command line prompt. Network professionals need to learn to work with these commands.

Getting to the Command Line

To get to the command line, click on the *Start* button and choose *Run*. Type either *cmd* and hit *OK* or *command* and then *OK*, depending on your version of Windows.

Command Line Rules

At the command line, you need to type everything exactly. You also need to hit Enter at the end of each line. It is also good to know that you can clear the command line screen by typing *cls[Enter]*.

Your Configuration

In Windows, you can find information about your own computer with ipconfig or winipconfig. In newer versions of Windows, type the command *ipconfig/all[Enter]*. Older versions of Windows require you to type the command *winipconfig[Enter]*. This will give you your IP address, your physical address (your Ethernet address), the IP addresses of your organization's or ISP's DNS hosts, and other information—some of which we will see in Chapter 8.

4. Use ipconfig/all or winipconfig.
   a) What is your computer's IP address?
   b) What is its Ethernet address?
   c) What are the IP addresses of your DNS hosts?

DNS Lookup

In this chapter, we saw that if you know the host name of the host to which you want to communicate, then your computer must look up the host's IP address by sending a DNS request message to your local DNS server. You can also do this yourself from the command line, using the nslookup command (DNS servers are also called name servers). For instance, type *nslookup www.google.com[Enter]* to find Google's IP address.

5. a) Do an nslookup DNS lookup on a host whose name you know and that you use frequently. What is its IP address?
   b) Now do an nslookup on that IP address. Do you get the host name?

Ping

To find out if you can reach a host and to see how much latency there is when you contact a host, use the **ping** command. You ping an IP address or host name much as a submarine pings a target to see if it exists and to see how far away it is. To use the command, type *ping* *hostname[Enter]* or *ping IPaddress[Enter]*. Ping may not work if the host is behind a firewall, because firewalls typically block pings.

6. Ping a host whose name you know and that you use frequently. What is the latency? If this does not work because the host is behind a firewall, do other hosts until you succeed.

Ping 127.0.0.1 (PC, Call Home)

Ping the address 127.0.0.1. This is your computer's **loopback address**. In effect, the computer's network program sends a ping to itself. If your PC seems to be having trouble communicating over the Internet, type *ping 127.0.0.1[Enter]*. If the ping fails, you know that the problem is internal, and you need to focus on your network software's configuration. If the ping succeeds, then your computer is talking to the outside world at least.

7. Ping 127.0.0.1. Did it succeed?

Tracert

The Windows **tracert** program is like a super ping. It lists latency not only to a target host but also lists each router along the way and lists latency to that router. Actually, it shows three latencies because it tests each router three times. To use tracert, type *tracert hostname[Enter]* or *tracert IPaddress[Enter]*. Again, hosts (and routers) behind firewalls will not respond.

8. Do a tracert on a host whose name you know and that you use frequently. You can stop the tracert process by hitting Control-C.
   a) What is the destination host?
   b) How many routers are there between you and the destination host? If this does not work because the host is behind a firewall, do other hosts until you succeed.

9. Distinguish between the information that ping provides and the information that tracert provides.

To Get Your IP and Ethernet Addresses with Windows XP

Do the following if you have an XP computer. This exercise will give you configuration information without your having to go to the command line. Choose *Start*, then *Control Panel*, then *Network and Internet Connections*, then *Network Connections*. In the window that appears, click on a network connection icon to select it. Choose *File, Status*. You will see the *Connection Status* dialog box for that connection. Select the *Support* tab to see your IP address. Click on *Details* while in the *Support* tab to see more information, including the physical (Ethernet) address of your network interface card (NIC).

10. If you have a Windows XP computer, find your IP address and the physical (Ethernet) address of your computer.

GETTTING CURRENT

Go to the book website's New Information and Errors pages for this chapter to get new information since this book went to press and to correct any errors in the text.

Case Study: Pat Lee's Home Network

Learning Objectives

By the end of this chapter, you should be able to discuss:

■ How to create a home PC network.

■ Applications for home PC networks.

■ Hardware for home PC networks.

■ The functions of access routers.

■ Wireless networking.

■ Costing out a home PC network.

INTRODUCTION

In this case study, you will learn how to create a home PC network. There are two good reasons for starting with these small networks. First, it will interest most students. Many students plan to build home PC networks, and quite a few have already done so. Second, it seems best to start studying small and familiar networks before learning about more complex and unfamiliar types of networks. In this chapter, we will not look at how to configure the software on the PCs to be networked. That is the subject of Chapter 1b.

THE INITIAL SITUATION

Pat Lee is the First Bank of Paradise's vice president for international marketing. Like most people in developed countries today, Pat has a computer at home. In fact, like many people, she has more than one PC at home. She has one desktop PC in her family's study. In addition, Pat's daughter Emily has a desktop computer in her room.

Initially, only the downstairs computer in the study was connected to the Internet. The family used its ordinary telephone connection and the telephone modem that came with that computer. The connection was miserably slow—only about 40 kbps on average—and family arguments often erupted when two people wanted to use the Internet at the same time. Of course, when someone was using the

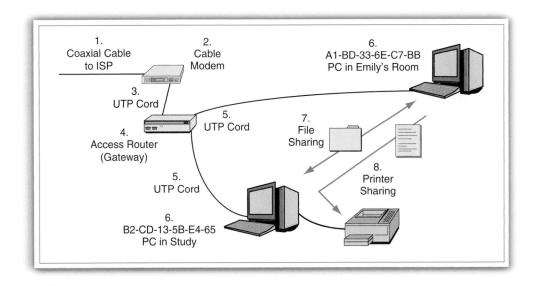

Figure 1a-1   Pat Lee's Initial Home Network

Internet, nobody could use the telephone, and vice versa. This was a special problem for Emily, who wanted to be able to be in constant contact with her friends using both instant messaging (IM) and the telephone.

The only printer in the house was a laser printer attached to the PC in the study. When Emily worked on her own computer, she had to copy files to a floppy disk and hope that nobody was working at the study computer, or, if they were, that they would let her do a "quick print."

One evening at dinner, the family decided that enough was enough. The next week, Pat took Yvonne Champion, the bank's network manager, to lunch. Yvonne listened to Pat's description of her needs, then listed what Pat would have to buy and do to build a home PC network. Figure 1a-1 shows the network that Yvonne sketched out.

TEST YOUR UNDERSTANDING

1. What problems were the members of the Lee family having with their computer systems?

APPLICATIONS

Before Yvonne sketched out the design, she asked Pat questions about applications—how Pat and her family wanted to use the network.

Internet Applications

Most obviously, the family will use the network to get to the Internet. They will surf webpages, send and receive e-mail, chat with friends using instant messaging, and do many other things. Pat's network design will give much faster Internet throughput—500 kbps or more. It also will allow people to use the telephone while others are using the Internet.

File Sharing

In addition, thanks to networking, the family members will be able to do **file sharing** between the two home PCs. The downstairs machine in the study is their main PC. As shown in Figure 1a-1, Emily, working on the computer in her room, will be able to retrieve files stored on the study PC's hard drive and will be able to write files to the computer. Currently, Emily often has no idea whether the copy of a document on the computer in the study or on her bedroom computer is the latest version. Now, there will only be one version—the one on the study PC. Pat had not even realized that file sharing was possible before talking with Yvonne.

Printer Sharing

Emily will also do **printer sharing**, which Figure 1a-1 also illustrates. The study machine has a high-speed laser printer. When Emily gives the print command on her computer, the network will send her print job to the downstairs computer, which will print it on the laser printer. Today, when Emily needed to print, she had to interrupt the person working at the study computer to get her file on a floppy disk printed.

TEST YOUR UNDERSTANDING

2. a) What benefits were sought for Internet access? b) How will the family use file sharing? c) How will it use printer sharing?

ACCESS ROUTER AND CABLE MODEM

Access Router

The network that Yvonne outlined is shown in Figure 1a-1. The heart of this network will be a device called an **access router** (sometimes called a **gateway**). The access router will tie together the various pieces of the network. We will look at access routers in depth a little later in this case study.

Cable Modem

For faster Internet access, Yvonne suggested using **cable modem service** provided by the local cable television company. (We will see other options for high-speed residential Internet access in Chapter 6.) The cable television company will install a small box called a **cable modem** in the home. Cable modem service will provide transmission from the Internet to Pat's network, averaging about 2 Mbps. This is the downstream throughput. Upstream throughput will be slower but will still be quite fast compared to Pat's current modem throughput.

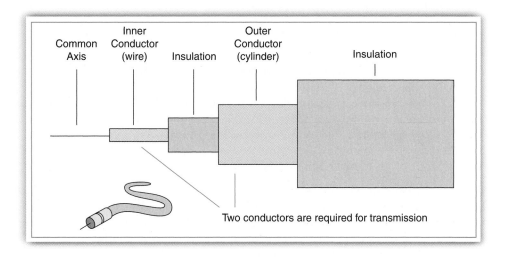

Common Axis · Inner Conductor (wire) · Insulation · Outer Conductor (cylinder) · Insulation

Two conductors are required for transmission

Figure 1a-2   Coaxial Cable

Coaxial Cable

The cable company will run a line from the cable modem out to the cable television cable running down the street. The line from the cable modem to the outside world is a **coaxial cable**. It is identical to the coaxial cable you use to connect a VCR to a television (see Figure 1a-2). It has a central conductor and a conducting mesh ring that has the same axis as the central conductor wire.

Pat will then run wiring from the cable modem to the access router. As we will see later, this will be a UTP (unshielded twisted pair) patch cord. Like a home telephone wire, a UTP patch cord comes premade, cut to a certain length and with connectors at the end. Pat will simply buy a three-foot (one-meter) patch cord, snap one connector into the cable modem's UTP jack, and snap the other end into the WAN jack on her access router.

TEST YOUR UNDERSTANDING

3. a) Distinguish between the access router and the cable modem. b) What is a gateway? c) What device will connect Pat Lee's network to the Internet? d) What are the two conductors in coaxial cable? e) Where will coaxial cable be used in Pat Lee's network?

4. a) What are the advantages of cable modems over telephone modems for Internet access? b) What type of transmission medium is used between your VCR and your television and by cable television service providers? c) What Internet download throughput has Pat's family received, and how will this change?

THE PERSONAL COMPUTERS

Network Interface Cards (NICs)

Pat will not need special PCs to create her network. The only hardware requirement will be for each computer to have a **network interface card (NIC)**. Figure 1a-3 shows an internal NIC for a desktop PC and a PC Card or ExpressCard NIC for a notebook PC.

Like most computers sold today, both PCs in Pat's house came with internal NICs, so there was nothing else to buy. However, if Pat had owned an older notebook computer, she probably would have needed to buy a PC Card or ExpressCard NIC.

Device Driver

As Figure 1a-4 shows, whenever you add a hardware device—such as a NIC, a hard drive, or a printer—you must add a piece of software called a device driver. The **device driver** converts general commands from the operating system into the detailed steps needed to get the device to carry out the operating system commands.

When you buy a computer, any installed NIC will have its device driver already installed. However, if you add a new NIC, you will also have to add a device driver. In some cases, the operating system will recognize the NIC and install the device driver automatically. However, always read the instructions that come with the NIC, which always includes a device driver on a disk.[1]

Networking Software

Both computers in the Lee household run the Windows XP Home operating system. This version of Windows (and most older versions of Windows still in use) are capable

Figure 1a-3   Network Interface Cards (NICs)

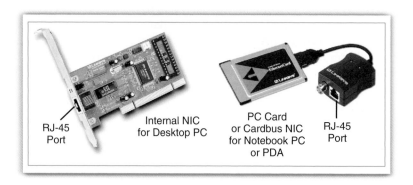

RJ-45 Port

Internal NIC for Desktop PC

PC Card or Cardbus NIC for Notebook PC or PDA

RJ-45 Port

---

[1]Another subtlety is that companies usually upgrade their device drivers over time. After installing the device driver that comes with the NIC, you should go to the NIC manufacturer's website and download the most recent version of the device driver. You should also do this with new peripherals (disk drives, printers, etc.) on new PCs, because the vendors may have created updated device drivers since the PC was produced.

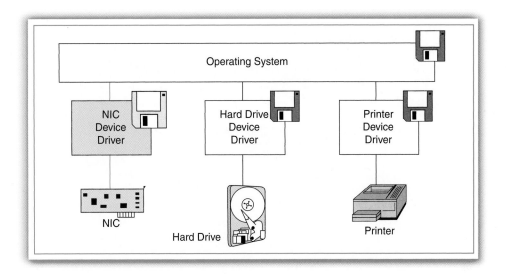

Figure 1a-4   Device Drivers

of handling file sharing, print service, and Internet access without the need for additional software. However, as Chapter 1b discusses, you do have to configure the two computers for file and printer sharing.

TEST YOUR UNDERSTANDING

5. a) Did Pat need special PCs to be able to network them? b) What hardware component might she have had to buy for her PCs? c) What is the role of device drivers? d) Could Pat's PCs handle file and print sharing without adding new software? e) Why or why not?

WIRES, CONNECTORS, AND JACKS

UTP Cords

Figure 1a-5 shows the main type of wiring that Pat will use in her home network.[2] (This also is the most common type of wiring used in corporate LANs.) It is called **unshielded twisted pair (UTP)** wiring. We will look at UTP in more detail in Chapter 3.

---

[2]Very large Ethernet networks also use another transmission medium, optical fiber, which sends signals as light pulses. Optical fiber can carry signals much farther than UTP.

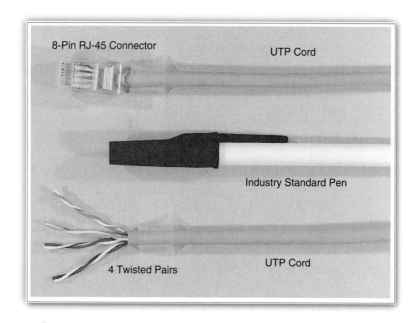

Figure 1a-5   Unshielded Twisted Pair (UTP) Cord with RJ-45 Connector

UTP wiring is about as thick as a pen and is rugged and flexible. A length of UTP is called a **cord**.

RJ-45 Connectors and Jacks

As Figure 1a-6 shows, a UTP cord terminates in an **RJ-45 connector**, which plugs into an **RJ-45 jack** (plug). RJ-45 connectors and jacks are similar to the RJ-11 connectors

Figure 1a-6   UTP Cord with RJ-45 Connector and Jack

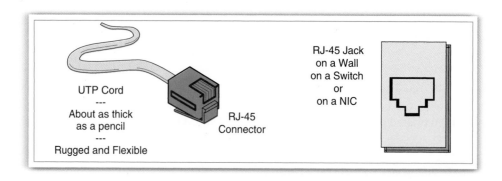

and jacks used by home telephone wiring. However, RJ-45 connectors and jacks are a little wider. RJ-45 connectors simply snap into RJ-45 jacks.

Patch Cords

To connect Pat's computers to the access router's built-in Ethernet switch and to connect the access router to the cable modem, Pat will need UTP cords of the right lengths. Fortunately, Pat will be able to buy 4-pair UTP patch cords of suitable lengths at her computer store.

Patch cords are UTP cords that come precut in a variety of lengths, with connectors attached. They are tested at the factory to ensure that they will work in the field. Although it is possible to buy bulk UTP cable and cut it to specific lengths, this takes special tools, including a tester. In addition, handmade cords not produced by experienced networking professionals often work poorly, if at all.

TEST YOUR UNDERSTANDING

6. a) What is a length of UTP wiring called? b) Compare RJ-45 connectors and jacks to home telephone connectors and jacks. c) What are UTP patch cords? d) Why are they attractive?

THE ACCESS ROUTER'S FUNCTIONS

The heart of Pat's home network will be her access router, which is shown in Figure 1a-7. This inexpensive device performs a number of important functions, as Figure 1a-8 illustrates.

The Access Router's Ethernet Switch

First, the access router will contain a 4-port **Ethernet switch**. This switch will allow the two computers to send frames to each other. The Ethernet switch will make Pat's home network a LAN.

Figure 1a-7   Home Access Router

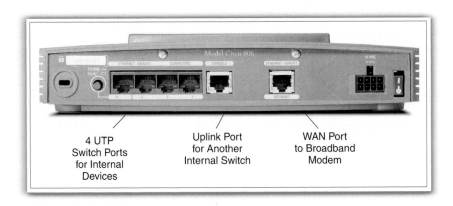

4 UTP
Switch Ports
for Internal
Devices

Uplink Port
for Another
Internal Switch

WAN Port
to Broadband
Modem

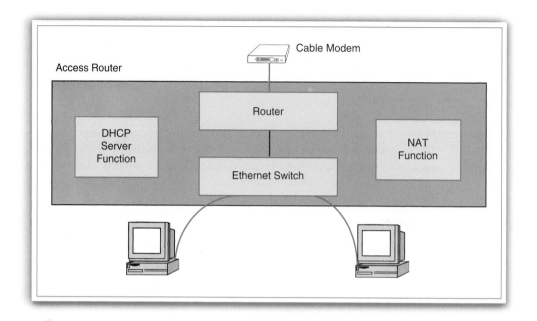

Figure 1a-8   Logical Functions of the Access Router

Each computer's NIC has an **Ethernet address**, as Figure 1a-9 illustrates. (This figure shows four computers instead of Pat's two to emphasize the generality of switching. Also, Pat's access router will have a 4-port Ethernet switch, so she will be able to add another two PCs if she wishes to do so.) As we saw in Chapter 1, a typical Ethernet address is something like A1-BD-33-6E-C7-BB. It has six two-character strings separated by dashes.

When the switch receives a frame addressed to one of these PCs, the switch looks up the Ethernet destination address in its switching table, which associates destination addresses with port numbers. It then sends the frame out of the port indicated for the destination address.

The Access Router's Router Function

Pat's home network will be a single network that follows the Ethernet standard. The telephone company's cable modem transmission line is another network. A router's job is to send packets (router messages are called packets) across different networks. Pat's router module in her access router will perform that essential router function, linking her home LAN to the Internet via her cable connection.

Routing is only one function of an access router.

The Access Router's DHCP Server

Each computer will need an Ethernet address, which is its address on its local network. It also will need an IP address, which is its address on the global Internet.

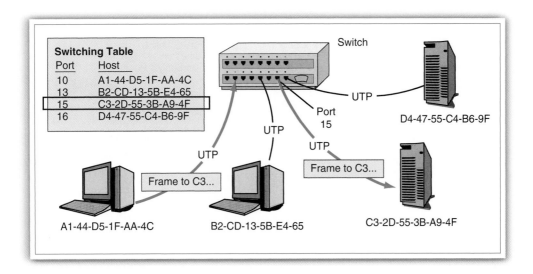

Figure 1a-9   Ethernet Switch Operation

Ethernet Addresses Are Assigned to NICs at the Factory

How does a computer get an Ethernet address? The answer is that every NIC that is sold has a unique Ethernet address assigned to it at the factory. Although this Ethernet address can be changed, users rarely do so.

IP Addresses

In Chapter 1, we saw that client PCs usually get their IP addresses automatically from DHCP servers. Internet service providers have DHCP servers, which provide a single IP address to each customer.

In Figure 1a-10, the IP address given to Pat Lee's house is 60.47.112.6. Pat's access router, however, will contain an internal DHCP server, which will give IP addresses to each of her internal PCs. In Figure 1a-10, Pat's access router's internal DHCP server gives her two PCs the internal addresses 192.168.0.2 and 192.168.0.3. The access router itself takes the internal IP address 192.168.0.1.[3]

The Access Router's Network Address Translation (NAT) Function

We have seen that Pat's ISP only gives her a single IP address and that her access router's DHCP server assigns each of her internal PCs an IP address—neither of which is the IP address assigned by the ISP.

---

[3]IP addresses beginning with 192.168 are private IP addresses that can only be used within private networks, such as Pat Lee's home network.

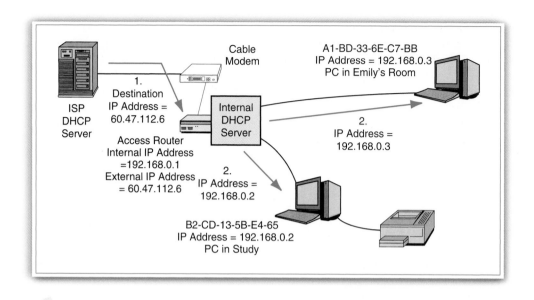

Figure 1a-10   Dynamic Host Configuration Protocol (DHCP)

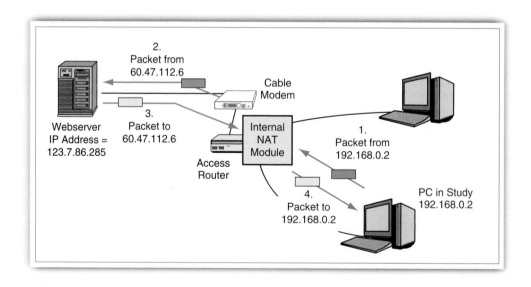

Figure 1a-11   Network Address Translation (NAT)

Figure 1a-11 shows that the access router will solve this problem by doing **network address translation (NAT)**. When internal host 192.168.0.2 sends a packet to a webserver, the access router's NAT module will capture the packet and replace 192.168.0.2 in the packet's source IP address field with 60.47.112.6—the IP address assigned by the ISP. The NAT function then sends the packet with source IP address 60.47.112.6 on to the ISP via the cable modem. The ISP will only accept packets from this source address.

When the server sends back an IP packet addressed to 60.47.112.6, the access router's NAT module will replace this destination IP address in the packet (60.47.112.6) with 192.168.0.2, then sends the packet on to the destination host.

TEST YOUR UNDERSTANDING

7. How does the switch decide which port to use to send the frame back out?

8. What will be the job of the router function in Pat's access router?

9. a) Who gives an Ethernet NIC its Ethernet address? b) How will Pat's home network get its single IP address? c) How will Pat's individual PCs get IP addresses? d) Why will NAT be needed in Pat's home network? e) How does NAT work?

ADDING WIRELESS TRANSMISSION

The Problem with Wires

Pat Lee installed the wired network shown in Figure 1a-1 and used it for several months. It worked well, but she ran into one nagging problem. The UTP patch cord running up to Emily's room had a tendency to trip people as they walked past Emily's room. In addition, the line running upstairs was unsightly. Something would have to be done about the ugly and foot-grabbing cord.

Things were brought to a head when Pat's family decided to move to a larger house. Pat decided to look into a different approach to networking technology. She decided to research wireless networking.

Figure 1a-12 shows the two potential networks that Pat Lee designed for her new house. The downstairs computer would be located in Pat's home office, while Emily's computer would still be in her room.

Access Router/Wireless Access Point Alternatives

For her access router, she had two choices, both of which are shown in Figure 1a-12. The first option is to keep her existing access router. She would then have to purchase a **wireless access point** and connect it via a short UTP patch cord to one of the Ethernet switch ports in her existing access router. The wireless access point will link wireless computers to the main Ethernet wired network via the access router.

The second option would be to purchase a new wireless access router, which would have all of the functions of Pat's original access router plus the functionality of a wireless access point. This would eliminate the need for a separate wireless access point.

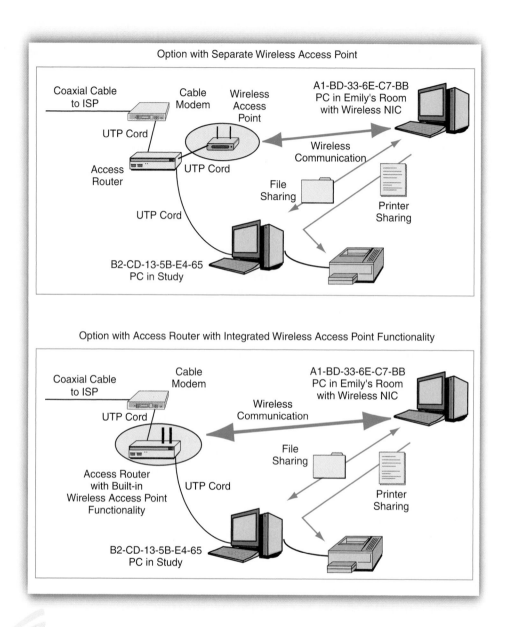

Figure 1a-12   Pat Lee's Wireless LAN

Wireless NICs

With either option for wireless transmission, Emily's computer would need a wireless NIC. As Figure 1a-13 shows, wireless NICs have antennas so that they can communicate with the wireless access point or with the access router's built-in wireless access point function.

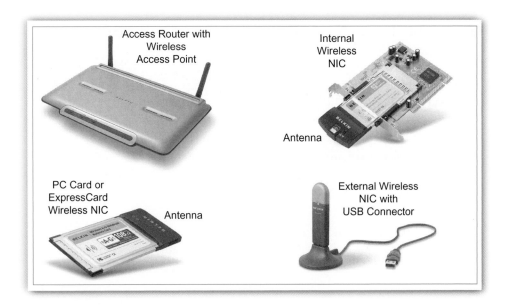

Figure 1a-13   Wireless NICs

The Downstairs PC

The access router in either case will be located in Pat Lee's office, only a few feet away from Pat's desktop computer. Consequently, there is no need to go to the expense of adding a wireless NIC to Pat's computer. She will still use UTP to connect her computer's existing wired Ethernet NIC to an RJ-45 port on the access router's Ethernet switch.

TEST YOUR UNDERSTANDING

10. a) For wireless transmission, what options did Pat Lee have for adding a wireless access point or wireless access point functionality? b) What did she have to add to Emily's computer? c) To the computer in her office?

REFLECTIONS ON PEER-TO-PEER NETWORKS VERSUS DEDICATED SERVERS

Peer-to-Peer Networks

In Pat Lee's home network, the client PCs provide services to one another. This is called **peer-to-peer service**.

Figure 1a-14   Peer-to-Peer Service Versus Dedicated Servers (Study Figure)

Peer-to-Peer Networks
>   Clients serving other clients
>
>   Inexpensive—no need to purchase a dedicated server
>
>   Operational problems for other users if a user PC is turned off or crashes
>
>   Poor security: No password or shared password for shared directories

Dedicated Servers
>   Servers that are not also used simultaneously as user PCs
>
>   Do not use standard client versions of Microsoft Windows (XP, and so forth)
>
>   They use special server operating systems
>>   Known for historical reasons as network operating systems (NOSs)
>>
>>   One popular NOS is Microsoft Windows (latest version is Windows Server 2003)
>>
>>   Another is Unix, which has versions for PCs (Linux, BSD, etc.)
>>
>>   NOSs are rich in functionality
>>
>>   They are designed to serve many users with many services
>>
>>   Have strong security
>
>   Unfortunately, they are very expensive
>
>   Installation requires specialized training
>
>   Make no sense for home use

Network Attached Storage (NAS) Units
>   Boxes cost $200 to $500
>
>   Contain a large shared hard drive
>
>   RJ-45 plugs allow the NAS to be connected to the switch in the access router via UTP
>
>   No mouse or keyboard; has a built-in webserver that can be managed remotely by a client PC
>
>   Do not lose availability when a user PC is turned off or crashes
>
>   Better security than PC file service
>
>   Backup is crucial

Inexpensive Networking

Peer-to-peer service makes sense for very small networks. It would be absurd, for example, for Pat Lee to spend $1,000 to purchase a third PC as a dedicated server to serve her two client PCs.

Operational Problems

However, as the number of PCs rises, operational problems inevitably begin to appear in peer-to-peer networks. To see why, suppose that a user turns off his or her PC or does something that causes the PC to crash. Then other users who rely on that PC's services will have their own applications crash, probably destroying any data currently being handled. Until the computer that crashed is rebooted, furthermore, nobody can use its services, including any shared data the other users might need to do their work. Given such operational problems, peer-to-peer service does not scale beyond about ten client PCs, and most analysts would set the cutoff point lower.

Poor Security

In addition, peer-to-peer security is poor. Often, shared directories are not even protected by passwords, and when they are, the passwords usually are shared by all users. Having no password is very dangerous if the user is connected to the Internet, especially if the home has an always-on high-speed connection, as Pat Lee's home does. Shared passwords may work in homes, but in businesses, not everybody should have equal access to every resource. Of course, you can reveal a directory's password to only some employees, but employees typically fail to keep shared passwords secret from unauthorized people "because everybody knows it, so it's not really a secret."

Dedicated Servers

Larger networks normally use dedicated servers, which are servers that are not also used simultaneously as user PCs. Servers do not use standard client versions of Microsoft Windows (XP, and so forth). Instead, they use special server operating systems, known for historical reasons as network operating systems (NOSs). One popular NOS is Microsoft Windows. The latest version of Windows is Windows Server 2003. Another popular operating system is Unix, including versions for PCs (Linux, BSD, and so forth).

NOSs are rich in functionality because they are designed to serve many users with many services and good security. However, rich functionality comes with a high price—both for purchasing the NOS and for learning how to use NOSs. Installing and using a dedicated server requires specialized training. For home use, it just does not make sense.

Network Attached Storage

One recent option is to purchase a **network attached storage (NAS)** unit. This is a box that costs between $200 and $500. It has a large hard drive that can be shared by multiple client PCs. It connects directly to the switch via UTP wire.

They have RJ-45 plugs that allow you to connect them to the Ethernet switch in your access router. They do not have a keyboard, mouse, or display. Instead, they have an internal webserver that allows you to manage them from one of your PCs.

NASs solve the operational problem of people turning off or crashing their PCs. Currently, NAS units for the home are early in their commercial development. They allow people to share files, but functionality and ease of use are still works in progress. As they mature, however, they probably will even offer enough functionality for use in small businesses.

NASs also have better security than simple peer-to-peer service. They provide more granular access control than peer PCs.

If you purchase a NAS, backup is absolutely critical because it contains so much of a family's or small business's data. If the NAS hard drive fails or if the NAS is stolen, the loss can be drastic. It is important to purchase a NAS with backup technology and to do backup very frequently.

TEST YOUR UNDERSTANDING

11. a) What is peer-to-peer service? b) What operational problems does it raise? c) What is the practical maximum number of user PCs for peer-to-peer networking? d) Why is peer-to-peer security usually poor? e) What is a dedicated server? f) What is a NOS? (Do not just spell it out.)

12. a) What is a NAS device? b) How is it connected to the network? c) What are its two advantages over peer-to-peer file sharing? d) Why is backup crucial for NASs?

CASE ANALYSIS

1. Cost out Pat Lee's original network on a spreadsheet. You can cut and paste the spreadsheet into your homework. For your analysis, have six columns:

   ➤ The general name of the component (access router, etc.)
   ➤ A manufacturer and product number (or other vendor designation) for a specific product
   ➤ Product details (e.g., for UTP, length)
   ➤ Unit price
   ➤ Number of units
   ➤ Item amount

   Give a final total purchase price. Do not include the cost of the cable modem. The cable modem typically is supplied by the cable operator as part of the service.

2. Repeat the cost analysis for the alternative in Figure 1a-12 that has an access router with an integrated access point.

Hands-On: Configuring Windows XP Home for Networking

Learning Objectives

By the end of this chapter, you should be able to discuss:

- The importance of Microsoft Windows XP Home.
- Setting up an Internet connection.
- Allowing peer-to-peer file sharing.
- Accessing shared files in the Shared Documents (SharedDocs) directory.
- Sharing additional directories.
- Making a printer available for peer-to-peer printing.
- Using a shared printer.

INTRODUCTION

In Chapter 1a, we looked at a small PC network in the home of Pat Lee, a vice president at the First Bank of Paradise. We saw that, with the major exception of using peer-to-peer service rather than dedicated servers, Pat Lee's home network is a microcosm of larger corporate networks.

In this chapter, we will look at how to configure a **Microsoft Windows XP Home** computer for home networking. XP Home is the dominant operating system today for residential PCs. It has all the functionality you need to set up a home network, including connecting to the Internet, peer-to-peer file sharing, and peer-to-peer printer sharing.

However, we will see that XP Home is limited to Simple File Sharing, which is easy to implement but offers no real security. **Microsoft Windows XP Professional** offers much better security, but it can only do this when it uses dedicated servers rather than peer-to-peer networking.

SETTING UP AN INTERNET CONNECTION

Initial Steps

The first step in setting up a Windows XP Home computer for home networking is to configure it to talk to the Internet. Figure 1b-1 shows the initial steps in doing this. These are the same initial steps needed for peer-to-peer file and printer sharing.

Hardware Installation

Before a computer can be configured for Internet communication, it needs to be physically connected to the Internet. Make sure that all hardware is connected properly, has electrical power, and is turned on.

The Start Button

Once the hardware is installed, hit the Start button. Choose *Control Panel*.

Control Panel

When the Control Panel appears, click on *Network and Internet Connections*.

Figure 1b-1   Initial Network Setup Process in Windows XP Home

---

0.
Install and Set Up Internet Connection Hardware

1.
Click on the Start Button
Choose "Control Panel"

2.
Control Panel
Click on "Network and Internet Connections"

3.
Network and Internet Connections
(Figure 1a-2)
Choices are:
"Set up or change your Internet Connection" [to set up or change an Internet connection]
"Create a connection to the network at your workplace" [for a virtual private network connection]
"Set up or change your home or small office network" [for file and printer sharing]

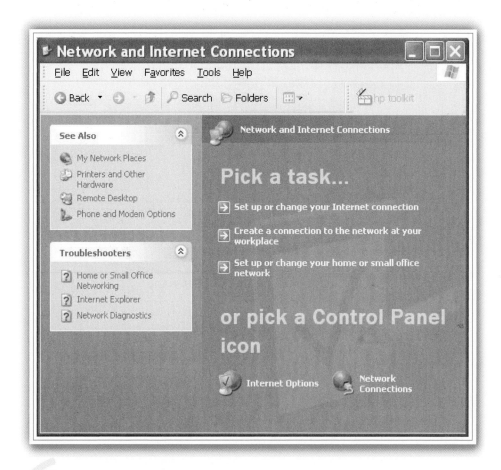

Figure 1b-2   Network and Internet Connections Dialog Box
in Windows XP Home

Network and Internet Connections Dialog Box

In the *Network and Internet Connections* dialog box, you will have three options, as shown
in Figure 1b-2.

> ➤ *Set up or change your Internet connection.* Choose this one.
> ➤ *Create a connection to the network at your workplace.* This is for setting up a virtual private
>   network (VPN). We will see VPNs in Chapter 7.
> ➤ *Set up or change your home or small office network.* We will return to this option later,
>   when we discuss setting up peer-to-peer file sharing.

Next Steps

Figure 1b-3 shows the remaining steps needed to set up an Internet connection.

```
1.
Internet Properties
Select the Connections tab
Click on "Setup"

2.
New Connection Wizard
Welcome to the New Connection Wizard
Click on "Next"

3.
New Connection Wizard
Network Connection Type
Select "Connect to the Internet"

4.
New Connection Wizard
Getting Ready
Options:
Choose from a list of Internet service providers (ISPs)
Set up my connection manually [Select this option]
Use the CD I got from an ISP

5.
New Connection Wizard
Internet Connection
Options:
Connect using a dial-up modem
Connect using a broadband connection that requires a user name and password [PPPoE]
Connect using a broadband connection that is always on [Choose this option]

6.
New Connection Wizard
Completing the New Connection Wizard
Click on "Finish"
```

Figure 1b-3   Setting Up an Internet Connection in Windows XP Home

Internet Properties

Selecting *Set up or change your Internet connection* will take you to the *Internet Properties* dialog box. When this dialog box is displayed, select the *Connections* tab if it is not selected. Click on *Setup* to set up your connection.

New Connection Wizard: Welcome to the New Connection Wizard

Now you begin working with the New Connection Wizard. At the Welcome screen, choose *Next* to get started.

New Connection Wizard: Network Connection Type

Select *Connect to the Internet*.

New Connection Wizard: Getting Ready

This dialog box gives you three options:

➤ *Choose from a list of Internet service providers.* You can choose this option if you do not already have an ISP.

➤ *Set up my connection manually.* This is the option we will follow.

➤ *Use the CD I got from an ISP.* Sometimes your ISP gives you a setup disk. If it does, use it.

New Connection Wizard: Internet Connection

This dialog box asks you to specify how you connect to the Internet.

➤ *Connect using a dial-up modem.* Select this option if you have a dial-up modem. You will be asked a number of modem-specific questions.

➤ *Connect using a broadband connection that requires a user name and password.* As soon as some people see the words *broadband connection,* they select this option. However, few broadband vendors use this approach. (Those that do use something called PPPoE—Point-to-Point Protocol over Ethernet.) PPPoE requires the users to log in each time they connect to the Internet.

➤ *Connect using a broadband connection that is always on.* This is the normal option for broadband connections. The provider knows where you are physically, so there is no need for you to log in. This is the option we will follow.

New Connection Wizard: Completing the New Connection Wizard

Click on *Finish.* The process of implementing your choices may take a few seconds.

ALLOWING PEER-TO-PEER DIRECTORY AND FILE SHARING

Now that the computer is connected to the Internet, the computer's owner may wish to share directories and files with others on the same SOHO (small office or home office) network. To allow peer-to-peer directory and file sharing, go through the initial steps in Figure 1b-1. In the last step, select *Set up or change your home or small office network.* This initiates the Network Setup Wizard, which is illustrated in Figure 1b-4.

Network Setup Wizard: Welcome to the Network Setup Wizard

Click on *Next* to continue.

Network Setup Wizard: Before You Begin

This dialog box has a checklist for your hardware. Go through it to be sure your hardware is set up correctly. Then click on *Next.*

Network Setup Wizard: Select a Connection Method

This option requires you to know that there are two basic ways to connect multiple computers to the Internet. Figure 1b-5 illustrates both.

Figure 1b-4   Setting up File and Folder Sharing on a Computer with Windows XP Home

4.
Network Setup Wizard
Welcome to the New Connection Wizard
Click on "Next"

5.
Network Setup Wizard
Before you continue...
Go through the checklist, click on "Next"

6.
Network Setup Wizard
Select a connection method
(Figure 1a-5)
Options:

This computer connects directly to the Internet. The other computers on my network connect to the Internet through this computer.

This computer connects to the Internet through another computer on my network or through a residential gateway *[Choose this option]*

Other

7.
New Setup Wizard
Your computer has multiple connections
If this appears, choose:
Determine the appropriate connections for me (Recommended)

8.
Network Setup Wizard
Give this computer a description and name
(Figure 1a-6)
Type a name and description for the computer
This is what other computers on the network will see when they access it.

9.
Network Setup Wizard
Name your network
(Figure 1a-7)
Type a workgroup name.
All computers on the network must have the same workgroup name.
Giving computers the same workgroup name creates a network.

10.
Network Setup Wizard
Ready to apply network settings
Select "Next." This may take some time.

11.
Network Setup Wizard
Finish

Figure 1b-5   Access Router (Gateway) Versus Internet Connection Sharing in Windows XP Home

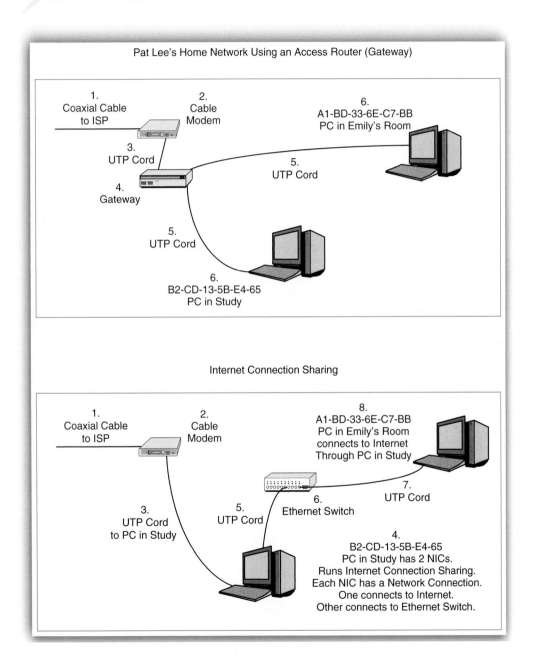

Using a Gateway (Access Router)

One option is to use a **gateway**, which is an obsolete term for *router* that Microsoft stubbornly continues to use. Some firms that sell access routers now call them gateways to be consistent with Microsoft terminology. Using a gateway is how Pat Lee's home network is implemented, as Figure 1b-5 shows. Access routers provide a good deal of security against attacks simply by implementing NAT.

Internet Connection Sharing (ICS)

Microsoft Windows XP also offers an **Internet connection sharing (ICS)** option, which also is illustrated in Figure 1b-5. Here one PC has two NICs. One NIC connects to a modem for Internet access. The other NIC connects to a desktop Ethernet switch, which connects to other PCs. ICS software on the PC connected directly to the Internet enables it to act as an access router.

Although ICS saves some money because access routers (gateways) are more expensive than desktop Ethernet switches, the saving is small. On the negative side, if the PC implementing ICS crashes or is turned off, all computers lose Internet access. In addition, ICS is a little complex to set up well. Without the access router for NAT security, it is important to implement a firewall on the PC implementing ICS. (Windows XP home has a built-in firewall discussed in Chapter 9a.) However, implementing a firewall on other computers can interfere with ICS operation.

Actually, ICS is only economical if a network has exactly *two* computers. In this case, there is no need for a switch. The second NIC on the computer connected directly to the Internet can be connected directly to the NIC in the other computer with a UTP **crossover cable**. NICs transmit on Pins 1 and 2 and listen on Pins 3 and 6. Connecting the two NICs with an ordinary UTP cord would mean that both would talk but neither would listen—not the recipe for a good relationship in technology (or the human realm either). A crossover cable connects Pins 1 and 2 on one computer to Pins 3 and 6 on the other computer, allowing communication.

Network Setup Wizard: Your Computer Has Multiple Connections

If your computer has multiple connections to the Internet, you see this dialog box: *Your computer has multiple connections.* If you see this dialog box, select *Determine the appropriate connections for me (Recommended).*

Network Setup Wizard: Give This Computer a Description and Name

This dialog box, which is shown a Figure 1b-6 is self-descriptive, but the figure is included to emphasize its importance. The name and associated description that you enter is how others on the network will see your computer.

New Connection Wizard: Name Your Network

The *Name Your Network* dialog box, which is illustrated in Figure 1b-7, is confusing to many users and is perhaps the biggest reason for failed file and directory sharing.

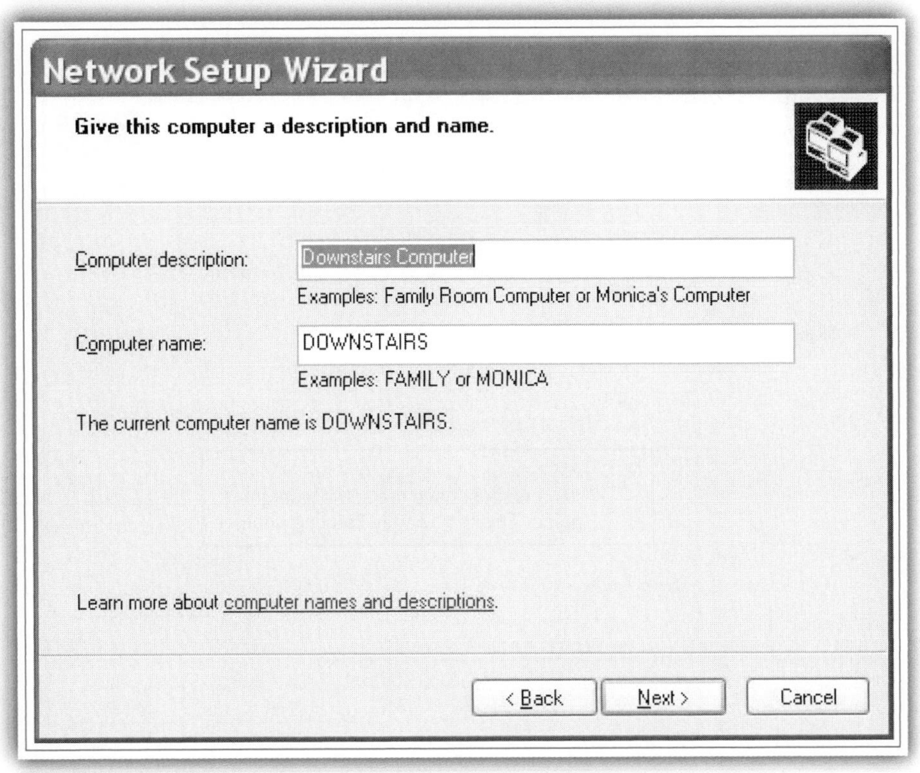

Figure 1b-6   Give This Computer a Description and Name

Although the dialog box does not make it clear, a network in Windows is a group of computers sharing the same **workgroup name**. The workgroup name is how computers find one another on a network. Giving several computers the same workgroup name automatically creates a **workgroup** (logical network).

Requiring all computers to have the same workgroup name seems silly in Pat Lee's home, where the physical network serves only a single logical network (group of users). However, in large corporate LANs, there may be several workgroups (logical groups of users) sharing the same physical network. They will be distinguished by their different workgroup names. However, given the poor security of Windows file and print sharing, many firms have forbidden the use of peer-to-peer networks on corporate LANs.

Network Setup Wizard: Ready to Apply Network Settings

Now the computer is ready to apply the network settings you have just specified. Select *Next*. Now wait. As the dialog box says, this may take some time to do. Do not interrupt the process.

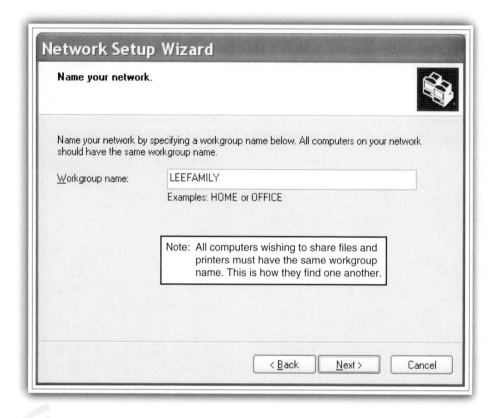

Figure 1b-7   Name Your Network

Network Setup Wizard: Finish

Your computer is set up for directory and file sharing. Select *Finish*.

ACCESSING SHARED FILES

Process

Once the computers on the network are set up for file sharing, users can access files on other computers. Figure 1b-8 shows how this is done. The process is dead simple.

First, click on the *Start* button. Then select *My Network Places*. A dialog box will appear showing which directories you can share on various computers. Figure 1b-9 shows this dialog box. It shows that **SharedDocs** (the **Shared Documents folder**) is available for sharing on both computers.

Shared Documents (SharedDocs)

By default, Windows XP only shares a single directory on each computer. This is the **Shared Documents (SharedDocs)** directory. (In older versions of Windows, *no* directory was shared by default.)

```
                              1.
                            Start
                   Choose My Network Places

                              2.
                    My Network Places
                       (Figure 1a-9)
                    Select a Directory
     Initially, only the Shared Directory (SharedDocs) is shared on each computer
        Files copied into the Shared Directory will be sharable over the network
  Files copied from the Shared Directory to other directories will not be sharable over the network
```

Figure 1b-8   Using a Shared Directory via a Network

Making Files Available for Sharing

To share a document on the network, a user can copy or move the document from one of his or her other directories (which cannot be seen over the network) into his or her Shared Documents directory. This makes the file available to other computers in the workgroup.

Saving to the Shared Document Directories on Other Computers

Other computers also can change files on the Shared Documents directory and can also save their own files to this directory.

Making Files Unavailable for Sharing

If someone else on the network writes a file into a user's Shared Documents directory, in turn, anyone in the workgroup can see it. To remove it from access by other computers on the network, the user can move it into another directory. This makes it invisible to the network.

Weak Security in Simple File Sharing

Note that there is only very weak security on files in Shared Documents folders. There is not even a simple password. Everyone in the workgroup can read them and even modify them. The only security is that people must know the workgroup names to read and change files, but this typically is easy to do. This weak security is called **Simple File Sharing**. Although Simple File Sharing is an option with Windows XP Professional, it is the only way to share files with Windows XP home.

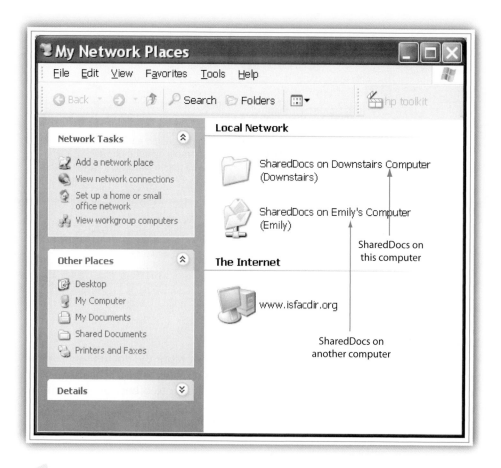

Figure 1b-9   My Network Places in Windows XP Home

SHARING ADDITIONAL DIRECTORIES

Simple File Sharing does allow additional directories besides Shared Documents to be shared. Figure 1b-10 shows how to share an additional directory besides Shared Documents.

Run the Network Setup Wizard

This process will only work after you have run the Network Setup Wizard, as described in an earlier section.

Select Another Directory You Wish to Share

Go to *My Computer* and find the directory you wish to share. Select it by right-clicking your mouse, and then select *Sharing and Security*.

0.
Run the Network Setup Wizard
The Shared Documents directory will be shared automatically

1.
Select Another Directory You Want to Share
Find it through My Computer
Right-click on the directory.
Select "Sharing and Security"

2.
In the Directory's Properties Dialog Box
Select the Sharing Tab.
(Figure 1a-11)
Under network sharing and security,
Click on "Share this folder on the network"

Enter a Share name

Click on "Allow network users to change my files" if desirable

---

Figure 1b-10   Sharing an Additional Directory in Windows XP Home

In the Directory's Properties Dialog Box

Once a directory is selected, everything else can be done from the directory's Properties dialog box. Figure 1b-11 shows the Properties dialog box for the My Music directory.

➤ Right-click on the directory to bring up its *Properties* dialog box.
➤ Select the *Sharing* tab.
➤ Under *Network Sharing and Security*, click on *Share this folder on the network*. Unless this is done, the folder will not be sharable.
➤ Enter a "share name" by which other computers will see this directory. (In Microsoft-speak, a **share** is something that is shared—usually a directory or a printer.)
➤ Check on *Allow network users to change my files* box if desirable. If you do not check this box, others will have only read-only access.

Still No Security

Although this approach allows directories to be made "read only," there still is no password or other security measure. Simple File Sharing, even when it is added to directories other than Shared Documents, is a security nightmare.

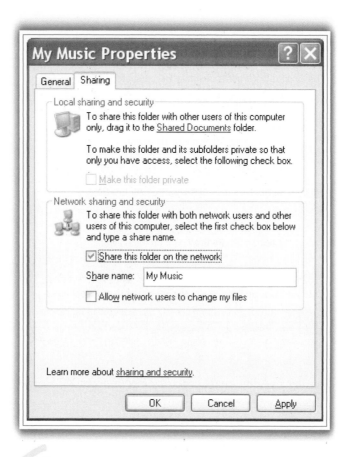

Figure 1b-11   My Music Properties Dialog Box
Sharing Tab in Windows XP Home

SHARING PRINTERS

Making a Printer Available for Sharing

Many users would also like to share printers. In Pat Lee's home network, for instance, the downstairs printer must be shared by Emily's computer in her bedroom. Figure 1b-12 shows how to share a printer.

Physically Set Up the Printer, Connect It to the Computer, and Turn It On

These initial steps seems obvious, but most problems in printer sharing configuration occur because the computer cannot "see" a printer that is powered off or not connected to the computer.

0.
Physically set up the printer, connect it to the computer, and turn it on

1.
Click on the Start Button
Choose "Printers and Faxes"

2.
Printers and Faxes
Click on the printer you wish to share.
In the Printer Tasks pane to the left,
Choose "Share this printer."

3.
Properties
(Figure 1a-13)
Select the Sharing tab
Click the "Share this printer" radio button
If other machines run diferent versions of Windows, you may need to install additional drivers.
Click on "OK"

Figure 1b-12   Sharing a Printer

Click on the Start Button

Click on the *Start* button and select *Printers and Faxes*.

Printers and Faxes

Click on the printer connected to your computer that you wish to share. In the left Printer Tasks pane, select *Share this printer*. Click on *OK*.

Printer Properties Dialog Box

This will take you to the printer's *Properties* dialog box (shown as Figure 1b-13). Click on the *Share this printer* radio button, and give the computer a share name by which other computers will know it.

When you install a printer on an XP computer, you install printer driver software that is specific to Windows XP. If other computers run older versions of Windows, you may have to install additional printer drivers for them. In the printer's dialog box, click on *Additional Drivers . . .* to install drivers for older versions of Windows.

Using a Shared Printer

Figure 1b-14 shows the steps a computer user (in the Pat Lee case study, Emily) would take to use a printer that someone else has made available for sharing.

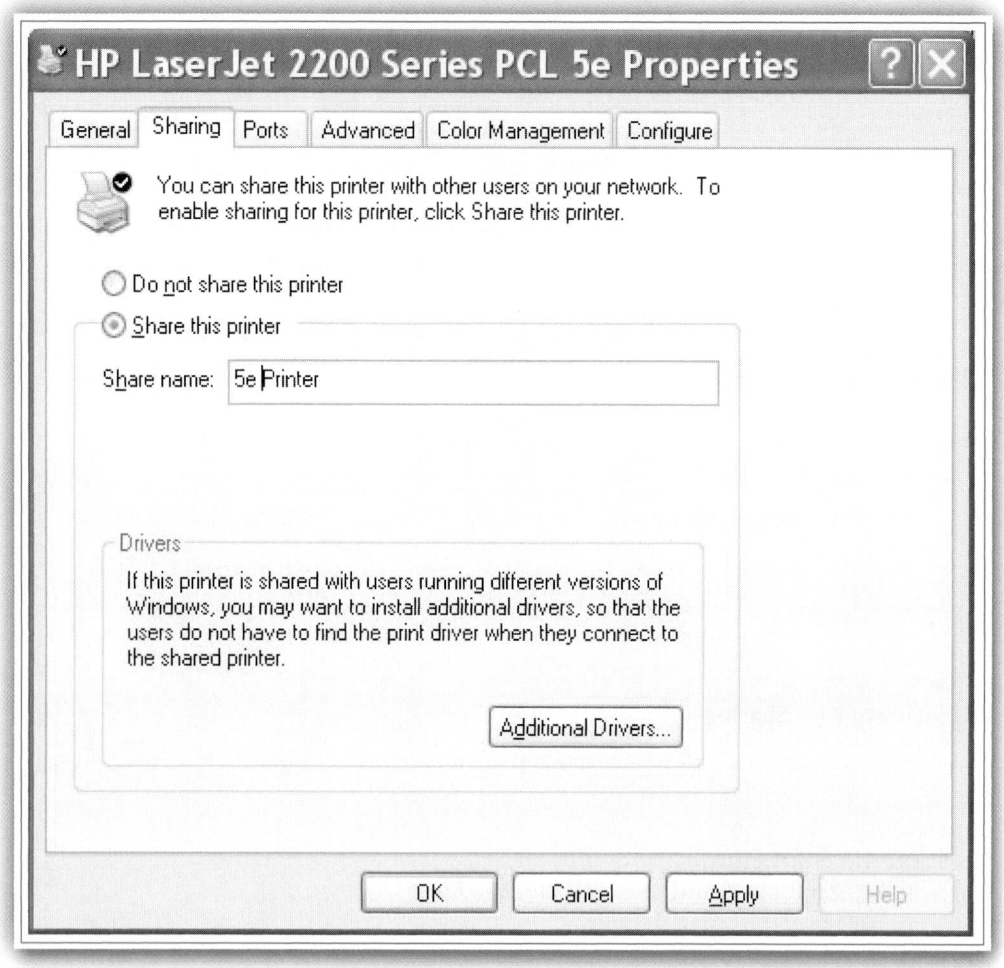

Figure 1b-13   Printer Properties Dialog Box / Sharing Tab in Windows XP Home

Printers and Faxes

To begin, hit the *Start* button. Then select *Printers and Faxes*. This will take you to the *Printers and Faxes* dialog box. In this dialog box, select *Add a printer*. This will start the Add Printer Wizard.

Add Printer Wizard: Welcome to the Add Printer Wizard

At the initial Add Printer Wizard dialog box, select *Next*.

Add Printer Wizard: Local or Network Printer

The next dialog box asks you if you will be adding a local or network printer. Select *A network printer, or a printer attached to another computer*. This indicates that you

1.
Start
Select "Printers and Faxes"

2.
Printers and Faxes
Choose "Add a Printer"

3.
Add Printer Wizard
Welcome to the Add Printer Wizard
Select "Next"

4.
Add Printer Wizard
Local or Network Printer
Click on "A network printer, or a printer attached to another computer"
Click on "Next"

5.
Add Printer Wizard
Specify a Printer
Select "Browse for a printer"
Click on "Next"

6.
Add Printer Wizard
Browse for a Printer
Select the printer you wish to use
Click on "Next"

...
Remaining steps are printer-specific.
You will be asked if you want to make the selected printer your default printer.

Figure 1b-14   Using a Shared Printer

want to use a computer that someone else has made available for sharing. Now click on *Next*.

Add Printer Wizard: Specify a Printer
At the *Specify a Printer* dialog box, select *Browse for a printer*. Then click on *Next*.

Add Printer Wizard: Browse for a Printer
At the next dialog box, browse *for the printer* you wish to use from a list of printers available on the network. After selecting the printer you want to use, click on *Next*.

Remaining Steps

The remaining steps are printer-specific but normally ask if you wish to make the selected printer your **default printer**—the printer to which your print jobs will be sent unless you specify a different printer.

TEST YOUR UNDERSTANDING

1. Which offers better security—Windows XP Home or Windows XP Professional?

2. a) What link in the Control Panel is used for many networking configuration actions? b) Explain the three options in the Network and Internet Connections dialog box.

3. a) What are "gateways" commonly called? b) How is Internet Connection Sharing less expensive than using an access router? c) Why is Internet Connection Sharing undesirable? d) When is a crossover UTP cord needed?

4. Explain why the workgroup name is important.

5. What is a *share* in Microsoft Windows XP Home?

6. a) When you set up a Windows XP Home PC to allow it to share directories and files, what directory or directories is/are available for sharing by default with Windows XP Home? b) In earlier versions of Windows? c) Using the default, how can you make files available for sharing? d) Can additional directories be made available for sharing? e) Can passwords be required for directory access with Windows XP Home? f) Can directories other than Shared Documents be made read-only?

7. How does a computer user see what files are available over the network?

8. If you want to print a particular document to a printer attached to another computer, what must have already been done?

Case Study: XTR Consulting: A SOHO Network with Dedicated Servers

Learning Objectives

By the end of this chapter, you should be able to discuss:

- Networks with dedicated servers.
- Peer-to-peer service versus the use of dedicated servers.
- (In a box) Server technology.
- XTR: The initial situation.
- A broad network design for XTR.
- Your detailed design for XTR.

INTRODUCTION

If you studied the Pat Lee case in Chapter 1a, you know how to set up a home network. If you studied Chapter 1b, you also know how to set up client PC software on a home network.

In this chapter, you will consider a network for XTR Consulting (name changed for confidentiality), which is a small environmental consulting company with sixteen professionals (including managers), plus a secretary. The company has an office suite in a large downtown office building. This is a SOHO (small office or home office)

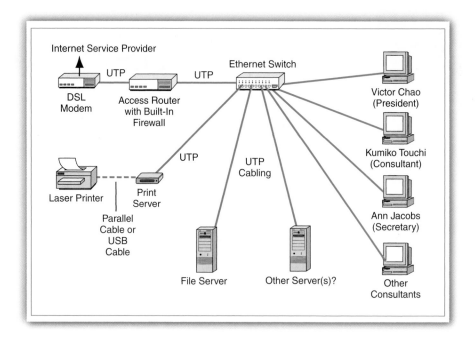

Figure 1c-1   XTR Consulting's Network

environment. The company is planning to build a LAN. It will be quite different from the large networks we will see in later chapters.

As Figure 1c-1 shows, this LAN also will be different from the small home LAN we saw in Pat Lee's house. Among these differences are the following:

➤ Most importantly, user PCs in Pat Lee's home act as servers for one another, providing both file sharing and printer sharing services. In the XTR network, however, there will be one or more **dedicated servers**—servers that do not act simultaneously as user PCs. In addition to being expensive to buy, dedicated servers require special skills to manage.

➤ Server administration is called **systems administration**. In small LANs with dedicated servers, systems administration takes far more work than the management of the rest of the network. In a small network, systems administration is the biggest part of ongoing networking costs. (In large networks, in contrast, networking and systems administration are separate functions.)

➤ In addition, the XTR network uses small electronic devices called print servers to feed printer output to shared printers. Thanks to print servers, shared printers no longer have to be attached to PCs, which may crash or be turned off accidentally.

➤ Finally, the functions of the Ethernet switch and router, which were combined in Pat Lee's inexpensive access router, are separated in the XTR network and are handled by a large Ethernet switch and by a separate access router. This access router will be more expensive than Pat Lee's because the XTR access router will have a built-in firewall function.

	Pat Lee's Home Network	XTR Consulting's Small Office Network
Number of Client PCs	2 PCs	17 user PCs (16 professionals and one secretary)
File Service	Peer-to-Peer	Dedicated Server Systems Administration
Print Service	Peer-to-Peer	Print Servers
Access Router and Ethernet Switch	Combined	Separate Boxes Access Router Has Firewall

Figure 1c-2   XTR Consulting's Network Versus Pat Lee's Network (Study Figure)

A dedicated server is a server that does not act simultaneously as a user PC.

In this chapter, you will learn about the XTR company and its needs. You will be told about an existing broad design for the XTR network. You will then create a detailed design for the network. Afterward, you will calculate the initial cost of the network. However, you will *not* have to calculate the annual ongoing cost for the network.

TEST YOUR UNDERSTANDING

1. a) What is a dedicated server? b) What is systems administration? c) How will XTR's network technology differ from Pat Lee's home network technology?

PEER-TO-PEER SERVICE

In Pat Lee's home network, the client PCs provide services to one another. This is called **peer-to-peer service**.

Inexpensive Networking

Peer-to-peer service makes sense for very small networks. It would be absurd, for example, for Pat Lee to spend $1,000 to purchase a third PC as a dedicated server to serve her two existing PCs.

Operational Problems

However, as the number of PCs rises, operational problems inevitably begin to appear in peer-to-peer networks. To see why, suppose that a user turns off his or her PC or does something that causes it to crash. Then other users who rely on that PC's services

Peer-to-Peer Service

    Clients serve other clients

    Inexpensive—no need to purchase a dedicated server

    Operational problems for other users if a user PC is turned off or crashes

    Poor security: No password or shared password for shared directories

Dedicated Servers

    Dedicated servers provide services while not being used simultaneously as client PCs

    Normally called, simply, servers

    Benefits

        Users do not accidentally crash the server or turn it off

        Strong security

        File server program access: install application programs once, on the server

            Users can use these programs from their client PCs

            Firm must buy multiuser licenses for sharable application programs

    Cost Concerns include:

        Servers must be purchased

        Hardware and operating system are more expensive than those of client PCs

        Systems administration is the management of one or more servers

        System administrators are called sys admins

        Systems administration labor costs to install and maintain a server are expensive

Figure 1c-3   Peer-to-Peer Service Versus Dedicated Servers (Study Figure)

may have their own applications crash, probably losing all data currently being handled. Until the computer that crashed is rebooted, furthermore, no other users can use its services, including any shared data they might need to do their work. Given such operational problems, peer-to-peer service does not scale (grow efficiently) beyond about ten client PCs,[1] and most analysts would set the cut-off point lower.

---

[1]Certification exams usually set the limit for peer-to-peer network size at about ten PCs. However, it tends to be suicide beyond three or four PCs.

Poor Security

In addition, peer-to-peer security is poor. Often, shared directories are not even protected by passwords, and when they are, the passwords usually are shared by all users. Having no password is very dangerous if the user is connected to the Internet, especially if the home has an always-on high-speed Internet connection, as Pat Lee's home does. Shared passwords might work in homes, but in businesses, not everybody should have equal access to every resource. Of course, you can reveal a directory's password to only some employees, but employees often fail to keep shared passwords secret "because everybody knows it."

TEST YOUR UNDERSTANDING

2. a) What is peer-to-peer service? b) What operational problems does it create? c) What is the practical maximum number of client PCs for peer-to-peer networking? d) Why is peer-to-peer security usually poor?

DEDICATED SERVERS

Given the limitations of peer-to-peer service, companies that have more than a few PCs use dedicated servers. Almost all servers in corporations are dedicated servers, so they are simply called **servers**.

Benefits and Problems

The benefits and problems of dedicated servers are largely the opposite of the benefits and problems of peer-to-peer services.

Lack of Operational Problems

A major benefit of dedicated servers is the very fact that they are not used simultaneously as client PCs. Consequently, individual users rarely can crash or accidentally turn off servers.

Good Security

While peer-to-peer service has very poor security, servers have excellent security. Different access permissions can be given to each individual employee for each file in each directory. In addition, servers have audit trails that allow the systems administrator to check on what individual users have done if misbehavior is suspected.

Managing Application Programs on the Server

Servers also offer more functionality than peer-to-peer service can provide. Most importantly, the systems administration can install application programs such as Microsoft Office once on the server and make them available to users without having to install software on their individual PCs. This greatly reduces the work of installing applications software and installing subsequent upgrades.

To manage application software on a server, the organization cannot simply buy a single-user program and share it. They must purchase a multiuser version of the application at considerably higher cost. However, the total cost of the software, installation, and update labor is much lower when software is installed and maintained only on the central server than it would be if the company had to buy software for each employee's individual computer.

High Cost

The main problem with servers is cost. Peer-to-peer service is inexpensive because one does not have to purchase extra computers to act as servers. Of course, servers are exactly the extra computers that peer-to-peer service was created to avoid. In fact, because servers often must serve many users, a dedicated server tends to be substantially more expensive than a client PC.

In addition to purchase costs, servers have high ongoing labor costs. As noted earlier, in small LANs with dedicated servers, systems administration is far more work than the management of the rest of the network.

TEST YOUR UNDERSTANDING

3. a) Why are dedicated servers also called, simply, servers? b) What are the advantages of using servers? c) What are the disadvantages?

Server Technology

SERVER HARDWARE

Dedicated servers tend to be much more powerful than client PCs. There are three common types of dedicated servers: PC servers, workstation servers, and mainframe computers.

PC Servers and Network Operating Systems (NOSs)

The first type of server, the **PC server**, is an ordinary computer that follows the standard Windows or Macintosh hardware architecture. Many are designed from the ground up to be servers; compared to client PCs, PC servers typically have a great deal of RAM, very large and fast hard disk drives, and redundant power supplies and fans. Some have multiple microprocessors to increase their processing power. Computers with multiple microprocessors are called **multiprocessing computers**. Having a

backup system capable of backing up the server nightly is mandatory.

Dedicated PC servers cannot use ordinary client PC operating systems, such as Microsoft Windows 98, ME, 2000 Professional, or Windows XP Home. These client-based operating systems do not have the functionality or (usually) the reliability needed for dedicated servers. Dedicated PC servers use different operating systems, called network operating systems (NOSs). Popular PC server NOSs include Microsoft Windows Server, Linux, and Novell NetWare.

Workstation Servers and Unix

Specialized Multiprocessors Windows PCs use ordinary Intel or compatible mass-market microprocessors. Another type of server, the **workstation server**, uses custom-designed microprocessors. These microprocessors are

PC Servers and Network Operating Systems (NOSs)
>   Standard PC architectures with more RAM, large and fast hard disk drives, redundant power supplies and fans, and multiple processors (multiprocessing)
>
>   Network operating systems are server operating systems that have more functions and reliability than client operating systems

Workstation Servers
>   Fast (and expensive) custom microprocessors for an expensive computer
>
>   Run the Unix operating system
>
>>   Extremely reliable
>>
>>   Difficult to learn and use
>>
>>   Not standardized

Mainframe Servers
>   Faster, more reliable, and more expensive than workstation servers
>
>   Require a large systems programming staff

Figure 1c-4   Server Technology (Study Figure)

faster than popular microprocessors but also much more expensive because of the need to push the state of the art in microprocessor design and because of the limited number of these microprocessors that are sold. Basically, workstation servers are like racing cars in both performance and price.

Unix Workstation servers run vendor-specific versions of the **Unix** operating system. Unix is extremely reliable. In addition, Unix has a rich toolbox of management applications. Unix on a high-speed workstation server is the platform of choice for large enterprise servers such as public webservers.

However, Unix workstation servers would not make sense for XTR's small network. Most important, this small network will not need the high-power (or the high prices) of workstation servers.

Also, Unix is very difficult to learn and use because server administrators often have to type complex commands such as those you saw in Chapter 1 if you did the hands-on exercises that took you to the Windows command line. Although Unix vendors offer graphical user interfaces similar to that of Microsoft Windows, the functionality of these interfaces tends to be limited, so Unix administrators constantly have to drop down to the command line to give commands.

In addition, Unix is not a standardized operating system. Each vendor's version of Unix has proprietary (vendor-specific) features. Most

(continued)

	Microsoft Windows Server	Linux
Ease of Learning	Very Good	Poor
Ease of Use	Very Good	Poor
Availability of Consultants	Excellent	Modest
Reliability	Very Good in the Most Recent Versions	Excellent
Standardization	Excellent	Poor (Many Distributions)
Availability of Device Drivers	Excellent	Poor
Price	Moderate	Low or Free

Figure 1c-5   Popular PC Server Network Operating Systems (NOSs)

application programs written for Unix will run on most versions of Unix, but vendors vary widely in the management utilities they offer. Consequently, most companies tend to use only one or two versions of Unix to minimize relearning.

Mainframe Servers

The last major dedicated server technology is the **mainframe computer**, which is much more powerful than a workstation server. In addition, mainframes are even more reliable than Unix workstation servers. However, mainframe power is more expensive than a comparable amount of workstation server power because mainframe hardware is expensive and because a mainframe requires a large staff of systems programmers to keep it functioning. Large organizations such as banks typically implement their major transaction processing systems on mainframes.

XTR Consulting: PC Servers

For its dedicated server or servers, XTR Consulting will go with the PC server option. A PC server or a few PC servers will be adequate for XTR's needs and will be far less expensive than a workstation server or a mainframe computer.

TEST YOUR UNDERSTANDING

4. a) List the major server technologies in terms of increasing power and price. b) What is a NOS for a PC server? c) Distinguish between PC servers and workstation servers in terms of hardware and operating systems. d) Why will XTR Consulting use PC server technology?

NETWORK OPERATING SYSTEMS (NOSS) FOR PC SERVERS

PC server operating systems, for historical reasons, are called **network operating systems (NOSs)**. For PCs, there are three popular network operating systems: Linux, Novell NetWare, and server versions of Microsoft Windows.

Figure 1c-5 compares these network operating systems.

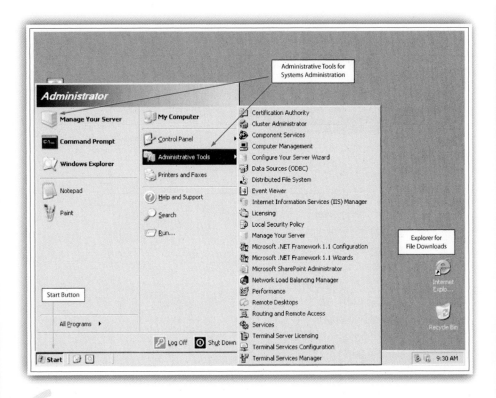

Figure 1c-6   Microsoft Windows 2003 Server User Interface

Microsoft Windows Server

For small businesses, the best choice usually is **Microsoft Windows Server**, which comes in three versions: NT, 2000, and 2003.

Ease of Learning and Operation Windows Server is the most popular NOS because it is the simplest NOS to learn and operate. As Figure 1c-6 shows, Windows Server 2003 looks almost exactly like client versions of Windows. In fact, server versions will execute ordinary client Windows application programs in client mode if this is required.

As the figure shows, most network management functions are located through the *Start* button in the *Administrative Tools* program group. In addition, most Windows management tools have similar user interfaces called **Microsoft Management Consoles (MMCs).** An MMC is shown in Figure 1c-7.

Reliability Early versions of Windows Server, through NT, had poor reliability. Newer versions have made Windows Server sufficiently reliable for departmental and small-business

---

[2]Linus Torvalds, who created the Linux kernel as an undergraduate student in Finland, pronounces Linux as "LEE-nucks." In English, it usually is pronounced with a short *i*, "LIH-nucks" (with a stress on the first syllable).

(continued)

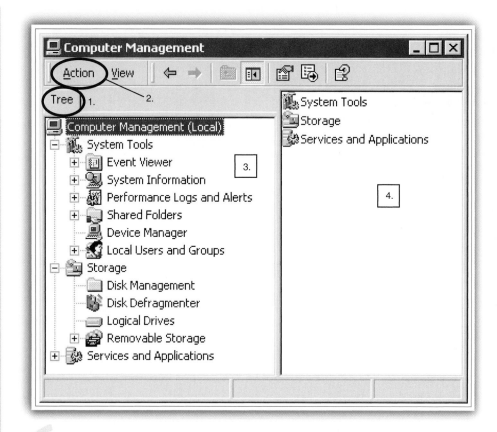

Figure 1c-7   Microsoft Management Console (MMC)

needs, although for central corporate servers, Unix still is the gold standard for reliability.

Linux

Linux was created as a freeware version of Unix.[2] Unlike most versions of Unix, which run on workstation servers, Linux is one of a handful of Unix variants that run on standard PCs.

Cost   A principle attraction of Linux is its cost. It can be downloaded for free, although boxed server versions with instructions and phone-in support tend to cost $200 or more. Even if an expensive boxed version is purchased, the disks inside the box can be used to install Linux on multiple servers, again bringing down the cost.

Also, because the Linux kernel is highly efficient, Linux can run on a smaller computer than Windows Server can for a comparable workload. This further contains costs.

Reliability   Another benefit is that Linux has the legendary reliability of Unix. Linux rarely crashes.

Diversity and Configuration Problems   When you buy Microsoft Windows Server, you know what you are getting. However, Linux really is only an operating system kernel. What you actually buy or download for free is a **Linux distribution** consisting of the Linux kernel plus a collection of many other programs. These other programs usually are taken from the GNU project, which produces open-source software to run on Unix kernels. Different distributions contain different GNU and non-GNU programs, causing endless confusion. For example, Linux offers two competing graphical user interfaces as well as a command-line language.

In addition, configuring Linux to run on a server can be very difficult. Often, there is no device driver for a particular NIC, or you may have to compile a device driver from source code.

Linux Overall   For small businesses, the low cost of Linux may be a false saving because of the learning, configuration, and maintenance headaches the business will have to face. This may change as Linux matures.

Not for XTR Consulting   XTR does not have a trained systems administrator to run its dedicated server or servers. However, everyone at XTR is familiar with Microsoft Windows. Under these circumstances, it will be much easier to train someone to do day-to-day systems administration with Windows Server than with Unix. Consequently, XTR will use Windows as its NOS.[3]

TEST YOUR UNDERSTANDING

5. a) What is the major benefit of Microsoft Windows Server NOSs? b) What are Linux distributions? c) Why do Linux distributions cause problems? d) What problems do Linux servers have for small businesses?

---

[3]Although nearly all organizations turn to either Windows Server or to Linux when they choose a NOS for a PC server, there are other choices. Novell NetWare used to be the most popular NOS and still has exceptional file and print service. However, its high price has greatly limited its market share. In addition, while Linux is the most popular version of Unix for PC servers, other PC versions of Unix exist—notably BSD, which in many ways is superior to Linux.

XTR: THE INITIAL SITUATION

Now we can finally get to the XTR network design. We will begin with the initial situation in the company.

PCs

When planning for the network began, each staff member had a good personal computer. This included XTR's sixteen professionals and one secretary.

Printers

Each staff member also had a printer. Victor Chao, XTR's president, had a laser printer. So did Ann Jacobs (the secretary) and one of the consultants. The other consultants had color ink jet printers because the cost of giving each a laser printer was seen as prohibitive.

Sneakernet

When a consultant with an ink jet printer needed a laser printout, he or she saved the file onto a floppy disk and gave it to Ann to print. Similarly, when consultants wanted to share a file, one had to save it to disk and walk it to the other consultant. Walking files around was jokingly called **sneakernet**. It wasted time and created confusion over who had the most current version of each file.

Remote Access

The consultants, who frequently are on the road, had to copy files they would need to the firm's one "loaner" notebook computer. If they needed an unexpected file on the road, there was no good way to retrieve it.

Internet Access

Although all PCs had modems, only one person could dial into the Internet at a time, and telephone access was very slow for the large maps that the consultants often had to download.

Maintenance

One of the employees, Kumiko Touchi, is very good with computers. However, there were many problems that Kumiko could not fix. Also, pulling Kumiko away from highly paid consulting work to fix a computer problem was absurd financially.

TEST YOUR UNDERSTANDING

6. a) Describe the computer situation at XTR before the network. b) Describe the printer situation at XTR before the network. c) Describe file sharing at XTR before the network. d) Describe remote access to files at XTR before the network. e) Describe Internet access at XTR before the network. f) Describe maintenance at XTR before the network.

BROAD NETWORK DESIGN

Given this situation, the firm naturally wanted to network its computers together and to connect the internal network to the outside world. Victor Chao hired a network consultant, Robert Blanco, to create a broad design for the network. Your job will be to flesh out Blanco's broad design, including its initial cost.

Labor Costs

XTR will hire a company to do the actual installation. The company will charge $75 per hour.

Switch

As shown in Figure 1c-1, the firm will have an Ethernet switch to connect all of the elements. This switch will operate at 100 Mbps. It will need quite a few ports. This will be a very simple switch that can simply be plugged into a power outlet with no additional installation work beyond physical installation. Installation will take about thirty minutes.

Wires

A UTP cord will run between the switch and each device. The company will run patch cords (precut UTP cords of approximately the correct length for each run). Patch cords will average $40 apiece.

The cords will run under carpets rather than neatly through false ceilings or walls. Neater but more expensive installation will not be done because the firm might be moving soon, and a neat installation would take more than four hours per UTP connection to the switch in XTR's building. Running the cords under carpets but leaving the cords otherwise exposed will only take about thirty minutes per UTP connection to the switch.

Network Interface Card (NIC)

The firm will have to install a NIC in three of the firm's current desktop PCs, now renamed client PCs. The other desktops came with adequate NICs when they were purchased. NICs, like the switch, will operate at 100 Mbps. Installation of a NIC will take about fifteen minutes. Setting up a PC with a NIC to run on the network will take an average of thirty minutes.

Dedicated Servers

In Mr. Blanco's design, the firm will purchase one or more new PCs to be used as dedicated servers. They will run the Windows 2003 Server network operating system instead of the desktop versions of Windows that the client computers use.

Pricing for the server NOS depends upon the number of users who will share the server. Assume an average purchase price of $2,000 for Microsoft Windows on each server. In addition, each server will require six hours of installation time.

File Service

One server task will be to provide **file service**, meaning that the consultants can store their files on the server, as Figure 1c-8 shows. Consequently, the main server is called a **file server**. File service is good because the server is backed up nightly.

Figure 1c-8   File Service for Data Files

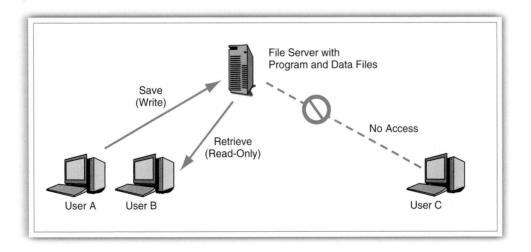

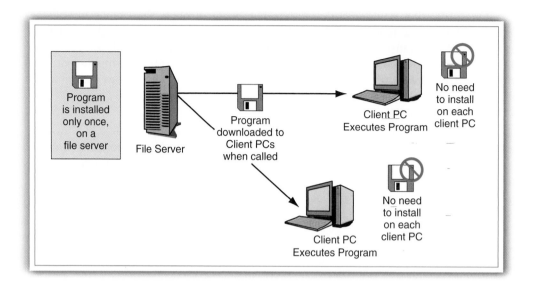

Figure 1c-9   File Server Program Access

As the figure shows, one user can save a file to a directory on a file server. Other authorized users can later retrieve the file and read it or can even change it and resave it if they are authorized to do so. However, unauthorized users cannot even see the file. Assigning and changing access permissions in various directories to the various users of a file server is a constant chore for server administrators, as noted earlier.

File Server Program Access

We have seen that dedicated programs let you store application programs on a dedicated server so that all users can access them. This is called file server program access. XTR will use file server program access. As Figure 1c-9 shows, the program is stored on the file server. When the user wants to run a program, the server downloads a copy to the user's client PC. It is far less expensive to install a program only once, on the file server, than to install it individually on all of the client PCs. Assume that the licenses for all the firm's application programs (other than database processing, which will be discussed later) will cost $1,500. Also assume that the initial installation of the programs will take ten hours.

Dedicated Print Servers

The network will replace the firm's diverse printers with the three existing high-capacity laser printers that will be spread around the office area for easy access by users. Pat Lee's network in Chapter 1 uses peer-to-peer print service. In contrast, as Figure 1c-10 shows, larger firms use dedicated **print servers**. When client users print, their printout will go to a print server. The print server will then feed the print job to the attached printer.

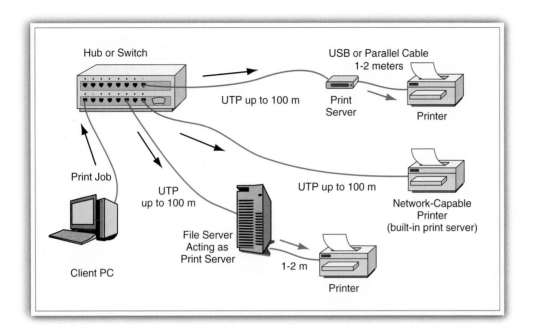

Figure 1c-10   Print Server Operation

Although print servers are called servers, they are not full computers. They are simple electronic devices that cost only $50 to $300 and have only the processing power and software needed to receive print jobs and feed them to the printer attached to them. A print server also has a built-in NIC to allow it to talk to the PCs it serves.

Each print server connects to a switch with a UTP cord and to its printer through an ordinary parallel cable or USB cord. Parallel cables and USB cords are very short—only one or two meters. UTP cords, in contrast, can be up to 100 meters long. Consequently, print servers sit right next to the printer, and there is a long UTP cord running to the switch that connects the print server to the network.

Each print server takes about thirty minutes to set up, including configuration. To configure the print server, the installer runs an installation program on a client PC. This program on the client PC communicates across the network with the print server.

Internet Access

For Internet access, the firm will replace its slow telephone access with high-speed DSL service (see Chapter 6) from its local telephone company. Several client PCs can use this access line simultaneously. This will require purchasing an access router. One end of the access router will plug into the DSL modem via a UTP cord. The other end will plug into the switch via another UTP cord. (In Pat Lee's home network, the access

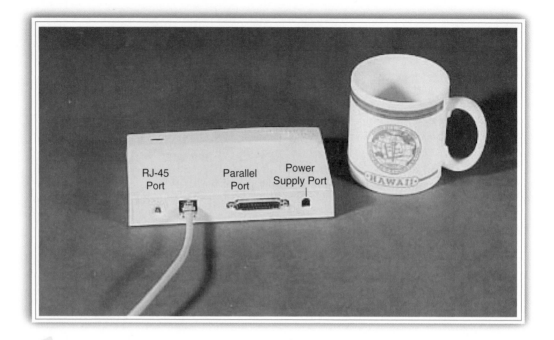

Figure 1c-11   Print Server

router had an internal Ethernet switch; this is not practical for this larger network, which needs many more switch ports.)

The access router has a built-in webserver. To configure the access router, the installer runs a browser on a client PC. The installer then types the IP address of the access router to connect the browser to the built-in webserver. Physical installation and setup will take about thirty minutes.

Firewall

The access router has a built-in firewall. Setting up the firewall will require about 12 hours. The major part of this time will be working with XTR employees to determine what traffic should be blocked and what traffic should be permitted.

Database Processing

The consultants have collectively developed a large database of environmental conditions in their area. They have been running the database on one of the consultant's PCs. They want to move the database to a server and allow multiple consultants to access the database simultaneously by installing an advanced database management program. The company can either run the database service software on the file server or purchase a separate database server. The e-database software will cost $3,000 and will take about 10 hours to install and configure.

Remote Access Service (RAS)

One issue is whether to install **remote access service (RAS)**, which would allow employees to connect to the network via the Internet. For remote access, a virtual private network (VPN) service (see Chapter 7) would have to be implemented. This would require activating and configuring VPN service on the remote access server. This would also require implementing authentication service on a file server or dedicated authentication server. Installing remote access service would take about five hours on the server. The company will not install remote access service initially but may decide to do so at some later time.

YOUR DETAILED DESIGN

Based on this information, you will flesh out the network design for the company. To guide you, answer the following questions. (Hand them in to your teacher.)

Design Questions

1. Should the company use separate file and e-mail servers, or should it use one server for both? Justify your answer.
2. Do you think the company should purchase the server or servers you listed in the previous question; or should it save money by taking away existing PCs from employees and using them as dedicated servers?
3. How many print servers should the company use—one per printer or just one for all three printers? Justify your number.
4. How many UTP cords will be needed? Justify your number.
5. How many ports will be needed on the switch? Justify your answer.
6. Switches can be purchased with 12, 24, 36, and 48 ports. Which switch should the company purchase? Justify your decision.
7. Cost out your PC server or servers, using Dell.com. Provide a detailed listing of your server's or servers' features. The server should have Microsoft Windows Server 2003. You will need one server customer access license (CAL) for each employee. You will not need high-end survey technology or an expensive monitor, but you will need a backup drive, a large amount of RAM, and a large hard drive.
8. Cost out the full installation cost that XTR must face. Use a spreadsheet model. Cite specific products (including product numbers and technical details) and sources of data. This is a really big task. It is also a very realistic task. It is the kind of thing you will have to do often as a network professional. Do it right.
9. What are the least expensive components of this network's cost?
10. What are the most expensive components of this network's cost?
11. Repeat parts 8–10 for the neat wiring installation.
12. Do you think the company should implement remote access? Cite reasons on both sides of the issue and give your choice, justifying it.

Network Standards

Learning Objectives

By the end of this chapter, you should be able to discuss:

■ Core standards concepts: message semantics, syntax, reliability, and connection-oriented versus connectionless service.

■ Layered standards architectures.

■ Standards at Layers 1 and 2 (the physical and data link layers) and how Ethernet works at these layers.

■ Layer 3 (internet layer) standards and how IP works at this layer.

■ Layer 4 (transport layer) standards and how TCP and UDP work at this layer.

■ Layer 5 (application layer) standards and how HTTP works at this layer.

■ Vertical communication among layer processes on the same device.

■ Common layered standards architectures and the dominance of the hybrid TCP/IP–OSI standards architecture.

INTRODUCTION

In this chapter, we will look at **standards**, which are rules of operation that allow two hardware or software processes to work together. In this chapter, we will look at network standards in more depth. Nearly everything in networking revolves around standards. To master networking, you must learn to think precisely about standards.

> Standards are rules of operation that allow two hardware or software processes to work together.

In this chapter, we often refer to standards as **protocols**. Strictly speaking, not all standards are protocols,[1] but all of the standards we will see in this book truly are protocols, so we will use the terms *standard* and *protocol* interchangeably. In fact, *protocol* is in the names of many of the standards we will see in this book, including the Hypertext

---

[1]Technically, protocols are standards between two hardware or software processes at the same layer on different devices. (Layers are discussed later in this chapter.) There also are standards for vertical communication between processes on the same machine but at different layers. These standards are not protocols. We will not look at any of these vertical standards in the book.

Transfer *Protocol*, the Internet *Protocol*, the Transmission Control *Protocol*, and the User Datagram *Protocol*.

TEST YOUR UNDERSTANDING

1. a) What are standards? b) In this book, will we use the terms *standards* and *protocols* interchangeably?

STANDARDS GOVERN THE EXCHANGE OF MESSAGES

Standards govern the exchange of messages between two hardware or software processes. For instance, in Figure 2-2, the two processes are a browser on a desktop PC

Figure 2-1   Standards Govern the Exchange of Messages (Study Figure)

Basics
- Standards are rules of operation that allow two hardware or software processes to work together
- Standards govern the exchange of messages between two hardware or software entities
- Standards govern message semantics and syntax
- Standards are called protocols

Message Semantics (Message Meaning)
- There are only a few message types because computers do not have the intelligence to handle open-ended communication
- In HTTP, there are request and response messages (Figure 2-2)

Message Syntax (Message Organization)
- Message cannot be freely structured like human sentences
- Messages are rigidly structured
    - In HTTP, lines of text (Figure 2-3)
    - Most lines are of the form "Keyword: Information"
- General Message Organization (Figure 2-4)
    - Three primary components
        - Data Field (content to be delivered)
        - Header (everything before the data field)
        - Trailer (everything after the data field)
- Header and trailer are further divided into fields
- Trailers are uncommon and come mostly at the data link layer
- Some messages only have a header

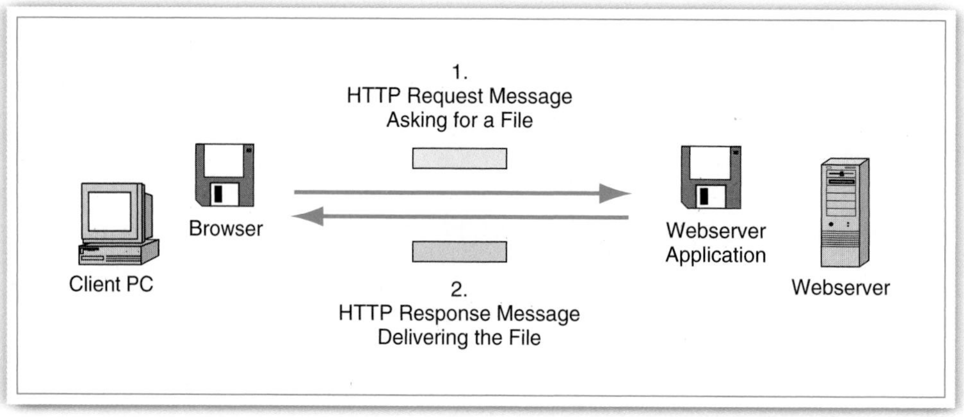

Figure 2-2   Hypertext Transfer Protocol (HTTP) Interactions

and a webserver application program on a webserver. The messages they exchange follow the Hypertext Transfer Protocol (HTTP) standard.

Standards govern the exchange of messages between two hardware or software processes.

Message Semantics (Meaning)

Standards govern the **semantics** of message exchanges—that is, the meanings of all messages. For instance, in Figure 2-2, the browser on the client PC transmits a message requesting a particular file on the webserver. The webserver responds with a message that either contains the requested file or explains why the requested file could not be delivered. Although HTTP has a few other message types, it offers nothing like the breadth of meanings in human communication. Computers lack the flexibility of human intelligence. Protocol semantics have to be limited to only a few message types.

Semantics describes the meaning of messages.

Message Syntax

Standards also govern message **syntax**—that is, how messages are organized internally. In human languages, sentences are organized by grammatical rules, although these rules are sometimes vague. In contrast, network standards need extremely precise and rigid rules for structuring messages because hardware and software processes are not intelligent and cannot deal with ambiguity.

Syntax describes how messages are organized internally.

Semantics and Syntax

    Semantics

        The meanings of messages

        HTTP request message: "Please give me a file."

        HTTP response message: "Here is the file" (or an error message).

    Syntax

        Organization of messages

HTTP Request Message

    GET /reports/project1/final.htm HTTP/1.1[CRLF]

    Host: Voyage.cba.hawaii.edu[CRLF]

HTTP Response Message

    HTTP/1.1 200 OK[CRLF]

    Date: Tuesday, 20-JAN-2006 18:32:15 GMT[CRLF]

    Server: *name of server software*[CRLF]

    MIME-version: 1.0[CRLF]

    Content-type: text/plain[CRLF]

    [CRLF]

    file to be downloaded

Syntax of Fields After the First Line:

    Keyword: contents [CRLF]

Note: [CRLF] is a carriage return followed by a line feed. This is how typewriters start a new line, and the terminology has survived.

Figure 2-3   Syntax of HTTP Request and Response Messages

HTTP Request Message

For instance, in Figure 2-3, the *HTTP request message* consists of two lines of **plaintext** (keyboard characters). The first line terminates with a carriage return/line feed [CRLF]. This indicates that a new line should begin.

There is rigid structure within each line. For example, the first line must have a method (in this case, GET) that describes what the other side is to do (get a file). A single space[2] comes next, followed by the path to the requested file (/reports/project1/final.htm). There is another single space, followed by the HTTP version the browser implements (1.1).

---

[2]Okay, the figure contains two spaces rather than one, but this is just to make the space more apparent.

Each subsequent line (there is only one subsequent line in this example) has a keyword, a colon (:), the value of the keyword, and a [CRLF]. For instance, the Host keyword, followed by a colon, precedes the host name of the webserver.

HTTP Response Message

Figure 2-3 also shows the *HTTP response message*, which begins with an indication of which HTTP version the webserver understands (Version 1.1). It then has a 200 code, which tells the browser that the GET request was successful. The *OK* on this line says the same thing for human readers.

Next, we see several more lines. Each contains a keyword, a colon, a value for the keyword, and a [CRLF]. A single blank line follows these lines. (Two carriage return/line feeds produce a blank line.) After this single blank line comes the file that the message is delivering. The file is a long string of ones and zeros organized into bytes.

General Message Organization

Figure 2-4 shows that messages in general may consist of three parts—a header, a data field, and a trailer. The header and trailer may be further divided into smaller units called fields.

Data Field

The **data field** contains the content delivered by a message. In an HTTP response message, the data field is the file the message is delivering.

The *data field* contains the content delivered by a message.

Header

The message **header**, quite simply, is everything that comes before the data field. For the HTTP request message, the entire message is the header. There is no data field. In the HTTP response message, the header is everything before the file the client requested.

The message *header*, quite simply, is everything that comes before the data field.

Trailer

Some messages also have **trailers**, which consist of everything coming after the data field. HTTP messages do not have trailers. They have nothing after the data field.

The message *trailer* is everything that comes after the data field.

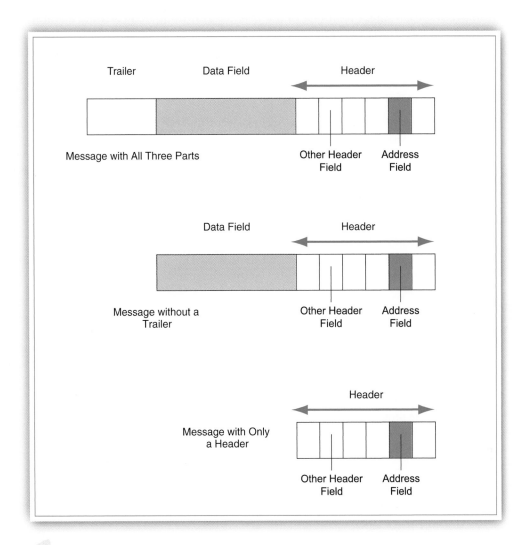

Figure 2-4   General Message Organization

Not All Messages Have All Three Parts

HTTP messages demonstrate that only a header is present in all messages. Data fields are not always present but are very common. Trailers are not common.

Fields in Headers and Trailers

The header and trailer usually contain smaller sections called **fields**. In HTTP, the first line of a request message has the method, path, and version fields. The first line of a response message consists of three fields. In both HTTP request and response messages, each subsequent line of the header (consisting of a keyword, a colon, content, and a [CRLF]) is a field.

The header and trailer usually contain smaller sections called fields.

TEST YOUR UNDERSTANDING

2. a) What two things about messages do standards govern? b) Distinguish between semantics and syntax.

3. a) What are the three general parts of messages? b) What does the data field contain? c) What is the definition of a header? d) Is there always a data field in a message? e) What is the definition of a trailer? f) Are trailers common? g) Distinguish between headers and header fields.

RELIABILITY AND CONNECTIONS

Two general characteristics apply to all standards. The first is whether the standard is reliable or unreliable. The second is whether the standard is connection-oriented or connectionless.

Reliability

A **reliable** protocol corrects lost or damaged messages by resending them. Protocols are either reliable or unreliable. Reliable protocols resend lost or damaged messages. Unreliable protocols do not correct errors.

Reliable protocols correct errors by resending lost or damaged messages.
Unreliable protocols do not correct errors.

Unreliable Protocols

HTTP is an **unreliable** protocol. It does not do error correction.

Reliable Protocols

Acknowledging Correctly Received Segments   Figure 2-5 shows how an important standard called the *Transmission Control Protocol (TCP)* implements reliability. Every time a TCP process receives a correct TCP segment (TCP messages are called **TCP segments**), it sends back an **acknowledgement(ACK)** segment. If the original sender receives the acknowledgement for a segment, it knows that its segment arrived correctly. See Segments 4 and 5 in Figure 2-5 for an example of a transmission and an acknowledgement.

Not Acknowledging Incorrect or Not-Received Segments   However, the receiving TCP process does not send an acknowledgement if the segment was damaged or (obviously) if the segment never arrived (see Segment 8). If the sending TCP process does not receive an acknowledgement for a segment promptly, it knows that the segment did not arrive at the other side. It resends the segment (see Segment 9). This process corrects the transmission error, giving reliability. Note that the TCP process

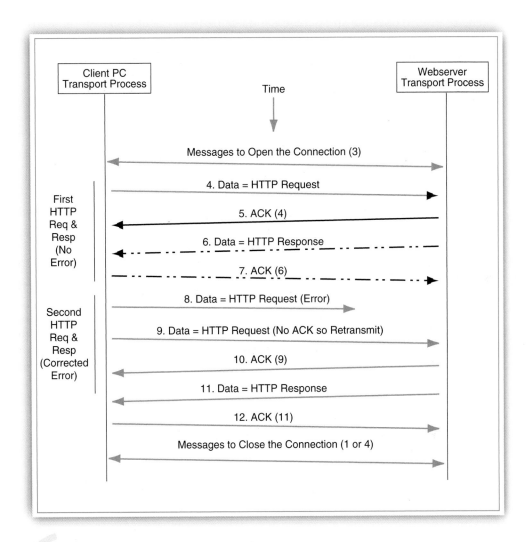

Figure 2-5   Reliable Transmission Control Protocol (TCP) Session

that originally sends a TCP segment—not the receiving TCP process—decides whether to resend it.

The Expense of Reliability

Reliability gives clean information, but it is extremely expensive. Consider the computer processing cycles that are needed for reliability. The heaviest aspect of reliability is doing the calculation needed to determine if an error has occurred. The sender treats the entire message as a very large binary number and does a lengthy computation on it. This computation yields a brief number that is included with the message.

The receiver redoes the computation and compares its calculation with the transmitted number. This requires far more expensive processing cycles than any other aspect of protocol functioning.

TEST YOUR UNDERSTANDING

4. a) What is reliability? b) How does TCP implement reliability? c) In TCP, what is the receiver's role in reliability? d) In TCP, what is the sender's role in reliability? e) What is the disadvantage of reliability?

Connection-Oriented and Connectionless Protocols

Another general characteristic of protocols is whether they are connection-oriented or connectionless.

Connection-Oriented Protocols

When you call someone on the telephone, you do not just begin speaking when the other party picks up the phone. There is at least a tacit initial negotiation to check that the called person is willing to speak. In addition, at the end of a conversation, it is rude simply to hang up without both sides indicating that they wish to end the call. In networking, as Figure 2-6 illustrates, **connection-oriented** standards work this way too. They have explicit openings and closings. (In Figure 2-5, note that TCP is a connection-oriented protocol.)

Connection-oriented standards have explicit openings and closings.

Figure 2-6   Connection-Oriented and Connectionless Protocols

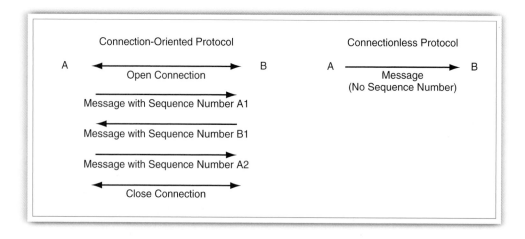

Advantages

> Connection-oriented protocols give each message a sequence number.

> Thanks to sequence numbers, the parties can tell if a message is lost. (There will be a gap in the sequence numbers.)

> Error messages, such as ACKs, can refer to specific messages according to the sequence numbers of these messages.

> Long messages can be fragmented into many smaller messages that can fit inside packets. The fragments will be given sequence numbers so that they can be assembled at the other end. Fragmentation followed by reassembly is an important concept in networking.

> Messages can refer to earlier messages by sequence number. This is important in database-based transaction processes where several messages must be exchanged to make a purchase, record a transaction, or do some other common business task.

Disadvantages

> Connection-oriented protocols place a heavy load on networks and on computers connected to the network.

Figure 2-7   Advantages and Disadvantages of Connection-Oriented Protocols (Study Figure)

Connectionless Protocols

As Figure 2-6 also shows, **connectionless** protocols do not establish a connection before transmitting. When you send someone an e-mail, for instance, you do not call him or her ahead of time to ask if you may send the e-mail message or call him or her afterward to ask if you can stop sending messages.

Advantages of Connection-Oriented Protocols

Figure 2-6 also shows that each message that is transmitted is given a **sequence number** to indicate its transmission order during the connection. This has several benefits:

> ➤ Thanks to sequence numbers, the parties can tell if a message is lost. (There will be a gap in the sequence numbers.)

> ➤ Error messages, such as ACKs can refer to specific messages according to the sequence numbers of these messages.

> ➤ Long messages can be fragmented into many smaller messages that can fit inside packets. The fragments will be given sequence numbers so that they can be assembled at the other end. **Fragmentation** followed by **reassembly** is an important concept in networking.

➤ Messages can refer to earlier messages by sequence number. This is important in database-based transaction processes where several messages must be exchanged to make a purchase, record a transaction, or do some other common business task.

Disadvantages of Connection-Oriented Protocols

Although connection-oriented protocols (thanks largely to their sequence numbers) are useful, they have one major disadvantage. They place a heavy burden on the network and on the computers attached to the network. Opens, closes, acknowledgements, and other supervisory messages can consume a good deal of bandwidth, and doing the work needed to create and use sequence numbers consumes a good deal of processing power. Connection-oriented protocols are referred to as heavyweight protocols.

In contrast, connectionless protocols do not create comparable burdens on networks and on computers attached to the network. Connectionless protocols are lightweight protocols.

Connectionless and Unreliable Protocols Dominate

Given the need to keep costs low, almost all of the protocols we will see in this book are connectionless and unreliable. The main exception to this is the connection-oriented Transmission Control Protocol, which we will see again later in this chapter. (We will also see why it is the exception to the pattern.)

Given the need to keep costs low, almost all of the protocols we will see in this book are connectionless.

TEST YOUR UNDERSTANDING

5. a) Distinguish between connectionless and connection-oriented protocols. b) Which can have sequence numbers? c) What are the advantages that sequence numbers bring to connection-oriented protocols? d) Explain fragmentation and reassembly. e) What is the disadvantage of connection-oriented protocols? f) Are most protocols connectionless or connection-oriented? g) Are most protocols reliable or unreliable?

LAYERED STANDARDS ARCHITECTURES

Up to now, we have been talking about the characteristics of individual standards. In networking, there are dozens of standards that do different things, just as different rooms in a house have different functions.

Architectures

To continue the house example, you do not design a house by building one room, then another, and then another, without any plan. Rather, you first create an **architecture**—a broad plan that specifies what rooms the house will have and how these rooms will relate to each other in terms of uses and traffic flow. The architecture ensures that the rooms will collectively provide everything the owner needs. Only after the architecture is finished will the architect begin to design individual rooms in detail.

Layer	Name	Specific Function	Broad Function
5	Application	Application layer standards govern how two applications work with each other, even if they are from different vendors.	Interoperability of application programs
4	Transport	Transport layer standards govern aspects of end-to-end communication between two end hosts that are not handled by the internet layer. These standards also allow hosts to work together even if the two computers are from different vendors or have different internal designs.	Transmission across an internet
3	Internet	Internet link layer standards govern the transmission of packets across an internet—typically by sending them through several routers along the route. Internet layer standards also govern packet organization, timing constraints, and reliability.	
2	Data Link	Data link layer standards govern the transmission of frames across a single network—typically by sending them through several switches along the data link. Data link layer standards also govern frame organization, timing constraints, and reliability.	Transmission across a single network
1	Physical	Physical layer standards govern transmission between adjacent devices connected by a transmission medium.	

Figure 2-8   Hybrid TCP/IP-OSI Architecture

TCP/IP–OSI

Similarly, data network standards are not created in isolation. A **network architecture** is a broad plan that specifies everything necessary for two application programs on different networks on an internet to be able to work together effectively. Figure 2-8 illustrates the most popular standards architecture for networking today, the **Hybrid TCP/IP–OSI Architecture.** Later in this chapter, we will discuss its odd name. For now, we will focus on its organization.

A network architecture is a broad plan that specifies everything needed for two application programs on different networks on an internet to be able to work together effectively.

Layers

The architecture has a series of layers. Each layer provides services to the layer immediately above it. For example, when you travel by car, the road provides service for your tires (support), and tires provide support for your car. Your car, of course, provides support for you.[3]

In a layered standards architecture, each layer provides services to the layer above it.

TEST YOUR UNDERSTANDING

6. a) What is a network architecture? b) What is the most popular network architecture today? c) In layered standards architectures, to what layer or layers does a layer provide service?

Layer 1 and Layer 2 Standards for Single Networks (LANs and WANs)

The bottom two layers (physical and data link) govern transmission across a single network—either a single LAN or a single WAN. Figure 2-9 compares these two layers. It shows a single network. In this network, Host A and Router R1 are separated by two switches—X1 and X2.

Figure 2-9 Physical and Data Link Layer Standards in a Single Network

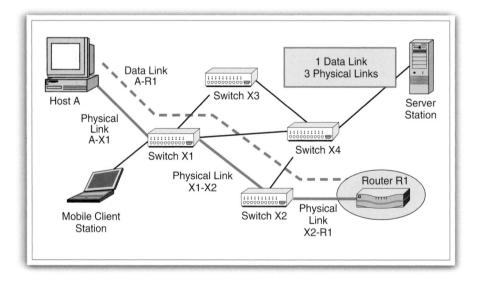

---

[3]To give another example, if you have a cat, food provides sustenance for the cat, and the cat provides services for you. Okay, bad example.

Physical Links

Physical layer (Layer 1) standards govern transmission between adjacent devices connected by a transmission medium. Such connections are **physical links**. In the figure, there are three physical links between Host A and Router R1: from Host A to the first switch, from the first switch to the second switch, and from the second switch to Router R1. The physical layer provides transmission between devices so that higher layers do not have to worry about this.

Physical layer (Layer 1) standards govern transmission between adjacent devices connected by a transmission medium.

Data Links

The **data link layer (Layer 2)** standards, in turn, govern the transmission of frames all the way from Host A to Router R1 across two switches (X1 and X2). The path that a frame takes across the network is the frame's **data link.** There is only one data link between the source and destination computers on a single network.

Data link layer (Layer 2) standards govern the transmission of frames across a single network—typically by sending them through several switches along the data link. Data link standards also govern frame organization, reliability, and other matters.

Data link layer (Layer 2) standards govern the transmission of frames across a single network—typically by sending them through several switches along the data link. Data link layer standards also govern frame organization, reliability, and other matters.

Many Single Network Standards

There are many types of single networks, including Ethernet for LANs and Frame Relay for WANs, to name just two. Each network standard specifies both physical layer standards and data link standards. There are many types of single networks, so most of the network standards we will see in this book will be physical and data link standards.

Single networks (LANs and WANs) are governed by physical and data link layer standards.

TEST YOUR UNDERSTANDING

7. a) What devices does a physical link connect? b) What is a data link? c) Five switches separate two computers on a network. How many physical links are there between the two computers? d) How many data links are there between them? e) What do data link layer standards govern? f) Which layers govern LAN transmission? g) Which layers govern WAN transmission?

Standards for Internet Transmission

Initially, there were only standards for single networks. However, as networks began to proliferate, companies needed new standards to link two or more single networks together into **internets**, which, as we saw in Chapter 1, are groups of networks connected by routers so that any application on any host on any network can communicate with any application on any other host on any other network. Standards at the internet and transport layers collectively govern transmission across an internet.

The Internet and Data Link Layers

Many people have a hard time differentiating between the data link layer and the internet layer. An example may help clarify this. In Figure 2-10, there are three networks in an internet. Host A in Network X is transmitting to Host B in Network Z. The connection linking the two hosts involves three networks, so there are three data links (A to R1, R1 to R2, and R2 to B).

In turn, the path that the packet takes across its internet is its **route**. There is only one route between the source and destination hosts (Host A and Host B). The main standard for internet transmission is the *Internet Protocol (IP)*.

Standards at the **internet layer (Layer 3)** govern the transmission of packets, hop by hop, *across an entire internet*. Standards at the internet layer specify what each router along the way does with packets. (Routers act individually in sequence to forward packets to the destination host.) Standards at the internet layer govern how each router along the way passes packets on to the next router on the route to the destination host. There is only one route across the internet in the figure.

Standards at the internet layer (Layer 3) govern the transmission of packets, hop by hop, *across an entire internet*.

Note that we do not capitalize *internet* when describing the internet layer. Consequently, when *internet* is spelled with a lowercase *i*, this either indicates an internet in general or the internet layer. As noted in Chapter 1, when *Internet* is spelled with an uppercase *I*, this designates the global Internet. (At the beginning of sentences or in titles, however, internet is always capitalized.)

When *internet* is spelled with a lowercase *i*, this either indicates an internet in general or the internet layer. As noted earlier, when *Internet* is spelled with an uppercase *I*, this designates the global Internet. (At the beginning of sentences or in titles, however, internet is always capitalized.)

The Internet Layer and Transport Layer

The Internet Layer   Figure 2-11 reiterates that the internet layer governs the transmission of packets, hop by hop, *across an entire internet*. Many routers are involved in the transmission of a packet over a large internet.

The Transport Layer   In turn, **transport layer (Layer 4)** standards govern the aspects of end-to-end communication between the two end hosts that are *not* handled by the

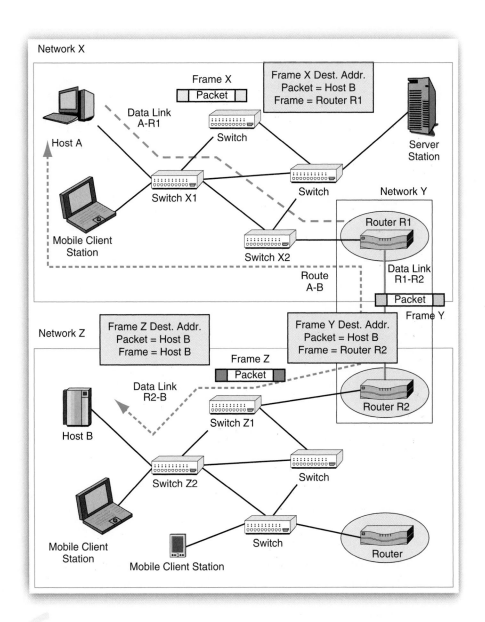

Figure 2-10   Internet and Data Link Layers in an Internet

internet layer. The many routers along the way are not involved with the transport layer. Only the two hosts are involved at this layer.

Transport layer (Layer 4) standards govern the aspects of end-to-end communication between the two end hosts that are *not* handled by the internet layer.

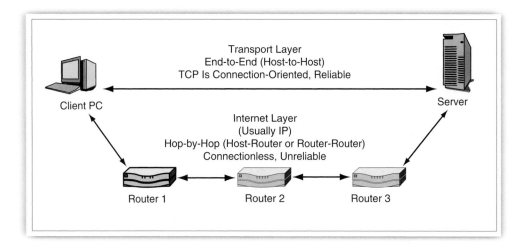

Figure 2-11   Internet and Transport Layers Standards

Typically, the transport layer standard (usually TCP) is reliable, fixing any errors created at the transport layer or lower layers and delivering clean data to the application program. However, later in this chapter, we will see in the discussion of UDP that transport layer protocols are not always reliable.

TEST YOUR UNDERSTANDING

8. a) What do the internet and transport layers do collectively? b) Distinguish between what the internet and transport layer standards govern. c) What is the main internet layer standard? d) What errors does the transport layer usually fix?

Standards for Applications

At the highest layer, **application layer (Layer 5)** standards govern how two applications work with each other, even if they are from different vendors. For example, a Microsoft Internet Explorer browser can work with an open-source Apache webserver application program.

Application layer (Layer 5) standards govern how two applications work with each other, even if they are from different vendors.

In Figure 2-2, we saw the Hypertext Transfer Protocol (HTTP) application layer standard. HTTP is only one of many application protocols used on the Internet. E-mail, FTP, and other applications use different application protocols. There are

---

Application Layer Standards
> Govern how two applications work with each other, even if they are from different vendors

Many application layer standards because there are many applications
> HTTP
>
> E-Mail
>
> Database
>
> Instant Messaging
>
> FTP
>
> Etc.

There are more application layer standards than any other type of standards

---

Figure 2-12 Application Layer Standards (Study Figure)

many applications, so there are more application standards than there are standards at any other layer.

TEST YOUR UNDERSTANDING

9. a) What do application layer standards govern? b) Which layer has the most standards? Why is this the case?

Why Layered Architectures?

BREAKING UP LARGE TASKS INTO SMALLER TASKS

Why divide networking standards into five pieces (layers)? The first answer is that whenever you have a major task, it is a good strategy to break it up into smaller pieces and attack the pieces individually. This strategy also works in standards development, which is a very large task.

SPECIALIZATION IN STANDARDS DESIGN

In addition, if a team is doing the work, team members should receive individual tasks that suit their skills. In networking standards development, for instance, electrical engineers usually create physical layer standards, while specialists in a particular application usually

(continued)

create application layer standards for that application.

SIMPLIFICATION IN STANDARDS DESIGN

Another benefit of layering is that development at one layer can ignore concerns at other layers. Application standards designers can design new application standards without having to worry about how to get messages between the two hosts. Physical layer standards designers, in turn, do not have to worry about which applications will use a particular physical link.

IF YOU CHANGE A STANDARD AT ONE LAYER, YOU DO NOT HAVE TO CHANGE STANDARDS AT OTHER LAYERS

A fourth reason for layering is that it allows standards to be updated or changed at various layers independently. If you switch from one LAN standard to another, say from Ethernet to an 802.11 wireless LAN, or if you upgrade from one version of Ethernet to a newer version, you do not have to change standards above the data link layer. In addition, if you switch from handling e-mail to browsing webservers (these are application layer functions), you do not need to use different lower-layer (Layer 1–4) standards.

TEST YOUR UNDERSTANDING

10. Why do standards architectures break down the standards development process into layers?

Figure 2-13   Why Layer? (Study Figure)

Breaking Up Large Tasks into Smaller Tasks is a Good General Strategy

Allows Specialization in Standards Design

Electrical engineers develop physical layer standards.

Specialists in an application develop application standards for that application.

Allows Simplification in Standards Design

Designers only have to focus on issues relevant to that layer.

If You Change a Standard at One Layer, You Do Not Have to Change Standards at Other Layers

LAYERS 1 (PHYSICAL) AND 2 (DATA LINK) IN ETHERNET

Having looked at layering in general, we will now begin to look at individual layers in more detail, beginning with Layers 1 and 2, which together govern individual LANs and WANs.

Ethernet Physical Layer Standards

We will see in Chapter 3 that Ethernet physical layer transmission can also be done using optical fiber cabling, which sends bits as light flashes. At the physical layer, there are no messages. Bits travel individually as voltage changes, light flashes, radio pulses, or other discrete signaling events.

Ethernet Frames

Messages at the data link layer are called **frames**. Data link standards dictate the semantics and syntax of frame transmission within a single network. As we saw in Chapter 1, Ethernet switches work with Ethernet frames. Figure 2-14 illustrates the standard **Ethernet frame**, which, formally speaking, is the **802.3 MAC layer frame**. In Chapter 4, we will look at Ethernet frames in detail. For now, we will only focus on a few fields.

Messages at the data link layer are called frames.

Figure 2-14   Ethernet Frame

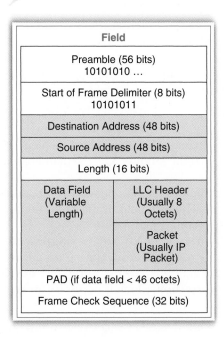

Octets

The Ethernet header and trailer are divided into fields. Field lengths can be measured in bits. Another common measure for field lengths in networking is the octet. An **octet** is a group of eight bits. Isn't that a byte? Yes, exactly. *Octet* is just another name for *byte*. It is widely used in networking, however, so you need to become familiar with the term.[4]

An octet is a group of eight bits.

Ethernet Addresses

48-Bit Ethernet Addresses   Ethernet frames have Ethernet data link layer source addresses and destination addresses that identify the sending and receiving computers, respectively. Each Ethernet network interface card (NIC) has a unique 48-bit Ethernet address set at the factory before the card ships.

Hexadecimal Notation   As Chapter 4 discusses, Ethernet addresses often are written in hexadecimal (Base 16) notation. In "hex" notation, a typical 48-bit **Ethernet address** is A7-BF-23-D4-33-99.

Ethernet Switches and Ethernet Addresses   As we saw in Chapter 1, switches between the source and destination hosts read the destination Ethernet address in every arriving frame. They look up the Ethernet address in the switching table. The line containing this address contains a port number. The switches send the frame back out this indicated port number.

The Ethernet Data Field

In the TCP/IP–OSI architecture, an Ethernet frame's data field begins with an LLC subheader, which is discussed in Chapter 4. More important, the data field usually (but not always) contains an IP packet. In the first chapter, we saw that frames encapsulate packets. Figure 2-14 shows how Ethernet implements this encapsulation by showing the position of the packet in the Ethernet frame.

Frame Check Sequence Field: Unreliable Operation

The last field in an Ethernet frame is the **frame check sequence field**. This four-octet field holds a binary number that the sending NIC calculates based on the bits in other fields in the frame.

The receiving NIC recomputes the number and compares its result to the value contained in the frame check sequence field. If the two do not match, an error must have occurred during transmission.

If there is an error, the receiving NIC's data link process simply discards the frame. There is no request for retransmission. Having no means of error correction, the Ethernet protocol at the data link layer is unreliable despite detecting errors. Error detection is not error correction, which is necessary for reliability.

---

[4] *Octet* actually makes more sense than *byte*, because *oct* means "eight." We have octopuses, octagons, and octogenarians. What is the eighth month? (Careful!)

Error detection is not error correction, which is necessary for reliability.

TEST YOUR UNDERSTANDING

11. What is an octet?

12. a) How long are Ethernet addresses? b) When are Ethernet addresses set on NICs? c) In what notation are they typically written for human reading? d) What device in a network besides the destination host reads the Ethernet address? e) What is its purpose in doing so?

13. What does the Ethernet data field usually contain?

14. a) How many *bits* long is the Ethernet frame check sequence field? b) What is its purpose? c) How does the receiving NIC use it? d) What happens if a receiving NIC detects an error? e) Does this error detection and discarding process make Ethernet a reliable standard?

Ethernet Characteristics

Ethernet Is Unreliable and Connectionless

In addition to being unreliable (as we have just seen), Ethernet is connectionless. NICs send Ethernet frames without opens, closes, acknowledgements, or sequence numbers.

TEST YOUR UNDERSTANDING

15. a) Is Ethernet connectionless or connection-oriented? Explain. b) Is Ethernet reliable or unreliable? Explain.

LAYER 3: THE INTERNET PROTOCOL (IP)

Internet layer standards govern the transmission of messages called packets across an internet. As noted earlier, the Internet Protocol (IP) is the most common standard at Layer 3, the internet layer.

Layer 2 Versus Layer 3

Figure 2-10 illustrated how the data link layer and the internet layer are related. Put simply, the data link is the path a frame takes through a single network. In turn, the internet layer path, called a route, is the path a packet takes from the source host to the destination host across an internet.

Figure 2-10 also showed how frames and packets are related. As a packet travels through an internet, it travels in the data field of a frame within each network. If three networks are involved in the transmission from the source to the destination host, there will be one packet that will travel in three different frames. To give an analogy, if you mail a letter, the letter goes all the way from you to the receiver, like a packet. Along the way, however, it will travel in a series of trucks and airplanes, which are analogous to frames.

The figure showed how addressing is done in frames and packets. The packet always has the same Layer 3 internet destination address: the IP address of Host B.

However, the three frames have Layer 2 data link layer destination addresses that are the endpoints in their individual networks.

➤ The destination address in Frame X in Network X is the data link layer address of Router R1.

➤ The destination address in Frame Y in Network Y is the data link address of Router R2.

➤ The destination address in Frame Z in Network Z is the data link address of the destination host, Host B.

TEST YOUR UNDERSTANDING

16. a) Four networks are involved in transmissions from the source to the destination host. How many packets will there be along the way when the source host transmits a packet? b) How many frames will there be? c) How many routers will there be along the route? (Hint: Draw a picture showing the hosts, networks, and routers.) d) How many routes will there be? e) How many data links will there be? f) How many destination IP addresses will there be? g) How many data link layer destination addresses will there be? h) In the data link layer address of the frame in the first network, the destination address is the destination address of which device? i) What will be the destination IP address of the packet contained in that frame?

The IP Packet

In Figure 2-14, we saw an Ethernet frame at Layer 2. We saw that an Ethernet frame typically carries an IP packet in its data field. Figure 2-15 shows the organization of an **Internet Protocol (IP)** packet.

Illustrated with 32 Bits per Line

An IP packet, like an Ethernet frame, is a long string of bits (1s and 0s). Unfortunately, drawing the packet this way would require a page several meters wide. Instead, Figure 2-15 shows an IP packet as a series of rows with 32 bits per row. In binary counting, the first bit is zero. Consequently, the first row is bits 0 through 31. The next row is bits 32 through 63. This is a different way of showing syntax than we saw with the Ethernet frame and with HTTP messages, but it is a common way of showing syntax, so you need to be familiar with it.

32-Bit Source and Destination Addresses

Like an Ethernet frame, an IP packet has source and destination addresses. These **IP addresses** are 32 bits long. (In contrast, we saw earlier in this chapter that Ethernet addresses are 48 bits long.) While an Ethernet address gives a host's address on its single network, an IP address gives a host's internet layer address on an internet consisting of multiple single networks.

For human comprehension, it is normal to express IP addresses in **dotted decimal notation**. As we saw in Chapter 1, a typical IP address in dotted decimal notation is

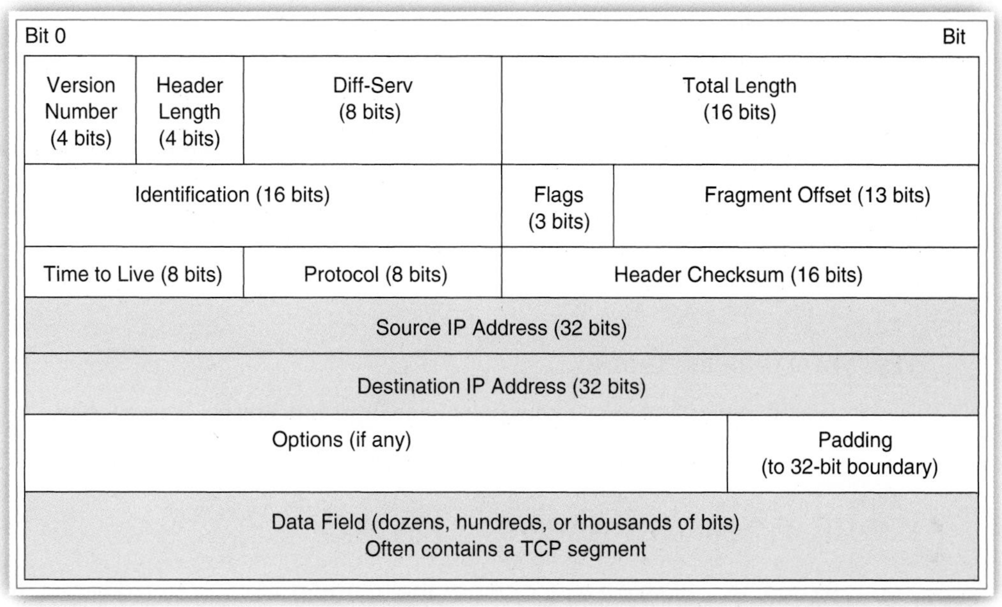

Bit 0				Bit
Version Number (4 bits)	Header Length (4 bits)	Diff-Serv (8 bits)	Total Length (16 bits)	
Identification (16 bits)			Flags (3 bits)	Fragment Offset (13 bits)
Time to Live (8 bits)		Protocol (8 bits)	Header Checksum (16 bits)	
Source IP Address (32 bits)				
Destination IP Address (32 bits)				
Options (if any)			Padding (to 32-bit boundary)	
Data Field (dozens, hundreds, or thousands of bits) Often contains a TCP segment				

Figure 2-15 Internet Protocol (IP) Packet

Notes:
Bits 0–3 hold the version number.
Bits 4–7 hold the header length.
Bits 8–15 hold the Diff-Serv information.
Bits 16–31 hold the total length value.
Bits 32–47 hold the Identification value.

128.171.17.13—four numbers separated by dots. The numbers have to be between 0 and 255.

Ethernet switches within a single network read the Ethernet destination address in the Ethernet header in a frame to learn where to send the frame. Similarly, routers along the way read the IP address in the destination IP address field of each packet. Based on this address, the router forwards the IP packet to the next router or, if the destination host is on a network connected to the router, to the destination host itself.

TEST YOUR UNDERSTANDING

17. a) How many octets long is an IP header if there are no options? (Look at Figure 2-15.) b) What is the bit number of the first bit in the destination address? (Remember that the first bit in binary counting is Bit 0.) c) How long are IP addresses? d) You have two addresses: B7-23-DD-6F-C8-AB and 217.42.18.248. Specify what kind of address each

address is. e) What device in an internet besides the destination host reads the destination IP address? f) What is this device's purpose in doing so?

IP Characteristics

Like Ethernet, IP is a connectionless protocol. What about reliability? As Figure 2-15 shows, the IP packet has a header checksum field,[5] which the receiver uses to check for errors in the IP header (but not its body). As in Ethernet, if the receiver detects an error, it simply discards the packet. There is error detection but no error correction, so IP is an unreliable protocol.

TEST YOUR UNDERSTANDING

18. a) Is IP connectionless or connection-oriented? b) Is IP reliable or unreliable?

LAYER 4: THE TRANSPORT LAYER

In this section, we will take a closer look at the transport layer. As noted earlier, transport layer (Layer 4) standards govern the aspects of end-to-end communication between the two end hosts that are *not* handled by the internet layer. The internet and transport layers work together to implement internetworking, just as the physical and data link layers work together to implement transmission through a single network (LAN or WAN).

> The internet and transport layers work together to implement internetworking, just as the physical and data link layers work together to implement transmission through a single network (LAN or WAN).

Layers 3 and 4

Hop-by-Hop Layers

Figure 2-11 showed the relationship between the internet and transport layers. Note that the internet layer is a **hop-by-hop layer**. Although it gets packets from the source host to the destination host, it does this by governing what each router does along the way. It governs internet layer processes on the source host, on each intermittent router, and on the destination host. Similarly, data link layer standards govern hop-by-hop transmission across multiple switches.

End-to-End Layers

In contrast, the transport layer is an **end-to-end layer**. It governs communication between the transport process on the source host and the transport process on the

---

[5]The figure actually shows the packet header for IP Version 4, which is the dominant version of the Internet Protocol in use today. The newer IP Version 6, which is beginning to spread, does not have a header checksum. It does neither error detection nor error correction.

destination host. The application layer we will see after this section also is an end-to-end layer.

TEST YOUR UNDERSTANDING

19. Ten routers separate two hosts. a) How many internet layer processes will be active on the two hosts and the devices between them? b) How many transport layer processes will be active? (The answer is not directly in the book. You will have to think about this one a little.) c) Which layers are hop-by-hop layers? (The physical layer is not considered to be either a hop-by-hop or an end-to-end layer.) d) Which layers are end-to-end layers? (The physical layer is not considered to be either a hop-by-hop or an end-to-end layer.)

TCP: A Reliable Protocol

Most protocols are unreliable. However, TCP, which operates at the transport layer, is reliable, as we saw earlier. As Figure 2-8 showed, the transport layer is the highest layer apart from the application layer. Making TCP reliable means that any errors made at the transport layer or at lower layers will be caught and corrected by TCP. This gives the application layer clean data.

Caution: the following discussion is difficult but extremely important.

Why not simply make all layers reliable? The answer is that reliability is expensive. It requires considerable processing and storage requirements on each device to hold copies of outgoing messages and to decide whether to resend a message. In fact, error correction consumes far more processor cycles per message than any other process in switching or routing.

Reliability is expensive. In fact, error correction consumes far more processor cycles per message than any other process in switching or routing.

TCP is a very complex protocol. We will look at it in detail in Chapter 8. However, we have already seen that extensive traffic is generated by openings, closings, acknowledgements, and retransmissions. TCP places heavy burdens on the sending and receiving hosts and on the network's traffic requirements.

One reason to make TCP reliable at the transport layer is that the transport layer is immediately below the application layer. Error correction at this layer automatically corrects errors at all lower layers. Doing error correction at only one layer—the highest layer before the application layer—provides error-free data to the application program at minimal cost compared to doing error correction at all layers.[6]

---

[6]It is also possible to make the application layer the only layer where error correction is done. However, by making TCP reliable at the transport layer, there is no need for each application program writer to have to develop error correction code. As we will see later, another transport layer protocol, UDP, does *not* do error correction. This makes UDP ideal for applications that do not need error correction or that prefer to do their own error handling.

A second reason for doing error correction only at the transport layer is that TCP is an end-to-end layer. This means that error correction is only done on the two hosts. In contrast, if error correction occurred on each hop between switches at the data link layer and on each hop between routers at the internet layer, the costs of switches and routers would be far higher than they are. Furthermore, incurring this cost at each switch and router would be extremely wasteful because transmission errors are rare today.

TEST YOUR UNDERSTANDING

20. a) Why are most standards unreliable? b) Why is making TCP reliable a good choice?

The User Datagram Protocol (UDP)

TCP is widely used at the transport layer, but it is a heavyweight protocol. It consumes many computer processing cycles doing the calculations needed for error correction. It also consumes extensive network capacity because it sends many supervisory messages (ACK segments, opening messages, closing messages, and so forth).

For applications that do not need error correction, there is another popular protocol at the transport layer. This is the **User Datagram Protocol (UDP)**. Figure 2-16 compares these two protocols.

The figure shows that both protocols work at the transport layer. They are complementary, and application developers can specify either TCP or UDP for use at the transport layer with their applications. While TCP is connection-oriented, reliable, and burdensome on the two hosts and on the network, UDP is connectionless, unreliable, and places a lighter load on the two hosts and the network.

What applications use UDP? Voice over IP (VoIP) uses UDP because voice packets must arrive with minimal delay. There is no time to wait for retransmissions if there is an error.

The Simple Network Management Protocol (SNMP) also uses UDP. SNMP must send queries constantly to many devices in a network. Using UDP greatly reduces the load on the network. In addition, occasional lost messages simply mean that the management

Figure 2-16   TCP and UDP at the Transport Layer

	TCP	UDP
Layer	Transport	Transport
Connection-orientation	Connection-Oriented	Connectionless
Reliable	Reliable	Unreliable
Burden on the two hosts	High	Low
Burden on the network	High	Low

program's information about a few of the network's devices will be very slightly out of date. Error correction is simply not worth the cost.

TEST YOUR UNDERSTANDING

21. Compare TCP and UDP in terms of layer of operation, connection-orientation, reliability, and burden (network traffic and processing on devices).

LAYER 5: HTTP AND OTHER APPLICATION STANDARDS

The highest layer is the application layer (Layer 5). Standards at this layer govern how application programs talk to one another. In our examples so far, we have used HTTP most of the time. However, as noted earlier, there are many application layer standards—more than there are standards at any other layer. After network professionals master the network and internetwork standards that this course presents, they spend much of the rest of their careers mastering application standards.

HTTP is a very simple application layer protocol. The browser sends HTTP request messages, and the webserver sends back HTTP response messages. Figure 2-17 shows a much more complex application protocol, the Simple Mail Transfer Protocol (SMTP). We will see this protocol in detail in Chapter 10. It is merely included in this chapter to illustrate that application layer standards can be complex and to emphasize that although we used HTTP in our early examples in this chapter, HTTP is not the only application layer standard.

TEST YOUR UNDERSTANDING

22. a) Is the application layer standard always HTTP? b) Which layer has the most standards? c) At which layer would you find standards for instant messaging? (The answer is not explicitly in this section.)

VERTICAL COMMUNICATION ON HOSTS, SWITCHES, AND ROUTERS

In this chapter so far, we have looked at horizontal communication at a single layer, between processes on different hosts, switches, and routers. Indeed, this kind of horizontal communication will be the focus of most of this book. However, communication also needs to take place within a single host, router, or switch. More specifically, a layer process on a device often needs to communicate vertically with the process one layer above it (Layer N+1) and the process one layer below it (Layer N−1). So a Layer 3 protocol has to communicate with Layer 2 (N−1) and Layer 4 (N+1) processes on the same computer.

Layered Communication on the Source Host

Figure 2-18 looks at vertical communication within a single host computer. Here the computer is a client PC with a browser.

Actor	Sends	Comment
Beforehand		Sending TCP process opens a connection to the receiving SMTP process.
Receiving SMTP Process	220 Mail.Panko.Com Ready	When a TCP connection is opened, the receiver signals that it is ready.
Sending SMTP Process	HELO *voyager.cba.hawaii.edu*	Sender asks to begin sending a message. Gives own identity. (Yes, HELO, not HELLO.)
Receiver	250 Mail.Panko.Com	Receiver signals that it is ready to begin receiving a message.
Sender	MAIL FROM: *Pukanui@ voyager.cba.hawaii.edu*	Sender identifies the sender (mail author, not SMTP process).
Receiver	250 OK	Accepts author. However, may reject mail from others.
Sender	RCPT TO: Ray@Panko.com	Identifies first mail recipient.
Receiver	250 OK	Accepts first recipient.
Sender	RCPT TO: Lee@Panko.com	Identifies second mail recipient.
Receiver	550 No such user here	Does not accept second recipient. However will deliver to first recipient.
Sender	DATA	Message will follow.
Receiver	354 Start mail input; end with <CRLF>.<CRLF>	Gives permission to send message.
Sender	*When in the course . . .*	The message. Multiple lines of text. Ends with line containing only a single period: <CRLF>.<CRLF>
Receiver	250 OK	Receiver accepts message.
Sender	QUIT	Requests termination of session.
Receiver	221 Mail.Panko.Com Service closing transmission channel	End of transaction.

Figure 2-17 A Complex Application Protocol: The Simple Mail Transfer Protocol (SMTP)

At the Application Layer

The browser creates an HTTP request message intended for the webserver process on a webserver destination computer. The two application layer processes are on different computers, so they cannot communicate directly. Rather, they must use processes at other layers on their own computers and on intermediate switches and routers to carry messages between the two application programs.

Figure 2-18 shows that immediately after the browser at the application layer creates the HTTP message, it passes this application message down to the next-lower layer, which is the transport layer.

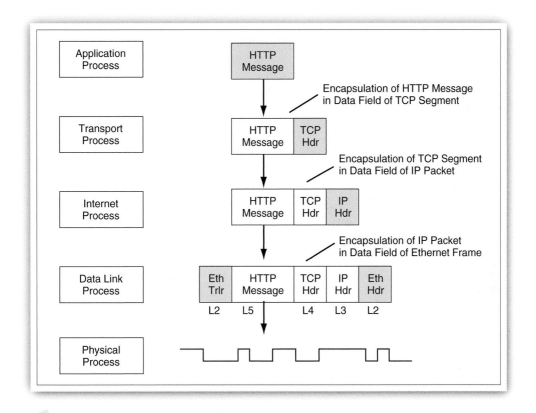

Figure 2-18   Layered Communication on the Source Host

At the Transport Layer

The transport layer process on the client PC then creates a TCP segment. It places the HTTP message in the body of the TCP segment and adds a header designed to be read by the transport process on the other host. A TCP segment carrying an application message, then, consists of a TCP header and the application message. As noted earlier in the chapter, placing a message in the data field of another message is *encapsulation*. The transport layer, in other words, encapsulates the HTTP message in the data field of a TCP segment. The transport layer then passes the TCP segment down to the internet layer.

At the Internet Layer

The internet layer process creates an IP packet by making the TCP segment the data field and adding an IP header. This packet now contains an HTTP message, a TCP header, and an IP header. Continuing the pattern, the internet layer process passes the IP packet down to the data link layer.

At the Data Link Layer

The data link layer takes the IP packet as its data field and adds a data link header and perhaps a data link trailer. The final message, then, consists of a data link header, an IP header, a TCP header, the HTTP message, and a data link trailer. If the network is an Ethernet network, the data link header is an Ethernet header and the data link trailer is an Ethernet trailer. This data link layer frame is the final message created on the source host.

Figure 2-18 lists the final frame with the layer numbers of its headers, messages, and trailers. There is a data link layer (L2) header, an IP (L3) header, a TCP (L4) header, an application layer (L5) message, and a data link layer (L2) trailer. Note the regular pattern—L2, then L3, then L4, then L5. The final element (L2) breaks the sequence. If you are confused about which protocol is used at each layer, remember the L2, L3, L4, L5, and L2 pattern.

At the Physical Layer

The data link layer passes the data link layer frame to the physical layer. The physical layer converts the ones and zeros of this frame into signals and transmits them to the next device, usually a switch.

A Simple Process, with Repetition

Some students have a difficult time with layered communication on source (and destination) hosts. If you are one of them, just keep in mind that there is a simple process repeated multiple times.

- ➤ When a layer N creates its message, the layer process passes the message down to the N–1 layer.
- ➤ The N–1 layer encapsulates the message in the data field of the Layer N–1 message and adds a Layer N–1 header and (at the data link layer only) perhaps a layer N–1 trailer. The Layer N–1 process then repeats the cycle.

The only exception is the physical layer, which receives data link layer frames, converts them into signals, and transmits them. And, of course, the layer that begins the transmission (in the example above, the application layer) does not encapsulate any messages from higher layers.

A Postal Analogy

To give an analogy, when you write a letter, you encapsulate it in an envelope, which the postal service delivers. Along the way, the postal service will encapsulate your message in mailbags for delivery between post offices.

At the other end, the post office decapsulates the envelope from its mail bag and delivers the envelope to your intended receiver. The recipient decapsulates the letter from the envelope and reads it.

TEST YOUR UNDERSTANDING

23. a) When a layer creates a message, what does it usually do immediately afterward?
    b) What does the layer below it usually do after receiving the next-higher-layer message?

c) What is encapsulation? d) With Web communication using HTTP, what message does IP encapsulate in packet data fields? e) What are the two steps after a layer process creates its layer message? f) What is the final frame if SMTP (an e-mail protocol that requires TCP) is used at the application layer and if Frame Relay (which has a header and a trailer) is used instead of Ethernet at the data link layer?

On the Destination Host

When the signal of the last frame finally reaches the destination host, the process of **decapsulation** on the destination host is the reverse of the encapsulation process on the source host, as Figure 2-19 shows.

6 ➤ The physical layer turns the signals into the bits of the frame and passes the frame to the data link layer.

Figure 2-19   Decapsulation on the Destination Host

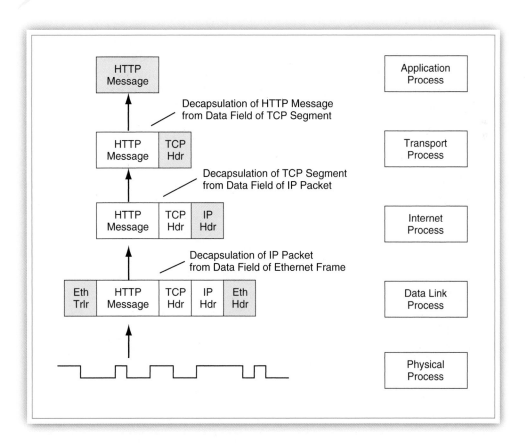

➤ The data link layer checks the frame for errors. If there are no errors, it decapsulates the IP packet from the frame and passes the packet up to the internet layer process.

➤ The internet layer checks the IP packet header for errors. If there are no errors, it decapsulates the TCP segment from the IP packet and passes the segment up to the transport layer process. (It also sends an acknowledgement.)

➤ The transport layer checks the TCP segment for errors. If there are no errors, it decapsulates the HTTP message and passes this message up to the application layer process.

What if there is an error at any layer? In that case, the layer process simply discards the message and does not send an error message. This is true for all layers above the physical layer.

TEST YOUR UNDERSTANDING

24. a) Which host decapsulates—the sending host or the receiving host? b) Describe what each layer's process does on the receiving host when the host receives an Ethernet frame containing an HTTP message.

On Switches and Routers Along the Way

So far, we have looked at layered communication only on the two hosts. However, layer processing also takes place on all intermediate switches and routers, as Figure 2-20 shows. Note that the highest layer on switches is the data link layer and that the highest layer on routers is the internet layer. This is why networking specialists call switches Layer 2 devices and call routers Layer 3 devices.

Figure 2-20   Layered End-to-End Communication

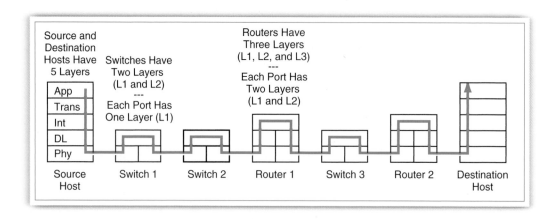

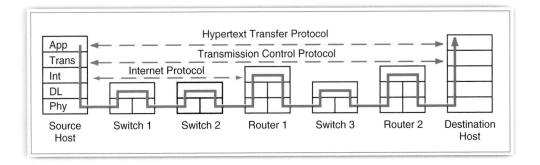

Figure 2-21   Combining Horizontal and Vertical Communication

TEST YOUR UNDERSTANDING

25. a) Why are switches called Layer 2 devices? b) Why are routers called Layer 3 devices? c) Do routers first encapsulate or decapsulate? (The answer is not explicitly in the text. Look at Figure 2-20.)

Combining Vertical and Horizontal Communication

In earlier parts of this chapter, we looked at *horizontal* communication between hardware or software processes at the *same layer* but on two *different* devices. In this section, we looked at *vertical* communication between *adjacent layer* processes on the *same* device. Figure 2-21 shows how the two views are related.

Vertical communication is necessary because hosts, switches, and routers only connect at the physical layer. For a process at any other layer, the only way to communicate with its peer process on another device is to pass its message down to the physical layer for transmission. The vertical communication process we have been examining does this in an orderly manner. In the examples shown in Figure 2-18 and Figure 2-19, the application process transmitted an entire message to its peer. Other layers simply added communication messages for their peers in the headers and perhaps trailers that they added during encapsulation. To continue the postal analogy, the address on an envelope is intended for the postal service to read, while the letter contained in the envelope is only intended for the recipient of the letter to read.

TEST YOUR UNDERSTANDING

26. To what software process is the transport layer message addressed?

MAJOR STANDARDS ARCHITECTURES

It might be nice if there were only one set of standards that governed all network equipment. The reality, however, is that there are several **standards architectures**, which are families of related standards that collectively allow an application program on one machine on an internet to communicate with another application program on another machine on that same internet.

Standards architectures are families of related standards that collectively allow an application program on one machine on an internet to communicate with another application program on another machine on that same internet.

Unfortunately, hardware and software processes cannot talk to each other if they use standards from different architectures. Consider one non-network example of multiple standards architectures and incompatibility: Different countries have different standards for their electrical systems (voltages, cycles per second, plug design, etc.). If you take your computer from one country to another, it may operate at the wrong voltage and with the wrong number of cycles per second. Plugging your PC into a wall socket might damage the computer beyond repair. Fortunately, you probably would not even be able to plug your computer into wall sockets because your power cord would not fit the wall jack.

TCP/IP and OSI Architectures

Although there are several major network standards architectures, two of them dominate actual corporate use: OSI and TCP/IP. Figure 2-22 illustrates both. Although they often are described as competitors, we will see that they actually work together in most networks. What corporations really use today is primarily a hybrid (combined) TCP/IP–OSI architecture.

Figure 2-22   The Hybrid TCP/IP-OSI Architecture

TCP/IP	OSI	Hybrid TCP/IP-OSI	Broad Purpose
Application	Application (Layer 7)	Application (Layer 5)	Applications
	Presentation (Layer 6)		
	Session (Layer 5)		
Transport	Transport (Layer 4)	Transport (Layer 4)	Internetworking
Internet	Network (Layer 3)	Internet (Layer 3)	
Use OSI	Data Link (Layer 2)	Data Link (Layer 2)	Communication within
Standards Here	Physical (Layer 1)	Physical (Layer 1)	a single LAN or WAN

Notes:

The Hybrid TCP/IP-OSI Architecture governs the Internet and dominates internal corporate networks.

OSI standards dominate the physical and data link layers (which govern communication within individual networks) almost exclusively.

TCP/IP governs 70–80 percent of all corporate traffic above the data link layer.

TEST YOUR UNDERSTANDING

27. a) What is a standards architecture? b) What are the two dominant network standards architectures? c) Are they competitors?

OSI

OSI is the "Reference Model of Open Systems Interconnection." *Reference model* is another name for *architecture*. An open system is one that is open to communicating with the rest of the world. In any case, OSI is rarely spelled out, which is merciful.

Standards Agencies: ISO and ITU-T

Standards architectures are managed by organizations called **standards agencies**. Figure 2-23 shows that OSI has two standards agencies.

➤ One is the **International Organization for Standardization (ISO)**, which generally is a strong standards organization for manufacturing, including computer manufacturing.[7]

Figure 2-23   OSI and TCP/IP

	OSI	TCP/IP
Standards Agency or Agencies	ISO (International Organization for Standardization) ITU-T (International Telecommunications Union–Telecommunications Standards Sector)	IETF (Internet Engineering Task Force)
Dominance	Nearly 100% at physical and data link layers	70% to 80% at the internet and transport layers
Documents Are Called	Various	Mostly RFCs (requests for comments)

Notes:
Do not confuse OSI (the architecture) with ISO (the organization).
The acronyms for ISO and ITU-T do not match their names, but these are the official names and acronyms.

---

[7]By the way, do not confuse OSI and ISO. OSI is an architecture. ISO is a standards agency.

Number	OSI Name	Description	Use
1	Physical	Physical connections betweens adjacent devices.	Nearly 100% dominant
2	Data Link	End-to-end transmission in single networks. Frame organization. Switch operation.	Nearly 100% dominant
3	Network	Generally equivalent to the TCP/IP internet layer. However, OSI network layer standards are not compatible with TCP/IP internet layer standards	Rarely used
4	Transport	Generally equivalent to the TCP/IP transport layer. However, OSI transport layer standards are not compatible with TCP/IP transport layer standards	Rarely used
5	Session	Initiates and maintains a connection between application programs on different computers.	Rarely used
6	Presentation	Designed to handle data formatting differences and data compression and encryption. In practice, a category for general file format standards used in multiple applications.	Rarely used as a layer. However, many file format standards are assigned to this layer.
7	Application	Governs remaining application-specific matters.	Some OSI applications are used

Figure 2-24   OSI Layers

> ➤ The other is the **International Telecommunications Union–Telecommunications Standards Sector (ITU-T)**[8] Part of the United Nations, the ITU-T oversees international telecommunications.

Although ISO or the ITU-T must *ratify* all OSI standards, other organizations frequently *create* standards for inclusion in OSI. For instance, we will see in Chapter 4 that the IEEE creates Ethernet standards. These standards are not official until the ITU-T or ISO ratifies them.

OSI's Dominance at Lower Layers (Physical and Data Link)

Although OSI is a seven-layer standards architecture (see Figure 2-22), standards from its five upper layers are rarely used. Figure 2-24 describes the seven OSI layers.

However, at the two lowest layers—the physical and data link layers—corporations use OSI standards almost universally in networks. These two layers govern transmission within a single network. Almost all single networks—both LANs and WANs—follow

---

[8]No, the names and acronyms do not match for ISO and ITU-T, but these are the official names and acronyms for these two organizations.

OSI standards at the physical and data link layers, regardless of what upper-layer standards they use. OSI standards are almost 100 percent dominant at the bottom two layers.

Almost all single networks—both LANs and WANs—follow OSI standards at the physical and data link layers, regardless of what upper-layer standards they use.

Other standards agencies, recognizing the dominance of OSI at the physical and data link layers, simply specify the use of OSI standards at these layers. They then create standards only for internetworking and applications.

OSI Network and Transport Layers

The network and transport layers of OSI correspond closely to the internet and transport layers of TCP/IP that we saw earlier in this chapter. However, actual OSI standards at these layers are incompatible with actual TCP/IP standards. More importantly, OSI standards are rarely used at the network or transport layers by real organizations.

OSI Session Layer

The **OSI session layer (OSI Layer 5)** initiates and maintains a connection between application programs on different computers. For instance, suppose that a single transaction requires a number of messages. If there is a connection break, the transmission can begin at the last session layer checkpoint. For example, if communication fails during a database transaction, the entire transaction does not have to be done over—only the work since the last rollback point.

OSI Presentation Layer

The **OSI presentation layer (OSI Layer 6)** is designed to handle data formatting differences between the two computers. For example, most computers format character data (letters, digits, and punctuation signs) using the ASCII code. In contrast, IBM mainframes format them using the EBCDIC code.

The OSI presentation layer is also designed to be used for compression and data encryption for application data. In practice, however, the presentation layer in practice is rarely used for either data format conversion or compression and encryption.

Rather, the presentation layer has become a category for general file format standards used in multiple applications, including MP3, JPEG, and many other general OSI file format standards.

OSI Application Layer

The **OSI application layer (OSI Layer 7)** governs remaining application-specific matters that are now covered by the session and presentation layers. The OSI application layer, freed from session and presentation matters, focuses on concerns specific to the application in use.

TEST YOUR UNDERSTANDING

28. a) What standards agencies are responsible for the OSI standards architecture? b) At which layers do OSI standards dominate usage? c) Name and describe the functions of OSI Layer 5. d) Name and describe the intended use of OSI Layer 6. e) How is the OSI presentation layer actually used? f) Beginning with the physical layer (Layer 1), give the name and number of the OSI layers.

TCP/IP

The **TCP/IP** architecture is mandatory on the Internet at the internet and transport layers. TCP/IP is also widely used at these layers by companies for their internal corporate networks.

The TCP/IP architecture is named after two of its standards, TCP and IP, which we have looked at briefly in this chapter. However, TCP/IP also has many other standards, including the UDP standard we have already seen. This makes the name TCP/IP rather misleading. Note that TCP/IP is the standards architecture while TCP and IP are individual standards within the architecture.

Note that TCP/IP is the standards architecture while TCP and IP are individual standards within the architecture.

The Internet Engineering Task Force (IETF)

TCP/IP's standards agency is the **Internet Engineering Task Force (IETF)**.[9] The IETF traditionally has been rather informal.[10] Its committees traditionally focus on consensus rather than on voting, and technical expertise is the source of most power within the organization. Although corporate participation has somewhat "tamed" the IETF, it remains a fascinating organization, although its members might argue that "*organization*" is too strong a word.

A great deal of the IETF's success is due to the fact that the IETF typically produces simple standards, then adds to their complexity over time. In fact, IETF standards often have the word *simple* in their name—for instance, the Simple Mail Transfer Protocol. Consequently, IETF TCP/IP standards are developed quickly. In addition, TCP/IP products can be developed quickly and inexpensively because they are simple.

---

[9]Traditionally, the IETF has been viewed as being in competition with ISO and ITU-T for standards development. However, in recent years, the IETF and these other organizations have begun to cooperate in standards development. For instance, the IETF is working closely with ITU-T for VoIP transmission standards.

[10]In 1992, IETF member Dave Clark summarized the situation this way: "We reject kings, presidents, and voting. We believe in rough consensus and running code." His last point is that the IETF normally will not create a standard unless there is working code that implements it. This avoids a frequent problem with OSI standards, which often are developed before any products exist—a tendency for standards implementation to be difficult because things that the standards developers found to be very clear turn out to be ambiguous during implementation.

Inexpensive and fast-to-market is almost always a good recipe for success. In contrast, OSI standards often take a very long time to be developed and often are so bloated with functionality that they are uneconomical.

Note that the success of TCP/IP is not primarily due to its use on the Internet. Corporations had already shifted many of their networks to TCP/IP before the Internet became a dominant force in the 1990s.

Requests for Comments (RFCs)

Most documents produced by the IETF have the rather misleading name **requests for comments (RFCs)**. Every few years, the IETF publishes a list of which RFCs are **Official Internet Protocol Standards**. Each list of standards adds some RFCs to the list and drops previously listed standards.

Dominance at the Internetwork Layers (Internet and Transport)

As noted earlier, physical and data link layer standards govern the transmission of data within a *single network*. We saw earlier that OSI standards are completely dominant at these layers.

TCP/IP internet and transport layer standards, in turn, govern transmission across an entire internet, ensuring that any two host computers can communicate. TCP/IP application standards ensure that the two application programs on the two hosts can communicate as well.

TCP/IP is dominant in the internetworking layers (internet and transport). However, it is less dominant at these layers than OSI standards are at the bottom two layers. In most organizations, TCP/IP standards govern 70 percent to 80 percent of internet and transport layer traffic, and this dominance is growing. In a few years, the use of other architectures at the internet and transport layers in new products will be increasingly rare.

TCP/IP is dominant in corporate networking at the internet and transport layers, although less dominant than OSI is at the physical and data link layers. In most organizations, TCP/IP standards govern 70–80 percent of internet and transport layer traffic.

TEST YOUR UNDERSTANDING

29. a) Which of the following is an architecture: TCP/IP, TCP, or IP? b) Which of the following are standards: TCP/IP, TCP, or IP? c) What is the standards agency for TCP/IP? d) Why have this agency's standards been so successful? e) What are most of this agency's documents called? f) At which layers is TCP/IP dominant? g) How dominant is TCP/IP today at these layers compared to OSI's dominance at the physical and data link layers?

The Application Layer

OSI is completely dominant at the physical and data link layers, and TCP/IP is very dominant at the internet and transport layers. What about the application layer? The answer here is highly complex. [11] Overall, it seems best to say that no standards agency or architecture dominates at the application layer, although the IETF is particularly strong, especially for popular standards such as e-mail and FTP.

Although many applications do not come from the IETF, they almost all run over TCP/IP standards at the internet and transport layers. This is even true for standards created by ISO and ITU-T.

At the application layer, in fact, there is growing cooperation between ISO, the ITU-T, and the IETF. In voice over IP, the ITU-T and the IETF have harmonized several key standards. ISO and the IETF, in turn, have been cooperating in file format standards.

TEST YOUR UNDERSTANDING

30. a) Is any standards architecture dominant at the application layer? b) Do almost all applications run over TCP/IP standards at the internet and transport layers?

TCP/IP *and* OSI: The Hybrid TCP/IP–OSI Standards Architecture

Although people sometimes view TCP/IP and OSI as competitors, most organizations use them together. The most common standards pattern in organizations is to use OSI standards at the physical and data link layers and TCP/IP standards at the internet and transport layers. This is very important for you to keep in mind because this **hybrid TCP/IP–OSI standards architecture**, shown in Figure 2-22, will form the basis for most of this book.

TEST YOUR UNDERSTANDING

31. a) What layers of the hybrid TCP/IP–OSI standards architecture use OSI standards? b) What layers use TCP/IP standards? c) Do LAN standards come from OSI or TCP/IP? (The answer is not explicitly in this section.) d) Do WAN standards come from OSI or TCP/IP? (Again, the answer is not explicitly in this section.)

---

[11]Many application protocols come from the IETF. These include such popular standards as e-mail protocols (SMTP, POP, IMAP, etc.), the FTP standards, and the Simple Network Management Protocol (SNMP) in network management.

Some standards come directly from OSI. This is particularly true of graphics file format standards.

Some standards came from OSI but were too complex for widespread use; the IETF then produced simpler versions of these OSI standards. A good example is the Lightweight Directory Access Protocol (LDAP) for access to directory servers. LDAP evolved from the OSI directory access protocol standard.

Increasingly, the IETF is cooperating with ISO or the ITU-T in the creation of specific standards. The IETF and ITU-T are cooperating closely in IP telephony, for instance.

Other standards agencies are also producing application layer standards. HTTP and HTML standards come from the World Wide Web Consortium (W3C), although the IETF is producing some WWW standards. Most confusingly, incompatible Service Oriented Architecture web services standards are being produced by several competing standards agencies.

Finally, many protocols are vendor-specific. Advanced database protocols usually fit into this category. I told you it was complex.

> **IPX/SPX**
>
> > Used by older Novell NetWare file servers for file and print service
> >
> > Sometimes used in newer Novell NetWare file servers for consistency with older NetWare servers
>
> **SNA (Systems Network Architecture)**
>
> > Used by IBM mainframe computers
>
> **AppleTalk**
>
> > Used by Apple Macintosh desktops and notebooks to talk to Macintosh servers

Figure 2-25   Other Major Standards Architectures

A Multiprotocol World at Higher Layers

At the same time, quite a few networking products (especially legacy products) in organizations follow other architectures shown in Figure 2-25. Real corporations live and will continue to live for some time in a multiprotocol world in which network administrators have to deal with a complex mix of products following different architectures above the data link layer. In this book, we focus on OSI and TCP/IP because they are by far the most important and are becoming ever more so. However, in a typical organization, 20–30 percent of all upper-layer traffic still uses protocols from other standards architectures.

IPX/SPX

The most widely used non-TCP/IP standards architecture found at upper layers in LANs is the **IPX/SPX architecture**. Older Novell NetWare file servers required this architecture. Many NetWare users are switching to TCP/IP.

Systems Network Architecture (SNA)

IBM Mainframe computers traditionally used the **Systems Network Architecture (SNA)** standards architecture, which actually predates OSI and TCP/IP. Most firms, however, are transitioning their mainframe communications from SNA to TCP/IP.

AppleTalk

Macintosh desktop and notebook computers are designed to use Apple's proprietary **AppleTalk architecture** when they talk to Macintosh servers. Macintoshes are rare in corporations today, so AppleTalk is not widely seen.

TEST YOUR UNDERSTANDING

32. a) Under what circumstances might you encounter IPX/SPX standards? b) SNA standards? c) AppleTalk standards?

STANDARDS AT THE FIRST BANK OF PARADISE

Physical and Data Link Layer Standards

At Layers 1 and 2, the First Bank of Paradise uses OSI standards almost exclusively—although the bank still has a few legacy systems built on data link layer standards that predate OSI.

However, this does not mean that selecting specific standards at these layers is simple. In LANs, Ethernet dominates, but the bank still has a few older legacy LANs as well. As we will see in Chapter 7a, the bank uses several different OSI standards for its WAN traffic.

Protocols at Higher Layers

At higher layers, there is nothing like the dominance of OSI. As in most other firms, TCP/IP standards govern more than 70 percent of the bank's traffic above the data link layer. However, the bank still has a good deal of SNA traffic because of its IBM mainframe traffic. The bank also has some upper-layer traffic that follows standards from other architectures.

In fact, upper-layer transmission for an average branch office used nine different internet and transport layer standards from three different architectures. A tenth upper-level standard used by the average branch was created before standards architectures emerged in the 1960s!

CONCLUSION

Synopsis

In this chapter, we looked broadly at standards. Most of this book (and the networking profession in general) focuses on standards, which are also called protocols.

Standards govern message exchanges. More specifically, they place constraints on message semantics (meaning) and message syntax (format).

Standards are connection-oriented or connectionless (see Figure 2-26). In connection-oriented protocols, there is a distinct opening before content messages are sent and a distinct closing afterward. There also are sequence numbers, which allow fragmentation and are used in supervisory messages (such as acknowledgements) to refer to specific messages by sequence numbers. In connectionless protocols, there are no such openings and closings. Connectionless protocols are simpler but lose the advantages of sequence numbers.

In turn, reliable protocols do error correction, while unreliable protocols do not (although unreliable protocols may do error detection without error correction). In general, standards below the transport layer are unreliable to reduce costs. The transport standard usually is reliable; this allows error correction processes on just the two

Layer	Protocol	Connection-oriented or Connectionless?	Reliable or Unreliable?
5 (Application)	HTTP	Connectionless	Unreliable
4 (Transport)	TCP	Connection-oriented	Reliable
4 (Transport)	UDP	Connectionless	Unreliable
3 (Internet)	IP	Connectionless	Unreliable
2 (Data Link)	Ethernet	Connectionless	Unreliable

Figure 2-26   Characteristics of Protocols Discussed in the Chapter

hosts to correct errors at the transport layer and at lower layers, giving the application clean data.

Standards are created within broad plans called standards architectures. Most networks use a five-layer architecture.

➤ The physical layer governs transmission between adjacent devices. There are no messages at the physical layer. Physical layer standards almost always come from OSI.

➤ The data link layer governs transmission between two devices on a single network. Messages at the data link layer are called frames. The path a frame takes through a single network is called a data link. Data link layer standards govern the operation of switches within a single network. Data link layer standards almost always come from OSI.

➤ The internet layer governs transmission between the source and destination hosts on an internet. Messages at the internet layer are called packets. The path a packet takes through an internet is called a route. Internet layer standards govern the operation of packets within an internet. Note that messages at the data link layer are frames, while messages at the internet layer are packets. If there are ten networks involved in a transmission between two hosts, there will be ten frames and ten data links along the way but only one packet and one route. Internet layer standards usually come from TCP/IP.

➤ The transport layer governs communication between the source and destination hosts in an internet. It usually corrects errors at lower layers. Transport layer standards usually come from TCP/IP.

➤ The application layer governs interactions between application programs. Application standards come from TCP/IP, OSI, and other standards architectures.

Transmission in single networks—both LANs and WANs—is governed by physical and data link layer standards, which almost always come from OSI. Ethernet is a fairly simple standard for physical and data link layer transmission in LANs. Ethernet is connectionless and unreliable. This simplicity leads to low costs, and low costs have brought Ethernet to dominance in LANs. Representations of the Ethernet frame's syntax usually show each field's length in octets. Ethernet addresses are 48 bits long. They are often expressed in hexadecimal notation for human reading.

Internetworking involves the internet and transport layer standards. At the internet layer, the Internet Protocol (IP) is a fairly simple connectionless and unreliable protocol. IP depends on TCP for error correction and even for the correct ordering of received packets. The IP packet's syntax usually is shown as a series of lines with 32 bits on each line. IP addresses are 32 bits long. Humans usually express them in dotted decimal notation.

The Transmission Control Protocol (TCP) is a complex transport layer protocol that is connection-oriented and reliable. The receiving transport process acknowledges every correct TCP segment. If a segment is not acknowledged promptly, the sender retransmits it. TCP corrects errors at all lower layers as well as at the transport layer, so it gives the application program clean data.

The User Datagram Protocol (UDP) is an alternative to TCP at the transport layer. It is a lightweight protocol that places a lower burden than TCP on devices and networks. However, it is connectionless and unreliable. It is up to the application layer program to deal with errors that occur.

HTTP is a simple connectionless and unreliable protocol that depends on TCP at the transport layer for reliable data transmission. HTTP has a simple text-based syntax for its headers.

Standards processes at each layer also communicate vertically with the process in the layer directly above them and the process in the layer directly below them on the same computer. On the sending device, a process usually creates a message and then passes the message down to the next-lower-layer process, which encapsulates the message in the data field of its own message. On the receiving process, the reverse process (decapsulation) is used. Hosts are Layer 5 devices, while switches are Layer 2 devices and routers are Layer 3 devices.

Standards are created by standards agencies, which first create standards architectures that guide the creation of individual standards. Standards from different architectures are incompatible. The TCP/IP architecture is managed by the IETF, while the OSI architecture is managed by two organizations, ISO and ITU-T. The dominant standards architecture used in organizations today is the hybrid TCP/IP–OSI architecture, with OSI standards being used at the bottom two (physical and data link) layers and TCP/IP standards being used at the upper (internet and transport) layers.

Again, application layer standards come from TCP/IP, OSI, and other standards architectures. Although many applications do not come from the IETF, they almost all run over TCP/IP standards at the internet and transport layers. This is even true for standards created by ISO and ITU-T.

Firms use OSI standards almost universally at the physical and data link layers. At higher layers, most firms are multiprotocol environments in which 20–30 percent of all traffic at upper layers comes from standards architectures other than TCP/IP—usually IPX/SPX (for some Novell NetWare file servers), SNA (for IBM mainframe communications), and AppleTalk (for Macintosh computers).

THOUGHT QUESTIONS

1. How do you think TCP would handle the problem if an acknowledgement were lost, so that the sender retransmitted the unacknowledged TCP segment, therefore causing the receiving transport process to receive the same segment twice?

2. a) In Figure 2-21, how many single networks, physical links, data links, and routes are shown?
   b) In Figure 2-21, how many data link, internet, transport, and application processes in total are involved in the transmission?

3. You can place both TCP/IP clients and servers and IPX clients and servers on the same Ethernet network, and each client will talk to its server. How do you think this is possible? (Hint: Consider the Ethernet frame in Figure 2-14.)

4. IP addresses are unique. What do you think would happen if two hosts had the same IP address?

5. Ethernet stations need Ethernet addresses. Do Ethernet switches need to have Ethernet addresses too? Explain your reasoning.

6. How can you make a connectionless protocol reliable? (Try to answer this one, but you may not be able to do so.)

7. Spacecraft exploring the outer planets need reliable data transmission. However, the acknowledgements would take hours to arrive. This makes an ACK-based reliability approach unattractive. Can you think of another way to provide reliable data transmission to spacecraft? (Try to answer this one, but you may not be able to do so.)

8. Figure 2-14 shows the fields in an Ethernet frame. Ethernet is the dominant standard in LANs. However, there are many other data link standards. One example is the Point-to-Point Protocol (PPP). This protocol is used at the data link layer to connect two routers using a point-to-point leased line from the telephone company. PPP frames begin and end with a one-octet flag field containing the content 01111110. These unambiguously signal the start of a new frame and the end of that frame, respectively. The second two octets always have the values 11111111 and 00000011. These are the address and control fields, respectively. They exist for historical reasons that are no longer important. Obviously, there is no need for an address field in a point-to-point connection, and the function of the control field has been replaced by the advanced use of the data field for supervisory communication. The next two octets form the protocol field, which describes the contents of the data field. If the PPP frame is delivering a packet, the protocol field contains the value 8021h. In PPP, this data field is called the information field. It can be up to 1500 octets long, although a shorter value can be negotiated. Next comes the frame check sequence field. As in Ethernet, this field is used to detect errors. If the receiver detects an error, it simply discards the frame. There are no acknowledgements whether or not the frame contains an error. a) Which fields form the PPP header? b) Which fields form the PPP trailer? c) Figure 2-18 shows the final frame when an HTTP application transmits an application message over an Ethernet network. Give the final frame if PPP is used instead of Ethernet. d) Give the final frame if the application is SNMP, which requires UDP at the transport layer. The protocol is still PPP at the data link layer. e) When TCP sends a pure acknowledgement, it transmits a TCP message that only has a header. The application layer is not involved at all in the acknowledgement process. Give the final frame when the packet travels over an Ethernet LAN.

GETTING CURRENT

Go to the book website's New Information and Errors pages for this chapter to get new information since this book went to press and to correct any errors in the text.

Physical Layer Propagation: UTP and Optical Fiber

Learning Objectives

By the end of this chapter, you should be able to discuss:

- Binary data representations for important types of data.
- Binary signaling (on/off signaling or using two possible voltage states).
- In the box on digital signaling: binary versus digital signaling, including the difference between bit rates and baud rates.
- Unshielded twisted pair (UTP) wiring, including relevant propagation effects that must be controlled by limiting cord length and by limiting the untwisting of pairs during connectorization.
- The differences between serial and parallel transmission, including the speed advantage of parallel transmission.
- Optical fiber cabling, including relevant propagation effects and different types of optical fiber cabling and signaling.
- Network topologies, including point-to-point connections, stars, extended stars (hierarchies), rings, meshes, and busses.

INTRODUCTION: THE PHYSICAL LAYER

Chapter 2 presented an overview of layered standards. Most of that chapter focused on the data link, internet, transport, and application layers. In this chapter, we will go down to Layer 1, the physical layer, which differs from upper layers in two ways:

- ➤ It is the only layer that does not use messages. It takes the bits of frames and turns them into signals.
- ➤ It alone deals with propagation effects, which change signals when they travel over transmission lines.

This chapter will cover physical layer signaling and two major transmission media: UTP and optical fiber. We will look at radio propagation in Chapter 5.

SIGNALS AND PROPAGATION

Propagation

Suppose that you and a friend are standing a few meters apart. You stretch a rope between you. Now you close your eyes. Your friend jiggles the rope. The disturbance **propagates** (travels) down the rope. When it arrives, you feel it.

Signals

Something like this happens in network transmission. As Figure 3-1 shows, the transmitter creates a disturbance in a transmission medium—wire, optical fiber, or radio. This disturbance is the signal. A **signal**, then, is a disturbance that propagates down a transmission medium to the other side, which reads the signal.

A signal is a disturbance that propagates down a transmission medium to the other side, which reads the signal.

Propagation Effects

Note that the received signal differs from the transmitted signal. This change is due to **propagation effects**—that is, changes in the signal during propagation. In the figure, the signal has **attenuated** (weakened). It also has been **distorted** (its shape has been changed). If propagation effects are too large, the receiver will not be able to interpret the signal correctly.

TEST YOUR UNDERSTANDING

1. a) What is a signal? b) What is propagation? c) What are propagation effects? d) Why are propagation effects bad?

Figure 3-1   Signal and Propagation

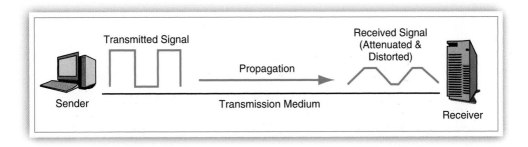

BINARY DATA REPRESENTATION

The messages that we saw in the previous chapter were long strings of bits. This type of data only has two possible values (ones and zeros), so it is **binary data** (from the Greek word for two).

In binary data, there are only two values.

Inherently Binary Data

As just noted, certain types of data are inherently binary. For instance, IP addresses are 32-bit binary strings, while Ethernet addresses are 48-bit binary strings.

Binary Numbers

Some message fields contain numbers. Senders represent whole numbers (integers) as simple **Base 2** or **binary numbers**. Figure 3-2 illustrates binary counting and arithmetic.

With binary numbers, counting begins with 0. This is a source of frequent confusion.

In counting, add 1 to each binary number to give the next binary number. There are four simple rules for addition in binary, as Figure 3-2 illustrates.

➤ If you add 0 and 0, you get 0.
➤ If you add 0 and 1, you get 1.
➤ If you add 1 and 1, you get 10 (carry the one).
➤ If you add 1, 1, and 1, you get 11 (carry the one).

Figure 3-2　Arithmetic with Binary Numbers

Counting Begins with 0, not 1 So the first three items are 0, 1, and 10 (10 is 2 in binary)						
Basic Rules					Examples	
				1	1000	8
0	0	1	1	+1	+1	+1
+0	+1	+0	+1	+1	=1001	=9
=0	=1	=1	=10	=11	+1	+1
					=1010	=10
					+1	+1
					=1011	=11
					+1	+1
					=1100	=12

These rules are simple to use, as the figure illustrates.

➤ For example, 8 is 1000.
➤ The number 9 adds a 1 to the final 0, giving a 1, so 9 is 1001.
➤ Adding 1 to the final 1 gives us 10, so 10 is 1010.
➤ The number 11 adds a 1 to the final 0, giving 1011.
➤ The number 12 adds a 1 to the final 1. With carries, this gives 1100.

Decimal numbers can also be converted into binary representations. There are several ways to do this. Generally, the representation contains two parts: the number itself and an indication of where the decimal point is.[1]

Encoding Alternatives

Sometimes a field represents one of several different **alternatives**, such as site names in a corporation or product numbers. How many possible alternatives can a field represent? The answer depends on the field's length. If a field is N bits long, it can represent 2^N possible alternatives. This is illustrated in Figure 3-3.

If a field is N bits long, it can represent 2^N possible alternatives.

➤ If the field is only one bit long, it can only represent 2^1 (2) alternatives. For instance, a 1-bit gender field might represent *female* by 1 and *male* by 0.
➤ If the field is two bits long, it can represent 2^2 (4) possibilities, representing each by 00, 01, 10, or 11. A 2-bit season field might represent *Spring* by 00, *Summer* by 01, *Autumn* by 10, and *Winter* by 11.

Figure 3-3   Binary Encoding for a Number of Alternatives

Encoding Alternatives (Number of Alternatives = 2^Number of Bits)	
Number of Bits in Field	Number of Alternatives Than Can Be Encoded
1	2
2	4
4	16
8	256
. . .	. . .

[1] In Chapter 1, we saw how to use the Microsoft Windows Calculator in scientific mode to convert between decimal, binary, and hexadecimal. You can also use it to check your binary calculations (obviously not on tests). First click on the Bin button to put yourself in binary mode. Then use the calculator normally. For example, to add two binary numbers, click on Bin, enter the first binary number, hit the plus button, type the second binary number, and click on the equal sign to see the total.

Need to Represent Text as Binary Data for Transmission

ASCII

Traditional way to represent text data in binary

Seven bits per character

2^7 (128) characters possible

Sufficient for all keyboard characters (including shifted values)

Capital letters (*A* is 1000001)

Lowercase letters (*a* is 1100001)

Digits (0 through 9) (*3* is 0110011)

Punctuation and other special characters (a period is 0101110)

Printing control (a carriage return is 0001101 and a line feed is 0001010)

Eighth bit in data bytes normally is not used

Extended ASCII

Used on PCs

8 bits per character

2^8 (256) characters possible

Extra characters can represent formatting in word processing, etc.

Text-to-ASCII and Text-to-Extended ASCII Calculators are Readily Available on the Internet

Figure 3-4 ASCII and Extended ASCII (Study Figure)

➤ A 1-octet (one-byte) field can represent 2^8 (256) alternatives.
➤ A 2-octet field can represent 2^{16} (65,536) alternatives.
➤ A 3-octet field can represent 2^{24} (over 16 million) alternatives.

Remember that binary counting begins with 0. Therefore, if you have eight bits, there are 256 possibilities. These begin with 0 and end with 255.

Text (ASCII and Extended ASCII)

Web pages use the **ASCII code**, whose individual symbols are each seven bits long but are usually stored as whole bytes. Seven bits gives 128 possibilities. This is enough for:

➤ capital letters (the letter *A* is 1000001)
➤ lowercase letters (the letter *a* is 1100001)

➤ digits (3 is 0110011)

➤ punctuation and other characters (a period is 0101110)

➤ printing control (a carriage return is 0001101 and a line feed is 0001010)

Seven-bit ASCII is sufficient for typing all keys on a PC keyboard. During transmission, the eighth bit of each byte usually is not used.[2]

However, PCs internally use **extended ASCII**, which uses all eight bits to represent text more richly. Going from seven to eight bits gives 128 extra character codes. Different application programs use these extra character codes differently. For instance, word processing programs typically use these extra codes to represent formatting.

If you go to a search engine, you can easily find converters to represent characters in both ASCII and extended ASCII.

Raster Graphics

In **raster graphics**, the screen is divided into a grid of dots called **pixels**. Graphics programs represent each pixel by one to three bytes. Using a single byte per pixel allows 256 colors. This option, used by **GIF** files, is not attractive to the human eye. In contrast, **JPEG** uses three octets per pixel—one octet each for red, green, and blue. This permits over 16 million colors. This is more than the human eye can distinguish and so gives very satisfying color.

Figure 3-5   Graphics Image and Conversion to Binary

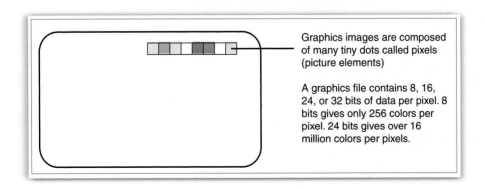

Graphics images are composed of many tiny dots called pixels (picture elements)

A graphics file contains 8, 16, 24, or 32 bits of data per pixel. 8 bits gives only 256 colors per pixel. 24 bits gives over 16 million colors per pixels.

---

[2]Early systems used the eighth bit as a "parity bit" to detect errors in transmission. This could detect a change in a single bit in the byte. At today's high transmission speeds, however, transmission errors normally generate multibit errors rather than single-bit errors. Consequently, parity is useless and is ignored.

In addition, JPEG and other graphics file mechanisms do file compression to reduce the size of files. Therefore, compressed graphics files allow the sender to transmit fewer than eight bits per pixel (GIF) or twenty-four bits per pixel (JPEG).

Computer screens have at least a half million pixels. Good consumer digital cameras create pictures with about 5 million pixels.

Overall, a graphics file can be thought of as a long string of bytes.

TEST YOUR UNDERSTANDING

2. a) Give the binary representations for 13, 14, 15, 16, and 17 by adding one to successive numbers (12 is 1100). b) Rounding off, about how many possible addresses can you represent with 32-bit IP addresses? (You probably will need a spreadsheet program to answer this question.) c) If you have four bits, how many possibilities can you represent? d) With four bits, what is the smallest non-negative binary number you can represent? e) What is its decimal equivalent? f) What is the largest binary number you can represent if you have four bits? g) What is its decimal equivalent?

3. a) How many bits does ASCII use to represent keyboard characters? b) If you transmit "Hello World!" (without the quotation marks) in ASCII, how many bytes must you transmit? c) Your computer screen has a resolution of 800 pixels horizontally and 600 pixels vertically. How many bytes will a JPEG screen image be if there is no compression? Express the file size in proper notation. Use B for bytes. d) How large would the file be with 20:1 compression (which is common)?

SIGNALING

Converting Data to Signals

So far, we have looked at how to encode *data* as a string of bits. For transmission, the sender must convert these bits into *signals* that will represent the bits. Note that most data must be converted twice—once into binary data and once into signals.

Most data must be converted twice—once into binary data and once into signals.

On/Off Signaling

The simplest way to signal is to divide time into brief **clock cycles** (periods of time) and to have each clock cycle represent one bit. As Figure 3-7 shows, the sender turns a signal on for a 1 during the clock cycle or off for a 0. Think of turning a flashlight I (*torch* in real English-speaking countries) on and off to send a signal. Optical fiber generally uses this type of **on/off signaling**.

Binary Signaling

In binary *data*, there are only two possible states. In **binary signaling**, there also are two possible states. It is easy to map binary data into binary signals. On/off signaling is an example of binary signaling, which is characterized by using two possible **states** (on or off) to represent binary data (1 or 0).

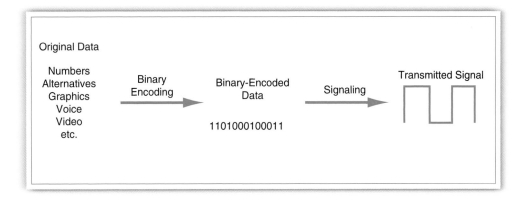

Figure 3-6   Data Encoding and Signals

Binary signaling uses two possible states to represent information or data (1s and 0s).

Binary Voltage Signaling

When signals travel over wires, it is common to use two different voltages to represent 1 and 0, as Figure 3-8 illustrates. This is also binary signaling.

Figure 3-7   On/Off Signaling

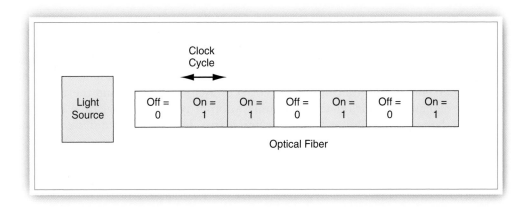

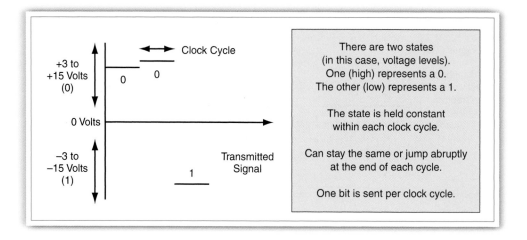

Figure 3-8   Binary Signaling in 232 Serial Ports

232 Serial Ports

In Figure 3-8, a high voltage is anything between 3 and 15 volts. A low voltage, in turn, is anything between negative 3 and negative 15 volts.

Now comes the strange part. A high voltage represents a 0, while a low voltage represents a 1. No, this is not a misprint. This is the way a **232 serial port** works on your PC.[3]

Constancy During Each Clock Cycle

As in on/off signaling, time is divided into brief clock cycles. The sender holds the signal constant within each clock cycle.[4] At the end of each clock cycle, the signal either stays the same or changes to the other voltage level (state).

Relative Immunity to Attenuation Errors

Binary signal transmission is attractive because it is relatively immune to attenuation errors (losses in signal intensity). If a signal starts at 12 volts and attenuates to 6 volts (a 50 percent loss), it will still be read correctly as a high voltage and therefore a 0. Binary signaling also is relatively immune to other types of propagation error. Of course, large propagation effects still cause errors, but with careful design, the **bit**

---

[3]Sometimes called RS-232-C serial ports, they actually follow the newer ANSI/TIA/EIA-232-F standard. In Europe, equivalent ports are specified by three standards: V.24, V.28, and ISO-2110.
[4]This constancy allows the receiver to read the voltage at any time during the clock cycle. Even if the receiver is slightly off on the timing of its read for a bit, the receiver will still read the value correctly.

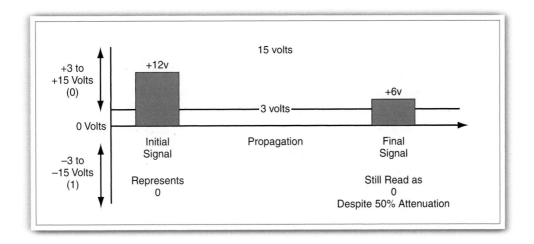

Figure 3-9 Relative Immunity to Errors in Binary Signaling

error rate or **BER** (the percentage of errors per thousand or million bits transmitted) will be very low.

Binary Signaling Versus Digital Signaling

Binary signaling is often called digital signaling. Although many professionals now consider the terms equivalent, the two concepts are not completely the same, as discussed in the box "Multistate Digital Signaling."

Concisely, while binary signaling is limited to two states (on/off, high/low voltage, etc.), **digital signaling** can have two states, four states, eight states,[5] or more. However, almost all signaling systems today are binary, and because digital signaling can involve just two states, it is correct to call all binary transmission systems digital transmission systems.

TEST YOUR UNDERSTANDING

4. a) In binary 232 serial port transmission for transmission over a binary transmission line, how are 1 and 0 represented? b) How does this give resistance to transmission errors? c) A signal is sent at 9 volts in a 232 serial port. What fraction of its strength can it lose before it becomes unreadable? d) Today, almost all signaling is binary. Is it correct to call all binary signaling "digital signaling?" e) Is it correct to call all digital transmission systems "binary transmission systems?"

---

[5]The number of states is always given by 2^N, where N is a small integer.

Multistate Digital Signaling

Figure 3-10 illustrates a slightly more complex form of signaling: digital signaling. In binary signaling, there are only two possible states (in the case of 232 serial ports, voltage levels) to represent information. In **digital signaling**, in contrast, there are a *few* possible states; the sender holds the state (voltage level in this example) constant during the clock cycle. The figure specifically shows digital signaling with four possible states. However, digital signaling can use eight, sixteen, thirty-two, or occasionally (but rarely) more states.

Note also that binary signaling is a special case of digital signaling. If *few* is *two* then digital signaling is binary.

In digital signaling, there are *a few* possible states. Binary signaling is a special case of digital signaling in which there are exactly two states.

Why use more than two possible states? The answer is that you can send multiple bits per clock cycle if you have more than two possible states. Binary transmission only sends one bit per clock cycle (a 1 or a 0). With four possible states, however, there can be four possibilities. If we let the four voltage levels represent 00, 01, 10, and 11, then we can send two bits per clock cycle—doubling the transmission rate.

Adding more possible states allows the sender to transmit even more bits per clock cycle. However, there are diminishing returns. Each doubling in the number of possible states allows the sender to transmit only one more bit per clock cycle. For instance, having eight possible states allows only three bits per clock cycle, and having sixteen possible states allows only four bits per clock cycle.

Figure 3-10   Four-State Digital Signaling

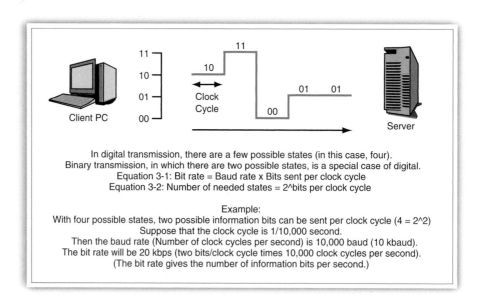

In digital transmission, there are a few possible states (in this case, four).
Binary transmission, in which there are two possible states, is a special case of digital.
Equation 3-1: Bit rate = Baud rate x Bits sent per clock cycle
Equation 3-2: Number of needed states = $2^{\wedge}$bits per clock cycle

Example:
With four possible states, two possible information bits can be sent per clock cycle ($4 = 2^{\wedge}2$)
Suppose that the clock cycle is 1/10,000 second.
Then the baud rate (Number of clock cycles per second) is 10,000 baud (10 kbaud).
The bit rate will be 20 kbps (two bits/clock cycle times 10,000 clock cycles per second).
(The bit rate gives the number of information bits per second.)

If there are too many possible states, furthermore, the possible states will be very close together. If the signal changes even slightly during transmission, the receiver will record the wrong state. This is why digital signaling only uses a *few* possible states.[6] In essence, sending more bits increases transmission rates but results in more errors. Beyond a small number of possible states, the net transmission rate actually falls because of the need to retransmit incorrect transmissions.

BIT RATES

In digital data transmission, the rate at which we transmit data is called the **bit rate**. It is measured in bits per second. This is what users care about.

BAUD RATE

In turn, the **baud rate** is the number of clock cycles the transmission system uses per second. If there are 1,000 clock cycles per second, the baud rate is 1,000 baud (not 1,000 bauds per second).

The bit rate is the rate at which we transmit data.
The baud rate is the number of clock cycles the transmission system uses per second.

AN EXAMPLE

To compute the bit rate in digital signaling, you must know two equations. The first is simple: the bit rate is the number of bits sent per clock cycle times the baud rate (Equation 3-1). For instance, if a transmission line changes its state one hundred times per second, the baud rate is 100 baud. If it can send three bits per clock cycle, then the bit rate is 300 bits per second.

Bit rate = Baud rate times the number of Bits
    sent per clock cycle   (Equation 3-1)

Second, the number of bits sent per clock cycle, in turn, is given by Equation 3-2. *Number of states* is the number of possible states, and *bits per clock cycle* is the number of bits that are sent per clock cycle. If you wish to send three bits per clock cycle, you will need 2^3 possible states, that is, 8. Alternatively, if you have four possible states, 2^2 is 4, so you can send 2 bits per second.

Number of States = $2^{\text{bits per clock cycle}}$

(Equation 3-2)

For example, if there are 10,000 clock cycles per second, the baud rate is 10,000 baud. If there are four possible states, then Equation 3-2 says that the sender transmits two bits per clock cycle. By Equation 3-1, the bit rate will be two bits per clock cycle times 10,000 baud (10 kbaud) or 20,000 bits per second (20 kbps).

TEST YOUR UNDERSTANDING

5. a) Distinguish between binary and digital transmission. b) Is binary transmission digital? c) What is desirable about having multiple possible states instead of just two? d) What is undesirable about having multiple possible states? e) How many more bits can you send per clock cycle every time you double the number of possible states?

6. a) Distinguish between the bit rate and the baud rate. b) When are the two equal? (You will have to think about this one.) c) If you have 10,000 clock cycles per second and transmit in binary, what is the baud rate? d) What is the bit rate? e) If instead you use sixteen voltage levels for digital signaling, what is the baud rate? f) What is the bit rate? g) To transmit 30 kbps over a 10 kbaud line, how many possible states will you need?

---

[6]Originally, digital signaling used ten states; it was called digital because our ten fingers are called digits.

UNSHIELDED TWISTED PAIR (UTP) WIRING

Having looked at propagation effects and signaling in general, we will now see how these concepts apply to UTP transmission. Later, we will see how they apply to optical fiber transmission.

4-Pair UTP and RJ-45

The 4-Pair UTP Cable

Ethernet networks typically use **4-pair unshielded twisted pair (UTP)** wiring.[7] The TIA/EIA-568 standard governs UTP wiring in the United States. In Europe, the comparable standard is ISO/IEC 11801.

This name 4-pair unshielded twisted pair (UTP) sounds complicated, but the medium is very simple. Figure 3-12 illustrates a 4-pair UTP cord with its four wire pairs showing.

- ➤ A length of UTP wiring is a **cord**.
- ➤ Each cord has eight copper wires.
- ➤ Each wire is covered with dielectric (nonconducting) **insulation**.[8] This prevents short circuits between the electrical signals traveling on different wires.
- ➤ The wires are organized as four pairs.
- ➤ Each pair's two wires are twisted around each other several times per inch.
- ➤ There is an outer plastic **jacket** that encloses the four pairs.

RJ-45 Connectors

At the two ends of a UTP cord, the wires must be separated and placed within an 8-pin **RJ-45 connector**, which also is shown in Figure 3-12. The RJ-45 connector at each end of a 4-pair UTP cord snaps into an **RJ-45 jack** (port) in the NIC, the switch, or the wall jack.[9]

Easy, Inexpensive, and Rugged

UTP is inexpensive to purchase, easy to **connectorize**[10] (add connectors to), and relatively easy to install. It is also rugged, so that if a chair runs over it accidentally, it probably will survive undamaged. Four-pair UTP dominates corporate usage in access links from the NIC to the first switch because of UTP's low cost and durability (access links are frequently exposed to harsh treatment in the office).

---

[7]Some types of wiring use shielding, in which a metal mesh is placed around each pair of wires and around the jacket. This reduces interference, which is discussed later in this chapter. However, shielding is expensive, so almost all UTP wiring used in organizations today is unshielded, although some USB cables are shielded.

[8]By the way, Benjamin Franklin coined the terms *conductor, insulation,* and many other terms in electricity (including *positive* and *negative*). He also created the theory of electricity flow, although he thought that electricity flowed from the positive end of a battery to the negative end. Today, we know that electrons flow from negative to positive.

[9]Home telephone connections use a thinner RJ-11 connector and jack. They were designed to terminate six wires but usually terminate only a single pair.

[10]Yes, *connectorize* is a really ugly term. Believe me, I didn't make it up.

Figure 3-11   Unshielded Twisted Pair (UTP) Wiring (Study Figure)

4-Pair UTP Cable

The TIA/EIA-568 standard governs UTP wiring in the United States

In Europe, the comparable standard is ISO/IEC 11801

Cord Organization (Figure 3-12)

A length of UTP wiring is a cord

Each cord has eight copper wires

Each wire is covered with dielectric (nonconducting) insulation. This prevents short circuits between the electrical signals traveling on different wires

The wires are organized as four pairs

Each pair's two wires are twisted around each other several times per inch

There is an outer plastic jacket that encloses the four pairs

Connector

RJ-45 connector is the standard connector

Plugs into an RJ-45 jack in a NIC, switch, or wall jack

Characteristics

Inexpensive and easy to purchase and install

Rugged: can be run over with chairs, etc.

Dominates media for access links

Attenuation and Noise

Attenuation is a problem (Figure 3-13)

Signal weakens during propagation

Signal decline is measured in decibels (Figure 3-14)

Noise is also a problem (Figure 3-13)

UTP Distance Limit

Limiting UTP runs to 100 meters limits attenuation and noise to an acceptable level

Electromagnetic Interference (EMI) (Figure 3-15)

EMI is electromagnetic interference from external sources

General EMI is controlled by twisting wires in each pair

Crosstalk EMI is one form of EMI (Figure 3-16)

Terminal crosstalk EMI is another type of crosstalk EMI

Terminal crosstalk interference is limited to an acceptable level by not untwisting wires more than a half inch (1.25 cm)

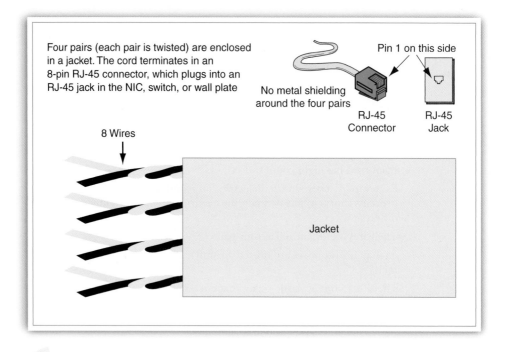

Four pairs (each pair is twisted) are enclosed in a jacket. The cord terminates in an 8-pin RJ-45 connector, which plugs into an RJ-45 jack in the NIC, switch, or wall plate

No metal shielding around the four pairs

Pin 1 on this side

RJ-45 Connector

RJ-45 Jack

8 Wires

Jacket

Figure 3-12   A 4-Pair UTP Cord with RJ-45 Connector

TEST YOUR UNDERSTANDING

7. a) What standards govern UTP? b) What is a length of UTP wiring called? c) In 4-pair UTP, how many wires are there in a cord? d) How many pairs? e) What surrounds each wire? f) How are the two wires of each pair arranged? g) What is the outer covering called?

8. Why is 4-pair UTP dominant in LANs for the access line between a NIC and the switch that serves the NIC?

Attenuation and Noise Problems

UTP signals change as they travel down the wires. If they change too much, they will not be readable. As noted earlier in this chapter, there are several types of propagation effects. We will now look at the most important propagation effects for UTP transmission, beginning with attenuation and noise.

Attenuation

As Figure 3-13 illustrates, when signals travel, they attenuate (grow weaker). To give an analogy, as you walk away from someone who is speaking, his or her voice will grow

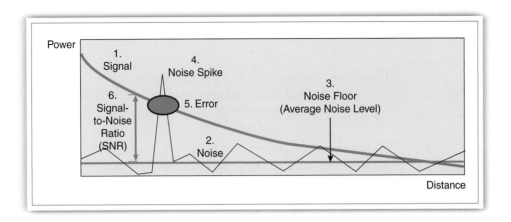

Figure 3-13   Attenuation and Noise

fainter and fainter. As noted earlier in this chapter, if a signal attenuates too much, the receiver will not be able to recognize it.

Decibels

Attenuation is measured in **decibels (dB)**. The equation for decibels in power attenuation is $dB = 10 \log_{10}(P_2/P_1)$, where the Ps are the initial (P_1) and final (P_2) powers. If P_2 is smaller than P_1, then the answer will be negative. For voltages, the equation is $dB = 20 \log_{10}(V_2/V_1)$.

$$dB = 10 \log_{10}(P_2/P_1) \text{ for power} \qquad \text{(Equation 3)}$$
$$dB = 20 \log_{10}(V_2/V_1) \text{ for voltages} \qquad \text{(Equation 4)}$$

To give an example, suppose that the initial power is 100 and the final power after propagation is 37.

➤ Then P_2/P_1 is 37/100 or 0.37.
➤ From Excel, LOG10(0.37) is −0.4318.
➤ Multiplying this by 10 and rounding off gives −4.3 dB.

Approximately Three Decibels Is a Halving in Power   Fortunately, you do not have to use this equation much in practice. You can work primarily with two facts. First, a decrease of half in power is a loss of approximately 3 dB. Each additional halving is another loss of approximately 3 dB. For example, a decrease to 1/4 of the original power would be approximately two 3 dB losses or 6 dB. A 9 dB loss would be a decline to approximately 1/8 the original power.

Attenuation Is Measured in Decibels (dB)

Equations

The equation for decibels is dB = $10 \log_{10}(P_2/P_1)$

Where P_1 is the initial power and P_2 is the final power after transmission

If P_2 is smaller than P_1, then the answer will be negative

For voltages, the equation is dB = $20 \log_{10}(V_2/V_1)$

In calculations, the Excel LOG10 function can be used

Example

Over a transmission link, power drops to 37 percent of its original value

P2/P1 = 37/100 = .37

LOG10(0.37) = −0.4318

10*LOG10(0.37) = −4.3 dB (the negative indicates power reduction through attenuation)

Two Simple Facts

3 dB loss is a reduction to 1/2 the original power

6 dB loss is a decrease to 1/4 the original power

9 dB loss is a decrease to 1/8 the original power

. . .

10 dB loss is a reduction to 1/10 the original power

20 dB loss is a decrease to 1/100 the original power

30 dB loss is a decrease to 1/1,000 the original power

. . .

Figure 3-14   Decibels (Study Figure)

Approximately Ten Decibels Is a Reduction to 1/10 the Original Power   Second, falling to 1/10 the initial power is a loss of approximately 10 dB. So falling to 1/100 the original power would be a loss of approximately 20 dB. Incredibly, 20 dB losses can occur in UTP transmission without making the signal unintelligible.

Noise

Electrons within a wire are constantly moving, and moving electrons generate random electromagnetic energy. This random electromagnetic energy is **noise**. Noise energy adds to the signal energy, so the receiver actually sees the total of the signal plus the noise.

Random electromagnetic energy is noise.

The mean of the noise energy is the **noise floor**—despite the fact that it is an average and not a minimum, as the name *floor* would suggest. Figure 3-13 shows a noise floor.

The mean of the noise energy is the noise floor.

As a consequence of noise being a random process, there are occasional **noise spikes** that are much higher or lower than the noise floor. As Figure 3-13 shows, if a noise spike is about as large as the signal, the combined signal and noise may be unrecognizable by the receiver.

Noise, Attenuation, and Propagation Distance

If a signal is far larger than the noise floor, then we have a high **signal-to-noise ratio (SNR)**. With a high SNR, few random noise spikes will be large enough to cause errors. However, as a signal attenuates during propagation, it falls ever closer to the noise floor. Noise spikes will equal the signal's strength more frequently, so errors will become more frequent. In other words, even if the noise level is constant, longer propagation distances create attenuation that results in a lower SNR and therefore more noise errors.

Even if the noise level is constant, longer propagation distances result in a lower SNR and therefore more noise errors.

Limiting UTP Cord Distance to Limit Attenuation and Noise Problems

Fortunately, installers can control attenuation and noise by limiting the length of UTP cords. The Ethernet standard currently limits UTP propagation distances to 100 meters at all speeds up to 1 Gbps. If UTP cords are restricted to 100 meters, the signal still will be comfortably larger than the noise floor when it arrives at the receiver, so there will be few noise errors.

The Ethernet standard limits UTP cords to 100 meters at all speeds up to 1 Gbps.

TEST YOUR UNDERSTANDING

9. a) Describe the attenuation problem and why it is important. b) A signal is 1/16 its initial value when it arrives at the receiver. How many decibels has it lost? c) A signal is 1/100 of its initial value when it reaches the receiver. How many decibels has it lost? d) Describe the noise problem. e) As a signal propagates down a UTP cord, the noise level is constant. Will greater propagation distance result in fewer noise errors, the same number of noise errors, or more noise errors? Explain.

10. a) What simple rule keeps UTP attenuation and noise errors to an acceptable level in Ethernet? b) What is the limit on UTP cord length in Ethernet standards?

Electromagnetic Interference (EMI) in UTP Wiring

General EMI

Noise is unwanted electrical energy within the propagation medium. In turn, **electromagnetic interference (EMI)**—or more simply, **interference**—is unwanted electrical energy coming from external devices, such as electrical motors, fluorescent lights, and even nearby UTP cords (which always radiate some of their signal). Like noise energy, interference energy adds to the signal energy and can make the received signal unreadable.

Using Twisted Pair Wiring to Reduce Interference

Fortunately, there is a simple way to reduce EMI to an acceptable level. This is to twist each pair's wires around each other several times per inch, as Figure 3-15 illustrates.

Consider what happens over a full twist. Over the first half of the twist, the interference might add to the signal. Over the other half, however, this same interference would subtract from the signal. The interference on the two halves would cancel out, and the net interference would be zero.

Does twisting really work this perfectly? No, of course not. However, twisting the wiring dramatically reduces interference, limiting it to an acceptable level. As a historical

Figure 3-15 Electromagnetic Interference (EMI) and Twisting

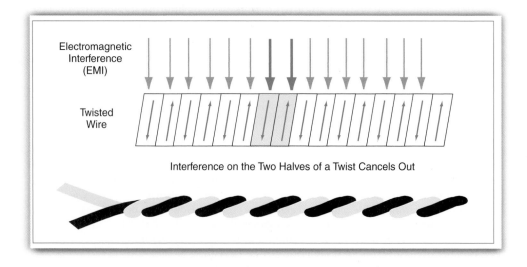

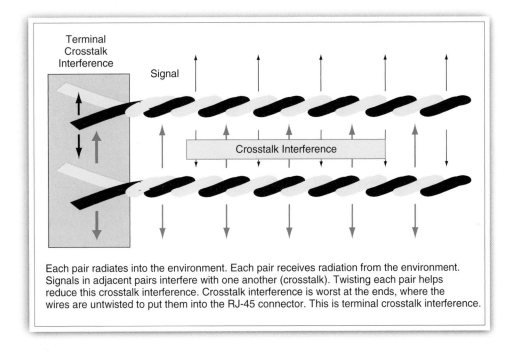

Each pair radiates into the environment. Each pair receives radiation from the environment.
Signals in adjacent pairs interfere with one another (crosstalk). Twisting each pair helps
reduce this crosstalk interference. Crosstalk interference is worst at the ends, where the
wires are untwisted to put them into the RJ-45 connector. This is terminal crosstalk interference.

Figure 3-16   Crosstalk Interference and Terminal Crosstalk Interference

note, Alexander Graham Bell himself patented twisted-pair wiring as a way to reduce
interference in telephone transmission.

Crosstalk Interference

As Figure 3-16 shows, individual pairs in a cord will radiate some of their energy, producing electromagnetic interference in other pairs within the cord. This mutual EMI
among wire pairs in a UTP cord is **crosstalk interference**. It is always present in wire
bundles and must be controlled. Fortunately, the twisting of each pair normally keeps
crosstalk interference to a reasonable level.

Terminal Crosstalk Interference

Unfortunately, when a UTP cord is connectorized, its wires must be untwisted to fit
into the RJ-45 connector, as shown in Figure 3-16. The eight wires are now parallel, so
there is no protection from crosstalk interference. Crosstalk interference at the ends
of the UTP cord, which is **terminal crosstalk interference**, usually is much larger than
the rest of the crosstalk interference over the entire rest of the cord.

Installers must be careful not to untwist UTP wires more than 1.25 cm (half an inch) when adding connectors. This precaution will not completely eliminate terminal crosstalk interference, but it will limit crosstalk interference to an acceptable level.

Installers must be careful not to untwist UTP wires more than 1.25 cm (half an inch) when adding connectors. This precaution will not completely eliminate terminal crosstalk interference, but it will limit crosstalk interference to an acceptable level.

TEST YOUR UNDERSTANDING

11. a) Distinguish between electromagnetic interference (EMI), crosstalk interference, and terminal crosstalk interference. b) How is EMI controlled? c) How is terminal crosstalk interference controlled in general? Explain. d) Does this precaution eliminate terminal crosstalk interference?

Serial and Parallel Transmission

Figure 3-17 shows an important distinction in wire communication: serial versus parallel transmission.

Figure 3-17   Serial Versus Parallel Transmission

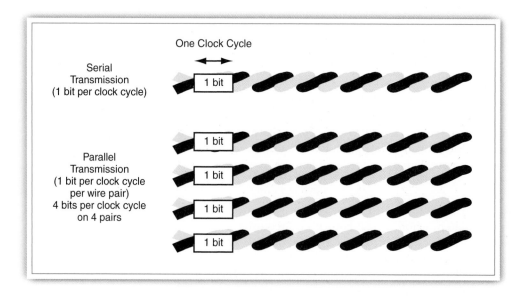

Serial Transmission

In the next chapter, we will look at Ethernet standards. In slower versions of Ethernet that run at 10 Mbps and 100 Mbps, a single pair in a UTP cord transmits the signal in each direction. Two-way transmission, then, uses two of the four pairs—one in each direction. The other two pairs are not used, although the standard calls for them to be present.

If one pair of wires is used to send a transmission, this is **serial transmission** because the transmitted bits must follow one another in series.

Parallel Transmission

For gigabit Ethernet, however, when the NIC or switch transmits, it transmits on all four pairs in each direction.[11] This means that it can transmit four bits at a time instead of just one. Sending data simultaneously on two or more transmission lines in the same direction is **parallel transmission**.

Sending data simultaneously on two or more transmission lines in the same direction is parallel transmission.

The benefit of parallel transmission is that it is faster than serial transmission for the same clock cycle duration. Speed is the key benefit of parallel transmission.

Note that parallel transmission does not mean the use of *four* transmitting pairs (or grounded wires). It means using more than a single pair of wires or one wire and a ground wire. For example, your computer's internal bus, which carries signals among components in your system unit, has about 100 wires for high-density parallel transmission. To give another example, parallel cables used to connect PCs to printers use eight wires to carry data in each direction.

Trend

In general, serial transmission has largely replaced parallel transmission in practice. Reducing the clock cycle in serial transmission has the same benefit as using more transmission paths, and it is generally cheaper. Parallel transmission survives only in some short-distance transmission applications such as gigabit Ethernet and PC parallel busses.

TEST YOUR UNDERSTANDING

12. a) Distinguish between serial and parallel transmission. b) What is the main benefit of parallel transmission? c) In parallel transmission, how many pairs (or single wires and ground wires) are used in each direction? d) Is serial or parallel transmission more widely used today?

---

[11]What if both sides transmit at the same time? Each knows what signal it sent. It subtracts this signal from the signal it hears on the wire. The remaining signal is the signal sent by the other side.

Wire Quality Standard Categories

Wire Quality Standards Categories

UTP cords vary in transmission quality. Wiring quality is rated through a series of **"categories"** with increasing ability to carry high-speed data. Higher-quality UTP cords have larger category numbers.

Standards Organizations

Two organizations set wiring quality standards. Fortunately, they usually harmonize their work, although one may lag behind the other for awhile. In the United States, wiring quality standards are set by three organizations: TIA, EIA, and ANSI. Their standards are designated as TIA/EIA/ANSI standards (although the order of the acronyms often varies). Internationally (especially in Europe), standards are set by ISO and IEC. In the United States, the **TIA/EIA/ANSI-568** standard governs UTP (and optical fiber). In Europe and many other parts of the world, UTP and optical fiber are governed by the **ISO/IEC 11801** standard.

Wiring Quality and Ethernet

Although wiring has uses other than Ethernet, Ethernet networking has been the driving force behind improvements in wire quality. In general, the goal has been to develop Ethernet standards that can transmit data up to 100 meters between a computer and a workgroup switch. As Ethernet speeds have increased from 10 Mbps to 1 Gbps, improvements have been needed in UTP wiring. Currently, wire quality standards are being developed to deliver 10 Gbps Ethernet over copper wires.

Categories 3 and 4

The earliest wiring quality standards were **Category 3** and **Category 4**. "Cat 3" and "Cat 4" wiring could only carry data up to 10 Mbps. This was fine for the earliest versions of Ethernet, but Ethernet today runs at much higher speeds. Many older buildings still have Cat 3 or Cat 4 wiring, preventing them from using newer versions of Ethernet.

Categories 5 and 5e

The next category of wiring, **Category 5**, could easily handle 100 Mbps versions of Ethernet. If installed properly, it could also handle 1 Gbps Ethernet. However, to be somewhat safer at gigabit speeds, the **Category 5e (enhanced)** standard was developed. Most UTP wiring sold today is "Cat 5e" wiring.

Category 6

The UTP wiring sold today that is not Cat 5e is almost entirely **Category 6** wiring. Category 6 is a rather new type of wiring and is not yet widely implemented.

Cat 6 wiring can handle much higher speeds than Cat 5e wiring. Unfortunately, the speed increases it can provide are not useful. For gigabit Ethernet, Cat 6 is no better than Cat 5e or even well-installed Cat 5. At the same time, Cat 6 is not good enough to carry 10 Gbps Ethernet to a distance of 100 meters. There simply is no good reason to install Cat 6 for Ethernet wiring, although Ethernet may develop a way to carry Ethernet over Cat 6 cable at distances shorter than the standard 100 meters.

Figure 3-18   Wire Quality Standards (Study Figure)

Wire Quality Standards
       Rated by Category (Cat) Numbers

Category Standards Are Set by ANSI/TIA/EIA and ISO/IEC
       Quality standards are driven by Ethernet networking

       Goal is to be able to carry Ethernet signals 100 meters

       In the United States, the TIA/EIA/ANSI-568 governs UTP and optical fiber standards

       In Europe and many other parts of the world, the standard is ISO/IEC 11801

Categories 3 and 4
       Early data wiring, which could only handle Ethernet speeds up to 10 Mbps

Categories 5 and 5e
       Most wiring installed today is Category 5e (enhanced)

       Cat 5e and Cat 5 (if well installed) can handle Ethernet up to 1 Gbps

       Most wiring sold today is Cat 5e

Category 6
       Relatively new

       No better than Cat 5 or Cat 5e at 1 Gbps

       Developed for higher Ethernet speeds of 10 Gbps

              But could not work at those speeds

       Cat 6 is widely sold, but less widely than Cat 5e

Next Steps
       Problem: Cat 6 was not able to handle 10 Gbps Ethernet

       Category 6A (augmented) that can handle 10 Gbps Ethernet is now being developed

       Category 7 STP is also being developed

              A more radical step in technology

              Shielded twisted pair (STP) rather than unshielded twisted pair (UTP)

                     Metal foil shield around each pair to reduce crosstalk interference

                     Metal mesh around all four pairs to reduce crosstalk from other cords

              STP is expensive

              Cat 7 will probably require a radically new connector

Next Steps: Category 6A UTP and Category 7 STP (Shielded Twisted Pair)

Once Cat 6's limitations were demonstrated, standards agencies began working on an improved version of Category 6. Instead of calling this new version Category 6e, to be parallel with the name Category 5e, standards agencies gave this improved version of Category 6 the name **Category 6A** (Augmented). This wiring should be able to handle 10 Gbps speeds. At the time of this writing, **Cat 6A** wiring is in the late stages of standardization. Although some vendors are selling wiring labeled as Cat 6A, this wiring is not likely to be compliant with the final standard.

In addition, standards agencies are now developing a radically new type of wiring, **Category 7 STP**. In this name, **STP** stands for **shielded twisted pair**. Each pair of wires in the 4-pair bundle is surrounded by a metal foil sheath. In addition, there is a metal mesh around all four pairs. The sheath and mesh reduce crosstalk interference dramatically so that Category 7 wiring can handle extremely high speeds easily. However, STP is very expensive compared to normal UTP (unshielded twisted pair) wiring. In addition, Cat 7 STP may require radically new connectors.

TEST YOUR UNDERSTANDING

13. a) What is the maximum length of UTP cords in Ethernet standards up to and including 1 Gbps? b) What wiring characteristic do UTP categories standardize? c) What two UTP quality categories dominate sales in the marketplace today? d) Cat 5e and Cat 6 are sufficient for Ethernet transmission speeds up to _____. e) What new categories of wiring are being developed for 10 Gbps Ethernet transmission?

OPTICAL FIBER

Light Through Glass

In the 1840s, scientists discovered that light would follow water flowing out of a hose. Where the water stream bent, the light would follow. This raised the possibility that light signals could be sent through glass rods. (Water was too difficult to control, and glass rods also bend light.) Simple *on/off signaling* could be used, with the light turned on to represent a 1 during a clock cycle and off to represent a 0. Unfortunately, scientists soon discovered that as soon as the glass rod touched anything, the light would stop bending.

Not until the 1960s did scientists realize that if the glass rod (called the core) was surrounded by a glass tube (called the cladding), then the combined core and cladding would be able to carry signals. (We will see later how claddings do this.)

Unfortunately, the cladding does nothing for attenuation. In early cores, attenuation rates of 1,000 dB/km were common. However, Corning developed ultra-pure glass in the 1970s that reduced attenuation to about 20 dB/km. This was enough to make optical fiber attractive telecommunications carriers. The market for carrier fiber boomed as manufacturers brought attenuation ever lower. Today, attenuation typically is only 0.5 dB/km to 3.0 dB/km.

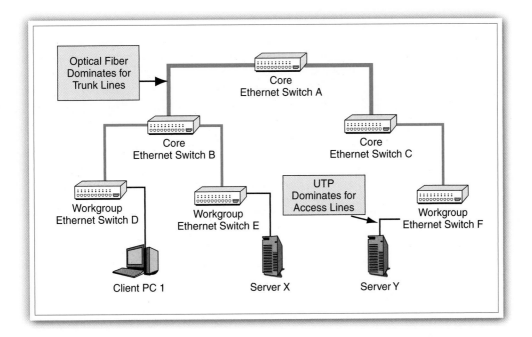

Figure 3-19   Roles of UTP and Optical Fiber in LANs

TEST YOUR UNDERSTANDING

14. a) How does optical fiber signaling represent 1s and 0s? b) What is a typical range for optical fiber attenuation today?

The Roles of Fiber and Copper

Although optical fiber is growing rapidly, it is not completely replacing UTP. Rather, as Figure 3-19 shows, the two play different roles in most LANs, so they are not direct competitors.

➤ UTP is dominant for access lines because UTP is less expensive than fiber and because access line distances normally are well within UTP's usual 100-meter distance limit and speed limits.

➤ In contrast, while UTP may be used for some trunk lines, most trunk lines are optical fiber. Trunk lines have greater speed and distance needs and so can justify the higher cost of optical fiber.

TEST YOUR UNDERSTANDING

15. In LAN transmission, what are the typical roles of UTP and optical fiber?

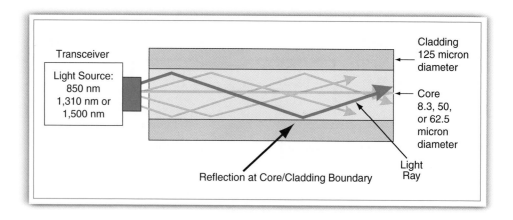

Figure 3-20 Optical Fiber Transceiver and Strand

Optical Fiber Construction and Operation

Figure 3-20 illustrates how an optical fiber strand is constructed and how it carries signals.

Cores in Multimode and Single-Mode Fiber

To send signals, the **transceiver** (sender/receiver) injects light into a very thin glass rod called the **core**. Typical core diameters are 8.3, 50, and 62.5 microns (millionths of a meter). In comparison, an average human hair is about 75 microns thick.[12]

Cladding and Perfect Internal Reflection

As noted earlier, surrounding the core is a thicker glass cylinder called the **cladding**. The cladding normally is 125 microns in diameter, regardless of the core diameter.

As Figure 3-20 shows, if a light ray enters at an angle, it hits the cladding and reflects back into the core with **perfect internal reflection** so that no light escapes into the cladding or beyond.[13] In contrast, UTP tends to radiate energy out of the wire bundle, causing rapid attenuation.

---

[12]Actually, human hair varies in thickness from about 40 microns to 120 microns. If hair is less than 60 microns thick, it is considered to be fine hair. If it is more than 80 microns thick, it is called thick or coarse.

[13]This is based on Snell's Law. The cladding has a slightly lower index of refraction than the core. This difference in index of refraction creates perfect internal reflection. By the way, if the fiber is bent too much, the angle between the core and cladding will become wrong for the light waves, and a great deal of light will be lost into the core. Of course, if optical fiber is bent even farther, it will crack. Glass is glass.

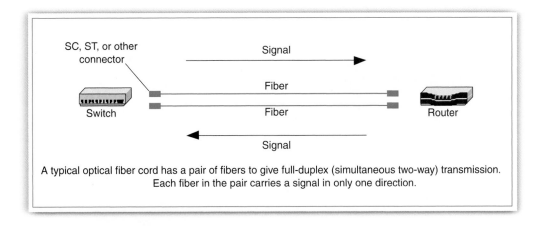

SC, ST, or other
connector

Signal

Fiber

Switch

Fiber

Router

Signal

A typical optical fiber cord has a pair of fibers to give full-duplex (simultaneous two-way) transmission.
Each fiber in the pair carries a signal in only one direction.

Figure 3-21   Full-Duplex Optical Fiber Cord with Two Strands

Strand Thickness

An opaque coating surrounds the cladding to keep out light and to strengthen the fiber. Part of this coating includes strands of yellow Aramid (Kevlar[14]) yarn to strengthen the fiber. The coating and outer jacket bring the outer diameter of a LAN fiber strand to about 900 microns (0.9 mm).

Two Strands for Full-Duplex Operation

Note in Figure 3-21 that an **optical fiber cord** normally has two **strands** of fiber—one for transmission in each direction. This gives **full-duplex communication** (simultaneous two-way communication).

Connectors

In UTP, there is only one type of connector—the RJ-45 connector. In optical fiber, there are two popular types of connectors. Figure 3-22 illustrates these two connectors.[15]

SC Connectors   The **SC connector** is square and snaps into an SC port. The SC connector is very popular and is now the recommended standard for use in new LANs.

ST Connectors   The **ST connector** is cylindrical. It pushes into an ST port and then twists to lock in place. ST is called a bayonet connector because bayonets use this type

---

[14]Yes, Kevlar is the stuff used to make bulletproof vests. If you cut optical fiber with a wire cutter built for UTP, you will dull the wire cutter very quickly.
[15]There also are several other connectors on the market. They usually are smaller than SC and ST connectors. The smaller size allows switches and routers of a given size to have more ports. These smaller connector types are not standardized.

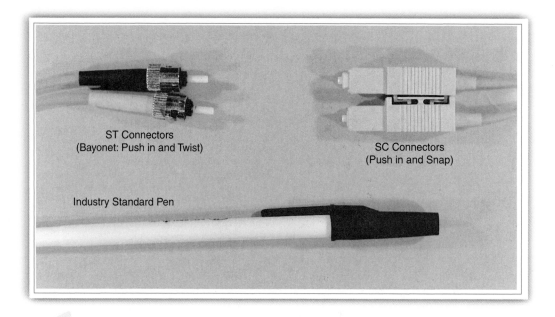

Figure 3-22   Full-Duplex Optical Fiber Cord with ST and SC Connectors

of push-and-twist connection. Although SC connectors are now recommended by the TIA/EIA-568 standard, ST remains widespread.

Switches and Routers   Fortunately, versions of almost all switches and routers can be purchased with either SC or ST ports for optical fiber connections. Therefore, fiber's lack of a single connector type is not a problem in practice.

Light Frequency and Wavelength

Figure 3-23 shows a pure light wave. The frequency is the number of times the wave goes through a complete cycle per second. Frequency is measured in hertz (Hz).

The **wavelength**, in turn, is the distance between comparable parts on two successive cycles—peak to peak, trough to trough, and so on. In light, wavelengths are measured in **nanometers (nm)**. A nanometer is one billionth of a meter. In LANs, wavelengths come in three main "windows" centered at 850 nm, 1,310 nm, and 1,550 nm. (See Figure 3-20.) These windows are approximately 50 nm wide.

Wavelength is important because longer wavelengths bring longer propagation distances and higher speeds. However, longer wavelengths also increase costs. Consequently, the goal is to select the shortest wavelength that will provide the speed and distance needed.

Longer-wavelength light can travel farther and faster, but longer-wavelength light sources are more expensive.

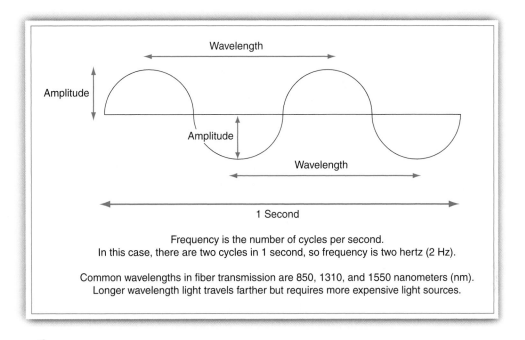

Wavelength

Amplitude

Amplitude

Wavelength

1 Second

Frequency is the number of cycles per second.
In this case, there are two cycles in 1 second, so frequency is two hertz (2 Hz).

Common wavelengths in fiber transmission are 850, 1310, and 1550 nanometers (nm).
Longer wavelength light travels farther but requires more expensive light sources.

Figure 3-23   Frequency and Wavelength

TEST YOUR UNDERSTANDING

16. a) In optical fiber, what are the roles of the core and the cladding? b) What is the ability to transmit in both directions simultaneously called? c) Why does a fiber cord normally need two fiber strands? d) What fiber connector is now recommended for new LANs? e) What other fiber connector is popular? f) Does the presence of two major connector standards for fiber cause problems for switch and router purchasing? Explain.

Carrier Fiber

Although optical fiber is widely used in LANs today, fiber was first used in long-distance carrier trunk lines. Carriers found that a single trunk line fiber could replace multiple existing copper lines.

Laser Light Sources

Carrier fiber has long used lasers as light sources. Lasers are extremely expensive but can send high-speed signals very far.

Figure 3-24 Carrier Fiber and LAN Fiber (Study Figure)

Carrier Fiber

    Carrier fiber must support long distances

    Uses expensive long-wavelength laser light sources

    Uses single-mode fiber with a very narrow core (8.3 microns)

    Main propagation problem is attenuation

        For 850 nm light, attenuation is around 2.5 dB/km

        At 1,310 nm, attenuation is lower—about 0.8 dB/km

        At 1,550 nm, attenuation falls even lower—about 0.2 dB/km

    Carrier fiber normally uses wavelengths of 1,310 or 1,550 nm

LAN Fiber

    Normally only need transmission distances of about 200 meters

    Uses inexpensive multimode fiber with core diameters of 50 or 62.5 microns

    Modal dispersion

        Light enters only at certain angles called modes

        Mode propagation straight through arrives quickly

        Modes that bounce many times arrive later

        Adjacent light pulses begin to overlap

        Limits the speed–distance product

    Graded-index multimode fiber

        The index of refraction decreases from the center of the core to the core's outer edge

        This slows the central mode and increases the speed of modes that bounce many times

    Multimode Fiber Quality

        Measured as modal bandwidth (MHz.km or MHz-km)

        More modal bandwidth is better

        Increases the speed–distance product

    Example: 1000Base-SX

        Uses inexpensive 850 nm light

        With 62.5 micron fiber and 160 MHz-km modal bandwidth, maximum distance is 220 m

        With 62.5 micron fiber and 200 MHz-km bandwidth, maximum distance is 275 m

        With 50 micron fiber and 400 MHz-km bandwidth, maximum distance is 500 meters

        Some vendors with higher-than-standard modal bandwidth can carry traffic farther

Noise and Electromagnetic Interference (EMI) Are Not Problems

    Noise from moving electrons cannot interfere with light signals

    EMI would have to be light signals

        Wrapping the cladding in an opaque covering prevents light from coming in

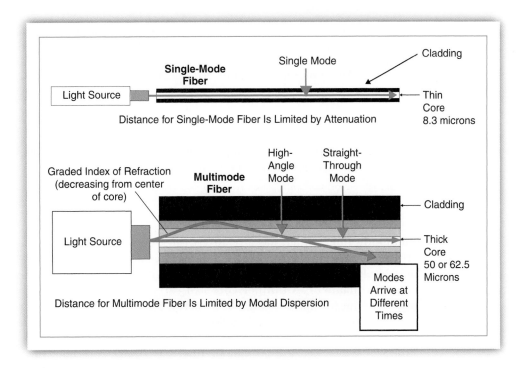

Figure 3-25   Single-Mode Fiber and Multimode Fiber

Single-Mode Fiber

In addition, carriers normally use a very expensive type of fiber called single-mode fiber. Figure 3-25 shows that **single-mode fiber** uses an extremely thin core—only 8.3 microns in diameter. Single-mode fiber can carry signals very far, but producing thin glass cores is very difficult and therefore expensive. Splicing and connectorizing single-mode fiber also is extremely difficult. (Try threading a needle with a very tiny eye.) However, for distances required in carrier trunk lines, single-mode fiber is necessary.

Attenuation

In single-mode fiber, the main propagation problem is attenuation.[16] Although fiber attenuation is far lower than copper wire attenuation, it is still a significant factor over long distances. For 850 nm light, attenuation is around 2.5 dB/km. At 1,310 nm, attenuation is lower—about 0.8 dB/km. At 1,550 nm, attenuation falls even lower—about 0.2 dB/km. Carrier fiber normally uses wavelengths of 1,310 or 1,550 nm.

---

[16]Attenuation comes from two sources. First, some of the light energy is absorbed by molecules in the fiber. Second, some of the light is scattered by impurities and connections. This light is not perfectly internally reflected because it hits the cladding at a high angle.

TEST YOUR UNDERSTANDING

17. a) What light-generating technology do carrier fiber systems normally use? b) Do carriers normally use single-mode fiber or multimode fiber? c) What is the characteristic of single-mode fiber? d) What is the advantage of increasing wavelength in optical fiber transmission? e) What is the disadvantage of increasing wavelength in optical fiber transmission? f) What wavelengths does carrier fiber usually use?

LAN Fiber

Carrier fiber can carry signals over very long distances—tens of kilometers. However, LAN trunk lines typically are less than 200 meters long. For LAN use, carrier fiber is overkill.

Multimode Fiber

LANs use **multimode fiber**, which has a relatively thick core, as Figure 3-25 shows. Initially, North American multimode fiber had a core diameter of 62.5 microns. In Europe, which developed fiber slightly later, the core diameter was a little thinner—only 50 microns in diameter. A thinner core can carry signals farther. Although 50-micron fiber is no more expensive than 62.5-micron fiber today, most U.S. organizations continue to standardize on 62.5-micron fiber, while European companies primarily use 50-micron fiber.

As Figure 3-25 shows, because multimode fiber has a thick core light rays can enter over a wide range of angles. Light traveling straight through the core arrives fastest. In contrast, light entering at high angles will zig-zag through the core many times. It will travel much farther and so will arrive later.

This difference in arrival times causes a problem called **modal dispersion**, in which light from successive light pulses overlaps. If the cord length is too great, light from successive light pulses will overlap so much that the signal will be unreadable.

Actually, light *cannot* enter at just any angle. Light is limited to entering at a few angles called **modes**. This is why the fiber is called multimode fiber. The thicker the core, the more modes can exist and the larger their angles can be.

The Speed–Distance Product

One way to limit modal dispersion to an acceptable level is to limit speed. This lengthens the duration of each pulse, giving more time between successive pulses. This reduces pulse overlap.

The other is to limit distance. Modal dispersion increases with distance because the time differences of arriving modes increase as signals propagate farther.

Modal dispersion, then, limits the **speed–distance product**—the combination of speed and distance of travel. One can reduce modal dispersion by limiting speed, limiting distance, or a combination of the two.

Graded-Index Multimode Fiber

To reduce modal dispersion, fiber manufacturers today only build **graded-index multimode fiber**, in which the index of refraction decreases from the center of the core to the core's outer edge. This slows light traveling down the center compared to light farther out the radius. Consequently, light going straight through along the center is slowed down, while light zig-zagging through the core is speeded up during its time away from the center. This reduces the time lapse between the direct mode and other modes, thus reducing modal dispersion.

Multimode Fiber Quality

Modal Bandwidth (MHz-km)   Another thing that fiber manufacturers do is to offer higher-quality multimode fiber. Higher-quality fiber can carry signals faster and/or farther than lower-quality fiber. In fiber, quality is measured by **modal bandwidth** and is measured as **MHz-km**,[17] which is sometimes written as **MHz.km**. There is not a precise relationship between the speed–distance product and MHz-km, but higher MHz-km means a greater speed–distance product. In general, multimode fiber can carry signals at tens of gigabits per second over distances of several hundred meters.

In fiber, quality is measured by modal bandwidth, which is measured as MHz-km.

1000Base-SX with 62.5/125 Fiber   For example, gigabit Ethernet, which carries signals at 1 Gbps, is dominated by the 1000Base-SX standard, which transmits light at 850 nm over 62.5/125 multimode fiber. By transmitting light at the lowest feasible wavelength and using widely deployed 62.5/125 fiber, 1000Base-SX offers acceptable performance at reasonable prices. With 160 MHz-km modal bandwidth, 1000Base-SX can transmit gigabit Ethernet signals over a distance of 220 m (the length of two football fields). With 200 MHz-km fiber, the distance rises to 275 m.

1000Base-SX with 50/125 Fiber   Few companies need longer distances than 62.5/125 multimode fiber can provide for their trunk lines. However, if do, they can use 50/125 rather than 62.5/125 fiber. Thinner fiber offers higher modal bandwidth. With a modal bandwidth of 400 MHz-km, 50/125 fiber can carry 1000Base-SX signals up to 500 meters.

Nonstandard Modal Bandwidths   The modal bandwidths described in the last two paragraphs are official Ethernet standards. However, most vendors offer fiber with higher modal bandwidths than the standards specify. For example, 62.5/125 fiber with higher modal bandwidths can carry 1000Base-SX signals 300 meters or even 500 meters.

---

[17]Speed is roughly related to bandwidth, which is the range of frequencies over which a signal spreads. For example, suppose that the modal bandwidth is 200 MHz-km. Then a signal width of 200 MHz can be sustained over one kilometer. Continuing the example, a signal bandwidth of 100 MHz can be sustained over 2 km, while a signal with a bandwidth of 400 MHz can be sustained only over half of a kilometer. Unfortunately, because the relationship between bandwidth and speed is not very precise, modal bandwidth cannot be used to forecast speed/distance limits in practice. Simply put, more modal bandwidth is better.

TEST YOUR UNDERSTANDING

18. a) Do LANs normally use multimode fiber or single-mode fiber? b) What is the main characteristic distinguishing multimode fiber from single-mode fiber? c) Why is multi-mode fiber used in LANs? (Give a complete explanation.) d) What are typical core diameters for multimode fiber? e) What are modes? f) What is modal dispersion? g) Explain the speed–distance product. h) What is the advantage of graded-index multi-mode fiber? i) Of what is modal bandwidth a measure? j) In what units is modal band-width expressed? k) In what two ways can businesses select multimode fiber to transmit 1000Base-SX signals farther?

Noise and Electromagnetic Interference

In fiber, attenuation and modal dispersion are important limitations. However, noise and electromagnetic interference, which are serious problems in UTP, are *not* prob-lems for fiber.

Noise

There is no noise energy in fiber. Electrons randomly moving around within the trans-mission medium generate electromagnetic energy called noise. However, electrons do not generate light energy that adds to the light signal.

Electromagnetic Interference

In UTP, EMI is an important concern. In optical fiber, this concern vanishes. The only type of electromagnetic interference applicable to fiber is light coming into the fiber from the outside. Fiber prevents this completely by having an opaque coating around the cladding.

TEST YOUR UNDERSTANDING

19. Are noise and interference major propagation problems for optical fiber propagation? Explain.

NETWORK TOPOLOGIES

The term **network topology** refers to the physical arrangement of a network's comput-ers, switches, routers, and transmission lines. Topology, then, is a physical layer concept. Different network (and internet) standards specify different topologies. Figure 3-26 shows the major topologies found in networking. Some are seen only in older legacy LANs using obsolete technology.

Network topology is the physical arrangement of a network's computers, switches, routers, and transmission lines.

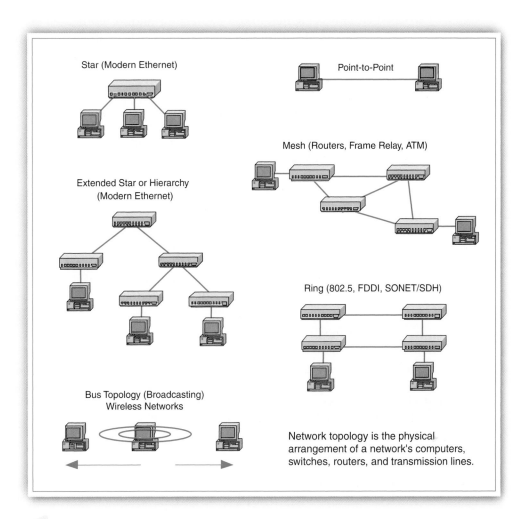

Figure 3-26   Major Topologies

Point-to-Point Topology

The simplest network topology is the **point-to-point topology**, in which two nodes are connected directly. Although some might say that a point-to-point connection is not a network, WANs often are built of point-to-point private leased lines provided by the telephone service, and dial-up telephone connections effectively provide point-to-point connections between users and the Internet.

Star Topology and Extended Star (Hierarchy) Topology

Modern versions of Ethernet, which is the dominant LAN standard, use the star and extended star topologies. In a **simple star topology**, all wires connect to a single switch. The Pat Lee and XTR networks Chapters 1a and 1c both used simple star topologies. In an **extended star (or hierarchy) topology**, there are multiple layers of switches organized in a hierarchy. We will see Ethernet hierarchies in the next chapter.

Mesh Topology

In a mesh topology, there are many connections among switches, so there are many alternative routes to get from one end of the network to the other. We will see **mesh topologies** with ATM and Frame Relay in Chapter 7 and with routers in Chapter 8.

Ring Topology

In a **ring topology**, computers are connected in a loop. Messages pass in only one direction around the loop. Eventually, all messages pass through all computers. In LANs, the obsolete 802.5 Token-Ring Network and FDDI network technologies discussed in Chapter 4a used a ring topology. In addition, the worldwide telephone network increasingly uses rings to connect its switches using the SONET/SDH technology, as we will see in Module B.

Bus Topologies

In a **bus topology**, when a computer transmits, it broadcasts to all other computers. Wireless LANs, which we will see in Chapter 5, use a bus topology by broadcasting signals. So do Ethernet hubs, which we will see in Chapter 4. The obsolete Ethernet 10Base5 and 10Base2 technologies also used a bus topology.

TEST YOUR UNDERSTANDING

20. a) What is a network topology? b) At what layer do we find topologies? c) List the major network topologies, and give the defining characteristics for each one. Present each topology in a separate paragraph. d) What technology is associated with each topology?

CONCLUSION

Synopsis

Chapter 2 discussed standards in general. It focused on the data link layer through the application layer because these layers all operate in the same general way—by sending messages. The physical layer, which was the focus of this chapter, is very different. It sends individual bits instead of messages, and it alone governs transmission media and propagation effects.

In this chapter we looked at UTP and optical fiber—the two transmission media that traditionally have dominated in LANs and WANs. We also looked at network topology and building wiring. In Chapter 6, we will look at radio transmission.

For physical transmission, data must be represented as strings of bits (1s and 0s).

➤ Whole numbers (integers) typically are represented as binary numbers. Binary counting begins with 0. You should know how to count in binary by adding 1 to each previous value.

➤ You should also know that a field with N bits allows you to represent 2^N alternatives.

➤ For text, 7-bit ASCII and 8-bit extended ASCII normally are used to represent characters in binary.

➤ Other forms of data, including graphics and the human voice, can also be represented in binary.

After conversion, these binary data streams must then be converted into signals to propagate down the transmission medium. In simple on/off signaling in optical fiber, the sender turns on during a clock cycle for a 1 and off for a 0. On/off signaling is binary signaling, in which there are two possible states or line conditions (on and off). Binary signaling can also use two voltage ranges on a wire. One voltage range represents a 0; the other, a 1.

In the box on digital signaling, we saw that in digital signaling, there are a few possible states (2, 4, 8, 16, etc.). Adding more possible states allows the sender to transmit more bits per clock cycle, but doing so decreases immunity to attenuation propagation errors. Binary transmission is a special case of digital transmission.

In unshielded twisted pair wiring, a cord consists of four twisted wire pairs. There is an RJ-45 connector at each end. UTP is rugged and inexpensive and so dominates the access links that connect computers to workgroup switches.

The two wires of each pair in a UTP cord are twisted around each other to reduce electromagnetic interference (EMI) problems. Two simple installation expedients keep propagation problems to acceptable levels. First, restricting UTP cord lengths to 100 meters usually prevents serious attenuation and noise errors. Second, limiting the untwisting of wires to no more than 0.5 inches (1.25 cm) usually keeps terminal crosstalk interference to an acceptable level.

Earlier versions of Ethernet transmitted serially—sending on only one wire pair in each direction. Gigabit Ethernet transmits in parallel, sending on all four wire pairs when it transmits. Other forms of parallel transmission use more than four transmission paths. Parallel transmission is faster than serial transmission for a given clock cycle but is more expensive, so serial transmission now dominates in the marketplace.

There are different grades (called categories) of UTP quality. Almost all UTP sold today is Category 5e or Category 6 wiring. This is sufficient for up to 1 Gbps in Ethernet.

For trunk lines, optical fiber dominates in LAN transmission and will grow even more dominant as speed requirements increase. In fiber, a transceiver injects signals into a thin glass core that is either 62.5 microns, 50 microns, or 8.3 microns in diameter. The transceiver uses simple binary on/off signaling. An optical fiber cord has two strands for full-duplex communication. Fiber normally uses SC connectors but can use ST connectors.

Carriers use single-mode fiber, which has a very thin core that is only 8.3 microns thick. Single-mode fiber is very expensive but can carry high-speed signals over the very long distances needed by carriers (tens of kilometers). Single-mode fiber is limited by attenuation, which is very low but is a significant problem over long distances. There are three major propagation windows centered around 850 nm, 1,310 nm, and 1,550 nm. Attenuation is lower at longer wavelengths, so carrier fiber normally uses 1,310 nm or 1,550 nm light.

Multimode fiber, which has a "thick" diameter of 62.5 or 50 microns, dominates in LANs because it is less expensive than single-mode fiber. Although it cannot carry signals as far as single-mode fiber, it can easily carry light 200 meters or even more. This is more than adequate for nearly all LAN trunk lines. Multimode fiber propagation is limited by modal dispersion. Higher-quality multimode fiber, which is characterized by a higher modal bandwidth (measured as MHz-km), can carry signals farther than lower-quality multimode fiber. In addition, multimode fiber with a thinner core diameter (50 microns instead of 62.5 microns) can carry signals farther.

A network's topology describes the way that transmission lines connect computers, switches, and routers. Examples of topologies are the point-to-point, star, hierarchy (extended star), mesh, ring, and bus topologies. As you work through this book, you will see these topologies and their implications for performance and reliability.

THOUGHT QUESTIONS

1. In binary, 35 is 100011. Compute 36 through 40 in binary. (The number 40 is 101000.)
2. a) A field is 8 bits long. How many values can it represent?
    b) Repeat for 1, 4, 16, 32, 48, and 64 bits. Do not use a spreadsheet program. (Hint: Each bit doubles the number of possible alternatives.)
3. The clock cycle is one millionth of a second. There is eight-level digital signaling.
    a) What is the baud rate?
    b) How many bits are sent per clock cycle?
    c) What is the bit rate?
    d) If your clock cycle is 1/10,000 of a second and you want a bit rate of 50 kbps, how many possible states will you need per clock cycle?
4. a) If power falls to 40 percent of its initial value through attenuation, how many decibels is this loss?
    b) If voltage drops to 40 percent of its initial value through attenuation, how many decibels is this? You may wish to use a spreadsheet program to compute the logarithm.
5. What type of interference is most likely to create problems in UTP transmission?
6. When a teacher lectures in class, is the classroom a full-duplex communication system or a half-duplex communication system?
7. In the author's college, the wiring has been described as "Cat 3 on a good day." What Ethernet speeds can it carry?
8. a) How many possible paths are there between any two computers in a point-to-point topology?
    b) In a hierarchical topology? (Hint: Draw a picture.)
    c) In a mesh topology with four switches (without back-tracking)? (Hint: Draw a picture.)

TROUBLESHOOTING QUESTIONS

1. A tester shows that a UTP cord has too much interference. What might be causing the problem? Give at least two alternative hypotheses, and then describe how to test them.
2. What kinds of errors are you likely to encounter if you run a length of UTP cord 200 meters? (Recall that the standard calls for a 100-meter maximum distance.)

HANDS-ON EXERCISES

Do this hands-on exercise if you have a lot of extra money or a very nice teacher. Chapter 3a discusses how to connectorize bulk UTP cabling. To try it out, you will need a box of bulk UTP cabling, a wire cutter, a wire stripper, a crimper, a bag of RJ-45 connectors, and a tester (because only about half of connections done by novices work). All of this will set you back about $300. Knowing this, the price of UTP patch cables, which are cut, connectorized, and tested at the factory, seems more reasonable, doesn't it?

GETTING CURRENT

Go to the book website's New Information and Errors pages for this chapter to get new information since this book went to press and to correct any errors in the text.

Hands-On: Cutting and Connectorizing UTP[1]

INTRODUCTION

Chapter 3 discussed UTP wiring in general. This chapter discusses how to cut and connectorize (add connectors to) solid UTP wiring.

SOLID AND STRANDED WIRING

Solid-Wire UTP Versus Stranded-Wire UTP

The TIA/EIA-568 standard requires that long runs to wall jacks use **solid-wire UTP**, in which each of the eight wires really is a single solid wire.

However, patch cords running from the wall outlet to a NIC usually are **stranded-wire UTP**, in which each of the eight "wires" really is a bundle of thinner wire strands. So stranded-wire UTP has eight bundles of wires, each bundle in its own insulation and acting like a single wire.

Relative Advantages

Solid wire is needed in long cords because it has lower attenuation than stranded wire. In contrast, stranded-wire UTP cords are more flexible than solid-wire cords, making them ideal for patch cords—especially the one running to the desktop—because they can be bent more and still function. They are more durable than solid-wire UTP cords.

Adding Connectors

It is relatively easy to add RJ-45 connectors to solid-wire UTP cords. However, it is very difficult to add RJ-45 connectors to stranded-wire cords. Stranded-wire

---

[1]This material is based on the author's lab projects and on the lab project of Prof. Harry Reif of James Madison University.

Solid-Wire UTP
> Each of the eight wires is a solid wire
> Low attenuation over long distances
> Easy to connectorize
> Inflexible and stiff—not good for runs to the desktop

Stranded-Wire UTP
> Each of the eight "wires" is itself several thin strands of wire within an insulation tube
> Flexible and durable—good for runs to the desktop
> Impossible to connectorize in the field (bought as patch cords)
> Higher attenuation than solid-wire UTP—Used only in short runs
>> From wall jack to desktop
>> Within a telecommunications closet (see Chapter 3)

Figure 3a-1   Solid-Wire and Stranded-Wire UTP (Study Figure)

patch cords should be purchased from the factory precut to desired lengths and preconnectorized.

In addition, when purchasing equipment to connectorize solid-wire UTP, it is important to purchase crimpers designed for solid wire.

CUTTING THE CORD

Solid-wire UTP normally comes in a box or spool containing 50 meters or more of wire. The first step is to cut a length of UTP cord that matches your need. It is good to be a little generous with the length. This way, bad connectorization can be fixed by cutting off the connector and adding a new connector to the shortened cord. Also, UTP cords should never be subjected to pulls (strain), and adding a little extra length creates some slack.

STRIPPING THE CORD

Now the cord must be stripped at each end using a **stripping tool** such as the one shown in Figure 3a-2. The installer rotates the stripper once around the cord, scoring (cutting into) the cord jacket (but not cutting through it). The installer then pulls off the scored end of the cord, exposing about 5 cm (about two inches) of the wire pairs.

It is critical not to score the cord too deeply, or the insulation around the individual wires may be cut. This creates short circuits. A really deep cut also will nick the wire, perhaps causing it to snap immediately or later.

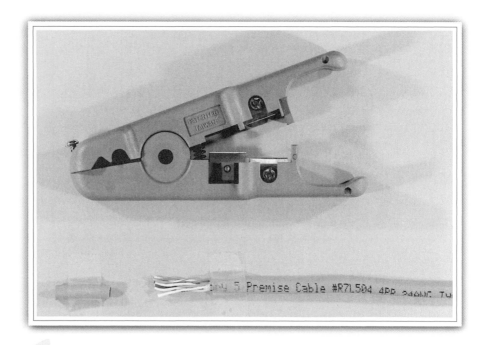

Figure 3a-2   Stripping Tool

WORKING WITH THE EXPOSED PAIRS

Pair Colors

The four pairs each have a color: orange, green, blue, or brown. One wire of the pair usually is a completely solid color. The other usually is white with stripes of the pair's color. For instance, the orange pair has an orange wire and a white wire with orange stripes.

Untwisting the Pairs

The wires of each pair are twisted around each other several times per inch. These must be untwisted after the end of the cord is stripped.

Ordering the Pairs

The wires now must be placed in their correct order, left to right. Figure 3a-3 shows the location of Pin 1 on the RJ-45 connector and on a wall jack or NIC.

Which color wire goes into which connector slot? The two standardized patterns are shown in Figure 3a-4. The T568B pattern is much more common in the United States.

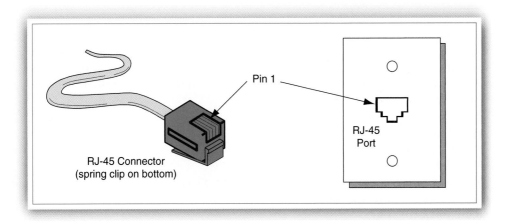

Figure 3a-3   Location of Pin 1 on an RJ-45 Connector and Wall Jack or NIC

The connectors at both ends of the cord use the same pattern. If the white-orange wire goes into Pin 1 of the connector on one end of the cord, it also goes into Pin 1 of the connector at the other end.

Pin*	T568A	T568B
1	White-Green	White-Orange
2	Green	Orange
3	White-Orange	White-Green
4	Blue	Blue
5	White-Blue	White-Blue
6	Orange	Green
7	White-Brown	White-Brown
8	Brown	Brown

Note: Do not confuse T568A and T568B
pin colors with the TIA/EIA-568 Standard.

Figure 3a-4   T568A and T568B Pin Colors

Cutting the Wires

The length of the exposed wires must be limited to 1.25 cm (half an inch) or slightly less. After the wires have been arranged in the correct order, a cutter should cut across the wires to make them this length. The cut should be made straight across, so that all wires are of equal length. Otherwise, they will not all reach the end of the connector when they are inserted into it. Wires that do not reach the end will not make electrical contact.

ADDING THE CONNECTOR

Holding the Connector

The next step is to place the wires in the RJ-45 connector. In one hand, hold the connector, clip side down, with the opening in the back of the connector facing you.

Sliding in the Wires

Now, slide the wires into the connector, making sure that they are in the correct order (white-orange on your left). There are grooves in the connector that will help. Be sure to push the wires all the way to the end or proper electrical contact will not be made with the pins at the end.

Before you crimp the connector, look down at the top of the connector, holding the tip away from you. The first wire on your left should be mostly white. So should every second wire. If they are not, you have inserted your wires incorrectly.[2]

Some Jacket Inside the Connector

If you have shortened your wires properly, there will be a little bit of jacket inside the RJ-45 connector.

CRIMPING

Pressing Down

Get a really good **crimping tool** (see Figure 3a-5). Place the connector with the wires in it into the crimp and push down firmly. Good crimping tools have ratchets to reduce the chance of your pushing down too tightly.

Making Electrical Contact

The front of the connector has eight pins running from the top almost to the bottom (spring clip side). When you **crimp** the connector, you force these eight pins through the insulation around each wire and into the wire itself. This seems like a crude electrical connection, and it is. However, it normally works very well. Your wires are now connected to the connector's pins. By the way, this is called an **insulation displacement connection (IDC)** because it cuts through the insulation.

---

[2]Thanks to Jason Okumura, who suggested this way of checking the wires.

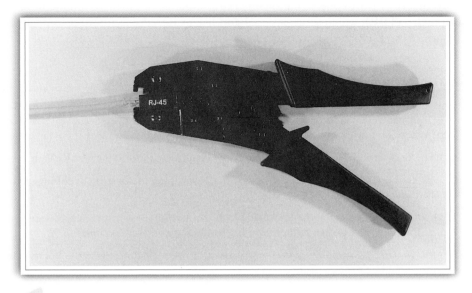

Figure 3a-5   Crimping Tool

Strain Relief

When you crimp, the crimper also forces a ridge in the back of the RJ-45 connector into the jacket of the cord. This provides **strain relief**, meaning that if someone pulls on the cord (a bad idea), they will be pulling only to the point where the jacket has the ridge forced into it. There will be no strain where the wires connect to the pins.

TESTING

Purchasing the best UTP cabling means nothing unless you install it properly. Wiring errors are common in the field, so you need to test every cord after you install it. Testing is inexpensive compared to troubleshooting subtle wiring problems later.

Testing with Continuity Testers

The simplest testers are **continuity testers**, which merely test whether the wires are arranged in correct order within the two RJ-45 connectors and are making good electrical contact with the connector. They cost only about $100.

Testing for Signal Quality

Better testers cost $500 to $2,000 but are worth the extra money. In addition to testing for continuity problems, they send **test signals** through the cord to determine whether the cord meets TIA/EIA-568 signal quality requirements. Many include **time domain reflectometry (TDR)**, which sends a signal and listens for echoes in order to measure the length of the UTP cord or to find if and where breaks exist in the cord.

TEST YOUR UNDERSTANDING

1. a) Explain the technical difference between solid-wire UTP and stranded-wire UTP. b) In what way is solid-wire UTP better? c) In what way is stranded-wire UTP better? d) Where would you use each? e) Which should only be connectorized at the factory?

2. If you have a wire run of 50 meters, should you cut the cord to 50 meters? Explain.

3. Why do you score the jacket of the cord with the stripping tool instead of cutting all the way through the jacket?

4. a) What are the colors of the four pairs? b) If you are following T568B, which wire goes into Pin 3? c) At the other end of the cord, would the same wire go into Pin 3?

5. After you arrange the wires in their correct order and cut them across, how much of the wires should be exposed from the jacket?

6. a) Describe RJ-45's insulation displacement approach. b) Describe its strain relief approach.

7. a) Should you test every cord in the field after installation? b)For what do inexpensive testers test? c) For what do expensive testers test?

Ethernet LANs

Learning Objectives

By the end of this chapter, you should be able to discuss:

- Ethernet physical layer standards and how they affect network design.
- The Ethernet data link layer and the Ethernet MAC layer frame.
- Basic Ethernet data link layer switch operation.
- Advanced aspects of Ethernet switch operation.
- Ethernet switch purchasing criteria.

AND THE WINNER IS . . .

According to Nortel Networks, 95 percent of wired LAN ports were Ethernet ports in 2002. That percentage is even higher today. Indeed, when people talk about LANs without referring to technology, they usually mean Ethernet. In this chapter, we will look at Ethernet in detail. In the next chapter, we will look at the other main LAN technology today—wireless LAN technology. Although wireless LAN technology is still small, it is growing explosively.

Ethernet became the dominant LAN technology because of its simple and therefore inexpensive data link layer operation, which we saw in Chapter 1 and which we will look at in more detail in this chapter. This cost advantage, coupled with adequate performance, has driven competing technologies out of the corporate LAN market.

Ethernet became the dominant LAN technology because of its simple and therefore inexpensive data link layer operation combined with adequate performance.

TEST YOUR UNDERSTANDING

1. a) What is the dominant LAN technology today? b) Why did it become dominant?

A SHORT HISTORY OF ETHERNET STANDARDS

Prehistory: Xerox, Intel, and Digital Equipment

Metcalfe and Boggs created Ethernet technology at the Xerox Palo Alto Research Center in the mid-1970s.[1] In the early 1980s, Xerox, Intel, and Digital Equipment Corporation teamed up to produce the first two commercial standards for Ethernet: Ethernet I and Ethernet II.

The 802 Committee

After creating Ethernet II, the three companies passed responsibility for Ethernet standards to the newly created **802 LAN/MAN Standards Committee** of the **Institute for Electrical and Electronics Engineers (IEEE)**. The "802 Committee," as everybody calls it, is broadly responsible for creating local area network standards and metropolitan area network standards.

The 802.3 Ethernet Working Group

The 802 Committee delegates the actual work of developing standards to specific working groups. The 802 Committee's **802.3 Working Group**, for example, creates Ethernet-specific standards. We will use the terms *Ethernet* and *802.3* interchangeably in this book.

We will use the terms *Ethernet* and *802.3* interchangeably in this book.

Other Working Groups

The 802 Committee has several other working groups. For example, the 802.11 Working Group creates the wireless LAN standards we will see in the next chapter. In turn, the 802.16 Working Group is creating the WiMax standards for wireless subscriber access within a city. The 802.1 Working Group creates general standards.

Ethernet Standards Are OSI Standards

Ethernet standards are LAN standards, so they are Layer 1 (physical) and Layer 2 (data link) standards. Recall from Chapter 2 that standards at the lowest two layers are always OSI standards. Although the 802.3 Working Group creates Ethernet standards, these standards are not official OSI standards until ISO ratifies them later. In practice, however, as soon as the 802.3 Working Group releases an 802.3 standard, vendors begin building products based on the specification.

TEST YOUR UNDERSTANDING

2. a) What working group creates Ethernet standards? b) To what committee does this working group report? c) In what organization is this committee? d) Are there other

---

[1]Bob Metcalfe has noted that he got the idea for Ethernet by visiting the University of Hawai'i's packet radio Alohanet project. The Alohanet project sent packets over radio and handled the problem of controlling when stations could transmit. Metcalfe realized that the same could be done over coaxial cable. See Bob Metcalfe, "Internet Fogies Reminisce and Argue at Interop Confab," *Infoworld* (September 21, 1992), p. 45.

Early History of Ethernet Standards

>> Developed at the Xerox Palo Alto Research Center by Metcalfe and Boggs

>> Standardized by Xerox, Intel, and Digital Equipment Corporation

>> Developed the Ethernet I and Ethernet II standards in the early 1980s

The 802 Committee

>> Development passed to the Institute for Electrical and Electronics Engineers (IEEE)

>> IEEE created the 802 LAN/MAN Standards Committee for LAN standards

>> This committee is usually called the 802 Committee

>> The 802 Committee creates working groups for specific types of standards.

>>> 802.1 for general standards

>>> 802.3 for Ethernet standards

>>> 802.11 for wireless LAN standards

>>> 802.16 for WiMax wireless metropolitan area network standards

The 802.3 Working Group

>> This group is in charge of creating Ethernet standards

>> The terms *802.3* and *Ethernet* are interchangeable today

>> Figure 4-2 shows Ethernet physical layer standards

>> Ethernet also has data link layer standards (frame organization, switch operation, etc.)

Ethernet Standards are OSI Standards

>> Layer 1 and Layer 2 standards are almost universally OSI standards

>> Ethernet is no exception

>> ISO must ratify them

>> In practice, when 802.3 finishes standards, vendors begin building compliant products.

Figure 4-1   A Short History of Ethernet Standards (Study Figure)

working groups? e) If so, what do they do? f) Does this book use *Ethernet* and *802.3* interchangeably? g) Why would you expect Ethernet standards to be OSI standards? h) When do vendors begin developing products based on Ethernet standards?

ETHERNET PHYSICAL STANDARDS

Ethernet defines standards at the physical and data link layers. We will look first at Ethernet physical layer standards.

Major Ethernet Physical Layer Standards

As just noted, Ethernet is a LAN technology, so standards must be set at both the physical and data link layers. We will look at 802.3 physical layer standards first.

When the 802.3 committee first created physical layer Ethernet standards, it used technologies that are no longer in use. Figure 4-2 shows the Ethernet physical layer standards that have been ratified.

Figure 4-2 shows Ethernet *physical* layer standards.

Venders have stopped producing products based on the oldest standards, and for higher speeds, vendors are only producing products for some standards. In addition, some vendors provide optical fiber of a higher quality than standards specify. These can carry Ethernet signals over longer distances. If you are designing an Ethernet network, you will need to conduct timely research on what is available.[2]

Baseband Transmission

As the figure shows, most Ethernet physical layer standards have *BASE* in their names. This is short for *baseband*. In **baseband** transmission, the transmitter simply injects signals into the transmission medium, as Figure 4-3 illustrates. For UTP, signals consist of voltage changes that propagate down the wires. For fiber, signals are light pulses.

Broadband Transmission

In contrast, in **broadband** transmission, the sender transmits signals in radio channels. However, radio-based broadband transmission is more expensive than baseband transmission. Although the 802.3 Working Group came up with early broadband LAN standards, these standards did not thrive because of their high cost.

Transmission Speed

The names of Ethernet physical layer standards also indicate transmission speeds—10 Mbps, 100 Mbps, or more. These are the speeds of NICs and switch ports. For example, a 12-port gigabit Ethernet switch will be able to send and receive at 12 Gbps across all of its ports.

10 Mbps Physical Layer 802.3 Standards

The slowest Ethernet physical layer standards in use today operate at 10 Mbps. The 802.3 10BASE-T standard normally uses 4-pair UTP wiring. The 10BASE-T standard is no longer commonly used today.

---

[2]In Chapter 3, we saw standards for optical fiber. Ethernet standards build on these optical fiber standards, adding light source standards and signaling methods.

Physical Layer Standard	Speed	Maximum Run Length	Medium
UTP			
10BASE-T	10 Mbps	100 meters	4-pair Category 3 or higher
100BASE-TX	100 Mbps	100 meters	4-pair Category 5 or higher
1000BASE-T	1,000 Mbps	100 meters	4-pair Category 5 or higher
Optical Fiber			
100BASE-FX	100 Mbps	2 km	62.5/125 multimode, 1,310 nm, switch.
1000BASE-SX	1 Gbps	220 m	62.5/125 micron multimode, 850 nm. 160 MHz-km modal bandwidth.
1000BASE-SX	1 Gbps	275 m	62.5/125 micron multimode, 850 nm. 200 MHz-km modal bandwidth.
1000BASE-SX	1 Gbps	500 m	50/125 micron multimode, 850 nm. 400 MHz-km modal bandwidth.
1000BASE-SX	1 Gbps	550 m	50/125 micron multimode, 850 nm. 500 MHz-km modal bandwidth.
1000BASE-LX	1 Gbps	550 m	62.5/125 micron multimode, 1,310 nm.
1000BASE-LX	1 Gbps	5 km	9/125 micron single mode, 1,310 nm.
10GBASE-SR/SW	10 Gbps	65 m	62.5/125 micron multimode, 850 nm.
10GBASE-LX4	10 Gbps	300 m	62.5/125 micron multimode, 1,310 nm, wave division multiplexing.
10GBASE-LR/LW	10 Gbps	10 km	9/125 micron single mode, 1,310 nm.
10GBASE-ER/EW	10 Gbps	40 km	9/125 micron single mode, 1,550 nm.
40 Gbps Ethernet	40 Gbps	Under Development	9/125 micron single mode.

Notes:

For 10GBASE-x, LAN versions (X and R) transmit at 10 Gbps. WAN versions (W) transmit at 9.95328 Gbps for carriage over SONET/SDH links (see Chapter 6).

The 40 Gbps Ethernet standards are still under preliminary development.

Figure 4-2   Ethernet Physical Layer Standards

100 Mbps Physical Layer 802.3 Standards

Next, the 802.3 Working Group produced 100 Mbps standards for UTP (T) and optical fiber (F). The **100BASE-TX** standard is the dominant Ethernet standard for connecting stations to switches today. **100BASE-FX**, in contrast, has almost entirely disappeared in favor of faster fiber-based Ethernet standards.[3] Another name for the 100 Mbps Ethernet standard is **Fast Ethernet**.

> Standard 100BASE-TX is the dominant Ethernet standard for connecting stations to switches today.

[3]Why TX and FX instead of T and F? The 802.3 Working Group created other 100 Mbps Ethernet standards, but only the TX and FX standards saw market acceptance.

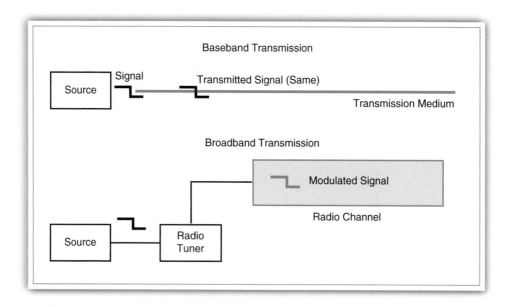

Figure 4-3   Baseband Versus Broadband Transmission

These standards are sometimes called **10/100 Ethernet** because 100BASE-TX and 100BASE-FX NICs and switches can do **autosensing**, which means that if they detect a 10BASE-x NIC or switch at the other end of the connection, they will slow down to 10 Mbps. However, they are full 100 Mbps technologies.

Gigabit Ethernet (1000BASE-x)

Advancing by another factor of 10, the 802.3 Working Group then produced **gigabit Ethernet (1000BASE-x)**. One gigabit per second is the dominant speed for connecting switches to switches, switches to routers, and routers to routers. However, companies are increasingly using it to connect servers and some desktops to the switches that serve them. Gigabit Ethernet equipment that does autosensing is sometimes called **10/100/1000** Ethernet.

A UTP version, **1000BASE-T**, can be used to bring gigabit Ethernet to the desktop. It can also be used to connect switches to other switches and switches to routers. Optical fiber connections tend to be three times as expensive as UTP connections, so 1000BASE-T is attractive.

However, most firms use fiber versions of gigabit Ethernet. Although fiber is more expensive to install, today's fiber should be able to carry much faster future versions of Ethernet. There are two fiber versions of gigabit Ethernet. The **1000BASE-SX** (short wavelength) version transmits at 850 nm using inexpensive laser signaling and multimode fiber. This standard has a maximum distance of 220 meters for older 62.5 micron fiber with a modal bandwidth of 160 MHz-km and to 275 m for newer 62.5 micron fiber with a modal bandwidth of 200 MHz-km. In addition, some fiber vendors offer ultra-high modal bandwidth fiber that can extend 1000BASE-SX to nonstandard but reliable lengths of 300–500 meters. Overall, 1000BASE-SX is the dominant gigabit Ethernet standard and is the most widely used standard for connecting switches to other switches in organizations.[4]

> Standard 1000BASE-SX is the most widely used standard for connecting switches to other switches in organizations.

10GBASE-x

The next step, 10 Gbps technology, uses optical fiber almost exclusively. Although the 802.3 Working Group is developing copper wiring standards,[5] the 10 Gbps Ethernet standards in widespread use today are fiber standards. Figure 4-2 shows that the 802.3 Working Group created quite a few 10 Gbps fiber standards.

R and W   Several of these standards come in two versions. LAN versions (R) operate at 10 Gbps. WAN versions (W) run over SONET/SDH transmission lines. These use a speed of 9.95328 Gbps, which is the closest SONET/SDH speed to 10 Gbps. The X standards also run at a true 10 Gbps. The 802.3 Working Group developed WAN versions first.

Why focus on SONET/SDH speeds? The answer is that the 802.3 Working Group developed the 10 Gbps Ethernet for WANs, or, more correctly, metropolitan area networks (MANs) within a city. However, corporate LANs also use 10 Gbps Ethernet today.

S, L, and E   We saw in Chapter 3 that the transceiver's wavelength is very important for propagation distance. In these standards, S indicates 850 nm, L indicates 1,310 nm, and E (extremely long wavelength) indicates 1,550 nm.

40GBASE-x

The 802.3 Working Group is now working on the next generation of physical layer Ethernet standards, 40GBASE-x. These standards will depart from the traditional practice of increasing speed by a factor of ten in each generation. Like 10GBASE-x, the 802.3 Working Group is developing them first for WAN carrier networks.

TEST YOUR UNDERSTANDING

3. a) At what layer is the 100BASE-TX standard? b) What can you infer from the name 100BASE-TX? c) Distinguish between baseband and broadband transmission. d) Why does baseband transmission dominate for LANs? e) What is 10/100 Ethernet? f) What is

---

[4]The 1000BASE-LX (long wavelength) version uses more expensive lasers to transmit at 1,310 nm. It can send data twice as far as SX using multimode fiber. With single-mode fiber, it can send data 5 km. However, 1000BASE-SX is used far more widely than 1000BASE-LX.
[5]The 802.3 Working Group is developing the 10GBASE-CX4 standard for runs of less than 15 meters. The 10GBASE-CX4 standard uses eight wires, but these are not arranged as twisted pairs, and there is metal shielding around the wiring. This will only be useful for switch-to-switch connections in wiring cabinets and server-to-switch connections in data centers. 10GBASE-CX4 uses adaptations of the Infiniband connectors and cabling created for storage area networks.
As noted in the last chapter, the 802.3 Working Group is now developing a 10GBASE-T standard using Cat 6A UTP and Cat 7 STP.

autosensing? g) What is Fast Ethernet? h) What is the most widely used 802.3 physical layer standard for connecting stations to switches today?i) What is the most widely used 802.3 physical layer standard for connecting switches to other switches today? j) Which versions did the 802.3 Working Group develop initially for WANs?

Link Aggregation (Trunking)

Ethernet transmission capacity usually increases by a factor of ten. What should you do if you only need somewhat more speed than a certain standard specifies? For instance, suppose that you have gigabit Ethernet switches and need a switch-to-switch link of 1.5 Gbps instead of 10 Gbps.

Figure 4-4 illustrates that sometimes two or more trunk lines connect a single pair of switches. This requires the switches to implement the **802.3ad** standard. The IEEE calls this **link aggregation**. Networking professionals also call this **trunking** or **bonding**.

Link aggregation allows you to increase trunk speed incrementally by a factor of two or three, instead of by a factor of ten. This incremental growth uses existing ports and usually is inexpensive compared to upgrading a switch to the next higher Ethernet speed. In contrast, moving to the next higher Ethernet speed usually involves purchasing new switches or at least new port modules for existing switches.

However, after two or three aggregated links, the company should compare the cost of link aggregation with the cost of a 10-fold increase in capacity by moving up to the next Ethernet speed. Going to a single faster trunk line will also give more room for growth.

The incremental growth that link aggregation brings usually is inexpensive compared to upgrading a switch to the next higher Ethernet speed. However, after two or three aggregated links, the company should compare the cost of link aggregation with the cost of a 10-fold increase in capacity by moving up to the next Ethernet speed.

TEST YOUR UNDERSTANDING

4. a) What is link aggregation (trunking or bonding)? b) Why may link aggregation be more desirable than installing a single faster link? c) Why may it not be desirable if you will need several aggregated links to meet capacity requirements?

Ethernet Physical Layer Standards and Network Design

Using Figure 4-2

Note that if you know the speed you need (100 Mbps, 1 Gbps, and so forth) and if you know what distance you need to span, Figure 4-2 will show you what type of transmission link you need. If link aggregation is also available with your switches, you have even more choices.

For instance, if you need a speed of 1 Gbps, and if your two switches are 130 meters apart, you would select 1000BASE-SX multimode fiber to minimize cost.

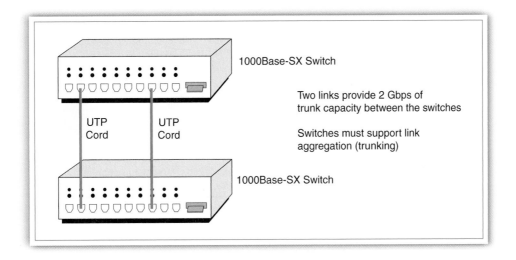

Figure 4-4   Link Aggregation (Trunking or Bonding)

Although 1000BASE-LX would also do the job, 1000BASE-SX is more than sufficient. Generally speaking, picking the shortest-distance standard that will do the job will minimize cost.

Alternatively, if you are designing a network from scratch, say for a new facility, the options in Figure 4-2 will allow you to consider alternative placements for your switches. If you can place your switches farther apart on average, for instance, you can reduce the total number of switches, and this can save money—although each of the switches in a more dispersed network will cost more to purchase because each will have to handle more traffic.

As noted earlier, however, Figure 4-2 lists standards that have been ratified. Some of these standards have been ignored by vendors, and some vendors have products that use superior fiber and so can cover long distances based on the same standard.

Switches Regenerate Signals to Extend Distance

The 100-meter limit for UTP and the longer distance limits for fiber shown in Figure 4-2 only apply to connections *between a pair of devices*—for example, a station and a switch, two switches, or a switch and a router.

The 100-meter limit for UTP and the longer distance limits for fiber shown in Figure 4-2 only apply to connections *between a pair of devices*, not to end-to-end connections between stations across multiple switches.

What should you do if a longer distance separates the source host and the destination host? Figure 4-5 shows a data link with two intermediate switches. In addition to

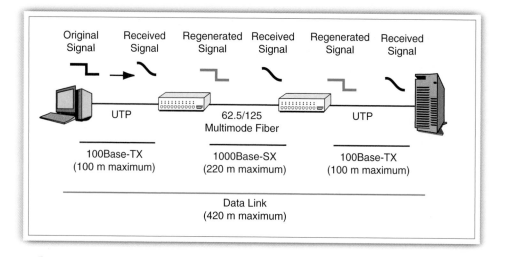

Figure 4-5   Data Link Using Multiple Switches

the two 100-meter maximum length UTP access links, there is a 220-meter maximum length 1000BASE-SX optical fiber link (using 62.5/125-micron 160-MHz-km modal bandwidth fiber) between the two switches. This setup can span a maximum of 420 meters.

Each switch along the way **regenerates** the signal. If the signal sent by the source host begins as a 1, it is likely to be distorted before it reaches the first switch. The first switch recognizes it as a 1 and generates a clean new 1 signal to send to the second switch. The second switch regenerates the 1 as well.

The key point is that Figure 4-2 shows maximum distances between pairs of devices, not end-to-end transmission distances. To deliver frames over long distances, intermediate switches regenerate the signal. There is no maximum end-to-end distance between pairs of stations in an Ethernet network. Although cumulative delay might be a problem with a dozen or more intermediate switches, this rarely is a problem in real networks.

There is no maximum end-to-end distance between pairs of stations in an Ethernet network.

TEST YOUR UNDERSTANDING

5. a) How could you use Figure 4-2 in network design? b) If more than one type of Ethernet standard in Figure 4-2 can span the distance you need, what would determine which one you choose? c) In Figure 4-2, is the distance the maximum for a single physical link or for the end-to-end distance between two stations across multiple switches? d) At what layer or layers is the 802.3 100BASE-TX standard defined—physical, data

link, or internet? e) How does regeneration allow a firm to create LANs that span very long distances? f) If you need to span 300 meters using 1000BASE-SX, what options do you have? (Include the possibility of using an intermediate switch.) g) How would you decide which option to choose?

THE ETHERNET FRAME

Layering

The Logical Link Control Layer

When the 802 Committee assumed control over Ethernet standardization, it realized that it would have to standardize non-Ethernet LAN technology as well. Consequently, the 802 Committee divided the data link layer into two layers, as Figure 4-6 illustrates.

➤ The lower part of the standard—the media access control layer—is specific to the particular LAN technology. For example, there are separate media access control layer standards for Ethernet and 802.11 wireless networks.

➤ The upper layer—the **logical link control (LLC)** layer—adds some functionality on top of technology-specific functionality. Unfortunately, time has proven the added functionality of LLC to be of little value, so it is now largely ignored. As we will see below, it adds an LLC subheader to each 802.3 frame. There is only a single LLC standard, **802.2**.

The 802.3 MAC Layer Standard

As just noted, the lower part of the data link layer is the MAC layer. *MAC* stands for **media access control**. The MAC layer defines functionality specific to a particular LAN technology.

Note in Figure 4-6 that while Ethernet (802.3) has many physical layer standards, it only has a single media access control layer standard, the **802.3 MAC Layer Standard**. This standard defines Ethernet frame organization and NIC and switch operation.

TEST YOUR UNDERSTANDING

6. a) Distinguish between the MAC and LLC layers. b) Does Ethernet have multiple physical layer standards? c) Does it have multiple MAC standards? d) What is the name of its single MAC standard?

The Ethernet Frame's Organization

Figure 4-7 shows the Ethernet MAC layer frame. We saw it briefly in Chapter 2. We will now look at the Ethernet frame in more depth.

Preamble and Start of Frame Delimiter Fields

Before a play in American football, the quarterback calls out something like "Hut one, hut two, hut three, hike!" This cadence synchronizes all of the offensive players.

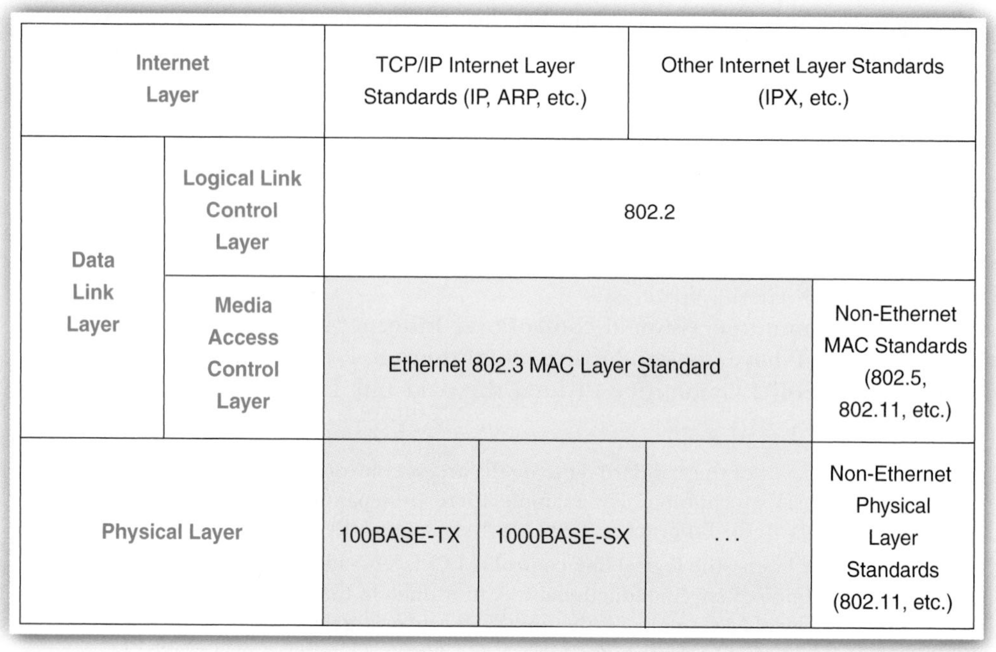

Internet Layer		TCP/IP Internet Layer Standards (IP, ARP, etc.)			Other Internet Layer Standards (IPX, etc.)
Data Link Layer	Logical Link Control Layer	802.2			
	Media Access Control Layer	Ethernet 802.3 MAC Layer Standard			Non-Ethernet MAC Standards (802.5, 802.11, etc.)
Physical Layer		100BASE-TX	1000BASE-SX	. . .	Non-Ethernet Physical Layer Standards (802.11, etc.)

Figure 4-6   Layering in 802 Networks

In the Ethernet MAC frame, the **preamble** field (7 octets) and the **start of frame delimiter** field (1 octet) synchronize the receiver's clock to the sender's clock. These fields have a strong rhythm of alternating 1s and 0s. The last bit in this sequence is a 1 instead of the expected 0, to signal that the synchronization is finished.

Source and Destination Address Fields

Hex Notation   We saw in Chapter 2 that the source and destination Ethernet address fields are 48 bits long and that while computers work with this raw 48-bit form, humans normally express these addresses in Base 16 **hexadecimal (hex) notation**.

> ➤ First, divide the 48 bits into twelve 4-bit units, which computer scientists call nibbles.
>
> ➤ Second, convert each nibble into a hexadecimal symbol, using Figure 4-8.
>
> ➤ Third, write the symbols as six pairs with a dash between each pair—for instance B2-CC-67-0D-5E-BA. (Each pair represents one octet.)

MAC Layer Addresses   Ethernet addresses exist at the MAC layer, so Ethernet addresses are **MAC addresses**. They are also called **physical addresses** because physical devices (NICs) implement Ethernet at the physical, MAC, and LLC layers.

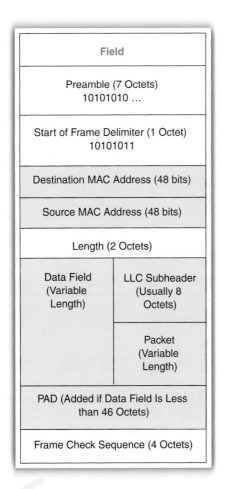

Figure 4-7   The Ethernet MAC-Layer Frame

Length Field

The **length** field contains a binary number that gives the length of the data field (not of the entire frame) in octets. The maximum length of the data field is 1500 octets.[6] There is no minimum length for the data field.

Data Field

The **data** field contains the information that the frame is delivering. The data field usually is far longer than all other fields combined.

---

[6]Many NICs and switches today can handle nonstandard *jumbo frames*, which have data fields up to 9,000 octets in length. This allows long messages to be sent with fewer frames. Handling fewer frames per message makes NICs and switches more efficient. However, jumbo frames are bad for VoIP because their length creates more latency at each switch.

4 Bits (Base 2)*	Decimal (Base 10)	Hexadecimal (Base 16)	4 Bits (Base 2)*	Decimal (Base 10)	Hexadecimal (Base 16)
0000	0	0 hex	1000	8	8 hex
0001	1	1 hex	1001	9	9 hex
0010	2	2 hex	1010	10	A hex
0011	3	3 hex	1011	11	B hex
0100	4	4 hex	1100	12	C hex
0101	5	5 hex	1101	13	D hex
0110	6	6 hex	1110	14	E hex
0111	7	7 hex	1111	15	F hex

Note: 2^4=16 combinations.
For example, A1-34-CD-7B-DF hex begins with 10100001 for A1.

Figure 4-8   Hexadecimal Notation

LLC Subheader   The data field begins with the **logical link control layer (LLC) sub-header**. This normally is eight octets long. The purpose of the LLC subheader is to describe the type of packet contained in the data field. For instance, if the LLC sub-header ends with the code 08-00 hex, the data field contains an IP packet.[7]

Encapsulated Packet   The packet encapsulated in the data field usually is an IP packet. However, it could also be a packet from another standards architecture, say an IPX packet. As long as the source and destination stations understand the packet format, there is no problem.

PAD Field
Although there is no minimum length for 802.3 MAC layer frame data fields, if the data field is less than 46 octets long, the sender must add a PAD field so that the total length of the data field and the PAD field is exactly 46 octets long. For instance, if the data field is 26 octets long, the sender will add a 20-octet PAD field. If the data field is 46 octets long or longer, the sender will not add a PAD field.

> There is no minimum length for the data field, but if the data field is less than 46 octets long, a PAD field must be added to bring the total length of the data and pad fields to 46 octets.

---

[7]The LLC subheader has several fields. In the SNAP version of LLC, which is almost always used, the first three octets are always AA-AA-03 hex. The next three octets are almost always 00-00-00 hex. The final two octets constitute the Ethertype field, which specifies the kind of packet in the data field. Common hexa-decimal Ethertype values are 0800 (IP), 8137 (IPX), 809B (AppleTalk), 80D5 (SNA services), and 86DD (IP version 6).

Frame Check Sequence Field

As noted in Chapter 2, the last field in the Ethernet frame is the frame check sequence field, which permits error detection. This is a four-octet field. If the receiver detects an error in a transmitted frame, the receiver simply discards the frame.

TEST YOUR UNDERSTANDING

7. a) What is the purpose of the preamble and start of frame delimiter fields? b) Why are Ethernet addresses called MAC addresses or physical addresses? c) What are the steps in converting 48-bit MAC addresses into hex notation? d) The length field gives the length of what? e) What are the two parts of the data field? f) What is the purpose of the LLC subheader? g) What type of packet is usually carried in the data field? h) What is the maximum length of the data field? i) Who adds the PAD field—the sender or the receiver? j) Is there a minimum length for the data field? k) If the data field is 40 octets long, how long a PAD field must the sender add? l) If the data field is 400 octets long, how long a PAD field must the sender add? m) What is the purpose of the frame check sequence field? n) What happens if the receiver detects an error in a frame? o) Convert 11000010 to hex.

BASIC DATA LINK LAYER SWITCH OPERATION

In this section, we will discuss the basic data link layer operation of Ethernet switches. This is also governed by the 802.3 MAC layer standard. In the section after this one, we will discuss other aspects of Ethernet switching that a firm may or may not use.

Frame Forwarding with Multiple Ethernet Switches

Figure 4-9 shows an Ethernet LAN with three switches. Larger Ethernet LANs have dozens of switches, but the operation of individual switches is the same whether there are only a few switches or many. Each individual switch between the source and destination host reads the address of an incoming frame, looks up an output port in its switching table, and sends the frame out that port.

In a multiswitch LAN, the switch may be forwarding the frame to another switch on the data link, instead of directly to the destination station. However, switches do not know if they are forwarding the frame to the destination station or to another switch. They merely send the frame out the indicated port.

For example, suppose that Station A1-44-D5-1F-AA-4C on Switch 1 transmits a frame destined for Station E5-BB-47-21-D3-56, which attaches to Switch 3. The frame will have to pass through Switch 2 along the way.

Switch 1 will look at its switching table and note that Station E5-BB-47-21-D3-56 is out Port 5. The switch will send the frame out that port. The link out Port 5 will carry the frame to Switch 2 instead of directly to the destination station.

TEST YOUR UNDERSTANDING

8. a) In a single-switch LAN, the switch reads the address of an incoming frame, looks up an output port in the switching table, and sends the frame out that port. Do individual switches work differently in multiswitch LANs? Explain. b) What happens on Switch 2? c) What happens on Switch 3?

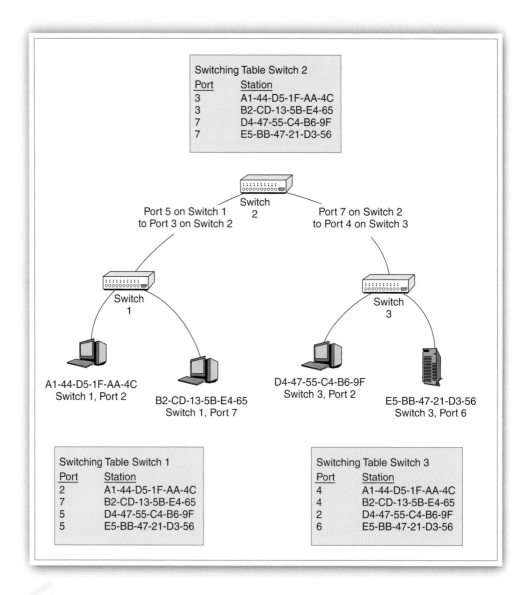

Figure 4-9 Multiswitch Ethernet LAN

Hierarchical Switch Topology
Hierarchical Switch Organization
Note that the switches in Figure 4-10 form a **hierarchy**, in which each switch has only one parent switch above it. In fact, the Ethernet standard *requires* a **hierarchical topology** for its switches. Otherwise, loops would exist, causing frames to circulate endlessly

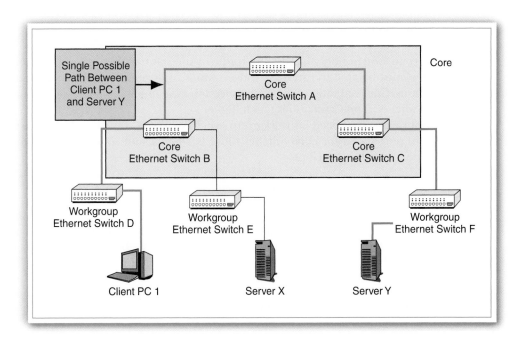

Figure 4-10   Hierarchical Ethernet LAN

from one switch to another around the loop or causing other problems. Figure 4-10 shows a larger switched Ethernet LAN organized in a hierarchy.

Ethernet *requires* a hierarchical switch hierarchy.

Single Possible Path Between End Stations

In a hierarchy, there is only a single possible path between any two end stations. (To see this, select any two stations at the bottom of the hierarchy and trace a path between them. You will see that only one path is possible.)

In a hierarchy, there is only a single possible path between any two end stations.

Workgroup Versus Core Switches

In a hierarchy of Ethernet switches, there are workgroup switches and core switches. Figure 4-10 illustrates these two types of switches.

  ➤ **Workgroup switches.** Switches that connect computers to the network via access lines are called workgroup switches (Switches D, E, and F in Figure 4-10).

  ➤ **Core switches.** Switches farther up the hierarchy (Switches A, B, and C in Figure 4-10) that carry traffic via trunk lines between pairs of switches, switches and routers, and pairs of routers are called core switches. The collection of all core switches plus the trunk lines that connect them is the network's **core**.

Workgroup switches only handle the traffic of the stations they serve. However, core switches must be able to carry the conversations of dozens, hundreds, or thousands of stations. Consequently, core switches need to have much higher capacity than workgroup switches. Their cost also is much higher.

The dominant port speed for workgroup switches today is 100 Mbps. In contrast, the dominant port speed for core switches today is 1 Gbps, and some core switches already use port speeds of 10 Gbps.

TEST YOUR UNDERSTANDING

9. a) How are switches in an Ethernet LAN organized? b) Because of this organization, how many possible paths can there be between any two stations? c) In Figure 4-10, what is the single possible path between Client PC 1 and Server Y? d) Between Client PC 1 and Server X?

10. a) Distinguish between workgroup switches and core switches in terms of which devices they connect. b) How do they compare in terms of switching capacity? Explain. c) How do they compare in terms of port speeds? Explain.

Only One Possible Path: Low Switching Cost

We have just seen that a hierarchy only allows one possible path between any two hosts.

If there is only a single possible path between any two stations, it follows that in every switch along the path, the destination address in a frame will appear only once in the switching table—for the specific outgoing port needed to send the frame on its way.

This allows a simple table lookup operation that is very fast and therefore costs little per frame handled. This is what makes Ethernet switches inexpensive. As noted in the introduction, simple switching operation and therefore low cost has led to Ethernet's dominance in LAN technology.

The fact that there is only a single possible path between any two end stations in an Ethernet hierarchy makes Ethernet switch forwarding simple and therefore inexpensive. This low cost has led to Ethernet's dominance in LAN technology.

In Chapter 8, we will see that routers have to do much more work when a packet arrives because there are multiple alternative routes between any two hosts. Each of these alternative routes appears as a row in the routing table. Therefore, a router must first identify all possible routes (rows) and then select the best one—instead of simply finding a single match. This additional work per forwarding decision makes routers very expensive for the traffic load they handle.

TEST YOUR UNDERSTANDING

11. a) What is the benefit of having a single possible path? Explain in detail. b) Why has Ethernet become the dominant LAN technology?

ADVANCED ETHERNET SWITCH OPERATION

Now that we have discussed basic Ethernet switch operation involved in frame forwarding, we will begin looking at additional aspects of Ethernet switch operation that are important in larger Ethernet networks.

802.1D: The Spanning Tree Protocol (STP)

Single Points of Failure

Having only a single possible path between any two stations allows rapid frame forwarding and, therefore, low switch cost. Unfortunately, having only a single possible path between any two computers also makes Ethernet vulnerable to **single points of failure**, in which the failure of a single component (a switch or a trunk line between switches) can cause widespread disruption.

> Having only a single possible path between end stations in a switched Ethernet network reduces cost but creates single points of failure, meaning that a single failure can cause widespread disruption.

To understand this, suppose that Switch 2 in Figure 4-11 fails. Then the stations connected to Switch 1 will not be able to communicate with stations connected to

Figure 4-11   Single Point of Failure in a Switch Hierarchy

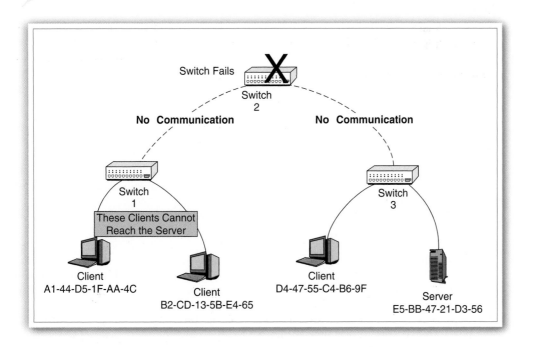

Switch 2 or Switch 3. Consider a second example: if the link between Switch 1 and Switch 2 fails, the network also will be broken into two parts.

Although the two parts of the network might continue to function independently after a failure, many firms put most or all of their servers in a centralized server room. Clients on the other side of the broken network would lose much of their ability to continue working. For example, in the figure, Client A1-44-D5-1F-AA-4C, which connects to Switch 1, cannot reach Server E5-BB-47-21-D3-56, which connects to Switch 3. External connections also tend to be confined to a single network point for security reasons. Computers on the wrong side of the divide after a breakdown would lose external access.

Loops

Another problem is that it is very easy to create accidental loops among switches in large networks. Ethernet frame forwarding cannot tolerate loops because loops cause frames to circulate endlessly.

802.1D Spanning Tree Protocol (STP)

Fortunately, the **802.1D Spanning Tree Protocol (STP)**,[8] which Figure 4-12 illustrates, addresses both single points of failure and loops.

Deactivating Loops

In the **Spanning Tree Protocol (STP)**, the switches constantly talk to one another. If they detect a loop, they communicate intensively and find a way to restore a hierarchy by deactivating links that create loops. See this in the top half of Figure 4-12.

Redundancy

STP also allows redundancy in a network. The network design can use disabled links to be standby links, as shown in the bottom half of Figure 4-12. Here, Switch 2 has failed. The Spanning Tree Protocol allows the switches to detect a break and reconfigure the network. Here, the reactivated link bypasses the failed switch. Users of this switch are locked out of the network. However, if a single trunk line leading to the switch had failed, the Spanning Tree Protocol would have recreated a complete hierarchical network among the Ethernet switches.

Rapid Spanning Tree Protocol

The problem with STP is that when a failure occurs, the network converges (reorganizes itself) rather slowly—typically taking 30 to 60 seconds. A newer version of STP, the **Rapid Spanning Tree Protocol (RSTP)** converges in only about a second. Most switches today support RSTP.

TEST YOUR UNDERSTANDING

12. a) Why is having a single possible path between any two stations in an Ethernet network dangerous? b) What is a single point of failure? c) Why are loops bad in Ethernet? d) What standard allows redundancy in Ethernet networks? e) What is

---

[8]In Chapter 3, we saw that STP at the physical layer refers to shielded twisted pair wiring. The spanning tree protocol is STP at the data link layer.

Figure 4-12   802.1D Spanning Tree Protocol (STP)

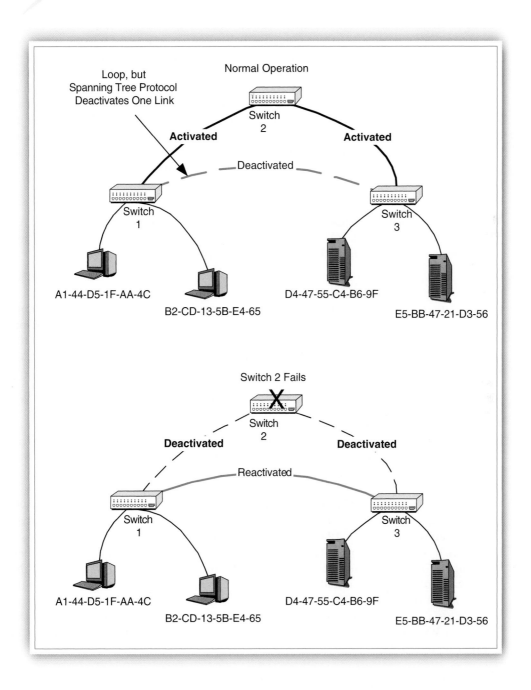

convergence in the context of STP and RSTP? f) How can STP's slow convergence be remedied?

Virtual LANs and Ethernet Switches

Broadcasting

Ethernet NICs normally wish to **unicast**—that is, send a frame to only one other station. However, sometimes stations wish to **broadcast** messages, that is, send them to all other stations, as Figure 4-13 illustrates. Most notably, Novell NetWare servers may advertise their presence every sixty seconds or so by broadcasting a server advertisement message that should go to all other stations. The server that wishes to broadcast will set the frame's destination MAC address to 48 ones (FF-FF-FF-FF-FF-FF). When an Ethernet switch sees this MAC address in the destination address of a frame, it broadcasts the frame out all other ports, like a hub. All NICs, in turn, process frames addressed to FF-FF-FF-FF-FF-FF as if it were their own address.

Congestion

Broadcasting is fine in small networks. However, in a large switched Ethernet LAN with many servers, broadcasting will produce a tremendous amount of traffic and therefore congestion. Quite simply, broadcasting does not work in large networks.

Virtual LANs

As Figure 4-13 illustrates, most Ethernet switches allow stations to be grouped into closed collections of servers and the clients they serve. These collections are **virtual LANs (VLANs)**. When Server E (on VLAN 1) transmits, its frames go only to the clients on its own VLAN (Client A and Client C). This reduces congestion.

VLANs are needed to control congestion due to frame broadcasting.

Standardizing VLANs

Until recently, there was no standard for VLANs, so if you used VLANs, you had to buy all of your Ethernet switches from the same vendor. However, as Figure 4-14 shows, the **802.1Q** standard is extending the Ethernet MAC layer frame to include two optional **tag fields**.

The first tag field (**Tag Protocol ID**) has the two-octet hexadecimal value 81-00, which simply indicates that this is a tagged frame. The second tag field (**Tag Control Information**) contains a 12-bit VLAN ID that it sets to 0 if the firm does not use VLANs. If the firm does use VLANs, it will give each VLAN a different VLAN ID. When a station on a VLAN transmits, the station adds the VLAN ID of its own VLAN to the Tag Control Information field. The switches will read the VLAN ID to determine how to forward the frame. (The destination Ethernet address is set to forty-eight 1s in broadcasts, so a switch can use only the VLAN ID to determine how to forward the frame.) With 12-bit VLAN IDs, there can be 4,095 (2^{12}-1) different VLANs on an Ethernet network.

802.1Q is the standard for frame tagging.

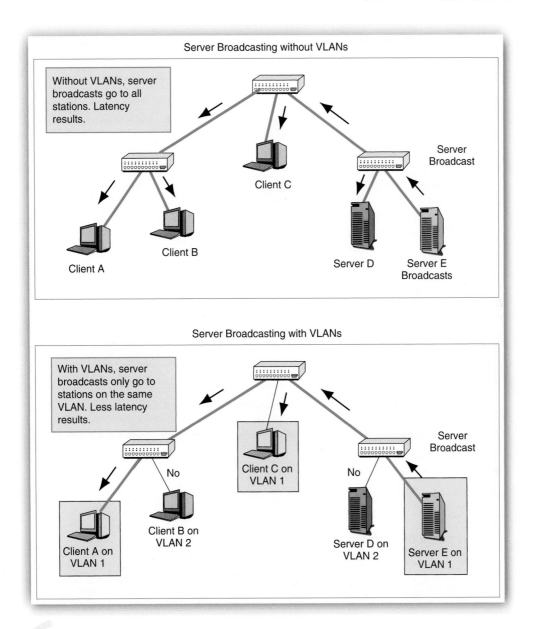

Figure 4-13   Virtual LAN (VLAN) with Ethernet Switches

With VLANs, switches do not use their switching tables that contain MAC address–port pairs. Rather, they use a VLAN switching table that associates VLAN ID numbers with one or more ports. Switches from different vendors can all build their VLAN switching tables using standardized VLAN ID numbers. This will allow them to interoperate.

Basic 802.3 MAC Frame		Tagged 802.3 MAC Frame
Preamble (7 Octets)		Preamble (7 Octets)
Start of Frame Delimiter (1 Octet)		Start of Frame Delimiter (1 Octet)
Destination Address (6 Octets)		Destination Address (6 Octets)
Source Address (6 Octets)		Source Address (6 Octets)
Length (2 Octets) Length of Data Field in Octets 1,500 (Decimal) Maximum	By looking at the value in the 2 octets after the addresses, the switch can tell if this frame is a basic frame (value less than 1,500) or a tagged (value is 33,024).	Tag Protocol ID (2 Octets) 1000000100000000 81-00 hex 33,024 decimal Larger than 1,500, So not a Length Field
Data Field (variable)		Tag Control Information (2 Octets) Priority Level (0 to 7) (3 bits) VLAN ID (12 bits) 1 other bit
PAD (If Needed)		Length (2 Octets)
Frame Check Sequence (4 Octets)		Data Field (variable)
		PAD (If Needed)
		Frame Check Sequence (4 Octets)

Figure 4-14   Tagged Ethernet Frame (Governed by 802.1Q)

TEST YOUR UNDERSTANDING

13. a) Distinguish between unicasting and broadcasting. b) What problem do VLANs address? c) How do they address it? d) When a server on a VLAN broadcasts, what stations receive its message? e) Describe the VLAN tagging standard, 802.1Q.

Handling Momentary Traffic Peaks

Momentary Traffic Peaks

If traffic volume is comfortably below a network's traffic capacity, traffic should get through promptly. However, sometimes there are **momentary traffic peaks** that briefly exceed the network's capacity, as Figure 4-15 illustrates.

During momentary traffic peaks, the switch will not be able to handle all of the frames that arrive. Some frames will be delayed. In networking, delay is called **latency**. During momentary traffic peaks, delayed frames will be held in a memory area called the switch's buffer. If traffic peaks last beyond a certain time, the buffer

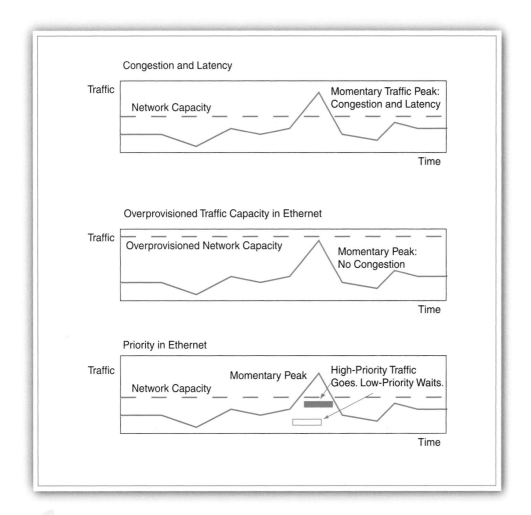

Figure 4-15 Handling Momentary Traffic Peaks with Overprovisioning and Priority

will become full. Subsequent frames that cannot be delivered will be dropped entirely.

Momentary traffic peaks create congestion that leads to latency and may even cause frame loss.

Although these peaks normally last only a fraction of a second to a few seconds, they can be highly disruptive for some applications, especially voice and video. These are called **latency-intolerant** applications. In contrast, the users of **latency-tolerant** applications, such as e-mail, will not even notice brief delays.

Overprovisioning Ethernet

Most organizations have discovered that the least expensive way to get around peak traffic congestion today is simply to **overprovision** the Ethernet LAN—that is, to install much more capacity in switches and trunk lines than will be needed most of the time. If 10BASE-T would be sufficient most of the time, for example, they install 100BASE-TX. When there are brief traffic bursts, these bursts will very rarely exceed capacity. Although this method wastes capacity most of the time, it works without adding to the cost of switch management. This is why overprovisioning currently is the most economical way of dealing with momentary traffic peaks.

Overprovisioning currently is the most economical way to deal with momentary traffic peaks in Ethernet networks.

Priority in Ethernet

Another way to address momentary traffic peaks is to give **priority** to certain traffic, meaning that high-priority traffic will go first. In commercial air travel, for example, people with children and disabilities and first-class passengers are given priority in boarding flights.

Figure 4-14 showed that 802.1Q Ethernet frame tagging can give priority to individual frames. The Tag Control Information field contains not only a 12-bit VLAN ID, but also a 3-bit **priority level** to give a frame one of eight priority levels from 000 (low) to 111 (high). The definition of these eight priority levels is in the **802.1p** standard.[9]

In switching, priority is based on the tolerance of traffic for latency. When brief traffic peaks occur, latency-intolerant traffic, such as voice and video, will be given high priority and so will be switched first. Of course, latency-tolerant applications will be delayed, but users probably will not even notice brief delays during momentary traffic peaks. Priority is also used to guarantee that network control messages get through, which may be crucial during periods of high congestion.

Most switches today support priority. However, priority can be difficult to manage. Its management costs have made priority substantially more expensive than overprovisioning Ethernet. In addition, prioritizing traffic can lead to pitched political battles within a firm over whose traffic should have the highest priority.

Momentary Versus Chronic Lack of Capacity

Note that we have been discussing momentary traffic peaks in a network that has sufficient capacity nearly all of the time. This is very different from **chronic lack of capacity**, in which the network lacks adequate capacity much of the time. In such cases, the

---

[9]In addition to the twelve VLAN ID bits and the three priority bits, the 16-bit Tag Control Information field has a 1-bit canonical format bit. This bit is set to 1 for all networks except 802.5 Token-Ring Networks and FDDI, for which it is set to 0. Both Token-Ring Networks and FDDI are now extremely rare. In canonical format, the rightmost bit in each byte is sent first. In 802.5 and FDDI, the leftmost bit in each byte is sent first. The canonical format bit is rarely used.

Number and Speeds of Ports
>Buyers must decide on the number of ports needed and the speed of each

>Buyers often can buy a prebuilt switch with this configuration

Switching Matrix Throughput (Figure 4-18)
>Aggregate throughput: total speed of switching matrix

>Nonblocking capacity: switching matrix sufficient even if there is maximum input on all ports

>Less than nonblocking capacity is workable

>>For core switches, at least 80 percent

>>For workgroup switches, at least 20 percent

Store-and-Forward Versus Cut-Through Switching (Figure 4-19)
>Store-and-forward Ethernet switches read whole frame before passing the frame on

>Cut-through Ethernet switches read only some fields before passing the frame on

>Cut-through switches have less latency, but this is rarely important

Manageability
>Manager controls many managed switches (see Figure 4-20)

>Polling enables managers to collect data and diagnose problems

>Switches can be fixed remotely by changing their configurations

>Manager provides the network administrator with summary performance data

>Managed switches are substantially more expensive than unmanaged switches

>However, in large networks, the savings in labor costs and rapid response are worth it

Figure 4-17   Switch Purchasing Considerations (Study Figure)

PURCHASING SWITCHES

We will end this chapter with a discussion of the issues you will have to deal with when purchasing Ethernet switches. Purchasing an Ethernet switch is a complex task.

Number and Speeds of Ports

The most basic issue is how many ports you will need to have and what their individual speeds need to be. For instance, you might need a workgroup switch with 12 or 24 100BASE-TX ports. To give another example, you might need a core switch with four gigabit Ethernet SC optical fiber ports and two 10GBASE-SX SC optical fiber ports. Fortunately, you can buy switches with a fixed number of ports in almost any port and speed configuration you wish. In addition, many switches are modular, meaning that you can buy the basic chassis and insert cards with the ports you require.

TEST YOUR UNDERSTANDING

16. a) What is the first issue to consider in switch purchases? b) Do you have many choices in port numbers and speeds?

Switching Matrix Throughput

As Figure 4-18 illustrates, a switch has a switching matrix that connects input ports to output ports.

Aggregate Throughput

A critical consideration in Ethernet switch selection is the switching matrix's **aggregate throughput**—that is, the total speed of the switching matrix. For example, suppose you have a 4-port 100BASE-TX switch, as shown in Figure 4-18. In the worst case, all ports may receive data simultaneously at 100 Mbps each, giving a total of 400 Mbps.

Nonblocking Capacity

Switches with aggregate throughput large enough to handle even their highest possible input load (maximum input on all ports) are said to be **nonblocking** because they will not block incoming traffic regardless of how much comes in. There is nothing

Figure 4-18   Switching Matrix

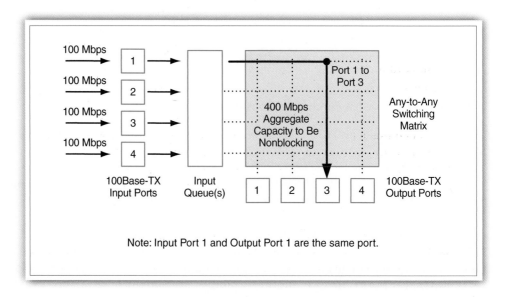

Note: Input Port 1 and Output Port 1 are the same port.

complex about the concept of nonblocking capacity. A switch that has four 100BASE-TX ports must have an aggregate throughput of 400 Mbps to be nonblocking.

Switches with aggregate throughput large enough to handle even their highest possible input load (maximum input on all ports) are said to be nonblocking.

The aggregate capacities of most switches are not fully nonblocking because it is not likely that all ports will be receiving simultaneously. However, if a switching matrix's aggregate throughput is too far below nonblocking capacity, there will be frame delays and even frame loss during traffic peaks.

Switching matrix throughput is especially important for switches high in the hierarchy. Each port on such switches is likely to carry traffic to and from many individual stations, so it is common to find most ports sending and receiving at any given moment. Core switches high in the hierarchy should be nonblocking or close to nonblocking (80–90 percent). Even workgroup switches should have aggregate throughput that is at least 20–30 percent of nonblocking capacity.

TEST YOUR UNDERSTANDING

17. a) What happens if a switch cannot handle the input traffic? b) What is a nonblocking switch? c) A switch has eight gigabit Ethernet ports. What aggregate switch matrix capacity does it need for nonblocking capacity? Show your calculations. d) To give 80 percent of nonblocking capacity? Show your calculations.

Store-and-Forward Versus Cut-Through Switching

One capability that many vendors tout is the ability to do store-and-forward or cut-through switching. We saw earlier that an Ethernet frame contains multiple fields and that the data field alone can be as large as 1,500 octets long.

Store-and-Forward Ethernet Switches

As Figure 4-19 illustrates, some Ethernet switches wait until they have received the entire frame before sending it out. This is **store-and-forward** switching. This approach allows them to check each frame for errors and to discard incorrect frames to reduce traffic. Frames often are hundreds or thousands of octets long, so store-and-forward switching adds a slight delay to frame transmission at each switch.

Cut-Through Ethernet Switches

In contrast, **cut-through** Ethernet switches examine only a few bits in a frame before sending the bits of the frame back out. This allows switches to begin sending out the bits they first received, despite the fact that they have not yet received all the bits of the frame.

➤ Obviously, as shown in Figure 4-19, switches must at least read the destination address, in order to know which port to use to send the frame back out. This requires reading the preamble, start of frame delimiter, and destination address— a total of only 14 octets.

➤ Handling VLANs and priority also requires the reading of tag fields if they are used.

➤ Finally, some cut-through switches, in the "extreme" case, wait for 64 octets of data because a smaller frame, called a runt, would violate the Ethernet standard.

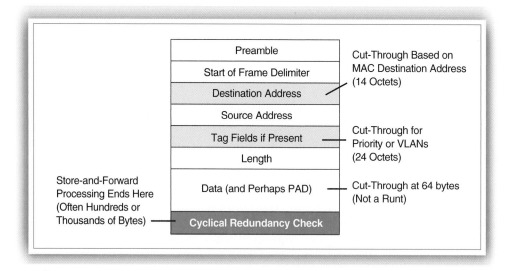

Figure 4-19   Store-and-Forward Versus Cut-Through Switching

By examining only a few dozen octets at most, then, cut-through switching can reduce latency at each switch compared to store-and-forward switching, which typically has to examine hundreds or thousands of octets.

Perspective

Although vendors once touted cut-through operation as a major advantage, the greater amount of latency added by store-and-forward switching tends to be negligible today. In addition, most switches today can do both cut-through and store-and-forward operations. Many offer cut-through operation as the default but sample full frames occasionally and change to store-and-forward operation if the error rate becomes too high. Cut-through versus store-and-forward operation is no longer a significant criterion for switch purchasing. However, you need to know these terms to read the vendor literature, and network managers tend to ask about these concepts in job interviews.

TEST YOUR UNDERSTANDING

18. a) Which is likely to have less latency—a cut-through switch or a store-and-forward switch? Explain. b) What is the advantage of the other mode of operation? c) Is determining which mode of operation a switch uses a major purchasing criterion today?

Manageability

The First Bank of Paradise has more than 500 switches. If there is a switch problem, discovering which switch is malfunctioning can be very difficult. Fixing the problem, furthermore, may require traveling to the switch to change its configuration.

Managed Switches and the Manager

As Figure 4-20 shows, the bank mitigates these problems by using only **managed switches**. As the name suggests, these switches have sufficient intelligence to be

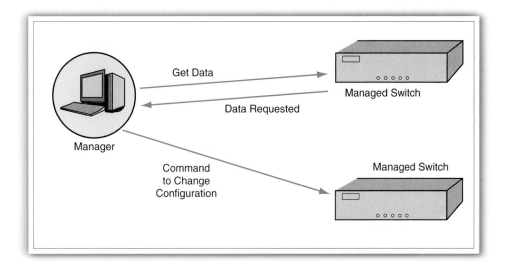

Figure 4-20   Managed Switches

managed from a central computer called the **manager.** In most cases, management communication uses the Simple Network Management Protocol discussed in Chapter 10.

Polling and Problem Diagnosis
Every few seconds, the manager polls each managed switch and asks for a copy of the switch's configuration parameters. If a problem occurs, the manager can discover quickly which switches are not responding and so can narrow down the source of the problem. In many cases, the status data collected frequently from the switches can pinpoint the cause of a problem.

Fixing Switches Remotely
In some cases, the network administrator can use the manager to fix switch problems remotely by sending commands to the switch. For instance, the manager can command the switch to do a self-test diagnostic. To give another example, the manager can tell the switch to turn off a port suspected of causing problems.

Performance Summary Data
At the broadest level, the manager can present the status data to the network administrator in summarized form, giving the administrator a good feeling for how well the network is functioning and for whether changes will be needed to cope with expected traffic growth.

The Cost of Manageability
Manageability is not cheap. Managed switches are much more expensive than nonmanaged switches. However, in firms with many switches, central management reduces management labor, which is considerable. This labor cost reduction more

than offsets its higher purchase cost. The main benefit of network management is to reduce overall management costs.

Managed switches are more expensive than nonmanaged switches, but they reduce management labor in large networks enough to more than offset managed switch purchase costs.

TEST YOUR UNDERSTANDING

19. a) What are managed switches? b) What benefits do they bring? c) Do managed switches increase or decrease total management costs?

Advanced Purchasing Considerations: Physical and Electrical Features

PHYSICAL SIZE

Almost all switches are 19 inches (48 cm) wide. This allows them to fit into standard 19-inch-wide telecommunications racks long used in telephony and later used for data switches and routers. In equipment racks, one U is 1.75 inches (4.4 cm) in height. Most switches, although not all, are multiples of U. For instance, a 2U switch is 3.50 inches tall.

PORT FLEXIBILITY

There are four basic types of switch organization, each giving a different degree of flexibility over how many ports you may have.

- Fixed-port switches, as their name suggests, give no port flexibility. The ports you buy them with are the ports you will have to live with for the life of the switch. They are one or two U tall. Most workgroup switches are fixed-port switches.

- Stackable switches, like fixed-port switches, also are 1 or 2U tall and have a fixed number of ports. However, as the name suggests, they can be stacked on top of one another. A special interconnect bus connects them at speeds that are higher than port-to-port Ethernet connections would permit. With stackable switches, companies can add ports in increments as few as twelve.

- Modular switches also are 1 or 2U tall but do not have a fixed number of ports. They have one or more slots for modules containing one to four ports.

- Chassis switches are several U tall. The box has expansion slots into which a firm can place modular expansion boards. The expansion boards contain six to twelve ports. The box itself contains a high-speed backplane bus that links the ports on all of the expansion cards together. Most core switches are chassis switches.

UPLINK PORTS

Ethernet NICs transmit on Pins 1 and 2 and listen on Pins 3 and 6. Normal Ethernet RJ-45 switch ports, in turn, transmit on Pins 3 and 6 and listen on Pins 1 and 2. If you connect two normal RJ-45 ports on different switches via a UTP cord, they will not hear each other. To address this problem, most switches have at least one **uplink port**, which transmits on Pins 1 and 2 and listens on Pins 3 and 6. You can use a standard UTP cable to connect a UTP uplink port on one switch to any normal port on its parent switch. In a growing number of switches, all ports automatically act as normal ports or uplink ports by detecting what type of port it is connected to.

Figure 4-21   Physical and Electrical Features (Study Figure)

Physical Size

    Switches fit into standard 19-in (48-cm) wide equipment racks

    Switch heights usually are multiples of 1U (1.75 in or 4.4 cm)

Port Flexibility

   Fixed-port switches

      No flexibility: the number of ports is fixed

      1 or 2U tall

      Most workgroup switches are fixed-port switches

   Stackable switches

      Fixed number of ports

      1 or 2U tall

      High-speed interconnect bus connects stacked switches

      Ports can be added in increments as few as 12

   Modular switches

      1 or 2U tall

      Contain one or a few slots

      Each slot module contains 1 to 4 ports

   Chassis switches

      Several U tall

      Contain several expansion slots

      Each expansion board contains 6 to 12 ports

      Most core switches are chassis switches

Uplink Ports

   Normal Ethernet RJ-45 switch ports transmit on Pins 3 and 6 and listen on Pins 1 and 2

   If you connect two normal ports on different switches via UTP cords, they will not be able to communicate

   Most switches have an uplink port, which transmits on Pins 1 and 2. You can use an ordinary UTP cord to connect a UTP uplink port on one switch to any normal port on a parent switch

Electrical Power

   Switches require electrical power

   Under the 802.3af standard, switches can provide electrical power over the UTP cord

   Because they are only 12.95 watts, they are sufficient for wireless access points (Chapter 5) and voice over IP telephones (Chapter 6) but not sufficient for computers

(*continued*)

ELECTRICITY

Ethernet switches require electrical power. With the new **802.3af** standard, they also can provide electrical power to attached devices over the ordinary UTP cord that stations already use to attach to the switch. This power is very limited—only 12.95 watts at 48 volts. This is sufficient for most of the wireless access points[10] discussed in Chapter 5, for voice over IP telephones discussed in Chapter 6, and for simple surveillance cameras. However, it is not sufficient for computers. Switches providing power can detect an incompatible device automatically and will not attempt to send it electrical power.

TEST YOUR UNDERSTANDING

20. a) Is it usually difficult to find an Ethernet switch with approximately the number of ports you need? b) How wide are most Ethernet switches? Why is this so? c) Distinguish between fixed-port switches, stackable switches, modular switches, and chassis switches. d) How tall are most Ethernet switches? e) Why are uplink ports needed on Ethernet switches? f) How do they work? g) What does the 802.3af standard permit? h) For what types of devices is this sufficient and not sufficient?

[10]Many of the newer wireless access points discussed in the next chapter need somewhat more power, so do biometric access controls, point-of-sale terminals, panning and zooming surveillance, and thin clients. The 802.3 Working Group now has a task force looking at the possibility of providing more power over Ethernet. The goal is to provide two to three times the 12.95 watts of power currently provided by 802.3.af switches.

ETHERNET SECURITY

Until recently, few organizations worried about the security of their wired Ethernet networks, presumably because only someone within the site can get access to the network, and security should be strong within the site. Unfortunately, experience has shown that attackers can easily get into sites, especially if a site has public areas.

Port Access Control (802.1X)

One threat to Ethernet is that any attacker can plug his or her notebook PC into any Ethernet wall jack and have unfettered access to the network. To thwart this attack, companies can implement **802.1X**, which is a standard for **port control**. By default, switch ports are in an *unauthorized* state. While ports are in the unauthorized state, people who connect to the port cannot get access to the rest of the network. However, 802.1X will require any device that attaches to the port to send authentication credentials to prove its identity and to prove its permission to use the network. If the authentication and authorization credentials are accepted, the port changes to an *authorized* state. The device attached to the port can then transmit and receive freely. By controlling access to individual switch ports on workgroup switches, 802.1X provides a first line of defense. We will see more about 802.1X in Chapter 5.

Media Access Control (MAC) Security (802.1AE)

A more subtle threat to an Ethernet network comes from management protocols, such as the Spanning Tree Protocol (802.1D). We saw in this chapter that if a switch or link between switches fails, then the switches will reconverge to a new stable hierarchy.

However, suppose that an attacker pretends to be a switch. The attacker can then send an STP management frame to all switches, indicating that it has detected a problem. This will cause all of the switches to stop handling traffic briefly, communicate with one another, elect a new root switch (the switch at the top of the hierarchy), and then reconfigure a new strict hierarchy.

Normally, this brief delay during convergence does little damage. However, if the attacker constantly transmits frames that require reconfiguration, it can keep the network in chaos. Causing many successively STP convergence processes will effectively stop all traffic flowing through the network.

Or, the attacker who uses his or her PC as a switch can "rig" the election so that it is elected as the root switch. This will allow the attacker to read a good fraction of the traffic traveling through the network. If the attacker runs a sniffer program, he or she can learn a great deal of sensitive information.

In addition, a PC probably will not have the capacity to handle the large amount of traffic normally handled by root servers. This will cause a good deal of traffic to be lost. In fact, the attacker "switch" can "black hole" (drop) *all* frames that reach it.

MAC security (802.1AE) attempts to thwart attacks using STP or other management protocols by creating security between each pair of switches. A switch will not accept management messages from another switch unless the sending switch has already authenticated itself to the receiving switch. In addition, 802.11AE has other cryptographic protections that we will see in Chapter 9, including the encryption of all messages passing between pairs of switches that use 802.1AE.

TEST YOUR UNDERSTANDING

21. a) What threat does 802.1X address? b) How does it address it? c) What threats does 802.1AE address? d) How does it attempt to thwart them? d) Did the working group that creates Ethernet standards create the 802.1X and 802.1AE standards? Explain.

CONCLUSION

Synopsis

This chapter looked in some depth at Ethernet local area networking. Ethernet is the dominant technology for corporate LANs today. Ethernet's only serious competitor is wireless LANs, which we will see in the next chapter. However, we will see that wireless LANs are not direct competitors to wired Ethernet LANs but rather usually work in conjunction with wired Ethernet LANs.

The IEEE 802 LAN/MAN Standards Committee creates many LAN standards. The Committee's 802.3 Working Group specifically creates Ethernet standards. Like all networking standards, Ethernet standards exist at both the physical and data link layers. Therefore, they are OSI standards.

The 802.3 Working Group has created many physical layer Ethernet standards and is still creating better physical layer standards. Speeds range from 10 Mbps to 10 Gbps and are still moving higher. These standards use both 4-pair UTP and optical fiber.

The dominant Ethernet standard for access lines from stations to switches is 100BASE-TX, while the dominant standard for switch-to-switch trunk lines is gigabit

Ethernet using optical fiber. The newest and fastest standards (10GBASE-x and beyond) are being created first for metropolitan area networks (MANs) but are moving into LANs as well. Chapter 7 discusses Ethernet MANs.

Although transmission links have maximum lengths, switches regenerate signals. Regeneration allows firms to send frames across many switches connected by trunk lines with little degradation.

The 802 Committee subdivided the data link layer into two layers. The media access control layer is specific to a particular technology, such as Ethernet or 802.11 wireless LANs. The logical link control layer deals with matters common to all LAN technologies. Ethernet has only a single MAC standard—the 802.3 Media Access Control standard. This standard specifies frame organization and switch operation.

The Ethernet frame has multiple fields. The preamble and start of frame delimiter fields synchronize the receiver's clock with the sender's clock. The destination and source MAC address fields are each 48 bits long, and NIC vendors assign Ethernet addresses to NICs at the factory. Because of human memory limitations (and to simplify writing), Ethernet MAC addresses usually are written in hexadecimal format, such as B2-CC-67-0D-5E-BA. The length field specifies the length of the data field (not of the frame as a whole). The data field has two parts: the LLC subheader, which describes the type of packet contained in the data field, and the packet itself. The PAD field is added if the data field is less than 46 octets long in order to make the data field plus the PAD field exactly 46 octets in length. The receiving NIC uses the frame check sequence field to check for errors. If the receiver finds an error, it simply discards the frame.

Firms must organize their Ethernet switches in a hierarchy. This simplifies switching, making Ethernet switches inexpensive. Switches that connect stations to the network are workgroup switches. Switches higher in the hierarchy are core switches. There must not be loops among switches because this would break the hierarchy. The Spanning Tree Protocol (802.1D) automatically detects and disables accidental loops. STP can also provide backup links in case of link or switch failures. The newer Rapid Spanning Tree Protocol converges faster than the original STP.

Servers often broadcast information to all devices in a network, and other types of broadcasting also occur. This can create a high level of traffic in networks. Virtual local area networks (VLANs) constrain broadcasting to the clients of particular servers in order to reduce broadcasting traffic. To standardize VLANs (and priority), two tag fields are added to the Ethernet frame, right after the source address. The Tag Control Information field has a 12-bit VLAN number to indicate to which VLAN a particular frame belongs.

Even networks that have sufficient capacity most of the time will experience momentary traffic peaks that exceed their capacity. Overloaded switches may have to drop frames, and congestion will cause latency (delay). The least expensive way to address momentary traffic peaks today is to overprovision the network—that is, to install much larger Ethernet lines and switches than are needed most of the time. A more efficient way to manage resources is to give latency-intolerant applications, such as voice, high priority so that they will go first during periods of congestion, minimizing their latency. Priority management uses the 3-bit priority level in the Tag Control Information field to indicate the priority levels of specific Ethernet frames. Unfortunately, priority is management-intensive.

(From the box Hubs and CSMA/CD.) Some older LANs still use Ethernet hubs instead of Ethernet switches. Hubs broadcast incoming bits, so only one station may transmit at a time. Consequently, NICs that use hubs must use CSMA/CD media access control, which only allows NICs to transmit if no other NIC is transmitting and which handles retransmission if there is a collision. NICs that use switches turn off CSMA/CD, giving them full-duplex (simultaneous two-way) transmission.

Purchasing switches is very complex. The most basic issue is the number and speeds of the ports needed. Core switches should have nonblocking or nearly non-blocking capacity, meaning that even if each port is receiving at its maximum speed, the switching matrix will have the capacity needed to switch the input traffic.

Store-and-forward switches forward frames only after receiving the entire frame. In contrast, cut-through switches start sending the frame back out after receiving only a few octets. Cut-through switches reduce latency at each switch, but this is rarely important in practice.

Managed switches are more expensive than other switches, but companies can manage them remotely. Using managed switches saves money overall by reducing management labor.

(From the box Advanced Purchasing Considerations: Physical and Electrical Features.) Switches come in various sizes, with varying basic numbers of ports and varying expandability. Some even provide electrical power to the stations they serve.

THOUGHT QUESTIONS

1. NICs transmit on Pins 1 and 2 and listen on Pins 3 and 6. Switch ports transmit on Pins 3 and 6 and listen on Pins 1 and 2. Uplink ports allow you to connect two switches. Can you think of a way to connect normal RJ-45 ports on two switches?
2. NICs can tell whether an arriving frame is tagged or not simply by looking at it. How can they do so? (Hint: They look at the value in the two octets following the address fields.)
3. If the sender adds a PAD field to an Ethernet frame, the combined data field and PAD will be 46 octets long. How can the receiving NIC tell which part is the data field?

DESIGN QUESTIONS

1. Two switches are 47 meters apart. They need to communicate at 600 Mbps. What Ethernet physical layer standard should you use?
2. Two switches are 200 meters apart. They need to be able to communicate at 1.7 Gbps. What Ethernet physical layer standard should you use?
3. Site Q attaches to Site R, which attaches to Site S. Site Q needs to be able to communicate with Site R at 45 Mbps. Site R needs to be able to communicate with Site S at 2 Gbps. Site Q needs to be able to communicate with Site S at 300 Mbps. a) Draw a picture of the situation. b) What traffic must the trunk line between Site Q and Site R be able to carry? c) What traffic must the trunk line between Site R and Site S be able to carry?
4. You will create a design for a network connecting four buildings in an industrial park. Hand in a picture showing your network. There will be a core switch in each building.
   - Building A is the headquarters building.
   - Building B is 85 meters south and 90 meters east of the headquarters building.
   - Building C is 150 meters south of the headquarters building.
   - Building D is 60 meters west of Building C.

- Computers in Building A need to communicate with computers in Building B at 60 Mbps.
- Computers in Building A need to be able to communicate with computers in Building C at 300 Mbps.
- Computers in Building A must communicate with computers in Building D at 50 Mbps.
- Computers in Building C must communicate with computers in Building D at 75 Mbps.
- Building A will connect directly to Buildings B and C.
- Building C will connect directly to Building D.

a) Specify the standard you will use to connect Building A to Building B.

b) Specify the standard you will use to connect Building A to Building C.

c) Specify the standard you will use to connect Building C to Building D.

HANDS-ON EXERCISES

Binary and Hexadecimal Conversions

If you have Microsoft Windows, the Calculator accessory shown in Chapter 1 can convert between binary and hexadecimal notation. Go to the *Start* button, then to *Programs* or *All Programs*, then to *Accessories*, and then click on *Calculator*. The Windows Calculator will then pop up.

Binary to Hexadecimal

To convert eight binary bits to hexadecimal (hex), first choose *View* and click on *Scientific* to make the Calculator a more advanced scientific calculator. Click on the *Bin* (binary) radio button, and type in the 8-bit binary sequence you wish to convert. Then click on the *Hex* (hexadecimal) radio button. The hex value for that segment will appear.

Hexadecimal to Binary

To convert hex to binary, go to *View* and choose *Scientific*. Click on *Hex* to indicate that you are entering a hexadecimal number. Type the number. Now click on *Bin* to convert this number to binary.

One additional subtlety is that Calculator drops initial 0s. So if you convert 1 hex, you get 1. You must add three initial 0s to make this a 4-bit segment: 0001.

1. a) Convert 1100 to hexadecimal.
   b) Express the following MAC address in binary: B2-CC-67-0D-5E-BA, leaving a space after every eight bits.
   c) Express the following MAC address in hex: 11000010 11001100 01100111 00001101 01011110 10111010.

GETTING CURRENT

Go to the book website's New Information and Errors pages for this chapter to get new information since this book went to press and to correct any errors in the text.

Chapter   4 a

Token-Ring
Networks

INTRODUCTION

Certification exams still require you to know about the 802.5 and FDDI (Fiber Distributed Data Interface) token-ring network technologies, despite the fact that the last hardware for these networks was produced around 1998 and also despite the fact that they have almost never been seen in organizations since the turn of the century. If you are going to take a certification exam, however, you have to learn about token-ring networks.

Before you read this chapter, you should read the box "Hubs and CSMA/CD" in Chapter 4. The token passing access control method used in token-ring networks serves a similar function to that served by CSMA/CD.

TOKEN-RING TECHNOLOGY

The term **token-ring network** involves two things.

➤ One is the topology of the network, which is a ring topology rather than the hierarchical topology that Ethernet uses whether switches or hubs are used.

➤ Second, a box in Chapter 4 discussed how in Ethernet hub networks, only one station may transmit at a time across the entire network. This limitation is also true in token-ring networks. Ethernet hub networks control when stations may transmit using CSMA/CD. Token-ring networks use a process called token passing to control when stations may transmit.

Ring Networks

Figure 4a-1 shows the **ring topology** used in 802.5 and FDDI. The network is laid out in a ring (loop), with transmission lines connecting a number of access units. Stations attach to these access units.

The figure shows that both technologies actually use a double ring. In normal operation, either both rings are used for transmission or one is left in standby mode. Frames travel in one direction around the active ring or rings.

The figure also shows that if a break occurs between access units, the ring is wrapped in a way that allows the two rings to become a single longer loop. Frames take

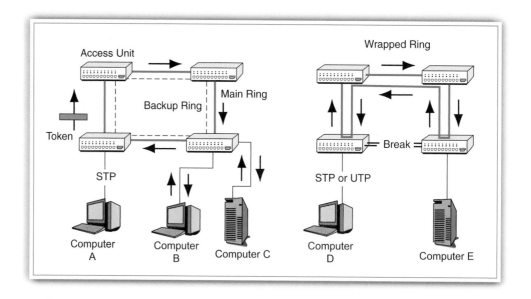

Figure 4a-1   Ring Network

longer to get around the ring, but all access units continue to communicate with one another.

This **ring wrapping** makes ring networks exceptionally reliable. There is no single point of failure for transmission lines as there is in Ethernet. Even if an access unit fails, only the stations attached to it are out of service.

However, ring wrapping technology to implement ring wrapping electronically rather than manually is quite expensive. Even adding manual ring wrapping adds to expense. In addition, a large amount of wiring must be laid if a ring topology is used.

TEST YOUR UNDERSTANDING

1. a) How many rings are used in a ring topology? b) Why are ring topologies reliable? c) What is the disadvantage of ring topologies?

Token Passing

As the box on hubs and CSMA/CD in Chapter 4 discussed, when hubs are used in Ethernet, only one station can transit at a time. As the number of stations on an Ethernet hub network increases, delay (latency) grows. Beyond about 100 stations, this latency becomes problematic.

In ring networks, a different access control method called **token passing** is used. When no station is transmitting, a special frame called a **token** circulates around the ring continuously. When a station wishes to transmit, it captures the token when the token reaches the station's position. The station may then transmit. After the transmission ends, the station releases the token again.

In networks with heavy traffic capacity, token-passing is more efficiency than CSMA/CD, allowing networks to work closer to capacity. However, when switches are used, there is even higher efficiency than there is with either CSMA/CD or token passing, and today, switches dominate.

Also, token passing is expensive to implement. The basic idea is straightforward, but token passing has many subtleties. It is said that the devil is in the details. In token passing, there are a surprisingly large number of details. Token passing is much more expensive to implement than CSMA/CD.

TEST YOUR UNDERSTANDING

2. a) Why is token passing needed? b) What is the advantage of token passing compared to CSMA/CD? c) What is the disadvantage of token passing compared to CSMA/CD?

EARLY ETHERNET AND 802.5 TOKEN-RING NETWORKS

Early Ethernet: CSMA/CD–Bus Networks

Figure 4a-2 illustrates (in a simplified way) that early versions of Ethernet used a **bus topology**. All stations on a segment connected to the segment. When one station transmitted, the signal traveled in both directions, passing all other stations. Essentially, the

Figure 4a-2   Early Ethernet Bus Topology

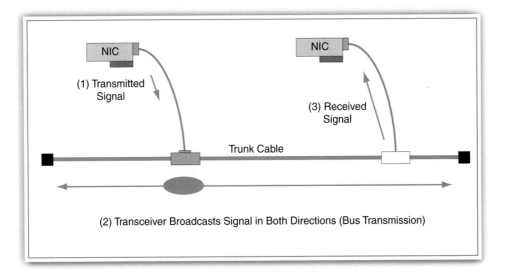

station broadcast its frame to all other stations. These early Ethernet systems used CSMA/CD for access control, so they were called CSMA/CD–bus networks.[1]

TEST YOUR UNDERSTANDING

3. a) What topology did early Ethernet networks use? b) What access control method did early Ethernet networks use?

802.5 Token-Ring Networks Appear

Ethernet technology was created before the 802 LAN/MAN Standards Committee came into existence. When the committee was created, most people thought that it would simply accept Ethernet or a slightly modified version of Ethernet as its LAN standard.

However, when the committee formed, IBM introduced and pushed its technology for a token-ring network. The 802 LAN/MAN Standards Committee failed to select between them. Instead, it released standards for both. Ethernet standards, as noted in Chapter 4, were created by the 802.3 Working Group (and still are). In contrast, the **802.5 Working Group** was created to standardize Token-Ring Network (TRN) technology. (Yes, *Token-Ring Network* is always capitalized when referring to 802.5.)

Given the complexity of token-ring technology, by the time the standard was specified and products began selling, Ethernet was already beginning to be widely installed. In addition, when 802.5 products were finally sold, the complexity of Token-Ring Networks meant that they were twice as expensive as Ethernet products. This was important because NICs in the 1980s often cost $100 to $500.

TEST YOUR UNDERSTANDING

4. Why were 802.5 Token-Ring Networks not successful when they came out?

Ethernet Wins

For a time, many companies felt that it made sense to install 802.5 LANs. This was especially true for companies that used large IBM mainframes, which worked very well with 802.5 networks.

Another reason for going with 802.5 technology was speed. Early versions of Ethernet could only operate at 10 Mbps, while TRNs worked at a whopping 16 Mbps (after a very short time at 4 Mbps). These speed differences seem trivial today, but they were very pervasive then.

However, 802.5 market penetration was always small. When Ethernet moved to 100 Mbps speeds and later to switches (switches do not need access control mechanisms), 802.5 Token–Ring Networks lost their advantages.[2]

---

[1] The figure shows a single segment. Several segments could be linked together, but the repeaters that connected them carried the broadcast signal across all segments, maintaining the broadcasting seen in Figure 4a-2. Adding more segments to Figure 4a-2 would complicate the figure without adding explanatory power.

[2] Although the 802.5 Working Group eventually defined 100 Mbps operation and switches, this development came too late to save Token-Ring Networks. Even before these developments were finalized, IBM ceased its participation in the 802.5 Working Group.

In addition, Ethernet's market share lead generated economies of scale in manufacturing. This increased the price gap between Ethernet and 802.5 networks.

Vendors stopped shipping 802.5 Token-Ring Networks in the late 1990s, and in today's network world of 100 Mbps or more to the network, almost every last company that used TRN has replaced it with Ethernet.

TEST YOUR UNDERSTANDING

5. a) At what speed did 802.5 Token-Ring Networks operate? b) What Ethernet developments killed 802.5 networks? c) With switching, do you need either CSMA/CD or token passing?

Shielded Twisted Pair Wiring

Chapter 3 noted that Category 7 wiring is shielded twisted pair wiring rather than UTP. There is a foil shield around each pair, and there is a metal mesh shield just inside the jacket. This almost completely eliminates interference. In fact, the 802.5 standard specified STP wiring, although optical fiber could also be used. The STP wiring for 802.5 was quite thick, heavy, and expensive.

TEST YOUR UNDERSTANDING

6. What type of wiring was 802.5 networks designed to use?

FIBER DISTRIBUTED DATA INTERFACE (FDDI)

By the mid-1980s, individual companies often had many 10 Mbps Ethernet networks and 16 Mbps Token-Ring Networks. These companies needed a way to link them all together into a larger site LAN. As Figure 4a-3 shows, this backbone network had to be much faster than the individual networks in order to be able to carry cross traffic.

In response to this need, the American National Standards Institute (ANSI) (rather than the IEEE 802 LAN/MAN Standards Committee) created the X3T9.5 **Fiber Distributed Data Interface (FDDI)** standard. As its name suggests, FDDI was defined from the beginning to use optical fiber. Fiber allowed FDDI to operate at 100 Mbps.

FDDI also is a token-ring network. It is similar to 802.5, primarily because it borrowed heavily from the earlier 802.5 specification. However, instead of beginning as a LAN standard, FDDI actually began as a metropolitan area network standard. Even with multimode fiber, there could be 2 km between access units (which FDDI calls concentrators). The entire loop could be 100 km in circumference with normal operation. Although FDDI was rarely used as a metropolitan area network, its ability to span longer distances made it ideal as a backbone to connect Ethernet hub networks and 802.5 networks, which both had similar distance limitations.

Although FDDI was ideal when it came out, Ethernet speeds rapidly grew from 10 Mbps to 100 Mbps. At that point, the 100 Mbps speed limitation of FDDI became insufficient for its backbone role. Within a short period of time, companies that had installed FDDI backbones began to remove them.

By the turn of the century, the production of FDDI components had stopped. With the demise of FDDI, even the concept of backbone networks connecting smaller

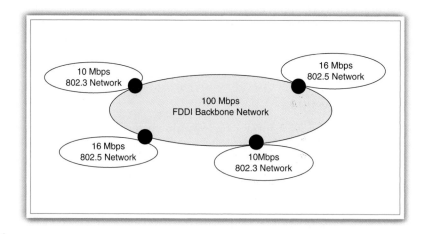

Figure 4a-3   Fiber Distributed Data Interface (FDDI) Backbone Network

networks of limited size disappeared. With Ethernet, there usually is a single hierarchy of Ethernet switches connecting all stations.

Ironically, the growth of Ethernet speeds from 10 Mbps to 100 Mbps that doomed FDDI was due to the 802.3 Working Group's "borrowing" of FDDI technological components at the physical layer adapting these components to a switched Ethernet topology and the 802.3 MAC layer protocol at the data link layer.

TEST YOUR UNDERSTANDING

7. a) Compare 802.5 TRNs and FDDI in terms of speed and ring circumference. b) In local area networks, what role did FDDI take? c) What killed FDDI?

RETURN OF THE RING

Although ring networks passed out of favor for LANs, the reliability of the dual ring topology reappeared in wide area networking, especially metropolitan area networking. The SONET/SDH technology discussed in Module C is a dual ring network. However, it is used to connect switches, so there is no need for token passing access control at the data link layer. We will not look at SONET/SDH because it use used almost exclusively in carrier network cores and is rarely used by corporations.

TEST YOUR UNDERSTANDING

8. What current carrier transmission technology uses a dual ring topology at the physical layer?

Wireless LANs (WLANs)

Lesson Objectives

By the end of this chapter, you should be able to discuss:

- Radio signal propagation, including spread spectrum transmission for resistance to propagation problems and resistance to interference between stations.
- Spread spectrum transmission methods.
- 802.11 wireless LAN (WLAN) operation.
- 802.11 transmission standards.
- (Box) Controlling 802.11 transmission.
- 802.11 security.
- 802.11 WLAN management.
- Bluetooth and ultrawideband (UWB) personal area networks (PANs).

INTRODUCTION

Today Ethernet technology dominates corporate LANs. Unfortunately, an Ethernet station must plug into a wall jack or directly into an Ethernet switch. This is a problem for the growing number of notebook computers, personal digital assistants, and other mobile devices used in organizations. To serve mobile users, a new type of local area network is emerging—the **wireless LAN (WLAN)**, which uses radio[1] for physical layer transmission.

Wireless LANs (WLAN) use radio for physical layer transmission.

802.11 Wireless LANs

The IEEE, which creates Ethernet standards through the 802.3 Working Group of the 802 LAN/MAN Standards Committee, also creates wireless LAN standards through

---

[1]In addition to radio, it is possible to use infrared light for transmission. (Your television remote control works by infrared transmission.) However, infrared transmission is too slow for corporate WLANs.

Physical-Layer Transmission
>   Uses radio transmission

802.11 Wireless LANs
>   The dominant WLAN technology today
>
>   Standardized by the 802.11 Working Group
>
>   Wireless computers connect to access points (Figure 5-2)
>
>   Speeds up to 54 Mbps with a distance of 30–100 meters
>>   Soon, under 802.11n, to be 100 Mbps or more
>   Supplement wired LANs
>>   Access points connect to LANs so that wireless stations can reach servers and Internet access routers on the Ethernet LANs.
>   Organizations can provide coverage throughout a building or a university campus by the judicious installation of many access points

Bluetooth
>   For personal area networks
>
>   Cable replacement technology
>
>   Limited to about 10 meters
>
>   Limited to 3 Mbps with a slower reverse channel today

Other Local Wireless Technologies
>   Ultrawideband: Up to 250 Mbps over a distance of 10 meters
>
>   ZigBee for almost-always-off sensor networks at low speeds
>
>   RFIDs: like UPC tags but readable remotely
>
>   Mesh networking: multiple access points can route frames to their destinations (Figure 5-4)

Figure 5-1   Local Wireless Technologies (Study Figure)

another working group, the **802.11 Working Group**. The 802.11 standards created by this group are the dominant WLAN standards today.

Rather than being a competitor for wired Ethernet LANs, **802.11 WLANs** today primarily *supplement* wired LANs, not replace them. Figure 5-2 shows that mobile users typically connect by radio to devices called **wireless access points** or simply **access points**. These wireless access points link the mobile user to the firm's wired Ethernet LAN.

This link to the firm's main wired Ethernet LAN is needed because the servers that mobile client devices need, as well as the firm's Internet access router, usually are on the wired LAN. In other words, although clients need to be mobile, the resources they need to work with typically are on the firm's main wired LAN.

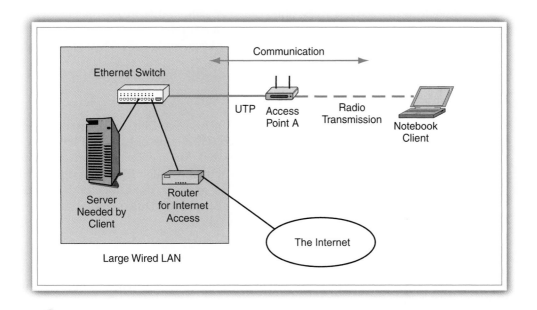

Figure 5-2   Wireless LAN (WLAN) Wireless Access Point

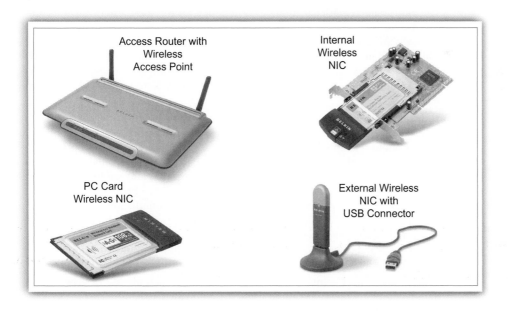

Figure 5-3   Access Router with Wireless Access Point and Wireless NICs

A single 802.11 wireless access point can serve stations that are 30–100 meters away at rated speeds of up to 54 Mbps today. By placing wireless access points judiciously throughout a building, a company can build a large 802.11 WLAN that can serve mobile users anywhere in the building.

Bluetooth Personal Area Networks

A less common and more limited wireless LAN technology, **Bluetooth**, has a different purpose. It is designed for *personal area networks (PANs)* that only serve a few devices carried by a person or around a desk. With a normal distance limit of 10 meters and a rated speed of only 3 Mbps with a slower reverse channel today, Bluetooth is primarily a technology for replacing cable connections. For instance, using Bluetooth, you can walk near a printer with your personal digital assistant (PDA) and print without physically connecting your PDA to the printer with a cable.

Emerging Local Wireless Technologies

Today, 802.11 WLANs dominate corporate planning for local wireless technology, and Bluetooth already has some corporate importance. There also are four interesting local wireless technologies on the horizon.

➤ **Ultrawideband (UWB)** transmission will have distance limits similar to those of Bluetooth (about 10 meters) but will provide speeds up to 250 Mbps. This is fast enough to send television signals locally.

➤ The oddly-named **ZigBee** technology is designed for wireless monitoring and control systems in businesses and homes. While Bluetooth is an always-on technology, ZigBee is an almost-always-off technology for sensors that rarely send signals. In addition, when sensors and other ZigBee devices do transmit signals, they can only send them at very slow speeds (up to 250 kbps, but usually slower). Such low performance actually has a benefit; it leads to extremely long battery life—months or even years.

➤ Today, bar-coded products must be run carefully over a laser scanner. In contrast, new **radio frequency ID (RFID)** tags can be used in place of UPC tags and only have to be brought *near* an RFID scanner to be read. An RFID reader sends a probing radio signal, and the RFID tag responds with the information it contains. There are several RFID technologies. Active RFID tags have batteries and can be read tens of feet away. They can be used to record such things as when a firm's delivery trucks arrive and leave. Passive RFID tags derive their power from the radio signal sent by the reader. Passive RFID tags can only absorb a little power from the signal, so when they respond, their signals will not travel more than a few inches to about four feet. Passive ID tags are placed on pallets and boxes, but they are still much too expensive ($0.20 to $0.30 apiece) to be placed on most individual products.

➤ One possibility for the future is **mesh networking**, in which wireless devices route frames among themselves, without using the company's wired Ethernet LAN.

➤ Figure 5-4 shows how 802.11 access points could form a mesh network. It also is possible to create a mesh network using individual wireless clients and servers. Mesh networks show considerable promise, but many concerns about reliability, coverage, and other matters still need to be addressed. The 802.11s Working Group is currently working to develop mesh networking for 802.11 WLANs.

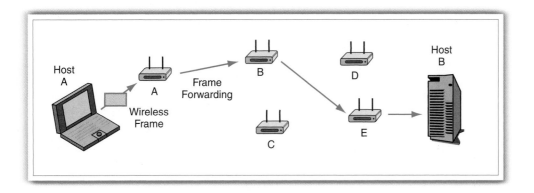

Figure 5-4   Mesh Network of Access Points

➤ In the more distant future, we will see even more radical developments. One of these is beam forming, which will allow a wireless access point to focus its transmission power toward multiple users simultaneously. Another is software-defined radio, which will allow a wireless device to switch between 802.11, Bluetooth, ZigBee, and other wireless standards.

TEST YOUR UNDERSTANDING

1. a) What type of computer primarily benefits from WLANs today? b) What are the dominant WLAN standards today? c) Are WLANs competitors for wired Ethernet LANs today? d) Why is a link to the main wired LAN needed in wireless networks? e) How can a firm create a large 802.11 WLAN?

2. a) Contrast the normal uses of 802.11 and Bluetooth WLANs. b) Compare 802.11 and Bluetooth distances.

3. a) Compare the speeds of 802.11, Bluetooth, UWB, and ZigBee. b) Compare the distance limits of 802.11, Bluetooth, and UWB. c) What technology could replace universal product code (bar code) tags on products? d) Describe mesh networking in 802.11.

RADIO SIGNAL PROPAGATION

Frequencies

WLAN radio signals propagate as waves. We looked at waves in Chapter 3. We saw that optical fiber waves are described by their wavelength. In contrast, the radio waves used in wireless LANs are measured in terms of their frequency.

A wave's **frequency** is the number of complete cycles the wave goes through per second. In sound, frequency corresponds to pitch. One cycle per second is one **hertz (Hz)**. Useful radio frequencies for WLAN transmission (and data networking in

---

Frequency
>   Radio waves are measured in terms of frequency
>   Measured in hertz (Hz)—the number of complete cycles per second

Measuring Frequencies
>   Frequency increases by factors of 1,000 (not 1,024)
>   Kilohertz (kHz)
>   Megahertz (MHz)
>   Gigahertz (GHz)

Most Common Frequency Range for WLANs
>   High megahertz to low gigahertz range

Figure 5-5   Frequency Measurement (Study Figure)

general) come in the high **megahertz (MHz)** to low **gigahertz (GHz)** range. As with transmission speeds, metric names increase by a factor of 1,000, not 1,024.

Frequency is used to describe the radio waves used in WLANs.

TEST YOUR UNDERSTANDING

4. a) What is a hertz? b) Are wavelengths or frequencies normally used to describe WLAN transmission?

Antennas

Radio transmission requires an antenna. Figure 5-6 shows that there are two types of radio antennas: omnidirectional antennas and dish antennas.

- **Omnidirectional antennas** transmit signals equally strongly in all directions and receive incoming signals equally well from all directions. Consequently, the antenna does not need to point in the direction of the receiver. However, because the signal spreads in all directions, only a small fraction of the energy transmitted by an omnidirectional antenna reaches the receiver.
- **Dish antennas,** in contrast, point in a particular direction, which allows them to focus stronger outgoing signals in that direction for the same power and to receive weaker incoming signals from that direction.

Dish antennas are good for long distances because of their focusing ability, but they need to know the direction of the other party. Also, omnidirectional antennas are easier to use. (Imagine if you had to carry a dish with you whenever you carried your cellular phone. You would not even know where to point the dish!)

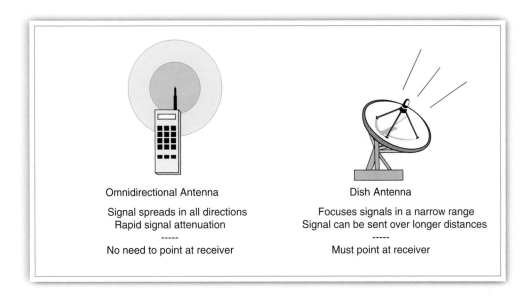

Figure 5-6   Omnidirectional and Dish Antennas

3b

WLANs use omnidirectional antennas almost exclusively. Distances are short and users do not always know the location of the nearest access point.

TEST YOUR UNDERSTANDING

5. a) Distinguish between omnidirectional and dish antennas in terms of operation. b) Under what circumstances would you use an omnidirectional antenna? c) Under what circumstances would you use a dish antenna? d) What type of antenna normally is used in WLANs? Why?

Wireless Propagation Problems

Although wireless communication gives mobility, wireless transmission is not very predictable, and there often are serious propagation problems.

Figure 5-7 illustrates four common wireless propagation problems.

Inverse Square Law Attenuation

4b

Compared to signals sent through wires and optical fiber, radio signals attenuate very rapidly. When a signal spreads out from any kind of antenna, its strength is spread over the area of a sphere. (In omnidirectional antennas, power is spread equally over the sphere, while in dish antennas, it is concentrated primarily in one direction on the sphere.) The area of a sphere is proportional to the square of its radius, so signal strength in any direction weakens by an **inverse square law** $(1/r^2)$, as Equation 5-1 illustrates.

$$S_2 = S_1/r^2$$ (Equation 5-1)

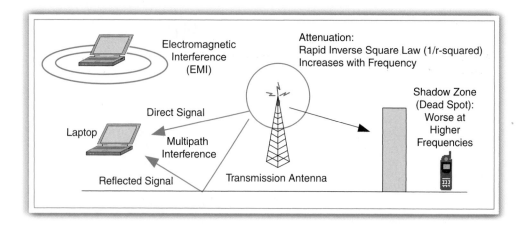

Figure 5-7   Wireless Propagation Problems

To give an example, if you triple the distance (r), the signal strength (S_2) falls to one-ninth ($1/3^2$) of its original strength (S_1). With radio propagation, you have to be relatively close to your communication partner unless the signal strength is very high, an omnidirectional antenna is used, or both.

Shadow Zones (Dead Spots)

To some extent, radio signals can go through and bend around objects. However, if there is a large or dense object (such as a brick wall), blocking the direct path between the sender and receiver, the receiver may be in a **shadow zone (dead spot)**, where it cannot receive the signal. If you have a cellular telephone and often use it within buildings, you probably are familiar with this problem.

Multipath Interference

In addition, radio waves tend to bounce off walls, floors, ceilings, and other objects. As Figure 5-7 shows, this may mean that a receiver will receive two or more signals—a direct signal and one or more reflected signals. The direct and reflected signals will travel different distances and so may be out of phase when they reach the receiver (one may be at its highest amplitude while the other is at its lowest, giving an average of zero). This **multipath interference** may cause the signal to range from strong to nonexistent within a few centimeters (inches).[2] If the difference in time between the direct and reflected signal is large, some reflected signals may even interfere with the

---

[2]Wireless access points often have two antennas to combat multipath interference. Many wireless NICs, in turn, have an antenna that looks like a fan. This really is a "rake" antenna, which gets this name because it has many small antennas side by side, like the tines in a garden rake.

next direct signal. Multipath interference is the most serious propagation problem at WLAN frequencies.

4d

Multipath interference is the most serious propagation problem at WLAN frequencies.

Electromagnetic Interference (EMI)

A final common propagation problem in wireless communication is *electromagnetic interference (EMI)*. As we saw in Chapter 3, electrical motors and many other devices produce EMI at frequencies used in data communications. Among these devices are cordless telephones, microwaves, and especially devices in other nearby wireless networks.

Frequency-Dependent Propagation Problems

Two propagation problems are affected by frequency.

4e

➤ First, higher-frequency waves attenuate more rapidly with distance than lower-frequency waves because they are absorbed more rapidly by moisture in the air, leafy vegetation, and other water-bearing obstacles. Consequently, as we will see later in this chapter, WLAN signals around 5 GHz attenuate more rapidly than signals around 2.4 GHz.

➤ Second, shadow zone problems grow worse with frequency. As frequency increases, radio waves become less able to go through and bend around objects.

4e

TEST YOUR UNDERSTANDING

6. a) Which offers more reliable transmission characteristics—UTP or radio transmission? b) Which attenuate more rapidly with distance—signals sent though wired media or radio signals? c) If the signal strength from an omnidirectional radio source is 8 milliwatts (mW) at 30 meters, how strong will it be at 120 meters? d) How are shadow zones (dead spots) created? e) Why is multipath interference very sensitive to location? f) What is the most serious propagation problem in WLANs? g) List some sources of EMI. h) What propagation problems become worse as frequency increases?

Bands and Bandwidth

The Frequency Spectrum and Service Bands

5a

Before going on, we need to discuss some basic radio transmission terminology. Most fundamentally, the **frequency spectrum** consists of all possible frequencies from zero hertz to infinity, as Figure 5-8 shows.

5b

Service Bands

The frequency spectrum is divided into **service bands** that are dedicated to specific services. For instance, in the United States, the AM radio service band lies between 535 kHz and 1,705 kHz. The FM radio service band, in turn, lies between 88 MHz and 108 MHz. The 2.4 GHz unlicensed band that we will see later for wireless LANs extends from 2.4000 GHz to 2.4835 GHz.

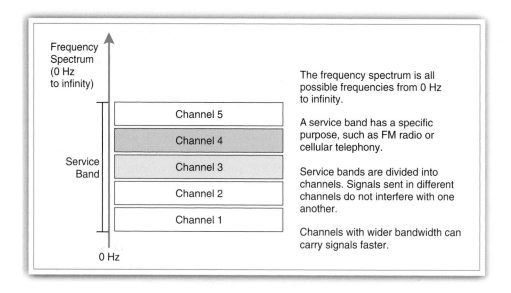

Figure 5-8   The Frequency Spectrum, Service Bands, and Channels

Channels

Service bands are subdivided into smaller frequency ranges called **channels**. A different signal can be sent in each channel because signals in different channels do not interfere with one another.[3] This is why you can receive different television channels successfully.

Signal and Channel Bandwidth

Figure 5-10 shows that signals do not operate at a single wavelength. Rather, signals spread over a range of frequencies. This range is called the signal's **bandwidth**. Signal bandwidth is measured by subtracting the lowest frequency from the highest frequency.

A channel also has a bandwidth. For instance, if the lowest frequency of a channel is 89.0 MHz and the highest frequency is 89.2 MHz, then the **channel bandwidth** is 0.2 MHz (200 kHz). AM radio channels are 10 kHz wide, FM channels have bandwidths of 200 kHz, and television channels are 6 MHz wide.

The relationship between possible transmission speed in a channel and channel bandwidth was quantified by Shannon, who found that the maximum possible transmission speed (C) in bits per second when sending data through a channel is directly proportional to the channel's bandwidth (B) in hertz, as shown in the **Shannon Equation** (Equation 5-2).[4] The signal-to-noise (S/N) ratio discussed in Chapter 3 is also important, but it is very difficult to modify in practice.

$$C = B \, [\text{Log}_2 \, (1 + S/N)] \qquad \text{(Equation 5-2)}$$

---

[3]Well, not much, anyway. There is always a small amount of cross-channel interference.
[4]Claude Shannon, "A Mathematical Theory of Communication," *Bell System Technical Journal* (July 1938), pp. 379–423, and (October 28, 1938), pp. 623–56.

Figure 5-9 Channel Bandwidth and Transmission Speed (Study Figure)

Signal Bandwidth

Chapter 3 discussed a wave operating at a single frequency

However, most signals are spread over a range of frequencies (Figure 5-10)

The range between the highest and lowest frequencies is the signal's bandwidth

The maximum possible transmission speed increases with bandwidth

Channel Bandwidth

Channel bandwidth is the highest frequency in a channel minus the lowest frequency (Figure 5-10)

An 88.0 MHz to 88.2 MHz channel has a bandwidth of 0.2 MHz (200 kHz)

Higher-speed signals need wider bandwidths

Shannon Equation

$C = B \, [\text{Log}_2 \, (1 + S/N)]$

C = Maximum possible transmission speed in the channel (bps)

B = Bandwidth (Hz)

S/N = Signal-to-Noise Ratio

Note that doubling the bandwidth doubles the maximum possible transmission speed

Increasing the bandwidth by X increases the maximum possible speed by X

Wide bandwidth is the key to fast transmission

Increasing S/N helps slightly but usually cannot be done to any significant extent

Broadband and Narrowband Channels

Broadband means wide channel bandwidth and therefore high speed

Narrowband means narrow channel bandwidth and therefore low speed

Narrowband is below 200 kbps

Broadband is above 200 kbps

The Golden Zone

Most organizational radio technologies operate in the golden zone in the high megahertz to low gigahertz range

Golden zone frequencies are high enough for there to be large total bandwidth

At higher frequencies, there is more available bandwidth

Golden zone frequencies are low enough to allow fairly good propagation characteristics

At lower frequencies, signals propagate better

Channel Bandwidth and Spectrum Scarcity

Why not make all channels broadband?

There is a limited amount of spectrum at desirable frequencies

Making each channel broader than needed would mean having fewer channels or widening the service band

Service band design requires tradeoffs between speed requirements, channel bandwidth, and service band size

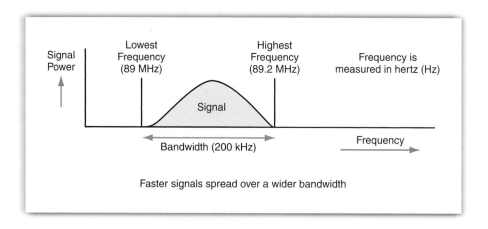

Faster signals spread over a wider bandwidth

Figure 5-10   Signal Bandwidth

The maximum possible speed is directly proportional to bandwidth, so if you double the bandwidth, you can potentially transmit up to twice as fast. However, *C* is the *maximum* possible speed for a given bandwidth and signal-to-noise ratio. *Real transmission throughput* will always be less.

To transmit at a given speed, you need a channel wide enough to handle that speed. For example, video signals produce many more bits per second than audio signals, so television uses much wider channels than AM radio (6 MHz versus 10 kHz in AM radio transmission).

Channels with large bandwidths are called **broadband** channels. They can carry data very quickly. In contrast, channels with small bandwidths, called **narrowband** channels, can only carry data slowly.

Although the terms broadband and narrowband technically refer only to the width of a channel, broadband has come to mean "fast," while narrowband has come to mean "slow." In terms of transmission speed, the dividing line between broadband and narrowband speeds is 200 kbps.

The dividing line between broadband and narrowband speeds is 200 kbps.

The Golden Zone

Commercial mobile services operate in the high megahertz to low gigahertz range (approximately 800 MHz to 6 GHz). This is the **golden zone**. At lower frequencies, the spectrum is limited and has been almost entirely assigned. At higher frequencies, radio waves attenuate more rapidly with distance and cannot flow through or around objects as they do at lower frequencies. Consequently, the sender and receiver must have a **clear line of sight** (unobstructed direct path) between them. Even at the high end of the golden zone, absorption and shadow zone propagation problems are substantial.

↗ 8a

The golden zone for commercial mobile services is the high megahertz to low gigahertz range.

TEST YOUR UNDERSTANDING

7. Distinguish between
   a) the frequency spectrum, b) service bands, and c) channels. d) In radio, how can you send multiple signals without the signals interfering with one another?

8. a) Does a signal usually travel at a single frequency, or does it spread over a range of frequencies? b) What is channel bandwidth? c) If the lowest frequency in a channel is 1.22 MHz and the highest frequency is 1.25 MHz, what is the channel bandwidth? d) Why is large channel bandwidth desirable? e) What do we call a system whose channels have large bandwidth?

9. a) What is the Shannon equation? b) What happens to the maximum possible propagation speed in a channel if the bandwidth is tripled while the signal-to-noise ratio remains the same? c) Given their relative bandwidths, about how many times as much data is sent per second in television than in AM radio? d) What is the dividing line between narrowband and broadband speeds?

10. a) What is the golden zone in commercial mobile radio transmission? b) Why are lower frequencies not used? c) For what two reasons is operating at higher frequencies unattractive? d) What is a clear line-of-sight limitation?

Normal and Spread Spectrum Transmission
Unlicensed Radio Bands

9a ↗

Both 802.11 wireless LANs and Bluetooth personal area networks, which we will see in some detail later in this chapter, operate in **unlicensed radio bands**, which get this name because individual stations do not have to be licensed to be set up or moved. (In licensed bands, every station must be licensed separately, and the license must be changed each time it moves.) WLANs today use two unlicensed bands. One is the 2.4 GHz band. The other is the 5 GHz band.

↗ 9b

Both 802.11 WLANs and Bluetooth PANs operate in unlicensed radio bands.

↗ 9c

The problem with unlicensed radio bands is that users of unlicensed radio bands must tolerate interference from others. If your neighbor sets up a wireless LAN next door to yours, you have no recourse but to negotiate with him or her for such matters as which channels each of you will use. At the same time, the law prevents you from creating unreasonable interference—for instance by using high transmission power.

Unlicensed Bands

> You do not need a license to have or move your stations
>
> You must tolerate interference from other users of the band
>
> You must not cause unreasonable interference
>
> Two unregulated bands are widely used: the 2.4 GHz band and the 5 GHz band

Spread Spectrum Transmission

> You are required by law to use spread spectrum transmission in unlicensed bands
>
> Spread spectrum transmission reduces propagation problems
>
> > Especially multipath interference
>
> Spread spectrum transmission reduces interference between nearby devices operating in the same channel
>
> Spread spectrum transmission is NOT used for security in WLANs

Normal Transmission Versus Spread Spectrum Transmission (Figure 5-12)

> Normal transmission uses only the channel bandwidth required by your signaling speed
>
> Spread spectrum transmission: uses channels much wider than signaling speed requires

Several Spread Spectrum Transmission Methods (Figure 5-13)

> Frequency Hopping Spread Spectrum (FHSS) can be used up to 2 Mbps
>
> Direct Sequence Spread Spectrum (DSSS) is used at 11 Mbps
>
> Orthogonal Frequency Division Multiplexing (OFDM) is used at 54 Mbps

Figure 5-11   Spread Spectrum Transmission (Study Figure)

Why Spread Spectrum Transmission?

At the frequencies used by WLANs, there are numerous and severe propagation problems. In these unlicensed bands, regulators mandate the use of a form of transmission called spread spectrum transmission.

They mandate the use of spread spectrum transmission primarily to minimize propagation problems—especially multipath interference. (If the direct and reflected signals cancel out at some frequencies within the range, they will be double at other frequencies.)

A second reason for requiring spread spectrum transmission is resistance to mutual interference between nearby stations transmitting in the same channel. With normal radio transmission, if two nearby stations transmit in the same channel, interference will ruin both of their transmissions. With spread spectrum transmission, only some damage will result and both signals are likely to get through. This obviously is important in unlicensed radio bands.

In commercial transmission, security is *not* a reason for doing spread spectrum $\rightarrow 9f$ transmission. The military uses spread spectrum transmission for security, but it does so by keeping certain parameters of its spread spectrum transmission secret. Commercial spread spectrum transmission methods must make these parameters publicly known in order to make it easy for two parties to communicate.

In wireless LANs, spread spectrum transmission is used to reduce propagation problems and to reduce mutual interference between nearby stations transmitting in the same channel, not to provide security.

How wide are spread spectrum channels? In 802.11 wireless LANs, the channel bandwidth is about 20 MHz and may soon be twice as wide. In turn, ultrawideband (UWB) transmission, which was mentioned at the beginning of this chapter, will have enormous channels that are wider than several entire *service bands*.

TEST YOUR UNDERSTANDING

11. a) Do WLANs today use licensed or unlicensed bands? b) What is the advantage of using unlicensed bands? c) What is the disadvantage? d) In unlicensed bands, what type of transmission method is required by regulators? e) What are the two benefits of spread spectrum transmission for business communication? f) Is spread spectrum transmission done for security reasons in commercial WLANs?

Spread Spectrum Transmission Methods

Normal Versus Spread Spectrum Transmission

As noted earlier in our discussion of the Shannon equation, if you need to transmit at a given speed, you must have a channel whose bandwidth is sufficiently wide.

To allow as many channels as possible, channel bandwidths in *normal radio transmission* are limited to the speed requirements of the user's signal, as Figure 5-12 illustrates. For a service that operates at 10 kbps, regulators would only permit enough channel bandwidth to handle this speed.

In contrast to normal radio transmission, which uses channels just wide enough for transmission speed requirements, **spread spectrum transmission** takes the original signal, called a **baseband signal**, and spreads the signal energy over a much broader channel than is required. As noted earlier, all wireless LAN systems are required by law to use spread spectrum transmission.

Frequency Hopping Spread Spectrum (FHSS)

The simplest form of spread spectrum transmission is **frequency hopping spread spectrum (FHSS)**. As Figure 5-13 illustrates, the signal in FHSS uses only the bandwidth

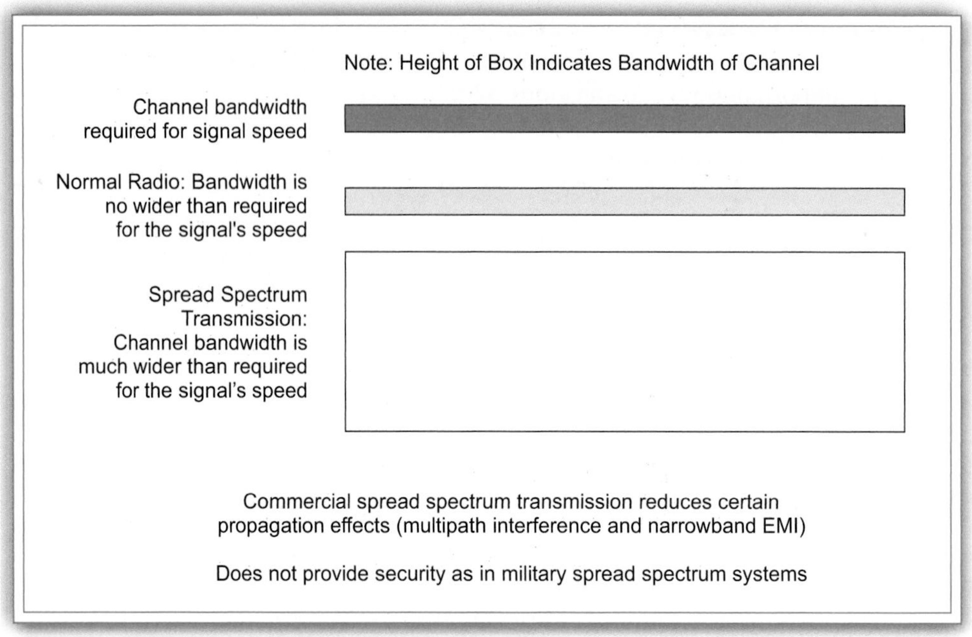

Note: Height of Box Indicates Bandwidth of Channel

Channel bandwidth
required for signal speed

Normal Radio: Bandwidth is
no wider than required
for the signal's speed

Spread Spectrum
Transmission:
Channel bandwidth is
much wider than required
for the signal's speed

Commercial spread spectrum transmission reduces certain
propagation effects (multipath interference and narrowband EMI)

Does not provide security as in military spread spectrum systems

Figure 5-12   Normal Radio Transmission and Spread Spectrum Transmission

required by the signal but hops frequently within the spread spectrum channel. If the signal runs into strong EMI or multipath interference in one part of the broad channel, that part of the message will be lost and must be retransmitted, but parts of the message in other parts of the channel will get through.

FHSS is only useful for relatively low speeds—up to 2 Mbps.[5] Consequently, as we will see later, the 802.11 Working Group for wireless LANs only specified frequency hopping spread spectrum transmission for speeds at or below about 2 Mbps. Few 802.11 LANs operating at these low speeds were purchased. Bluetooth, also discussed later, currently uses FHSS, which is sufficient for Bluetooth's low speed of 3Mbps today.

Direct Sequence Spread Spectrum (DSSS)

Another spread spectrum technique shown in Figure 5-13 is **direct sequence spread spectrum (DSSS)** transmission, in which a signal is spread over the entire bandwidth of a channel. Interference and multipath interference will affect only small parts of

---

[5]This speed limitation exists because the transmitter must be retuned with each frequency hop. This takes a small but significant amount of time, slowing the transmission rate.

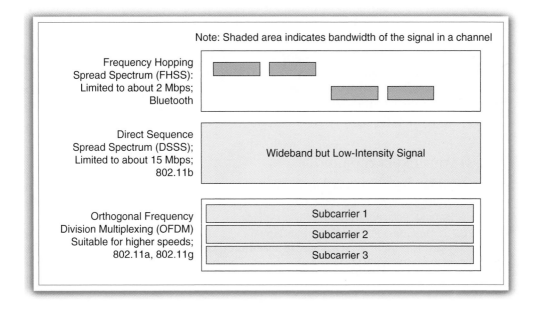

Note: Shaded area indicates bandwidth of the signal in a channel

Frequency Hopping
Spread Spectrum (FHSS):
Limited to about 2 Mbps;
Bluetooth

Direct Sequence
Spread Spectrum (DSSS);
Limited to about 15 Mbps;
802.11b

Wideband but Low-Intensity Signal

Orthogonal Frequency
Division Multiplexing (OFDM)
Suitable for higher speeds;
802.11a, 802.11g

Subcarrier 1
Subcarrier 2
Subcarrier 3

Figure 5-13   Spread Spectrum Transmission Methods

the signal, allowing most of the signal to get through for correct reception. To give an analogy, if an ocean wave hits an obstacle such as a pier, it will still hit the shore at almost full strength.

Although DSSS is more complex than FHSS, DSSS can support speeds up to about 15 Mbps and is used in the 11 Mbps 802.11b wireless LANs we will see later in this chapter.[6] However, 802.11b WLANs are rapidly being replaced by faster WLAN technologies that do not use DSSS.

Orthogonal Frequency Division Multiplexing (OFDM)

As transmission speeds move above about 15 Mbps, another form of spread spectrum transmission dominates. This is **orthogonal frequency division multiplexing (OFDM)**, which Figure 5-13 also illustrates.

In OFDM, each broadband channel is divided into many smaller subchannels called **subcarriers**. Parts of each frame are transmitted in each subcarrier.[7] OFDM

---

[6]Note that 802.11b also has some very-low-speed fallback modes that use FHSS.
[7]In the 802.11a and 802.11g wireless LAN standards discussed later, each 20 MHz channel is divided into 52 subcarriers, each 312.5 kHz wide. Of the 52 subcarriers, forty-eight are used to send data and four are used to control the transmission.

sends data redundantly across the subcarriers, so if there is impairment in one or even a few subcarriers, all of the data usually will still get through.

OFDM is complex and therefore expensive. However, sending data over a single very large channel reliably with DSSS is very difficult. In contrast, OFDM can be used at very high speeds because it is easier to send many slow signals reliably in many small subcarriers than it is to send one signal very rapidly over a very wide-bandwidth channel. Both of the 54 Mbps 802.11 wireless LAN standards discussed below (802.11a and 802.11g) use OFDM.[8]

TEST YOUR UNDERSTANDING

12. a) In normal radio operation, how does channel bandwidth usually relate to the bandwidth required to transmit a data stream of a given speed? b) How does this change in spread spectrum transmission?

13. a) Describe FHSS. b) What is its limitation? c) Describe DSSS. d) For what WLAN standard is it used? e) What spread spectrum transmission method is used for 54 Mbps 802.11g WLANs? f) Describe it.

802.11 WLAN OPERATION

As noted at the beginning of this chapter, wireless LANs replace signals in wires with radio waves. WLANs allow mobile workers to stay connected to the network as they move through a building. In some cases, wireless LANs are less expensive to install than wired LANs, but this certainly is not always the case.

Typical Operation

As noted at the start of the chapter, and as Figure 5-14 shows, an 802.11 wireless LAN typically is used to connect a small number of mobile devices to a large wired LAN—typically, an Ethernet LAN—because the servers and Internet access routers that mobile client stations need to use usually are on the wired LAN.[9]

Stations

Each mobile station must have a **wireless NIC**. Mobile stations tend to use PC Card NICs, which simply snap into the station. Fixed stations normally use internal NICs. Both types of stations also can use external USB wireless NICs, which sit outside the PC and plug into USB ports.

---

[8]The DSL services discussed in Chapter 6 generally also use OFDM, although in DSL service, OFDM is called discrete multitone (DMT) service.

[9]There is a rarely used 802.11 ad hoc mode, in which no wireless access point is used. In ad hoc mode, computers communicate directly with other computers. (In contrast, when an access point is used, this is called 802.11 infrastructure mode.) In addition, 802.11 can create point-to-point transmission over longer distances than 802.11 normally supports. This approach, which normally is used to connect nearby buildings, uses dish antennas and higher power levels authorized for this purpose.

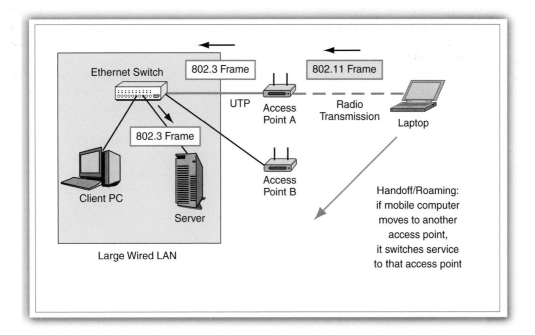

Figure 5-14   Typical 802.11 Wireless LAN Operation
with Wireless Access Points

Wireless Access Points

When a wireless station wishes to send a frame to a server, it transmits the frame to a wireless access point.

Technically, an access point is a *bridge* between wireless stations and the wired LAN. **Bridges** connect two different types of 802 LANs—in the case of 802.11 access points, an 802.11 wireless LAN and an 802.3 wired LAN.[10] Bridges convert between both physical layer signals and data link layer frame formats.

Bridges connect two different types of LANs.

As Figure 5-14 shows, when a wireless NIC transmits to a server on the wired LAN, it places the packet for the server into an 802.11 frame.[11] The wireless access point removes the packet from the 802.11 frame and places the packet in an 802.3

---

[10]Do bridges sound like routers? Routers can connect any two single networks (LANs or WANs), while bridges can only connect different LANs—specifically, 802 LANs. Also, routers can forward packets across complex internets, while bridges only forward packets and do this forwarding simply and with low functionality. Fortunately, these limitations make bridges much less expensive than routers. For 802.11 access points, bridging is sufficient and inexpensive.
[11]Note that 802.11 frames are much more complex than 802.3 Ethernet frames. Much of this complexity is needed to counter wireless propagation problems.

frame. The access point sends this 802.3 frame to the server, via the wired Ethernet LAN. When the server replies, the wireless access point receives the 802.3 frame, removes the packet from the frame, and forwards the packet to the wireless station in an 802.11 frame.

The wireless access point also controls stations. It assigns transmission power levels to stations within its range and performs a number of other supervisory chores.

Handoff/Roaming

When a mobile station travels too far from a wireless access point, the signal will be too weak to reach the access point. However, if there is a closer access point, the station can be **handed off** to that access point for service. In WLANs, the ability to use handoffs is also called **roaming**.[12] This aspect of 802.11 WLANs was standardized as 802.11F in 2003, but vendor interoperability has been limited.

Sharing a Single Channel

As Figure 5-15 shows, the access point and all of the wireless stations it serves transmit and receive in a single channel. When a station or the access point transmits, all other devices must wait. (If two devices transmit in the same channel at the same time, their

Figure 5-15   Stations and Access Points Transmit in a Single Channel

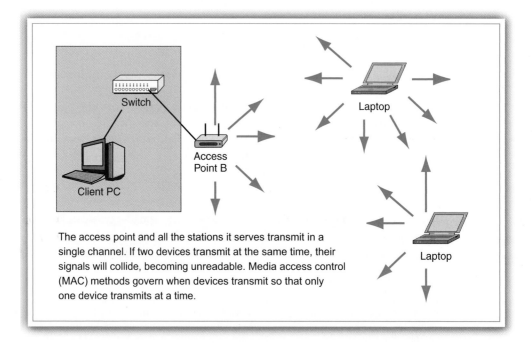

The access point and all the stations it serves transmit in a single channel. If two devices transmit at the same time, their signals will collide, becoming unreadable. Media access control (MAC) methods govern when devices transmit so that only one device transmits at a time.

---

[12]In cellular telephony, which we will see in the next chapter, the terms *handoff* and *roaming* mean different things.

signals will interfere with each other.) As the number of stations served by an access point increases, individual throughput falls. The box "Controlling 802.11 Transmission" discusses how **media access control** methods govern when stations and access points may transmit so that collisions can be avoided.

The access point and all of the wireless stations it serves transmit and receive in a single channel. When a station or the access point transmits, all other devices must wait. → _116_

TEST YOUR UNDERSTANDING

14. a) List the elements in a typical 802.11 LAN today. b) Why is a wired LAN usually still needed if you have a wireless LAN? c) Is a wireless access point a bridge or a router? d) Why must the access point remove an arriving packet from the frame in which the packet arrives and place the packet in a different frame when it sends the packet back out? e) What is a handoff in 802.11? f) What is the relationship between handoffs and roaming in WLANs? g) When there is an access point and several wireless clients, why may only one device transmit at a time?

Controlling 802.11 Transmission

MEDIA ACCESS CONTROL

As noted in the body of the text, the access point and the stations it serves all transmit in the same channel. If two 802.11 devices (stations or wireless access points) transmit at the same time, their signals will be jumbled together and will be unreadable.

The 802.11 standard has two mechanisms for **media access control**—ensuring that stations and the access point do not transmit simultaneously. The first, CSMA/CA + ACK, is mandatory and is normally used. The second, RTS/CTS, is optional except in one special case.

TEST YOUR UNDERSTANDING

15. a) What is the purpose of media access control? b) Does media access control limit the actions of wireless stations, the access point, or both?

CSMA/CA+ACK MEDIA ACCESS CONTROL

Problems in Hearing Collisions

We saw in the Chapter 4 box, "Hubs and CSMA/CD," that Ethernet hubs use carrier sense multiple access with collision detection for media access control. Unfortunately, wireless LANs cannot use collision detection. Although all wireless stations can hear the access point, stations cannot necessarily hear one another. They may be in dead spots relative to one other, or they may be too far apart. Although CSMA—controlling media access by listening to (sensing) the carrier is still possible, collision detection is not.

CSMA/CA

Instead of using CSMA/CD, 802.11 LANs use **carrier sense multiple access with collision**

(continued)

CSMA/CA (Carrier Sense Multiple Access with Collision Avoidance)
Sender listens for traffic

If there is traffic, waits

If there is no traffic:

If there has been no traffic for less than the critical time value, waits a random amount of time, then sends if still no traffic

If there has been no traffic for more than the critical value for time, sends without waiting

ACK (Acknowledgement)
Receiver immediately sends back an acknowledgement

If sender does not receive the acknowledgement, retransmits using CSMA/CA

Figure 5-16   CSMA/CA+ACK in 802.11 Wireless LANs

avoidance (CSMA/CA). Note that collision *detection* is replaced by collision *avoidance*. Figure 5-16 illustrates CSMA/CA.

CSMA, as discussed in Chapter 4, requires that a station refrain from transmitting if it hears traffic. This is a very simple rule.

If there is no traffic, collision avoidance comes into play.

- If the station does not hear traffic, it considers the last time it heard traffic. If the time since the last transmission exceeds a critical value, the station may transmit immediately.
- However, if the time is less than the critical value, the station sets a random timer and waits. If there still is no traffic after the random wait, the station may send.

If the last two points seem odd, remember that the goal is to avoid collisions as much as possible. Two stations are most likely to transmit at the same time if they have both been waiting for another station to finish

transmitting. Without the random delay, both will transmit at the same time, causing a collision.

ACK

More specifically, 802.11 uses **CSMA/CA+ACK**. Collisions and other types of signal loss are still possible with CSMA/CA. When a wireless access point receives a frame from a station, or when a station receives a frame from an access point, the receiver *immediately* sends an acknowledgement frame, an **ACK**. A frame that is not acknowledged is retransmitted. Note that there is no wait when transmitting an ACK. This ensures that ACKs get through while other stations are waiting.

Note also that retransmission makes 802.11 a reliable protocol. We saw in Chapter 2 that very few protocols are reliable because reliability usually costs more than it brings in benefits. The low error rates in wired media simply do not justify implementing reliability in Ethernet and other wired LAN protocols. However, wireless transmission has many errors, so a reliable protocol is required for reasonably good operation.[13]

Thanks to CSMA/CA, 802.11 is a reliable protocol.

Inefficient Operation

CSMA/CA+ACK works well, but it is inefficient. Waiting before transmission wastes valuable time. Sending ACKs also is time-consuming. Overall, an 802.11 LAN can only deliver throughput (actual speed) of about half the rated speed of its standard—that is, the speed published in the standard.

This throughput, furthermore, is aggregate throughput that is shared by the wireless access point and all of the stations sharing the channel. Individual station throughput will be substantially lower.

TEST YOUR UNDERSTANDING

16. a) Describe CSMA/CA+ACK. b) Is CSMA/CA+ACK transmission reliable or unreliable? Explain. c) Why is CSMA/CA+ACK inefficient?

Figure 5-17   Request to Send/Clear to Send (RTS/CTS)

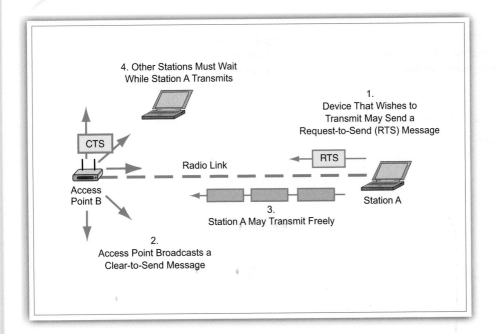

---

[13]In addition, 802.11 uses forward error correction. It adds many redundant (extra) bits to each frame. If there is a small error, the receiver can use these redundant bits to fix the frame. If the receiver can make the repair, it does so and then sends back an ACK. This process makes wireless NICs more expensive than Ethernet NICs, but wireless transmission errors are so common that it makes economic sense to correct errors at the receiver in order to minimize retransmissions.

(continued)

REQUEST TO SEND/CLEAR TO SEND (RTS/CTS)

Although CSMA/CA+ACK is mandatory, there is another control mechanism called **request to send/clear to send (RTS/CTS)**. Figure 5-17 illustrates RTS/CTS. As noted earlier, the RTS/CTS protocol is optional except in one special case we will see later. Avoiding RTS/CTS whenever possible is wise because RTS/CTS is much less efficient and therefore slower than CSMA/CA+ACK.

When a station wishes to send and is able to send because of CSMA/CA, the station may send a **request-to-send (RTS)** message to the wireless access point. This message asks the access point for permission to send messages.

If the access point responds by broadcasting a **clear-to-send (CTS)** message, then other stations must wait. The station sending the RTS may then transmit, ignoring CSMA/CA.

Although RTS/CTS is widely used, keep in mind that it is only an option, while CSMA/CA is mandatory for at least initial communication. Also, tests have shown that RTS/CTS reduces throughput when it is used.

The one special situation in which RTS/CTS is mandatory rather than optional is when 802.11b stations operating at 11 Mbps and 802.11g stations operating at 54 Mbps share an 802.11g wireless access point. In this case, stations must use request to send/clear to send.

TEST YOUR UNDERSTANDING

17. a) Describe RTS/CTS. b) Is CSMA/CA+ACK usually required or optional? c) Is RTS/CTS usually required or optional? d) Is RTS/CTS or CSMA/CA+ACK more efficient?

802.11 TRANSMISSION STANDARDS

As Figure 5-18 shows, the 802.11 Working Group has created several WLAN transmission standards.

How Fast Are 802.11 Networks?

Figure 5-18 shows rated speed and throughput for 802.11 transmission standards.

➤ The figure shows that the *rated speeds* of 802.11 WLANs today lie between 11 Mbps and 54 Mbps. (This will soon be more than doubled.) However, these rated speeds are misleading.

➤ As Figure 5-18 also shows, actual *throughput* usually is considerably lower than rated speeds and falls off rapidly with distance.

➤ Furthermore, this 802.11 throughput is *aggregate throughput* that is shared by all stations that wish to transmit at the same time. For instance, if the aggregate shared throughput is 5 Mbps, stations using a wireless access point serving 10–20 stations might see individual throughput of only one or two megabits per second, despite the fact that only a few stations are likely to be transmitting at any given moment.

TEST YOUR UNDERSTANDING

18. Distinguish between rated speed, aggregate throughput, and individual throughput in 802.11 WLANs.

	802.11a	802.11b	802.11g	802.11g if 802.11g access point serves an 802.11b station
Unlicensed Band	5 GHz	2.4 GHz	2.4 GHz	2.4 GHz
Rated Speed	54 Mbps	11 Mbps	54 Mbps	Not Specified
Actual Throughput, 3 m	25 Mbps	6 Mbps	25 Mbps	12 Mbps
Actual Throughput, 30 m	12 Mbps	6 Mbps	20 Mbps	11 Mbps
Is Throughput Shared by All Stations Using an Access Point?	Yes	Yes	Yes	Yes
Number of Nonoverlapping Channels (varies by country)	12 to 24 in most countries	3	3	3

Source for throughput data: Broadcom.com.

Notes: The number of nonoverlapping channels is important because nearby access points should operate *136* on different channels.

For 802.11b and g, the nonoverlapping channels are 1, 6, and 11. →*13 a*

For 802.11a in the United States, there are now 24 nonoverlapping channels, and this number is growing.

Figure 5-18   Specific 802.11 Wireless LAN Standards

802.11a

When the base 802.11 specification was ratified in 1997, it only permitted a transmission speed up to 2 Mbps in the 2.4 GHz wireless band. At this low speed, access points could only serve a handful of stations. Unfortunately, 802.11a had two problems that stunted its adoption.

In 1999, the 802.11 Working Group released its first revision, **802.11a**. This standard supports 54 Mbps transmission in the 5 GHz unlicensed band. Unfortunately, 802.11a had two problems that stunted its adoption.

First, general radio technology for the 5 GHz band was new in 1999 and therefore expensive. In addition, 802.11a requires OFDM, which requires complex (and therefore more expensive) NICs and access points. High prices for 802.11a greatly limited its initial adoption—especially because, as we will see next—the 802.11 Working Group also introduced a less expensive 802.11 standard the same day it introduced 802.11a.

Another problem with 802.11a that continues to this day is that while the 2.4 GHz band is available in nearly all countries, room in the 5 GHz region for unlicensed operation is not. This greatly complicates the development of radios for 802.11a because these radios must operate at different frequency ranges in different countries if they can operate at all. In addition, there are differences in allowed power levels and other matters, and these further complicate 802.11a radio development.

TEST YOUR UNDERSTANDING

19. a) What is the rated speed of 802.11a? b) In what band does 802.11a operate? c) Why was 802.11a not popular when it first appeared?

802.11b

On the same day the 802.11 Working Group ratified 802.11a, it also ratified 802.11b. The 802.11b standard has a rated speed of only 11 Mbps, but it operates in the 2.4 GHz band and uses DSSS. These are important because 2.4 GHz radio technology is cheaper than 5 GHz technology and because DSSS is simpler and less expensive than OFDM.

Although 802.11b is slower than 802.11a, 11 Mbps was considered to be fast enough by most firms in 1999, and 802.11b's low price was very attractive. While the market for 802.11a equipment stagnated, the market for 802.11b wireless NICs and access points grew explosively.

TEST YOUR UNDERSTANDING

20. a) What was the first widely used 802.11 LAN standard? b) What is the rated speed of 802.11b? c) In what band does 802.11b operate? d) What was the advantage of 802.11b over 802.11a?

802.11g: Today's Dominant Technology

Many analysts expected companies to move to 802.11a once 11 Mbps became too slow for growing wireless LANs. However, in 2001, the 802.11 Working Group ratified the 802.11g standard. This was another 54 Mbps standard using OFDM.

While 802.11a operates in the 5 GHz band, 802.11g operates in the 2.4 GHz un-licensed band. This confers three major advantages on 802.11g compared to 802.11a.

➤ First, as noted earlier, radio technology is cheaper in the 2.4 GHz band than in the 5 GHz band, allowing 802.11g to be less expensive than 802.11a equipment.

➤ Second, attenuation increases with frequency. Although both 802.11a and 802.11g have the same *rated speed*, 802.11g has better *throughput* at distance, as Figure 5-18 shows.

➤ Third, and most important, 802.11g is **backward-compatible** with 802.11b, which operates in the same 2.4 GHz band. This means that if you have an 802.11g access point, you can serve both 802.11b and 802.11g wireless clients. (Or, if you buy a new 802.11g wireless NIC, it will work with existing 802.11b access points at 11 Mbps until the company upgrades its access points to 802.11g.) Because it is backward-compatible with older equipment, 802.11g is a seamless upgrade. There is no need to throw away all existing equipment, as there would be in a shift to 802.11a.

The higher speed of 802.11g caused many companies to increase their spending on WLAN equipment. Very soon, 802.11g dominated sales. Soon after that, it became the most-widely installed 802.11 technology.

The most widely installed 802.11 technology is 802.11g.

Many firms are phasing out their 802.11b equipment aggressively. As Figure 5-18 shows, if even a single 802.11b device associates with an 802.11g access point, throughput plummets for *all* devices associated with the access point.[14]

TEST YOUR UNDERSTANDING

21. a) What 802.11 standard has the largest market share today? b) How is 802.11g better than 802.11b? c) Can you use 802.11b stations with an 802.11g access point? d) Is there a speed penalty for using 802.11b stations with an 802.11g access point? e) What disadvantages does 802.11a have compared to 802.11g? f) Is 802.11a backward-compatible with 802.11b or 802.11g?

802.11a Redux?

Although 802.11g further stymied demand for 802.11a, 802.11b and 802.11g share a major problem. The 2.4 GHz band is fairly small, so there is only room for three nonoverlapping channels—1, 6, and 11.[15]

Having only three nonoverlapping channels is a problem because nearby wireless access points will interfere with each other if they operate on the same channel. Figure 5-19 illustrates this situation.

Figure 5-19   Interference Between Nearby Access Points Operating on the Same Channel

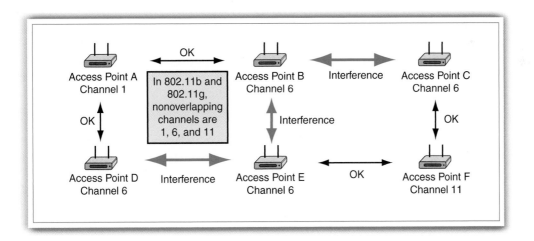

---

[14]This occurs because when an 802.11b device associates with an 802.11g access point, transmission control is equired to change from CSMA/CA+ACK to RTS/CTS. This greatly reduces throughput for 802.11g stations.
[15]Although there are eleven center frequencies for channels, 802.11 channel bandwidths (20 MHz) are wider than the differences between these center frequencies (5 MHz). Center frequencies have to be selected so that channel bandwidths do not overlap. This odd state of affairs is a holdover from the original 802.11 FHSS standard, which hopped between the original eleven small channels. Moving from 2 Mbps to 54 Mbps required much wider channels for 802.11a.

In some cases, access point channels can be set so that nearby access points do not use the same channel. However, in a large three-dimensional building with many access points, it usually is impossible to arrange access points without having interference in 802.11b and 802.11g.

The 5 GHz band is much wider than the 2.4 GHz band, allowing many possible nonoverlapping channels. Originally, there were 12 standard channels in the United States.[16] More have been added since, and today there are more than 20.[17] Even more are likely to be added later. With so many nonoverlapping channels, it is very easy to assign different channels to different nearby access points even in a building with many access points.

In addition, access points and their stations operate today in a single channel. In the future, however, it is likely that each 802.11a access point will be able to operate on multiple channels, with each channel serving many wireless clients. This will greatly increase throughput for each access point.

The major driver for 802.11a in the future may be voice over IP. VoIP phones would connect through access points to the firm's wired VoIP system. The 802.11a standard can provide multiple channels at each access point, giving the capacity necessary for good voice communication and allowing particular channels to be reserved for voice communication.

TEST YOUR UNDERSTANDING

22. a) How many nonoverlapping channels do 802.11b and 802.11g support? b) Why is the number of nonoverlapping channels that can be used important? c) How many nonoverlapping channels does 802.11a support?

802.11n and MIMO

The 802.11 Working Group has recently drafted a new transmission standard, **802.11n**.[18] Figure 5-18 does not list 802.11n because it is not yet an approved standard. However, draft standards usually do not change much within the 802 LAN/MAN Standards Committee. Consequently the final version of 802.11n will almost certainly have the following characteristics.

First, instead of using 20 MHz channels like today's versions of 802.11, 802.11n will allow the use of either 20 MHz or 40 MHz channels. This alone will roughly double the maximum speed.

More spectacularly, 802.11n will use **multiple input/multiple output (MIMO)** transmission, which sends two or more radio signals in the same channel between two

---

[16]These were 36, 40, 44, 48, 52, 56, 60, 64, 149, 153, 157, and 161.
[17]These are 100, 104, 108, 112, 116, 120, 124, 128, 136, and 140.
[18]A number of WLAN NICs and wireless access points are now being sold with the designation, "pre-standard 802.11n." This is highly misleading. Usually, *pre-standard* means that the standard is near completion and that the pre-standard equipment can be easily upgraded when the full standard is available. In contrast, "pre-standard 802.11n" products are being sold long before the 802.11 Working Group has even selected what type of MIMO technology it will use. The probability that "pre-standard 802.11n" products will be upgradeable later to the full standard is not good. These are pure proprietary products, not true pre-standard products.

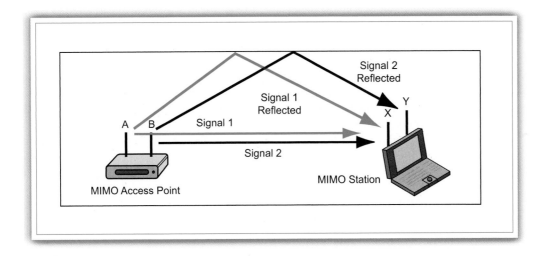

Figure 5-20   Multiple Input/Multiple Output (MIMO) Transmission

or more different antennas on access points and wireless NICs. Figure 5-20 illustrates MIMO transmission.

The two signals, being in the same channel, will interfere with each other. However, using special detection and separation methods based on differences in arrival times for direct signals and reflections, the receiver can separate the different signals in the same channel and read them both. Even with only two radio signals and two antennas on the sender and receiver, this can substantially increase throughput. Using more antennas and radio signals can increase throughput even more. MIMO also substantially increases propagation distance. The MIMO standard will permit 2, 3, or 4 antennas on each device.

Overall, 802.11n will have a rated speed of 100–600 Mbps. Throughput will be lower, but it will come much closer to its rated speed than earlier versions of 802.11 because of enhancements at the MAC layer. The 802.11n standard will also substantially increase transmission range. At the same time, 802.11n will be interoperable with earlier 802.11 standards.

The 802.11n draft standard goes beyond physical layer improvements. It also includes a major revision of the 802.11 MAC layer standard. The revised standard brings much greater efficiency to data link layer operation. Consequently, 802.11n's actual throughput will be much closer to its rated speed than earlier 802.11 standards.

Finally, the 802.11 standard will be the first 802.11 standard to work in both the 2.4 GHz and 5 GHz band.

TEST YOUR UNDERSTANDING

23. a) What are the two benefits of MIMO? b) What will be 802.11n's rated speed? c) In what two ways will 802.11n increase throughput? d) How does MIMO work? e) Why will

the throughput of 802.11n be much closer to its rated speed than earlier 802.11 standards? f) In which band will 802.11n operate?

802.11e Quality of Service (QoS)

Transmission speed and throughput are important, but for some applications, guaranteed throughput is even more important. The **802.11e** standard will govern quality of service (QoS) for 802.11 WLANs. Primarily, this will allow good-quality voice over IP. An 802.11e access point will reserve capacity for voice traffic so that voice will get the throughput it needs even if there is heavy data traffic. This is needed to prevent disruptions in telephone service. The QoS capability of 802.11e will also be useful for streaming audio, streaming video, and even videoconferencing.

TEST YOUR UNDERSTANDING

24. a) Why would 802.11e QoS standards be welcome? b) What application is likely to benefit the most from 802.11e?

802.11 WLAN SECURITY

WLAN Security Threats

For most companies, the biggest problem with 802.11 wireless LANs has been security. There are four major security threats to 802.11 WLANs:

- ➤ Most seriously, **drive-by hackers** park just outside a company's premises and eavesdrop on the firm's data transmissions. They can also mount denial-of-service attacks; send viruses, worms, and spam into the network; and do other mischief. Using readily downloaded attack software, drive-by hackers can succeed easily against many WLANs.

- ➤ Less importantly, **war drivers** are people who, as the name suggests, drive around a city looking for working access points that are unprotected. Only if they try to break in do they become drive-by hackers.

- ➤ Drive-by hackers can configure their computers to act as access points. These **evil twin access points** operate at high power, enticing internal clients to associate with them rather than with legitimate internal access points. The evil twin then relays traffic between the duped wireless client and a legitimate access point. It can read the encrypted traffic because it knows the key used in encryption.

- ➤ Finally, many departments and individual people set up unauthorized access points. These are called **rogue access points**. They often have poor security and provide entry points for drive-by hackers who could not otherwise break into the network. They also frequently operate at high power, attracting many stations to their poor-security service.

TEST YOUR UNDERSTANDING

25. a) Distinguish between war drivers and drive-by hackers. b) Distinguish between evil twin access points and rogue access points. c) What is an evil twin access point? d) What is a rogue access point?

Drive-By Hackers

> Sit outside the corporate premises and read network traffic
>
> Can send malicious traffic into the network
>
> Easily done with readily available downloadable software

War Drivers

> Merely discover unprotected access points—become drive-by hackers only if they break in

Evil Twin Access Points

> Drive-by hacker sets up an access point outside walls of firm
>
> Internal clients: associate with the evil twin access point
>
> Evil twin: intercepts authentication credentials, associates with real access point
>
> Decrypts message traffic, reads it, re-encrypts it, passes it on to a legitimate access point
>
> Does the same in the other direction

Rogue Access Points

> Unauthorized access points that are set up by a department or an individual
>
> Often have very poor security, making drive-by hacking easier
>
> Often operate at high power, attracting many clients to their low-security service

Figure 5-21   WLAN Security Threats (Study Figure)

WEP Security

Problems with 802.11 security began when the first version of the standard was released in 1997. The standard only included a very rudimentary security method called **wired equivalent privacy (WEP)**.[19]

Good security methods give every station a unique secret key and change this key frequently. In contrast, WEP had everyone who was sharing an access point use the same key, and WEP had no mechanism for changing this key. To provide some protection, each frame contained a clear text (unencrypted) 24-bit **initialization vector (IV)**. Most of the frame was then encrypted with a *per-frame key* consisting of the IV plus the shared key. The receiver would read the IV in the arriving frame, recreate the per-frame

---

[19]The WEP specification was only ten pages long. In contrast, the specification for 802.11i security (discussed later) is 200 pages long.

Figure 5-22   802.11 Security Standards (Study Figure)

Wired Equivalent Privacy (WEP)

    Initial security provided with 802.11 in 1997

    Everyone shared the same secret encryption key

    WEP protected the key with a poorly implemented initialization vector (IV)

    Not even turned on by default on early products

    Because secret key was shared, it does not seem to be secret

        Users often give out freely

    Key initially could be cracked in 1–2 hours; now can be cracked in 3–10 minutes using readily available software

    By 2001, WEP security was in crisis

Wireless Protected Access (WPA)

    The Wi-Fi Alliance

        Normally certifies interoperability of 802.11 equipment

        Created WPA as a stop-gap security standard in 2002 until 802.11i was finished

    Designed for upgrading old equipment

        Old equipment has limited memory and processing power

        WPA uses a subset of 802.11i that can run on older wireless NICs and access points

        WPA added simpler security algorithms for functions that could not run on older machines

    Equipment that cannot be upgraded to WPA should be discarded

802.11i (WPA2)

    Uses AES-CCMP with 128-bit keys for confidentiality and key management

    In Robust Security Networks (RSN), all devices use 802.11i exclusively

802.1X Mode (Figure 5-23)

    Uses a central authentication server for consistency

    Authentication server also provides key management

    Wi-Fi Alliance calls this *enterprise mode*

    802.1X standard protects communication with an extensible authentication protocol

        Several EAP versions exist with different security protections

        Firm implementing 802.1X must choose one

        Protected EAP (PEAP) is popular because Microsoft favors it

Pre-Shared Key (PSK) Mode: Stations Share a Key with the Access Point

    Access point does all authentication and key management

    All users must know an initial pre-shared key (PSK)

    Each, however, is later given a unique key

    If the pre-shared key is weak, it is easily cracked

    Pass phrases that generate key must be at least 20 characters long

key by adding this IV to the shared key, and decrypt the frame. Unfortunately, there were severe weaknesses in the way that WEP implemented the per-frame keying mechanism.[20] This made it relatively easy for drive-by hackers to learn the shared key.

WEP had other problems as well. For example, WEP was turned off by default in early products. Unless user organizations took specific action, they did not even have WEP protection.

Another problem was that if a firm had many access points and users, it normally gave all access points the same WEP key. Everybody in the firm was told the WEP key, so many employees thought it was not really secret and were willing to tell unauthorized users.

By 2001, because software that would crack WEP keys quickly was readily available, 802.11 security was in crisis. Initially, cracking a WEP key with one of these programs took one or two hours. Today, it often takes only about 10 minutes. Companies began putting the brakes on WLAN implementation, and many pulled out their existing access points.[21]

TEST YOUR UNDERSTANDING

26. a) When 802.11 was created, what security protocol did it offer? b) How long does it take to crack WEP today? c) When products that offered WEP were initially sold, was WEP turned on or off by default?

WPA (Wireless Protected Access)

The **Wi-Fi Alliance** is an industry trade group that certifies 802.11 products for interoperability. Normally, the Wi-Fi Alliance leaves standards creation to the 802.11 Working Group. However, when WEP's fatal flaws were discovered in 2000 and 2001, the market for wireless products began to falter. Furthermore, the 802.11i security standard being developed by the 802.11 Working Group was going to take years to develop.

As a stop-gap measure until 802.11i could be developed, the Wi-Fi Alliance created an interim security standard, **Wireless Protected Access (WPA)**. It announced this standard in 2002 and began certifying products for compliance in early 2003.

The alliance decided to keep protection fairly simple so that many older NIC and access point products, which had limited memory and little processing power, could be upgraded to WPA via software only. Older products would not be upgradeable to full

---

[20]For example, the initialization vector was too short (only twenty-four bits long). More seriously, many IV values "leak" information about the key. By analyzing frames encrypted with these "interesting" IV values, readily downloadable software can quickly crack the key.

[21]Some companies began taking other steps, like hiding the SSID (Service Set Identifier) of the access point. Users need to know this SSID to use an access point even if WEP is not used. Another common step was to only accept computers whose wireless NICs had registered MAC addresses. (All 802 LANs have 48-bit MAC addresses.) Unfortunately, these measures take a great deal of work, and they are easily cracked by readily available hacking software. They make sense only if you are only concerned about unsophisticated but nosy neighbors at home.

In Chapter 7, we will see that virtual private networks provide client–server security even if the underlying network is not secure. Some companies have implemented virtual private networks for all wireless transmission. Unfortunately, setting up virtual private networks for all clients is expensive.

802.11i security, which requires more memory and processing power in wireless NICs and access points. The ability to upgrade many existing products meant that WPA protected the installed base of WLAN equipment for corporations. More specifically, WPA2 consists of the parts of 802.11i that would fit on most existing products, so that installed products could be updated to WPA. For other parts of 802.11, the alliance chose weaker processes that were easier to implement.

WPA provides far stronger security than WEP. Firms that use WPA should discard legacy wireless NICs and access points that cannot be upgraded to WPA.

TEST YOUR UNDERSTANDING

27. a) Who created WPA? b) What is WPA's advantage over 802.11i? c) What should companies do if they have access points or NICs that cannot be upgraded to WPA?

802.11i (WPA2)

In 2004, the 802.11 Working Group finally ratified the **802.11i standard**. Most important, the 802.11i standard uses the extremely strong **AES-CCMP** encryption with 128-bit keys and a key management method that was too processing intensive to include in WPA. Confusingly, the Wi-Fi Alliance refers to the 802.11i standard as **WPA2**.

Today, 802.11i is the gold standard in WLAN security. Many corporations are now restricting their purchases of products that do not support 802.11i. They also require the discarding of all existing wireless LAN products that do not have WPA and cannot be upgraded to WPA.

Even supporting both WPA and 802.11i components is only a temporary expedient. Many firms are setting dates by which *all* components must comply with 802.11i. When all components comply with 802.11i, the network is called a **Robust Security Network (RSN)**.

TEST YOUR UNDERSTANDING

28. a) What is the strongest security protocol for 802.11 today? b) What does the Wi-Fi Alliance call 802.11i? c) What encryption method does 802.11i use? d) What is a Robust Security Network (RSN)?

802.1X Mode Operation

Figure 5-23 illustrates that 802.11i and WPA normally use the **802.1X** (*not* 802.11X) authentication and key management standard. The Wi-Fi Alliance refers to 802.1X mode as **enterprise mode**.[22]

Using an Authentication Server

In 802.1X, the company has a central **authentication server**. Most authentication servers use the RADIUS standard.

---

[22]Actually, 802.1X was first developed for wired Ethernet LANs. Without authentication, anyone can walk into a building, plug his or her computer into an untended Ethernet wall jack, and do whatever he or she wishes. Companies that implement 802.1X for both WLANs and wired LANs will have strong LAN site security.

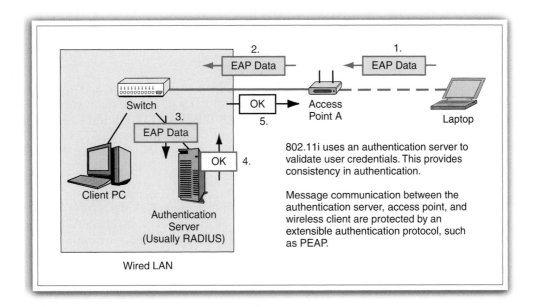

Figure 5-23   802.11i Security in 802.1X (Enterprise) Mode

When a client attempts to connect to a wireless access point, the wireless access point requests certain credentials, such as a username and password. The wireless access point passes these credentials to the authentication server, which checks them. The authentication server sends the access point a message that tells the wireless access point whether or not the credentials are valid. The wireless access point then accepts or rejects the client.

The access point also provides **key management**. It sends an encryption key for the access point and the station to use when communicating with each other.

Using a central authentication server provides *consistency* in authentication. No matter what access point a user approaches, 802.11i will use the same authentication server to check the credentials, and the authentication server will always send back the same reply. Attackers cannot try different wireless access points until they find one that is improperly configured with the wrong authentication data.

Using a central authentication server provides *consistency* in authentication.

Extensible Authentication Protocol (EAP) Types

EAP   The 802.1X standard uses the **Extensible Authentication Protocol (EAP)** to handle communication between the client, the access point, and the authentication server. EAP has the *extensible* in its name to indicate that it can support a wide variety of specific authentication mechanisms. This flexibility allows companies to decide what type of authentication server to use and what specific authentication methods to use on the authentication server.

EAP Types   In addition to this basic flexibility, there are several basic EAP types from which to select. Different EAP types give different levels of protection at correspondingly different levels of cost. These include EAP-TLS, EAP-TTLS, and PEAP, among several others. A company using 802.11i must select an EAP type that vendors offer and that is appropriate for the firm. Microsoft has focused its support on **Protected EAP (PEAP)**.

Specific Authentication Mechanisms   In addition, most EAP types offer multiple authentication mechanism options (passwords, smart cards, and so forth). After selecting an EAP type, a company needs to pick a specific authentication method.

TEST YOUR UNDERSTANDING

29. a) In what mode of 802.11i and WPA operation is a central authentication server used? b) What does the Wi-Fi Alliance call 802.1X mode? c) What is the benefit of using an authentication server? d) What benefit does 802.1X provide beyond authentication? e) What standards does 802.1X use for authentication communication? f) Which Extensible Authentication Protocol type does Microsoft favor? g) Do most EAP types have a single authentication method or multiple authentication methods? h) Along what two dimensions do extensible authentication protocols vary?

Pre-Shared Key (PSK) Mode

For homes and small businesses, which cannot afford a separate authentication server, 802.11i and WPA offer a simpler operating mode, **pre-shared key (PSK)** mode. PSK does all authentication and key management. The Wi-Fi Alliance calls this **personal mode**.

In this mode, normally used when there is only a single access point, the access points and stations begin with a shared 64-bit key. Everybody allowed to use the access point is told the shared key. This sounds like WEP, but after authentication, the wireless access point gives each authenticated user a new unique key to use while on the Internet. It also changes this key frequently.

Although PSK mode can be very strong, if the organization implements a weak key as its pre-shared key, the key can be cracked even faster than a WEP key. To create the pre-shared key, the company usually creates a long **pass phrase** that the access point and client use to generate the key. This pass phrase must be at least twenty characters long to provide adequate security.

TEST YOUR UNDERSTANDING

30. a) How does PSK mode differ from 802.1X mode? b) What is a potential weakness of PSK mode? c) How long should pass phrases be with PSK?

802.11 WIRELESS LAN MANAGEMENT

Until recently, the term *WLAN management* was almost an oxymoron. Large WLANs were like major airports without air traffic control towers. To a considerable extent, this condition is still true today, but there has been some progress.

Access Point Placement

To provide WLAN service throughout a building, it is crucial to determine where to place access points. Otherwise, there will be many dead spots, interference between many access points, or both.

The first step is to determine how far signals should travel. In many firms, a good radius is 30–50 meters. If the radius is too great, many stations will be far from their access points. Stations far from the access point must drop down to lower transmission

Figure 5-24   Wireless LAN Management (Study Figure)

Access Points Placement in a Building
    Must be done carefully for good coverage and to minimize interference between access points

    Lay out 30-meter to 50-meter radius circles on blueprints

    Adjust for obvious potential problems such as brick walls

    In multistory buildings, must consider interference in three dimensions

    Install access points and do site surveys to determine signal quality

    Adjust placement and signal strength as needed

Remote Access Point Management
    The manual labor to manage many access points: can be very high

    Centralized management alternatives (Figure 5-25)

        Smart access points

        Dumb access points, with intelligence in WLAN switches

    Desired functionality

        Notify the WLAN administrators of failures immediately

        Support remote access point adjustment

        Should provide continuous transmission quality monitoring

        Allow software updates to be pushed out to all access points or WLAN switches

        Work automatically whenever possible

speeds, and their frames will take longer to send. This will reduce the access point's effective capacity. If the radius is too small, however, the firm will need many more access points to cover the space to be served.

Once an appropriate radius is selected, say 30 meters, the company gets out its building blueprints and begins to lay out 30-meter circles with as little overlap as possible. Where there are thick walls or other obstructions, shorter propagation distances must be assumed. In addition, in a multistory building, this planning must be done in three dimensions. In addition, planners must install channels to access point positions to minimize interference.

Next, the access points are installed in the indicated places. However, the implementation work has just begun. When each access point is installed, a **site survey** must be done of the area around the access point to discover if there are any dead spots or other problems. This requires a signal analyzer, which can be a personal digital assistant (PDA) or a notebook computer with signal strength analysis software.

When areas with poor signal strength are found, surrounding access points must be moved appropriately, or their signal strengths must be adjusted until all areas have good signal strength.

TEST YOUR UNDERSTANDING

31. a) Describe the process by which access point locations are selected. b) After access points are installed, what must be done?

Remote Management: Smart Access Points and Wireless Switches

Large organizations have hundreds or even thousands of 802.11 wireless access points. Traveling to each one for manual configuration and troubleshooting would be extremely expensive. To keep management labor costs under control, organizations need to be able to manage access points remotely, from a central management console. Figure 5-25 illustrates two approaches to centralized wireless access point management.

Smart Access Points

The simplest approach architecturally is to add intelligence to every access point. The central management console can then communicate directly with each of these **smart access points**[23] via the firm's Ethernet wired LAN. However, adding management capacity raises the price of access points considerably. Using smart access points is an expensive strategy.

Wireless LAN Switches

A second approach illustrated in Figure 5-25 is to use **WLAN switches**. As the figure shows, multiple access points connect to each wireless LAN switch. The management

---

[23]Smart access points are also called fat access points.

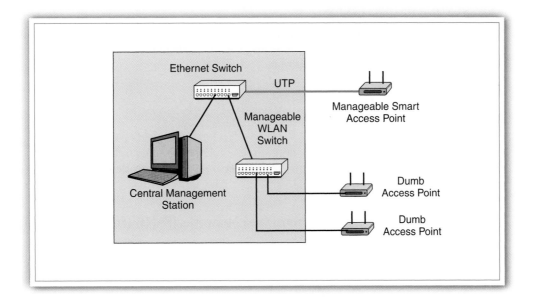

Figure 5-25   Wireless Access Point Management Alternatives

intelligence is placed in the WLAN switch rather than in the access points themselves. Vendors who sell WLAN switches claim that this approach reduces total cost because only inexpensive **dumb access points** are needed. Of course, smart access point vendors dispute these cost comparisons.

Wireless LAN Management Functionality

Although technological approaches to centralized WLAN management vary, vendors generally agree on the types of functionality these systems should provide.

➤ These systems should notify the WLAN administrators of failures immediately so that malfunctioning access points can be fixed or replaced rapidly.

➤ They should allow remote adjustment—for instance telling nearby access points to increase their power to compensate for an access point failure. Such adjustments are also needed over time as furniture is moved (creating different shadow zones) or as the number of users in an area changes.

➤ They should provide continuous transmission quality monitoring to allow WLAN administrators to adjust access point operating parameters constantly.

➤ They should allow software updates to be pushed out to all access points or WLAN switches, bypassing the need to install updates manually.

➤ The management software should be able to work automatically, taking as many actions as possible without human intervention.

TEST YOUR UNDERSTANDING

32. a) Why is centralized access point management desirable? b) What are the two technologies for remote access point management? c) What functions should remote access point management systems provide?

BLUETOOTH PANs

Personal Area Networks (PANs) for Cable Replacement

Although 802.11 is good for fairly large wireless LANs, another wireless networking standard, **Bluetooth**,[24] was created for wireless **personal area networks (PANs)**, which are

Figure 5-26   Bluetooth Personal Area Networks (PANs) (Study Figure)

For Personal Area Networks (PANs)
    Devices on a person's body and nearby (cellphone, PDA, notebook computer, etc.)
    Devices around a desk (computer, mouse, keyboard, printer)

Cable Replacement Technology
    For example, with a Bluetooth PDA, print wirelessly to a nearby Bluetooth-enabled printer
    Does not use access points
        Uses direct device-to-device communication

Disadvantages Compared to 802.11
    Short distance (10 meters)
    Low speed (3 Mbps today with a slower reverse channel)

Advantages Compared to 802.11
    Low battery power drain, so long battery life between recharges
    Application profiles (printing, etc.)
        Somewhat rudimentary
        Devices typically only automate a few

Bluetooth Trends
    Bluetooth Alliance is enhancing Bluetooth
    One option is likely to offer UWB transmission at 100 Mbps or more at a distance of 10 meters. This is fast enough and far enough for home video transmission.

---

[24]Bluetooth is named after King Harald Bluetooth, a Scandinavian king of the tenth century. As you might guess, Bluetooth was developed in Sweden, although it is now under the control of an international consortium.

intended to connect devices used by a single person. Bluetooth basically offers *cable replacement*—a way to get rid of cables between devices. It is not designed for full WLANs.

Using Bluetooth, a notebook computer can print wirelessly to a printer and synchronize its files wirelessly with those on a desktop computer. To give another example, a cellphone can print to the same wireless printer and place a call through the firm's telephone system instead of paying to make a cellular call. Bluetooth does not use access points. Rather, it uses direct device-to-device communication.

Disadvantages Compared to 802.11

Limited Distance

While 802.11i normally has propagation distances up to 100 meters, 30–50 meters is a more realistic range in practice. Bluetooth, however, is normally limited to 10 meters or less.[25] For cable replacement around a desk or among the devices carried by a person, there is no need for longer distances. For a home or office WLAN, this distance is insufficient.

Low Speed

Bluetooth was not designed to handle heavy transmission loads. It currently offers a speed of only 3 Mbps with a slower reverse channel. This is sufficient for printing and most other Bluetooth applications, but it is not fast enough for WLANs.

Advantages Compared to 802.11

Long Battery Life

Although Bluetooth offers only low speeds and short distances, these limitations mean that radio transmission power is low, so battery life is quite long. This is very important for small portable devices.

Application Profiles

Bluetooth has one very important capability that 802.11 does not—**application profiles**, which are application-layer standards designed to allow devices to work together automatically, with little or no user intervention. For instance, you may be able to take a Bluetooth-enabled notebook computer to a Bluetooth-enabled printer and print as soon as the two devices recognize each other. The 802.11 standard has nothing like this currently. Unfortunately, the Bluetooth application profiles introduced to date have been rudimentary. In addition, most devices implement only a few of these application profiles, so there is no guarantee that two Bluetooth devices that you wish to connect will be able to work together.

Bluetooth Trends

The Bluetooth Alliance, which creates Bluetooth standards, will be enhancing the standard in the future. The Alliance is likely to offer a UWB Bluetooth option capable of moving video and other broadband information at 100 Mbps or more over a distance of 10 meters.

---

[25]This with the standard 2.5 milliwatts (mW) of power. There is an option for 100 mW power, which can raise the maximum propagation distance to 100 meters. This option is rarely built into Bluetooth products.

TEST YOUR UNDERSTANDING

33. a) Contrast how 802.11 and Bluetooth are likely to be used in organizations. b) What is a PAN? c) Why are Bluetooth application profiles attractive? d) Why do they not always fulfill their promise? e) What are the speeds of Bluetooth transmission today? f) What is the normal maximum distance for Bluetooth propagation? g) What benefit do low speeds and short distances bring? h) What speed will the next generation of Bluetooth devices provide?

CONCLUSION

Synopsis

The mantra of networking has always been "anything, anywhere, any time." With the advent of wireless data transmission, this promise is finally being extended to mobile users. This chapter focused on 802.11 WLANs and, to a lesser extent, on Bluetooth. However, other local wireless technologies are appearing, including RFIDs, ultrawideband (UWB) transmission, ZigBee, and mesh networking.

Wireless networks predominantly use radio transmission. Radio waves are described by frequency (hertz). Real radio signals contain a mix of frequencies. The range of frequencies between the lowest frequency and the highest frequency of a signal is the signal's bandwidth.

Radios send and receive using antennas. Dish antennas concentrate incoming and outgoing signals for long-distance transmission but are bulky and require the receiver to know the direction of the other party. In contrast, omnidirectional antennas send and receive equally well in all directions. If the other party is not very far away, as is the case in WLANs, omnidirectional antennas are attractive because they do not require users to know where access points are (or carry around a dish antenna).

We saw in Chapter 3 that propagation problems with copper wires and optical fiber are mild and can be controlled with good installation discipline. In contrast, we saw in this chapter that radio propagation problems are serious and difficult to control. First, radio waves attenuate very rapidly, following an inverse square law. Other problems are electromagnetic interference from nearby devices (including other wireless stations), multipath interference because of reflections off floors, walls, and ceilings, and shadow zones (dead spots) where signals cannot reach. Shadow zones are more pronounced at higher frequencies, and attenuation increases with frequency.

The frequency spectrum consists of all frequencies from 0 Hz to infinity. The frequency spectrum is divided into service bands for particular types of services. Service bands are further divided into channels. Different signals can be sent at the same time if they are sent in different channels.

The maximum possible transmission speed within a channel is directly proportional to the channel's bandwidth. Normally, channel bandwidth is set only wide enough to meet transmission speed requirements. However, spread spectrum transmission uses a much higher bandwidth than the signal requires. Spread spectrum transmission is done to reduce propagation problems, which often occur only at certain frequencies. It also reduces mutual interference between nearby devices transmitting in the same channel. Most wireless 802.11 WLAN standards today use orthogonal frequency division multiplexing (OFDM) spread spectrum transmission, which divides the broadband channel into many smaller subcarriers, each of which carries part of the signal.

The 802.11 Working Group sets most wireless LAN (WLAN) standards. Normally, 802.11 wireless LANs serve users through access points, which connect wireless stations to resources on the company's wired LAN. The most widespread WLAN technology today is 802.11g, which has a rated speed of 54 Mbps. Actual throughput (speed delivered to users) is about half of the rated speed near the wireless access point and falls off with distance. In addition, all stations using an access point share this throughput, so individual throughput is even lower.

There also is a 54 Mbps 802.11a standard. 802.11g signals travel farther than 802.11a signals because 802.11g operates in the lower-frequency 2.4 GHz band, while 802.11a operates in the higher-frequency 5 GHz band. In addition, 802.11g equipment is less expensive than 802.11a equipment, and 802.11g access points can serve older 802.11b stations, while 802.11a access points cannot.

On the plus side, 802.11a offers many more nonoverlapping channels, which is important in terms of placing wireless access points so that nearby access points do not interfere with each other by operating on the same channel.

The 802.11n technology, which is currently a draft standard, will use MIMO technology and perhaps wider channels. Compared to older standards, 802.11n will produce both much faster communication and longer propagation distances.

The box entitled "Controlling 802.11 Transmission" demonstrated that the access point and the wireless stations it serves must share a single channel. Only one device may transmit at any time. This means that as the number of wireless stations increases, individual throughput goes down. To control when stations may transmit, the access point and stations implement either the CSMA/CA+ACK or RTS/CTS media access control (MAC) method. Apart from one special case, CSMA/CA+ACK is mandatory while RTS/CTS is optional.

The first 802.11 LANs used weak wired equivalent privacy (WEP) security, and many users did not even turn on this anemic protection. Even with WEP enabled, drive-by hackers could easily eavesdrop on conversations and send attack packets into a network. The 802.11 Working Group finally created a robust security standard, 802.11i, but the development took several years, and older access points and wireless NICs cannot be upgraded to 802.11i. The interim WPA standard has aspects of 802.11i that can be applied to older wireless NICs and access points. Both 802.11i and WPA can operate in 802.1X (enterprise) mode, which uses a central authentication server and extensible authentication protocol communication. These two standards also can work in pre-shared key (PSK) mode, which uses a shared key based on a pass phrase. If the pass phrase is too short (fewer than 20 characters), security will be weaker than it was with WEP.

Wireless LANs need extensive management. The first concern is where to place access points in a building to provide good service. In addition, there now are technologies to manage all of a site's access points from a central location. Some vendors do remote management using expensive smart access points. Others use traditional "dumb" access points, and the management intelligence is placed in wireless LAN switches.

Bluetooth today is a low-speed, short-distance personal area network (PAN) technology designed to replace wired connections between devices within a few meters of each other. In the future, UWB versions of Bluetooth should give much higher speeds but will continue to limit propagation distance.

THOUGHT QUESTIONS

1. Telephone channels have a bandwidth of about 3.1 kHz, as we will see in the next chapter.
   a) If a telephone channel's signal-to-noise ratio is 30 dB, how fast can a telephone channel carry data? Note: You need to convert decibels into the absolute signal-to-noise ratio to use the Shannon equation. (Check figure: Telephone modems operate at about 30 kbps, so your answer should be roughly this speed.)
   b) How fast could a telephone channel carry data if the SNR were increased to 40 dB?
   c) With an SNR of 30 dB, how fast could a telephone channel carry data if the bandwidth were increased to 4 kHz? Show your work or no credit.

2. In a home network, would you use 802.11a or 802.11g? Justify your answer.

3. Suppose that 802.11a access points have only half the range of 802.11g access points. In a multistory building, if you need thirty 802.11g access points, roughly how many 802.11a access points will you need?

4. What advice would you give a company about WLAN security?

5. a) Do you think that 802.11g and Bluetooth might interfere with each other if they are used in the same office? Explain your reasoning.
   b) Do you think that 802.11a and Bluetooth might interfere with each other if they are used in the same office? Explain your reasoning.

DESIGN QUESTION

1. Consider a one-story building that is a square. It will have an access point in each corner and one in the center of the square. All access points can hear one another.
   a) Assign access point channels to the five access points if you are using 802.11g. Try not to have any access points that can hear each other use the same channel. Available channels are 1, 6, and 11.
   b) Were you able to eliminate interference between access points?
   c) Repeat the first two parts of the question, this time using 802.11a. Available channels are 36, 40, 44, 48, 53, 56, 60, 64, 149, 153, 157, and 161, but many NICs and access points only support channels below 100.

TROUBLESHOOTING QUESTIONS

1. When you set up an 802.11g wireless access point in your small business, your aggregate throughput is only about 6 Mbps. List at least two possible reasons for this low throughput. Describe how you would test each. Describe what you would do if each proved to be the problem.

2. Wal-Mart is perhaps the most famous user of RFID tags. Vendors must place RFID tags on individual boxes and on pallets carrying groups of boxes. The tags contain two pieces of information. The first is an electronic variant of the UPC bar code that we now see on individual products. The second is something UPC codes do not have—a serial number for the individual product. This allows the tracking of individual items of the same type. When Wal-Mart brings a pallet into a distribution center or store, the pallet passes by an RFID reader, which attempts to read the tags on the pallet and on the individual boxes on the pallet. Unfortunately, only 60–80 percent

of the tags typically are read when the pallet passes near the reader! The main problem is radio propagation difficulties. Radio signals do not propagate well through water or metal. Consequently, signals from the reader's antenna may not reach the tags, or the responses may not reach the reader. How might Wal-Mart deal with this problem?

INTERNET EXERCISE

1. Home wireless access points today are inexpensive, but enterprise access points cost much more. Go to cnet.com and compare prices for Cisco's residential Linksys access points and Cisco's Aironet enterprise access points. List your findings.

PROJECT

Write a short report on a new wireless technology—UWB, ZigBee, mesh networking, or 802.11n.

GETTING CURRENT

Go to the book website's New Information and Errors pages for this chapter to get new information since this book went to press and to correct any errors in the text.

Telecommunications

Learning Objectives

By the end of this chapter, you should be able to discuss:

- ☐ Telecommunications.

- ☐ The technology of the public switched telephone network (PSTN), including customer premises equipment, the access system, the transport core, and signaling.

- ☐ Circuit switching.

- ☐ The digital nature of the PSTN, except for the analog local loop to residential customer premises.

- ☐ (In a box) PCM conversion of customer signals at the end office.

- ☐ Cellular telephony.

- ☐ Voice over IP (VoIP).

- ☐ Residential Internet access technologies.

INTRODUCTION

Telecommunications and the PSTN

In Chapter 1, we looked at the difference between data networking and telecommunications. Telecommunications is the transmission of voice and video—principally telephony and the delivery of television and radio signals to stations and cable television companies. Telecommunications includes other services as well, such as videoconferencing. In this chapter, we will look at telecommunications.

The Public Switched Telephone Network (PSTN)

The worldwide telecommunications network is officially called the **public switched telephone network (PSTN)**. Every time you place a telephone call anywhere in the world, your call travels over the PSTN. Although the PSTN carries video as well as voice traffic, it is still called the public switched *telephone* network.

Telecommunications Carriers and Wide Area Networks

Why are we looking at telecommunications at this point in the book? The answer is that we need a transition between local area networks, which we saw in Chapters 4 and 5, and wide area networks, which Chapter 7 discusses. Telephony begins taking us outside of the corporate walls.

More fundamentally, we will see in Chapter 7 that wide area data networks normally use the existing telecommunications transmission system for data transport—adding switching and other functionality to be able to handle data. The carriers that provide telephone service to your home and company either are the same carriers that provide data service or support those carriers.

TEST YOUR UNDERSTANDING

1. a) What is the name of the worldwide telecommunications network? b) Does the PSTN only handle telephone traffic? Explain. c) Why are we looking at the PSTN in this chapter?

The Four Elements of the PSTN

Figure 6-1 shows the four technical elements of today's worldwide public switched telephone network: customer premises equipment, access, transport, and signaling.

Customer Premises Equipment

Equipment owned by the customer is called **customer premises equipment**. For some reason, *customer premises* is always written in plural.

Figure 6-1   Elements of the Public Switched Telephone Network (PSTN)

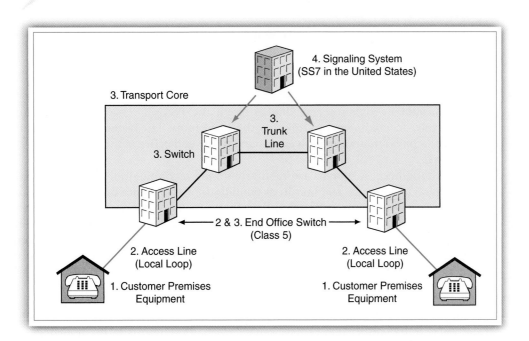

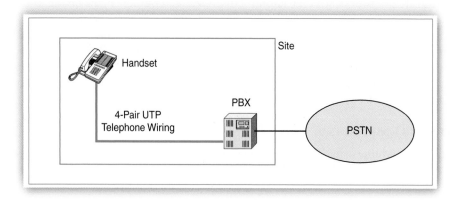

Figure 6-2   Customer Premises Equipment

Figure 6-2 shows that there are three elements to customer premises equipment—the telephone handsets, wiring, and a device called a private branch exchange (PBX).

The PBX is like an internal telephone switch. The PBX routes internal calls between handsets at the site, and it routes calls between the firm and public switched telephone networks.

Business telephone wiring uses 4-pair UTP. In fact, 4-pair UTP was created for business telephone usage and was used for business telephony many years before it was used to carry data. Given UTP's ubiquity in firms, it simply made sense to use 4-pair UTP for LAN data transmission.

Wiring is the most expensive component in customer premises equipment. Fortunately, once wiring is laid—at the cost of several hundred dollars per wall jack—maintenance is usually modest.

Access

The customer needs an **access line** to reach the PSTN's central transport core. Collectively, access lines are known as the **local loop**. The **access system** includes both access lines and **termination equipment** in the **end office** at the edge of the transport core.

Although access systems are relatively simple technologically, they represent a huge capital investment. The hundreds of millions of access lines that run to customer premises cost much more collectively than the trunk lines that run between the internal switches in the transport core. Similarly, there are many more end office switches in the PSTN than there are internal switches. The huge capital investment in today's access system is an impediment both to change and to the entry of new access competitors.

Transport

Transport means transmission—taking voice signals from one subscriber's access line and delivering them to another customer's access line. Internally, the **transport core**

consists of trunk lines and switches. The end office switch is the transition point between the access system and the transport core, and it is a member of both.

While changes in access line technology have been slow, changes in the transport core have been very rapid (at least by telephony's standards). Changing the transport core represents a smaller investment than changing the access system, and changes in the transport core can save carriers a great deal of money.

Signaling

Finally, **signaling** means the controlling of calling, including setting up a path for a conversation through the transport core, maintaining and terminating the conversation path, collecting billing information, and handling other supervisory functions.

In the PSTN, *transport* is the transmission of voice communication. In contrast, *signaling* is the process of supervising voice communication sessions.

TEST YOUR UNDERSTANDING

2. What are the four technical elements in the PSTN?

3. a) What is customer premises equipment? b) What is the purpose of the PBX? c) What type of wiring does business telephony use? d) What is the most expensive part of customer premises equipment to purchase and install?

4. a) What is the local loop? b) What is the function of the transport core? c) What are the two elements of the transport core? d) Which is changing more rapidly—the access system or the transport core? e) Explain why.

5. a) What is signaling? b) In telephony, distinguish between transport and signaling.

Ownership of the PSTN

The public switched telephone network normally works so well that most people do not realize it really is a linked collection of smaller telephone networks owned by different carriers. Generally speaking, these carriers fall into three categories:

➤ Local carriers provide access lines and handle transport within a city or other small area.

➤ Long-distance domestic (within a country) carriers transport traffic between different local areas.

➤ International carriers transport traffic between countries.

To complicate matters, many companies fit into multiple categories, offering two or even three layers of service. We are even beginning to see carriers operating in multiple countries.

In Chapter 1, we saw a similar situation—the organization of the Internet. There are many ISPs. However, they all follow the same technical standards (TCP/IP), and they all connect together at network access points. Similarly, all telephone companies

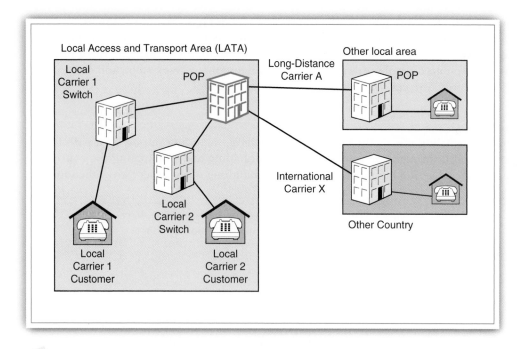

Figure 6-3 Points of Presence (POPs)

follow international standards, and they are all interconnected. In the United States, these interconnection points are called **points of presence (POPs).**

TEST YOUR UNDERSTANDING

6. a) What are the three tiers of carriers in the PSTN? b) What are connection points between carriers called in the PSTN?

CIRCUIT SWITCHING

Circuits

In contrast to the packet-switched networks that we saw in previous chapters, the telephone system has traditionally offered **circuit switching**, in which capacity for a voice conversation is reserved on every switch and trunk line end-to-end between the two subscribers (see Figure 6-4). Although it may be difficult to get a dial tone during natural disasters or on Mother's Day, once a **circuit** (a two-way connection with reserved capacity) is set up, there is no slowing of speech or delay when you talk.

A circuit is a two-way connection with reserved capacity.

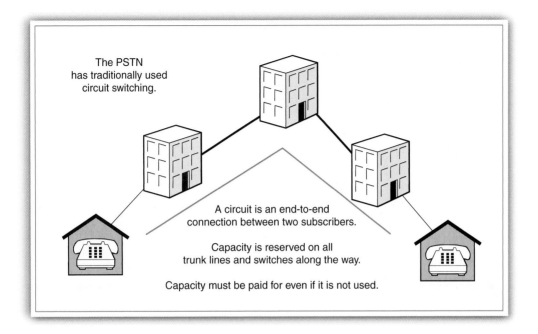

The PSTN
has traditionally used
circuit switching.

A circuit is an end-to-end
connection between two subscribers.

Capacity is reserved on all
trunk lines and switches along the way.

Capacity must be paid for even if it is not used.

Figure 6-4   Circuit Switching

Voice Versus Data Traffic

Circuit switching works well for voice. As Figure 6-5 illustrates, voice traffic is fairly constant. In a conversation, one side or the other is talking most of the time. Usually, about 30 percent of the capacity of each full-duplex (two-way) telephone circuit is actually used. Relatively little reserved capacity is wasted.

In contrast, data traffic is **bursty**, with short, high-speed bursts separated by long silences. For instance, when you are using a website, your request message is very brief. The response message takes a bit longer to transmit, but, particularly on a broadband connection, transmitting the response message only takes a few seconds. After receiving a webpage, you are likely to look at it for 30–60 seconds on average. During this time, no data is transmitted in either direction. Other data applications are similarly bursty. Reserved capacity in circuit switching is extremely wasteful for data transmission, which typically uses only 5 percent of capacity.

Dial-Up Circuits

The PSTN provides two types of circuits. From your personal experience, you probably are only familiar with **dial-up circuits**. When you place a call, the PSTN sets up a circuit. When you finish this call, your circuit is ended, and reserved capacity is released for other circuits. You also know that modem-based data transmission over a dial-up telephone circuit is very slow.

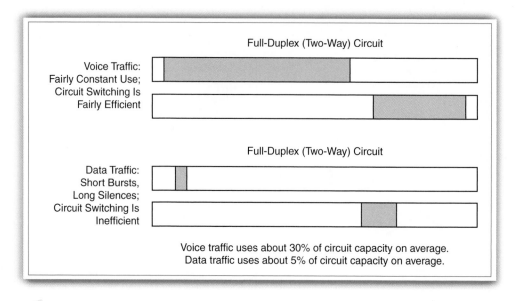

Figure 6-5   Voice and Data Traffic

Leased Line Circuits

Figure 6-6 compares the dial-up circuit with the other type of circuit offered by telephone carriers. This is the **leased line circuit**, also called the **private line circuit**.

Always-on

In contrast to dial-up circuits, a leased line circuit is permanent and **always on**. Once a leased line is provisioned (set up) by the telephone company, it is always available for transmission.

	Dial-Up Circuits	**Leased Line Circuits**
Operation	Dial-up. Separate circuit for each call.	Permanent circuit, always on
Speed for Carrying Data	Up to 56 kbps	56 kbps to gigabit speeds
Number of Voice Calls	One	Several due to multiplexing

Figure 6-6   Dial-Up Circuits Versus Leased Line Circuits

High Data Speed

Leased line circuits also carry data much faster than dial-up circuits. Even the slowest leased line circuits carry data at 56 kbps or 64 kbps. The fastest carry data at several gigabits per second.

Multiplexing Multiple Voice Calls

At home, you use dial-up circuits. In contrast, businesses primarily use leased line circuits. These circuits typically connect a corporate PBX to the nearest end office switch of the public switched telephone network. In doing so, they **multiplex** (mix together on the same line) multiple voice circuits. For instance, the most popular leased line, the T1 line, multiplexes 24 voice circuits. In Chapter 7, we will see how leased lines carry data traffic as well as voice traffic. We saw in Chapter 1 that packet switching uses multiplexing. In contrast, leased line circuits use a less efficient multiplexing method called time division multiplexing. Module B discusses time division multiplexing. In Chapter 7, we will see how these lines can be used to carry data.

TEST YOUR UNDERSTANDING

7. a) What is circuit switching? b) Why does circuit switching make sense for voice communication? c) What does it mean that data transmission is bursty? d) Why is burstiness bad for circuit switching?

8. a) What are the differences between dial-up and leased line circuits? b) What is multiplexing in the context of telephone calls and leased lines?

THE ACCESS SYSTEM

The PSTN's access system is the only part of the PSTN that corporations work with directly. Consequently, we will look at it in the most detail.

The Local Loop

As noted earlier, the local loop, although fairly simple, represents an enormous capital investment and so is very difficult to change. Figure 6-7 shows that three main technologies

Figure 6-7   Local Loop Technologies

Technology	Use	Status
1-Pair Voice-Grade UTP	Residences	Already installed
2-Pair Data-Grade UTP	Businesses for high-speed access lines	Must be pulled to the customer premises (this is expensive)
Optical Fiber	Businesses for high-speed access lines	Must be pulled to the customer premises (this is expensive)

dominate the local loop, although radio-based local loops and fiber to the home (FTTH) for residential customers may also be important in the future.

Single-Pair Voice-Grade UTP

Traditionally, the telephone system has brought a single pair of voice-grade UTP to each subscriber home and office. **One-pair voice-grade** copper has much lower transmission quality than the 4-pair UTP used in LANs.

2-Pair Data-Grade UTP

Even for the slowest leased lines, telephone carriers have to run higher-quality access lines, namely **2-pair data-grade** access lines. Note that two pairs are used—one for communication in each direction. In addition, the wiring is of higher quality than voice-grade UTP. This allows it to carry signals much faster.

Although 2-pair data-grade wiring is very good, the telephone carrier has to pull two new pairs of data-grade wiring UTP to each customer who needs it. The labor to do this is very expensive, and this labor cost translates into high monthly prices. In fact, customers must sign leases for certain periods of time to allow the telephone carrier to recoup its investment. It may also take several weeks to **provision** (install and set up) a 2-pair data-grade UTP access line.

Optical Fiber

For leased lines running faster than about 2 Mbps, the telephone carrier has to pull an even more expensive two-strand optical fiber cord to the customer premises. The cost of running fiber to the customer premises is even higher than the cost of running 2-pair data-grade wiring.

TEST YOUR UNDERSTANDING

9. a) Distinguish between the 4-pair UTP wiring used in Ethernet and the UTP wiring in the residential local loop. b) Distinguish between the UTP wiring in the residential local loop and the UTP wiring used for lower-speed leased lines. c) What technology do the highest-speed leased lines use? d) What is provisioning?

The End Office Switch

The access line runs from the customer premises to the nearest switch of the telephone company. As Figure 6-1 showed, this is called an **end office switch**. It is sometimes called a **Class 5 switch** because the telephone network uses a five-class switch hierarchy, and end office switches are the lowest switches in the hierarchy.

TEST YOUR UNDERSTANDING

10. a) What is an end office switch? b) Why is it called a Class 5 switch?

Analog–Digital Conversion for Analog Local Loops

Analog Voice Signals

In Chapter 3, we saw digital signals. However, traditional telephones produce a different type of signal, an analog signal. Figure 6-8 shows that when a person speaks into a telephone mouthpiece, his or her sound waves (which are pressure waves) cause a

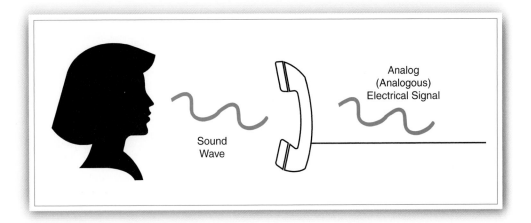

Figure 6-8   Analog Telephone Transmission

diaphragm inside the mouthpiece to vibrate. This generates an analogous electrical disturbance that propagates down the local loop to the nearest switching office. This **analog signal** rises and falls in intensity smoothly, with no clock cycles and no limited numbers of states as in digital signaling.

An analog signal rises and falls in intensity smoothly, with no clock cycles and no limited numbers of states as in digital signaling.

Mostly Digital

As Figure 6-9 shows, the PSTN transport core, which was originally completely analog, is almost entirely digital today. Almost all of its switches are digital, as are almost all of its trunk lines. Large businesses even get digital access lines for their local loop communication.

Codecs: Analog-to-Digital and Digital-to-Analog Conversion

On the local loop that connects residential customers to the nearest end office, the customer's telephone sends and receives analog signals, so the end office switch needs equipment to convert between the analog local loop signals and the digital signals of the end office switch.

Figure 6-10 shows that this termination equipment is called a **codec**. Incoming signals from the subscriber go through an **analog-to-digital conversion (ADC)** process, which is called *coding*. In turn, the codec converts digital signals from the switch into analog signals for subscribers. This is the **digital-to-analog conversion (DAC)** process, which is called decoding. (Hence the name *codec*.)

Leased Lines

Leased lines do not need codecs because they carry digital customer signals. Although this eliminates the need for analog–digital conversion, selecting leased lines

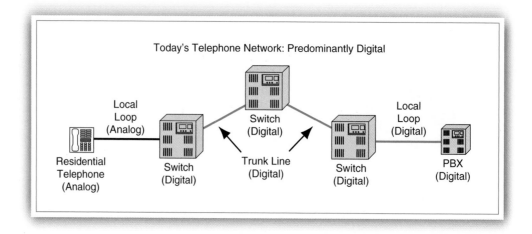

Figure 6-9   The PSTN: Mostly Digital with Analog Local Loops

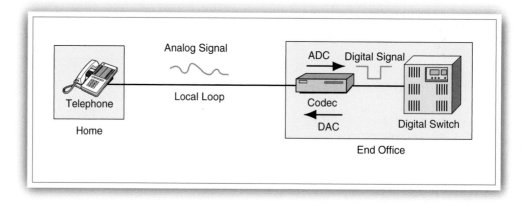

Figure 6-10   Codec at the End Office Switch

is complex because they come in a wide range of speeds, as we will see in the next chapter.

TEST YOUR UNDERSTANDING

11. a) Distinguish between analog and digital signals. b) What parts of the telephone system are largely digital today? c) What parts of the telephone system are largely analog today? d) What is the role of the codec in the end office switch?

Codec Operation

This box looks in more detail at the analog-to-digital and digital-to-analog conversion processes discussed in the chapter text.

ANALOG-TO-DIGITAL CONVERSION

Analog-to-digital conversion is the more complex of the two processes.

ADC Step 1: Bandpass Filtering

Microwave radio was once used heavily for trunk lines. As Figure 6-11 shows, microwave transmission uses **frequency division multiplexing (FDM)**, in which the microwave bandwidth is subdivided into channels, with each carrying a single circuit.

How wide should a microwave channel be? Figure 6-12 shows the frequency spectrum for the human voice. Human hearing can range up to 20 kHz, although for most people, the maximum is substantially lower. Most voice energy, furthermore, comes at frequencies below 4 kHz, so using 20 kHz channels would do fairly little to improve sound quality.

Instead, microwave channel bandwidths were set to 4 kHz. This allowed five times as many voice signals to be carried by a microwave system than a 20 kHz-channel system would have permitted.

To limit voice bandwidth to 4 kHz, termination equipment in the access system passes

Figure 6-11   Frequency Division Multiplexing (FDM) in Microwave Transmission

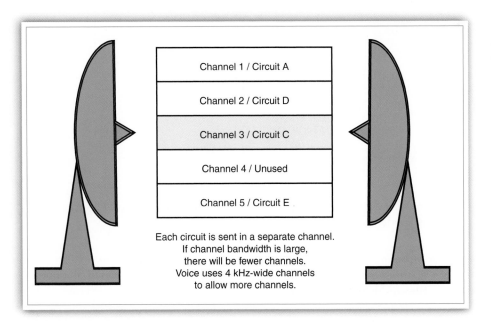

Channel 1 / Circuit A

Channel 2 / Circuit D

Channel 3 / Circuit C

Channel 4 / Unused

Channel 5 / Circuit E

Each circuit is sent in a separate channel.
If channel bandwidth is large,
there will be fewer channels.
Voice uses 4 kHz-wide channels
to allow more channels.

(continued)

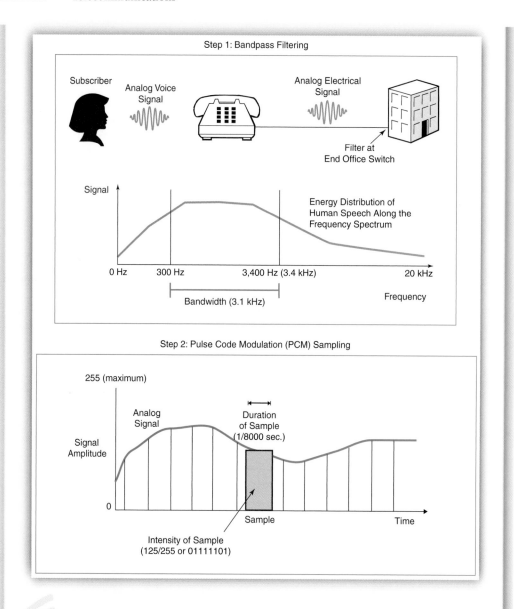

Figure 6-12   Analog-to-Digital Conversion (ADC): Bandpass Filtering and Pulse Code Modulation (PCM)

subscriber incoming signals through a codec only *after* first passing the signals through a **bandpass filter**, which filters out all signals between 300 Hz and about 3.4 kHz. This gives guard bands around the signal—one below 300 Hz and one between 3.4 kHz and 4 kHz.

Although microwave trunk lines are rarely used today, this bandpass filtering continues.

ADC Step 2: Sampling
To digitize voice, the codec ADC **samples** (reads the intensity of) the bandpass-filtered

voice signal 8,000 times per second, as Figure 6-12 illustrates. Nyquist showed that if you sample at twice the highest frequency in the signal, you can reproduce the signal with no loss of information.[1] This is why we need 8,000 samples per second (twice 4,000 Hz after bandpass filtering).

During each sampling period, the codec measures the intensity of the signal. The ADC represents the intensity of each sample by a number between 0 and 255. For instance, a signal of half the maximum intensity would be represented by 127. With 256 possible values, a single octet of binary data is needed to store each sample's value.

If you multiply 8 bits per sample times 8,000 samples per second, you get 64,000 bits per second. In other words, using this analog-to-digital conversion technique, called **pulse code modulation (PCM)**, ADCs produce a data stream of 64 kbps for voice. Consequently, most telephone

lines and equipment are built around 64 kbps channels.[2]

64 kbps Versus 56 kbps

In many cases, the telephone carrier will "steal" 8 kbps from each channel for supervisory signaling, leaving 56 kbps for transmission. This is why the telephone system is built around units of 56 kbps or 64 kbps.

DIGITAL-TO-ANALOG CONVERSION (DAC)

ADCs are used for transmissions from the customer premises to the end office switch. In contrast, digital-to-analog converters (DACs) are for converting transmissions from the digital telephone network's core to signals on the analog local loop (see Figure 6-10).

Figure 6-13 shows that as the DAC reads each sample, it puts a signal on the local loop that has the intensity indicated for that sample.

Figure 6-13   Digital-to-Analog Conversion (DAC)

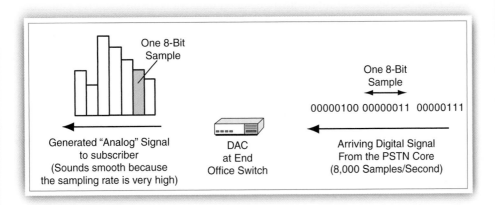

[1]Harry Nyquist, "Certain Topics in Telegraph Transmission Theory," *Trans. AIEE*, Vol. 47 (April 1928), pp. 617–44.
[2]The full PCM process is even more complex, but additional details add only marginally to sound quality.

(continued)

It keeps the intensity the same for 1/8000 of a second. If the time period per intensity level is very brief, the amplitude changes will sound smooth to the human ear.

Is the resultant signal really analog? Precisely speaking, it still is digital. However, to the human ear, the sampling and playback rates are so high that the choppiness of the signal shown in Figure 6-13 is not apparent at all. The final signal *sounds* analog to users, so it is considered to be an analog signal.

TEST YOUR UNDERSTANDING

12. a) Explain why bandpass filtering is done. b) Explain how the ADC generates 64 kbps of data for voice calls when it uses PCM. c) Why do we need DACs? d) How do they work?

CELLULAR TELEPHONY

Cellular Service

Nearly everybody today is familiar with cellular telephony. In most industrialized countries, half or more of all households now have a cellular telephone.[3] Many people now *only* have a cellular telephone.

Today, cellular telephony is used primarily for voice communication. Many users also do text messaging (**texting**), in which they type short messages and send them to other cellular subscribers. Texting is particularly attractive during peak periods, when voice calling rates are higher. Many people text during the day but call after peak hours. Texting has developed a rich shorthand to save thumb movements. For example, *you* has devolved into *U*.

It is also common for cellular subscribers to take pictures on built-in cameras and transmit these pictures to others. With new "3G" technologies, cellular telephony can even be used for moderately high-speed data transmission when a cellphone connects to a computer with a cellular data modem.

Cells

Cells and Cellsites

Figure 6-14 shows that cellular telephony divides a metropolitan service area into smaller geographical areas called **cells**.

The user has a cellular telephone (also called a **cellphone**, mobile phone, or mobile). Near the middle of each cell is a **cellsite**, which contains a **transceiver** (transmitter/receiver) to receive cellphone signals and to send signals out to the cellphone. The cellsite also supervises each cellphone's operation (setting its power level, initiating calls, terminating calls, and so forth).

---

[3]Although cellular telephony was first developed in the United States, the United States has slightly lower market penetration than most other countries. One reason is that normal telephony is inexpensive in the United States, so moving to cellular service is an expensive choice. Another reason is that when someone calls a cellular phone in the United States, the cellular owner pays; in most countries, the caller pays. These two factors increase the relative price of using a cellular phone compared to using a landline phone. A third factor is that U.S. cellular carriers give inadequate coverage, even in large metropolitan areas. In most countries, dropped calls and dead spots are rare.

Mobile Telephone Switching Office (MTSO)

All of the cellsites in a cellular system connect to a **mobile telephone switching office (MTSO)**, which connects cellular customers to one another and to wired telephone users.

The MTSO also controls what happens at each of the cellsites. It determines what to do when people move from one cell to another, including which cellsite should handle a caller when the caller wishes to place a call. (Several cellsites may hear the initial request at different loudness levels; if so, the MTSO selects a service cellsite on the basis of signal loudness—not necessarily on the basis of physical proximity.)

TEST YOUR UNDERSTANDING

13. a) In cellular technology, what is a cell? b) What is a cellsite? c) What are the two functions of the MTSO? d) Trace the path of a call between a cellular subscriber and a wireline (normal telephone) subscriber.

Why Cells?

Why not use just one central transmitter/receiver in the middle of a metropolitan area instead of dividing the area into cells and dealing with the complexity of cellsites?

Channel Reuse

The answer is **channel reuse**. The number of channels permitted by regulators is limited, and subscriber demand is heavy. Cellular telephony uses each channel multiple times, in different cells in the network. This multiplies the effective channel capacity, allowing more subscribers to be served with the limited number of channels available.

Cellular technology is used because it provides channel reuse—the ability to use the same channel in different cells. This allows cellular systems to support more subscribers.

Traditionally, No Channel Reuse in Adjacent Cells

With traditional cellular technologies, such as the GSM technology discussed later, you cannot reuse the same channel in adjacent cells because there will be interference. For instance, in Figure 6-14, suppose you use Channel 47 in Cell A. You cannot use it in Cells B or C. This reduces channel reuse. In general, the number of times you can reuse a channel is only about the number of cells divided by seven. In other words, if you have 20 cells, you can only reuse each channel about 3 (20/7) times.

Channel Reuse in Adjacent Channels with CDMA

Some cellular systems in the United States use a new cellular technology, **code division multiple access (CDMA)**. CDMA is a form of spread spectrum transmission. In contrast to the types of spread spectrum transmission used in 802.11 wireless LANs, which allow only one station to transmit at a time in a channel, CDMA allows multiple stations to transmit at the same time in the same channel. Furthermore, these channels are very wide, so several stations can transmit at the same time.

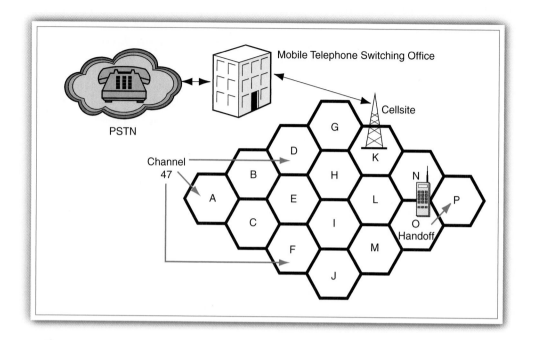

Figure 6-14   Cellular Technology

In addition, CDMA permits stations in adjacent cells to use the same channel without serious interference. In other words, if you have twenty cells, with CDMA, you can reuse each channel twenty times. This allows you to serve far more customers with CDMA than you can with older forms of cellular telephony.

If CDMA is so good, why do only some systems use it? The answer is that it is new. The first CDMA cellular systems were not built until 1993, and even then, they represented a technological and economic risk. However, CDMA has now proven itself, and all future cellular telephone standards will use CDMA.

TEST YOUR UNDERSTANDING

14. a) Why does cellular telephony use cells? b) What is the benefit of channel reuse? c) If I use Channel 3 in a cell, can I reuse that same channel in an adjacent cell with traditional cellular technology? d) Can I reuse Channel 3 in adjacent cells if the cellular system uses CDMA transmission?

Handoffs Versus Roaming

Handoffs

If a subscriber moves from one cell to another within a system, the MTSO will implement a **handoff** from one cellsite to another. For instance, Figure 6-14 shows a handoff from Cell O to Cell P. The cellphone will change its sending and receiving channels during the handoff, but this occurs too rapidly for users to notice.

Roaming

In contrast, if a subscriber leaves a metropolitan cellular system and goes to another city or country, this is called **roaming**. Roaming requires the destination cellular system to be technologically compatible with the subscriber's cellphone. It also requires administration permission from the destination cellular system. Roaming is as much a business and administrative problem as it is a technical problem.

> In cellular telephony, handoffs occur when a subscriber moves between cells in a local cellular system. Roaming occurs when a subscriber moves between cellular systems in different cities or countries.

Handoffs and Roaming in 802.11 WLANs

Recall from Chapter 5 that handoffs and roaming mean the same thing in 802.11 WLANs—moving from one access point to another within the same WLAN. In other words, the terms *handoff* and *roaming* are used differently in cellular telephony and in WLANs.[4]

TEST YOUR UNDERSTANDING

15. Distinguish between handoffs and roaming in cellular telephony.

Cellular Telephone Standards

First-Generation and Second-Generation Cellular Technologies

The **first-generation (1G)** cellular systems that appeared in the 1980s were relatively primitive. For example, they used analog voice signaling. Today's cellular telephone systems use **second-generation (2G)** cellular technology, which uses digital transmission.

GSM Cellular Systems

Nearly the entire world standardized on **GSM (Global System for Mobile communication)** technology for 2G service. This widespread adoption allows roaming across most of the world with a GSM cellphone.

GSM uses 200 kHz channels—much wider than the 30 kHz channels used in most 1G systems. GSM divides each second into many time slots. It assigns these time slots in order to up to eight stations. For instance, one subscriber in the channel gets slot 1, 9, 17, and so forth. This assignment of capacity within channels is time division multiplexing (TDM).

Code Division Multiple Access (CDMA)

In the United States, the Federal Communications Commission decided not to mandate the use of GSM. It decided to let each carrier select the technology it would offer

---

[4]Wouldn't it be nice if there were a networking terminology court that could punish this sort of thing?

to its customers. This decision has been a constant source of chaos in the United States, but it did have one good effect. It let carriers introduce a more advanced form of cellular technology, CDMAone (IS-95), which is much more efficient. The specific technology selected uses 1.25 MHz channels.[5]

"Cells" in Wireless LANs

In a sense, enterprise wireless LANs with many access points are like cellular technologies. They allow you to use the limited number of frequencies available in WLANs many times within a building.

TEST YOUR UNDERSTANDING

16. a) What are the two major cellular telephone standards in use today? b) Which is used through most of the world? c) Which is more efficient?

VOICE OVER IP (VoIP)

Basic Operation

One of the newest areas in telephony is **voice over IP (VoIP)**, which is the transmission of telephone signals over IP internets instead of over circuit-switched networks. VoIP is also called **IP telephony**. Both terms are widely used.

Figure 6-15 shows two clients. One is a client PC with multimedia hardware (a microphone and speakers) and VoIP software. The other is an **IP telephone**, which has the electronics to encode voice for digital transmission and to handle packets over an IP internet. With VoIP, their two users can talk with each other.

In addition, **media gateways** connect IP telephones to ordinary telephones on the public switched telephone network. Media gateways do not simply make connections. They also convert between the signaling (call setup, etc.) formats of the IP telephone system and the PSTN.

Although "VoIP" has traditionally meant *voice* over IP, it is beginning to get a second meaning—**video over IP**. By adding a camera, any multimedia PC can support video over IP. Although the term *video over IP* usually brings to mind videoconferencing, in which people can see their communication partners as well as hear them, video over IP is more likely to involve the downloading of video programs.

TEST YOUR UNDERSTANDING

17. a) What is VoIP? b) What is another name for VoIP? c) What is an IP telephone? d) What is a media gateway? e) What is the second meaning of VoIP?

---

[5]What standard does your cellphone carrier use? For a full list of U.S. and other cellular carriers, go to *www.cellular-news.com/coverage*. Among the U.S. cellular vendors using GSM are Cingular and T-Mobile. CDMA vendors include Sprint PCS, US Cellular, and Verizon.

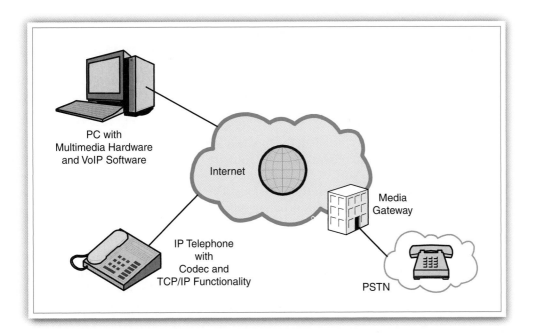

Figure 6-15   Voice over IP (VoIP)

Corporate VoIP Alternatives

When companies plan for VoIP they have two separate issues. One is how to provide VoIP between sites. The other is how to provide VoIP within sites.

VoIP Between Sites

Most companies begin experimenting with VoIP between sites. The reason for this is simple economics. Long-distance telephone calling is expensive, and international telephone calling is much more expensive.

One approach is to place a PBX at each site and get leased lines to connect sites together. Most companies already connect their PBXs at multiple sites with leased lines to reduce the cost of telephone calls without VoIP. The company simply has to add a VoIP module to each PBX. PBX–PBX VoIP is attractive because it does not affect anything inside the sites. The VoIP module in the PBX translates between external and internal telephone signaling.

In addition, many carriers are beginning to offer VoIP services directly to firms. These **carrier VoIP services** typically are not limited to transmissions between the firm's sites. Companies can place any long-distance or international call at attractive prices. Carrier VoIP services are possible because many carriers are replacing their traditional circuit-switched transport cores with IP packet-switched cores designed for VoIP.

VoIP Within Sites

More controversial is using VoIP within sites. In LANs, transmission costs per bit are low, so no major cost savings result from using VoIP within sites. In fact, the cost of installing VoIP within sites would probably raise internal telephony costs. The main benefit of internal VoIP for corporations is the ability to create applications that integrate voice and data. For instance, when a customer calls, information about the customer can be brought up on a salesperson's computer screen before the salesperson answers the phone.

With a LAN already installed, the firm has to purchase IP telephones or upgrade PCs with multimedia equipment and VoIP software. The biggest technical issue is how to handle mobile users. VoIP needs very good quality of service, and wireless LANs create too much latency (delay) in transmissions. The 802.11e standard discussed in the previous chapter may address this problem successfully.

VoIP Carriers

Although corporations can implement VoIP internally, many carriers are beginning to offer VoIP service to both residences and businesses. These include both traditional telephone carriers and new entrants such as cable television companies, Internet service providers, and companies like Skype that provide service over any ISP.

TEST YOUR UNDERSTANDING

18. a) If a company already has a multisite PBX network installed for site-to-site voice service, what must it add for site-to-site VoIP? b) Do many carriers offer VoIP services to business customers? c) Can a company save more money with long-distance VoIP or with VoIP within the company's sites? d) What is the main advantage of internal VoIP? e) Is it easier to implement VoIP on wired LANs or WLANs? f) What carriers provide VoIP service?

Corporate Concerns with VoIP

Although corporations are implementing VoIP widely, they still have some serious concerns about their VoIP systems.

Cost Savings?

The traditional promise of VoIP is that it can save money by sending voice over efficient packet-switched networks rather than over inflexible and inefficient circuit-switched networks. However, VoIP will require upgrades to existing packet-switched networks because voice requires quality-of-service guarantees. This will eliminate at least some potential savings. In addition, the long-distance and international telephone calling rates against which VoIP costs must be compared have been falling very rapidly. Whether VoIP will achieve major cost savings is not entirely clear.

Maintaining Voice Quality and Availability

Corporate telephone staffs are concerned with maintaining voice quality and availability. They have long been able to deliver voice signals of high quality 99.999 percent of the time. IP telephone networks will provide lower quality and significantly lower availability.

TEST YOUR UNDERSTANDING

19. a) Why may VoIP not reduce corporate telephone costs? b) What two concerns do corporate telephone staffs have about VoIP?

VoIP Technology

This section looks at some details of VoIP that are useful in comparing VoIP options.

SPEECH CODECS

As discussed earlier, **speech codecs** convert analog voice signals into digital bit streams. We looked at PCM, which creates 64 kbps data streams with high auditory quality. These codecs follow the G.711 standard. Cellular telephony also uses speech codecs. The GSM codec, for example, produces a 13 kbps data stream (although this data stream requires 22.4 kbps to transmit because of overhead in the transmission protocol). For VoIP, the default codec standard is G.723.1, which sends voice at 5.3 kbps or 6.3 kbps.

As Figure 6-16 shows, several other speech codecs have been defined by the ITU-T. Some speech codecs compress voice more, reducing traffic transmission requirements and, therefore, costs. However, these codecs usually have lower voice quality.[6]

The fact that there are so many speech codecs is good because it gives organizations more options. However, this flexibility can create problems for interoperability unless planning and vendor selection is done carefully.

Figure 6-16   Speech Codecs

Codec	Transmission Rate
G.711	64 kbps
G.721	32 kbps
G.722	48, 56, 64 kbps
G.722.1	24, 32 kbps
G.723	5.33, 6.4 kbps
G.723.1A	5.3, 6.3 kbps
G.726	16, 24, 32, 40 kbps
G.728	16 kbps
G.729AB	8 kbps

TEST YOUR UNDERSTANDING

20. a) What do speech codecs do? b) What is the tradeoff to consider when selecting a speech codec standard for use in a VoIP system? c) What is the drawback of having many speech codecs from which to select?

TRANSPORT

Recall that *transport* means transmission in telephony. Figure 6-17 shows the packet used in VoIP transport. We will look at it piece by piece.

---

[6]Another issue in codec design is latency (delay). In voice communication, a latency of 250 microseconds creates serious problems in turn-taking in conversations. (Note how awkward interactions are between CNN anchors and correspondents halfway around the world.) Some codecs provide very good compression and decent voice quality but have too much latency to be useful over international distances.

(continued)

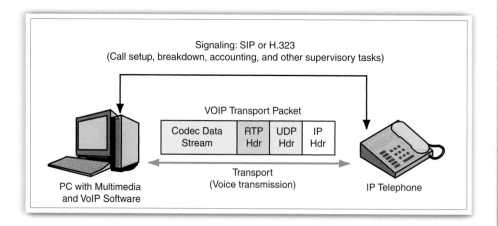

Figure 6-17   VoIP Protocols

TCP Versus UDP

In Chapters 1 and 2, we saw that TCP is widely used at the transport layer. TCP is a reliable protocol, correcting errors at the transport layer and lower layers as well. However, to do this, TCP has to be a heavyweight protocol requiring openings, closings, and ACKs.

In VoIP, it is not feasible to correct errors through retransmission. The delay would completely disrupt the voice stream. Instead, if a packet is lost, the receiver either replays the previous packet's sound or interpolates what the lost packet probably contained based on the data contents of earlier and later packets.

Given the impossibility of error correction, VoIP uses a simpler protocol at the transport layer. This is the User Datagram Protocol (UDP), which we saw in Chapter 2 and which we will see in more detail in Chapter 8. UDP is connectionless and unreliable. UDP messages are called UDP datagrams.

Real Time Protocol (RTP)

Although UDP is a lightweight protocol, it is not perfect for VoIP. It does not guarantee that

packets will arrive in order, and the timing between consecutive UDP datagrams on arrival may be different than it was during transmission. This results in jitter.

Consequently, as Figure 6-17 shows, VoIP adds a **Real Time Protocol (RTP)** header after the UDP header. RTP headers contain sequence numbers to ensure that the UDP datagrams are placed in proper sequence, and they contain time stamps so that jitter can be eliminated. The receiver collects several packets in a section of RAM called the jitter buffer and plays them out with timing dictated by their RTP time stamps.

Payload

The payload (data field) in the packet is a stream of codec data octets.

TEST YOUR UNDERSTANDING

21. a) Draw an IP packet's headers and application message for VoIP transport. b) Why is UDP used instead of TCP at the transport layer in VoIP? c) Why is an RTP header added? d) What is in the data field of the packet?

SIGNALING IN VoIP

RTP is used for the *transport* of voice communication. For *signaling* (supervision), a different protocol is needed. In practice, there are two signaling protocols for VoIP. The **H.323** signaling protocol, which was created by the ITU-T, was popular in earlier systems. Newer systems, while still supporting H.323, also offer the simpler **Session Initiation Protocol (SIP)** created by the IETF.[7] SIP is likely to dominate in the future due to its simplicity and therefore its lower management cost.

TEST YOUR UNDERSTANDING

22. a) What two signaling protocols are used in VoIP? b) Why is SIP likely to be dominant in the future?

---

[7] There is another signaling protocol of note. It does not provide for signaling directly; rather it is a way of *controlling* the components of signaling systems. This standard was developed jointly by the IETF and ITU-T. The IETF calls it MEGACO, while ITU-T calls it H.248. But it is a single standard. H.248/MEGACO permits the centralized management of large IP telephone systems with many signaling elements.

RESIDENTIAL INTERNET ACCESS

In Chapter 7, we will see how wide area network vendors create complex data networks on top of the PSTN. However, in this chapter, we will look at how home users can get Internet access. In the business context, remote workers can get access to the Internet using these techniques when they are at home or on the road.

Telephone Modems

Since the 1970s, people have been using telephone modems to connect to distant computers. Figure 6-19 illustrates a telephone modem connection.

As discussed earlier in this chapter, the telephone system expects analog signals from home subscribers. However, computers generate digital signals. A translation

Figure 6-18   Residential Internet Access Services

Telephone Modems

Asymmetric Digital Subscriber Line (ADSL)

Cable Modem Service

3G Cellular Data Service

WiMAX (802.16d and 802.16e)

Broadband over Power Lines

Fiber to the Home (FTTH)

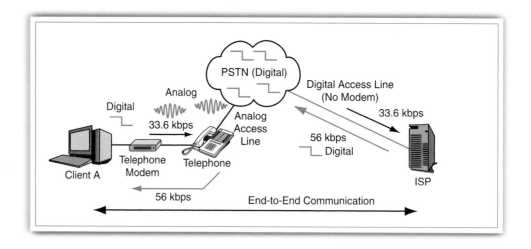

Figure 6-19   Telephone Modem Connection to an ISP

device—the **telephone modem**—is needed to translate between digital computer signals and analog local loop signals.

Note the strangeness here. The modem converts digital computer data into analog signals that travel over the local loop to the end office switch. There, the analog signal is converted back to digital again to travel over the core of the telephone network!

Telephone modems **modulate** digital computer signals—that is, they convert them to analog signals that can travel over the analog local loop. They also **demodulate** (convert from analog to digital) the analog signals coming from the telephone carrier to the customer's digital computer. This is why they are called modems.

Figure 6-20 shows a simple form of modulation called **amplitude modulation**. In this approach, the modem transmits one of two analog signals—a high-amplitude (loud) signal or a low-amplitude (soft) signal. Suppose that the high-amplitude signal represents a 1 and the low-amplitude signal represents a 0. To send 1011 in four successive clock cycles, the modem would transmit loud-soft-loud-loud. Modern modems use more complex forms of modulation. However, such details are hidden from both users and corporate network professionals. (Module B has some of these details.)

As Figure 6-19 illustrates, only one of the two communicating partners—the user—has an analog access line. The modem allows the user to transmit at 33.6 kbps. (The way the codec at the end office switch does analog-to-digital conversion creates this limitation.) The other side—the ISP—must have a digital leased access line to the telephone network. This allows the ISP to transmit at 56 kbps, because there is no codec on digital leased access lines.

One big problem with telephone modems, of course, is their low speed. A telephone modem is suitable for e-mail, but it is painful for World Wide Web applications and for large file transfers.

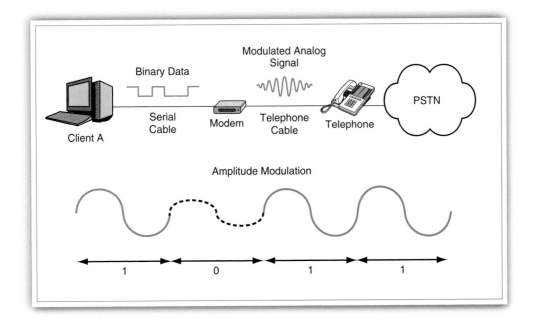

Figure 6-20   Amplitude Modulation

The other big problem with modems is that they tie up your telephone line. If you need to call someone, you must first disconnect from the Internet. If someone calls you, in turn, you may get kicked off your Internet connection. And, of course, members of your family who wish to use the telephone have to wait until you get off.

TEST YOUR UNDERSTANDING

23. a) What is modulation? b) What is demodulation? c) How are 1s and 0s represented in amplitude modulation? d) In telephone modem communication, does the user have a modem at home? e) Does the ISP have a modem at its premises? f) What are the two big problems with telephone modems?

Digital Subscriber Lines (DSLs)

If telephone modems tie up your telephone line and provide only low transmission speed, why not bring a leased line to your home? The answer is that leased lines are extremely expensive because new transmission media have to be pulled to residences. Even for the lowest-speed leased lines, physically installing the required 2-pair data-grade UTP is very expensive. This initial expense leads to extremely high monthly rates—far too high for residential customers.

Instead, what about sending high-speed data over the single pair of voice-grade UTP that already runs to each residential subscriber's premises? This would eliminate the high cost of pulling new cabling.

Until recently, sending high-speed data over these low-quality existing wires was impossible. However, new technologies now allow this. This new technology is called **digital subscriber line (DSL)** transmission because it involves sending digital signals over the residential customer's existing single-pair UTP voice-grade access line.

A digital subscriber line provides digital data signaling over the residential customer's existing single-pair voice-grade UTP access line.

There are several different types of DSL lines.[8] The type designed to go into residential homes is the **asymmetric digital subscriber line (ADSL)**, which offers broadband downstream speeds of up to about 3 Mbps at the time of this writing but limited upstream speeds of up to about 512 kbps. (Actual throughputs will be lower because residential DSL service is not guaranteed.) This asymmetry is fine for World Wide Web access and FTP downloading. For most other services, such as e-mail, upstream speeds are sufficient.

As Figure 6-21 shows, the ADSL customer plugs a splitter into each telephone wall jack. The splitter separates data signals and voice signals. This permits simultaneous voice and data transmission.

At the end office of the telephone company, there is a DSL access multiplexer (DSLAM), which sends voice signals to the ordinary PSTN and sends data to a data network, such as an ATM network.

Although DSL carriers emphasize that the access line to the customer is not shared, multiple ADSL users do share the capacity of the DSLAM and the capacity of the trunk line going from the DSLAM to the Internet. Most ADSL carriers do not install enough capacity in the DSLAM and the trunk line to give all users their maximum speed if user traffic is heavy. Consequently, ADSL subscribers often find their throughput falling during peak usage periods.

Telephone companies are now beginning to install **ADSL2+** equipment in their DSLAMs. ADSL2+ could give download speeds up to 15 Mbps. This would be enough for video transmission. At the time of this writing, vendors have not announced plans for ADSL2+ service.

TEST YOUR UNDERSTANDING

24. a) How do leased lines and DSLs differ in terms of transmission media? b) Describe ADSL speeds. c) Describe the physical components of DSL technology. d) Does ADSL disable your telephone line when you are using the Internet? e) Does sharing affect ADSL speed? f) What download speeds will ADSL2+ make possible?

---

[8]In terms of proper English, *digital subscriber lines* should be *DSLs* rather than *DSL lines*.

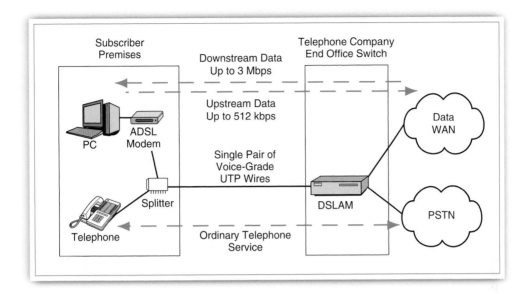

Figure 6-21   Asymmetric Digital Subscriber Line (ADSL)

Cable Modem Service

Telephone companies are not the only carriers that deliver broadband service to households. Cable television operators, besides bringing television into homes, also offer high-speed Internet access, as Figure 6-22 indicates. From the cable television company's operations building, called the head end, optical fiber runs out to neighborhoods with about five hundred households apiece. Within the neighborhood, a standard coaxial television cable comes into the subscriber's house.

The coaxial cable coming into the home plugs into a device called a cable modem. The cable modem has a coaxial cable port plus either an RJ-45 port or a USB port to connect to your PC or access router.

Cable modem speed is shared by all users in a neighborhood, so rated speed is not very descriptive. In practice, cable modem service today normally provides real downstream throughput of about 5 Mbps. In general, individual cable modem throughput is faster than ADSL throughput, but cable modem throughput depends heavily on how many users in the neighborhood are sharing the aggregate capacity at any moment.

TEST YOUR UNDERSTANDING

25. a) Describe the physical components of cable modem technology. b) What is typical cable modem throughput? c) Compare speed reductions in DSL service and cable modem service because of sharing.

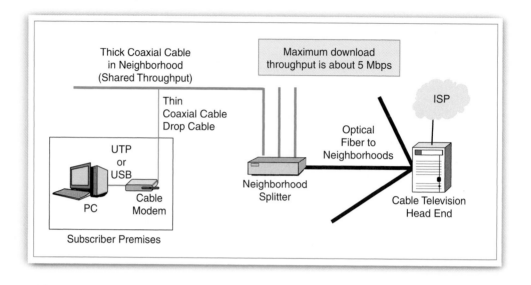

Figure 6-22   Cable Modem Service

3G Cellular Data Service

Another carrier that provides service to residences is third-generation (3G) cellular data service. The GSM and CDMA technologies are capable of transmitting data through special **cellular modems**. However, both services can only transmit data at 10 kbps—far lower than even telephone modem speeds.

However, both GSM and CDMAone's creators are now developing faster **third-generation (3G)** cellular telephone services that are specifically designed to carry data. As Figure 6-23 shows, these services vary widely in speed. In fact, the slowest of these services are sometimes called second-and-a-half generation cellular systems. Not surprisingly, faster services cost more. The slowest of these services provide throughputs equal to those of telephone modems. The fastest provide low ADSL-like speeds.

TEST YOUR UNDERSTANDING

26. Generally, 3G throughputs are comparable to throughputs in what two traditional residential Internet access services?

WiMax (802.16) Service

Although 3G cellular service is now available and is experiencing modest success, it will soon face competition. The IEEE is working on several terrestrial wireless access standards. The most developed is **802.16**, which is widely known as **WiMAX**.

The original WiMAX standard (**802.16d**) was designed to serve fixed customers. It was designed to provide an aggregate speed of 75 Mbps over a distance of up to 50 km (30 miles). Of course, individual customers will only get a fraction of this throughput.

GSM Family

    200 kHz channels have 8 time slots per cycle

    GPRS and EDGE give each user multiple time slots

        GPRS (General Packet Radio Service) can offer a data throughput near that of a telephone modem with typical speeds of about 20–30 kbps

        EDGE (Enhanced Data Rates for GSM Evolution) offers even higher speeds in GSM channels: 80–125 kbps

    Wideband CDMA (W-CDMA) will use CDMA technology

CDMAone Family

    1x means the use of a single 1.25 MHz CDMA channel

    CDMA2000 1x offers speeds of up to 144 kbps

        The effective throughput is about 30–50 kbps

    CDMA2000 1x EV-DO will offer speeds of 300 kbps to about 1 Mbps

        In practice, users typically will get download speeds of about 100–500 kbps

    CDMA2000 3x will use three 1.25 MHz channels to triple throughput

Perspective

    GPRS offers low telephone modem throughput, while EDGE offers very low DSL throughput

    1x offers telephone modem throughput, while 1x EV-DO offers low DSL throughput

Figure 6-23   Third-Generation (3G) Cellular Data Services

Services based on 802.16d will be useful for large corporate customers, 802.11 hot spots, and, eventually, individual homes.

The newer **802.16e** WiMAX standard will extend WiMAX service to mobile users, providing aggregate speeds of 3–16 Mbps. Neither 802.16 nor 802.16e are available now, and service for mobile users will lack the availability of fixed-location service.

TEST YOUR UNDERSTANDING

27. a) Describe the service that 802.16 WiMAX will provide. b) Describe the service that 802.16e WiMAX will provide.

Broadband over Power Lines

Even electrical power companies are exploring the provision of broadband service. **Broadband over power lines** service sends data over existing electrical lines, directly to homes. Experiments have shown that it is technically possible to send data at broadband speeds over power lines. One question is whether data signals traveling down unshielded power lines will interfere with radio equipment.

TEST YOUR UNDERSTANDING

28. Describe broadband over power lines.

Fiber to the Home (FTTH)

For really high speeds, carriers are likely to provide **fiber to the home (FTTH)** technology. This could bring speeds of tens of megabits per second to individual subscribers—enough for services like television on demand.

However, to provide fiber to even a small fraction of all homes and businesses would require an enormous investment in fiber and installation labor. This would lead to high prices. In addition, the entire transport core would have to be upgraded to support the traffic if there were many FTTH users. When FTTH arrives on the market, it is not likely to be cheap.

In addition, several different FTTH services are possible. Strict fiber to the home would bring fiber all the way to the house. Fiber to the curb would only bring fiber to the outside of the house, and it would require using copper to bring data the rest of the way into the home. Fiber to the neighborhood would bring fiber to within about a block of the home, but again, it would require using copper to finish the connection. The more copper is involved, the slower speeds will be but the less expensive the installation will be.

Perspective on Speeds and Prices

In this chapter, we have given speeds and prices that were current at the time the book was written. However, speeds have been increasing over time, while price for a given speed has generally decreased. This has been especially true in the two leading broadband services—DSL and cable modem service.

TEST YOUR UNDERSTANDING

29. a) What is the potential benefit of FTTH? b) What is deterring FTTH's rapid widespread implementation? c) Rank the three types of FTTH in order of increasing speed and cost.

30. What have the trends been in broadband speeds and prices?

CONCLUSION

Synopsis

Telecommunications traffic—voice and video—normally travels over the worldwide telephone network, which is officially called the Public Switched Telephone Network (PSTN). The PSTN has four technological elements:

➤ Customer premises equipment includes the PBX, telephones, and transmission lines in the customer's buildings.

➤ The access system is the way customers connect to the PSTN. The access system is the most expensive part of the PSTN, and it is the only part of the PSTN that corporations see directly. The subscriber access line is called the local loop.

➤ The transport core carries signals between customer access lines across distances ranging from less than a mile to halfway around the world.

➤ Signaling is the way the PSTN sets up connections, breaks down connections, provides billing information to carriers, and handles other supervisory chores.

Almost all data networks use packet switching, but the PSTN uses circuit switching, in which capacity is reserved at the start of a call on all switches and trunk lines along the path (circuit) of the call. Circuit switching is reasonably efficient for voice conversations, in which one side or the other usually is talking. However, it makes little sense for data transmission, which is bursty, with short traffic bursts separated by long silences. Data transmission must pay for reserved capacity even during these long silences.

You personally are most familiar with dial-up circuits, which are set up at the start of a call and broken down afterward. However, most corporations use leased lines, which are circuits that are always on, can multiplex many voice calls, and can carry high-speed data.

The PSTN access system consists of single pairs of voice-grade UTP to residential homes and two pairs of data-grade UTP or an optical fiber cord to businesses for leased lines. These carry customer signals to the PSTN carrier's end office switch. The PSTN is almost entirely digital internally, but residential customers send and receive analog signals, which rise and fall smoothly in intensity over time.

At the end office switch, as the box entitled "Codec Operation" stated, a device called a codec converts residential analog subscriber signals into digital signals that the transport core can carry. This is analog-to-digital conversion (ADC). In ADC, the subscriber's signal is sent through a bandpass filter to filter out all frequencies lower than about 300 Hz and higher than about 3.4 kHz. Pulse code modulation (PCM) samples the bandpass filtered voice signal 8,000 times per second and sends an 8-bit signal for each sample, resulting in a 64 kbps data stream. (This is sometimes 56 kbps because some carriers steal 8 kbps for signaling.) The codec has a digital-to-analog converter (DAC) that reverses the PCM process for telephone systems going to residences.

Cellular networks divide a region into multiple small areas called cells. This arrangement allows the same channel to be used in multiple cells, permitting more subscribers to be served with a limited number of channels. Traditional FDM and TDM cellular systems cannot reuse a channel in adjacent cells, but CDMA systems can, thus allowing more channel reuse. Most current cellular networks are GSM networks, but future cellular technologies will be based on CDMA. Today's cellular systems primarily use second-generation (2G) technologies, which are digital but cannot carry data rapidly.

Today, corporations have separate packet-switched networks for data and circuit-switched networks for voice. However, VoIP (also called IP telephony) promises to integrate all networking via IP transmission over packet-switched networks. Several codecs are available for converting analog voice to digital signals. For transport, these codec data streams are divided into IP packets containing an RTP header, a UDP header, and several bytes of codec data. Signaling technologies include H.323 and the newer and simpler SIP.

For residential Internet access, there now are several alternatives, and options are increasing rapidly. Telephone modems provide very slow access. ADSL lines provide much higher speeds over the same residential telephone wires, and cable modem service provides even higher speeds over cable television systems. New third-generation (3G) cellular telephone systems will allow mobile users to send and receive data at telephone modem and DSL/cable modem speeds. In the future, WiMAX will provide even more wireless access choices. In the more distant future, we can expect fiber to the home, and we will even be able to send data over electrical power lines.

THOUGHT QUESTIONS

1. Beings of the planet Zamco can hear frequencies up to 30 kHz. However, they can only hear two loudness levels—soft and deafening. The Zamconian telephone system uses PCM codecs. a) How many bits per second will a Zamconian telephone call generate? Do your work in Excel and paste your results. b) How many bytes will it take to store an hour of a Zamconian telephone conversation? (Hint: the answers are 60 kbps and 26 MB).

2. In this chapter, you saw how PCM generates 64 kbps of data when it digitizes voice. For music CDs (which store information digitally), a PCM-like algorithm was also used. However, instead of cutting off sounds above 3.4 kHz, music digitization uses a 20 kHz cutoff to capture the higher-pitched sounds of musical instruments. Music digitization also uses 16 bits per sample instead of the 8 bits per sample used by voice to give more precise volume representation. Furthermore, music is presented in stereo, so there are two 20 kHz channels to digitize. Audio CDs were designed to store one hour of digitized music. Compute how big audio CDs need to be. Remember to convert your bit rates into bytes per second, and remember that there are 1,024 bytes in a kilobyte and 1,024 kilobytes in a megabyte. (Hint: The first CD-ROM disks, which were based on audio disk technology, had 550 MB of capacity. You should get a number reasonably close to this.) Present your answer as a spreadsheet. Copy and paste the spreadsheet into your answer page.

3. Another Internet access method is the communication satellite. Unfortunately, launching satellites is extremely expensive, so satellite Internet access service tends to be costly for the speed it provides. Another issue is delay, which causes problems for FTP. Acknowledgements take a long time, so the sender often times out and resends before an acknowledgement arrives. Geosynchronous satellites orbit about 36 km above the earth but appear to be stationary in the sky, so users can employ dish antennas that point in a fixed direction. Low-earth orbit satellites orbit about 500 km above the earth, allowing the use of omnidirectional antennas but requiring high signal length. The speed of light is 300,000,000 meters per second. a) What is the two-way (up then down) latency (time delay) for geosynchronous satellites? b) For low earth orbit satellites?

HANDS-ON EXERCISES

1. How fast is your Internet connection? See for yourself by going to *www.pitstop.com* and *http://reviews.cnet.com/7004-7254_7-0.html*. Both provide a test of your Internet download speed. What was your download speed? What form of Internet access did you use?

GETTING CURRENT

Go to the book website's New Information and Errors pages for this chapter to get new information since this book went to press and to correct any errors in the text.

C h a p t e r   7

Wide Area Networks (WANs)

Learning Objectives

By the end of this chapter, you should be able to discuss:

- Differences between LANs and WANs, including the high cost of WANs per bit transmitted and, consequently, the dominance of low-speed transmission (56 kbps to a few megabits per second) in WAN service.

- The three purposes of WANs: remote individual access, site-to-site corporate networking, and Internet access.

- Leased line networks.

- Public Switched Data Networks (PSDNs): Frame Relay, ATM, and metropolitan area Ethernet.

- Virtual private networks (VPNs) using IPsec and SSL/TLS.

INTRODUCTION

Chapter 6 began to take us beyond the customer premises, to telephone services provided by carriers. It also looked at individual Internet access technologies and services. This chapter looks at carrier services for wide area transmission.

LANs are single networks. Wide area networks (WANs) also are single networks, although very large single networks. Consequently, WANs are governed by physical and data link layer standards, which come from OSI.

WANs and the Telephone Network

Many of these **wide area network (WAN)** services are built on top of the telephone network's technology that we saw in the last chapter. Sometimes, end-user companies lease circuits from the telephone company to carry their internal data. In other cases, WAN carriers lease telephone circuits, add their own switching, and offer data networking services, including management, to end-user corporations.

Wide Area Networks (WANs)
>   Single networks connect different sites
>
>   As single networks, they are governed by physical and data link layer standards
>
>   Standards come from OSI

WANs and the Telephone Network
>   Use the PSTN transport system for transmission
>
>   Add switching and management to create a WAN

WAN Purposes
>   Provide remote access to individuals who are off site
>
>   Link sites within the same corporation
>
>   Provide Internet access

Site-to-Site Transmission Within a Firm
>   Leased line networks
>
>   Public switched data networks (PSDNs)
>
>   Virtual Private Networks (VPNs)

High Costs and Low Speeds
>   High cost per bit transmitted compared to LANs
>
>   Consequently, lower speeds (most commonly 128 kbps to a few megabits per second)

Carriers
>   Beyond their physical premises, companies must use the services of regulated carriers for transmission
>
>   Companies are limited to whatever services the carriers provide
>
>   Prices for carrier services change abruptly and with technological reasons
>
>   Prices and service availability vary from country to country

Figure 7-1   Wide Area Networks (WANs) (Study Figure)

Reasons to Build a WAN

There are three main purposes for WANs.

> ➤ The first is to provide remote access to customers or to individual employees who are working at home or traveling.
>
> ➤ The second is to link two or more sites within the same corporation. Given the large amount of site-to-site communication in most firms, this is the dominant WAN application.
>
> ➤ The third is to provide corporate access to the Internet.

In Chapter 6, we looked at data transmission alternatives for providing remote access to customers or to individual employees who are working at home or traveling. In this chapter, we will look at WAN technologies for site-to-site networking and corporate Internet access. We will see that corporations have three major alternatives for these two needs:

➤ Networks of leased lines.

➤ Public switched data networks (PSDNs).

➤ Virtual private networks (VPNs).

High Costs and Low Speeds

Most LAN users are accustomed to at least 100 Mbps unshared speed to the desktop. In contrast, long-distance communication is much more expensive per bit transmitted, so companies usually content themselves with slower transmission speeds in WANs. Most WAN communication links operate at between 128 kbps and a few megabits per second, and this throughput often is shared by multiple simultaneous users.

Most WAN communication links operate at between 128 kbps and a few megabits per second, and this throughput often is shared by multiple simultaneous users.

Carriers

A company can build its own LANs because these LANs run through the company's own buildings and land. However, you cannot lay wires through your neighbor's yard, and neither can corporations. Transmission beyond the customer premises requires the use of regulated **carriers**.

One shock that companies face when dealing with carriers is pricing. With LAN technology, prices closely follow costs, and prices change gradually as technology matures. However, with carriers, there often is little relationship between prices and costs. For instance, until recently, companies could purchase Frame Relay WAN service confident that it would be less expensive than leased line networking. Recently, however, many carriers abruptly and dramatically raised their Frame Relay prices and slashed their leased line prices. This created chaos in corporate WAN planning.

Another shock is service limitations. Usually, there only a few competing carriers that a firm can use, and these carriers often offer only a few service options. There is nothing like the freedom companies have when they create LANs.

Global companies, furthermore, find that pricing and service options vary widely around the world. Options that are widely available in the United States and Europe often are rare in other parts of the world, and prices almost everywhere are higher than they are in the United States.

TEST YOUR UNDERSTANDING

1. a) How are telephony and wide area networking related? b) What are the three main purposes for WANs? c) Compare LAN and WAN transmission speeds. d) Why are they different? e) What are carriers, and why must they be used? f) How are prices and costs

related in carrier WAN services? g) Does a company have more service options with LANs or WANs? h) Are service options and prices similar around the world?

POINT-TO-POINT LEASED LINE NETWORKS

So far, we have been looking at services for individual Internet access. Now we will begin looking at technologies for building complete corporate WANs. We will start with networks built with leased lines, which we saw briefly in the last chapter. Leased lines provide point-to-point, permanent, always-on, and fast service.

Leased Line Networks for Voice and Data

Private Telephone Networks

Figure 7-2 shows that companies have traditionally used leased lines to connect their PBXs at various sites. This allows any telephone at any site to call any other telephone at any other site. Although leased lines are expensive, this arrangement is almost always much cheaper than using normal dial-up service to place long-distance calls between sites.

Leased Line Data Networks

Figure 7-2 also shows an internal corporate data network using leased lines. If the voice and data parts of the figure seem similar, this reflects the fact that data networking using leased lines is based on the technology used for leased line telephone networks. The main difference is that data networks use routers at each site rather than PBXs.

TEST YOUR UNDERSTANDING

2. Distinguish between the technologies of leased line voice networks and data networks.

Leased Line Network Topologies

Should many or all pairs of sites be connected to each other, or should there be as few connections as possible? How the organization links its sites to one another is the network's topology. Figure 7-3 shows two topological extremes for building leased line networks.

Full Mesh Topology Leased Line Networks

The first is a **full mesh topology**, which provides direct connections between every pair of sites. This provides many redundant paths so that if one site or leased line fails, communication can continue unimpeded.

Unfortunately, as the number of sites increases, the cost of a full mesh grows exponentially. For example, if there are N sites, a pure mesh will require $N*(N-1)/2$ leased lines. So a 5-site pure mesh will require $5*(5-1)/2$ (10) leased lines, a 10-site pure mesh will require 45 leased lines, and a 20-site pure mesh will require 190 leased lines. Full meshes, while reliable, are prohibitively expensive if a company has many sites.

Figure 7-2 Leased Line Networks for Voice and Data

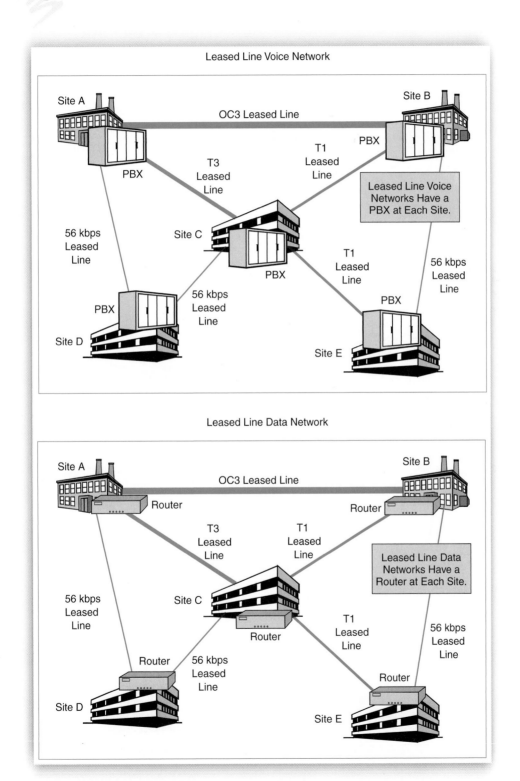

Figure 7-3 Full Mesh and Pure Hub-and-Spoke Topologies for Leased Line Data Networks

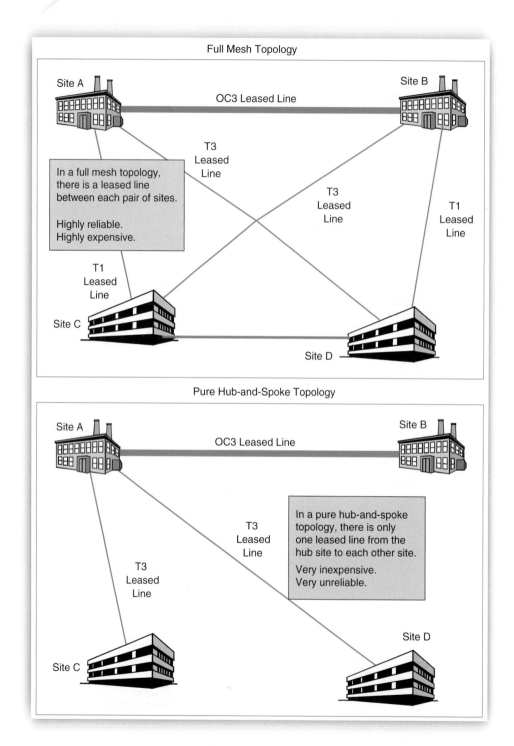

Hub-and-Spoke Leased Line Networks

The second extreme topology for building leased line networks is the **pure hub-and-spoke topology**. This also is illustrated in Figure 7-3. In a pure hub-and-spoke topology, all communication goes through one site. This dramatically reduces the number of leased lines required to connect all sites compared to a full mesh, and so this kind of topology minimizes cost. However, it also reduces reliability. If a line fails, there are no alternative paths for reaching an affected site. More disastrously, if the hub site fails, the entire network goes down.

Mixed Designs

As you might suspect, full meshes and pure hub-and-spoke topologies represent the extremes of cost and reliability. Most real networks use a mix of these two pure topologies. Real networks must trade off reliability against cost.

TEST YOUR UNDERSTANDING

3. a) What is the advantage of a full mesh leased line network? b) What is the disadvantage? c) What is the advantage of a pure hub-and-spoke leased line network? d) What is the disadvantage? e) Do most leased line networks use a full mesh or a pure hub-and-spoke topology?

Leased Line Speeds

Leased line speeds vary from 56 kbps to several gigabits per second. We will now specifically look at the types of leased lines actually offered by telephone carriers.

Figure 7-4 shows that different parts of the world use different standards for leased lines below 50 Mbps. The figure shows lower-speed leased lines in the United States and Europe. There also are differences in other countries.

56 kbps and 64 kbps

The lowest-speed lines in these hierarchies operate at 56 kbps or 64 kbps. This is barely higher than telephone modem speeds, and these leased lines are rarely used today.

T1 and E1 Leased Line

At the next level of the hierarchy, the T1 line in the United States operates at 1.544 Mbps. The comparable European E1 line operates at 2.048 Mbps.

Fractional T1/E1 Leased Lines

The gap between 56 kbps/64 kbps and 1.544 Mbps/2.048 Mbps is large, so many U.S. carriers offer **fractional T1** leased lines operating at 128 kbps, 256 kbps, 384 kbps, 512 kbps, or 768 kbps. These provide intermediate speeds at intermediate prices. Similarly, carriers that offer E1 lines offer fractional lines.

T1/E1 and fractional T1/E1 lines provide speeds in the range of greatest corporate demand for WAN transmission—128 kbps to a few megabits per second. Consequently, T1/E1 and fractional T1/E1 lines are the most widely used leased lines.

T1/E1 and fractional T1/E1 lines are the most widely used leased lines.

North American Digital Hierarchy

Line	Speed	Typical Transmission Medium
56 kbps or 64 kbps	56 kbps or 64 kbps	2-Pair Data-Grade UTP
T1	1.544 Mbps	2-Pair Data-Grade UTP
Fractional T1	128 kbps, 256 kbps, 384 kbps, 512 kbps, 768 kbps	2-Pair Data-Grade UTP
Bonded T1s (multiple T1s acting as a single line)	Small multiples of 1.544 Mbps	2-Pair Data-Grade UTP
T3	44.736 Mbps	Optical Fiber

CEPT Hierarchy

Line	Speed	Typical Transmission Medium
64 kbps	64 kbps	2-Pair Data-Grade UTP
E1	2.048 Mbps	2-Pair Data-Grade UTP
E3	34.368 Mbps	Optical Fiber

SONET/SDH Speeds

Line	Speed (Mbps)	Typical Transmission Medium
OC3/STM1	155.52	Optical Fiber
OC12/STM4	622.08	Optical Fiber
OC48/STM16	2,488.32	Optical Fiber
OC192/STM64	9,953.28	Optical Fiber
OC768/STM256	39,813.12	Optical Fiber

Figure 7-4   Leased Line Speeds

Bonded T1s

Sometimes, a firm needs somewhat more than a single T1 line but does not need the much higher speed of the T3 line (discussed next). Often, a company can **bond** a few T1s to get a few multiples of 1.544 Mbps. This is like link aggregation in Ethernet, which we saw in Chapter 4. Bonding is also done with E1 lines, although this is not shown in the figure.

T3 and E3 Leased Lines

The next level of the hierarchy is the T3[1] line in the United States. It operates at 44.736 Mbps. The comparable E3 line operates at 34.368 Mbps.

SONET/SDH

Beyond T3/E3 lines, the world has nearly standardized on a single technology or, more correctly, on two compatible technologies. These are **SONET (Synchronous**

---

[1]Although there are T2 and E2 standards, they are not offered commercially.

Optical Network) in North America and **SDH (Synchronous Digital Hierarchy)** in Europe. Other parts of the world select one or the other.

Figure 7-4 shows that SONET/SDH speeds are multiples of 51.84 Mbps, which is close to the speed of a T3 line. SONET speeds are given by **OC (optical carrier)** numbers, while SDH speeds are given by **STM (synchronous transfer mode)** numbers.

The slowest offered SONET/SDH speed is 155.52 Mbps. Its speeds range up to several gigabits per second. Note that the SONET speed nearest to 10 Gbps is 9,953.28 Mbps. Ethernet uses this speed for WAN usage so that it can transmit data over physical layer SONET lines.

TEST YOUR UNDERSTANDING

4. a) Below what speed are there different leased line standards in different parts of the world? b) At what speeds do the slowest leased lines run? c) What is the exact speed of a T1 line? d) What are the speeds of comparable leased lines in Europe? e) Why are fractional T1 and E1 speeds desirable? f) List common fractional T1 speeds. g) What are the most widely used leased lines? h) What leased line standards are used above 50 Mbps?

Digital Subscriber Lines (DSLs)

In the last chapter, we saw digital subscriber lines. While leased lines up to T1 and E1 use 2-pair data-grade UTP, DSLs send data over 1-pair voice-grade UTP.

Single-pair voice-grade UTP is attractive for carrying data because these lines are already in place. In contrast, services that use 2-pair data-grade UTP and optical fiber require new wiring or fiber to be pulled to the customer. This is very expensive. Unfortunately, single-pair voice-grade UTP lines were not designed to carry data at high speeds, and not all 1-pair voice grade UTP lines can carry DSL signals.

The last chapter looked at asymmetric digital subscriber lines (ADSL lines), which provide high downstream (from the ISP) speeds but lower upstream (from the PC) speeds. This is fine for residential users, but businesses with site-to-site and Internet access requirements need symmetric high speeds. They also want guaranteed throughput.

HDSL

Fortunately, several business-oriented DSLs are available, as Figure 7-5 indicates. The most popular business DSL is the **high-rate digital subscriber line (HDSL)**. This standard allows symmetric transmission at 768 kbps (approximately half of a T1's speed) in both directions. A newer version, **HDSL2**, transmits at 1.544 Mbps in both directions. Like all DSLs, both use a single voice-grade twisted pair. Businesses find HDSL and HDSL2 attractively priced compared to T1 and fractional T1 lines.

SHDSL

The next step in business DSL is likely to be **SHDSL (super-high-rate DSL)**, which can operate symmetrically over a single voice-grade twisted pair and over a speed range of 384 kbps to 2.3 Mbps. In addition to offering a wide range of speeds and

	HDSL	HDSL2	SHDSL
Uses Existing 1-Pair Voice-Grade UTP Telephone Access Line to Customer Premises?*	Yes	Yes	Yes
Downstream Throughput	768 kbps	1.544 Mbps	384 kbps–2.3 Mbps
Upstream Throughput	768 kbps	1.544 Mbps	384 kbps–2.3 Mbps
Symmetrical Throughput?	Yes	Yes	Yes
Target Market	Businesses	Businesses	Businesses
QoS Throughput Guarantees?	Yes	Yes	Yes

*By definition, ALL DSLs use 1-pair voice-grade UTP residential access lines.

Figure 7-5   Business-Class Symmetric Digital Subscriber Line (DSL) Services

a higher top speed than HDSL2, SHDSL also can operate over somewhat longer distances.

Quality-of-Service (QoS) Guarantees

Generally, there are no hard guarantees for ADSL speeds, which are aimed at the tolerant home market. However, throughputs for HDSL, HDSL2, and SHDSL generally come with strong quality-of-service guarantees because they are sold to businesses, which require predictable service. Meeting these guarantees requires more stringent engineering and management by the carrier and so increases carrier costs. This leads to higher prices for HDSL, HDSL2, and SHDSL.

TEST YOUR UNDERSTANDING

5. a) How do leased lines and DSL lines differ in terms of transmission media? b) Describe HDSL and HDSL2 in terms of speed. c) Describe SHDSL in terms of speed. d) Which DSL services usually offer performance guarantees?

PUBLIC SWITCHED DATA NETWORKS (PSDNs)

Leased Lines in Leased Line Data Networks

Earlier, we looked at two topologies for building leased line data networks—mesh and hub-and-spoke topologies. Both approaches use many leased lines, and these leased lines must span long distances—all the way between sites. This is very expensive. In addition, each country must design and operate its leased line network.

Leased Line Data Networks
    Use many leased lines, which must span long distances between sites

    This is very expensive

    Company must design and operate its leased line network

Public Switched Data Networks
    PSDN carrier does most of the work

    Subscriber only needs a single leased line from each site to the PSDN's nearest point of presence (POP)

    PSDN core network is drawn as a cloud to indicate that subscribers do not have to understand it

Costs
    Carriers benefit from economies of scale in building and managing the large PSDN network

    Consequently, the price to most companies is less than the cost of a network of leased lines

Service Level Agreements (SLAs)
    Guarantees for services

    Throughput, availability, latency, error rate, and other matters

    An SLA might guarantee a latency of no more than 100 milliseconds 99.99 percent of the time

Figure 7-6 Public Switched Data Networks (PSDNs) (Study Figure)

Public Switched Data Network (PSDN) Access Lines

In contrast, Figure 7-7 illustrates a **public switched data network (PSDN)**. Using a PSDN, the user needs only one leased line per site. This leased line only has to run from the site to the PSDN's nearest access point, called a **point of presence (POP)**.[2]

This means that if you have ten sites, you only need ten leased lines. Furthermore, most PSDN carriers have many POPs, so the few leased lines that are needed tend to span only short distances.

The PSDN Cloud

The PSDN's transport core usually is represented as a **cloud**. This reflects the fact that although the PSDN has internal switches and trunk lines, the customer does not have

[2]In Chapter 6, we saw that the term point of presence (POP) is also used in telephony as a place where various carriers interconnect.

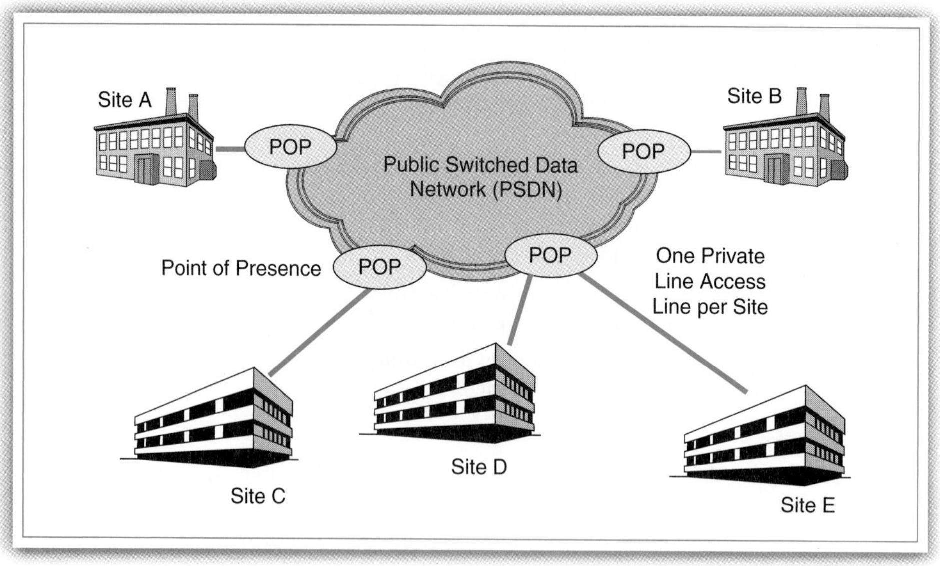

Figure 7-7 Public Switched Data Network (PSDN)

to know how things work inside the PSDN cloud. The PSDN carrier handles almost all of the management work that customers have to do when running their own leased line networks. Customers merely have to send data to and receive data from the PSDN cloud in the correct format. Although PSDN carrier prices reflect their management costs, there are strong **economies of scale** in managing very large PSDNs instead of individual corporate leased line networks. It is cheaper to manage the traffic of many firms than of one firm. There also are very large economies of scale in switching and leased line technologies. These economies of scale allow low PSDN prices compared to the costs of running leased line networks.

OAM&P: Operation, Administration, Maintenance and Provisioning

All carriers must provide OAM&P. This is an acronym for operation, administration, maintenance and provisioning.

➤ Operation is the day-to-day provision of service.

➤ Administration is accounting, billing, and things of this nature.

➤ Maintenance is the work of fixing problems and doing preventative work.

➤ Provisioning is the providing of service to a new customer. This may include taking the order, running wire out to the customer, installing customer premises equipment, configuring the customer premises equipment, turning on the service at the POP, and testing the connection. Provisioning can also involve changing a customer's setup and terminating a customer.

The cost of OAM&P usually is substantially larger than the cost of technology in a PSDN.

Service Level Agreements (SLAs)

Most PSDNs offer **service level agreements (SLAs)**, which are quality-of-service guarantees for throughput, availability, latency, error rate, and other matters. For instance, an SLA may guarantee a latency of no more than 25 milliseconds 99.99 percent of the time. Although SLAs are very nice to have, they add considerably to the price of a service because PSDN vendors need to allocate more resources to the customer to ensure that SLA guarantees are met.

TEST YOUR UNDERSTANDING

6. a) Describe the physical components of PSDN technology. b) Do customers need leased lines if they use PSDNs? c) Compare leased line costs for leased line networks and PSDNs. d) Which usually is less expensive overall—leased line data networks or PSDN transmission? e) Why is the PSDN transport core drawn as a cloud? f) Why do PSDNs tend to cost less than leased line networks? g) For what is OAM&P and abbreviation? h) What is provisioning? i) What things do SLAs guarantee? j) Why would an SLA guarantee maximum latency rather than minimum latency?

Virtual Circuit Operation

Figure 7-8 shows that PSDN switches usually are connected inside the cloud in a mesh topology. In any mesh topology, whether partial or full, there are multiple alternative paths for frames to use to go from a source POP to a destination POP.

Selecting Best Possible Paths Through Meshes

Selecting the best possible path for each frame through a PSDN mesh would be complex and, therefore, expensive. In fact, if the best possible path had to be computed for each frame at each switch along its path, PSDN switches would have to do so much work that they would be prohibitively expensive.

Virtual Circuits

Instead, most PSDNs select the best possible path between two sites *before transmission begins*. The actual transmission will flow along this path, called the **virtual circuit**. As Figure 7-8 shows, the switch merely makes a switching decision based upon the virtual circuit number in the frame's header. This virtual circuit lookup is very fast compared to the work needed to select the best path for each frame.

PSDN Frame Headers Have Virtual Circuit Numbers Rather Than Destination Addresses

Note that PSDNs that use virtual circuits do not have destination addresses in their frame headers. Rather, each frame has a virtual circuit number in its header.

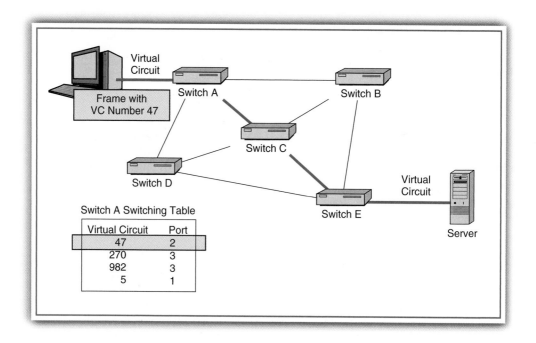

Figure 7-8   Virtual Circuit Operation

TEST YOUR UNDERSTANDING

7. a) Why are virtual circuits used? b) With virtual circuits, on what does a switch base its forwarding decision when a frame arrives? c) Do PSDN frames have destination addresses or virtual circuit numbers in their headers?

FRAME RELAY

The Most Popular PSDN

The most popular PSDN service today is Frame Relay. Frame Relay operates at 56 kbps to about 40 Mbps, with most customers operating well below that top speed. This is consistent with the needs of most corporations—128 kbps to a few megabits per second. Furthermore, when Frame Relay service is compared to networks of leased lines, Frame Relay usually is less expensive.

Components

Figure 7-10 shows the main elements of a Frame Relay network: access devices, access lines, ports at POPs, permanent virtual circuits (PVCs), and management.

The Most Popular PSDN Service Today
>   56 kbps to 40 Mbps. This fits the range of greatest corporate demand for WAN speed
>
>   Usually less expensive than networks of leased lines

Components of a Frame Relay Network (Figure 7-10)
>   Access device: router or Frame Relay Access Device (FRAD) on the customer premises
>
>   CSU/DSU to connect the access device to the leased line also on the customer premises
>
>   Leased access line to the nearest carrier POP
>
>   Port speed at the POP (usually the biggest cost component)
>
>   Virtual circuits between sites (usually the second-biggest cost component)
>
>   Management (FR carriers always provide basic management, can even manage your customer premises devices for extra speed)

In Frame Relay, Virtual Circuit Numbers: DLCIs
>   Data Link Control Indicators (pronounced "DULL-sees")
>
>   Normally 10 bits long

Types of Virtual Circuits
>   Permanent Virtual Circuits (PVCs): Set up once, used for weeks, months, or years
>
>   Switched Virtual Circuits (SVCs): Set up before each connection

Figure 7-9   Frame Relay (Study Figure)

Access Devices

Each user site needs an access device to convert between internal and Frame Relay signaling. This is either a router or a dedicated **Frame Relay Access Device (FRAD)**.

CSU/DSU

The port on the router or FRAD that terminates the leased access line going to the Frame Relay network must have a physical layer device called a **CSU/DSU**. The **CSU (channel service unit)** is designed to protect the telephone network from improper voltages. In turn, the **DSU (data service unit)** formats the data in the way the leased line requires. A CSU/DSU is needed whenever a company sends data over a leased line.

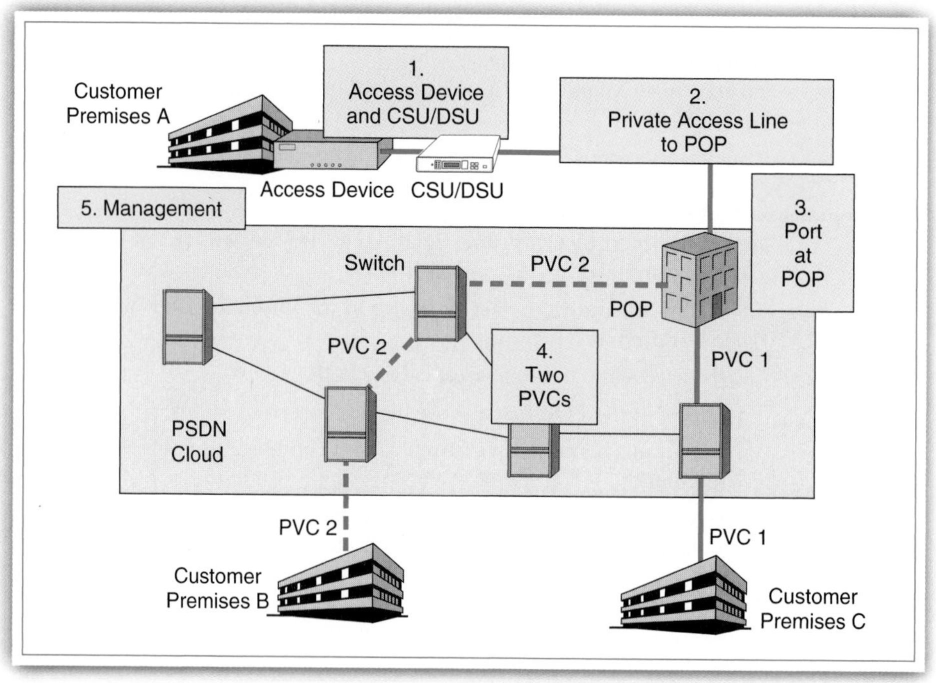

Figure 7-10 Frame Relay Network

Access Lines and Points of Presence (POP)

From the customer premises, the customer needs a leased line to use as an **access line** to the nearest **point of presence (POP)** of the Frame Relay network. The POP is the entry point to the Frame Relay network. If a carrier has many POPs, then access lines will be relatively short and, therefore, relatively inexpensive.

Port Speed

The POP contains a switch that contains multiple ports of different speeds. At the POP, user transmission speed is limited by port speed. To transmit at a particular speed, the user has to select a port speed suitable for his or her transmission needs. As you would suspect, using faster ports costs more. In fact, port speed usually is the most expensive pricing element in Frame Relay service. Selecting a port speed that is sufficient but not extravagant is critical in Frame Relay network design.

Port speed usually is the most expensive pricing element in Frame Relay service.

Virtual Circuits

Between each pair of sites that wish to communicate, there must be a virtual circuit. Collectively, virtual circuit charges usually are the second most expensive element in Frame Relay prices.

Management

Most Frame Relay vendors offer **managed Frame Relay** networks. Although PSDN carriers automatically do internal management, managed Frame Relay services also take on most of the remaining management tasks that customers must still do. They provide traffic reports and actively manage day-to-day traffic to look for and fix problems. They also manage corporate access devices.

TEST YOUR UNDERSTANDING

8. a) List the technical components in a Frame Relay network. b) Briefly explain the purpose of each. c) Which usually is the most expensive component in Frame Relay pricing? d) Which usually is the second most expensive component?

Frame Relay Virtual Circuits

Virtual Circuits and DLCIs

Recall that most PSDNs use virtual circuits. If they do, their frame headers have virtual circuit numbers rather than destination addresses. This virtual circuit number in Frame Relay is the **Data Link Control Identifier** or **DLCI** (pronounced "DULL-see"). A DLCI is 10 bits long.[3] The switch looks up this DLCI in its virtual circuit switching table and sends the frame out the indicated port

Permanent Virtual Circuits (PVCs) and Switched Virtual Circuits

Normally, the virtual circuit between corporate sites is set up once and kept in place for weeks, months, or years at a time. Such virtual circuits are called **permanent virtual circuits (PVCs)**. Many Frame Relay vendors also offer **switched virtual circuits (SVCs)** that are set up just before a call and last only for the duration of the call. SVCs require more carrier work per call and so are more expensive.

TEST YOUR UNDERSTANDING

9. a) What is the name of the Frame Relay virtual circuit number? b) How long is it usually? c) How many virtual circuits does this number of bits allow? d) Distinguish between PVCs and SVCs. e) Which are more expensive?

---

[3]Stations also have true Frame Relay addresses governed by the E.164 standard. These addresses are used to set up virtual circuits. Consequently, if an equipment failure renders a virtual circuit inoperable, a new virtual circuit can be set up using the E.164 addresses.

ASYNCHRONOUS TRANSFER MODE (ATM)

For PSDN service at speeds greater than Frame Relay can provide, corporations can turn to **asynchronous transfer mode (ATM)** service. ATM services reach gigabits per second. They may extend down to 1 Mbps, but most usage will be much faster.

Not a Competitor for Frame Relay

It might seem that Frame Relay and ATM are competitors. In practice, however, almost all carriers offer both Frame Relay and ATM. Carriers recommend Frame Relay for

Figure 7-11   ATM (Study Figure)

For Speeds Greater Than Frame Relay Can Provide
> 1 Mbps up to several gigabits per second

Not a Competitor for Frame Relay
> Most carriers provide both FR and ATM

> May even interconnect the two services

Designed to Run over SONET/SDH

Cell Switching
> Most frames have variable length

> All ATM frames, called cells, are 53 octets long

>> 5 octets of header

>> 48 octets of data (payload)

> Using fixed-length frames is called cell switching

> Short length minimizes latency (delay) at each switch

ATM Has Strong Quality of Service (QoS) Guarantees for Voice Traffic
> Not surprising because ATM was created for the PSTN's transport core

> For pure data transmission, ATM does not provide QoS guarantees

Manageability, Complexity, and Cost
> Very strong management tools for large networks (designed for the PSTN)

> Too complex and expensive for most firms

ATM's Future?
> May flourish after firms outgrow Frame Relay speeds

> However, metropolitan area Ethernet should be a strong competitor

customers with lower-speed needs and ATM for customers with higher-speed needs. In fact, some vendors have interconnected ATM and Frame Relay networks so that customers can connect low-speed sites with Frame Relay and high-speed sites with ATM.

Designed for SONET/SDH

ATM was designed to run over SONET/SDH at the physical layer. Although ATM can run over other physical layer technologies, SONET/SDH supports the high speeds that are ATM's forte.

Cell Switching

Most network protocols have variable-length data fields. This gives flexibility, but switches must do a number of calculations when dealing with variable-length frames. This adds to the work a switch must do and, therefore, its cost. It also creates a bit of latency at each switch.

Short, Fixed-Length Cells to Reduce Switch Costs and Latency

To reduce switch processing costs and latency, ATM uses short, fixed-length frames. Short fixed-length frames are called **cells**, so ATM is referred to as a **cell-switching** technology.

Short Cells to Reduce Latency

ATM cells are 53 octets long. They consist of a 5-octet header[4] and a 48-octet data field, which ATM calls the **payload**. This makes ATM cells much shorter than typical frames in Frame Relay, Ethernet, or other network protocols. Having short cells reduces latency. Often, switches must process entire frames before sending them back out. Shorter frames can be sent back out more quickly.

ATM Quality-of-Service Guarantees

ATM supports several different classes of service that receive different guarantees. For voice, ATM can set strict limits on latency and jitter (variable in latency). This makes ATM ideal for voice traffic. Data, however, usually are given no guarantees. In fact, the capacity that has to be reserved to give QoS guarantees to voice means that data traffic gets only leftovers. For pure data transmission, ATM's ability to provide QoS guarantees is not a benefit.

Manageability, Complexity, and Cost

ATM was created to become the transport mechanism for the worldwide PSTN. In fact, most long-distance telecommunications companies have already moved at least partway to having ATM transport cores.

The requirement to be able to manage the entire worldwide telephone network required the creation of an extremely sophisticated set of ATM management protocols. This sophistication, of course, results in complexity and high cost. For most firms, ATM is prohibitively expensive.

---

[4]ATM has a two-part hierarchical virtual circuit number consisting of a virtual path identifier (VPI) and a virtual channel identifier (VCI). A specific VPI might be a path to a particular site. VCIs associated with that VPI might represent paths to specific computers at that site.

Market Strengths

As just noted, ATM has become very important in the telephone system's transport core. As corporate demands for WAN speeds increase as a result of growing needs and falling prices, many Frame Relay users may migrate to ATM. However, for speeds higher than Frame Relay can provide, many firms are considering another PSDN, metropolitan area Ethernet.

TEST YOUR UNDERSTANDING

> 10. a) Compare Frame Relay and ATM speed ranges. b) Are Frame Relay and ATM competitors? Explain. c) In ATM, what is a cell? d) How long are ATM headers and payloads? e) Why does ATM use short cells? Explain your answer. f) Compare what ATM has to offer to voice and data service. g) Why does ATM have strong management tools? h) Why is ATM's sophistication good? i) Why is it problematic? j) Why is ATM usage likely to grow in the future?

METROPOLITAN AREA ETHERNET

Metropolitan Area Networking

Ethernet dominates local area networking. However, the newest versions of Ethernet—10 Gbps Ethernet and 40 Gbps Ethernet—are being designed first for WAN use. More specifically, they are being used in **metropolitan area networks (MANs)**, which span single urban areas, including their suburbs. In fact, the 10 Gbps version of Ethernet was developed first for metropolitan area networking, and the 40 Gbps version is also being developed first for metropolitan area networking. **Metropolitan area Ethernet**, also called **metro Ethernet**, is still very new, but it is already beginning to spread rapidly.

E-Line and E-LAN

Metro Ethernet is offered in two forms.

> ➤ **E-line** services provide point-to-point connections, like leased lines.
> ➤ In turn, **e-LAN** services link multiple sites simultaneously.

To the switches at each site, e-LAN service simply looks like a set of additional trunk lines linking the sites.

Attractions of Metropolitan Area Ethernet

Low Cost

Although there are several aspects of metropolitan area Ethernet that are attractive, the most important is its low cost. As it does in LANs, Ethernet's simplicity reduces switching costs in MANs. Overall, metro Ethernet is much cheaper than Frame Relay or ATM for comparable speeds.

High Speeds

In addition, metropolitan area Ethernet offers very high speeds. While Frame Relay offers speeds up to a few tens of megabits per second, metro Ethernet offers speeds up

Metropolitan Area Network (MAN)

> A carrier network limited to a large urban area and its suburbs
>
> Metropolitan area Ethernet (metro Ethernet) is available for this niche
>
> Metro Ethernet is new but is growing very rapidly

Services

> E-Line Service
>
> > Provides point-to-point connections between sites, like leased lines
>
> E-LAN Service
>
> > Links multiple sites simultaneously

Attractions of Metropolitan Area Ethernet

> Low Prices
>
> High Speeds
>
> Familiar Technology for Networking Staff
>
> Rapid Provisioning

Carrier Class Service

> Basic Ethernet standards are insufficient for large wide area networks
>
> Quality of service and management tools: must be developed
>
> The goal: provide carrier class services that are sufficient for customers
>
> 802.3ad standard
>
> > Ethernet in the First Mile
> >
> > Standard for transmitting Ethernet signals over PSTN access lines
> >
> > 1-pair voice-grade UTP, 2-pair data-grade UTP, optical fiber

Figure 7-12   Metropolitan Area Ethernet (Study Figure)

to 10 Gbps at only slightly higher cost and will soon offer 40 Gbps. In addition, transmission speed can be purchased in small increments, so companies order only the transmission capacity they actually need.

Familiar Technology

A third advantage of metropolitan area Ethernet is that firms can use the standard Ethernet interface they already know well instead of having to master Frame Relay, ATM, or other new interfaces. A site only needs an Ethernet switch, not a router.

Rapid Provisioning

Provision is the setting up of service. Once a customer is set up by a metro Ethernet carrier, most carriers can change a customer's setup in a few hours, providing additional speed whenever special circumstances require it.

Carrier Class Service

However, metro Ethernet has not completely developed the quality-of-service and traffic management tools needed to offer true **carrier class service**. Until these tools are finished, corporations will be hesitant to use Ethernet for very large metro networks.

➤ First, metro Ethernet must have much better reliability than LAN versions of Ethernet. This may require the use of a mesh or ring topology.

➤ Second, there must be strong quality-of-service guarantees for voice, not simply priority levels.

➤ Third, there must be management tools to gain central control of large metropolitan LANs.

So far, only one major aspect of metro Ethernet has been standardized. This is the 802.3ad standard for Ethernet in the First Mile. This standard describes how to transmit Ethernet signals over PSTN local loop technologies. These include 1-pair voice-grade UTP, 2-pair data-grade UTP, and optical fiber. The 802.3ad standard specifically describes how to do signaling over these lines.

TEST YOUR UNDERSTANDING

11. a) What is metropolitan area Ethernet? b) Distinguish between e-line and e-LAN service. c) Why is metro Ethernet attractive? d) Why are companies hesitant to create large metro Ethernet MANs?

Carrier IP Networks

Traditional PSDNs—Frame Relay, ATM, and Metro Ethernet—operate at Layer 2. The Internet provides low-cost and universally available service at Layer 3 but has poor security and problems with congestion.

Vendors are now beginning to provide Layer 3 **carrier IP networks** that are based on IP. They effectively are private versions of the Internet. They are closed networks, so adversaries would have a difficult time attacking them. In addition, because these carrier IP networks are provided not by many poorly coordinated ISPs but by a single company, good traffic engineering can provide strong SLA guarantees.

Even companies that wish to stay with their traditional Layer 3 VPNs may find that they cannot. Most PSDN carriers have invested heavily in their carrier IP networks and want their customers to migrate to IP service. In 2005, for instance, Sprint told its customers that they would have to migrate within four years.

TEST YOUR UNDERSTANDING

12. a) Why are carrier IP networks attractive compared to the Internet? b) Compare carrier support for carrier IP networks with their support for traditional Layer 2 PSDN networks.

VIRTUAL PRIVATE NETWORKS (VPNs)

The Attractiveness of Internet Transmission

Most firms already have all of their sites connected to the Internet. The fees paid to ISPs are very attractive per bit transmitted compared to those paid to PSDN vendors. Consequently, companies would like to use the Internet for WAN transmission.

However, the Internet is a nonsecure environment, so corporate transmission over the Internet has to be cryptographically protected. As Figure 7-14 shows, **virtual private networks (VPNs)** use the Internet with added security for data transmission.

Virtual private networks (VPNs) use the Internet with added security for data transmission.

Figure 7-13   Virtual Private Networks (VPNs) (Study Figure)

Virtual Private Networks (VPNs)
Use the Internet with added security for data transmission

The Attractiveness of Internet Transmission
Low cost per bit transmitted
Universal access to communication partners

Management
Self-managed corporate VPNs
VPNs managed by carriers

Types of VPNs (Figure 7-14)
Remote access VPNs to link a remote user to a corporate site
Site-to-site VPNs to link LANs at different sites
Host-to-host VPNs to link pairs of hosts directly

VPN Security Technologies
IPsec for any type of VPN with high security (Figure 7-15)
SSL/TLS for low-cost transmission (Figure 7-16, Figure 7-17)
Browser–server secure transmission
Remote access VPNs

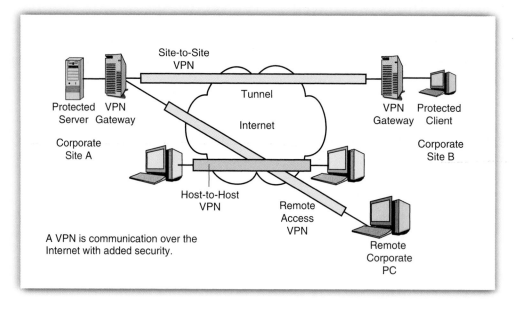

Site-to-Site
VPN

Tunnel

Internet

Protected   VPN
Server   Gateway

VPN   Protected
Gateway   Client

Corporate
Site A

Corporate
Site B

Host-to-Host
VPN

Remote
Access
VPN

Remote
Corporate
PC

A VPN is communication over the
Internet with added security.

Figure 7-14   Virtual Private Networks (VPNs)

VPNs, then, should offer much lower costs than leased line networks or PSDNs, while offering adequate security.

Companies can build their own VPNs by adding equipment at their sites and then actively managing their VPNs. Alternatively, they can get **managed VPNs** from carriers. Carriers install and do active management for these VPNs; essentially, managed VPNs allow companies to outsource their VPNs.

There are three basic types of VPN. Most firms use all three.

➤ Remote Access VPNs connect an individual user to a corporate site.

➤ Site-to-site VPNs connect LANs at different sites. They carry the traffic of many users. Consequently, site-to-site VPNs will eventually dominate VPN usage.

➤ Host-to-Host VPNs are set up directly between two hosts. This allows two employees to communicate securely.

TEST YOUR UNDERSTANDING

13. a) What is a VPN? b) Why are VPNs attractive? c) Why are managed VPNs attractive? d) What is a remote access VPN? e) What are site-to-site VPNs? f) Why are site-to-site VPNs likely to become the largest corporate use for VPNs? g) What are host-to-host VPNs?

IPsec

There are two standards families for virtual VPN security. The most sophisticated VPN technology is a set of standards collectively called **IP security (IPsec).**[5] As its name suggests, IPsec operates at the internet layer. It provides security to all upper layer protocols transparently, protecting everything carried in the IP packet's data field.

Pros and Cons

IPsec offers the strongest security and should eventually dominate remote access VPN transmission, site-to-site VPN transmission, and internal IP transmission as well.

However, IPsec requires clients to have digital certificates. As we will see in Chapter 9, giving each client computer a digital certificate is expensive and difficult to manage.

Transport Mode

Figure 7-15 shows that IPsec has two modes of operation. In **transport mode**, the two computers that are communicating implement IPsec. This gives strong end-to-end security, but it requires IPsec configuration *and* a digital certificate on all machines. For PCs with versions of Windows older than Windows 2000, transport mode also requires an operating system upgrade or the addition of IPsec software.

Tunnel Mode

In contrast, in **tunnel mode**, the IPsec connection extends only between **IPsec gateways** at the two sites. This provides no protection within sites, but the use of tunnel mode IPsec gateways offers simple security. The two hosts do not have to implement IPsec security and, in fact, do not even have to know that IPsec is being used between the IPsec gateways. Most importantly, there is no need to install digital certificates on individual hosts. Only the two IPsec gateways need to have digital certificates.

TEST YOUR UNDERSTANDING

14. a) At what layer does IPsec operate? b) What layers does it protect? c) Describe IPsec tunnel mode. d) What is the main advantage of tunnel mode? e) What is the main disadvantage of tunnel mode? f) Describe IPsec transport mode. g) What is the main advantage of transport mode? h) What is the main disadvantage of transport mode? i) Describe IPsec authentication in transport mode. j) Describe IPsec authentication in tunnel mode. k) Is IPsec used for remote access or site-to-site VPNs?

SSL/TLS

The simplest VPN security standard to implement is **SSL/TLS**. This standard was originally created as **Secure Sockets Layer (SSL)** by Netscape. It was later taken over by the

---

[5] *IPsec* is pronounced "eye-pea-SEK."

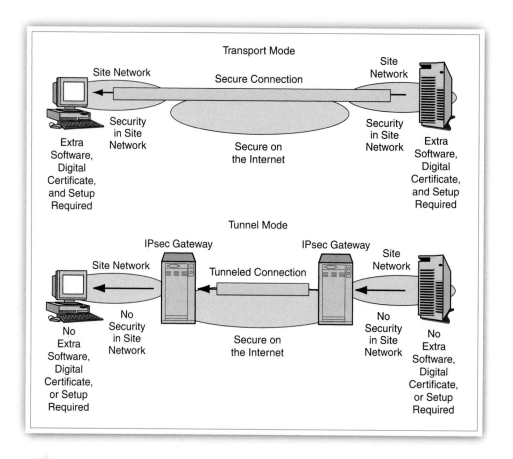

Figure 7-15   IPsec Transport and Tunnel Modes

IETF and renamed **Transport Layer Security (TLS)**. We will call it SSL/TLS because it is still called by both names.

Nontransparent Protection

As Figure 7-16 shows, SSL/TLS provides a secure connection at the transport layer. This protects all applications above it. However, SSL/TLS only protects applications that are **SSL/TLS-aware**—that is, modified to work with SSL/TLS. All browsers and webservers are SSL/TLS-aware. Some e-mail systems also are SSL/TLS-aware. Few other applications are.

Although traditional SSL/TLS is limited to a few applications, many firms need only remote Web access. These firms are likely to use SSL/TLS, which is easy to implement because every browser and webserver application program has SSL/TLS built in.

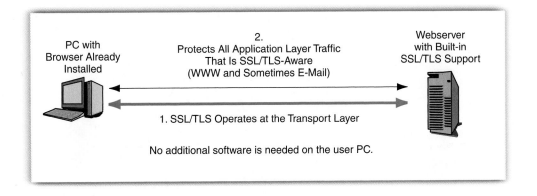

Figure 7-16   SSL/TLS for Browser–Webserver Communication

Authentication Options

In SSL/TLS, one issue is how to authenticate the user—that is, require the user to prove his or her identity. One SSL/TLS option for corporations is to do no authentication for the client; this opens SSL/TLS-based systems to many attacks. Webserver application programs can supplement this SSL/TLS weakness by adding passwords themselves, but password security is not strong.

The other option is for corporations to use a digital certificate for each client. This provides very strong security, but as mentioned earlier, implementing client digital certificates is very difficult.

SSL/TLS Gateways

Initially, SSL/TLS protected direct connections between a client and a webserver. However, as Figure 7-17 shows, several vendors have begun to produce SSL/TLS gateways to let an authenticated user reach any internal webserver to which he or she should have access. It turns SSL/TLS into a true VPN technology. The user has a single SSL/TLS connection—to the SSL/TLS gateway. The gateway provides access to internal webservers.

Although SSL/TLS normally is limited to HTTP, most SSL/TLS gateway vendors are able to "**webify**" some other applications—converting screen images into webpages that browsers can read. This has greatly expanded the ability of remote access users to reach nonweb applications, but not all applications can be webified.

Some gateway vendors even provide add-ins that can be downloaded to browsers. These add-ins provide additional access to internal applications.

TEST YOUR UNDERSTANDING

15. a) How is SSL/TLS limited? b) Why is it attractive? c) Without an SSL/TLS gateway, under what circumstances is SSL/TLS likely to be used? d) When an SSL/TLS gateway is

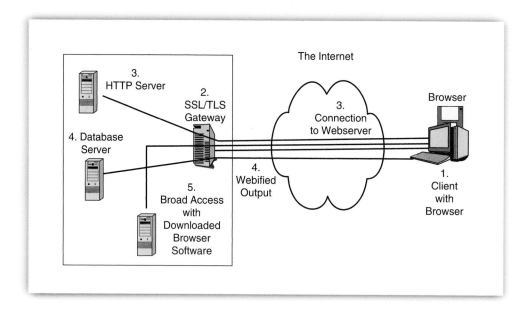

Figure 7-17 SSL/TLS VPN with a Gateway

used, how many SSL/TLS connections does the client have? e) What is webification? f) What is webification's benefit?

16. a) Of the two VPN security technologies in this section, which provides transparent security to higher layers? b) Which tends to require the installation of software on many client PCs? c) Which has the strongest security? d) Which would you use for an intranet that gives employees remote access to a highly sensitive webserver via the Internet? (This is not a trivial question.) Justify your answer.

MARKET PERSPECTIVE

In this chapter, we have covered several WAN technologies. It is important to understand their relative importance in planning for the future. We will look at them one more time in terms of their future importance.

Leased Line Networks

Leased line networks emerged in the 1960s and dominated corporate WAN technology until the 1990s. Since then, leased line sales have stagnated, and leased lines have primarily been an access technology to link sites to PSDN POPs. However, sharp drops in vendor pricing around 2002 created a spurt in the market share of leased lines. For the long term, however, leased lines are likely to be only access line technologies.

Leased Line Networks

    Dominated WAN transmission until the 1990s

    But difficult to set up and expensive to run

    Recent spurt in use because of reduced leased line prices and rising Frame Relay prices

    Needed for access lines in PSDNs and VPNs anyway

Frame Relay

    Grew explosively in the 1990s

    Became very widely used

    FR prices have risen recently in an effort by carriers to increase their profit margins

    Widely used and familiar, but now considered a legacy technology

Metro Ethernet

    Price and speed are very attractive

    Growing very rapidly

    Limited to metropolitan area networking

    Still somewhat immature technically

Carrier IP Networks

    PSDN vendors are beginning to offer IP service to their customers

    Essentially, private Internets

    Provide better security and congestion control than the Internet

    Most vendors want their customers to transition to IP offerings

    Sprint will force this change by 2009

Virtual Private Networks (VPNs)

    IP is an attractive technology base for everything

    Internet transmission is relatively inexpensive

    Security and performance issues can be addressed

    Growing rapidly

    Dominates planning for the future in most firms

Figure 7-18   Market Perspective (Study Figure)

Frame Relay

PSDNs have been around since the 1970s, but they really came into their own in the 1990s when Frame Relay began to grow explosively. Frame Relay was ideal because it allowed companies to get wide area network service without investing extensively in

WAN technology or WAN expertise. Routers, dedicated Frame Relay Access Devices, CSU/DSUs, and leased lines were all that companies needed. For an additional fee, Frame Relay vendors would even provide and manage them actively.

Frame Relay prices were very low, but this resulted in low profit margins for carriers. Around 2002, many carriers simultaneously raised Frame Relay prices and dropped leased line prices. Although pricing may change again, Frame Relay is now viewed as a legacy technology rather than as a technology for the future.

Metropolitan Area Ethernet

Many corporations have strong needs for metropolitan area transmission. Although metro Ethernet is still immature, its low costs and high speeds have already brought high market growth.

Virtual Private Networks (VPNs)

Most corporations now believe that IP transmission over the Internet via VPNs is the wave of the future. IP is an attractive technology, and the Internet offers very attractive pricing and adequate security with proper technology.

TEST YOUR UNDERSTANDING

17. a) Which technologies that we saw in this chapter should be considered as legacy technologies that are not likely to see rapid growth in the future and that may actually see decline?
    b) Which technologies are growing rapidly?

CONCLUSION

Synopsis

Corporations build wide area networks (WANs) for individual remote access, site-to-site transmission, and Internet access. Among the technologies they use are telephone modems for low speeds, networks of leased lines, public switched data networks (PSDNs), metropolitan area radio transmission (rarely), and virtual private networks (VPNs).

Your personal experience probably has been limited primarily to LAN transmission, where cheap transmission leads to high speeds. You must adjust your thinking for wide area networks (WANs), where long distances make the price per transmitted bit very high, which in turn leads to companies limiting themselves primarily to low speeds—most typically between 128 kbps and a few megabits per second. Although faster transmission systems exist, 128 kbps to a few megabits per second is the range of greatest corporate demand.

For site-to-site networking, companies have traditionally turned to networks of leased lines. They did this first for telephone services, using leased lines to connect PBXs at different sites. For data networking, they replaced the PBXs with routers. Most leased line networks mix the characteristics of full mesh topologies, which are reliable but expensive, and pure hub-and-spoke topologies, which are inexpensive but have many single points of failure.

Companies that use leased lines typically use 56 kbps/64 kbps leased lines, T1/E1 leased lines operating at 1.5 Mbps to 2 Mbps, and fractional leased lines below T1/E1 speeds. However, if they have some connections that require much higher speeds, they can use T3/E3 lines operating at roughly 30 Mbps to 50 Mbps, or SONET/SDH lines operating at 156 Mbps to several gigabits per second. In addition, many firms use HDSL, HDSL2, or SHDSL. These are digital subscriber line services, but they offer high symmetrical speeds and throughput guarantees.

With public switched data networks (PSDNs), the PSDN carrier does most of the transmission and management work. Companies merely need access devices (typically routers) at their sites and a single leased line from each site to the PSDN carrier's nearest point of presence. Frame Relay provides speeds of 56 kbps to 40 Mbps, with most corporations using the lower end of this range.

ATM offers speeds of 1 Mbps to several gigabits per second, with low-megabit speeds being fairly uncommon. For voice traffic, ATM offers stringent latency and jitter control, but it offers no special QoS SLA guarantees for data traffic. In addition, ATM is extremely expensive.

Both Frame Relay and ATM use virtual circuits to simplify the operation of switches and, therefore, minimize switching costs. Switches base forwarding decisions on virtual circuit numbers rather than on destination addresses.

Metropolitan area Ethernet, which extends Ethernet beyond the corporate borders for transmission within an urban area, is very new. It offers the potential to slash transmission costs compared to ATM. However, it may not thrive until quality-of-service standards and general management standards are created to allow Ethernet to work in the large but highly price-sensitive world of WAN transmission.

An option for both remote access and site-to-site networking is the virtual private network (VPN), which uses the Internet to lower transmission costs but adds security to protect sensitive conversations. For remote access, SSL/TLS VPNs can work if the company is primarily using Web-based services, although SSL/TLS gateways have recently extended the number of applications that can use SSL/TLS. Every browser already has the ability to work with SSL/TLS. The IPsec standard offers much better security than SSL/TLS and so should eventually dominate for both remote access and site-to-site transmission. However, IPsec in transport mode requires that digital certificates be provided to all clients, and this is expensive.

THOUGHT QUESTION

Several Internet access systems are asymmetric, with higher downstream speeds than upstream speeds. a) Is this good for client PC access to webservers? Explain. b) Does it matter for client access to e-mail servers? c) Is it good for a file server? Explain. d) Is it good for videoconferencing? Explain.

PROJECTS

Getting Current. Go to the book website's New Information and Errors pages for this chapter to get new information since this book went to press and to correct any errors in the text.

Case Study: First Bank of Paradise's Wide Area Networks

INTRODUCTION

The First Bank of Paradise (FBP) is a mid-sized bank that operates primarily within the state of Hawai'i, although it has one affiliate office on Da Kine Island in the South Pacific.

FBP is a mid-sized bank, but it is not a small company. The bank has annual revenues of $4 billion. It has 50 branches and 350 ATMs. It has more than 500 switches, 400 routers, 2,000 desktop and notebook PCs, 200 Windows servers, 30 Unix servers, and 10 obsolete Novell NetWare file servers. Its information systems staff has 150 employees.

ORGANIZATIONAL UNITS

Major Facilities

Figure 7a-1 shows that FBP has three major facilities, all located on the island of Oah'u.

> ➤ **Headquarters** is a downtown office building that houses the administrative staff.
> ➤ **Operations** is a building in an industrial area that houses the bank's mainframe operations and other back-office technical functions. It also has most of the bank's IT staff, including its networking staff.
> ➤ **North Shore** is a backup facility. If Operations fails, North Shore can take over within minutes. North Shore is located in an otherwise agricultural area.

Branches

Although branches are small buildings, they are technologically complex, primarily because the devices there use diverse network protocols. The automated teller

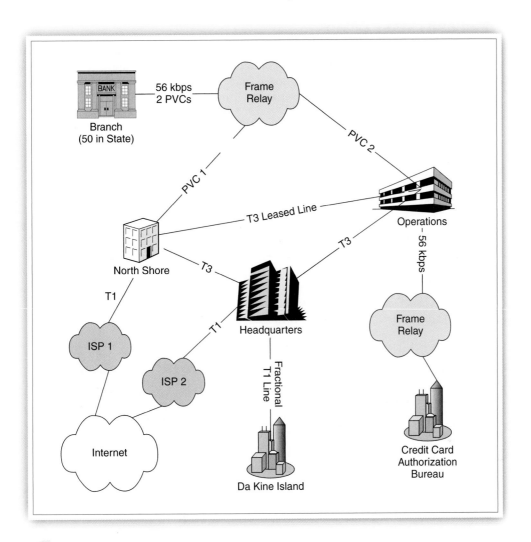

Figure 7a-1   First Bank of Paradise Wide Area Networks

machine at a branch uses SNA protocols to talk with the mainframe computer at Operations. The teller terminals use different SNA protocols to talk to the Operations mainframe. File servers require IPX/SPX communication, and branch offices that need Internet access require TCP/IP.

At each branch, there is a Cisco 2600 router to connect the branch to Operations and North Shore (its backup). This is a multiprotocol router capable of handling the many protocols used at the internet and transport layers in branch office communication.

External Organizations

First Bank of Paradise has to deal with several organizations outside the company. Figure 7a-1 shows only one of these—a connection to a credit card authorization bureau. In fact, FBP deals with more than a dozen outside support vendors, each in a different way. Fortunately, the credit card authorization firm uses TCP/IP, which simplifies matters.

THE FBP WIDE AREA NETWORK (WAN)

Figure 7a-1 shows the complex group of WANs that the bank uses to hold together this geographically dispersed and technologically diverse collection of sites.

T3 Lines

A mesh of T3 lines connects major facilities, as Figure 7a-1 shows. T3 private lines operate at 44.7 Mbps, providing "fat pipes" between these facilities.

Branch Connections

Branches are connected to the major facilities in two ways. Most of the time, they communicate via a Frame Relay network. For each branch, there are two 56 kbps PVCs. One PVC leads to Operations, the other to North Shore.

Da Kine Island Affiliate Branch

For the Da Kine Island affiliate branch, the firm has a 128 kbps fractional T1 digital private line.

Credit Card Service

FBP connects to the credit card processing company using a 56 kbps Frame Relay network connection. This gives adequate speed.

Branch LANs

Branch offices have Ethernet networks. Each branch has a single 48-port 100Base-TX switch connected to the branch's Cisco 2600 border router.

Internet Access

For Internet access, FBP uses two separate ISPs, connecting to each via a T1 private line.

ANTICIPATED CHANGES

Outsourcing

The bank is anticipating two major changes. First, it plans to outsource about 60 percent of its internal operations to a bank processing company in Northridge, California.

Fractional T1 Lines to Branches

Also, in a reversal of past trends, Frame Relay vendors in Hawai'i have been raising their rates in recent years to seek higher profit margins. At the same time, the local telephone company has been dropping its rates on private lines dramatically in response to a strong long-term drop in demand for these circuits. The bank believes that it can bring a 256 kbps fractional T1 connection to each branch economically.

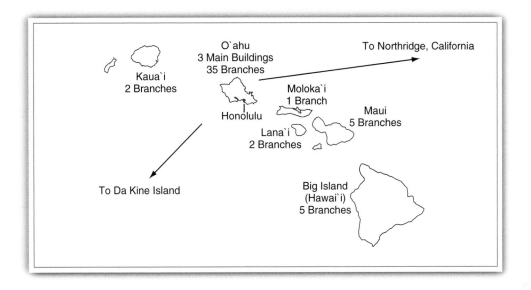

Figure 7a-2   First Bank of Paradise Locations

The bank's main buildings are located on the island of O'ahu. The bank also has 35 branch offices on O'ahu, which is the most populous island. The bank also does business on five "outer islands"—Maui, Kaua'i, Moloka'i, Lana'i, and the Big Island (the Island of Hawai'i). Maui and the Big Island have five branches each. Moloka'i has one branch.

TEST YOUR UNDERSTANDING

1. a) List all examples of redundancy in the FBP network. b) What is the goal of redundancy?
2. a) Why do you think two access points were created instead of one? b) Why are there only two access points to the Internet?

3. Do you think the bank uses the same Frame Relay network to connect its branches as it uses to connect to its credit card processing center?

4. a) Why do you think the bank uses a fractional T1 line to its Da Kine Island branch instead of a full T1 line? b) Instead of a Frame Relay connection?

5. Why do you think the bank uses T3 lines to link its major facilities instead of using ATM?

6. Why do branches need highly capable routers?

DESIGN QUESTIONS

1. What type of connection do you think the bank should have to Northridge, California?
2. Create a rough design for a private line network that would bring a 256 kbps private line to each of the bank's fifty branch offices. Be economical, but ensure that there is redundancy in interisland connections. Assume that connections within an island do not need redundancy because of the high traditional reliability of private lines.

TCP/IP
Internetworking

Learning Objectives

By the end of this chapter, you should be able to discuss:

■ TCP/IP, IP, TCP, and UDP.

■ Hierarchical IP addresses, networks and subnets, border and internal routers, basic router operation, and multiprotocol routing.

■ (In a box) How routers make routing decisions for incoming packets using a routing table.

■ Other important TCP/IP standards, including dynamic routing protocols, the Address Resolution Protocol, MPLS, DNS, ICMP, and DHCP.

■ IPv4 fields and IPv6 fields.

■ TCP fields, session openings and closings, and port numbers.

■ UDP.

■ The differences between IP routers, Layer 3 switches, Layer 4 switches, and application switches (Layer 5 and Layer 7 switches).

INTRODUCTION

In Chapters 4, 5, and 7, we looked at single LANs and WANs. However, most corporations have many networks and must connect them into corporate-wide internets. These corporate internets link clients and servers on different networks across the firm. Then, of course, there is the global Internet, which has revolutionized information exchange around the world. Many of the Internet's thousands of networks are themselves large internets.

Corporate internets link clients and servers on different networks across the firm.

In this chapter, we will look at internetworking using TCP/IP. Although most routers also have to route IPX/SPX, SNA, and other non-IP packets, networking professionals spend most of their time managing TCP/IP internetworking. In Chapter 10, we will look at some additional aspects of TCP/IP internetworking.

TCP/IP RECAP

The TCP/IP Architecture and the IETF

We first looked at TCP/IP in some depth in Chapter 2. Recall from that chapter that the Internet Engineering Task Force (IETF) sets TCP/IP standards. TCP/IP is an architecture for setting individual standards. Figure 8-1 shows a few of the standards the IETF has created within this architecture. Some of the standards are shaded in this figure. These are the standards we will look at in this chapter.

Simple IP at the Internet Layer

Recall also from Chapter 2 that internetworking operates at two layers. The internet layer moves packets from the source host to the destination host across a series of routers. Figure 8-1 shows that the primary standard at the internet layer is the Internet Protocol (IP). Figure 8-2 shows that IP is a simple (connectionless and unreliable) standard. This simplicity minimizes the work that each router has to do along the way, thereby minimizing routing costs.

Reliable Heavyweight TCP at the Transport Layer

In turn, TCP at the transport layer corrects any errors at the internet layer and lower layers as well. As we saw in Chapter 2, when the transport process on a destination host receives a TCP supervisory or data segment, it sends back an acknowledgement. If the transport process on the source host does not receive an acknowledgement for a TCP segment, it resends the segment. TCP is both connection-oriented and reliable, making it a heavyweight protocol. However, the work of implementing TCP only occurs on

Figure 8-1   Major TCP/IP Standards

5 Application	User Applications			Supervisory Applications		
	HTTP	SMTP	Many Others	DNS	Routing Protocols	Many Others
4 Transport	TCP			UDP		
3 Internet	IP			ICMP	MPLS	ARP
2 Data Link	None: Use OSI Standards					
1 Physical	None: Use OSI Standards					

Note: Shaded protocols are discussed in this chapter.

Protocol	Layer	Connection-Oriented/ Connectionless	Reliable/ Unreliable	Lightweight/ Heavyweight
TCP	4 (Transport)	Connection-oriented	Reliable	Heavyweight
UDP	4 (Transport)	Connectionless	Unreliable	Lightweight
IP	3 (Internet)	Connectionless	Unreliable	Lightweight

Figure 8-2   IP, TCP, and UDP

the source and destination hosts, not on the many routers between them. This keeps the cost of reliability manageable.

Unreliable Lightweight UDP at the Transport Layer

In Chapters 2 and 6, we saw that TCP/IP offers an alternative to heavyweight TCP at the transport layer. This is the User Datagram Protocol (UDP). Like IP, UDP is a simple (connectionless and unreliable) and lightweight protocol.

TEST YOUR UNDERSTANDING

1. a) Compare TCP and IP along the dimensions in Figure 8-2. b) Compare TCP and UDP along the dimensions in Figure 8-2.

IP ROUTING

In this section, we will look at how routers make decisions about forwarding packets—in other words, how a router decides which interface to use to send an arriving packet back out to get it closer to its destination. (In routers, ports are called **interfaces**.) This forwarding process is called **routing**. Router forwarding decisions are much more complex than the Ethernet switching decisions we saw in Chapters 1 and 4. As a consequence of this complexity, routers do more work per arriving packet than switches do per arriving frame. Consequently, routers are more expensive than switches for a given level of traffic. A widely quoted network adage reflects this cost difference: "Switch where you can; route where you must."

When routers forward incoming packets closer to their destination hosts, this is called routing.

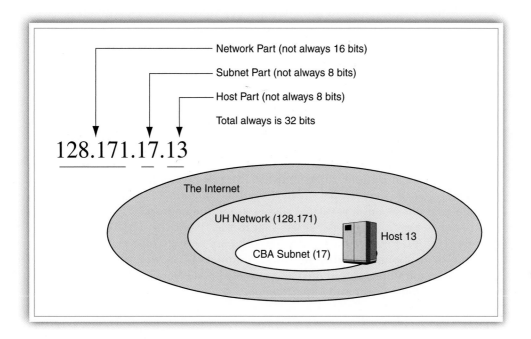

Figure 8-3   Hierarchical IP Address

Hierarchical IP Addressing

To understand the routing of IP packets, it is necessary to understand IP addresses. In Chapter 1, we saw that IP addresses are 32 bits long. However, IP addresses are not simple 32-bit strings.

Hierarchical Addressing

As Figure 8-3 shows, IP addresses are **hierarchical**. They usually consist of three parts that locate a host in progressively smaller parts of the Internet. These are the network, subnet, and host parts. We will see later in this chapter that hierarchical IP addressing simplifies routing tables.

Network Part

First, every IP address has a **network part**, which identifies the host's network on the Internet. **Internet networks** are owned by single organizations, such as corporations, universities, and ISPs. In the IP address shown in Figure 8-3, the network part is 128.171. It is 16 bits long. This happens to be the network part for the University of Hawai'i Network on the Internet. All host IP addresses within this network begin with 128.171. Different organizations have different network parts that range from 8 to 24 bits in length.

Note that "network" in this context does not mean a single network—a single LAN or WAN. The University of Hawai'i Network itself consists of many single networks and routers at multiple locations around the state. In IP addressing, *network* is an organizational concept—a group of hosts, single networks, and routers owned by a single organization.

> In IP addressing, *network* is an organizational concept—a group of hosts, single networks, and routers owned by a single organization.

Subnet Part

Most large organizations further divide their networks into smaller units called **subnets**. After the network part in an IP address come the bits of the **subnet part**. The subnet part bits specify a particular subnet within the network.

For instance, Figure 8-3 shows that in the IP address 128.171.17.13, the first 16 bits (128.171) correspond to the network part, and the next eight bits (17) correspond to a subnet on this network. (Subnet 17 is the College of Business Administration subnet within the University of Hawai'i Network.) All host IP addresses within this subnet begin with 128.171.17.

Host Part

The remaining bits in the 32-bit IP address identify a particular host on the subnet. In Figure 8-3, the **host part** is 13. This corresponds to a particular host, 128.171.17.13, on the College of Business Administration subnet of the University of Hawai'i Network.

Variable Part Lengths

In the example presented in Figure 8-3, the network part is 16 bits long, the subnet part is 8 bits long, and the host part is 8 bits long. This is only an example. In general, network parts, subnet parts, and host parts vary in length. For instance, if you see the IP address 60.47.7.23, you may have an 8-bit network part of 60, an 8-bit subnet part of 47, and a 16-bit host part of 7.23. In fact, parts may not even break conveniently at 8-bit boundaries. The only thing you can tell when looking at an IP address by itself is that it is 32 bits long.

Routers, Networks, and Subnets

Border Routers Connect Different Networks

As Figure 8-4 illustrates, networks and subnets are very important in router operation. Here we see a simple site internet. The figure shows that a **border router's** main job is to connect different networks. This border router connects the 192.168.x.x network within the firm to the 60.x.x.x network of the firm's Internet service provider.

> A border router's main job is to connect different networks.

Internal Routers Connect Different Subnets

The site network also has an **internal router**. An internal router, as Figure 8-4 demonstrates, connects different subnets within a firm—in this case, the 192.168.1.x,

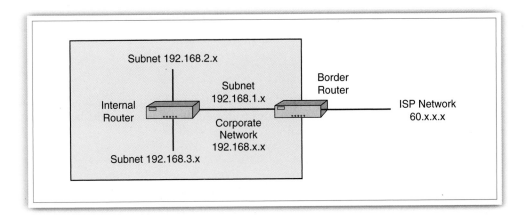

Figure 8-4   Border Router, Internal Router, Networks, and Subnets

192.168.2.x, and 192.168.3.x subnets. Many sites have multiple internal routers to link the site's subnets.

An internal router only connects different subnets within a firm.

TEST YOUR UNDERSTANDING

2. a) What is routing? b) What are the three parts of an IP address? c) How long is each part? d) What is the total length of an IP address? e) Connecting different networks is the main job of what type of router? f) What type of router only connects different subnets?

Network and Subnet Masks

When you look at a 32-bit IP address, how can you tell the sizes of the network, subnet, and host parts? As discussed in Module A, IP addresses were once handed out in ways that would let you look at the first few bits and be able to tell the size of the IP address' network part, but that process has not been used for some time. Furthermore, even when that process was used, it would not tell you how many bits were in an IP address' subnet part and host parts.

Masks Are Binary

To allow the sizes of network and subnet parts to be communicated, the IETF uses a process called masking. A **mask** is a 32-bit string of 1s and 0s. The mask has a certain number of initial 1s. The remaining bits are 0s.

A mask is a 32-bit string of 1s and 0s. The mask has a certain number of initial 1s. The remaining bits are 0.

Masks in Dotted Decimal Notation

Masks are sometimes written in dotted decimal notation. Eight ones is 255 in decimal, and 8 zeros is 0. So a mask with 16 ones followed by 16 zeros would be written as 255.255.0.0 in dotted decimal notation.

Masks in Prefix Notation

There also is a **prefix notation** for describing masks, based on the number of initial 1s. A mask with sixteen 1s followed by sixteen 0s would be designated as /16 in prefix notation.

Network Mask

The first type of mask created by the IETF was the **network mask**, in which there are 1s in the bits of the network part and 0s for all subsequent bits. If you are told that a network's mask is 255.255.0.0 and that an IP address is 128.171.17.13, you know that there are sixteen bits in the network part. Consequently, the network part is 128.171. Or, if you are told that 127.171.17.13 /16 is an IP address and its network mask, you know the same thing.

In network masks, the initial 1s correspond to the network part.

Subnet Mask

Subnets were created after the Internet and network masks had been in use for some time. The IETF finally decided to create **subnet masks** that had 1s in both the network and subnet parts, followed by 0s in the host part. So if you have an IP address 128.171.17.13 with a subnet mask of 255.255.255.0, you know that the combined network and subnet parts are 128.171.17 (24 bits). Therefore, the host part must be 8 bits long. However, you do not know individually the sizes of the network and subnet parts. Their total length is 24 bits, but this could mean 8 bits in the network part and 16 bits in the subnet part, 16 bits in the network part and 8 bits in the subnet part, or several other combinations.

In subnet masks, the initial 1s indicate the combined network and subnet parts.

No Difficulties in Routing

Routers use masks to make routing decisions, as Chapter 8b discusses. To do its work, the router never needs to know whether a mask is a network part or a subnet part, so the inability to separate network and subnet parts in subnet masks causes no difficulties in routing.

TEST YOUR UNDERSTANDING

3. a) How many bits are there in a mask? b) List the bits in the mask 255.255.255.0.
   c) What are the bits in the mask /14? d) If /14 is the network mask, how many bits are
   there in the network part? e) If /14 is the network mask, how many bits are there in the
   subnet and host parts? f) If /14 is the subnet mask, how many bits are there in the network
   part? g) If /14 is the subnet mask, how many bits are there in the subnet part? h) If /14 is
   the subnet mask, how many bits are there in the host part?

Multiprotocol Routing

We have been focusing on IP routing. In the real world, of course, most routers must
be **multiprotocol routers** that can handle not only TCP/IP internetworking protocols,
but also internetworking protocols from IPX/SPX, SNA, and other standards architectures, as Figure 8-5 shows. As noted earlier, we will look only at TCP/IP routing in
this chapter. However, multiply the complexity of the next section by a factor of three
to five to understand the complexity of real-world routing (and another reason why
routers are much more expensive than switches).

Figure 8-5   Multiprotocol Routing

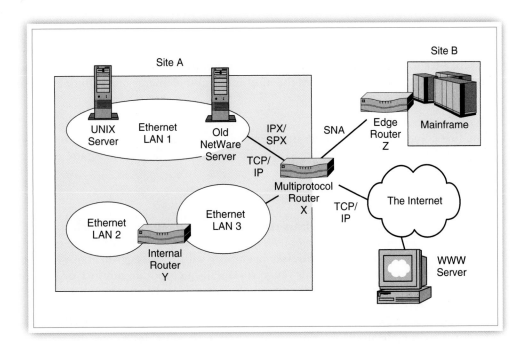

TEST YOUR UNDERSTANDING

4. a) What are multiprotocol routers? b) Why are multiprotocol routers more complex (and, therefore, more expensive) than IP-only routers?

HOW ROUTERS PROCESS PACKETS

Switching Versus Routing

In Chapters 1 and 4, we saw that Ethernet switching is very simple. As Figure 8-6 shows, each row in an Ethernet switching table has a single Ethernet address. This row tells the switch which port to send the frame back out. This single row can be found quickly, so an Ethernet switch does little work per frame. This makes Ethernet switching inexpensive.

In contrast, routers usually are organized in meshes. This gives more reliability because it allows many possible alternative routes between endpoints. Figure 8-6 shows that in a routing table, each alternative route for a packet is represented by a different row. Consequently, to **route** (forward) a packet, a router must first find all rows representing alternative routes that a packet can take. It must then pick the best alternative route from this list. This requires quite a bit of work per packet, making routing more expensive than switching.

TEST YOUR UNDERSTANDING

5. Why are routing tables more complex than Ethernet switching tables?

A Simplified Routing Table

Figure 8-6 shows a simplified routing table that has four columns. Although this routing table is simplified, it illustrates the most important elements of all routing tables.

Row Number

The first column is a route (row) number. Routing actually does not use this column. We include it to allow us to refer to specific rows in our discussion. Again, each row specifies a route to a destination.

IP Address Range

The second column is an **IP address range**—not a single IP address. Each row represents a route for *all IP addresses within this range*. For example, in Row 1 in the table, the IP address is 60.3.x.x—all IP addresses beginning with 60.3, regardless of what their following bits are. Sometimes, this range represents a corporate network or a subnet within a corporate network. In other cases, the range is an IP address range served by a specific ISP.

Again, each row represents a route. Now we can be more specific. Each row represents a route to be used for a range of destination IP addresses. Often, the route is to

Figure 8-6   Ethernet Switching Versus IP Routing

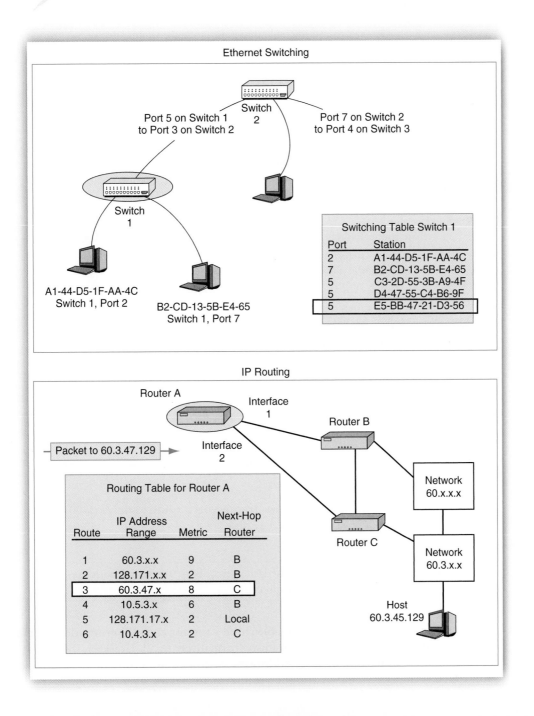

Routing

Processing an individual packet and passing it on its way is called *routing*

The Routing Table

Each router has a routing table that it uses to make routing decisions

Routing Table Rows

Each row represents a route to a range of IP addresses—often a network or subnet

There are several routing table columns

Row (route) number

IP address range governed by the row

Metric for the quality of the route

Next-hop router that should get the packet next if the row is selected as the best match

A Routing Decision

The router looks at the destination IP address in an arriving packet

The router determines which rows match (have an IP address range containing the packet's destination IP address)

The router must check all rows for possible matches

The router then determines the best match

It selects the row with the longest length of match

If two or more rows tie for the longest length of match, router uses the metric column

The router sends the packet on to the next-hop router indicated in the best-match row

Figure 8-7   The Routing Process (Study Figure)

a network or subnet. In Figure 8-6, Row 1 represents a route to network 60.3.x.x, and Row 3 represents a route to subnet 60.3.47.x.

Each row represents a route to be used for a range of destination IP addresses. Often, the route is to a network or subnet.

In contrast, Ethernet switching tables have a row for each Ethernet address. This is fine in Ethernet networks, which are usually relatively small. However, the Internet will soon have literally billions of IP addresses. Having a row in routing tables for each individual IP address would be completely unworkable.

Metric Column

Some routes are better than others. Consequently, a routing table usually includes a **metric** column that quantifies the desirability of a particular route. Sometimes, a larger metric value is better—for example if the metric represents throughput. In other cases, a smaller metric value is better—for instance if the metric represents cost.

Next-Hop Router

The last column lists the next-hop router for the route represented by the row. Although the row represents a route to a range of IP addresses, individual routers do not know the entire route through the Internet. They only know the **next-hop router** in a route—the router they should send the packet to next to move it closer to its destination.

TEST YOUR UNDERSTANDING

6. a) What is routing? b) What are the four columns in the simplified routing table? c) In a routing table, what does each row represent? d) In a routing table, are there entries for individual IP addresses or ranges of IP addresses? e) Why is this good? f) Does the router know the packet's entire route through the Internet? g) What is the purpose of the metric column? h) What is the next-hop router?

A Routing Decision

Forwarding Is Routing

As noted earlier, processing an individual packet and passing it on its way is called routing. We will use the simplified routing table in Figure 8-6 to illustrate the routing process.

Finding All Matching Rows

Suppose that Router A receives a packet with the destination IP address 60.3.47.129. To know what to do with the packet, it must know which rows in the table match the IP address. Looking at the figure, you can see that two rows match the IP address. The first matching row is Row 1, whose IP address range is 60.3.x.x. This is a match because the packet's destination IP address is in this range. The second matching row is Row 3, whose IP address range is 60.3.47.x.

Human beings like you are good at pattern matching. You can simply glance down the rows and see quickly which rows match. Routers cannot do that. Being dumb computers, routers must look at each row to see if the destination IP address matches the row's IP address range.

The router cannot stop when it finds a match because there are likely to be multiple matches. The router cannot even stop when it reaches the last matching row because it has no way of knowing whether it has found the last matching row. The router must look at every row, beginning with Row 1 and ending with the last row. This means that routers must do much more work per arriving packet than Ethernet switches do per arriving frame.

Finding the Best Match

After finding all matching rows (Rows 1 and 3 in this example), the router must identify the *best* match. A basic rule in routing is that the best route is the one that gets a packet closest to its destination host. From Figure 8-6, you can see that the route in Row 1 only gets the packet to a particular network, 60.3.x.x. The route in Row 3 is better, getting the packet to a particular subnet (60.3.47.x) within that network.

The router will decide that Row 3 is the best-match row. In general, the longest match (the most numbers before the x) will represent the best possible route.

However, in some cases, two or more rows will have the same length of match. In such cases, the general quality of the route is used to break ties. The metric column gives a value for the route's quality. If the metric is cost, for instance, the cheaper route would be selected. To give another example, if the metric is reliability, the route with a higher reliability value would be chosen.

Forwarding the Packet

Now that the router has selected Row 3, it is time to forward the packet to the next-hop router along the packet's route to its destination host. The fourth column in the best-match row says that Router A should pass the packet on to Router C. When Router A does so, it is finished with the packet and can start processing the next packet.

TEST YOUR UNDERSTANDING

> 7. a) When a packet arrives, how many rows in the routing table must the router examine to find matches? b) After a router identifies all matches, what is the next thing it must do? c) After a router identifies the best match, what will it do?

Perspective

Note how much work routers have to do for each arriving packet. They have to compare the packet's destination IP address with the address range in *every row*. In the Internet core, routers have hundreds of thousands of rows, so this matching process takes a long time. Even after the router finds all matches, it still is not finished. It must do additional calculations to find the best-match row (route).

In contrast, Ethernet switches only have to find a single row match for each frame's destination MAC address. There will only be a single match, so the table can be implemented in a tree structure for very fast matching. In addition, once a switch finds that single match, the switch forwards the frame out the indicated port immediately. There is no need to find the best match.

A final point is that this discussion of routing has been simplified. More details on how routers actually work are available in the box "Two Routing Table Details."

Two Routing Table Details

This box explains additional details about how routing operates. The first concerns the address range in the routing table. The second concerns the next-hop router column.

IS THE DESTINATION IP ADDRESS IN A ROW'S ADDRESS RANGE?

Figure 8-6 shows an IP address range column. If the destination IP address of the arriving packet is in a row's IP address range, then the row is a match. Unfortunately, routers have no hardware to compute whether an IP address is within a range. Routers actually use a different method involving masking.

Destination Value and Mask

Figure 8-8 illustrates this method. The figure shows that routing tables actually have two columns for the IP address range—a single IP address (**destination**) and a **mask**. In Row 1, the destination is 10.7.3.0, and the mask is 255.255.255.0. Although it may not seem like it, this combination actually represents the address range 10.7.3.0 to 10.7.3.255. Note that the destination is the bottom IP address in the range.

An IP Address in the Range

Suppose that an arriving packet has a destination IP address in the range—10.7.3.47. How can we tell if the row is a match?

- As Figure 8-8 shows, the first step is to apply the mask in the row (255.255.255.0) to the destination IP address. The result is 10.7.3.0.
- The second step is to compare the masking result with the destination value, 10.7.3.0. The two match, so the row is a match.

In fact, when *any* IP address in the range is masked with the mask in the row, the result will be 10.7.3.0, which is the destination value.

An IP Address out of the Range

Now suppose that a packet arrives with destination IP address 10.7.4.33. This is slightly outside the row's IP address range.

- Again, as Figure 8-8 shows, the first step is to apply the mask in the row (255.255.255.0) to the destination IP address. The result is 10.7.4.0.
- The second step is to compare the masking result with the destination value, 10.7.3.0. This time, the two do *not* match, so the row is not a match.

Perspective

This matching method is clumsy for humans to do. However, the two operations it uses—masking and bit string matching—are very easy for computers. Computer processors have special hardware for these two operations, so doing them is very fast.

Sending the IP Packet Back Out

The chapter body said that after a router finds the best-match row for the packet's IP destination address, it sends the packet back out, directing it to the next-hop router indicated in the row. Actually, the situation is a little more complicated.

First, real routing tables have an important column that Figure 8-6 does not show. This is the interface column. As noted earlier, an interface is a port. If the row is selected as the best-match row, the router sends the packet out the indicated port.

With an Ethernet switch, the switch merely sends the frame out a port. There is either a computer or another switch out that port. However, as Figure 8-9 shows, there is an entire subnet attached to each router interface. Consequently, it is not enough for a routing protocol to send a packet out a particular interface.

(continued)

Routing Table

Row	Destination	Mask	...	...	...
I	10.7.3.0	255.255.255.0	...	...	...
2	...	...	...	...	...
3	...	...	...	...	...

Masking

If a data 1 is masked by a 1, the result is a 1

If a data 0 is masked by a 1, the result is a 0

If a data 1 is masked by a 1, the result is a 0

If a data 0 is masked by a 1, the result is a 0

So when the mask bit is a 1, the data bit is returned

Also, when the mask bit is a 0, the result is always 0

Eight 0s is 0 in decimal

Eight 1s is 255 in decimal

Example 1: A Destination IP Address That Is in the Range

Destination IP Address of Arriving Packet	10.7.3.47
Apply the Mask	255.255.255.0
Result of Masking	10.7.3.0
Destination Column Value	10.7.3.0
Does Destination Match the Masking Result?	Yes
Conclusion	The row is a match.

Example 2: A Destination IP Address That Is NOT in the Range

Destination IP Address of Arriving Packet	10.7.5.47
Apply the Mask	255.255.255.0
Result of Masking	10.7.5.0
Destination Column Value	10.7.3.0
Does Destination Match the Masking Result?	No
Conclusion	The row is NOT a match.

Figure 8-8 Detailed Row-Matching Algorithm

The router also has to know to which host or router on that subnet the packet should be sent. Instead of just having a next-hop router column, routing tables have both an interface column and a next-hop router column. If the row is selected as the best match, the router will send the packet out the interface to the indicated next-hop router.

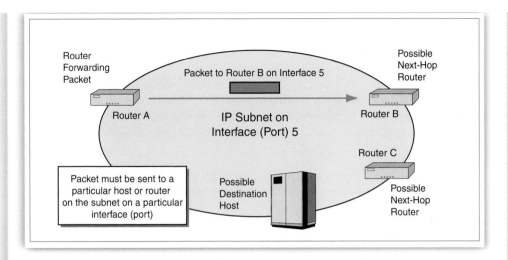

Figure 8-9   Interface and Next-Hop Router

What if the destination host is on one of the subnets attached to the router? Then the router will not send the packet out the interface to a next-hop router. Rather, it will send the packet out the indicated interface in the best-match row directly to the destination host.

In Figure 8-6, one row has the notation *Local* in the next-hop column. This indicates that the router should not send the packet to another router but rather to the destination host.

TEST YOUR UNDERSTANDING

8. a) Describe the process by which the router determines whether the destination IP address in a packet is in a row's IP address range. b) What does the router have to know to send an IP packet back out to the next-hop router?

OTHER INTERNET LAYER STANDARDS

In this section, we will look briefly at several other internet layer TCP/IP standards that are related to IP.

Dynamic Routing Protocols

How does a router get the information in its routing table? One possibility is to enter routes manually. However, that approach does not scale to large internets. Instead, as

Figure 8-11 shows, routers constantly exchange routing table information with one another using **dynamic routing protocols**.

Routing

Note that TCP/IP uses the term **routing** in two different but related ways. First, we saw earlier that the process of forwarding arriving packets is called routing. Second, the process of exchanging information for building routing tables is also called **routing**.

> In TCP/IP the term *routing* is used in two ways—for packet forwarding and for the exchange of routing table information through dynamic routing protocols.

Autonomous Systems and Interior Dynamic Routing Protocols

Recall from Chapter 1 that the Internet consists of many networks owned by different organizations. Within an organization's network, which is called an **autonomous system**, the organization owning the network decides which dynamic routing protocol to use among its internal routers, as shown in Figure 8-11. For internal use, the organization is free to choose among available **interior dynamic routing protocols**. There are three popular interior dynamic routing protocols. Each has different strengths and weaknesses.

Routing Information Protocol (RIP)

The simplest interior dynamic routing protocol created by the IETF is the **Routing Information Protocol (RIP)**. RIP's simplicity makes it attractive for small internets. Management labor is relatively low. On the negative side, RIP is not very efficient because its metric is merely the number of router hops needed to get to the destination host. However, this is not a serious problem for small internets. The one serious problem with RIP in small internets is poor security. If attackers take over a firm's interior dynamic routing protocol communications, they can maliciously reroute the internet's traffic.

Open Shortest Path First (OSPF)

For larger autonomous systems, or if security is a serious concern, the IETF created the **Open Shortest Path First (OSPF)** dynamic routing protocol. OSPF is very efficient, having a complex metric based on a mixture of cost, throughput, and traffic delays. It also offers strong security. It costs much more to manage than RIP, but unless a corporate internet is very small, OSPF is the only IETF dynamic routing protocol that makes sense.

EIGRP

Cisco Systems is the dominant manufacturer of routers. Cisco has its own proprietary interior dynamic routing protocol for large internets—the **Enhanced Interior Gateway Routing Protocol (EIGRP)**. The term **gateway** is another term for *router*. EIGRP's metric is very efficient because it is based on a mixture of interface bandwidth, load on the interface (0 percent to 100 percent of capacity), delay, and reliability (percentage of packets lost). EIGRP is comparable to OSPF, but many companies use it instead of

Figure 8-10   Dynamic Routing Protocols (Study Figure)

Routing

Routers constantly exchange routing table information with one another using dynamic routing protocols.

Note that the term routing is used in two ways in TCP/IP

For IP packet forwarding and

For the exchange of routing table information through routing protocols

Autonomous System

An organization's internal network (internet)

Interior Dynamic Routing Protocols

Within an autonomous system, firms use interior dynamic routing protocols

The organization can freely select an interior dynamic routing protocol

Routing Information Protocol (RIP)

Simple interior dynamic routing protocol from the IETF

Low-cost management

Poor efficiency: metric is merely the number of router hops to the destination host

Poor security

Only useful in very small firms

Open Shortest Path First

Sophisticated IETF interior dynamic routing protocol

Very efficient, having a complex metric based on a mixture of cost, throughput, and traffic delays

Strong security

High management costs

The only IETF interior dynamic routing protocol that makes sense for all but the smallest networks

Enhanced Interior Gateway Routing Protocol (EIGRP)

Proprietary interior dynamic routing protocol from Cisco Systems

"Gateway" is an obsolete term for *router*

Very efficient because it is based on a mixture of interface bandwidth, load on the interface (0 percent to 100 percent of capacity), delay, and reliability (percentage of packets lost)

Only dynamic interior routing protocol that supports multiprotocol routing (not just TCP/IP): IPX/SPX, SNA, etc.

To use it, a company has to buy all Cisco routers

Exterior Dynamic Routing Protocols

Between autonomous systems, companies use an exterior dynamic routing protocol

An organization must select the required exterior routing protocols

Border Gateway Protocol (BGP) is the main exterior routing protocol

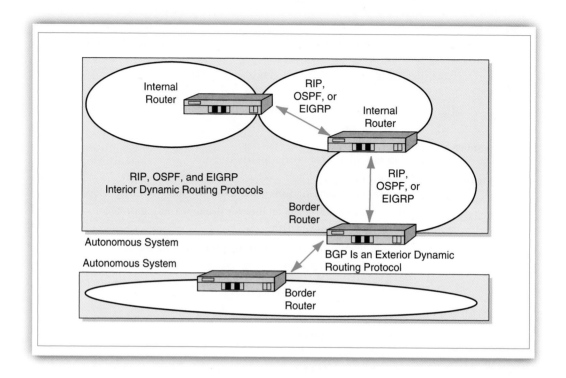

Figure 8-11   Dynamic Routing Protocols

OSPF because it can route SNA and IPX/SPX traffic as well as IP traffic. On the negative side, EIFRP is a proprietary protocol, and using it forces the company to buy only Cisco routers.

Exterior Dynamic Routing Protocols

For communication outside the organization's network, the organization is no longer in control. It must use whatever **exterior dynamic routing protocol** the external network to which it is connected requires. The almost universal exterior dynamic routing protocol is the **Border Gateway Protocol (BGP)**. BGP is designed specifically for the exchange of routing information between autonomous systems.

TEST YOUR UNDERSTANDING

9. a) What is the purpose of dynamic routing protocols? b) In what two ways does TCP/IP use the term *routing*?

10. a) What is an autonomous system? b) Within an autonomous system, can the organization choose its interior routing protocol? c) What are the two TCP/IP interior dynamic routing protocols? d) Which IETF dynamic routing protocol is good for small internets that do not have high security requirements? e) Which IETF dynamic routing protocol is good for large businesses that have high security requirements? f) What is the main benefit of EIGRP compared to OSPF as an internal dynamic routing protocol? g) When might you use EIGRP as your interior dynamic routing protocol? h) May a company select the routing protocol its border router uses to communicate with the outside world?

Address Resolution Protocol (ARP)

As discussed earlier, if the destination host is on one of the subnets directly attached to the router, then the router delivers the IP packet in a frame that follows the subnet's data link layer protocol.

To do its work, the router's interface must know the data link layer address of the destination host. Otherwise, the router's interface will not know what to place in the destination address field of the frame.

The internet layer process may only know the IP address of the destination host. If the router's interface is to deliver the frame containing the packet, the internet layer process must discover the data link layer address of the destination host.

Address Resolution on an Ethernet LAN with ARP

Determining a data link layer address when you know only an IP address is called **address resolution**. Figure 8-12 shows the **Address Resolution Protocol (ARP)**, which provides address resolution on Ethernet LANs. There are other address resolution protocols for other subnet technologies.

ARP Request Message

Suppose that the router receives an IP packet with destination address 10.19.8.17. Suppose also that the router determines from its routing table that it can deliver the packet to a host on one of its Ethernet subnets.

➤ First, the router's internet layer process creates an ARP request message that essentially says, "Hey, device with IP address 10.19.8.17, what is your 48-bit MAC layer address?" The router then broadcasts this ARP packet to all hosts on the subnet.[1]

➤ Second, the internet layer process on every host examines the ARP request message. If the target IP address is not that of the host, the host's internet layer process ignores the ARP request message. However, host 10.19.8.17 composes an ARP

---

[1]Actually, the router passes the packet down to the data link layer process on the subnet's interface. It tells the data link layer process to broadcast its ARP packet. If the subnet standard is Ethernet, the data link layer process places the packet into a frame with the destination Ethernet address FF-FF-FF-FF-FF-FF (forty-eight 1s). This is the Ethernet broadcast address. Switches will send frames with this broadcast address to all stations, and all stations will accept it as they would a frame addressed to their specific Ethernet address.

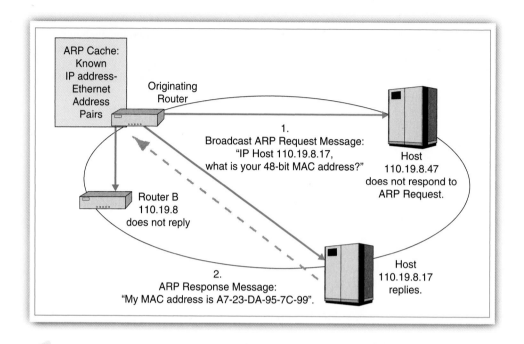

Figure 8-12   Address Resolution Protocol (ARP)

response message that includes its 48-bit MAC layer address (A7-23-DA-95-7C-99). The target host sends this ARP response message back to the router.

➤ Third, the router's internet layer process now knows the subnet MAC address associated with the IP address. It will deliver the packet to that host.

The ARP Cache

The internet layer process on the router saves the IP address–data link layer address information in its **ARP cache** (section of memory). Afterward, whenever an IP packet comes for this IP destination address, the router will send the IP packet down to its NIC, together with the required MAC address. The NIC's MAC process will deliver the IP packet within a frame containing that MAC destination address.

Using ARP for Next-Hop Routers

We have looked at how routers use ARP when they deliver packets to destination hosts. A router also needs to know the data link layer destination addresses of next-hop routers. Routers use ARP to find the data link layer destination addresses of both destination hosts and other routers.

Finally, Another Internet Layer Protocol!

In this book so far, we have only seen a single protocol at the internet layer—the Internet Protocol (IP). However, ARP is also a protocol at the internet layer, and ARP messages are called packets. ARP packets are encapsulated directly in frames, just like IP packets.

TEST YOUR UNDERSTANDING

11. A router wishes to send an IP packet to a host on its subnet. It knows the host's IP address. a) What else must it know? b) Why must it know it? c) What message will it broadcast? d) What device will respond to this broadcast message? e) Does a router have to go through the ARP process each time it needs to send a packet to a destination host or to a next-hop router? Explain. f) Is ARP used to find the destination data link layer destination addresses of destination hosts, routers, or both? g) At what layer does the ARP protocol operate?

Multiprotocol Label Switching (MPLS)

Problems with IP

Routers are extremely costly per packet forwarded because they have to compare the packet's destination address to every row in the long routing table and then must pick the best-match row. Another problem with traditional router forwarding is that there is no way to do **traffic engineering** that controls the details of transmission paths. For example, there is no way to prevent certain connections between routers from becoming overloaded or to give special priority to voice traffic or other time-sensitive traffic.

Label Header

A majority of ISPs are now using a traffic management tool called **multiprotocol label switching (MPLS)** for at least some of the traffic they carry. As Figure 8-13 shows, MPLS places a **label header** before the IP header (and after the frame header).

Label Switching for Cost Reduction

When a labeled packet arrives, a **label-switching router** does not go through the traditional routing calculation processes. Instead, it merely reads the **label number** from the label header. It then looks into the **label-switching table** to find the interface associated with the label number. It sends the packet out that interface. This is extremely fast compared to traditional routing calculations because there is only a single row for each label number. This simplicity dramatically lowers the cost of routing. Lowering router costs is the main attraction of MPLS, but there are other advantages as well.[2]

---

[2]In Chapter 7, we saw that PSDNs cope with their mesh topologies by setting up virtual circuits. MPLS does something very similar for routers.

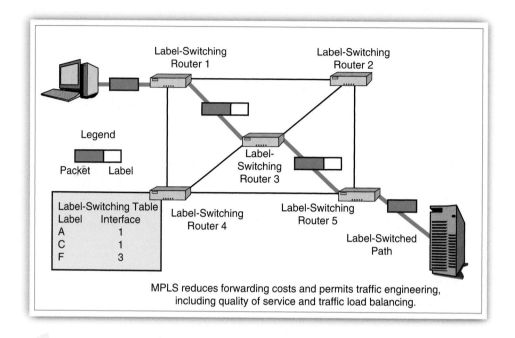

Legend

Packet   Label

Label-Switching Table
Label	Interface
A	1
C	1
F	3

MPLS reduces forwarding costs and permits traffic engineering, including quality of service and traffic load balancing.

Figure 8-13   Multiprotocol Label Switching (MPLS)

One Label Number, Many Packets

All packets between two host IP addresses could be assigned the same label number. This would be like creating a virtual circuit at the internet layer. In fact, all traffic between two sites might be assigned a single label number because it would all be going to and from the same site.

Quality of Service

Another possibility is that traffic between two sites might be assigned one of two different label numbers. One label number might be for VoIP, which is latency-intolerant, and the other might be for latency-tolerant traffic between the sites. For latency-intolerant traffic, it is even possible to reserve capacity at routers along the selected path.

Traffic Load Balancing

MPLS can also be used to balance traffic—for instance, to move some traffic from a heavily congested link between two routers to an alternative route that uses different and less-congested links. MPLS does this by setting up multiple label-switched routes ahead of time and by sending traffic based on the congestion along different label-switched routes.

TEST YOUR UNDERSTANDING

12. a) How does MPLS work? b) What is MPLS's main attraction? c) What are its other attractions? d) How can MPLS provide quality of service? e) Can MPLS provide traffic load balancing?

Domain Name System (DNS)

As we saw in Chapter 1, if a user types in a target host's host name, the user's PC will contact its local Domain Name System (DNS) server. The DNS server will return the IP address for the target host or will contact other DNS servers to get this information. The user's PC can then send IP packets to the target host.

What Is a Domain?

Figure 8-14 shows that the **Domain Name System (DNS)** and its servers are not limited to providing IP addresses for host names. More generally, DNS is a general way of naming domains. A **domain** is any group of resources (routers, single networks, and hosts) under the control of an organization. The figure shows that domains are hierarchical, with host names being at the bottom of the hierarchy.

Figure 8-14   Domain Name System (DNS) Hierarchy

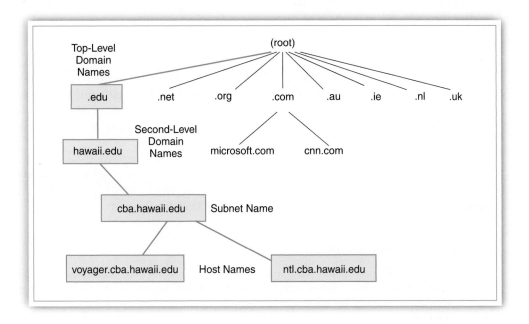

A domain is any group of resources (routers, single networks, and hosts) under the control of an organization.

Root DNS Servers

At the top of the hierarchy is the **root**, which consists of all domain names. Under the root are **top-level domains** that categorize the domain by organization type (.com, .net, .edu, .biz, .info, etc.) or by country (.uk, .ca, .ie, .au, .jp, .ch, etc.).

Second-Level Domains

Under top-level domains are **second-level domains**, which usually specify a particular organization (microsoft.com, hawaii.edu, cnn.com, etc.). Sometimes, however, specific products, such as movies, get their own second-level domain names. Competition for good second-level domain names is fierce.

Getting a second-level domain name is only the beginning. Each organization that receives a second-level domain name must have a DNS server to host its domain name record. Large organizations have their own internal DNS servers that contain information on all subnet and host names. Individuals and small businesses that use webhosting services depend on the webhosting company to provide this DNS service.

Further Qualifications

Domains can be further qualified. For instance, within hawaii.edu, which is the University of Hawai'i, there is a cba.hawaii.edu domain. This is the College of Business Administration. Within *cba.hawaii.edu* is *voyager.cba.hawaii.edu*, which is a specific host within the college.

Hierarchy of DNS Servers

To implement this naming hierarchy, the domain name system maintains a hierarchy of DNS servers. At the root level, there are 13 **DNS root servers** that contain information about DNS servers for top-level domains (.com, .edu, .ca., .ie, etc.). Having multiple DNS root servers provides reliability. Each top-level domain itself maintains multiple DNS servers.

Companies with second-level domain names are required to have their own DNS servers and almost always maintain two or more DNS servers for their own second-level domain name. For small businesses that have their websites hosted by a webhosting service, the webhosting service also maintains their DNS function.

TEST YOUR UNDERSTANDING

13. a) Is the Domain Name System only used to send back IP addresses for given host names? b) What is a domain? c) Which level of domain name do corporations most wish to have? d) What are DNS root servers? e) How many DNS root servers are there?

Internet Control Message Protocol (ICMP) for Supervisory Messages at the Internet Layer

Supervisory Messages at the Internet Layer

IP is only concerned with packet delivery. For supervisory messages at the internet layer, the IETF created the **Internet Control Message Protocol (ICMP)**. IP and ICMP work closely together. As Figure 8-15 shows, IP encapsulates ICMP messages in the IP data field, delivering them to their target host or router. There are no higher-layer headers or messages.

Error Advisement

IP is an unreliable protocol. It offers no error correction. If the router or the destination host finds an error, it discards the packet. Although there is no retransmission, the router or host that finds the error may send an **ICMP error message** to the source device to inform it that an error has occurred, as Figure 8-15 illustrates. This is **error advisement** (notification) rather than error correction. There is no mechanism within IP or ICMP for the retransmission of lost or damaged packets. ICMP error messages are only sent to help the sending process or its human user diagnose problems. One important subtlety is that sending error advisement messages is not mandatory. For security reasons, many firms do not allow error advisement messages to leave their internal internets because hackers can exploit the information contained in them.

Echo (Ping)

Perhaps the most famous ICMP error message type is the **ICMP echo** message. One host or router can send an echo request message to another. If the target device's internet process is able to do so, it will send back an echo reply message.

Figure 8-15   Internet Control Message Protocol (ICMP) for Supervisory Messages

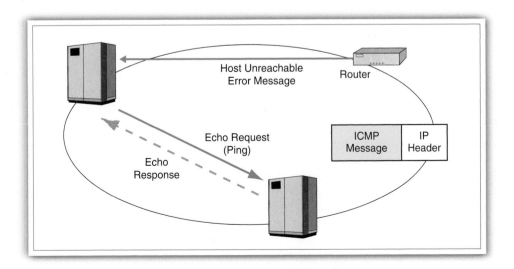

Sending an echo request is often called **pinging** the target host, because it is similar to a submarine pinging a ship with sonar to see if it is there. In fact, the most common program for pinging hosts is called **ping**.[3] Echo is a good diagnostic tool because if there are network difficulties, a logical early step in diagnosis is to ping many hosts and routers to see if they can be reached.

TEST YOUR UNDERSTANDING

14. a) For what general class of messages is ICMP used? b) How are ICMP messages encapsulated? c) An Ethernet frame containing an ICMP message arrives at a host. List the frame's headers, messages, and trailers at all layers. List them in the order in which they will be seen by the receiver. For each header or trailer, specify the standard used to create the header or message (for example, Ethernet 802.3 MAC layer header). Hint: remember how ICMP messages are encapsulated. d) Explain error advisement in ICMP. e) Explain the purpose of ICMP echo messages. f) Sending an ICMP echo message is called _____ the target host.

DHCP

In Chapter 1, we saw that the Dynamic Host Configuration Protocol (DHCP) gives a PC a temporary IP address when it first boots up. The DHCP's job actually is more complex than this, but we needed the information in this chapter before we could discuss the other configuration information that DHCP sends to PCs at boot-up. Simply put, DHCP gives a PC not only a temporary IP address but also a subnet mask to use in interpreting addresses. It also sends the IP addresses of the company's or ISP's DNS servers (most companies have two or more DNS servers) and a default router to send packets to.

Although PCs could be configured manually, they would have to be manually reconfigured every time a company changed its masks or the IP addresses of the DNS servers. When DHCP is used, only the DHCP servers have to be updated.

TEST YOUR UNDERSTANDING

15. What configuration information does a DHCP server send to a PC when the PC boots up and sends out a DHCP request?

IPv4 Fields

Today, most routers on the Internet and private internets are governed by the **IP version 4 (IPv4)** standard. (There were no versions 0 through 3.) Figure 8-17 shows the IPv4 packet. Its first four bits contain the value 0100 (binary for 4) to indicate that the packet is formatted according to IPv4. Although we have looked already at some of the fields in IPv4, here we will look at fields that we have not seen yet.

---

[3]The echo reply message also gives the latency for the reply—the number of milliseconds between echo messages and echo reply messages. This is useful in diagnosing problems.

DHCP Provides to Each Client PC at Boot-Up:

A temporary IP Address

A subnet mask

The IP addresses of local DNS servers

Better Than Manual Configuration

If subnet mask or DNS IP addresses change, only the DHCP server has to be updated manually

Client PCs are automatically updated when they next boot up

Figure 8-16   Dynamic Host Configuration Protocol (DHCP) (Study Figure)

Time to Live (TTL)

In the early days of the ARPANET, which was the precursor to the Internet, packets that were misaddressed would circulate endlessly among packet switches in search of their nonexistent destinations. To prevent this, IP added a **time to live (TTL)** field that is given a value by the source host. Different operating systems have different TTL defaults. Most insert TTL values between 64 and 128. Each router along the way decrements the TTL field by 1. A router decrementing the TTL to 0 will discard the packet, although it may send back an ICMP error advisement message to the source host.

Protocol

The **protocol** field tells the contents of the data field. If the protocol field value is 1, the IP packet carries an ICMP message in its data field. TCP and UDP have protocol values 6 and 17, respectively. After decapsulation, the internet layer process must pass the packet's data field to another process. The protocol field value designates which process should receive the data field.

Identification, Flags, and Fragment Offset

If a router wishes to forward a packet to a particular network and the network's maximum packet size is too small for the packet, the router can fragment the packet into two or more smaller packets. Each fragmented packet receives the same **identification** field value that the source host put into the original IP packet's header.

The destination host's internet process reassembles the fragmented packet. It places all packets with the same identification field value together for sorting. It then places them in order of increasing **fragment offset** size. The more fragments bit is set (equal to 1) in all but the last fragment. Not setting it in the last fragment indicates that there are no more fragments.

Fragmentation is uncommon in IP today and is suspicious when it occurs because it is rarely used legitimately and is often used by attackers.

Figure 8-17   IPv4 and IPv6 Packets

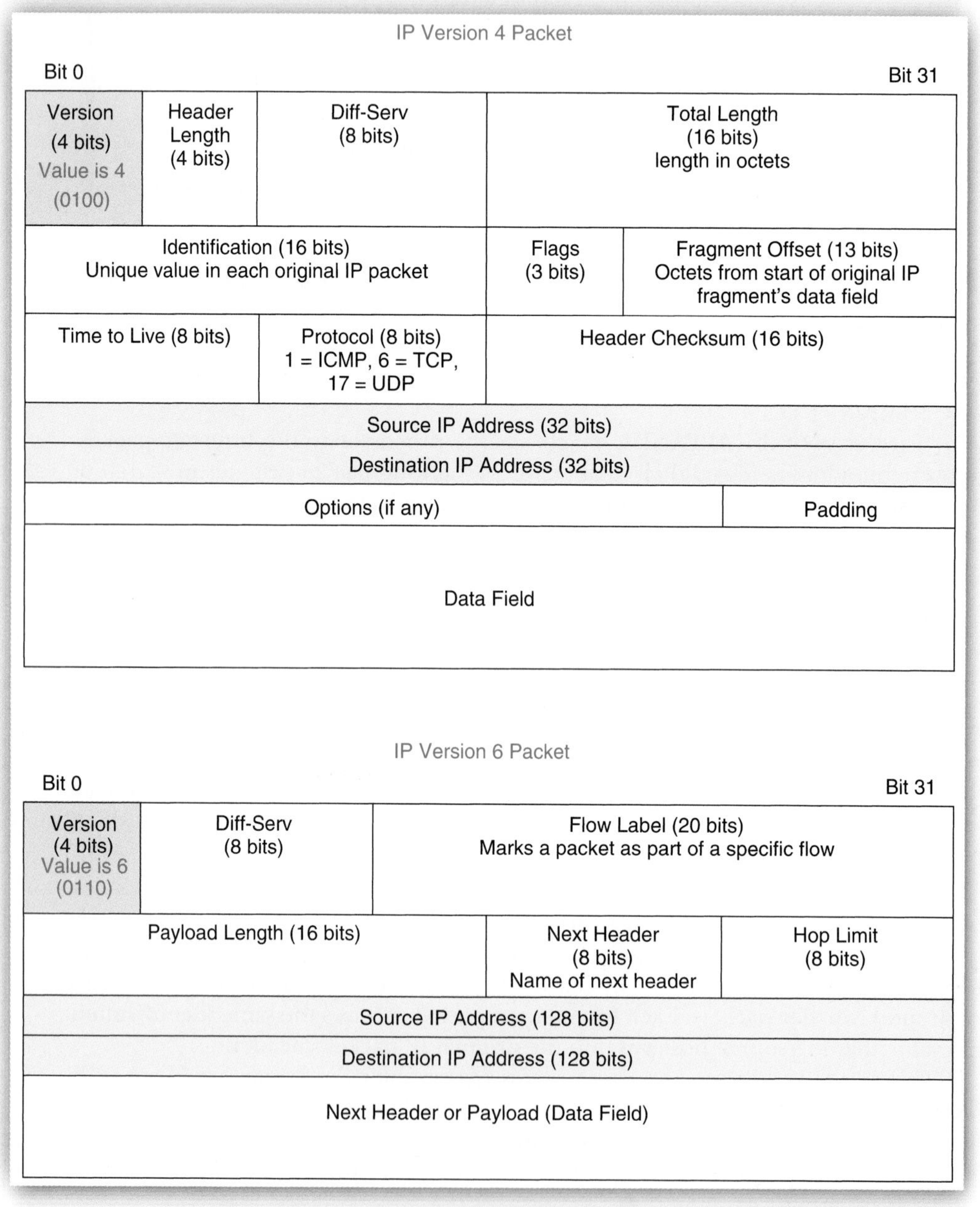

IP Version 4 Packet			
Bit 0			Bit 31

Version (4 bits) Value is 4 (0100)	Header Length (4 bits)	Diff-Serv (8 bits)	Total Length (16 bits) length in octets
Identification (16 bits) Unique value in each original IP packet		Flags (3 bits)	Fragment Offset (13 bits) Octets from start of original IP fragment's data field
Time to Live (8 bits)	Protocol (8 bits) 1 = ICMP, 6 = TCP, 17 = UDP	Header Checksum (16 bits)	
Source IP Address (32 bits)			
Destination IP Address (32 bits)			
Options (if any)			Padding
Data Field			

IP Version 6 Packet		
Bit 0		Bit 31

Version (4 bits) Value is 6 (0110)	Diff-Serv (8 bits)	Flow Label (20 bits) Marks a packet as part of a specific flow
Payload Length (16 bits)	Next Header (8 bits) Name of next header	Hop Limit (8 bits)
Source IP Address (128 bits)		
Destination IP Address (128 bits)		
Next Header or Payload (Data Field)		

Options

Similarly, **options** are uncommon in IP today and also tend to be used primarily by attackers. If an option does not end at a 32-bit boundary, **padding** is added up to the 32-bit boundary.

Diff-Serv

The **Diff-Serv** field can be used to label IP packets for priority and other service parameters. MPLS is likely to be used instead of this field.

TEST YOUR UNDERSTANDING

16. a) What is the main version of the Internet Protocol in use today? b) What does a router do if it decrements a TTL value to 0? c) What does the protocol field value tell the destination host? d) Under what circumstances would the identification, flags, and fragment offset fields be used in IP? e) Why is fragmentation suspicious? f) Why are options suspicious?

IPv6 Fields

The IETF has standardized a new version of the Internet Protocol, **IP version 6 (IPv6)**. As Figure 8-17 shows, IPv6 also begins with a version field. Its value is 0110 (binary for 6). This tells the router that the rest of the packet is formatted according to IPv6.

Address Field

The most important change from IPv4 to IPv6 is an increase in the size of IP address fields from 32 bits to 128 bits. The number of possible IP addresses is 2 raised to a power that is the size of the IP address field. For IPv4, this is 2^{32}. For IPv6, this is 2^{128}— an enormous number. IPv6 will support the huge increase in demand for IP addresses that we can expect from mobile devices and from the likely evolution of even simple home appliances into addressable IP hosts.

Slow Adoption

IPv6 has been adopted only in a few geographic regions because its main advantage, permitting far more IP addresses, is not too important yet. However, IPv6 is beginning to gather strength, particularly in Asia and Europe, which were short-changed in the original allocation of IPv4 addresses.[4] In addition, the explosion of mobile devices accessing the Internet will soon place heavy stress on the IPv4 IP address space. Fortunately, IPv6 packets can be tunneled through IPv4 networks by placing them within IPv4 packets, so the two protocols can (and will) coexist on the Internet for some time to come.

TEST YOUR UNDERSTANDING

17. a) How is IPv6 better than IPv4? b) Why has IPv6 adoption been so slow? c) What forces may drive IPv6's adoption in the future? d) Must IPv6 replace IPv4 all at once? Explain.

---

[4]North America has 74 percent of all IPv4 addresses. In fact, Stanford University has more IPv4 addresses than China, which now has fewer IP addresses than it has Internet users.

THE TRANSMISSION CONTROL PROTOCOL (TCP)

Fields in TCP/IP Segments

Chapter 2 looked at the **Transmission Control Protocol (TCP)**. In this section, we will look at this complex protocol in even more depth. When IP was designed, it was made a very simple "best effort" protocol (although its routing tables are complex). The IETF left more complex internetwork transmission control tasks to TCP. Consequently, network professionals need to understand TCP very well. Figure 8-18 shows the organization of TCP messages, which are called **TCP segments**.

TEST YOUR UNDERSTANDING

18. a) Why is TCP complex? b) Why is it important for networking professionals to understand TCP? c) What are TCP messages called?

Sequence Numbers

Each TCP segment has a unique 32-bit sequence number that increases with each segment. This allows the receiving transport process to put arriving TCP segments in order if IP delivers them out of order.

Acknowledgement Numbers

In Chapter 2, we saw that TCP uses acknowledgements (ACKs) to achieve reliability. If a transport process receives a TCP segment correctly, it sends back a TCP segment acknowledging the reception. If the sending transport process does not receive an acknowledgement, it transmits the TCP segment again.

The **acknowledgement number** field indicates which segment is being acknowledged. One might expect that if a segment has sequence number X, then the acknowledgment number in the segment that acknowledges it would also be X. As Module A notes, the situation is more complex, but the acknowledgement number is at least based on the sequence number of the segment being acknowledged.

Flag Fields

TCP has six single-bit fields. Single-bit fields are called **flag fields**, and if they have the value 1, they are said to be **set**. These fields allow the receiving transport process to know the kind of segment it is receiving. We will look at four of these flag bits.

➤ If the ACK bit is set, then the segment acknowledges another segment. If the ACK bit is set, the acknowledgement field must be filled in to indicate which message is being acknowledged.

➤ If the SYN (synchronization) bit is set (has the value 1), then the segment requests a connection opening.

➤ If the FIN (finish) bit is set, then the segment requests a normal connection closing.

➤ If the RST (reset) bit is set, then the segment announces an abrupt connection closing.

Openings and Normal Closings

In Chapter 2, we saw that TCP is a connection-oriented protocol. Connection-oriented protocols have formal openings and closings. Figure 8-19 illustrates these openings and closings.

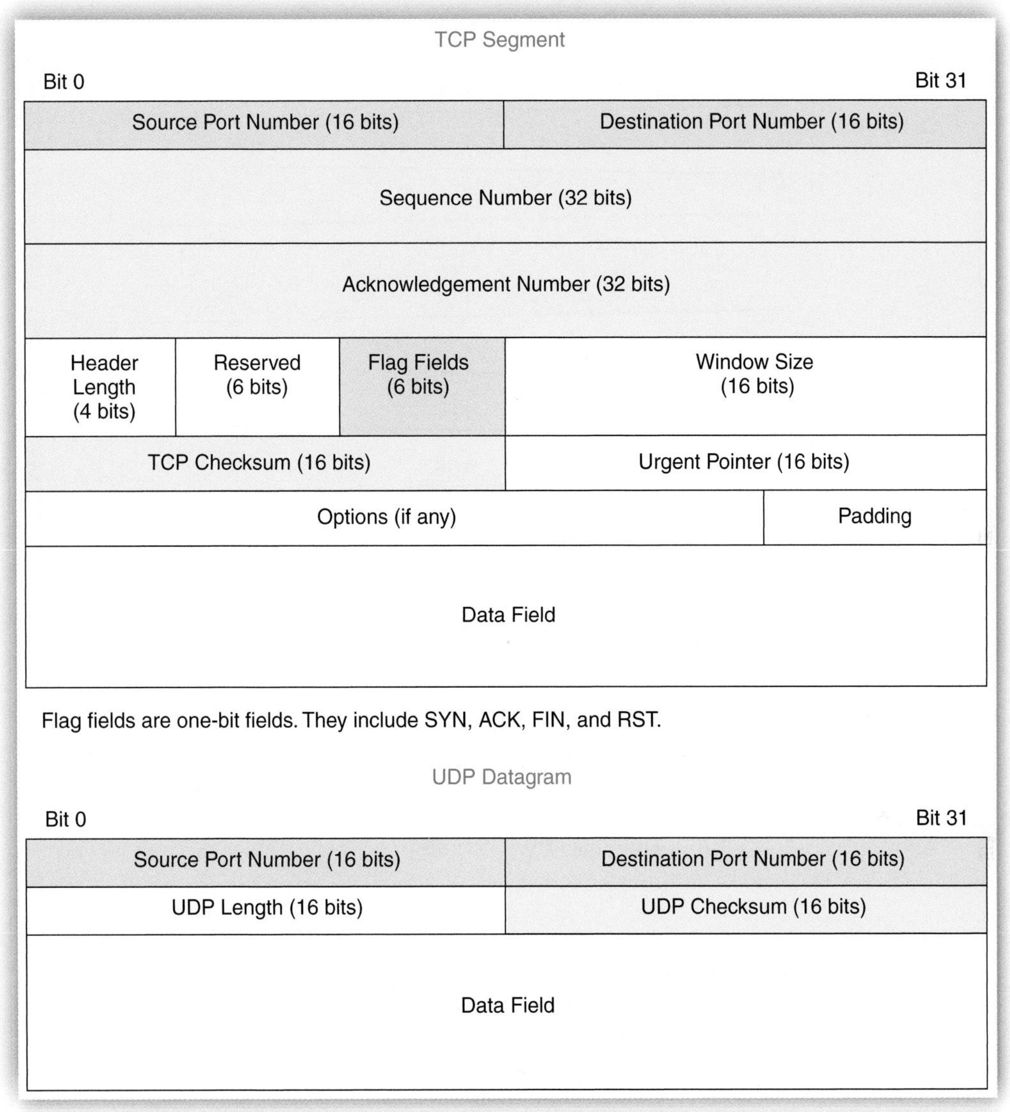

TCP Segment

Bit 0   Bit 31

Source Port Number (16 bits)	Destination Port Number (16 bits)
Sequence Number (32 bits)	
Acknowledgement Number (32 bits)	

Header Length (4 bits)	Reserved (6 bits)	Flag Fields (6 bits)	Window Size (16 bits)

TCP Checksum (16 bits)	Urgent Pointer (16 bits)

Options (if any)	Padding

Data Field

Flag fields are one-bit fields. They include SYN, ACK, FIN, and RST.

UDP Datagram

Bit 0   Bit 31

Source Port Number (16 bits)	Destination Port Number (16 bits)
UDP Length (16 bits)	UDP Checksum (16 bits)

Data Field

Figure 8-18   TCP Segment and UDP Datagram

Openings with SYN Segments

Opening a TCP connection requires an interaction called a **three-way handshake**.

> ➤ First, one transport process sends a SYN (synchronization) message to open the connection. A synchronization message consists of a header without a body. In a synchronization message, the **SYN bit** is set.

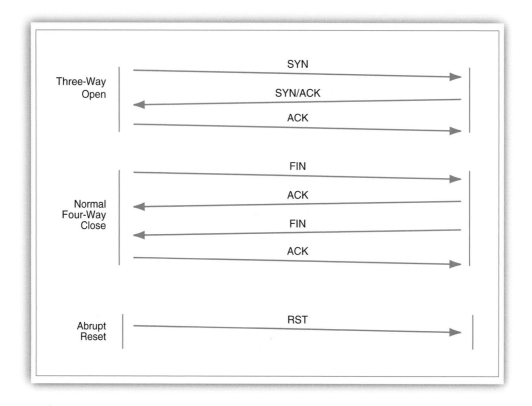

Figure 8-19   TCP Session Openings and Closings

➤ The other transport process sends back a SYN/ACK. In this message, the SYN and ACK bits are both set. In addition, the acknowledgement number field indicates which segment is being acknowledged (in connection openings, the initial SYN segment).

➤ Finally, the side that initiated the connection opening sends back an ACK segment.

Normal Closes with FIN Segments

Each side normally ends a TCP connection by sending a FIN message in which the FIN bit is set. This closing is called a **four-way close** because four segments must be sent, as Figure 8-19 illustrates.

➤ First, one side initiates the close by sending a FIN (finish) segment. This is a TCP segment whose **FIN bit** is set. The TCP segment is only a header and has no data field.

➤ The other side responds with an ACK segment that acknowledges receiving the FIN segment. This also is a header-only TCP segment.

➤   Later, the other side sends a FIN segment, which the side that initiates the close acknowledges. The connection is now closed.

When the side that initiates the close sends the FIN segment, it signals that it has no more information to send. However, the other side may continue to send TCP segments containing information, and the side that initiated the close will continue to send back ACK segments. When the other side finishes sending information segments, it sends its own FIN message, which the side that initiated the close acknowledges.

Abrupt Resets

Figure 8-19 shows that TCP also allows a second way to close connections. This is the abrupt reset. It is like hanging up during the middle of a telephone conversation. Either side can send a reset message with the **RST bit** set. This is a one-way close. There is no acknowledgement or response from the other side.

TEST YOUR UNDERSTANDING

19. a) Why are sequence numbers good? b) What are 1-bit fields called? c) If someone says that a flag field is set, what does this mean? d) If the ACK bit is set, what other field must be filled in? e) What is a SYN segment? f) Describe three-way openings in TCP. g) Distinguish between four-way closes and abrupt resets. h) Do SYN and FIN segments have data fields? i) After a side sends a FIN segment, will it respond to further messages from the other side? Explain.

Port Numbers

As Figure 8-18 shows, both TCP and UDP have **port number** fields. These fields are used differently by clients and servers. In both cases, however, they tell the transport process what application process sent or should receive the data in the data field. This is necessary because computers can run multiple applications at the same time.

Server Port Numbers

For servers, the port number field indicates which application program on the server should receive the message. Major applications have **well-known port numbers** that are usually (but not always) used. These well-known port numbers are from 0 to 1023.

➤   For instance, the well-known TCP port number for HTTP is 80.
➤   For FTP, TCP Port 21 is used for supervisory communication with an FTP application program, and TCP Port 20 is used to send and receive data segments.
➤   Telnet uses TCP Port 23.
➤   TCP Port 25 is for Simple Mail Transfer Protocol (SMTP) messages in e-mail.
➤   UDP has its own well-known port numbers. The well-known UDP port numbers also run from 0 to 1023.

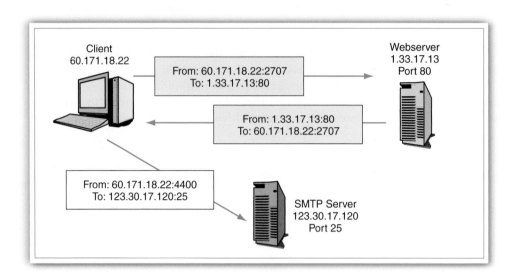

Figure 8-20   Use of TCP (and UDP) Port Numbers

Figure 8-20 shows that every time the client sends a message to a server, the client places the port number of the server application in the destination port number field. In this figure, the server is a webserver, and the port number is 80. When the server responds, it places the port number of the application (80) in the source port number field.

Client Part Numbers

Clients do something very different. Whenever a client connects to an application program on a server, the client creates a random **ephemeral port number**, which it only uses for a single TCP session with a single server. According to IETF rules, this port number should be between 49153 and 65535. However, many operating systems ignore these rules and use other ephemeral port numbers. For instance, Microsoft Windows, which dominates the client PC operating system market, uses the ephemeral port number range 1024 to 4999.

Microsoft Windows uses the ephemeral port number range 1024 to 4999.

In Figure 8-20, the ephemeral port number is 2707 for client communication with the webserver. When the client transmits, it places 2707 in the source port field of the TCP or UDP header. The server, in return, places this ephemeral port number in all destination port number fields of TCP segments or UDP datagrams it sends to the client.

A client may maintain multiple connections to different application programs on different servers. In Figure 8-20, for example, the client has a connection to an SMTP mail server as well as to the webserver. The client will give each connection a different ephemeral port number to separate the segments of the two connections. For the SMTP connection in Figure 8-20, the client has randomly chosen the ephemeral port number to be 4400.

Sockets

The combination of an IP address and a port number designates a specific connection to a specific application on a specific host. This combination is called a **socket**. It is written as an IP address, a colon, and then a port number—for instance, 128.171.17.13:80.

> A socket is written as an IP address, a colon, and then a port number. It designates a specific application on a specific host.

TEST YOUR UNDERSTANDING

20. a) What type of port number do servers use? b) What type of port number do clients use? c) What is the port range for well-known port numbers? d) What is the official range for ephemeral port numbers? e) What is the range of Microsoft ephemeral port numbers?

21. A Windows host sends a TCP segment with source port number 25 and destination port number 2404. a) Is the source host a server or a client? Explain. b) If the host is a server, what kind of server is it? c) Is the destination host a server or a client? Explain.

22. a) What is a socket? b) What specifies a particular application on a particular host in TCP/IP? c) How is it written? d) When the SMTP server in Figure 8-20 transmits to the client PC, what will the source socket be? e) The destination socket?

THE USER DATAGRAM PROTOCOL (UDP)

We saw in Chapter 2 that UDP is a simple (connectionless and unreliable) protocol. We saw in Chapter 6 that VoIP uses UDP to carry voice packets because there is no time to wait for retransmissions. In Chapter 10, we will see that the Simple Network Management Protocol uses UDP for a different reason—to reduce network traffic. UDP does not have openings, closings, or acknowledgements, and so it produces substantially less traffic than TCP.

As a consequence of UDP's simple operation, the syntax of the UDP datagram shown in Figure 8-18 is very simple. After two port number fields, which we just saw in the previous section, there are only two more header fields.

There is a **length** field so that the receiving transport process can process the datagram properly.

There also is a **UDP checksum** field that allows the receiver to check for errors in this UDP datagram. If an error is found, the UDP datagram is discarded. There is no mechanism for retransmission.

TEST YOUR UNDERSTANDING

23. a) What are the four fields in a UDP header? b) Describe the third. c) Describe the fourth. d) Is UDP reliable? Explain.

LAYER 3 AND LAYER 4 SWITCHES

In Chapters 1 and 4, we saw why Ethernet switches are so fast and inexpensive. In this chapter, we saw why routers are so slow and expensive. However, just as nature abhors a vacuum, technology abhors a sharp distinction. New devices called Layer 3 switches sit between routers and traditional Layer 2 (data link layer) switches for single networks in terms of speed and price.

Layer 3 Switches

First, we need to get one thing clear. **Layer 3 switches** are true routers. They are *not* switches. They forward IP packets using routing tables, implement routing protocols to exchange routing table information, and do other things that routers do. In other words, the term "switch" is highly inaccurate—a "gift" of marketers who used the term "switch" because switches traditionally have been faster than routers.

Layer 3 switches are true routers. They are *not* switches.

Layer 3 Switches Are Fast and Relatively Inexpensive

Layer 3 switches are fast primarily because they do almost all processing in hardware. Hardware-based routing is much faster than traditional software-based routing.[5] Largely as a consequence, Layer 3 switches are less expensive to purchase than traditional software routers for a given traffic level. Layer 3 switches cost only about as much as Ethernet switches and are almost as fast.

However, the labor cost of managing any router—including Layer 3 switches—is much higher than the cost of managing Ethernet switches. The total cost of Layer 3 switches therefore lies between the total cost of Ethernet switches and traditional software routers.

---

[5]Programs consist of multiple statements. Often, dozens of program statements may need to be loaded and run to accomplish a simple task. If the task can be done in hardware, in contrast, no time is needed to "load" software statements or write out results to memory. In addition, parallel processing usually allows hardware to do functions in fewer steps than software implementations. On the negative side, it is far more expensive to create hardware to implement required functionality than to write a program to do the work. The technology that makes Layer 3 switches possible is the application-specific integrated circuit (ASIC). This is a production integrated circuit custom-made for a particular application (in this case, routing).

Layer 3 Switches Have Limited Functionality
However, there are limits today on what can be done in hardware. Consequently, Layer 3 switches today do not have all of the functionality of full routers. Instead of being full multiprotocol routers, for example, they often handle only IP or perhaps IP and IPX. In addition, they often have only Ethernet interfaces.

Roles in Site Networks
For many organizations, such as banks, which have multiple internal protocols from different architectures, Layer 3 switches cannot be used at all. However, where the limited functionality of Layer 3 switches is sufficient for an organization, they are ideal.

For instance, Layer 3 switches are often used as internal routers in organizations that have standardized on TCP/IP for internal communication. Figure 8-21 shows that in many site networks, Layer 3 switches are pushing routers to the edges of the site because the ability of routers to support multiple WAN protocols is crucial at borders. In contrast, within the site, the low cost of Layer 3 switches usually makes them dominant in the core above the workgroup switch. For workgroup switches, in turn, labor costs usually are too high to replace Ethernet switches with Layer 3 routers.

Layer 4 Switches
As noted earlier in this chapter, TCP and UDP headers have port number fields that indicate the application that created the encapsulated application layer message and the application layer program that should receive the encapsulated application message.

Figure 8-21   Layer 3 Switches and Routers in Site Internets

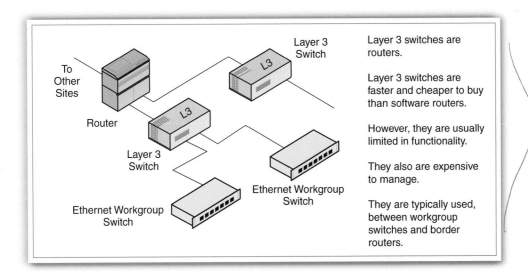

Layer 4 switches examine the port number field of each arriving packet's encapsulated TCP segment. This allows them to switch packets based on the application they contain. Specifically, this allows Layer 4 switches to give priority to or even to deny forwarding to IP packets from certain applications. For example, TCP segments to and from an SMTP mail server (Port 25) might be given low priority during times of congestion because e-mail is insensitive to moderate latency.

Application Switches (Layer 5 or Layer 7 Switches)

Finally, some switches are application switches. They are also called Layer 5 or Layer 7 switches. Layer 5 is the application layer in the hybrid TCP/IP–OSI architecture, and Layer 7 is the application layer in the OSI architecture. Whatever they are called, application switches make switching decisions based on the content of application messages. For instance, for 'Web traffic', switching may be done on the basis of URLs in request messages. Application switches may determine where the application message goes and what priority the message should be given.

TEST YOUR UNDERSTANDING

24. a) Are Layer 3 switches really routers? b) How are they better than traditional software-based routers? c) How are they not as good? Give a full explanation. d) When would you often use Layer 3 switches? e) Where would you not use Layer 3 switches? f) What do Layer 5 and Layer 7 look at to determine what to do with arriving messages?

25. a) What are Layer 4 switches? b) What field do Layer 4 switches examine? c) Why are Layer 4 switches good? d) What layer name is given to application switches?

CONCLUSION

Synopsis

TCP/IP is a family of standards created by the Internet Engineering Task Force (IETF). IP is TCP/IP's main standard at the internet layer. IP is a lightweight (unreliable and connectionless) protocol. At the transport layer, TCP/IP offers two standards: TCP, which is a heavyweight protocol (reliable and connection-oriented), and UDP, which is a lightweight protocol like IP.

IP addresses are hierarchical. Their 32 bits usually are divided into a network part, a subnet part, and a host part. All three parts vary in length. Subnet masks and network masks help devices know which bits in an IP address are the network part, the subnet part, the host part, or the total of two parts.

Routers forward packets through an internet. Border routers move packets between the outside world and an internal site network. Internal routers work within sites, moving packets between subnets. In the Internet backbone, core routers handle massive traffic flows. Ports in routers are called interfaces. Different interfaces may connect to different types of networks—for instance, Ethernet or Frame Relay networks. Most routers are multiprotocol routers, which can handle not only TCP/IP internetworking protocols, but also internetworking protocols from IPX/SPX, SNA, and other architectures.

Routers are designed to work in a mesh topology. This creates alternative routes through the internet. Alternative routes are good for reliability. However, the router has to consider the best route for each arriving packet, and this is time consuming and therefore expensive.

To make a routing decision (deciding which interface to use to send an incoming packet back out), a router uses a routing table. Each row in the routing table represents a route to a particular network or subnet. All packets to that network or subnet are governed by the one row. Each row (route) has an IP address range field, a metric field, and a next-hop router row. If the destination IP address in an arriving packet is in a row's range, that range is a match. After finding all matches in the routing table, the router finds the best-match row on the basis of match length and metric values. Once a best-match route (row) is selected, the router sends the packet out to the next-hop router in that row.

The box entitled "Two Routing Table Details" adds two refinements to this picture of router operation. First, it describes how a row's IP address range is expressed in terms of an IP address and a mask. Second, it notes that the router really sends the packet out an interface (port) to a next-hop router or destination host on the subnet out the interface.

Routers build their routing tables by listening to other routers. Routers frequently exchange messages, giving information stored in their routing tables. These messages are governed by one of several available dynamic routing protocols.

When a packet arrives, the routing table tells the router the IP destination address of the next-hop router or destination host. To deliver this packet, the router also has to know the data link layer address of the next-hop router or destination host in order to put the packet into a frame for delivery. The router uses the Address Resolution Protocol (ARP) to find the required data link layer address. The router then puts the IP address and corresponding data link layer address in its ARP cache.

Selecting the best route for each arriving packet is very time-consuming and expensive. ISPs and some firms are beginning to implement multiprotocol label switching (MPLS), which essentially creates virtual circuits to reduce costs. MPLS adds a label before the IP packet, and label-switching routers base forwarding decisions on the label's value, which they look up in a simple label-switching table. In addition to reducing router costs, MPLS can be used to provide quality of service for voice and other time-critical traffic flows. MPLS can also be used to do load balancing across different routes for efficiency.

Servers have both host names and IP addresses. Domain name system (DNS) servers provide IP addresses for users who know only a target host's host name. However, DNS is a broader service. It is a hierarchical system for naming domains, which are collections of resources on the Internet. Second-level domains, such as cnn.com, typically are prized by corporations.

IP itself does not have supervisory messages. For internet layer supervisory messages, hosts and routers use the Internet Control Message Protocol (ICMP). We looked at two types of ICMP messages—error advisement messages and echo messages (ping). ICMP messages are carried in the data fields of IP packets.

In Chapter 1, we saw that DHCP provides a temporary IP address to client PCs when they first boot up. In this chapter, we saw that DHCP also sends other configuration information to the PC—a mask and the IP addresses of local DNS hosts.

IP version 4 has a number of important fields besides the source and destination address fields. The time to live (TTL) field ensures that packets that are misaddressed do not circulate endlessly around the Internet. The protocol field describes the contents of the data field—ICMP message, TCP segment, UDP datagram, and so forth. IP version 6 will offer many more addresses thanks to its 128-bit address fields.

The Transmission Control Protocol (TCP) has sequence numbers that allow the receiving transport process to place arriving TCP segments in order. The TCP header has several flag fields that indicate whether the segment is a SYN, FIN, ACK, or RST segment. Connection openings use a three-way handshake that uses SYN segments. Normal closes involve a four-way message exchange that use FIN segments. Resets close a connection with a single segment (RST) instead of the normal four.

Both TCP and UDP have 16-bit source and destination port number fields that tell the transport process which application process sent or should receive the contents in the segment data field. Major applications have well-known port numbers. For instance, the well-known server port number of HTTP is Port 80. Clients, in contrast, have ephemeral port numbers that they select randomly for each connection. Microsoft uses the ephemeral port number range 1024 to 4999.

Traditionally, there has been a sharp distinction between fast and inexpensive switches and slow and expensive routers. However, Layer 3 switches bridge this gap. They are true routers but operate in hardware rather than in software as traditional routers do. However, hardware operation can only implement some of the functionality of routers. Layer 3 switches are not multiprotocol routers. In addition, Layer 3 switches are routers and so are more costly to manage than Layer 2 switches. Layer 4 switches, in turn, base switching decisions on the content of transport layer messages, usually port number fields. Finally, application switches (Layer 5 or Layer 7 switches) base their switching decisions on the basis of the contents of application layer messages.

THOUGHT QUESTIONS

1. Give a non-network example of hierarchical addressing, and discuss how it reduces the amount of work needed in physical delivery.
2. A client PC has two simultaneous connections to the same webserver application program on a webserver. (Yes, this is possible, and in fact it is rather common.) What will be different between the TCP segments that the client sends on the two connections?
3. For security reasons, many organizations do not allow error reply messages to leave their internal internets. How, specifically, could hackers use information in echo reply messages to learn about the firm's internal hosts?
4. Continuing from the previous question, how could a hacker use the TTL field to learn about the organization of the firm's routers?

TROUBLESHOOTING QUESTION

1. You suspect that the failure of a router or of a transmission line connecting routers has left some of your important servers unavailable to clients at your site. How could you narrow down the location of the problem using what you learned in this chapter?

HANDS-ON EXERCISES

To get a second-level domain name, you need to go to an address registrar. Network Solutions is a well-known address registrar. Go to the Network Solutions website, *www.netsol.com*. Pick a second-level domain name for an imaginary business and see if it is available. If it is not, try other second-level domain names until you find one that is available.

ADVANCED ROUTING QUESTIONS

The following questions are based on information in the box "Two Routing Protocol Details." They refer to the detailed routing table in Figure 8-22.

1. a) If an arriving packet has the IP destination address 1.2.3.4, which row will match it? Why? b) This row is called the default row, and the next-hop router is called the default router. It will be used to forward any packet that does not match any other row. What is the default router?

Figure 8-22   Detailed Routing Table

Row	Destination Network or Subnet	Mask (/Prefix)	Metric (Cost)	Interface	Next-Hop Router
1	128.171.0.0	255.255.0.0 (/16)	47	2	G
2	172.30.33.0	255.255.255.0 (/24)	0	1	Local
3	60.168.6.0	255.255.255.0 (/24)	12	2	G
4	123.0.0.0	255.0.0.0 (/8)	33	2	G
5	172.29.8.0	255.255.255.0 (/24)	34	1	F
6	172.40.6.0	255.255.255.0 (/24)	47	3	H
7	128.171.17.0	255.255.255.0 (/24)	55	3	H
8	172.29.8.0	255.255.255.0 (/24)	20	3	H
9	172.12.6.0	255.255.255.0 (/24)	23	1	F
10	172.30.47.0	255.255.255.0 (/24)	9	2	Local
11	172.30.12.0	255.255.255.0 (/24)	3	3	Local
12	123.241.0.0	255.255.0.0 (/16)	16	2	G
13	0.0.0.0	0.0.0.0 (/0)	5	3	H

2. An arriving packet has the destination IP address 60.168.6.184.
a) What two rows will it match? b) What will be the best-match row? Justify your conclusion. c) What interface will the router send the packet out? d) To what next-hop router will the router forward the packet?

3. An arriving packet has the destination IP address 128.171.17.13. a) What three rows will it match? b) What will be the best-match row? Justify your answer. c) What interface will the router send the packet out? d) To what next-hop router will it send the packet?

4. Suppose that Rows 5 and 8 match an arriving packet's destination IP address.
a) Which row will be the best match? Why? b) How would your answer change if the metric column represented speed rather than cost?

5. Suppose that a packet arrives with the destination IP address 172.30.12.86 and that Row 11 is the best match row. Where will the router send the packet?

GETTING CURRENT

Go to the book website's New Information and Errors pages for this chapter to get new information since this book went to press and to correct any errors in the text.

Hands-On: Packet Capture and Analysis with WinDUMP and TCPDUMP

Learning Objectives

By the end of this chapter, you should be able to discuss:

■ The purpose of WinDUMP and TCPDUMP.

■ How to obtain and run WinDUMP.

■ How to read "simple" WinDUMP output.

■ How to read hexadecimal WinDUMP output.

WHAT ARE WINDUMP AND TCPDUMP?

WinDUMP and TCPDUMP are packet capture and analysis programs. As the names suggest, they capture packets entering and leaving your computer and afterward allow you to look at the contents of selected fields in individual packets.

More specifically, after these programs capture packets, they print one or more lines per packet, as Figure 8a-1 illustrates for an HTTP request–response cycle. The printout is dense and looks forbidding, but with a little practice, it becomes easily readable.

This detailed information can help you troubleshoot problems and detect hacker activity. Using WinDUMP/TCPDUMP is also a great way to solidify your understanding of TCP.

Historically, TCPDUMP was created to run on Unix machines, and it has been wildly popular among Unix administrators. TCPDUMP was ported to Windows

Command prompt>tcpdump www2.pukanui.com

7:50.10.500020 10.0.5.3.62030 > www2.pukanui.com.http: S 800000050:800000050(0) win 4086 <mss1460>

7:50.10.500030 www2.pukanui.com.http > 10.0.5.3.62030 : S 300000030:300000030(0) ack 800000051 win 8760 <mss1460>

7:50.10.500040 10.0.5.3.62030 > www2.pukanui.com.http: . ack 1 win 4086

7:50.10.500050 10.0.5.3.62030 > www2.pukanui.com.http: P 1:100(100)

7:50.10.500060 www2.pukanui.com.http > 10.0.5.3.62030 : . ack 101 win 9000

7:50.10.500070 www2.pukanui.com.http > 10.0.5.3.62030 : . 1:1000(999)

7:50.10.500080 10.0.5.3.62030 > www2.pukanui.com.http: . ack 1001 win 4086

7:50.10.500090 www2.pukanui.com.http > 10.0.5.3.62030 : P 1001:2000(999)

7:50.10.500100 10.0.5.3.62030 > www2.pukanui.com.http: . ack 2001 win 4086

7:50.10.500110 10.0.5.3.62030 > www2.pukanui.com.http: R

Figure 8a-1   ASCII WinDUMP Printout

computers as WinDUMP. Although WinDUMP is not as mature or as full-featured as TCPDUMP, it will run on the Windows clients that most students have.

WORKING WITH WINDUMP

Installing WinDUMP

To get a copy of WinDUMP, go to *http://www.tcpdump.org/*. This website has directions for downloading the program to your computer. Websites do not always remain alive, so if this website is not working, you might have to do an Internet search to find WinDUMP.

WinDUMP does not work by itself. It requires a library of packet capture programs collectively known as WinPCAP. Fortunately, websites that help you download WinDUMP also help you download WinPCAP. During installation, install WinPCAP first, then WinDUMP.

Running WinDUMP

As Figure 8a-1 shows, you begin a WinDUMP session by going to the command line. You do this by clicking Start, then Run, and then typing cmd or command. You can then give WinDUMP commands. In this example the command is the following:

Command prompt>tcpdump www2.pukanui.com -c 40

Note that the command is "tcpdump," not windump. TCPDUMP may have been ported over to WinDUMP, but its Unix commands have been kept.

If you simply type the command "tcpdump" without options, all packets going into and out of the computer interface will be captured. However, the tcpdump program has many options to control what packets are captured and how they are displayed. In the example shown in Figure 8a-1, for instance, only packets to and from the specified host, www2.pukanui.com, will be captured. The packet count, c, is set to 40, meaning that only the first 40 packets will be captured.

To get full information about TCPDUMP, do an Internet search for "tcpdump man page." This will take you to a detailed Unix manual page. Most of what you read there will work with WinDUMP.

Getting Data to Capture

Of course, if no packets go to or from *www2.pukanui.com*, there will be nothing to capture. Without closing your command prompt window, open your browser and go to a website. This will download the home page, giving you at least one HTTP request–response cycle. (If a page has graphics and other elements, each is a separate file, so several request–response cycles will be captured. In this case, capturing only 40 packets will show you only the connection opening and some of the subsequent packet exchanges.

READING WINDUMP OUTPUT

To see how WinDUMP works (and to help you solidify and extend your understanding of IP and especially TCP), we will look at the WinDUMP output in Figure 8a-1.

Opening the TCP Connection

The first three packets in Figure 8a-1 open a TCP connection between a client PC and a server. This is the classic SYN–SYN/ACK–SYN three-way handshake.

SYN

The first packet carries a SYN segment from the client PC running WinDUMP to a webserver.

> 7:50.10.500020 10.0.5.3.62030 > www2.pukanui.com.http: S 800000050:800000050(0) win 4086 <mss1460>

➤ The printout begins with a time stamp, 7:50.10.500020. This gives time to the millionth of a second.

➤ Next comes the source host's IP address and port number. The IP address is 10.0.5.3. The source host's port number, 62030, is an ephemeral port; so the source host must be a client PC. It is the computer running WinDUMP.

➤ Next comes the destination host's host name and port number. Unless you tell it otherwise, WinDUMP looks up the host name for the source and destination IP addresses and inserts them in the printout. The client, 10.0.5.3, does not have a host name, so its IP address is used in the packet printout. The destination host is *www2.pukanui.com*. The port number is the well-known port for http (80). Unless you tell it otherwise, WinDUMP substitutes protocol names when it sees well-known port numbers.

➤ The "S" indicates that the SYN flag is set. Flags except for ACK are shown in this position. If no flag is set, a period is shown instead of flags.

➤ Next comes the odd-looking 800000050:800000050(0). When a host begins a TCP session, it randomly generates an initial sequence number. The client has generated an initial sequence number of 800000050 for this session. A SYN message is a pure supervisory message containing no data. The 800000050:800000050(0) shows that the data field has a length of zero (0) because this is a supervisory segment containing no data.

➤ The win 4086 part of the printout shows that the client has told the server to use a window of 4,086 bytes. The server can transmit only 4,086 bytes of data before getting a window extension.

➤ Data within angle brackets describe options. Here the client advertises a maximum segment size (MSS) of 1460. This tells the receiver of the packet (the webserver) to place no more than 1,460 bytes of data in TCP data fields.

SYN/ACK

Now the webserver replies with its SYN/ACK message.

7:50.10.500030 www2.pukanui.com.http > 10.0.5.3.62030 : S 300000030:300000030(0) ack 800000051 win 8760 <mss1460>

➤ The host designations are reversed to indicate that the webserver is sending to the client.

➤ The S flag is again set.

➤ The webserver's initial sequence number is 300000030, and the packet carries no data.

➤ The "ack" indicates that this TCP segment contains an acknowledgement. The acknowledgement number is 800000051. The acknowledgement number is always one byte larger than the last data byte in the segment being acknowledged (800000050). It specifies the next byte of data that is expected after the segment being acknowledged.

➤ The window again indicates how many more bytes may be transmitted before the window size is increased. In this case, the window size is 8760. The client may transmit through byte 800000051 plus 8,760, or 800008811.

ACK

The client now sends back an ACK.

7:50.10.500040 10.0.5.3.62030 > www2.pukanui.com.http: . ack 1 win 4086

➤ Notice that there is no flag other than ack, so a period (.) is placed in the flags position.

➤ Also notice that the ack is 1, not 300000031, as you would expect (one more than the last data byte received). The packet really does have 300000031 as the acknowledgement. However, to make the printout easier to read, WinDUMP subtracts the initial sequence number, leaving 1. All subsequent TCP data indications will be based on the bytes sent by a transport process since the beginning of the session.

The HTTP Request Message

Now the client sends an HTTP request message. This consists of a single packet.

7:50.10.500050 10.0.5.3.62030 > www2.pukanui.com.http: P 1:100(100)

➤ The flags field shows P, for push. This tells the receiver that a full application message is contained in the message, and that the transport process should pass the application message to the application layer.

➤ The 1:100(100) says that the HTTP request message contains data bytes 1 through 100—100 bytes in total.

The webserver responds with an acknowledgement. The acknowledgement number, as always, gives the next data byte the webserver expects to see (101).

   7:50.10.500060 www2.pukanui.com.http > 10.0.5.3.62030 : . ack 101 win 9000

The HTTP Response Message

Now the webserver sends back an HTTP response message. This response message is too large to fit into a single packet. Consequently, the webserver sends the HTTP response message in two packets, each of which is acknowledged separately.

   7:50.10.500070 www2.pukanui.com.http > 10.0.5.3.62030 : . 1:1000(999)
   7:50.10.500080 10.0.5.3.62030 > www2.pukanui.com.http: . ack 1001 win 4086
   7:50.10.500090 www2.pukanui.com.http > 10.0.5.3.62030 : P 1001:2000(999)
   7:50.10.500100 10.0.5.3.62030 > www2.pukanui.com.http: . ack 2001 win 4086

➤ The packets containing the HTTP response message do not have any flag fields set, so a period (.) appears where you would see a flag if one had been included in the segment.

➤ Note that the first packet contains bytes 1 through 1000 of the HTTP response message, while the second packet contains remaining bytes, 1001 through 2000.

➤ Note also that the second packet containing the HTTP response message contains a P flag field. This is the push flag, which tells the receiving transport process that all data has been delivered, so that the data should be pushed up to the application program. The first response packet does not have a push flag because it only delivers the first part of the HTTP response message. A push is not needed again until all the data is received.

Ending the Connection

   7:50.10.500110 10.0.5.3.62030 > www2.pukanui.com.http: R

In Chapter 8, we saw how TCP connections should end with a four-way close in which FINs are sent and acknowledged. In Figure 8a-1, however, the client, for no obvious reason, has sent a reset message (flag R) to the webserver. A reset message abruptly terminates the connection. Neither side transmits again.

SOME POPULAR WINDUMP OPTIONS

Major Options

WinDUMP's tcpdump command has a large number of options. We have already seen two of them.

➤ Giving a hostname or IP address specifies that packets to or from only that address should be captured.

➤ The "-c" option specifies how many packets should be captured.

The following are a few other commonly used options. The tcpdump command has many more.

- ➤ e: Print the data link layer header fields on each line.
- ➤ i: Specify an interface (NIC) if a computer has more than one.
- ➤ n: Do not convert IP addresses into host names (reduces capture processing work).
- ➤ N: Print only the host part of a hostname. This makes output more condensed and perhaps easier to read.
- ➤ q: Quiet. Print less information for each packet in ASCII.
- ➤ s: Snaplen. Specifies how many octets will be shown for each packet. The default is 68.
- ➤ t: Do not print the time stamp on each line.
- ➤ v: Verbose output—more detail than the normal output. There also are vv and vvv options for more verbose and incredibly verbose output.
- ➤ w: Writes the raw packets to a file. A space and then a file name must follow the w option.
- ➤ r: Reads data from a file instead of capturing the data. Often used when the data was captured in a file with the w option.
- ➤ The -x option specifies that output should be in hex, while the -X option specifies that output should be in both ASCII and hex. We will see what this means in the next section.

Example

For example, suppose you give the following command.

    tcpdump www2.pukanui.com -c 1 -tN

This tells tcpdump to collect data only for packets going to and from *www2.pukanui.com*. It also tells tcpdump to suppress time stamps and to show only the host name. Finally, it tells tcpcump to capture only a single packet. The following shows the output you might see:

    10.0.5.3.62030 > www2.http: S 800000050:800000050(0) win 4086 <mss1460>

Expression

In the examples we have been using, we have included the name of a host, *www2.pukanui.com*. This type of option is called an expression. It specifies what packets will be captured and analyzed.

- ➤ Host expressions are the most common. They should be written as "host hostname", but host is the default, so it does not need to be added.
- ➤ The expression "port 80" tells TCPdump to look only at HTTP traffic. The more finely grained expression "src port 80" captures packets only from HTTP servers.
- ➤ It is even possible to have expressions that limit traffic to a particular network, as in "net 128.171", to capture traffic going to or from a particular network.

HEXADECIMAL PRINTOUT

ASCII versus Hex

The type of printout we have been seeing is called ASCII printout, because it contains alphanumeric characters (keyboard characters) stored in the ASCII format. WinDUMP also offers another way to store and see packet information—hexadecimal format. As discussed in Chapter 4, "hex" represents a group of four bits as a symbol from 0 through F. Hex output typically groups hex symbols in groups of two to represent a byte (octet) or in groups of four, to represent two-byte sequences. WinDUMP does the latter.

Hex Output

Figure 8a-2 shows hexadecimal output for a single packet. To turn on hex output, give the -x (lowercase x) option in a tcpdump command. To get both ASCII and hex output, give the -X (uppercase X) option.

IP Fields

To help you read this very dense output, the IP header is shown in boldface. In the following description, the most widely interpreted sequences are shown in boldface.

- ➤ **4500.** The 4 indicates that this is an IPv4 packet. The 5 indicates that the length of the header is 5 times 32 bits, or 20 octets. This is the header length of an IP header without options. Options are rare and suspicious, so anything other than a 5 for the header length should be seen as a caution sign. The 00 is the Diff-Serv octet, which normally is not used and so normally is set to 00. Almost all packets should start with 4500.
- ➤ **00c7.** This is the length of the entire IP packet (199 bytes).
- ➤ ff53 0000. This is the identification field value and other information used to reassemble fragmented packets. Fragmentation is rare.
- ➤ **8006.** The 80 is the one-byte time to live field value (128 in decimal). The 06 is the one-byte protocol field value. The 06 protocol is TCP. This field is needed to interpret the IP data field, which is not always a TCP segment. Protocol 01 is ICMP, for instance, while Protocol 17 is UDP.
- ➤ 3d5e. This is the header checksum.
- ➤ **b87a 3270.** This is the IP source address.
- ➤ **b87a c3d0.** This is the IP destination address.

TCP Fields

In Figure 8a-2, the TCP fields are underlined. The following are the TCP fields. Again, the most widely interpreted fields are shown in boldface.

Figure 8a-2   Hexadecimal Output from WinDUMP

```
4500 00c7 ff53 0000 8006 3d5e b87a 3270

b87a c3d0 F230 0050 0023 37d6 1d37 1302

5018 07d0 b329 0000 ...
```

➤ **F230.** This is the source port number (62000).

➤ **0050.** This is the destination port number (80 decimal).

➤ **0023 37d6.** This is the sequence number.

➤ **1d37 1302.** This is the acknowledgement number.

➤ **50.** 5 is the header length in 32-bit units; as in IP, 5 is the header length without options. In contrast to IP, options are common in TCP. The 0 is from reserved bits. It should always be 0.

➤ **18.** The 1 indicates that the ack bit is set. The 8 indicates that the push bit is set. These two symbols indicate which bits are set. Experienced WinDUMP users learn the most common combinations.

➤ **07d0.** This is the window size (2000 in decimal).

➤ **b329.** This is the checksum.

➤ **0000.** This is the urgent pointer. If the urgent (U) bit is set in the flags field, this pointer tells where urgent data begin in the TCP byte sequence.

GENERAL QUESTIONS

1. What does WinDUMP do?
2. Distinguish between WinDUMP and TCPDUMP.
3. Distinguish between ASCII and hex output.
4. What steps should you take to capture and display data?

For Each of the Following, Specify a Command to Do the Work

5. Show all packets.
6. Show the first 100 packets going to or from dakine.pukanui.com.
7. Repeat the preceding command, this time not showing a time stamp or the full host name.
8. Show all packets going to or from HTTP servers.

INTERPRETATION

1. Interpret the following ASCII printout.
   7:50.10.500099 db.pukanui.com.54890 > www2.pukanui.com.http: 1:21(21) ack 52 win 4086

2. The following hex printout shows an IP packet. a) What type of message is in its data field? b) What is the IP destination address?

4500	00c7	ff53	0000	8017	3d5e	b87a	3270
b87a	c3d0						

3. The following hex printout shows an IP packet containing a TCP segment. a) What is the source port (in decimal)? b) Is the ack bit set? (Tell how you can know.)

4500	00c7	ff53	0000	8006	3d5e	b87a	3270
b87a	c3d0	0060	0050	0023	37d6	0000	0000
5008	07d0	b329	0000	. . . .			

Security

Learning Objectives

By the end of this chapter, you should be able to discuss:

■ Security threats (worms and viruses, hacking, and denial-of-service attacks).

■ Types of attackers.

■ Why security is primarily a management issue, not a technical issue.

■ Security planning principles.

■ Access control, including authentication mechanisms: passwords, digital certificate authentication, and biometrics.

■ Firewall protection, including stateful inspection, IDSs, and IPS filtering.

■ The protection of dialogues by cryptographic systems. Encryption for confidentiality. The phases of cryptographic systems.

■ Responding to successful compromises.

INTRODUCTION

In the 1990s, the Internet blossomed, allowing people to reach hundreds of millions of servers around the world. Unfortunately, the Internet also gave attackers access to hundreds of millions of users. Security quickly became one of the most important IT management issues.

One thing that sets security apart from other aspects of IT is that the company must battle against intelligent adversaries, not simply against errors and other forms of unreliability. Companies today are engaged in an escalating arms race with attackers, and security threats and defenses are mutating at a frightening rate.

SECURITY THREATS

The first principle in security is this: First, understand the organization's needs. In security, this requires a solid knowledge of the **threat environment** the company faces. Before discussing how to prevent attacks, we will look at the main types of attacks that corporations face.

Had at Least One Security Incident in This Category (May have had several)	Percent Reporting an Incident in 1997	Percent Reporting an Incident in 2003	Number Reporting Quantified Losses in 2002	Average Reported Annual Loss per Firm (Thousands) in 1997	Average Reported Annual Loss per Firm (Thousands) in 2002
Viruses	82%	82%	254	$76	$200
Insider Abuse of Net Access	Not Asked	80%	180	Not Asked	$136
Laptop Theft	58%	59%	250	$38	$47
Unauthorized Access by Insiders	40%	45%	72	NA	$31
Denial of Service	24%	42%	111	$77	$1,427
System Penetration	20%	36%	88	$132	$56
Sabotage	14%	21%	61	$164	$215
Theft of Proprietary Information	20%	21%	61	$954	$2,700
Financial Fraud	12%	15%	61	$958	$329
Telecom Fraud	27%	10%	34	NA	$50
Telecom Eavesdropping	11%	6%	0	NA	NA
Active Wiretap	3%	1%	0	NA	NA

Survey conducted by the Computer Security Institute (www.gocsi.com).
Based on replies from 530 U.S. computer security professionals.
If fewer than twenty firms reported quantified dollar losses, data for the threat are not shown.

Figure 9-1   CSI/FBI Survey

Figure 9-1 looks at some key results from an annual survey of about 500 security professionals. The FBI and the Computer Security Institute *www.gocsi.com* conduct this survey jointly. The figure underscores the fact that security **compromises** (successful attacks) are widespread, varied, and expensive. Nearly all of the firms surveyed had experienced a compromise (also called an **incident** or **breach**) in the previous year. Although not all firms could or were willing to report dollar losses from these attacks, the limited data provided in the table make it clear that many compromises are extremely costly.

Compromises are widespread, varied, and costly.

TEST YOUR UNDERSTANDING

1. a) What is a compromise? b) Are compromises common or rare? c) Give two other names for compromises.

Viruses and Worms

The most widespread compromises identified in the CSI/FBI survey are virus and worm attacks. In the CSI/FBI survey, almost all of the firms experienced at least one compromise from virus and worm attacks—despite the fact that about 90 percent had antivirus systems in place.

Viruses and Virus Propagation

Propagation Within a Computer   **Viruses** are pieces of executable code that attach themselves to other programs. Within a computer, whenever an infected program runs (executes), the virus attaches itself to other programs.

Propagation Between Computers   Between computers, the virus spreads when an infected program is transferred to another computer via a floppy disk, an e-mail attachment, a webpage download, an unprotected disk share, a peer-to-peer file-sharing transfer, an instant message, or some other propagation vector. Once on another machine, if the infected program is executed, the virus spreads to other programs on the machine.

More than 90 percent of viruses today spread via e-mail. They find addresses in the infected computer's e-mail directories. They then send messages with infected attachments to all of these addresses. If a receiver opens the attachment, the infected program executes, and the receiver's programs become infected. In addition, instant messaging (IM) and peer-to-peer (P2P) file transfers are also becoming important ways for viruses and worms to spread.

To stop viruses, a company must protect its computers with **antivirus programs** that scan each arriving e-mail message or floppy disk for signatures (patterns) that identify viruses. These antivirus programs also scan for other types of **malware** (evil software).

Worms and Worm Propagation

Another important type of malware is worms. We have just seen that viruses are pieces of code that must attach themselves to other programs. In contrast, **worms** are full programs that operate by themselves. Both viruses and worms can create mass epidemics that infect hundreds or even millions of computers. However, they can spread in different ways.

Worms are capable of propagating like viruses, through e-mail attachments, IM, and P2P file transfers. These methods require human gullibility to succeed. Although human gullibility is widespread, it is not reliable. More importantly, human gullibility is rather slow. Until someone opens an e-mail attachment, nothing happens.

Unlike viruses, worms have another propagation vector (way to propagate). This is the exploitation of software vulnerabilities rather than human gullibility. Security vulnerabilities are discovered in most programs several times per year. Although software vendors usually issue patches, it usually takes some time to patch all vulnerable computers. Attackers use this window of vulnerability to launch **vulnerability-enabled** worms that exploit the vulnerability.

Figure 9-2   Malware (Study Figure)

Malware

    This is a general name for evil software

Viruses

    Pieces of code that attach to other programs

    Virus code executes when infected programs execute

    Infect other programs on the computer

    Spread to other computers by e-mail attachments, IM, peer-to-peer file transfers, etc.

    Antivirus programs are needed to scan arriving files

        Also scan for other malware

Worms

    Stand-alone programs that do not need to attach to other programs

    Can propagate like viruses through e-mail, etc.

        This requires human gullibility, which is slow

    Vulnerability-enabled worms jump to victim hosts directly

        Can do this because hosts have vulnerabilities

    Vulnerability-enabled worms can spread with amazing speed

    Vendors develop patches for vulnerabilities, but companies often fail or are slow to apply them

Payloads

    After propagation, viruses and worms execute their payloads

    Payloads erase hard disks, send users to pornography sites if they mistype URLs

    Trojan horses are exploitation programs that disguise themselves as system files

Attacks on Individuals

    Social engineering is tricking the victim into doing something against his or her interests

    Spam is unsolicited commercial e-mail

    Credit card number theft is performed by carders

    Identity theft involves collecting enough data to impersonate the victim in large financial transactions

    Adware pops up advertisements

    Spyware collects sensitive data and sends it to an attacker

    Phishing is a sophisticated social engineering attack in which an authentic-looking e-mail or website entices the user to enter his or her username, password, or other sensitive information

Vulnerability-enabled worms require no human intervention, so they can spread directly from computer to computer with incredible speed. In 2003, the Blaster worm infested 90 percent of all vulnerable hosts on the entire Internet within ten minutes. The nightmare scenario for security professionals is the prospect of a fast-spreading worm that exploits a vulnerability that damages a large percentage of all computers on the Internet.

Vulnerability-enabled worms require no human intervention, so they can spread with incredible speed.

Payloads

In war, when a bomber aircraft reaches its target, it releases its payload of bombs. Similarly, after they spread, viruses and worms may execute pieces of code called **payloads**. In malicious viruses and worms, these payloads can completely erase hard disks and do other significant damage. In some cases, they can take the victim to a pornography site whenever the victim mistypes a URL. In other cases, they can turn the user's computer into a spam generator or a pornography download site.

Often the payload installs a **Trojan horse** program on the user's computer. Once installed, the Trojan horse continues to exploit the user indefinitely. A Trojan horse does not spread by itself but rather relies on a virus, worm, hacker, or gullible user to install it on a computer. As its name suggests, a Trojan horse disguises itself as a system file; it typically replaces a legitimate system program, so it is difficult to detect.

Attacks on Individuals

Social Engineering   As technical defenses improve, a growing number of malware attacks today focus on **social engineering**, which is a fancy name for tricking the victim into doing something against his or her interests. Viruses and worms have long tried to do this with e-mail attachments, say by telling someone that they have won a lottery and need to open the attachment for the details. The range of social engineering attacks has expanded greatly in the last few years. The CSI/FBI survey tends to lump these attacks under "viruses," but it is important to understand them.

Spam   Perhaps the most annoying type of malware on a day-in, day-out basis is **spam**,[1] which is unsolicited commercial e-mail. Spammers send the same solicitation e-mail message to millions of e-mail addresses in the hope that a few percent of all victims will respond. Most users today have to delete about ten or more spam messages for every legitimate message they receive. In addition, many spam messages involve pornography or frauds.

---

[1] Except at the beginning of sentences, *spam* is spelled in lowercase. This distinguishes unsolicited commercial e-mail from the Hormel Corporation's meat product, Spam. In addition, Spam is *not* an acronym for *spongy pink animal matter*.

Credit Card Number Theft   In fraudulent spam, the message may convince the user to type a credit card number to purchase goods. The attacker will not deliver the goods. Instead, the **carder** (credit card number thief) will use the credit card number to make unauthorized purchases.

Identity Theft   In other cases, thieves collect enough data to impersonate the victim in large financial transactions. This impersonation is **identity theft**. It allows thieves to take out large loans and do other major damage.

Adware   A recent threat is **adware**—the installing of software that constantly pops up advertisements on the victim's computer.

Spyware   Another recent threat (and one related to adware) is **spyware**—a name given to programs that are installed on your computer **surreptitiously** (without your knowledge) to collect information about you and to send this information to the attacker. Some spyware programs collect information about your Web surfing habits and send this information to advertisers. More dangerous are **keystroke loggers**, which record your keystrokes, hoping to find passwords, social security numbers, and other information that can help the person who receives the keystroke logger's data commit credit card number theft or identity theft. **Data mining** spyware searches your hard drive for potentially useful information and sends this information to the attacker.

Phishing Attacks   **Phishing**[2] is a sophisticated social engineering attack in which an authentic looking e-mail or website entices the user to enter his or her username, password, or other sensitive information. Phishing is growing explosively.

TEST YOUR UNDERSTANDING

2. a) How do viruses propagate within computers? b) How do viruses propagate between computers? c) How can viruses be stopped? d) Distinguish between vulnerability-enabled worms and e-mail worms. e) Which can spread faster—viruses or vulnerability-enabled worms? Explain. f) How can vulnerability-enabled worms be stopped? g) What are payloads? h) What is malware? i) What are Trojan horses? j) How does a Trojan horse get on a computer?

3. a) What is social engineering? b) What is the definition of spam? c) Distinguish between credit card number theft and identity theft. d) What are carders? e) What is adware? f) What is spyware? g) What is a keystroke logger? h) What is phishing?

Human Break-Ins (Hacking)

Viruses and worms spread randomly with fixed attack methods. However, human attackers often wish to break into a specific company's computers manually. Human adversaries can attack a company with a variety of approaches until they find one that succeeds. This makes human break-ins much more likely to succeed than viruses.

[2]IT attackers often replace *f* with *ph*. For example, *phone freaking* (dialing long distance numbers illegally) became *phone phreaking* and later just *phreaking*.

Human Break-Ins
      Viruses and worms rely on one main attack method

      Humans can keep trying different approaches until they succeed

Hacking
      Hacking is breaking into a computer

      Hacking is intentionally using a computer resource without authorization or in excess of authorization

Scanning Phase
      Send attack probes to map the network and identify possible victim hosts

      The Nmap program is popular for scanning attacks (Figure 9-4)

The Exploit
      The term "exploit" is used in several ways

      Exploit (noun) can refer to the actual break-in

      Exploit (noun) can refer to the program used to make the break-in

      Attackers *exploit* (verb) the computer

After the Break-In
      The hacker becomes invisible by deleting log files

      The hacker creates a backdoor (way to get back into the computer)

            Backdoor account—account with a known password and superuser privileges

            Backdoor program—program to allow reentry; usually Trojanized

      The hacker can then do damage at his or her leisure

Figure 9-3   Human Break-Ins (Hacking) (Study Figure)

What is Hacking?

We will use the term *hacking* to mean breaking into a computer. More specifically, **hacking** is intentionally using a computer resource without authorization or in excess of authorization. Note that it is still hacking if the attacker is given an account and uses the computer for unauthorized purposes.

Hacking is intentionally using a computer resource without authorization or in excess of authorization.

The Scanning Phase

When a hacker begins an attack on a firm, he or she usually begins by **scanning** the network. This involves sending **probe packets** into the firm's network. Responses to these probe packets tend to reveal information about the firm's general network design and about its individual computers—including the operating systems and the applications these computers are running.

Figure 9-4 shows output from one popular scanning program, Nmap. In the figure, Nmap has identified several open ports on a server—port numbers that will accept connection attempts. If the attacker has an exploit (tailored attack method) for one of the services associated with these ports, the attacker can now attack the server. The scan has also fingerprinted the operating system of the server because many attacks are operating system-specific.

The Exploit

Once the attacker has identified a potential victim host, the next step is the break-in itself. There are many tools for breaking into a computer, including tools for cracking passwords and other laborious break-in work. However, like worms, most hackers exploit known vulnerabilities. They have break-in programs, called **exploits**(noun), which take advantage of one or more known vulnerabilities to give the user access to the computer. If the target computer has not been patched, the exploit can succeed in less than a second. Confusingly, when attackers break into a computer, it is said that they **exploit** (verb) the computer.

Exploits (noun) take advantage of one or more known vulnerabilities to give the user access to the computer. Confusingly, when attackers break into a computer, it is said that they exploit (verb) the computer.

After the Break-In

Erasing Log Files   After the attack, the hacker tries to erase the operating system's log files so that the computer's rightful owner cannot trace how the attacker broke in or gather evidence to find and prosecute the attacker. Unless attackers are stopped very quickly, they often become very difficult to stop.

Creating a Backdoor   To be able to exploit the computer later, even if the vulnerability that was exploited is fixed, the attacker must create a way to get back in. This is called a **backdoor**. It may simply be a new account with a known password and superuser privileges, or it may be a Trojan horse program that is difficult to detect.

Doing Damage   The attacker can now read all files on the computer, change them, delete them, or do almost anything else. Hackers often look for trade secrets that they can try to sell to competitors. They also tend to install **exploitation software** that continues to cause damage—for instance, turning the host into a pornography download site or installing software to attack other computers.

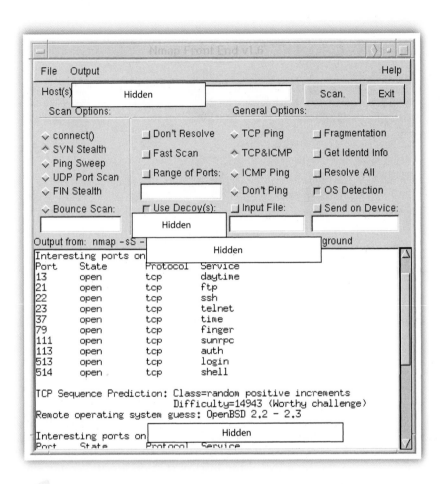

Figure 9-4   Nmap Scanning Output

TEST YOUR UNDERSTANDING

4. a) List the usual main phases in human break-ins (hacks). b) What is hacking? c) Why do hackers send probe packets into networks? d) What is an exploit (noun)? e) What is an exploit (verb)? f) Do most exploits take advantage of vulnerabilities? g) What steps does a hacker usually take after a break-in? h) What is a backdoor? i) What is host exploitation software?

Denial-of-Service (DoS) Attacks

Another type of attack, the denial-of-service attack, does not involve breaking into a computer, infecting it with a virus, or infesting it with a worm. Rather, the goal of **denial-of-service (DoS)** attacks is to make a computer unavailable to its users. As

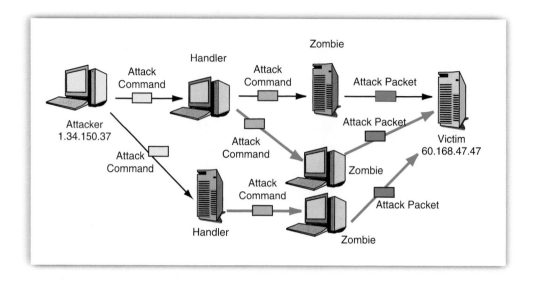

Figure 9-5   Distributed Flooding Denial-of-Service Attack

Figure 9-5 shows, most DoS attacks involve flooding the victim computer with irrelevant packets. The victim computer becomes so busy processing this flood of attack packets that it cannot process legitimate packets. The overloaded host may even fail. The attack shown in the figure is a **distributed DoS (DDoS)** attack. In this type of attack, the attacker first installs programs called bots on hundreds or thousands of PCs or servers. When the user sends these bots an attack command, they all begin to flood the victim with packets.

Bots

Bots are limited to DDoS attacks. Bots are general-purpose exploitation programs that can be remotely controlled after installation. The attacker can send commands to the bots and can even upgrade them remotely with new capabilities. Bots are extremely dangerous because they can engage in massive attacks that were previously possible only with relatively dumb and inflexible viruses and worms. Bots bring the flexibility of human thought into the attack, making them very dangerous. (See Figure 9-6.)

TEST YOUR UNDERSTANDING

5. a) What is the purpose of a denial-of-service attack? b) What are bots? c) How do distributed DoS attacks work?

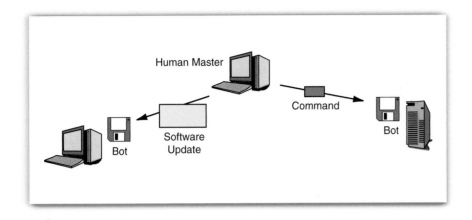

Figure 9-6   Bots

Attackers

As Figure 9-7 shows, there are many different types of attackers facing organizations today.

Traditional Attackers

When most people think of attackers, they normally have three pictures in their minds: hackers driven by curiosity, virus writers, and disgruntled employees and ex-employees. Indeed, these used to be the three most important types of attackers.

Hackers   Traditionally, some **hackers** have been motivated primarily by curiosity and the sense of power they get from breaking into computers. In many cases, they are also motivated by a desire to increase their reputation among their hacker peers by boasting about their exploits. This typically is the image of hackers presented in Hollywood movies. However, these are not the typical hackers today.

Virus Writers   **Virus writers**, as the name suggests, create viruses. They also create other types of automated malware. Virus writers appear to enjoy the excitement of seeing their programs spread rapidly. These virus writers tend to be blind to the harm that they do to people.

Script Kiddies   Experienced hackers and virus writers often developed small programs, called scripts, to automate parts of their attacks. Over time, these programs

Traditional Attackers

    Traditional Hackers

        Hackers break into computers

        Driven by curiosity, a feeling of power, and peer reputation

    Virus writers

    Script kiddies use scripts written by experienced hackers and virus writers

        They have limited knowledge and abilities

        But large numbers of script kiddies make them dangerous

    Disgruntled employees and ex-employees

Criminal Attackers

    Most attacks are now made by criminals

    Crime generates funds that criminal attackers need to increase attack sophistication

On the Horizon

    Cyberterror attacks by terrorists

    Cyberwar by nations

    Potential for massive attacks

Figure 9-7   Types of Attackers (Study Figure)

grew more sophisticated. More importantly, they grew easier to use. Many now have graphical user interfaces and have the look, feel, and reliability of commercial programs. This has led to the emergence of **script kiddie** attackers, who use these scripts developed by more experienced attackers. Although traditional attackers disparage the lack of skills of these script kiddies, there are far more script kiddies than traditional hackers and virus writers, and script kiddies collectively represent a great threat to corporations.

Disgruntled Employees and Ex-Employees   Other traditional attackers have been **disgruntled employees** and **disgruntled ex-employees** who attacked their own firms. Employee attackers have been few in number but tend to do extensive damage when they strike because they typically already have access to systems and have extensive knowledge of how systems work.

Criminal Attackers

In addition, there now are many **criminal attackers** who steal credit card numbers to commit credit card fraud, who extort firms, and who steal trade secrets to sell to competitors. In fact, today, more than half of all Internet attacks are committed by criminals motivated by money, and this fraction is rising rapidly.

Funded by their criminal gains, many criminals can afford to hire the best hackers and to enhance their own skills. Consequently, criminal attacks are not just growing in numbers; they also are growing very rapidly in sophistication.

Cyberterrorists and National Governments

On the horizon, there is the danger of far more massive **cyberterror** attacks created by terrorists and even worse **cyberwar** attacks by national governments. These could produce damages of hundreds of billions of dollars.

TEST YOUR UNDERSTANDING

6. a) Are most attackers today driven by curiosity and a sense of power? b) Why are employees dangerous? c) What type of attacker is the most common today? d) What are cyberterror and cyberwar attacks?

PLANNING

Security Is a Management Issue

People tend to think of security as a technological issue, but security experts are unanimous in noting that security is primarily a management issue. Unless a firm does excellent planning, implementation, and day-to-day operation, the best technology will be wasted. As Bruce Schneier, a noted security expert, has often said, "security is a process, not a product."

Security is primarily a management issue, not a technology issue.

TEST YOUR UNDERSTANDING

7. Why is security primarily a management issue, not a technology issue?

Planning Principles

Perhaps more than in any other aspect of IT, effective security depends on effective planning. Security planning is a complex process. We will only note three key principles that must be used in planning.

Risk Analysis

In contrast to military security, which often makes massive investments to stop threats, corporate security planners have to ask whether applying a protection against a particular threat is justified economically. For example, if the probable annual loss is

Security Is a Management Issue, Not a Technical Issue
        Without good management, technology cannot be effective

Risk Analysis
        Risk analysis is the process of balancing threats and protection costs
        for individual assets

Comprehensive Security
        An attacker only has to find one weakness

        A firm needs comprehensive security to close all avenues of attack

Defense in Depth
        Every protection breaks down sometimes

        An attacker should have to break through several lines of defense to
        succeed

        Providing this protection is called defense in depth

Figure 9-8   Planning Principles (Study Figure)

$100,000 and security measures to thwart the threat will cost $200,000, firms should not spend the money. Instead, they should accept the probable loss. **Risk analysis** is the process of balancing threats and protection costs for individual assets.

> Risk analysis is the process of balancing threats and protection costs for individual assets.

Comprehensive Security

Corporate security is an example of asymmetrical warfare in which the attacker has a clear advantage. A company must close off all vectors of attack. If it misses even one, and if the attacker finds it, the attacker will succeed. The attacker, in contrast, only has to find one security weakness. Although it is difficult to achieve **comprehensive security**, in which all avenues of attack are closed off, it is essential to come as close as possible.

Defense in Depth

Another critical planning principle is defense in depth. Every protection will break down occasionally. If attackers have to break through only one line of defense, they will succeed during these vulnerable periods. However, if an attacker has to break through two, three, or more lines of defense, the breakdown of a single defense technology will not be enough to allow the attacker to succeed. Having successive lines of defense is called **defense in depth**.

TEST YOUR UNDERSTANDING

8. a) List the three major planning principles. b) What is risk analysis? c) Why is comprehensive security important? d) What is defense in depth? e) Why is it necessary?

CONTROLLING ACCESS

Access Control Plans

Enumerating and Prioritizing Resources

A firm has a wide variety of resources on its client PCs and servers. Some of these resources are extremely crucial, others less so.

- ➤ One of the first things a company must do to have adequate security is to enumerate (identify and list) its resources.
- ➤ The next step is to rank these resources by sensitivity (security risk). Databases of customer information, for instance, would be ranked as very sensitive because the consequences of a security breach in which this information was stolen would be catastrophic.
- ➤ Finally, the company must develop an **access control plan** for each resource (or at least for each resource category).

Access Control Plan (AAA)

In general, access control plans have three key elements: authentication, authorization, and auditing. Collectively, they are known as AAA.

Figure 9-9   Access Control (Study Figure)

Enumerating and Prioritizing Assets
   Firms must enumerate and prioritize the assets they have to protect
   Otherwise, security planning is impossible

Companies Must Then Develop an Access Control Plan for Each Asset
   The plan includes the AAA protections
   Authentication is proving the identity of the person wishing access
   Authorization is determining what the person may do if he or she is authenticated
   Auditing is logging data on user actions for later appraisal

Authentication   **Authentication** is requiring someone wishing to use a resource to prove his or her identity. Grocery stores do this when they require you to show them identification when you want to cash a check.

Authorization   Just because a person has access to a resource does not mean that the person should be able to do anything he or she wishes. The person must have specific **authorizations**, which define specific actions that the person can take—for instance, deleting files.

Auditing   The final element of the access control plan is **auditing**—that is, collecting information about what people do and recording this information in log files for later analysis. Auditing serves roughly the same function as surveillance cameras. If people know that what they are doing is being recorded, they are less likely to misbehave.

TEST YOUR UNDERSTANDING

9. a) What are the three things that companies must do with assets? b) What does *AAA* stand for? c) Distinguish between authentication and authorization. d) What is auditing?

Authentication

The most complex element of access control is authentication. Figure 9-10 illustrates authentication. The user trying to prove his or her identity is the **applicant** (sometimes called the supplicant). The party requiring the applicant to prove his or her identity is the **verifier**. The applicant tries to prove his or her identity by providing **credentials** (proofs of identity) to the verifier.

As we saw in Chapter 5, there often is a third party, the **authentication server**, which stores data to help the verifier check the credentials of the applicant. Use of a central authentication server helps provide consistent security by ensuring that all verifiers use the same authentication information.

Use of a central authentication server helps provide consistent security by ensuring that all verifiers use the same authentication information.

The type of authentication tool that is used with each resource must be appropriate for the sensitivity of that particular resource. Sensitive personnel information should be protected by very strong authentication methods. For relatively nonsensitive data, less expensive and weaker authentication methods may be sufficient.

TEST YOUR UNDERSTANDING

10. a) What is authentication? b) Distinguish between the applicant and the verifier. c) What are credentials? d) Why are authentication servers used? e) Why must authentication be appropriate for the sensitivity of an asset?

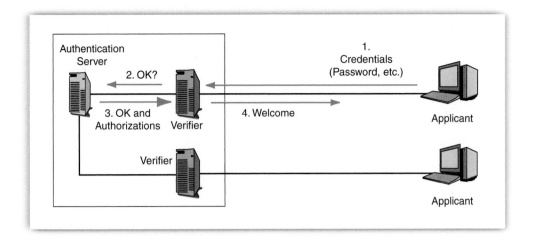

Figure 9-10   Authentication

Passwords

The most common authentication method is the **password**, which is a string of characters that a user types to gain access to the resources associated with a certain **username** (account) on a computer. It also is the weakest form of authentication, and it is only appropriate for the least sensitive assets.

Ease of Use and Low Cost

People find passwords familiar and relatively easy to use. In addition, passwords add no additional cost because operating systems and many applications have built-in password authentication.

Word/Name Passwords and Dictionary Attacks

The main problem with passwords is that most users pick very weak passwords. They often pick ordinary **dictionary words** or the **names** of family members, pets, sports teams, or celebrities. Dictionary-word and name passwords often can be **cracked** (guessed) in a few seconds if the attacker can get a copy of the password file (which contains an encrypted list of account names and passwords). The attacker uses a **dictionary attack**, trying all words or names in a standard or customized dictionary. There are only a few thousand dictionary words and names in any language, so dictionary attacks can crack dictionary-word and name passwords almost instantly.

The main problem with passwords is that most users pick very weak passwords.

Passwords
> Passwords are strings of characters
>
> They are typed to authenticate the use of a username (account) on a computer

Benefits
> Ease of use for users (familiar)
>
> Inexpensive because they are built into operating systems

Often Weak (Easy to Crack)
> Word and name passwords are common
>
> They can be cracked quickly with dictionary attacks

Passwords Should Be Complex
> They mix case, digits, and other keyboard characters ($, #, etc.)
>
> They can only be cracked with brute force attacks (trying all possibilities)

Passwords Also Should Be Long
> Passwords should have a minimum of eight characters
>
> Each added character increases the brute force search time by a factor of about 70

Other Concerns
> If people are forced to use long and complex passwords, they tend to write them down
>
> People should use different passwords for different sites
>
>> Otherwise, a compromised password will give access to multiple sites

Figure 9-11   Password Authentication (Study Figure)

Dictionary attacks also have **hybrid modes**, in which they look for simple variations on words, such as a word with the first letter capitalized, followed by a single digit (for instance, Dog1). Hybrid word or name passwords are cracked almost as quickly as simple words and names.

Complex Passwords and Brute Force Attacks

Dictionary attacks can be thwarted by making passwords more complex. Ideally, the password will be a random string of upper-case letters, lower-case letters, the digits from 0 to 9, and other keyboard symbols, such as & and #. Random or semi-random passwords can be cracked only by **brute force attacks** that try all possible combinations of characters. First, all combinations of a single character are tried, then all combinations of two characters, then all combinations of three characters, and so forth. Brute force attacks take far longer than dictionary attacks.

Ideally, the password will be a random string of upper-case letters, lower-case letters, the digits from 0 to 9, and other keyboard symbols, such as & and #.

Unfortunately, random or nearly random passwords are difficult for users to remember, so they tend to write them on a sheet of paper that they keep next to their computers. This makes passwords easy to steal so that there is no need to crack them by dictionary or brute force attacks.

Password Length

Increasing **password length** (the number of characters in the password) helps, too. If the password uses a combination of uppercase and lowercase letters, digits, and punctuation symbols, each additional character increases the time needed for a brute force attack by a factor of about 70.

Passwords should be at least eight characters long, and longer passwords are highly desirable.

Passwords should be at least eight characters long, and longer passwords are highly desirable.

Reusing Passwords at Multiple Sites

Another problem with passwords is that users often use the same password at multiple sites. This is very dangerous because if a password is cracked at one site, the attacker is likely to be able to impersonate the user at other sites.

TEST YOUR UNDERSTANDING

11. a) Distinguish between usernames and passwords. b) Why are passwords widely used? c) What types of passwords are susceptible to dictionary attacks? d) What is a brute force attack? e) What types of passwords can be broken only by brute force attacks? f) Why is password length important? g) How long should passwords be? h) Why are long and complex passwords not likely to be successful? i) Why is it dangerous if users use the same password at multiple sites?

12. Critique each of the following passwords regarding strength and the type of cracking attack that would be used to crack it. a) Viper1 b) R7%t& c) NeVeR.

Digital Certificate Authentication

The gold standard for authentication is digital certificate authentication. For extremely sensitive assets, digital certificate authentication is almost certainly necessary.

Public and Private Keys

    Each party will have both a public key and a private key

    A party makes its public key available to everybody

    A party keeps the private key secret

Digital Certificate

    Tamper-proof file that gives a party's public key

Operation

    Applicant performs a computation with his or her private key, which only he or she should know

    Verifier tests the calculation with the public key in the digital certificate of the true party—the party the applicant claims to be

    If the test is successful, the applicant is authenticated as knowing the true party's secret private key

    If the test fails, the applicant is rejected

Appraisal

    Digital certificate authentication is very strong

    However, it is very expensive because companies must set up the infrastructure for distributing public-private key pairs

    The firm must do the labor of creating, distributing, and installing private keys

---

Figure 9-12   Digital Certification Authentication (Study Figure)

Public Keys, Private Keys

In **digital certificate authentication**, each user is given a **public key**, which, as the name suggests, is not kept secret. This public key is paired with a **private key** that only the user should know.

Digital Certificate

The **digital certificate** is a tamper-proof file that gives the name of a subject (person or software process) and the subject's public key.

Operation

For authentication, the applicant uses his or her *private key* to do a calculation, which only the person who was given the private key should know.

    The verifier uses the *public key* contained in the digital certificate of the true party—the person the applicant claims to be—to test the calculation performed by the applicant. If the test is successful, then the applicant must know the private key of the true party. If the test fails, the applicant is an impostor and is rejected.

Strong Authentication

Digital certificate authentication is extremely strong because private keys are extremely long and perfectly random. There is no known way to calculate private keys from the public key in a digital certificate in a reasonable time period.

Expensive to Implement

Unfortunately, digital certificate authentication, also known as **public key authentication**, is expensive to implement. Each server and client PC must have digital certificate authentication software and a private key installed on it. This requires a great deal of expensive labor time. Many companies are reluctant to spend this much money on authentication despite the strength of digital certificate authentication.

TEST YOUR UNDERSTANDING

13. a) In digital certificate authentication, who should know a user's private key? b) Who should know a user's public key? c) What information does a digital certificate provide? d) Describe how digital certificates are used in authentication. e) In digital certificate authentication, what key does the applicant use to perform a calculation? f) What key does the verifier use to test the calculation performed by the applicant? g) Is digital certificate authentication strong? h) Why are companies reluctant to implement digital certificate authentication?

Biometrics

A relatively new form of authentication is **biometrics**, which is the use of bodily measurements to identify an applicant. The main promise of biometrics is the promise of eliminating passwords.

The main promise of biometrics is the promise of eliminating passwords.

Fingerprint Scanning

The least expensive (and unfortunately the weakest) form of biometric authentication is **fingerprint scanning**. In addition to having substantial **error rates** (normal misidentification rates that occur even when the subject is cooperating), many fingerprint scanners can be deceived fairly easily by impostors. This makes fingerprint authentication very weak.

Despite its limitations, fingerprint scanning is by far the most widely used biometric authentication method. Many firms feel that the balance between fingerprint scanning vulnerabilities and the weaknesses of passwords still tip the scale toward fingerprint scanning for noncritical applications.

Iris Scanners

At the other extreme of the strength and cost range, **iris scanners** use cameras that read the very complex pattern of the applicant's iris (colored part of the eye). Irises are extremely complex, so iris scanners have low error rates, making them suitable for

Biometric Authentication
> Authentication based on bodily measurements
>
> Promises to eliminate passwords

Fingerprint Scanning
> Dominates biometrics use today
>
> Simple and inexpensive
>
> Substantial error rate (misidentification)
>
> Often can be fooled fairly easily by impostors

Iris Scanners
> Scan the iris (colored part of the eye)
>
> Irises are complex, so iris scanning gives strong authentication
>
> Expensive

Face Recognition
> Camera: allows analysis of facial structure
>
> Can be done surreptitiously—that is, without the knowledge or consent of the person being scanned
>
> Very high error rate and easy to fool

Error and Deception Rates
> Error and deception rates are higher than vendors claim
>
> The effectiveness of biometrics is uncertain

Figure 9-13   Biometric Authentication (Study Figure)

sensitive applications. However, even iris scanners have small error rates and can be deceived, so their use in critical situations needs to be considered very carefully.

Face Recognition

Some airports and other public locations now have cameras with **face recognition** systems that scan passersby to identify terrorists or wanted criminals by the characteristics of their faces. This is controversial because it typically is done **surreptitiously**—that is, without the knowledge or explicit permission of passersby.

In surreptitious identification, the person is identified without his or her knowledge.

Error rates have been so high that many of these systems are now being removed. In nearly every case in which a face recognition identifies someone as a criminal or terrorist, the scanner is producing a false alarm. In addition, criminals and terrorists often can deceive face recognition systems.

Questions About Error Rates and Deception

As just noted, error rates refer to the percentage of mistakes made by a biometric system even when users are not practicing deception to fool the system. When an attacker intentionally uses deception, his or her probability of being falsely authenticated or not authenticated may be much higher than the error rate. How bad are biometric error rates and vulnerabilities to deception? This currently is an open question, but it is clear that error rates in practice are much higher than those stated by vendors and that many systems are vulnerable to deception. Biometric authentication must be used carefully.

TEST YOUR UNDERSTANDING

14. a) What is biometrics? b) What is its main promise? c) Give a pro and a con of fingerprint scanning. d) Give a pro and some cons of iris scanning. e) Give a pro and some cons of face recognition. f) What is surreptitious scanning? g) Distinguish between error rates and deception.

FIREWALLS, IDSs, AND IPSs

Firewalls

In hostile military environments, travelers must pass through one or more checkpoints. At each checkpoint, their credentials will be examined. If the guard finds the credentials insufficient, the guard will stop the arriving person from proceeding and note the violation in a checkpoint log.

Dropping and Logging Provable Attack Packets

Figure 9-14 shows that firewalls operate in similar ways. Whenever a packet arrives, the **firewall** examines the packet. If the firewall identifies a packet as a **provable attack packet**, the firewall discards it. The firewall also copies information about the discarded packet into a **log file**. Firewall managers should read the log file every day to understand the types of attacks coming into the resource that the firewall is protecting. On the other hand, if the packet is not a provable attack packet, the firewall allows it to pass.

If a firewall identifies a packet as a provable attack packet, the firewall discards it.

Ingress and Egress Filtering

When most people think of firewalls, they think of filtering packets arriving at a network *from the outside*. This is called **ingress filtering**. Figure 9-14 illustrates ingress filtering.

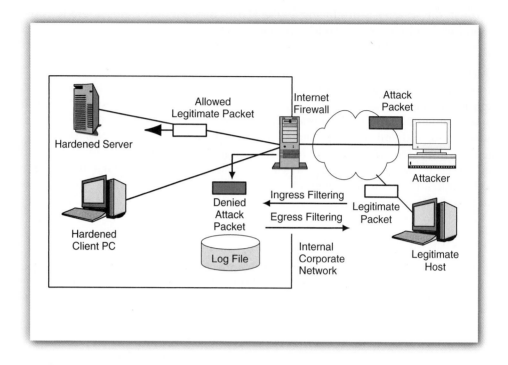

Figure 9-14   Firewall Operation

In addition, most firms also do **egress filtering**—that is, filter packets going from the network *to the outside*. Egress filtering makes the corporation a good citizen, ensuring that its computers are not used in attacks against outside firms. Egress filtering also attempts to prevent sensitive corporate information from being sent outside the firm.

TEST YOUR UNDERSTANDING

15. a) What does a firewall do when a packet arrives? b) Why is it important to read firewall logs daily? c) Distinguish between ingress and egress filtering.

Stateful Firewall Filtering

We have used the term firewall *filtering* without explaining it. We did this because firewalls use several different **filtering methods**. Most firewalls today, however, use stateful firewall filtering, which was invented in the early 1990s and has now become the dominant firewall filtering method.

Packets That Attempt to Open a Connection

Stateful firewalls have rules for evaluating packets that attempt to open a connection (such as packets containing TCP segments whose SYN bits are set). There are default

Figure 9-15   Stateful Firewall Filtering (Study Figure)

Stateful Firewall Filtering
> There are several types of firewall filtering
>
> Stateful inspection is the dominant filtering method today
>
> Stateful firewalls often use other filtering mechanisms as secondary mechanisms

Connection Initiation
> Packets attempt to open a connection
>> Example: packets with TCP segments whose SYN bits are set
>
> Default connection-initiation behavior (see Figure 9-16)
>> By default, all connections that are initiated by the outside are prevented
>>> This prevents outside clients from reaching internal servers
>>
>> By default, all connections that are initiated by an inside host to an outside host are permitted
>>> This allows clients to connect freely to external servers
>
> Stateful inspection access control lists (ACLs)
>> ACLs modify the default behavior for ingress or egress
>>
>> Ingress ACL rules allow access to selected internal servers
>>
>> Egress ACL rules prevent access to certain external server

Packets That Do Not Attempt to Open a Connection
> Most packets do not attempt to open a connection
>
> The rules governing these packets are very simple
>
> If the packet is part of an established connection, it is passed without further inspection (However, these packets can be filtered if desired)
>
> If the packet is not part of an established connection, it is dropped and logged
>
> This simplicity makes the cost of processing most packets minimal

Perspective
> Simple operation leads to inexpensive stateful firewall operation
>
> However, stateful inspection firewall operation is highly secure

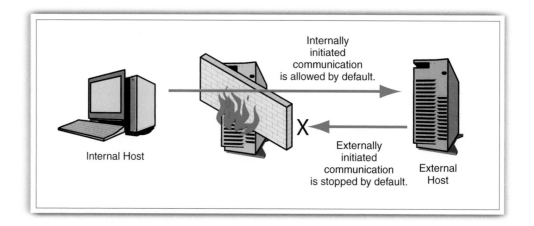

Figure 9-16   Default Stateful Firewall Behavior
for a Connection-Opening Attempt

rules that are automatically applied unless they are specifically overruled. In addition, there is a way to overrule these rules using access control lists.

Default Behavior   As Figure 9-16 shows, **stateful firewall filtering** is concerned with connections, not just individual packets. Its main work occurs when a host inside or outside attempts to open a connection.

➤ By default, all connections that are initiated by the outside are prevented. This prevents outside clients from reaching internal servers.

➤ By default, all connections that are initiated by an inside host going to an outside host are permitted. This allows clients to connect freely to external servers.

Access Control Lists (ACLs)   Although the default behavior of stateful firewalls provides both strong protection against outside attacks and easy access to the outside world, this default behavior is not always appropriate. In most firms, some outside clients need to get access to at least a few internal servers. In addition, firms may not want their internal client PCs to connect to all servers on the Internet.

Access control lists (ACLs) are sets of rules that modify the default behavior of stateful firewalls, allowing connections to some internal servers and preventing connections to some external servers. ACLs allow security administrators to tune how their stateful filtering mechanisms work.

Figure 9-17 shows a very simple ingress ACL. By default, all connection openings from the outside are forbidden. The last ACL rule ensures this default behavior.

1. If packet's source and destination sockets are in the connection table, PASS.

   If the packet is part of a previously established connection, pass it without further filtering.

2. If the packet's source and destination sockets are not in the connection table and the packet is not a connection-opening attempt, DROP and LOG.

   Drop any packet that is not a connection-opening attempt and that is not part of an established connection.

3. If protocol = TCP AND destination port number = 25, PASS and add connection to connection table.

   This rule permits external access to all internal mail servers.

4. If IP address = 10.47.122.79 AND protocol = TCP AND destination port number = 80, PASS and add connection to connection table.

   This rule permits access to a particular webserver (10.47.122.79).

5. Deny All AND LOG.

   If earlier rules do not result in a pass or deny decision, this last rule enforces the default rule of banning all externally initiated connection-opening attempts.

Figure 9-17   Ingress Access Control List (ACL) for a Stateful Inspection Firewall

Rules 3 and 4, however, permit externally-initiated connections to all internal mail servers and a specific FTP webserver, respectively.

Packets That Do Not Attempt to Open a Connection

Handling packets that attempt to open a connection are somewhat complicated in stateful inspection firewalls. However, very few packets attempt to open connections. For packets that do not attempt to open connections, there is a very simple pair of rules.

➤ If the packet is part of an established connection, it is passed without further inspection. (However, these packets can be filtered if desired.) Rule 1 in Figure 9-17 implements this behavior.

➤ If the packet is not part of an established connection, it is dropped and logged. Rule 2 in Figure 9-17 implements this behavior.

These rules are very simple to implement. Consequently, most packets are handled with very little processing power. This makes stateful firewalls very inexpensive.

Perspective

Although the simple operation of stateful inspection makes it inexpensive, stateful filtering provides a great deal of protection against attacks coming from the outside.

This combination of low cost and strong security is responsible for the dominance of stateful inspection today.

TEST YOUR UNDERSTANDING

16. a) What is the default behavior for stateful firewalls regarding connection opening attempts? b) Why are ACLs needed for stateful firewalls? c) When a packet that is part of an ongoing connection arrives at a stateful inspection firewall, what does the firewall do? d) When a packet that is not part of an ongoing connection and that does not attempt to open a connection arrives at a stateful inspection firewall, what does the firewall do? e) Why are stateful firewalls attractive? f) What type of firewalls do most corporations use for their main border firewalls?

Intrusion Detection Systems (IDSs)

Figure 9-18 compares firewalls and two other protection devices—intrusion detection systems (IDSs) and intrusion prevention systems (IPSs). Firewalls, as noted earlier, drop provable attack packets. To give an analogy, police officers may only arrest people if

Figure 9-18　Firewalls, Intrusion Detection Systems (IDSs), and Intrusion Prevention Systems (IPSs)

	Firewalls	IDSs	IPSs
Inspect Packets?	Yes	Yes	Yes
Action Taken	Drop and log individual proven attack packets based on individual packet or connection inspections	Log multipacket attacks based upon deep (multilayer) packet inspections of *streams* of packet flows. Notify an administrator of severe attacks but do not stop the attacks	Applies IDS processing methods—deep packet inspection and packet stream inspection. But actually stops some attacks
Processing Power Required	Modest	Heavy	Heavy
Maturity	Fairly mature	Still somewhat immature with too many false positives (false alarms). Tuning can reduce false positives, but this takes a great deal of labor	New. Only used to stop attacks that can be identified fairly accurately

they have probable cause—a reasonably high standard of proof. They cannot arrest anyone who is merely acting suspiciously.

Reporting Suspicious Packets

To continue the analogy, **intrusion detection systems (IDSs)** supplement firewalls by identifying *suspicious* packets that may indicate an attack. Although IDSs do not drop these suspicious packets, they do log them, and, if the attack looks serious, they notify a security administrator. To continue the law enforcement analogy, although police officers cannot arrest people for merely suspicious behavior, they can note it and investigate them.

Notification Speed and False Positives

Attack notification is important because unless security administrators identify attacks quickly, the attacker will be able to do extensive damage. Unfortunately, like car alarms, IDSs tend to create too many false alarms. (These are called **false positives** in IDS terminology.) Many firms "tune" their IDS to reduce false positives. For instance, they only have the IDS report attacks with high potential severity. To give another example, if a firm does not have servers running the Solaris operating system, it can turn off alarms over attacks against that operating system. However, many firms disconnect their IDSs after deciding that the benefits are not worth the tuning effort and that the volume of false positives that occur even after tuning is still too large for the IDS to be useful.

TEST YOUR UNDERSTANDING

> **17.** a) Distinguish between the types of packets that firewalls and IDSs seek. b) What type of filtering device is plagued by false alarms?

Intrusion Prevention System (IPS) Filtering

Based on IDS Filtering

Although stateful filtering provides strong security, it cannot stop some highly sophisticated attacks. A relatively new filtering method, **intrusion prevention system (IPS)** filtering is capable of stopping many complex attacks that can bypass even stateful firewall inspection. We discuss firewall IPS filtering after IDSs because most IPS filtering methods derive from IDS inspection methods. More specifically, IPS filtering uses two sophisticated filtering methods.

Deep Packet Inspection

First, IPSs use **deep packet inspection**, which examines internet, transport, and application layer content in an integrated way. This allows an IPS to detect certain types of attacks that other filtering methods cannot.

Inspecting Streams of Packets

Second, it examines patterns in *streams of packets*, not just individual packets. Again, this process can discover attacks that packet-by-packet inspection or asking whether the packet is part of a connection cannot.

Intensive Processing and ASICs

These two types of inspection are extremely processing-intensive. Earlier firewalls did not have the processing speed to implement them. Now, however, application-specific integrated circuits (ASICs) allow many computations that were previously done in software to be done in hardware. This greatly reduces processing time because hardware processing is much faster than software processing. Firewalls that use ASICs to do IPS filtering now have the processing speed they need.

What's in a Name?

The name *intrusion prevention system* is another unfortunate "gift" from marketers. *All* firewalls are systems to prevent intrusions, so all are IPSs in that sense. In fact, firewalls have long detected and automatically stopped denial-of-service attacks and several other complex attacks. However, the term *intrusion prevention system* today is only used for firewalls that do deep packet inspection and that inspect streams of packets to identify problems.

Choosing What Attacks to Stop

One problem with IPS filtering is that it is based on IDS inspection methods, which have a poor reputation for precision. Consequently, IPS filtering left unchecked has the potential to stop many legitimate traffic flows. In effect, IPSs could potentially generate a self-inflicted denial-of-service attack. To prevent the stopping of legitimate traffic, most firms only allow their IPSs to stop attacks that can be identified fairly accurately. This need to decide which attacks to stop means that firms must have a very good understanding of IPS filtering to use it effectively.

TEST YOUR UNDERSTANDING

18. a) What are the two characteristics of IPS filtering? b) Why must firms that use IPS filtering understand it very well?

Multimethod Firewalls

Although stateful packet inspection is the dominant firewall filtering methodology, most real firewalls supplement stateful inspection with other filtering methodologies. In addition, as noted earlier, firewalls usually stop several types of denial-of-service attacks and other complex attacks. This means that before firewalls filter specific traffic, they first decide what method to use to examine it.

On the other hand, firewalls rarely do antivirus filtering. They either ignore the problem or actively pass webpage downloads, e-mail messages with attachments, and other traffic that should be filtered to an antivirus filtering server.

TEST YOUR UNDERSTANDING

19. a) Do most firewalls provide only a single filtering method? b) What additional types of filtering do they do?

PROTECTION WITH CRYPTOGRAPHIC SYSTEMS

Cryptographic Systems

In Chapter 7, we saw that many companies use virtual private networks (VPNs), which transmit data over the nonsecure Internet with added security. We looked at two VPN standards: SSL/TLS and IPsec.

These two standards and many others are called cryptographic systems. **Cryptographic systems** provide security to dialogues that involve the exchange of many messages. At the beginning of each communication session, the two communication partners authenticate each other.

After this initial authentication, cryptographic systems provide protection to every message. First, each message is encrypted for confidentiality. If an attacker intercepts the message in transit, he or she will not be able to read it.

Cryptographic systems also provide message-by-message authentication by adding an electronic signature to each message. These authentication messages also provide message integrity, which is assurance that the message has not been changed in transit. (If the message has been changed, the electronic signature authentication will fail.)

TEST YOUR UNDERSTANDING

20. a) What do cryptographic systems protect? b) What three protections do cryptographic systems provide for individual messages?

Figure 9-19   Cryptographic Systems (Study Figure)

Cryptographic Systems
>   These systems provide security to multimessage dialogues

At the Beginning of Each Communication Session
>   The two parties authenticate each other

Message-by-Message Protection
>   After this initial authentication, cryptographic systems provide protection to every message

>   Encrypt each message for confidentiality so that eavesdroppers cannot read it

>   Adds an electronic signature to each message

>>   The electronic signature authenticates the sender

>>   It also provides message integrity: the receiver can tell if a message has been changed in transit

Encryption for Confidentiality

When most people think of cryptographic protection, they think of encryption for confidentiality. **Encryption** is the scrambling of messages so that communication is **confidential** (cannot be read by eavesdroppers). Encryption methods are called **ciphers**. The receiver **decrypts** (unscrambles) the message in order to be able to read it. Figure 9-20 illustrates encryption for confidentiality. More specifically, it illustrates two general types of ciphers.

Symmetric Key Encryption for Confidentiality

Most communication uses **symmetric key encryption** ciphers, in which the two sides use the same key to encrypt messages to each other and to decrypt incoming messages. As Figure 9-20 shows, symmetric key encryption ciphers only use a single key in two-way exchanges. Popular symmetric key encryption ciphers include DES, 3DES, and AES.

Public Key Encryption for Confidentiality

As Figure 9-20 also shows, in **public key encryption** ciphers, each side has a public key and a private key, so there are four keys in total.[3] The sender encrypts messages with the receiver's public key. The receiver, in turn, decrypts incoming messages with the receiver's own private key. Only the receiver knows his or her own private key, so only the receiver can decrypt the message. Popular public key encryption ciphers include RSA and ECC.

The Dominance of Symmetric Key Encryption

Nearly all encryption today uses symmetric key encryption because symmetric key encryption is very efficient. In contrast, public key encryption is very slow, placing a heavy processing burden on the sender and receiver. Public key encryption for confidentiality is used only for specific purposes. In contrast, all common applications use symmetric key encryption for message-by-message confidentiality.

> All common applications use symmetric key encryption for message-by-message confidentiality.

Key Length

Earlier, we looked at brute force password guessing. Symmetric and public/private keys also can be guessed by trying all possible keys. This is called **exhaustive search**. The way to defeat exhaustive key searches is to use long keys, which are merely binary strings.

- ➤ For symmetric key ciphers, lengths of 100 bits or greater are considered to be strong keys. DES only has a 56-bit key length, but 3DES doubles or triples this key length. AES supports multiple strong key lengths up to 245 bits.

---

[3]Yes, we saw these public and private keys earlier in the context of digital certificate-based authentication. Public key encryption can be used for both authentication and confidentiality.

Figure 9-20 Symmetric Key Encryption and Public Key Encryption for Confidentiality

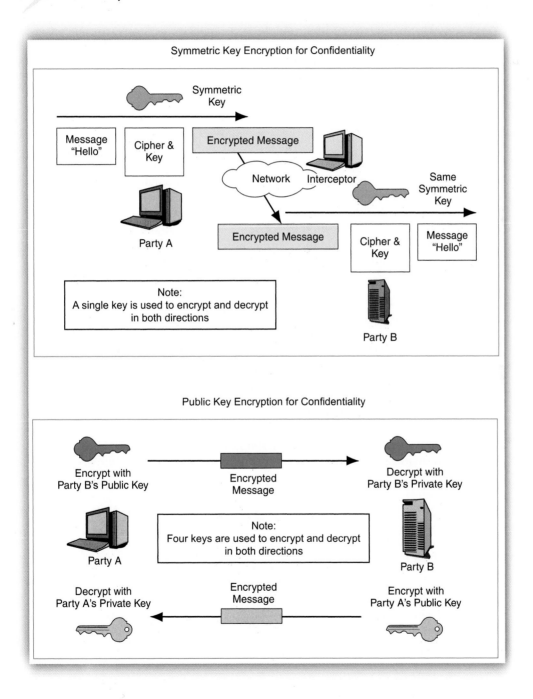

➤ In public key encryption, RSA key lengths need to be at least 1,024 bits to be considered strong. ECC key lengths can be smaller (around 512 bits) and still be strong.[4]

TEST YOUR UNDERSTANDING

21. a) What is a cipher? b) Distinguish between symmetric key encryption and public key encryption for confidentiality. c) In two-way dialogues, how many keys are used in symmetric key encryption? d) In public key encryption? e) What kind of encryption for confidentiality is used in all common applications? f) What is the minimum size for symmetric keys and public keys to be considered strong?

Electronic Signatures

Authentication and Message Integrity

In addition to encrypting each packet for confidentiality, cryptographic systems normally add **electronic signatures** to each packet. These are small bit strings that provide message-by-message authentication, much as people use signatures to authenticate written letters. Electronic signatures also provide message integrity, meaning that if the packet is changed in transit, the receiver will be able to detect that. Consequently, cryptographic systems provide three protections: message-by-message confidentiality, authentication, and message integrity.

Digital Signatures

There are two types of cryptographic signatures. **Digital signatures** use digital certificate authentication. Digital signatures provide very strong authentication, but they place a very heavy processing load on computers and are expensive to manage.

HMACs

Digital signatures are talked about a great deal in the popular press, but most cryptographic systems use **key-hashed message authentication codes** (HMACs) for authentication.[5] HMACs use a process called hashing, which is very fast. HMACs place a low processing load on computers and provide authentication and message integrity

---

[4]In symmetric key encryption, key length once was limited to 40 bits for exportable products. The RC4 encryption method usually was used with this strength limitation. The WEP security method used in wireless LANs uses the RC4 cipher.

For commercial products, however, 40-bit keys are far too short for symmetric key encryption. In the 1970s, businesses began adopting the DES encryption method, which had keys that were 56 bits long. Later, a variation of DES called 3DES was adopted. This raised key length to 112 or 168 bits. Today, many products are adopting the AES encryption method, which is more efficient (places a lighter processing burden on computers) than 3DES and offers superior key lengths.

For public key encryption, the RSA algorithm is dominant. However, a new public key encryption method, ECC, is growing in popularity because it is more efficient.

[5]No, it's not KHMAC, although it is occasionally kHMAC. Why not put in the *k* most of the time? I asked one of the creators of the IETF HMAC standard about this. His response was, "Well, obviously it uses a key, so why put that in the acronym?" When then asked why "key" is included in the name, he responded, "because it uses keys."

almost as strong as digital signatures. However, for legal transactions between organizations, HMACs have some limitations that may be crucial.

TEST YOUR UNDERSTANDING

22. a) What two protections do electronic signatures provide? b) What are the two popular types of electronic signatures? c) What methods do they use? d) Which type of electronic signature is more widely used? e) What is the relative advantage of HMACs over digital signatures? f) Which type of electronic signature is better for commercial transactions between organizations?

OTHER ASPECTS OF PROTECTION

Hardening Servers

Even if companies install several layers of firewalls to protect servers, some attack packets will inevitably get through. Consequently, servers have to be **hardened**—that is, set up to protect themselves.

Backup

The most basic computer protection of all is to keep data on servers backed up frequently. Recovery may be difficult or impossible unless the data on affected systems have been backed up very recently.

Vulnerabilities and Patching

As noted earlier in this chapter, security vulnerabilities are found frequently in both operating systems and application programs. When vulnerabilities are found, vendors develop patches (software updates). If companies install these updates, the companies will be immune to worms and hackers who can exploit these vulnerabilities.

Unfortunately, companies tend to be slow to install patches on servers and sometimes do not install them at all. In contrast, attackers are quick to develop exploits (programs that exploit known vulnerabilities). Consequently, hackers often have an easy time breaking into host computers, and worm writers often have massive success.

Host Firewalls

It is difficult to configure border firewalls and even internal firewalls because these devices must protect many internal servers, each of which has different requirements. Consequently, it makes sense to install firewalls on individual servers. Most servers only need one or two ports open, so firewall protection can be configured simply and adequately.

Hardening Client PCs

The same things that are important in server hardening—installing patches, having a firewall, and implementing backup—are important in client PC hardening as well. In addition, clients need to have good antivirus programs and antispyware programs.

Hardening Servers and Client PCs
> Setting up computers to protect themselves
>
> Server hardening
>> Back up so that restoration is possible
>>
>> Patch vulnerabilities
>>
>> Use host firewalls
>
> Client PC hardening
>> As with servers, patching vulnerabilities, having a firewall, and implementing backup
>>
>> Also, a good antivirus program that is updated regularly
>>
>> Client PC users often make errors or sabotage hardening techniques
>>
>> In corporations, group policy objects (GPOs) can be used to centrally manage security on clients

Vulnerability Testing
> Protections are difficult to set up correctly
>
> Vulnerability testing is attacking your system yourself or through a consultant
>
> There must be follow-up to fix vulnerabilities that are discovered

Figure 9-21   Other Aspects of Protection (Study Figure)

The problem with client security is that it usually is left to end users, who typically lack the knowledge and skills needed to make their computers secure. In addition, many end users actively sabotage security—for instance by turning off their antivirus programs to speed the transmission of attachments. Users may even install prohibited software, such as music file-sharing software, which attackers can use to compromise the computers.

Larger organizations can "lock down" their desktops by administering them remotely. This is particularly true for Microsoft Windows client computers, which dominate the corporate client base. Corporations that install Microsoft domain controllers can create **group policy objects (GPOs)**; these are sets of security policy rules. Domain controllers enforce GPOs on individual client PCs.

Group policy objects (GPOs) are sets of security policy rules that domain controllers enforce on individual client PCs.

TEST YOUR UNDERSTANDING

23. a) What is host hardening? b) What are the three steps in hardening servers? c) What are the steps in hardening client PCs? d) What are group policy objects (GPOs)?

Vulnerability Testing

One problem in creating protections is that it is easy to make mistakes when configuring firewalls and other protections. It is essential to do **vulnerability testing** after configuring protections such as firewall ACLs in order to catch those mistakes. In vulnerability testing, the company or a consultant attacks protections in the way a determined attacker would and notes which of those attacks that should have been stopped actually succeed.

Vulnerability testing must result in a report that leads to a plan to upgrade protections to remove vulnerabilities. There also must be follow-up to ensure that the vulnerability removal plan actually is carried out.

TEST YOUR UNDERSTANDING

24. a) What is vulnerability testing? b) Why is it important? c) Describe appropriate steps after vulnerability testing is completed.

RESPONSE

Inevitably, some attacks will succeed in getting through the company's protection systems. The amount of damage done in these compromises depends heavily on how quickly and how well the organization responds.

Stages

There are four general stages in responding to an attack.

Detecting the Attack

The first stage is detecting the attack. Detection can be done by the firm's IDS or simply by users reporting apparent problems. Obviously, until an attack is detected, the attacker will be able to continue doing damage. Companies need to develop strong procedures for identifying attacks quickly.

Stopping the Attack

The second stage is stopping the attack. The longer an attack has to get into the system, the more damage the hacker can do. Reconfiguring corporate firewall ACLs may be able to end the attack. In other cases, attack-specific actions will have to be taken.

Repairing the Damage

The third stage is repairing the damage. In some cases, this is as simple as running a cleanup program or restoring files from backup tapes. In other cases, it may involve the reformatting of hard disk drives and the complete reinstallation of software and data.

Stages

      Detecting the attack

      Stopping the attack

      Repairing the damage

      Punishing the attacker

Major Attacks and CSIRTs

      Major incidents

      Computer security incident response team (CSIRT)

            Must include members of senior management, the firm's security staff, members of the IT staff, members of functional departments, and the firm's public relations and legal departments

Disasters and Disaster Recovery

      Natural and humanly-made disasters

      Need a disaster recovery plan ahead of time

      Need a backup site and procedures to shift work there

      Need rehearsals to iron out difficulties and develop speed

Figure 9-22   Incident Response (Study Figure)

Punishing the Attacker?

The fourth general stage is punishing the attacker, if possible. This is easiest if the attacker is an employee because remote attackers can be extremely difficult to track down, and even if they are found, prosecution may be difficult or impossible.

If legal prosecution is a goal, it is critical to use proper **forensic procedures** to capture and retain data in ways that fit the rules of evidence in court proceedings. These rules are very complex, and it is important to use certified forensics professionals. Even if an employee is fired, it is important to use good forensic procedures to avoid a potential lawsuit.

Major Incidents and CSIRTs

Minor attacks can be handled by the on-duty IT and security staff. However, during **major incidents**, such as the theft of thousands of credit card numbers from a corporate host, the company must convene the firm's **computer security incident response team (CSIRT)**, which is trained to handle major incidents.

The key to creating CSIRTs is to have the right mix of talents and viewpoints. Major attacks affect large parts of the firm, so the CSIRT must include members of senior management, the firm's security staff, members of the IT staff, members of functional departments, and the firm's public relations and legal departments.

Disasters and Disaster Response

When natural disasters, terrorist attacks, or other catastrophes occur, the company's basic operations may be halted. This can be extremely expensive. Companies must have active disaster recovery plans to get their systems working quickly.

IT disaster recovery is the reestablishment of information technology operations. Many large firms have dedicated backup sites that can be put into operation very quickly, after data and employees have been moved to the backup site. Another option, if a firm has multiple server sites, is to do real-time data backup across sites. If one site fails, the other site can take over immediately or at least very rapidly.

More broadly, **business continuity recovery** goes beyond IT disasters to deal with disasters that affect enough of a firm to pause or stop the functioning of the business. IT security is only one player in business continuity recovery teams.

Rehearsals

"Practice makes perfect" is time-honored advice. It certainly is true for major attacks that must be handled by CSIRTs, and it equally true for disaster recovery. It is important to establish CSIRT and disaster teams ahead of time and to have them rehearse how they will handle major attacks and disasters. Although practice does not really make perfect, it certainly improves response speed and quality. During the first two or three rehearsals, team members will work together awkwardly, and there will be many mistakes. Rehearsals will also reveal flaws in the company's major attack and disaster response plans. It is far better to go through these problems before the firm is in a real crisis.

TEST YOUR UNDERSTANDING

25. a) What are the four response phases when attacks occur? b) What is the purpose of forensic tools? c) Why are CSIRTs necessary? d) Should the CSIRT be limited to security staff personnel? e) What is disaster recovery? f) Explain how firms use backup sites in disaster recovery. g) Why are CSIRT and disaster response team rehearsals necessary?

CONCLUSION

Synopsis

Attacks

Companies today suffer compromises from many different types of attacks.

> ➤ Viruses attach themselves to other programs and need human actions to propagate—most commonly by opening e-mail attachments that are infected programs. Worms are full programs; they can spread by e-mail, but vulnerability-enabled worms can propagate on their own, taking advantage of unpatched vulnerabilities in victim hosts. Some vulnerability-enabled worms can spread through the Internet host population with amazing speed. Many worms and viruses have damaging payloads. Often, payloads place a Trojan horse program or other

types of exploitation software on the victim computer. Malware is the general name for evil software.

➤ Viruses, worms, and Trojan horses are not the only attacks that are aimed at individuals. Spam deluges the victim with unsolicited commercial e-mail, and messages often are fraudulent. Spyware collects information about users and sends this information to an attacker. Adware pops up advertisements constantly. Phishing attacks use an official-looking e-mail message or website to trick users into divulging passwords and other special information. Attacks on individuals, including e-mail virus and worm attacks, often depend on social engineering—tricking the victim into doing something against his or her best interests. Two common goals of attacks on individuals are credit card number theft, in which a credit card number is stolen, and identity theft, in which enough private information is stolen to allow the attacker to impersonate the victim in large financial transactions.

➤ Hacking is intentionally using a computer resource without authorization or in excess of authorization. Hacking break-ins typically require a prolonged series of actions on the part of attacker.

➤ Denial-of-service (DoS) attacks overload victim servers so that they cannot serve users.

Attackers

Traditionally, most attackers were curiosity-driven hackers and disgruntled employees and ex-employees. Now, criminals dominate the attack world, and the money their crimes generate allows them to invest in new technology and hire top hackers. On the horizon, cyberterror attacks by terrorists and cyberwar attacks by national governments could do unprecedented levels of damage.

Security Management

Security is primarily a management issue, not a technical issue. Planning involves risk analysis (balancing the costs and benefits of protections), creating comprehensive security (closing all avenues of attack), and using defense in depth (establishing successive lines of defense in case one line of defense fails).

Access Control

Firms need to control access to their assets. The first step, obviously, is to enumerate (identify and list) assets. The second is to rate the sensitivity of each asset in terms of security risks. Then the firm must develop a specific asset control plan for each asset. This asset control plan must be appropriate to the sensitivity of each asset.

Access control plans require authentication (proving an applicant's identity to a verifier), authorization (specifying what the applicant can do to various resources), and auditing (recording actions when users work). This trio of actions is called AAA. The most complex aspect of access control is authentication. There are three main technologies for authentication.

➤ Passwords are inexpensive and easy to use, but users typically choose poor passwords that are easy to crack. Passwords should only be used for low-sensitivity resources.

➤ Digital certificate authentication at the other extreme gives very strong authentication, but it is complex and expensive to implement.

➤ Biometrics promises to use bodily measurements to authenticate applicants, replacing other forms of authentication. Concerns with biometrics include error rates and the effectiveness of deliberate deception by applicants.

Firewalls, IDSs, and IPSs

Firewalls examine packets passing through the firewall. If a firewall finds provable attack packets, it drops them and records them in a log file. Ingress filtering examines packets coming into the firm; egress filtering examines packets going out of the firm.

Most firewalls use stateful inspection, which controls which internally-initiated and externally-initiated connections will be allowed. By default, all connection-opening attempts from inside hosts to outside hosts are allowed, but all connection-opening attempts from outside hosts to inside hosts are prohibited. Access control lists (ACLs) can modify this default behavior.

Once a connection is established, subsequent packets in the connection usually are passed with little or no filtering. However, packets that are not connection-opening attempts or in established connections are dropped.

A firewall drops provable attack packets, but it does *not* drop packets that are merely suspicious. However, intrusion detection systems (IDSs) are designed to detect suspicious traffic. If an IDS finds suspicious traffic that indicates a serious attack, the IDS will notify the security manager. Although prompt discovery of an attack is crucial, IDSs create many false positives (false alarms). False positives can be reduced, but this takes a great deal of work.

Some new firewalls use intrusion prevention system (IPS) filtering, which is based on IDS filtering methods. IPS filtering can detect complex attacks that stateful inspection and other traditional firewall inspection methods cannot identify. To avoid the false positives problem of IDSs, IPS filtering is only used to stop attacks if there is a high degree of confidence that an attack has been identified.

Cryptographic Systems

Cryptographic systems provide protections to multimessage dialogues. One key protection is encryption for confidentiality, which encrypts messages to prevent attackers from reading any messages that they intercept. Encryption methods are called ciphers. There are two types of ciphers for confidentiality.

➤ In symmetric key encryption, both sides encrypt and decrypt with a single key.
➤ In public key encryption, each side has a private key and a public key.

Symmetric key encryption is the dominant encryption technology for confidentiality because it is very efficient. Symmetric key encryption is used in nearly all applications for confidentiality. Public key encryption for confidentiality is used only for special purposes. Symmetric keys must be at least 100 bits long to be considered strong keys today. As noted earlier, public/private keys need to be much longer—1,024 and 512 bits long for RSA and ECC, respectively.

In addition to providing message-by-message encryption, cryptographic systems also provide message-by-message authentication by adding an electronic signature to each message. This allows the receiver to be sure that each message he or she receives is from the true party. Electronic signatures also provide message integrity.

There are two types of electronic signatures. Digital signatures use digital certificate authentication; digital signatures are extremely strong, but they require a large amount of processing power and time-consuming management. Most electronic signatures are HMACs, which require much less processing power and require little management labor to implement. However, digital signatures are needed for many business-to-business transactions.

Host Hardening

Ongoing protection includes server and client hardening to protect them from attacks. Servers can be hardened by patching vulnerabilities, installing host firewalls, and backing up servers regularly. Client PC hardening includes the same protections, plus installing an antivirus program and an anti-spyware program. Spam filters and anti-adware filters also are desirable.

Vulnerability Testing

Protections are very difficult to set up and configure, so it is easy to make mistakes that make a firm vulnerable to attack. Consequently, firms should conduct vulnerability tests in which an employee or a consultant attempts to attack the firm (with permission), in order to identify security weaknesses.

Response

Protections occasionally break down. Response to successful compromises must be rapid and effective to limit damage. The stages in response to attack typically include identifying the attack, stopping the attack, recovering from the attack, and (sometimes) punishing the attacker. Major incidents require the convening of a computer security incident response team (CSIRT). IT disaster recovery requires getting IT back in operation at another site, while business continuity recovery involves getting the entire firm back in operation. It is important for recovery teams to conduct rehearsals before problems occur.

THOUGHT QUESTIONS

1. a) Suppose that an attack would do $100,000 in damage and has a 15 percent annual probability of success. Spending $9,000 on "Measure A" would cut the annual probability of success by 75 percent. Do a risk analysis comparing benefits and costs. Show your work clearly. b) Should the company spend the money? c) Should the company spend the money if Measure A costs $20,000 per year? Again, show your work.

2. a) What form of authentication would you recommend for relatively unimportant resources? Justify your answer. b) What form of authentication would you recommend for your most sensitive resources?

3. Critique each of the following passwords regarding strength and the type of cracking attack that would be used to crack it.
a) swordfish b) Processing1 c) SeAtTLe d) R7%t& e) 4h*6tU9$^l

GETTING CURRENT

Go to the book website's New Information and Errors pages for this chapter to get new information since this book went to press and to correct any errors in the text.

Hands-On: Windows XP Home Security

Learning Objectives

By the end of this chapter, you should be able to discuss:

■ Differences between Windows XP Home and Windows XP Professional.

■ Protections for client PCs.

■ Backup.

■ The Windows XP SP2 Security Center.

■ Automatic updates.

■ Internet options.

■ The Windows Firewall.

■ Antivirus programs.

■ Other common security methods: anti-spyware programs, anti-adware programs, spam blockers, NAT protection from access routers, and virtual private networks.

■ Advanced security with Windows XP Professional, including domains, domain controllers, and group policy objects (GPOs).

INTRODUCTION

Windows XP

Windows dominates the market for client PC operating systems, and **Windows XP** is the dominant version of Windows in both corporations and in homes. Therefore, it is important for you to understand how to deal with Windows XP security.

Windows XP comes in two versions: **Windows XP Home** for residential use and **Windows XP Professional** for corporate use. Most students have computers running XP Home rather than XP Professional, so we will focus on XP Home security. This will allow students to do hands-on exercises at home. Fortunately, both versions provide basic security in the same way and differ primarily in advanced areas we will cover at the end of this chapter.

Backing up critical files.

Updating Windows by downloading security patches.

Adding antivirus software and keeping it current.

Selecting appropriate Internet options.

Turning on a client firewall.

Adding anti-spyware software and perhaps other anti-malware software.

Setting up a virtual private network (VPN).

Figure 9a-1   Major Security Protections for Windows XP PCs

Service Pack 2

Microsoft does periodic major updates called **service packs**. Every user who runs Windows XP needs to install **Service Pack 2 (SP2)**, which brought serious security to Windows XP. If you have Windows XP, how can you tell if you have SP2 installed? Hit the *Start* button, and select *Control Panel*. You should see an icon with a colorful shield and the name *Security Center*. If you do, XP2 is installed.

Major Security Actions

Protecting client PCs is not a simple process. It requires a number of protections:

- ➤ Backing up critical files.
- ➤ Updating Windows by downloading security patches.
- ➤ Adding antivirus software and keeping it current.
- ➤ Selecting appropriate Internet options.
- ➤ Turning on a client firewall.
- ➤ Adding anti-spyware software and perhaps other anti-malware software.
- ➤ Setting up a virtual private network (VPN).

The Windows Security Center

Windows XP SP2 brought the **Windows Security Center**, which is shown in Figure 9a-2. This window, which is usually called the **Security Center**, is a single window for managing several security protections, including the Windows Firewall, automatic updates, Internet options, and checking that your virus protection is on and up to date. Note, however, that not all required security actions can be taken from the Security Center. This includes the first and arguably the most important protection—backing up critical files.

TEST YOUR UNDERSTANDING

1. a) Distinguish between Windows XP Home and Windows XP Professional. b) Why does this chapter deal with Windows XP Home? c) What is a service pack? d) What service

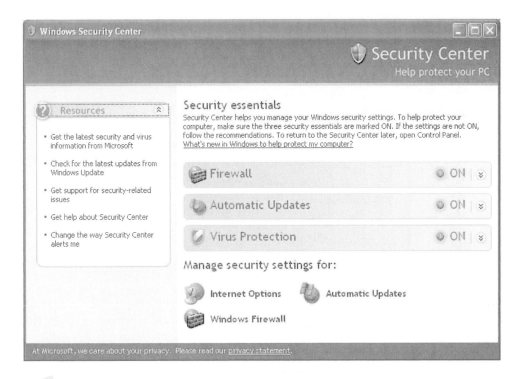

Figure 9a-2   The Windows Security Center

pack is needed in Windows XP for strong security? e) List the security actions that should be taken for client PCs. f) What is the central security control screen for Windows XP computers with SP2? g) Can all security actions be taken from this screen?

BACKUP

The Need for Backup

Most security professionals say that the most important action a user can take to secure a PC is to **backup** (copy and store) its crucial files regularly. First, mechanical breakdowns are more common than security attacks, and the most unreliable element in a computer is its hard drive. Second, from a security point of view, even the best security protections sometimes break down, leading to successful attacks. Any data that is not backed up is likely to be lost.

The Most Ignored Protection

Despite the enormous importance of backup, most PC users rarely if ever backup their computers. In nearly every case when a hard drive is lost, critical information is lost as

The Need for Backup

> Perhaps the most important thing a user can do
>
> Widely ignored by users because it is difficult and slow

Backup Technology

> Optical drive
>
>> Faster than traditional floppy backup
>>
>> Even with dual-layer DVDs, one disk may not be enough
>>
>> Slow writing speed
>
> Second hard drive
>
>> Faster than backup to optical drives
>>
>> If computer is damaged or stolen, the backup drive is lost
>>
>> A virus that wipes out the main drive also is likely to wipe out the backup drive
>>
>> Removable external drives: can reduce these problems

What to Backup

> Only data?
>
> All files?
>
> Recovery software that can bring the computer back to a previous condition

For Reinstallation, Keep Installation Disks for Software, Along with Keys

Managing Backups

> For client PCs, backups once a week are reasonable unless there is a critical project
>
> Backup media should be stored away from the computer to protect it if the computer is damaged

Dedicated Backup Software

> Allows a full backup followed by several fast incremental backups

Figure 9a-3   Backup (Study Figure)

well. The problem with backup is that it is difficult and slow. When users cannot do something easily, they are not likely to do it—especially when effort is frequent but the payoff is uncertain and rare.

> The problem with backup is that it is difficult and slow. When users cannot do something easily, they are not likely to do it—especially when effort is frequent but the payoff is uncertain and rare.

Backup Technology

One way to make backup easier is to improve the technology available to users. Once, users had to do backup on floppy disks. This was slow, messy procedurally, and resulted in a stack of disks to file away. When floppy drives were the only option, end users almost never did backup.

Optical Drives

Writable optical disks have made backup much easier and faster. Users with relatively little data may be able to back their data up on a single CD-R disk. For single-disk back-ups, which are important because disk-shuffling in multi-disk backup is clumsy and time consuming, users with normal amounts of data are likely to need a DVD writer. Even with DVD writers, it may be necessary to use a dual-layer DVD writer for one-disk backups.

Although optical drives can backup a large amount of data, they write rather slowly. Although writing speeds are increasing, optical drives are still very slow compared to hard drives. Backup on optical drives can be painfully slow, and most users are afraid to do other work when they are backing up their data.

Second Hard Drives

Another possible backup technology is using a second hard drive on each PC and using it only as a backup drive. This is relatively expensive, but it offers both fast back-ups and the freedom from dealing with optical disk storage.

Unfortunately, backup onto a second hard drive has an Achilles heel. If the computer is stolen or destroyed in a fire or flood, both drives are lost, including the "backed up" data. In addition, a virus that erases the main hard drive may also erase a second drive on the same computer. These problems can be minimized by using a portable hard drive that plugs into a USB or FireWire port.[1]

Network Attached Storage

It is even possible to purchase a network-attached storage device for small offices and homes. A network storage device attaches directly to the network rather than to a computer. It can backup several computers centrally. Again, however, if there is a fire or a flood, the central backup computer will be lost. In addition, it is important to backup the backup computer frequently so that its contents will not be lost.

Internet Backup

Perhaps the safest backup for home users it to backup their computers over the Internet. Online backup services store user backups securely and professionally away from the customer's premises. The problem is that even broadband connections have upload speeds that are far lower than the transfer speeds of disk drives and other local technologies.

---

[1]It is even possible to purchase a network-attached storage device for small offices and homes. A network storage device attaches directly to the network rather than to a computer. It can backup several computers centrally.

What to Backup

Data Backup

The most obvious thing to backup is data. It is common to backup all data frequently and to backup up all active data much more frequently.

Full System Recovery

Backing up the entire computer, including programs, requires more thought. Fortunately, most computers today come with **recovery software** to allow the computer to be restored to its last recorded configuration. **Full system recovery** backups take a great deal of time, so they are usually done only when new programs are added or heavily updated.

Keeping Installation Disks

If a system cannot be restored, it may be necessary to do a complete **reinstallation**. This is only possible if the user has saved all installation disks for the operating system and application software and has also saved installation keys.

Managing Backups

Schedule

It is important to have a schedule for backups. Doing backups once a week may be a reasonable goal for users. Losing a whole week's work would be bad, but it would not ordinarily be disastrous. Of course, if the user is in the middle of a major project, one week might be far too long. The basic question to ask is, "How bad would it be if all the work since the last backup was lost?"

Generations

Another question to ask is how long backups should be kept. When expensive tapes were used for storage, they often would be reused every few weeks or months. However, with backups on relatively inexpensive CDs or DVDs, reuse usually is not a serious issue. Keeping backups for many months or years often comes in handy when an old file that you deleted a long time ago becomes important again.

Storage Location

Where should backup disks be stored? The basic rule is that backup disks should always be stored away from the computer. This way, if the computer is damaged in a fire or flood, the backup disks hopefully will be fine. Even in computer thefts, thieves often steal all the disks they can find near the computer, including backup disks.

Backup Software

The simplest way to backup files onto a disk is to use the disk-burning software that came with your CD writer or DVD writer. You select the folders you wish to backup, and the software burns the software files to a disk. The process is very straightforward but rather slow.

You can also buy **dedicated backup software** designed specifically for that purpose. (In fact, Windows XP has a rudimentary backup program.) One major advantage of dedicated backup software is that it writes everything to a single compressed file, taking up less storage space. Another major advantage is that after a **full backup** is made, the user can do a series of **incremental backups** that only save files that were changed since the last full backup. This is much faster than doing a series of full backups by copying folders.

Perspective

Although things can be done to make backup faster and easier, backup is one of the least automatic protections for PCs, despite being arguably the most important. Users need to develop a disciplined routine for doing backups.

TEST YOUR UNDERSTANDING

2. a) What do most security professionals say is the most important thing that a user can do to secure his or her PC? b) What probably is the most-ignored security protection? c) What characteristics must backup technology have if users are to accept it? d) What are the advantages of optical drives for backup? e) What are the disadvantages? f) Why is backup to a second hard drive desirable? g) What problems does doing backup on a second hard drive have? h) What is the advantage of backing up active files to a USB thumb drive? i) What are the advantages and disadvantages of network attached storage (NAS) backup? j) What are the advantages and disadvantages of Internet backup?

3. a) What files can a user backup? b) What is full system recovery? c) What software must be used for full system recovery? d) Why is it important to keep the original installation disks for software? e) What is a good backup schedule for PC hard drives? f) Where should backup disks be stored? g) Why? h) Why is routine important?

WINDOWS SECURITY CENTER

Windows XP Service Pack 2 was primarily a security upgrade to XP. As noted earlier, the heart of SP2 was the creation of the Windows Security Center, which is shown in Figure 9a-2. To get to the Security Center, follow these three steps:

➤ Click on the *Start* button.
➤ Select the *Control Panel.*
➤ In the Control Panel, the *Security Center* icon is a colorful shield. Click on it to go to the Security Center.

TEST YOUR UNDERSTANDING

4. How can you get to the Windows Security Center?

The Windows Security Center
  Came with Service Pack 2 (SP2)

Three Status of Protections Bands
  Windows firewall
  Automatic updates
  Virus protection

Default Settings and Options
  Windows: good security defaults

Automatic Updates
  Updates
  Good automatic downloading and installation
  However, sometimes problems with updates, so testing is good
  Work-arounds
  Service packs
  Severity ratings
  Does not update applications
  User controls downloading and installation

Windows Firewall
  Stateful inspection firewall
  Can permit connections from the outside
    Based on port number or application name
  Cannot prevent connections to external hosts
    Users probably could not make good decisions on this
    However, it does not block Trojan horse communication with the outside world
  Can do logging, but turned off by default
  Incoming ICMP messages: can be permitted or denied
  Incoming pings allowed by default

Internet Options for Privacy and Security
  Internet Properties dialog box
  Security Options
    Protection by zones
    Internet—the default zone (medium-level security)
    Local intranet—medium-low
    Trusted sites—low
    Restricted sites—high level
    Levels can be replaced with custom security options, but this is difficult and dangerous
  Privacy Options (mostly cookies)
    Slide bar for privacy
    Medium: the default
    Pop-up blocker turned on by default

The Center

Protection Status Indicator Bands

Prominent on the Security Center window are three bands showing the status of the user's Windows Firewall, Automatic Updates, and Virus Protection. The bands tell you whether each protection is working. Normally, the bands are light blue. If there is a problem, a band changes to yellow or red to indicate the severity of the protection breakdown.

Default Configurations and User-Selectable Configurations

However, the bands do not tell you how these protections are configured. Nor do they tell you about your computer's Internet Options configuration. Internet Options cannot be turned off, so there is no point showing it as a band. However, the protection offered by Internet Options is very important to users and should not be overlooked.

The three items under the control of Windows—the Windows Firewall, Internet Options, and Automatic Updates—all have default settings that provide reasonably good security while still offering good usability. However, it is good to examine these default settings and modify them where it is reasonable to do so.

Reinforcing Your Security Knowledge

Another reason to be concerned with the Windows Security Center is that the center can help make the concepts in Chapter 9 more concrete for you. In particular, we will see how stateful firewalls are implemented (although the Windows Firewall cannot block outgoing traffic effectively).

TEST YOUR UNDERSTANDING

5. For what three things does the Security Center tell you the status?

Automatic Updates

Updates

As discussed in Chapter 9, when any piece of software ships, it is likely to have unknown *security vulnerabilities*. When a vulnerability is discovered, the software vendor releases an **update (patch)** to remove the vulnerability Users must download this update or be at risk for attack. This is not a theoretical concern. Vulnerability attacks are pandemic. Updating Windows is not a luxury.

Automatically downloading and installing updates as soon as they occur is the safest option. However, updates occasionally can be disruptive.[2] Many companies routinely delay the installation of updates in order to test them before widely installing them. This is understandable, but it leaves a company open to attacks during the testing period. The time between the availability of updates and the beginning of attacks can be less than a single day. For users, delaying updates is a bad choice.

Work-Arounds

In some cases, installing an update will not fix the security vulnerability. Instead, the company will have to engage in a **work-around**, in which manual changes will have to

---

[2]For instance, one Windows XP update in 2002 slowed computer operation dramatically. Microsoft did not issue another update to correct this problem for more than a month.

be made even after an update is installed. In some cases, the work-around involves potentially dangerous actions, such as modifying the system registry. While work-arounds are feasible on servers, which are administered by trained professionals, they make little sense for ordinary PC owners.

Service Packs and Severity Ratings

Microsoft issues both individual updates and service packs, which combine a number of individual updates into a single large update. On a newly installed computer, it is important to install service packs. There may be several, and they should be installed in order. This takes time, but it is much faster than installing many individual updates.

Software vendors often have **severity ratings** for their updates. Updates with high severity ratings correct severe security vulnerabilities. Updates for severe vulnerabilities should be installed promptly. Many users, however, may wait to install updates with low severity ratings.

Updating Applications

Although we have focused on Windows updating, individual application programs also have to be updated regularly. If an attacker can take over an application, he or she often can take over the entire computer. Unfortunately, every application vendor has a different mechanism for updating its programs. Updating applications can be more time consuming and difficult than updating Windows if a user has many applications. If fact, it may be difficult even to discover updates for many applications.

The Automatic Updates Dialog Box

At the bottom of the Security Center, there are three options for managing your security settings. We will look at the **Automatic Updates** icon first. Click on this option to bring up the *Automatic Updates* dialog box shown in Figure 9a-5.

The default choice is to download and install updates automatically. This is a very secure default, but it has one potential weakness. It looks for updates on certain days or times. You should be sure that your computer will be turned on and connected to the Internet when it is time to look for automatic updates. The Automatic Updates screen also offers three riskier options.

➤ One is to download updates to your computer but to wait for your permission to install them. Unfortunately, the user may delay or forget the installation.

➤ Another is to merely notify you when there are updates. This is good if you are highly disciplined, but it is a risky choice even for people who are disciplined.

➤ The third is to turn off automatic updates entirely. This is very risky as the text with this option indicates.

TEST YOUR UNDERSTANDING

5. a) Why is the automatic downloading and installation of updates important? b) Why is it dangerous? c) Distinguish between updates and work-arounds. d) What are service packs? e) What are severity ratings? f) Do Windows updates update your application programs? g) What choices do you have at the Automatic Updates dialog box?

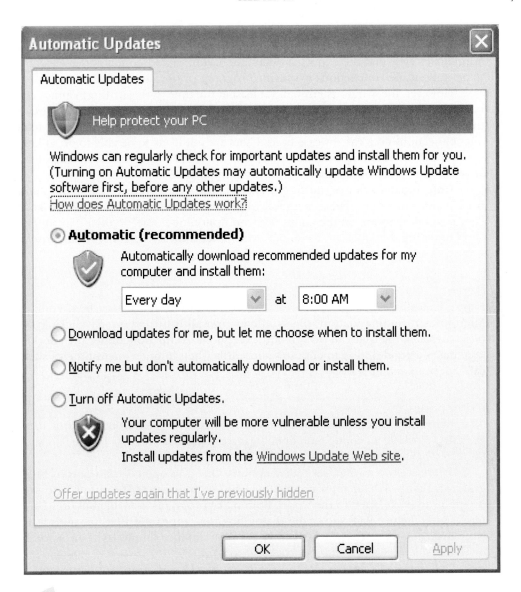

Figure 9a-5 Automatic Updates

Windows Firewall

A Limited Stateful Inspection Firewall

Before Service Pack 2, Windows XP had a rudimentary firewall. However, SP2 introduced the new **Windows Firewall**, which uses stateful inspection. Recall from Chapter 9 that stateful inspection firewalls by default block all connection-openings from the outside but permit all connection-openings from the inside. Access control lists (ACLs) can modify this default behavior for specific programs or port numbers. The Windows Firewall has the expected default behavior. In addition, it allows exceptions to permit outside connections to specific programs or port numbers.

However, the Windows Firewall (at least at the time of this writing) cannot block internal connection openings to outside sites. This is understandable because firewalls that can limit connection openings to the outside world must ask users whether to permit connections on a case-by-case basis. Users are not likely to be able to do so knowledgeably. By accidentally selecting poor choices, users can open their computers to attack or make certain necessary connections impossible.

Unfortunately, not permitting users to control outgoing connection openings has a major side effect. There is no way to prevent Trojan horses, bots, keystroke loggers, or other malware on the computer from "phoning home" to their controllers or from initiating denial-of-service attacks and other attacks. To address this problem, some users purchase third-party firewall programs.

General Tab

Figure 9a-6 shows the *General tab* on the Windows Firewall dialog box. Following Microsoft's recommendation, the Windows Firewall is turned on. By clicking *Don't allow exceptions*, the user can prevent any exceptions. As the note under the check box says, this is a good option to choose temporarily when in open environments such as café hot spots and airports.

Exceptions

As noted earlier, it is possible to create exceptions to the default behavior of stateful firewalls (blocking all connection openings from external sites). As Figure 9a-7 shows, the *Exceptions* tab can be used to create exceptions.

There are two ways to permit exceptions. One is to open certain ports. The program on that port can then receive external connections. The other is to select programs to make open to the world. Both make programs available but do so in different ways. Figure 9a-8 shows the dialog box that appears if the user adds a port. Note that the user must specify whether the port number should be allowed for TCP or UDP.

One especially interesting aspect of permitting exceptions to ports or programs is the *Change scope* button. As Figure 9a-9 shows, external access to a certain port or program will be permitted from any computer (including those on the Internet), computers on the user's subnet, or computers on a custom list of IP addresses. For file and printer sharing, the user should limit access to other computers on its subnet.

Advanced Settings

The Windows Firewall also has an *Advanced Settings* tab. This tab allows you to restore all defaults in case your specific configuration does not appear to be working well. (See Figure 9a-10.)

Chapter 9 noted that firewalls log dropped packets. Windows Firewall does not do this by default because few users will read such logs. However, users can turn on

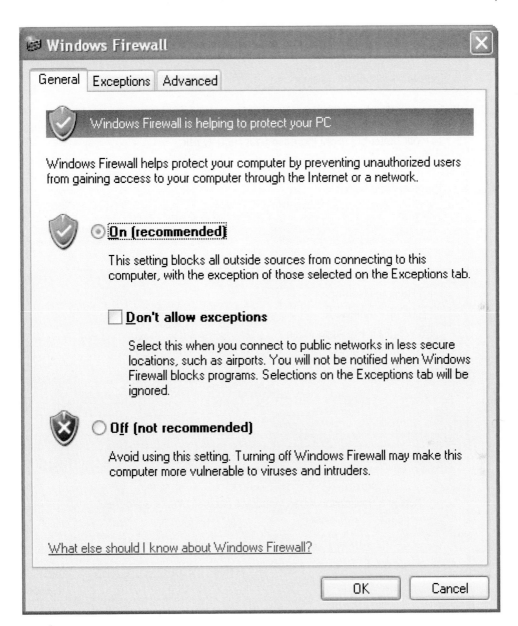

Figure 9a-6   Windows Firewall General Tab

logging. Figure 9a-11 shows that there are only two logging options: logging all dropped packets and logging successful connections. To prevent log files from taking over the computer's entire hard drive, there is a default log size of 4 MB. The user can also decide where to store the log file.

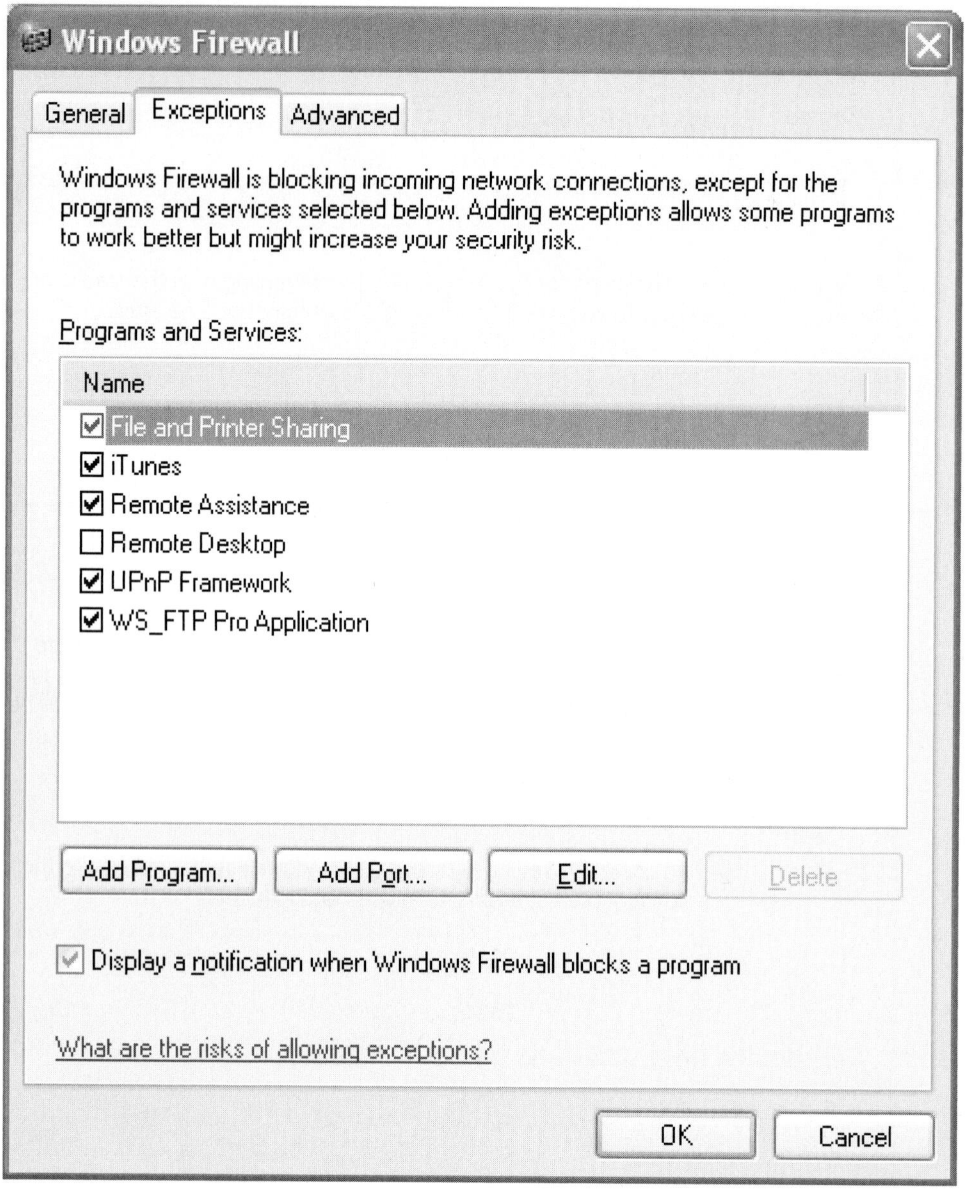

Figure 9a-7   Windows Firewall Exceptions Tab

As discussed in Chapter 8, the Internet Control Message Protocol (ICMP) is TCP/IP's internet layer supervisory protocol. The Advanced tab allows the user to fine-tune ICMP security settings. As Figure 9a-12 shows, most ICMP messages are dropped by default. However, the echo request messages used in pinging are

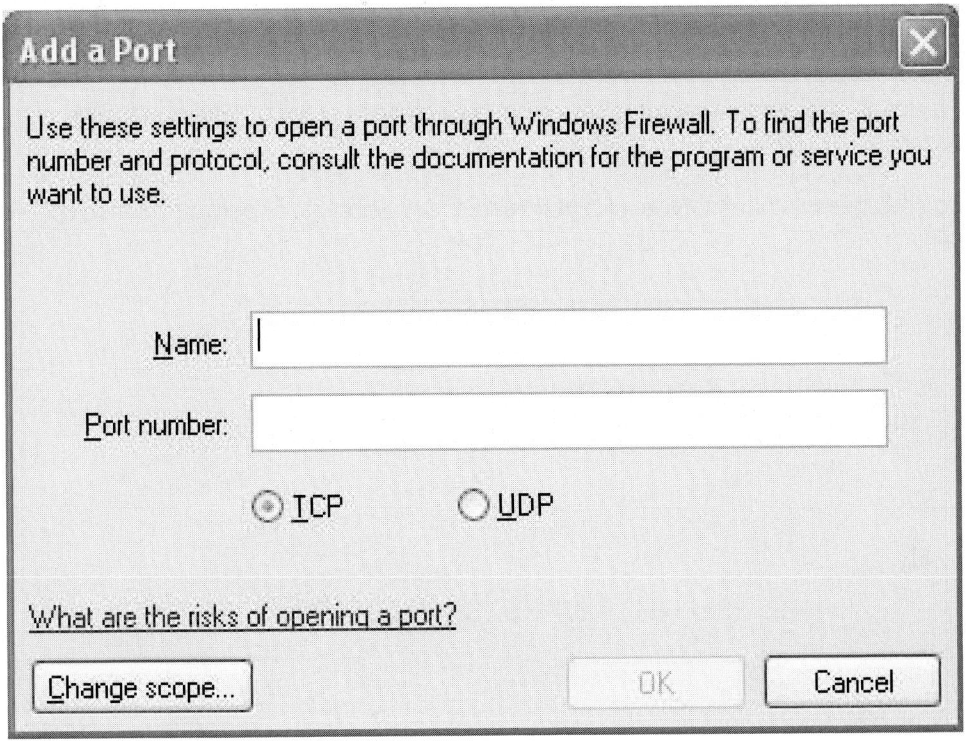

Figure 9a-8   Adding a Port

allowed, even if they come from the Internet. This permits attackers to determine which IP addresses have active hosts. This is useful surveillance information for an attack.

TEST YOUR UNDERSTANDING

6. a) What kind of firewall is the Windows Firewall? b) What limitation does it have? c) Why is this limitation undesirable? d) Why are exceptions needed? e) In what two ways can exceptions be specified? f) Does Windows Firewall allow logging? g) Does it do logging by default? h) By default, what ICMP message is allowed into the system?

Internet Options for Privacy and Security

One of the three configuration icons in the Security Center is **Internet Options**. Selecting this choice will take you to the **Internet Properties** dialog box shown in Figure 9a-13.

Figure 9a-9   Changing the Access Scope of a Port

Security Options

In this figure, the *Security* tab is selected. It lists four **content zones** for which different security policies can be set: By default, all domains are in the Internet zone. However, they can be moved to other zones.

➤ *Internet.* This is the default zone. The default security setting gives a reasonable balance between security and functionality.

➤ *Local intranet.* This content zone is for webservers inside a company's intranet. These webservers typically are protected by a firewall and other hardening measures, so lower security may be appropriate. Users can add local intranet websites to this zone. The default security level is lower than it is in the Internet zone.

➤ *Trusted sites.* These are highly trusted sites. They are given low security barriers. This is very risky, so sites should not be put into this zone unless the user is very certain of the site's security.

➤ *Restricted sites.* These are sites that should not be used or that should be used only with great caution. This zone has high security, which drastically reduces access and what the site can do. If you are about to use a site that raises suspicions, placing it in the Restricted zone is prudent.

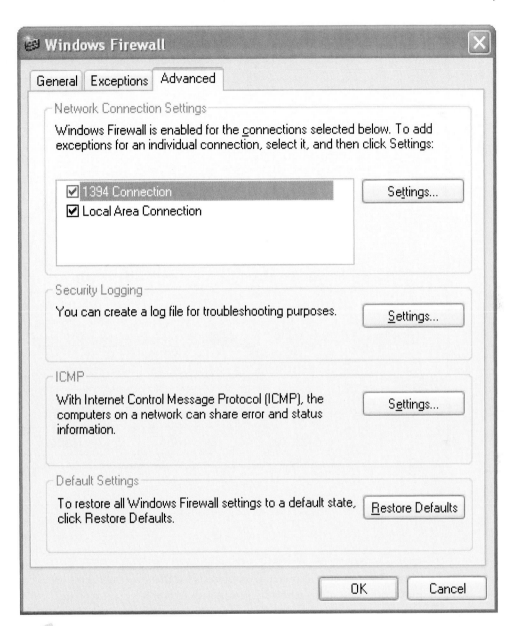

Figure 9a-10   Windows Firewall Advanced Settings Tab

Setting Security Options

Default zone security usually is appropriate. To change the specific security settings for a zone, click on the zone and then click on the *Custom Level* button. This will take you to the *Security Settings* dialog box shown in Figure 9a-14. This dialog box has a complex

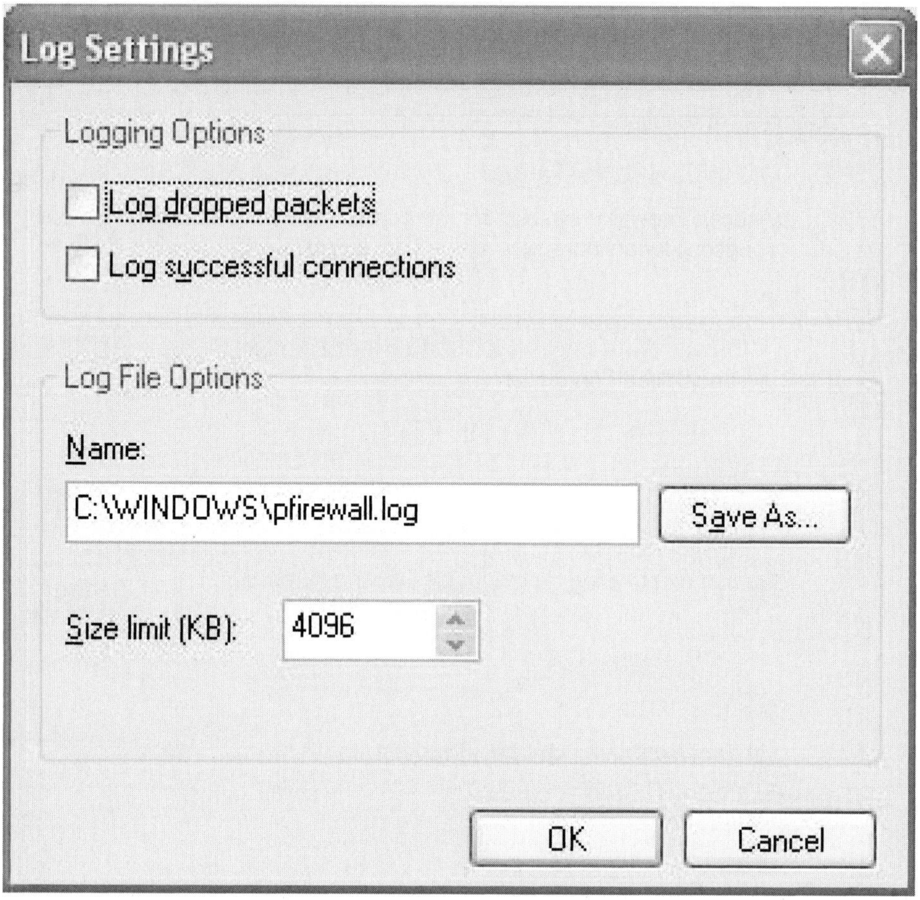

Figure 9a-11   Windows Firewall Log Settings

list of settings. Some corporations have checklists for these settings. Few users have the skills to modify these settings without getting into trouble.

Privacy Options: Cookies

Privacy settings are managed through the *Privacy* tab of the *Internet Properties* dialog box. This tab is primarily used to control cookies. A **cookie** is a small text string that a website places on the user's PC. The site that placed the cookie there can retrieve the cookie, but other sites cannot. Cookies have many legitimate uses, and many sites cannot be used without cookies. However, in some cases, cookies may store personally-identifiable information and other undesirable content.

As Figure 9a-15 shows, Windows XP provides a slider control that lets the user select more or less privacy in terms of cookie control. The default, medium privacy,

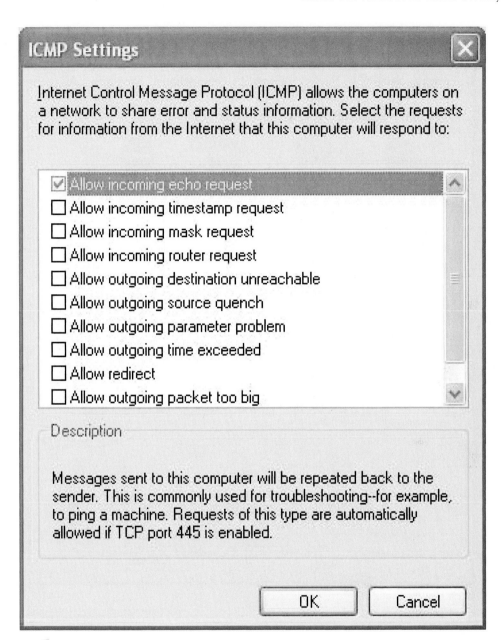

Figure 9a-12 ICMP Settings

generally is a good choice. It restricts personally identifiable information unless you have given at least implicit consent.

If desired, the *Advanced* button can allow the user to configure specific privacy options. There also is an option to override normal cookie handling from specific sites

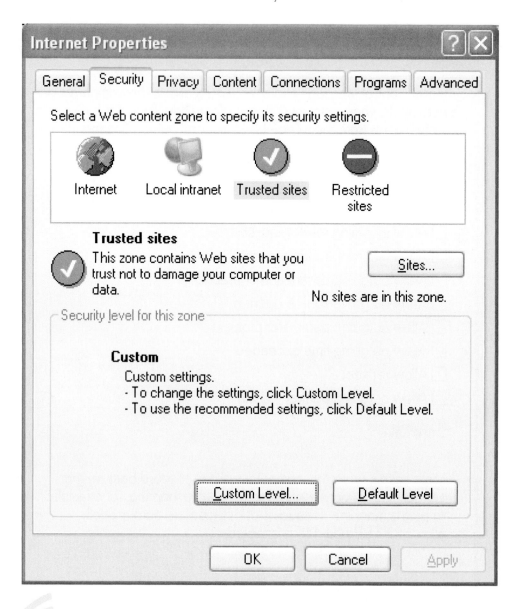

Figure 9a-13   Internet Properties Security Tab

and permit almost no cookie activity. (In fact, domains that have historically been problems are listed automatically under this option.)

Privacy Options: Pop-Up Blocker

The *Privacy* tab also has a **pop-up blocker**, and the default is to block all pop-ups. It is possible to allow pop-ups from certain sites, and it is possible to set the level of pop-up blocking.

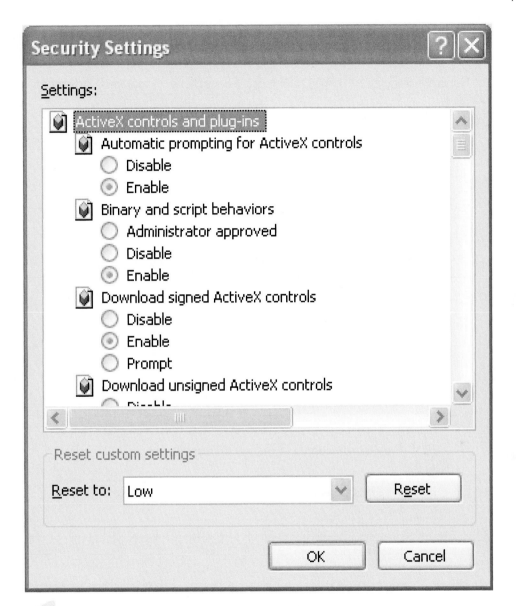

Figure 9a-14   Zone Security Settings

TEST YOUR UNDERSTANDING

7. a) How are security zones used in website security? b) What is the default zone for websites? c) Describe security in other zones. d) How can privacy settings be configured simply? e) What is the main thing that privacy settings control? f) Does SP2 have a pop-up blocker?

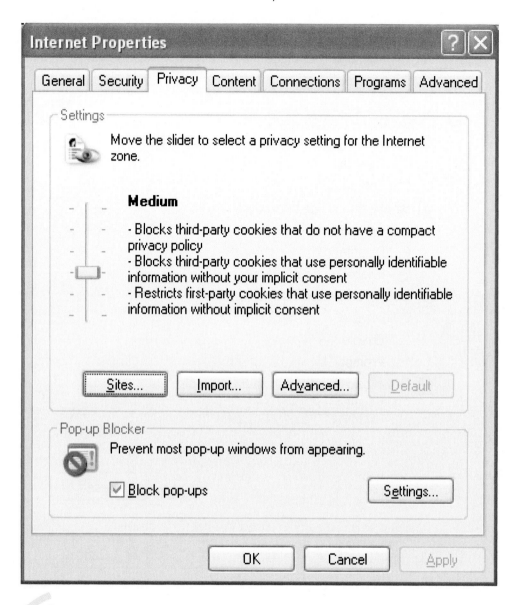

Figure 9a-15   Internet Properties Privacy Tab

ANTIVIRUS SCANNING

Updates primarily provide protection against vulnerability-driven worms and human hackers. They normally do little or nothing to protect against viruses and worms that arrive in e-mail attachments, through instant messaging, file transfer protocols, and other sources. As discussed in Chapter 9, malware attacks are extremely widespread. According to late-2005 statistics from MessageLabs (*www.messagelabs.com*), one to two percent of all e-mail messages contain malware, and this percentage has been roughly constant over time, with brief periods of much higher malware activity. Every client PC needs antivirus software, which also defends against worms that arrive in e-mail and other media.

It is difficult to talk specifically about antivirus scanning programs because they differ in their specific operation. However, all have some things in common.

Virus Definitions Updates

Most importantly, all programs need to be updated regularly. The antivirus program uses a **virus definitions database** to allow it to identify viruses. As new viruses are found, the virus definitions database must be updated. Otherwise, the antivirus program will provide no protection at all against new viruses. In fact, having a nonupdated antivirus program that is no longer effective may give the user a false sense of security.

All antivirus programs have an automatic updating mechanism. However, they vary in how automatic this updating is, and they typically leave it up to the user to decide how often updating is performed. Given the rate of spread of some new viruses, automatically checking for updates *every time the computer is turned on* is good policy.

Configuration and Breadth of Protection

All antivirus programs will filter e-mail, but the user has to configure the program by telling it what e-mail programs he or she uses. Most antivirus programs also filter website downloads. However, antivirus programs differ considerably in whether they filter peer-to-peer applications such as instant messaging and file downloading. Users need to consider what applications they use when selecting an antivirus program.

Problems with Updates

Even if an antivirus program is installed on a user's PC, users often subvert it. Sometimes they turn it off entirely if they think it is interfering with other programs. In other cases, they turn it off to speed up their computer's operation by not waiting for scanning. In yet other cases, users turn off (or do not turn on) automatic updating. More subtly, antivirus program subscriptions have to be paid for annually. Users who fail to pay for subscription extensions lose update protection. In addition to user subversion, virus and worm infections often turn off antivirus protection.

TEST YOUR UNDERSTANDING

8. a) Does updating Windows provide antivirus protection? b) What does? c) What are virus definitions databases? d) Why are updates needed for antivirus programs? e) What is a good schedule for updates to antivirus programs? f) Why must antivirus programs be configured? g) What kind of applications should antivirus programs filter? h) How may users subvert antivirus protection? i) How can viruses subvert antivirus protection?

OTHER COMMON SECURITY MEASURES

Although handling updates and virus checking is important and time consuming, companies may extend more security protection to Windows XP users.

Other Malware-Scanning Programs

Antivirus programs do a good job of scanning arriving files and doing periodic scans of the computer for malware. However, antivirus programs do not scan for all malware. Most users have to purchase one to three additional anti-malware programs.

Anti-Spyware Programs

Spyware is software that sits on a user's computer, gathers information about the user, and sends this information to an attacker. Some spyware programs scour the user's computer for credit security numbers, bank account numbers, and other sensitive information. Others log all of a user's keystrokes to capture passwords and other sensitive information. Although antivirus programs do, in fact, look for spyware, most

Figure 9a-16   Other Common Security Measures (Study Figure)

Other Malware Scanning Programs
- Anti-spyware programs
- Spam blockers
- Anti-adware programs

NAT Protection from Access Routers
- Provides a large amount of protection against attacks automatically

Establishing Virtual Private Networks
- Does not set up SSL/TLS VPNs, which are at the application layer
- Requires two connections
  - An Internet connection
  - A VPN connection to a VPN gateway or host
- Easy to set up
- After setup, most adjust properties
- Some VPN products have a validation program on the client PC
  - The validation program tells the VPN gateway the security status of the PC
  - Validation program operation and communication with VPN servers are not standardized

users find it better to purchase dedicated anti-spyware programs. When most users first run anti-spyware programs, they usually find twenty to eighty pieces of spyware on their systems. Many of the items detected are simply cookies that contain too much personal information, but keystroke loggers and data scouring programs are also found widely.

Spam Blockers

Spam is unsolicited commercial e-mail. Spammers send the same message to millions of e-mail addresses. The transmission is free, so if even a fraction of a percent of the addressees respond, an expert spammer can make a great deal of money. In addition, spammers also make money by selling their e-mail lists to unskilled spammers who create poor-quality messages but who still flood mailboxes with toxic junk mail.

Most users are now protected by their e-mail providers, who now almost universally filter spam. Still, vendor spam filtering is only somewhat effective; so many users also purchase a **spam blocking** program for their own computers.

Anti-Adware Programs

Another type of malware is the **adware** program. These annoying programs pop up advertisements constantly, take users to specific sites whenever the user mistypes a URL, and do other things to bring up advertisements on the user's screen. Special-purpose **anti-adware** programs do a better job screening out adware than do antivirus programs.

TEST YOUR UNDERSTANDING

9. a) What is malware? b) What is spyware? c) What will an anti-spyware program look for? d) Why may a user not need spam blocking on his or her PC? e) What is adware?

NAT Protection from Access Routers

Nearly all access routers use **network address translation (NAT)**. An access router receives a single IP address from the ISP. It then gives a different IP address to each internal PC. When an internal PC transmits, the access router changes the source IP address in the packet with the IP address given to the customer by the ISP. This is network address translation. Of course, NAT also works in the opposite direction. When a packet arrives from the outside, the access router changes the packet's destination IP address from that of the ISP to that of the target internal PC. (NAT also translates port numbers.)

NAT is done primarily to allow multiple internal PCs to share a single external IP address. However, NAT also provides a large amount of automatic security protection. With NAT, it is almost impossible for outside attackers or vulnerability-enabled worms to open connections to internal hosts.

TEST YOUR UNDERSTANDING

10. What protection does NAT provide?

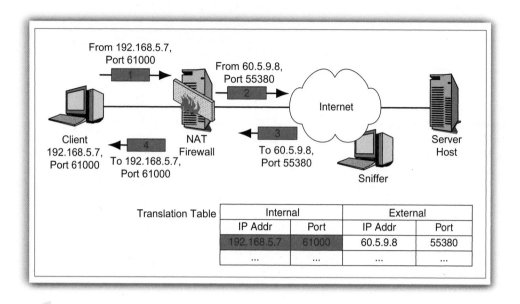

Figure 9a-17   Network Address Translation (NAT)

Establishing Virtual Private Networks

As discussed in Chapter 7, many corporations now use virtual private networks (VPNs), in which the transmission travels over the Internet with added security.

SSL/TLS VPNs

Windows does not provide a way to establish SSL/TLS VPNs because application programs, such as browsers and webserver application programs, handle SSL/TLS VPNs.

Two Connections

Windows XP permits internet-layer VPNs in a simple but somewhat confusing way. To create a VPN connection, *two* connections are needed, as Figure 9a-18 illustrates. First, the user needs a connection to the Internet. Second, once the Internet connection is established, the user establishes a second connection, this time to a security gateway or individual host at a corporate site.

To set up the second connection after you have an Internet connection, go to the *Network and Internet Connections* dialog box (Figure 9a-19). The second choice is *Create a connection to the network at your workplace*. Choosing this option is how you establish a VPN connection to a corporate server.

Setting up the Connection

Selecting this choice starts a New Connection Wizard. During this wizard, you will specify the host name (or IP address) of the host or VPN gateway to which you wish to connect. Windows will then set up the connection.

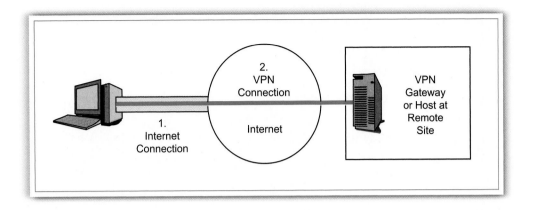

Figure 9a-18   Internet and VPN Connections

The next screen asks if you wish to have a dial-up connection to the network or if you wish to establish a virtual private network. We will select the VPN alternative, but the dial-up alternative is an important way for many users to get into their networks. The wizard ends with a connection screen.

Configuring the VPN Connection

Although the connection is set up, it may be desirable to configure the connection farther. In the *Network and Internet Connections* dialog box (Figure 9a-19), choose *Network Connections*. This will show your Internet connection or connections and the VPN connection you have just created.

Select your VPN connection and right-click on it. Choose *Properties*. You will then see a dialog box with the name of the connection. Under the *Networking* tab, there is an option labeled *Type of VPN*. The default is to allow the type of VPN to be negotiated automatically. Today, L2TP with IPsec is the most common choice. This is highly secure. Sometimes, the remote host or VPN gateway negotiates the less-secure PPTP option.

Validating the Client

Some VPN products add a validation agent to client PCs. The VPN gateway can query the validation agent about the status of the client PC's security before allowing a connection. For instance, the VPN gateway probably will deny the connection unless the user has up-to-date antivirus software. Unfortunately, while basic VPN protocols are standardized, validation agents and communication between validation agents and VPN gateways is not standardized.

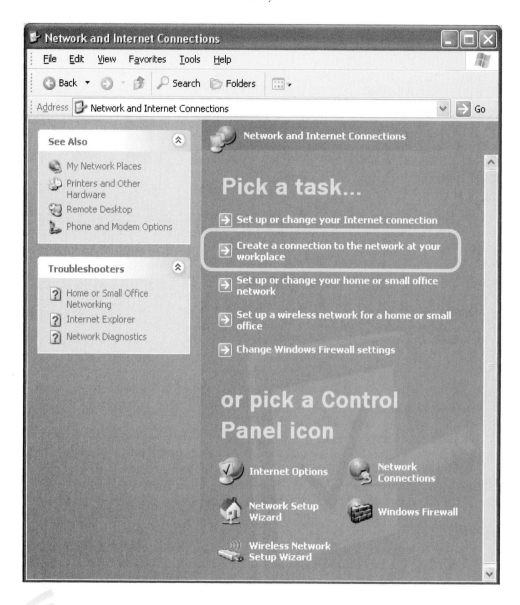

Figure 9a-19   Network and Internet Connections Dialog Box

TEST YOUR UNDERSTANDING

11. a) What is a VPN? b) Why does Microsoft Windows not implement SSL/TLS VPNs. c) What two connections are established to set up an internet-layer VPN? d) What can a user do after creating a VPN connection? e) Why do some VPN products place validation software on client PCs? f) Is validation software standardized?

WINDOWS XP PROFESSIONAL

Windows XP Home, as its name suggests, is designed for home users who connect to the Internet and who may want to share files and printers with other PC users in the same home.

In contrast, **Windows XP Professional** is designed to be used in the corporate environment. Consistent with the more heightened security environment in corporations than in homes, Windows XP Professional has a number of security advances over XP Home.

In corporate environments, PCs are parts of a larger infrastructure. As Figure 9a-20 shows, organizations arrange their clients and servers into groups of resources called **domains**. The computers in the domain are managed by one or more **domain controllers**. The domain's clients and other servers (called member servers) are managed by the domain controller.

This domain structure permits a network administrator to exert strong control over individual computers in the domain. In particular, the administrator can create **group policy objects (GPOs)**, which are policies that govern a specific type of resource, such as client PCs. With GPOs, network administrators can set many security parameters on all PCs within the zone. GPOs can even "lock down" the desktop, controlling what programs can be used and even controlling the layout of the user's desktop.

Figure 9a-20   Controlling Windows XP Professional Computers

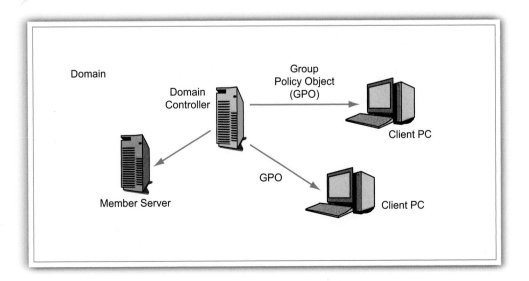

TEST YOUR UNDERSTANDING

12. a) What are domains? b) What are domain controllers? c) What are GPOs? d) How can GPOs be used to manage security on Windows XP client computers?

HANDS-ON EXERCISES

Do the following exercises on your home Windows XP Home computer or on a Windows XP Home computer in your lab.

1. a) How large is your *My Documents* directory? (Right-click on the My Documents folder and select *Properties*). b) How many CD disks (assume a 700 MB capacity) would be needed to back up My Documents? c) How many DVDs would be needed (assume a 4 GB capacity disk).

2. Check the computer's Windows updating.
a) What option is selected? b) Comment on the suitability of this option.

3. a) What antivirus program is on the computer? b) How does it update itself? (You may have to use the antivirus program's help function.) c) What applications is it configured to protect?

4. a) Place a domain in the Restricted zone. b) Remove it from the Restricted zone. c) What level of privacy protection does the computer have? d) Change this level. e) Then change it back to its original value.

5. a) Is the Windows Firewall turned on? b) If not, turn it on. c) Permit incoming WWW connections on Port 80. d) Reverse the previous step. e) If the computer is not yours, reverse the two previous steps.

6. a) Create a VPN connection to a mythical computer at a mythical site. b) Configure the VPN connection to use L2TP with IPsec.

Network Management

Learning Objectives

By the end of this chapter, you should be able to discuss:

- Total cost of ownership (TCO) analysis.
- Network simulation.
- Managing IP, including IP subnet planning, private IP addresses, DHCP, DNS, WINS, directory servers, and configuration for switches and routers.
- Network management tools for client PC connectivity, route analysis, and network mapping.
- Traffic management methods.

NETWORK MANAGEMENT

Up to this point, we have focused primarily on network technology. However, technology is worthless unless the network is well planned and managed. In this chapter we will look at some key issues and skills in network management.

The fact that network management comes late in the book should not be taken as an indication that it is unimportant. Rather, network management comes after discussions of technology because it is impossible to discuss network management in a comprehensive way until the student has a strong understanding of the technologies that network administrators must manage.

COST ANALYSIS

Demand Versus Budget

As Figure 10-1 illustrates, user demand for networking is growing rapidly, but network budgets are either stagnant or growing very slowly. This puts extreme cost pressure on each project. When considering candidate projects, it is critical to develop realistic cost projections.

Labor Costs

In most of this book, we have focused on technology because there are many technical concepts that you must know if you wish to work in networking. However, hardware, software, and carrier services are only a fraction of the total cost of running a network.

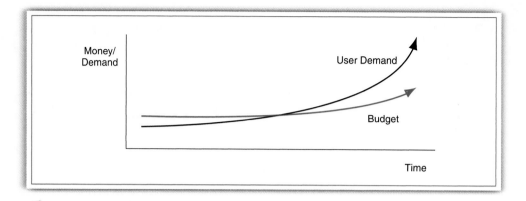

Figure 10-1   Network Demand Versus Budget Trends

The Importance of Costs
  Exploding demand
  Slow budget growth
  Falling hardware costs help, but software costs fall more slowly, and labor costs are rising
  Select the least expensive technology that will fully meet user needs

Non-Technology Costs
  Labor costs
      High, and unit labor costs are rising over time
  Carrier fees

Total Cost of Ownership
  Fully configured cost of hardware
  Fully configured cost of software
  Initial installation costs
      Vendor setup costs
      IT and end-user labor
  Ongoing costs
      Upgrades
      Labor costs often exceed all other costs
      Immature products have very high labor costs
  Total cost of ownership (TCO): total of all costs over life span

Figure 10-2   Cost Issues (Study Figure)

For instance, capital equipment purchases account for just under half of the average networking budget.[1]

Labor dominates nontechnology costs. A third of the average corporate networking budget is employee labor. It is expensive to plan and implement a complex new networking technology, and the long-term labor costs to operate a network system on a day-to-day basis are more expensive still. In addition, although hardware costs are falling rapidly, hourly labor costs actually tend to increase over time. Finally, the users who need the system to do their functional work will also have labor costs to implement and use the system.

Carrier Fees

If a company has wide area networks, it has to pay fees to carriers. These fees can be very substantial.

Total Cost of Ownership (TCO)

Although costs must be managed, this is difficult to do because costs are highly complex and take place over the multiyear time span of most projects. Even so, the costs of projects must be estimated accurately. Companies have lost patience with "guessti-mates" that end up in large cost overruns.

Figure 10-3 illustrates a typical cost analysis. Note that it includes several types of costs. Note also that these costs come over the entire life span of a project, not just during its initial planning and implementation stages.

The Fully Configured Cost of Products

We must first look at the **total purchase cost of network products**. Just as PCs are sold as collections of components, most network products, such as switches and routers, come as collections of hardware and software components. A **fully configured** switch or router often costs far more than the **base price** listed in catalogs. When comparing products from different vendors, it is critical to compare fully configured products. Services such as public switched data networks also tend to come with many options that can add considerably to the base price.

Although hardware is visible and, therefore, easy to appreciate, software costs are very important in the total purchase price. In many cases, software costs exceed hardware costs. As in the case of hardware, software often comes as a base price bundle plus many options.

Initial Installation Costs

In addition, there typically are substantial costs associated with **initial installation**. Some vendors, especially carriers, charge one-time **setup fees**.

There also are a company's own **initial labor costs** associated with installation. These include the costs of the network staff's labor, and they also include the labor

---

[1]Network budget percentages are from Sharon Gaudin, "Spending on the Rise," *Network World*, January 29, 2001. *http://www.nwfusion.com/research/2001/0129feat.html.*

	Year 1	Year 2	Year 3	Year 4	Total
Base Hardware	$200,000	15,000	15,000	15,000	245,000
Hardware Options	85,000	9,000	9,000	9,000	112,000
Base Software	$100,000	10,000	10,000	10,000	130,000
Software Options	50,000	10,000	10,000	10,000	80,000
Technology Subtotal	435,000	44,000	44,000	44,000	567,000
Planning and Development	75,000				75,000
Implementation	50,000				50,000
Ongoing IT Labor	100,000	75,000	75,000	75,000	325,000
Ongoing User Labor	50,000	25,000	25,000	25,000	125,000
Labor Subtotal	275,000	100,000	100,000	100,000	575,000
Total	710,000	144,000	144,000	144,000	1,142,000

Note: The total cost of ownership is $1,142,000.

Figure 10-3   Multiyear Cost Analysis: Total Cost of Ownership (TCO)

costs of end users.[2] End-user labor costs may rise dramatically during installation periods because of training and disruption. In general, the labor costs to create and implement a new network tend to be very high.

Ongoing Costs

Initial costs, as large as they are, often are far smaller than **ongoing costs**. These may come in the form of hardware or software upgrades over the life of the product selected or in the form of monthly payments to vendors. Also substantial are the ongoing labor costs to operate the system. Ongoing costs, especially ongoing labor costs, may be far larger than initial costs. As in the case of initial costs, the ongoing costs to end users must be taken into account.

Ongoing costs are especially high for new technologies that are not yet **mature**. It may take several years for technologies to become easy to install and use. Immature products often lack utilities that allow easy management; therefore, they require a great deal of expensive labor. It is a good idea to avoid new "bleeding edge" technologies if possible. Perversely, vendors and the networking trade press typically focus on such new and immature technologies, giving a rather distorted picture of the workable options available to network administrators.

---

[2]End users are employees in functional departments, such as marketing or finance, who use networking to perform their functional work more effectively.

Total Cost of Ownership (TCO)

In Figure 10-3, the total cost of the system over its expected four-year lifespan is $1,142,000. This is called the **total cost of ownership (TCO)**. This TCO is far higher than the initial base price of the system's hardware ($200,000). As is typical in many systems, labor costs are comparable to the costs of hardware and software. When comparing projects, it is important to compare TCOs.

TEST YOUR UNDERSTANDING

1. a) Why are base prices misleading? b) Why is multiyear analysis necessary? c) How important are labor costs? d) Why do immature products tend to lead to high labor costs? e) What is TCO? f) Why is it important? g) What are the elements of TCO?

NETWORK SIMULATION

As noted earlier in the chapter, designing a new network or a modified network is very difficult because the designer faces many alternatives and because network components tend to interact in unforeseen ways. Network simulation allows network designers to get a handle on this complexity. In addition, it is far more economical to simulate many alternatives than to build several real systems to study.

Network Simulation Purposes

There are several specific reasons to do network simulation.

➤ Comparing alternatives in order to identify the best one.

➤ Sensitivity analysis. This means choosing a most likely situation and seeing how changing ranges of configuration values will affect various performance measures.

➤ Anticipating problems. In the simulation, determining where bottlenecks (points of congestion) will appear.

➤ Planning for growth. Areas where the network will not continue to meet needs as traffic grows must be determined by extrapolating traffic.

TEST YOUR UNDERSTANDING

2. a) Why is network simulation attractive economically? b) For what purposes is network simulation done? c) What is sensitivity analysis?

Before the Simulation: Collecting Data

The best simulation analysis is worthless if the model does not include realistic data. Analysts use the acronym *GIGO*—"garbage in, garbage out"—to emphasize that if input data is bad, the results cannot be accurate. Networking simulation data is never perfect, but simulations are best if the firm collects actual data on its traffic—including how traffic varies by time of day and how much it fluctuates from second to second. Of course, simulations usually deal with the future, so traffic needs to be extrapolated to what it is likely to be in the future.

TEST YOUR UNDERSTANDING

3. a) Explain *GIGO*. b) How can a firm get good data for a simulation?

Simulation

    What-is versus what-if

    More economical to simulate network alternatives than to build them

    Purposes

        Comparing alternatives to select the best one

        Base case and sensitivity analysis to see what will happen if the values of variables were varied over a range

        Anticipating problems, such as bottlenecks

        Planning for growth, to anticipate areas where more capacity is needed

Before the Simulation, Collect Data

    Data must be good

    Otherwise, GIGO (garbage in, garbage out)

    Collect data on the current network

    Forecast growth

The Process

    Based on OPNET IT Guru

    Add nodes to the simulation work area (clients, servers, switches, routers, etc.)

    Specify the topology with transmission lines

    Configure the nodes and transmission lines

    Add applications, which generate traffic data

    Run the simulation for some simulated period of time

    Examine the output to determine implications

    Validate the simulation (compare with reality if possible to see if it is correct)

    What-if analysis

    Application performance analysis (OPNET ACE)

Figure 10-4   Network Simulation (Study Figure)

The Process

Once data is collected, the modeler can begin to create the simulation. We will discuss simulation using the popular **OPNET IT Guru** network simulation program.

Adding Nodes

The first step in building a simulation is to place **nodes** (items to be connected by transmission lines) on the simulation work area. These nodes can be clients, servers, switches, routers, and other types of devices. As Figure 10-5 shows, IT Guru has templates with icons of common nodes. You can drag and drop these icons onto the simulation work area.

Specifying the Topology

The next step is to specify the **topology**—how the nodes are linked together by transmission lines. IT Guru has a template with icons for transmission lines and networks. You select a transmission icon and then decide what nodes it will link. In this case, a

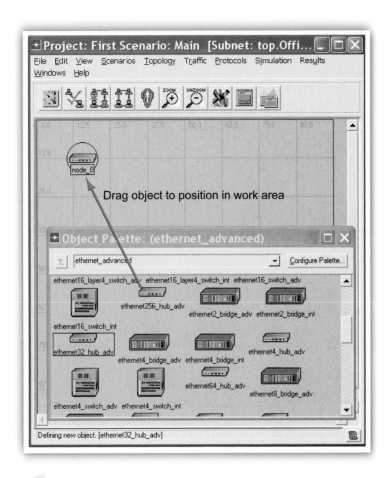

Figure 10-5   OPNET IT Guru Node Template

Frame Relay network will be used to connect the host computers. You now have something that looks very much like the network you are modeling.

Configuring Elements

However, the nodes and transmission links need to be configured before your simulation of them is complete. For instance, on a router, you will have to specify the speeds of various interfaces. You also will have to configure specific operating parameters, such as the window size field in TCP. Figure 10-6 shows a Frame Relay transmission link being configured so that its outgoing excess burst size (Be) is set to 64 kbps.

Adding Applications

Your nodes and lines are now ready to work, but you need to specify traffic. IT Guru has you do this by specifying applications, the traffic characteristics of these applications, and on which nodes they will run. This is realistic because traffic is created by applications,

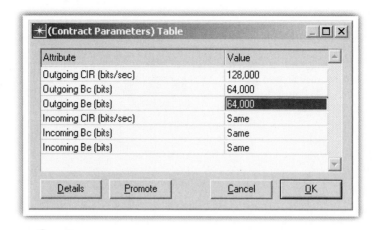

Figure 10-6   Configuring a Frame Relay CIR

not by the network.[3] Figure 10-7 shows the final configured simulation model after applications have been added.

Running the Simulation
Your simulation is now complete, so the next step is to run it. You can specify a time period over which the simulation is to run—say over an entire simulated day or during a simulated busy period. After you do this, IT Guru will run the simulation using sophisticated statistical and queuing theory methods.

Examining the Output
IT Guru gives you many alternatives for looking at your output. Graphical output is best for searching for trends or anomalies. You often can learn a great deal by looking at the simulation results in detail.

Validating the Simulation
If you are simulating a real network, you can **validate** the model by comparing its performance with that of the real network. If the model gives very different output, you need to revise the model and attempt to validate it again. Of course, for proposed networks, validation generally is impossible.

What-If Analysis
Now comes the real power of simulation—running what-if analyses to see how specific changes would change the results. You might change a single parameter on a single computer (such as a windows size field in TCP). You might change the speed of a transmission line or consider an upgrade for a router. You might see if adding a router

---

[3]Somewhat oddly, each application appears as an icon on the simulation working area. It is important not to confuse these software objects with the physical hardware and transmission line objects on the working area.

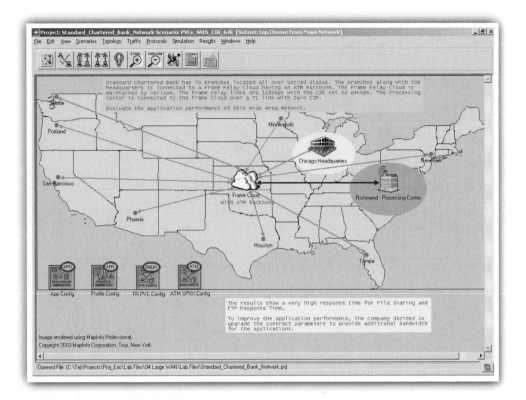

Figure 10-7   Configured Simulation Model

in a particular place would get rid of a bottleneck. The possibilities are endless. By trying many alternatives, you can develop a network solution that is optimized for the company's business needs.

Figure 10-8 shows a what-if analysis in which two PVC speeds are tried to determine the impact on response times for two applications—FTP and database queries. It shows that PVC committed information rate has a major impact on FTP response time but not on database response time.

Application Analysis

OPNET offers a product related to IT Guru. This is the **Application Characterization Environment (ACE)**. While IT Guru focuses primarily on network-level and internet-level performance, ACE allows the modeler to focus on application performance.

TEST YOUR UNDERSTANDING

4. a) What are nodes? b) What is a topology? c) List the steps in building a network simulation. d) What steps should be undertaken after running the simulation? e) What is validation, and why is it important? f) What is what-if analysis? g) Distinguish between IT Guru and ACE.

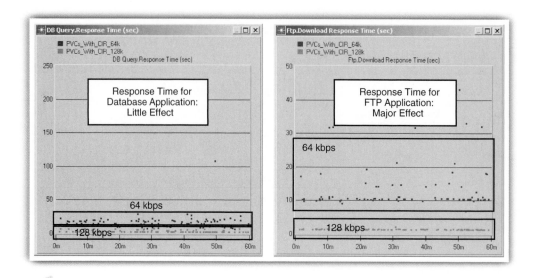

Figure 10-8   What-If Analysis

IP MANAGEMENT

If a firm uses TCP/IP as its internetworking protocol, it must do a considerable amount of work to build and maintain the necessary infrastructure of IP.

IP Subnet Planning

As Chapter 8 discussed, IP addresses are 32 bits long. Each organization is assigned a network part. We saw that the University of Hawai'i's network part (128.171) is sixteen bits long. It was up to the university to decide what to do with the remaining sixteen bits.

Subnetting at the University of Hawai'i

The university, like most organizations, chose to subnet its IP address space. It divided the 16 bits over which it has discretion into an 8-bit subnet part and an 8-bit host part.

The 2^N–2 Rule

With N bits, you can represent 2^N possibilities. Therefore, with 8 bits, one can represent 2^8 (256) possibilities. This would suggest that the university can have 256 subnets, each with 256 hosts. However, a network, subnet, or host part cannot be all 0s or all 1s. Therefore, the university can have only 254 (256–2) subnets, each with only 254 hosts. Figure 10-9 illustrates these calculations.

In general, if a part is N bits long, it can represent 2^N–2 networks, subnets, or hosts. For example, if a subnet part is 9 bits long, there can be 2^9–2, or 510, subnets. Or if a host part is 5 bits long, there can be 2^5–2, or 30, hosts.

In general, if a part is N bits long, it can represent 2^N–2 networks, subnets, or hosts.

Step	Description				
1	Total size of IP address (bits)	32			
2	Size of network part assigned to firm (bits)	16		8	
3	Remaining bits for firm to assign	16		24	
4	Selected subnet/host part sizes (bits)	8/8	6/10	12/12	8/16
5	Possible number of subnets (2^N-2)	254 (2^8-2)	62 (2^6-2)	4,094 ($2^{12}-2$)	254 (2^8-2)
6	Possible number of hosts per subnet (2^N-2)	254 (2^8-2)	1,022 ($2^{10}-2$)	4,094 ($2^{12}-2$)	65,534 ($2^{16}-2$)

Figure 10-9 IP Subnetting

Balancing Subnet and Host Part Sizes

The larger the subnet part, the more subnets there will be. However, the larger the subnet part is made, the smaller the host part must be. This will mean fewer hosts per subnet.

The University of Hawai'i's choice of 8-bit network and subnet parts was useful for many years because no college needed more than 254 hosts. However, many colleges now have more than 254 computers, and the limit of 254 hosts required by its subnetting decision has become a serious problem. Several colleges now have two subnets connected by routers. This is expensive and awkward.

The University would have been better served had it selected a smaller subnet part, say 6 bits. As Figure 10-9 shows, this would have allowed 62 college subnets, which probably would have been sufficient. A 6-bit subnet part would give a 10-bit host part, allowing 1,022 hosts per subnet. This would be ample for several years to come.

A Critical Choice

In general, it is critical for corporations to plan their IP subnetting carefully, in order to get the right balance between the sizes of their network and subnet parts.

Using Private IP Addresses

As just noted, companies are assigned network parts for their IP addresses. If this network part is large, then the organization will have comparatively few bits left over to use for subnets and hosts.

However, three IP address ranges have been designated as private IP addresses. These are the three ranges:

➤ 10.x.x.x
➤ 192.168.x.x
➤ 172.16.x.x through 172.31.x.x

Private IP addresses may not be used on the Internet itself. However, they may be used within a firm. Network address translation (NAT), which we saw in Chapter 1, allows internal private IP addresses to be translated into public IP addresses for transmission over the Internet.

The 10.x.x.x range of private IP addresses has only 8 bits in its network part. This leaves 24 bits for the subnet and host parts, allowing the firm to select large subnet parts and large host parts simultaneously.

For instance, as Figure 10-9 shows, if the network and subnet parts are both set at 12 bits, then the firm can have $2^{12}-2$ (4,094) subnets, each with up to 4,094 hosts. Alternatively, if the subnet and host parts had been 8 bits and 16 bits respectively, there could be up to 254 subnets, each with up to 65,534 hosts.

TEST YOUR UNDERSTANDING

5. a) Why is IP subnet planning important? b) If you have a subnet part of 9 bits, how many subnets can you have? c) Your firm has the 8-bit network part 60. If you need at least 250 subnets, what must your subnet size be? d) How many hosts can you have per subnet? e) Your firm has a 20-bit network part. What subnet part would you select to give at least 10 subnets? f) How many hosts can you have per subnet? g) How are private IP address ranges used? h) What are the three ranges of private IP addresses?

Administrative IP Servers

Managing IP also requires the organization to set up and manage several **administrative IP servers**, which are needed to support IP.

DHCP Servers

Most clients have temporary IP addresses delivered by DHCP servers. These DHCP servers have to be set up and operated by the firm. Some firms have each subnet manager maintain a DHCP server for his or her subnet. At the University of Hawai'i, a strong tradition of decentralization made this a logical choice. At the First Bank of Paradise, however, each site has a single DHCP server—even the headquarters site, which has many subnets. Each DHCP server has a configurable **scope** parameter which determines how many subnets it will serve.

DNS Servers

Large organizations with second-level domain names (such as *pukanui.com*) are responsible for maintaining a Domain Name System (DNS) server that lists all internal hosts that have host names. Most firms have a primary DNS server and a secondary DNS server for redundancy because losing DNS service will make the network useless for most users. Maintaining the firm's shifting use of host names on the DNS server is a full-time job in large organizations.

WINS

Before Windows 2000 Server, Windows had a different computer naming system associated with Microsoft's NETBIOS protocol. Just as DNS provides IP addresses for host names, **Windows Internet Name Service (WINS)** servers provide IP addresses for NET-BIOS computer names.

Suppose an older Windows client or server needs to send a packet to another computer whose NETBIOS name it knows. The computer sends a WINS request message to a WINS server giving the NETBIOS computer name of the target. The WINS server sends back a response message containing the IP address of the target.

Firms that have older clients and servers with older versions of Windows (and this is nearly all firms) need to support WINS servers as well as DNS servers.

Directory Servers and LDAP

Many firms now have directory servers, which centralize information about a firm.

Hierarchical Organization   As Figure 10-10 shows, information in a directory server is arranged hierarchically, much as entries in a DNS server are organized (see Chapter 8).

The figure shows the directory structure for the mythical University of Waikiki. The top level is the **organization**. Under the top level, there are schools (**organizational units**, in directory server terminology). In each school, there are faculty, staff, and router categories. Under the faculty category, there are the usernames of faculty members. At the bottom of the hierarchy are the **properties** of individual faculty members, including the faculty member's common name, e-mail address, and telephone extension.

Lightweight Directory Access Protocol (LDAP)   Most directory servers today permit query commands governed by the **Lightweight Directory Access Protocol (LDAP)**.

Figure 10-10   Hierarchical Directory Server Name Space

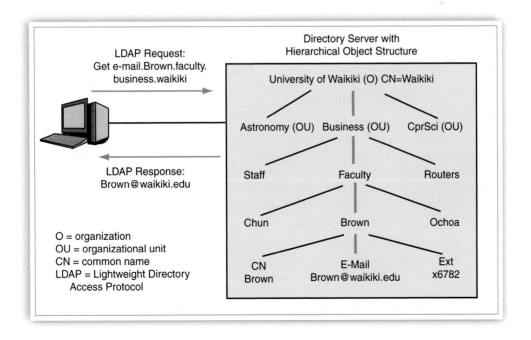

The figure shows that LDAP commands specify the path to a property, with individual nodes along the way separated by dots. This is why the request for Brown's e-mail address is specified as the following:

e-mail.brown.faculty.business.waikiki

Directory Servers and the Networking Staff Organizations store a great deal of information about themselves in directory servers, including a great deal of networking information. Creating a directory server requires a great deal of planning about what information an organization needs to store and how this information should be arranged hierarchically.

Although creating and managing a directory server goes well beyond networking, the networking staff is often given the task of leading directory server planning projects and managing the directory server on a daily basis.

TEST YOUR UNDERSTANDING

6. a) What major types of servers must be created and maintained to manage IP in a corporate environment? b) What are DHCP scopes? c) Why do most firms have both a primary and a secondary DNS server? d) What is the purpose of WINS? e) For what operating systems is WINS needed? f) How is information in directory servers organized? g) What is the purpose of LDAP? h) If Astronomy has a similar directory organization to Business (in Figure 10-10), give the specification for the telephone extension of Claire Williams (username cwilliams), who is an Astronomy staff member.

Device Configuration

Individual devices on the network—clients, servers, switches, and routers—need to be configured to work with TCP/IP. We saw how to configure Windows XP Home clients for networking in Chapter 1a.

Configuring IOS Devices

Cisco Systems, which dominates the market for switches and routers, has an operating system that it uses on all of its routers and all of its switches. This is the **Internetwork Operating System (IOS)**.

Initial Router Configuration

When you turn on a Cisco router for the first time, you are led through a sequence of configuration questions. This allows you to configure much of what needs to be configured about the router. However, although this extended configuration mode gets a router up and running, it does not do all configuration work.

In the initial configuration process, the user specifies many things about the router and its interface, including:

➤ A name for the router.

➤ An enable secret for privileged mode (which is needed to do most configuration tasks).

➤ Whether or not SNMP (discussed later) should be turned on to manage the router.

➤ Whether routing should be set up for IP, IPX, AppleTalk, and other protocols.

➤ For each interface, operating characteristics, an IP address, a subnet mask, and other information.

➤   Finally, whether the configuration should be saved in NVRAM (nonvolatile RAM) for permanent use (until changed).

The Command Line Interface (CLI)

To work with the limited processing power and memory of switches and routers, IOS has to be kept as small as possible. This has necessitated using a **command line interface (CLI)**, in which a user has to type highly structured commands, ending each command with Enter. Figure 10-11 shows some steps needed to configure a router in CLI mode rather than through initial configuration.

TEST YOUR UNDERSTANDING

7. a) List some configuration tasks for routers. b) What is Cisco's operating system? c) What is a CLI? d) What is the advantage of using a CLI? e) What happens when you first turn on a new Cisco router? f) Does extended configuration when you first turn on a new Cisco router handle all configuration chores? g) Must an IP address and subnet mask be configured for each router interface? h) What is the IOS CLI prompt in nonprivileged mode? i) What is the IOS CLI prompt in privileged mode?

NETWORK MANAGEMENT UTILITIES

As networks grow more complex and geographically dispersed, network administrators need tools to manage their networks. Fortunately, network administrators have a broad spectrum of **network management utilities** that help them manage their networks. We will discuss the broad categories of functionality into which these tools fall. We saw many of these programs in the hands-on exercises in Chapter 1, and we saw more about the ubiquitous ping utility in Chapter 8.

Security Concerns

Usage Policies

Although network management utilities are very useful, the tools that network managers use are the same tools that hackers use to plan their attacks on networks. Companies need **usage policies** for who may use various tools and how they may use them in order to ensure that they are not being used to attack the firm.

Firewalls and Network Management Tools

Another consequence of hacker interest in network management utilities is that border firewalls typically keep network management packets from entering sites. This makes managing multiple sites from a single location difficult.

TEST YOUR UNDERSTANDING

8. a) Why are usage policies for network tools important? b) Why do companies often configure their border firewalls to interfere with network management utilities?

Figure 10-11 Cisco Internetwork Operating System (IOS) Command Line Interface (CLI)

Command	Comment
Router>enable[Enter]	Router> is the prompt. The ">" shows that the user is in non-privileged mode. Enables privileged mode so that user can take supervisory actions. User must enter the enable secret. All commands end with [Enter]. Enter is not shown in subsequent commands.
Router#hostname julia	Prompt changes to "#" to indicate that user is in privileged mode. User gives the router a name, julia.
julia#config t	Enter configuration mode. The t is an abbreviation for terminal.
julia(config)#int e0	Prompt changes to julia(config) to indicate that the user is in configuration mode. User wishes to configure Ethernet interface 0. (Router has two Ethernet interfaces, 0 and 1.)
julia(config-if)#ip address 10.5.0.6 255.255.0.0	User gives the interface an IP address and a subnet mask. (Every router interface must have a separate IP address.) The subnet is 5.
julia(config-if)#no shutdown	This is an odd one. The command to shut down an interface is "shutdown". Correspondingly, "no shutdown" turns the interface on.
julia(config-if)# Ctrl-Z	User types Ctrl-Z (the key combination, not the letters) to end the configuration of e0.
julia(config)#int s1	User wishes to configure serial interface 1. (Router has two serial interfaces, 0 and 1.)
julia(config-if)#ip address 10.6.0.1 255.255.0.0	User gives the interface an IP address and subnet mask. The subnet is 6.
julia(config-if)#no shutdown	Turns on s1.
julia(config-if)# Ctrl-Z	Ends the configuration of s1.
julia# router rip	Enables the Router Initiation Protocol (RIP) routing protocol.
julia#disable	Takes user back to non-privileged mode. This prevents anyone getting access to the terminal from making administrative changes to the router.
julia>	

Host Diagnostic Tools

Network Setup Wizard

Figure 10-12 shows several categories of network management utilities. We will begin with host computers, which have to be configured for networking. Client configuration for Windows XP systems was discussed in Chapter 1b. Configuration for other client operating systems is broadly similar; the user or IT installer runs a network setup wizard. Most of the time, this works well and nothing else is necessary. Sometimes, however, more diagnostic help is needed.

Testing the Connection

After configuration, the installer typically tests the connection by double-clicking on the browser and seeing if he or she can go to a known website. It is even better to drop down to the command prompt (see Chapter 1) and ping a distant host. Ping, which we saw in Chapter 1, measures latency very precisely, giving potentially subtle indications of problems even if the browser connections succeed.[4] Tracert (Chapter 1) measures latency at various routers along the way to a target host, giving more detailed latency data.

Loopback Testing with Ipconfig or Winipconfig

If testing the connection causes problems or fails to work, it is important to get more diagnostic data. If running the browser, pinging, or tracert cannot get to the target host, the first step is to *ping 127.0.0.1*, which is your computer's **loopback interface**. Essentially, pinging 127.0.0.1 pings your own computer. If it fails, you know that there is a problem with your network setup.

The next logical step in diagnosing a Windows client is to drop down to the command prompt and run *ipconfig /all* or *winipconfig*, depending on your version of Windows. This will give you a great deal of information on your Internet connection, including your MAC address, IP address, DNS addresses, subnet mask, and other basic information. This might be enough to identify the problem and suggest how to fix it. For instance, if your computer cannot reach hosts, you may have the wrong IP address for your company's DNS hosts.

Checking the NIC

Another problem may be that the NIC is not functioning properly. To check on the NIC, hit the *Start* button. Then choose *Connect to,* and select *Show all connections.* This will take you to a list of connections.

Right-click on the connection you have established and select *Properties.* This will take you to a dialog box. Under the name of the NIC, click on the *Configure* button.

This takes you to a new configuration dialog box for the NIC, as shown in Figure 10-13. The *Device Status* box will tell you if the NIC is working properly. If the NIC is not working properly, the *Troubleshoot* button will take you through a wizard to help you diagnose the problem.

Packet Capture and Display Programs

For even more subtle problems, **packet capture and display programs** capture selected packets or all of the packets arriving at a NIC or going out of a NIC. Afterward, you can

---

[4]Joseph D. Sloan, *Network Troubleshooting Tools*, Sebastopol, California: O'Reilly & Associates, 2001.

Figure 10-12   Network Management Utilities (Study Figure)

Security
    Management tools can be used to make attacks
    Policies should limit these tools to certain employees and for certain purposes
    Firewalls block many network management tools to avoid attacks
Host Diagnostic Tools
    Network Setup Wizard works most of the time; need tools if it does not
    Testing the connection
        Open a connection to a website using a browser
        Ping a host to see if latency is acceptable
    Loopback testing and ipconfig/winipconfig
        Go to the command line
        Ping 127.0.0.1. This is the loopback interface (you ping yourself)
        For detailed information: ipconfig /all or winipconfig (older versions of Windows)
    Checking the NIC in Windows XP
        Right click on a connection and select Properties
        Under the name of the NIC, hit the Configuration button
        The dialog box that appears will show you the status of the NIC
        It also offers a Troubleshooting wizard if the NIC is not working
    Packet capture and display programs
        Capture data on individual packets
        Allows extremely detailed traffic analysis
        Look at individual packet data and summaries
        WinDUMP is a popular packet capture and display program on Windows
    Traffic summarization
        Shows statistical data on traffic going into and out of the host
        EtherPeek is a popular commercial traffic summarization program
    Connection analysis
        At the command line, Netstat shows active connections
        This can identify problem connections
Route Analysis Tools
    To test the route to another host
    Ping tests if a route to a host exists and what its latency is
    Tracert shows the routers along the way and latencies to them
Network Mapping Tools
    To understand how the network is organized
    Discovering IP addresses with active devices
    Fingerprinting them to determine their operating system (client, server, or router)
    A popular network mapping program is Nmap (Figure 10-6)
Simple Network Management Protocol (SNMP)
    Components: manager, managed devices, agents, objects, RMON probes
    Management information base (MIB)
    Commands, responses, traps
    Set command

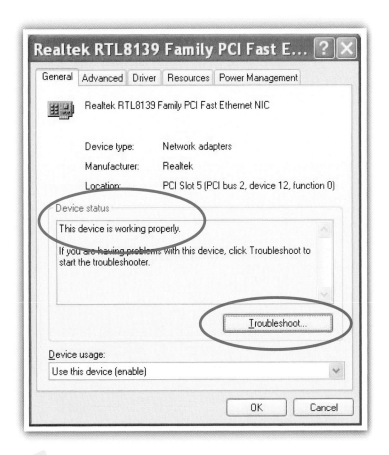

Figure 10-13   NIC Configuration Dialog Box

display key header information for each packet in greater or lesser detail. This packet-by-packet analysis gives you maximum information on traffic going into and out of your computer.

The most popular freeware packet-analysis program is **TCPDUMP** for Unix, which is available as **WinDUMP** for Windows computers.[5] The user runs the program and tells it to collect data for some period of time. TCPDUMP/WinDUMP then presents data on each packet. Chapter 8a discussed WinDUMP/TCPDUMP.

Traffic Summarization

While looking at individual packets can be helpful, it may also be good to go to the other extreme, looking at broad statistical trends over periods of time. Figure 10-14

---

[5]A good link for downloading WinDUMP (and the WinPCAP software you must download first to run WinDUMP) is *http://windump.polito.it/*. The site also has good documentation on WinDUMP.

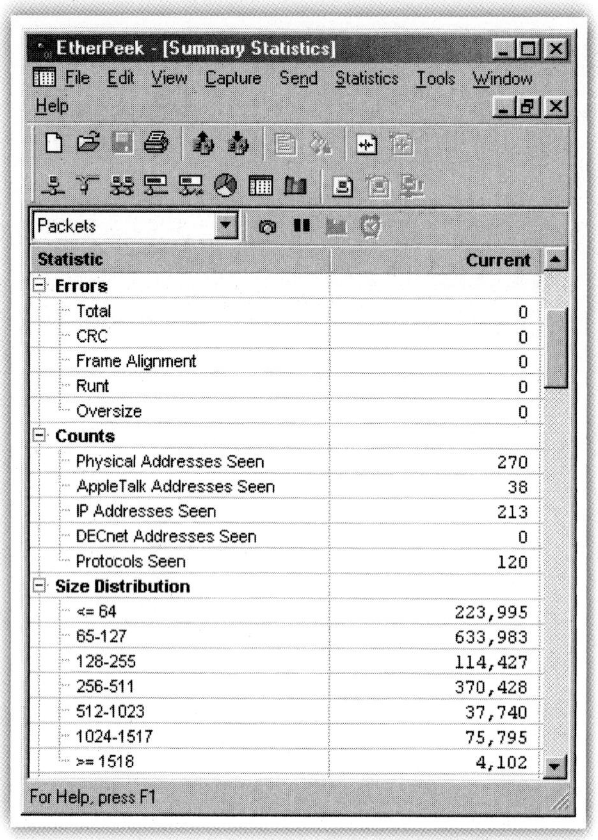

Figure 10-14   EtherPeek Packet Capture and
Summarization Program

shows some output from **EtherPeek**, a commercial traffic summarization program. EtherPeek works by capturing all packets arriving at and leaving a NIC, then providing a wide spectrum of summarization tools. EtherPeek can show overall trends and also can drill down to specifics.

Connection Analysis

Another popular tool, which is built into the operating system in both Unix and Windows, is **Netstat**. This program shows active connections. In Figure 10-15, there is a single TCP connection, on Port 3290. The connection is closed and in the wait mode. This might be an indication that the computer has a Trojan horse program installed on it. In addition to causing damage in general, Trojan horses can cause serious problems for network connections. Alternatively, this connection might be a legitimate connection.

Figure 10-15   Netstat Connections Analysis Program

TEST YOUR UNDERSTANDING

9. a) After you use the network setup wizard to create a network connection, with what two quick ways can you verify that the connection is working? b) How can pinging be used in two ways to test a connection? c) How do ipconfig /all and winipconfig assist in troubleshooting? d) What are the benefits of packet capture and display programs? e) What is a common freeware program for packet capture and display? f) What information do traffic summarization programs like EtherPeek provide? g) What information does Netstat tell you?

Route Analysis Tools

Once the operating system can talk to the outside world, the next problem may be a route to a particular host, such as a webserver or mail server. If there appears to be a problem with the route, the network troubleshooter has to perform **route analysis** to locate the problem.

Our old friends ping and tracert are good places to begin. Both give latencies. Ping gives latency to the host. If this latency appears to be high, tracert will give latencies at all routers along the route.

TEST YOUR UNDERSTANDING

10. a) What is the purpose of route analysis? b) How does ping support route analysis? c) How does tracert support route analysis?

Network Mapping Tools

Sometimes, network managers have a broader need, most commonly to map the layout of their networks, including what hosts and routers are active and how various devices are connected. **Network mapping** has two phases. The first is **discovering** hosts and subnets—that is, finding out if they exist. The second is **fingerprinting** hosts (determining their characteristics) to determine if they are clients, servers, or routers.

Although ping and tracert are useful for the host discovery phase, they are tedious to use. Network administrators typically turn to network mapping tools, including the free Nmap program that we saw in the previous chapter.

Nmap pings a broad range of possible host addresses to determine which IP addresses have active hosts. If ping will not work (or is blocked by firewalls), Nmap offers other ways to scan for active IP addresses.

Nmap also offers fingerprinting, which attempts to identify the specific operating system running on each host and sometimes even the version number of the operating system. For instance, a computer running Windows XP is almost certainly a client, while a computer running Windows Server 2003 or Solaris (the SUN version of Unix) probably is a server. Nmap can even fingerprint router operating systems to identify routers.

When network mapping is finished, the network manager should have a good understanding of how the network is organized and what parts are not working correctly.

TEST YOUR UNDERSTANDING

11. a) What is network mapping? b) Describe the two phases of network mapping. c) How can Nmap help in network mapping?

Simple Network Management Protocol (SNMP)

Although the tools we have been discussing all have their places, the Internet Engineering Task Force has developed a general way to collect rich data from various devices in a network. This is the **Simple Network Management Protocol (SNMP)**. Figure 10-16 shows the major elements of SNMP communications.

The Manager

The network administrator works at a central computer that runs a program called the **network management program**, or, more simply, the **manager**.

Managed Devices

The manager is responsible for many **managed devices**—devices that need to be administered, such as printers, hubs, switches, routers, application programs, user PCs, and other pieces of hardware and software.

Agents

Managed devices have pieces of software (and sometimes hardware) called **network management agents**, or, more simply, **agents**. In sports and entertainment, an agent acts on behalf of a person. Similarly, network management agents communicate with the manager on behalf of their managed devices. In other words, the manager does not communicate with the managed device directly, but rather with the device's agent.

The manager does not communicate with the managed device directly, but rather with the device's agent.

Objects

More specifically, the manager, through the agent, manages **objects** (properties of the managed device). Figure 10-17 shows the basic model for organizing SNMP objects. First, there is the system. This might be a computer, switch, router, or another device.

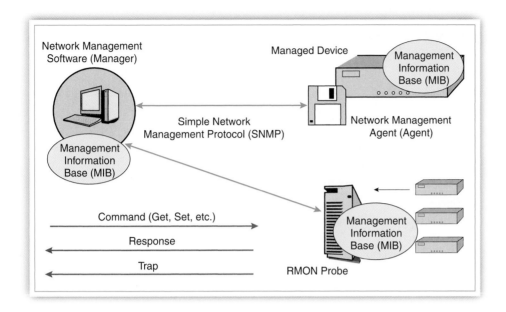

Figure 10-16   Simple Network Management Protocol (SNMP)

In addition, there are TCP, UDP, IP, and ICMP objects and objects for individual inter-faces. Each of these objects has categories under it, and those subcategories have fur-ther subcategories.

For example, if a router does not appear to be working properly, the manager can issue *Get* commands to collect appropriate router objects. A first step might be to check if the router is in forwarding mode. If not, it will not route packets. If this does not clarify the problem, the manager can collect more information, including error statistics and general traffic statistics of various types.

RMON Probes

One specialized type of agent is the **RMON probe** (remote monitoring probe). This may be a stand-alone device or software running on a switch or router. An RMON probe collects data on network traffic passing through its location instead of informa-tion about the RMON probe itself. The manager can poll the RMON probe to get summarized information about the distribution of packet sizes, the numbers of various types of errors, the number of packets processed, the ten most active hosts, and other statistical summaries that may help pinpoint problems. This generates far less network management traffic than polling many devices individually.

Management Information Base (MIB)

In a database, the **schema** describes the design of the database—that is, the specific types of information it contains. Similarly, network management requires a **management information base (MIB)** specification that defines what objects can exist

Figure 10-17   SNMP Object Model

System Objects
>   System name
>   System description
>   System contact person
>   System uptime (since last reboot)

IP Objects
>   Forwarding (for routers). Yes if forwarding (routing), No if not
>   Subnet mask
>   Default time to live
>   Traffic statistics
>   Number of discards because of resource limitations
>   Number of discards because could not find route
>   Number of rows in routing table
>   Rows discarded because of lack of space
>   Individual row data

TCP Objects
>   Maximum/minimum retransmission time
>   Maximum number of TCP connections allowed
>   Opens/failed connections/resets
>   Segments sent
>   Segments retransmitted
>   Errors in incoming segments
>   No open port errors
>   Data on individual connections (sockets, states)

UDP Objects
>   Error: no application on requested port
>   Traffic statistics

ICMP Objects
>   Number of errors of various types

Interface Objects (One per Interface)
>   Type (e.g., 69 is 100Base-FX; 71 is 802.11)
>   Status: up/down/testing
>   Speed
>   MTU (maximum transmission unit—the maximum packet size)
>   Traffic statistics: octets, unicast/broadcast/multicast packets
>   Errors: discards, unknown protocols, etc.

on each type of managed device and also the specific characteristics (attributes) of each object. Figure 10-17 shows a general MIB schema.

Besides the schema, you also have the database itself, which contains actual data in the form dictated by the schema. Unfortunately, this is also called the management information base, so you must be careful when hearing the term *MIB* to determine whether it means the database design or the database itself.

To add further confusion, there is a small MIB on each managed device that contains information about that device's objects, and there also is a complete MIB on the manager's computer to hold data collected from many managed devices.

Commands and Responses

Communication between the manager and the agents is governed by the Simple Network Management Protocol. Normally, SNMP communication between the manager and agents works through **command–response cycles**. The manager sends a command. The agent sends back a response confirming that the command has been met, delivering requested data, or saying that an error has occurred and that the agent cannot comply with the command.

In SNMP, *Get* commands tell the agent to retrieve certain information and return this information to the manager. In practice, the manager constantly polls all of its managed devices, collecting many pieces of data from each in every round of polling.

This can generate a great deal of traffic. Consequently, SNMP uses UDP rather than TCP at the transport layer. This eliminates the opening, closing, and acknowledging of messages that would occur with TCP. Although UDP is not reliable, losing an occasional status message from a managed device merely means that a small part of the manager's knowledge is out of date for at most a few seconds.

Traps

Sometimes, agents do not wait for commands to send information. If an agent detects a condition that it thinks the manager should know about, it can send a **trap** message to the manager, as Figure 10-16 illustrates. For instance, if a switch detects that a transmission line to which a certain port is connected appears to have failed, it might send the manager a trap to advise the manager of this situation. Traps are typically generated when a major event occurs (such as a cold restart when a system crashes) or when some statistic indicating problems rises to a certain predetermined level, such as the number of errors of a particular type. This threshold analysis is called trapping, which gives rise to the practice of calling these messages traps.

Set Commands

In addition to *Get* commands, the manager can send *Set* commands, which tell the agent to change a parameter on the managed device. For instance, a *Set* command may tell an agent to change an interface's condition from "on" to "off" or "testing." The former will cause the agent to turn off that port, while the latter will tell the agent to test that port.

Most firms are very reluctant to use *Set* commands because of security dangers. If setting is permitted and attackers learn how to send *Set* commands to managed devices, the results could be catastrophic. The original version of SNMP, SNMPv1, had almost no authentication at all, making this danger a distinct possibility. The manager and all managed devices merely had to be configured with the same **community name**. With hundreds or thousands of devices sharing the same community name, attackers could easily learn the community name and use it to attack the managed devices.

SNMPv3 has added passwords for each manager–agent pair, and these passwords are encrypted during transmission. In addition, each message is authenticated by the shared password. This requires a great deal of work to set up.

Given SNMP's poor security history, many firms are reluctant to use SNMP *Set* commands for changing object parameters. Most products today permit two SNMPv3 passwords—one for *Get* commands and another for *Set* commands.

TEST YOUR UNDERSTANDING

12. a) List the main elements in a network management system. b) Does the manager communicate directly with the managed device? Explain. c) Explain the difference between managed devices and objects. d) Is the MIB a schema or the actual database? (This is a trick question.) e) Where is the MIB stored? (This is a trick question.)

13. List one object in each of the following areas: the system, IP, TCP, UDP, ICMP, and an interface.

14. a) In SNMP, which device creates commands? b) Responses? c) Traps? d) Explain the two types of commands. e) What is a trap? f) Why are firms often reluctant to use *Set* commands? g) Describe SNMPv1's poor authentication method. h) Describe SNMPv3's good authentication method.

TRAFFIC MANAGEMENT METHODS

Even on LANs, high-speed transmission is expensive. On WANs, transmission capacity is very expensive. Consequently, companies need to manage their transmission capacity actively. Several traffic management methods that deal with traffic and capacity are available to network managers, as Figure 10-18 shows.

Momentary Traffic Peaks

In Chapter 4, we saw that congestion problems caused by momentary traffic peaks can be handled in Ethernet in two basic ways: overprovisioning and priority. ATM added a third way to deal with momentary traffic peaks: quality-of-service (QoS) guarantees.

Overprovisioning Ethernet LANs

Overprovisioning Ethernet LANs means adding much more switching and transmission line capacity than will be needed most of the time. With overprovisioning, it will be rare for momentary traffic peaks to exceed capacity and so produce congestion and latency. This means that no regular ongoing management is required. The downside of overprovisioning is that it is wasteful of capacity. Today, minimizing labor costs on LANs makes overprovisioning very attractive. On WANs, however, overprovisioning is too expensive to consider.

Priority

Priority, in turn, assigns high priority to latency-intolerant applications, such as voice, while giving low priority to latency-tolerant applications, such as e-mail. Whenever congestion occurs, high-priority traffic is sent through without delay. Low-priority traffic must wait until the momentary congestion clears. Priority allows the company to work with lower capacity than overprovisioning but requires more active management labor.

QoS Guarantees

ATM goes a step beyond priority, reserving capacity on each switch and transmission line for certain types of traffic. This allows firm quality-of-service (QoS) guarantees for minimum throughput, maximum latency, and even maximum jitter.

Traffic Management

> Capacity is expensive; it must be used wisely

> Especially in WANs

Traditional Approaches

> Overprovisioning

>> In Ethernet, install much more capacity than is needed most of the time

>> This is wasteful of capacity
>> Does not require much ongoing management labor

> Priority

>> In Ethernet, assign priority to applications based on sensitivity to latency

>> In momentary periods of congestion, sent high-priority frames through

>> Substantial ongoing management labor

> QoS Reservations

>> In ATM, reserve capacity on each switch and transmission line for an application

>> Allows strong QoS guarantees

>>> Minimum throughput, maximum latency, maximum jitter
>> Highly labor-intensive

Traffic Shaping

> The Concept

>> Control traffic coming into the network at access switches
>> Filter out unwanted applications

>> Give a maximum percentage of traffic to other applications

> Advantages and Disadvantages

>> Traffic shaping alone reduces traffic coming into the network to control costs

>> Very highly labor intensive

>> Creates political battles (as do priority and QoS reservations to a lesser degree)

Figure 10-18   Traffic Management Methods

QoS requires extremely active management. Traffic with no QoS guarantees only gets whatever capacity is left over after reservations. This may be too little, even for latency-tolerant traffic.

Traffic Shaping

Even with priority and overprovisioning, sufficient capacity must be provided for the total of all applications apart from momentary traffic peaks. Even more active management is needed to control the amount of traffic entering the network in the first place. Restricting traffic entering the network at access points is called **traffic shaping**.

Filtering

Traffic shaping has two components. The first is **filtering** out unwanted traffic at access switches. Some traffic generally has no business on the corporate network, such as the downloading of MP3 files, video files, and software.

Capacity Percentages

The second tool of traffic shaping is to assign certain **percentages of capacity** to certain applications arriving at access switches. Even if file sharing has legitimate uses within a firm, for instance, the firm may wish to restrict the amount of capacity that file sharing can use. Typically, each application or application category is given a maximum percentage of the network's capacity. If that application attempts to use more than its share of capacity, incoming frames containing the application messages will be rejected.

Perspective on Traffic Shaping

Overprovisioning, priority, and QoS guarantees merely attempt to deal with incoming traffic. Traffic shaping actually *reduces* the amount of incoming traffic. Only traffic shaping can dramatically reduce network cost.

Although traffic shaping is very economical in terms of transmission capacity, it is highly labor intensive. It is used today primarily on high-cost WAN links. However, as management software costs fall in price and require less labor to operate, traffic shaping should see increasing use.

Another issue that arises when traffic shaping is used is politics. Telling a department that its traffic will be filtered out or limited in volume is not a good way to make friends. Priority and QoS reservations also raise political problems, but in traffic shaping, these problems are particularly bad.

TEST YOUR UNDERSTANDING

15. a) List traffic management approaches in increasing order of effectiveness. b) Why are the most effective traffic management tools typically not used? c) How may this change? d) What are the strengths and weaknesses of overprovisioning? e) What are the strengths and weaknesses of priority? f) What are the strengths and weaknesses of QoS guarantees? g) What is traffic shaping? h) What are the two elements of traffic shaping? i) What are the strengths and weaknesses of traffic shaping?

CONCLUSION

Synopsis

Corporate networking functions face tight budgets in the face of rapidly growing network demand. Although declining prices for technologies help somewhat, companies must analyze their needs very carefully. For every project, companies must compute a multiyear total cost of ownership (TCO) that involves all costs—base hardware prices, fully configured hardware prices, base software prices, fully configured software prices, IT labor, and end-user labor. Initial costs in the first year are substantial, but ongoing costs over the several years of a network project's life may be much larger.

Often, several alternative designs for network projects will have to be considered. In addition, after a network is built, alternative changes may have to be considered to deal with ongoing problems. Obviously, creating several different networks and testing them would be completely uneconomical. With network simulation programs, a firm can design different models, run simulations on them, and consider the results. Many what-if analyses can be considered in a brief span of time. OPNET IT Guru is a widely used network simulation program. It has a drag-and-drop user interface for laying out the model's nodes and topologies.

The decision to use TCP/IP for internetworking is not a simple one because it requires many management actions. One of the most fundamental is deciding how to subnet the firm's IP addresses to have a sufficient number of subnets with a sufficient number of hosts in each. Many firms use private IP address ranges, which can only be used within their sites. This provides security benefits, and it usually provides more IP addresses and therefore more subnetting flexibility than a company's public IP address range.

In addition, the networking staff needs to set up and maintain a number of IP-related servers, including DHCP servers, DNS servers, and WINS servers. (WINS servers are like DNS servers for older Windows client and server operating systems.) The network staff typically is involved with corporate directory servers. The configuration of clients, servers, switches, routers, and other devices can be very time consuming, especially because router and switch operating systems tend to have command line interfaces.

To manage networks on an ongoing basis, network administrators use a wide variety of network management programs. These programs are also useful to attackers, so firms need strong usage policies for who may use these programs and what users may do with them. In addition, many firms have their border routers prevent the use of network management tools from computers outside a site.

One common source of network problems is the configuration of individual client PCs. When a host is connected to a network, the connection can be tested by using the browser to go to a known site or by pinging a known site to see if latency is excessive.

If a connection does not appear to be working, a user can ping 127.0.0.1, the computer's loopback interface. Essentially, this pings the user's own computer. More information can be collected with ipconfig and winipconfig. For really detailed information, packet capture and display programs can capture data from a stream of packets and allow the user to study individual packets. At the other end of the spectrum, traffic summarization tools give statistical summaries of traffic. Connection analysis tools such as Netstat can let the user see all of his or her computer's connections to other hosts on the Internet.

More broadly, users can use ping, tracert, and performance testing to determine if there are problems on the route between a user's PC and a specific host. More broadly still, network mapping tools help a network administrator discover active IP addresses and fingerprint the devices at these addresses to determine what types of devices they are. This provides a good understanding of the network's structure. A popular network mapping tool is the aptly named Nmap.

The Simple Network Management Protocol (SNMP) is a general way to collect data from many managed devices on a network in order to be able to analyze these data at a central point. Using SNMP *Get* commands, a central manager program can poll managed devices to collect data. Using the *Set* command, the manager can change how managed devices work. In addition, when managed devices experience problems, they can send trap messages to the manager on their own initiative. The management information base (MIB) specifies what objects (types of data) can be analyzed. Until SNMP Version 3, security was very poor.

Traffic management is needed to ensure that a firm has adequate capacity on its networks. Overprovisioning (increasing network traffic beyond what is needed most of the time), priority (allowing latency-sensitive traffic to go first during congestion), and QoS guarantees (reserving capacity for certain applications) all try to do their best given traffic coming into the network. Traffic shaping goes a step beyond them by examining traffic at access switches to filter out unwanted traffic and to ensure that applications do not take up their assigned percentage of capacity. Unfortunately, as effectiveness increases, management labor costs also increase.

THOUGHT QUESTIONS

1. You have the following prompt: "Router>". List the commands you would use to set up the router's first Ethernet interface. You wish the interface to have IP address 60.42.20.6 with a mask that has 16 ones followed by 16 zeros.
2. Assume that an average SNMP response message is 100 bytes long. Assume that a manager sends 20 SNMP *Get* commands each second. a) What percentage of a 100-Mbps LAN link's capacity would the resulting response traffic represent? b) What percentage of a 56-kbps WAN link would the response messages represent? c) What can you conclude from your answers to this question?
3. A firm is assigned the network part 128.171. It selects an 8-bit subnet part. a) Draw the bits for the four octets of the IP address of the first host on the first subnet. (Hint: Use Windows Calculator.) b) Convert this answer into dotted decimal notation. c) Draw the bits for the second host on the third subnet. (In binary, 2 is 10, while 3 is 11.) d) Convert this into dotted decimal notation. e) Draw the bits for the last host on the third subnet. f) Convert this answer into dotted decimal notation.

HANDS-ON EXERCISES

Note: For command line programs, click on *Start*. Then choose *Run*. Type *cmd* or *command* depending on your version of Windows. Then hit OK.

1. Do the following on a Windows or Unix computer. a) Ping a remote host. What is the latency? If ping does not work on that host, try others until you find one that does work. b) Do a tracert on the connection. How many routers separate your computer from the remote host? On a spreadsheet, compute the average latency increase between each pair of routers. Paste the latency into your answer. What connection between routers brings the largest increase in latency?
2. Do the following on a Windows computer. Give the winipconfig command or the ipconfig /all command. Describe what you learned.
3. Do the following on a Windows or Unix computer. Give the Netstat command. Describe what you learned.
4. Do the following on an XP computer if you have access to one. Check on a connection's properties to see if the NIC appears to be working. What did you find?

GETTING CURRENT

Go to the book website's New Information and Errors pages for this chapter to get new information since this book went to press and to correct any errors in the text.

Networked Applications

Learning Objectives

By the end of this chapter, you should be able to discuss:

■ The characteristics and limitations of host communication with dumb terminals.

■ Client/server architectures, including file server program access and client/server processing (including web-enabled applications).

■ Electronic mail standards and security.

■ World Wide Web and e-commerce (including the use of application servers), and e-commerce security.

■ Software as a service with SOAP/messages and XML syntax.

■ Peer-to-peer (P2P) computing, which, paradoxically, normally uses servers for part of the work.

INTRODUCTION

Networked Applications

Once, applications ran on single machines—usually mainframes or stand-alone PCs. Today, however, most applications spread their processing power over two or more machines connected by networks instead of doing all processing on a single machine.

Application Architectures

In this chapter, we will focus on **application architectures**—that is, how application layer functions are spread among computers to deliver service to users. Thanks to layering's ability to separate functions at different layers, most application architectures can run over TCP/IP, IPX/SPX, and other standards below the application layer. In turn, if you use TCP at the transport layer, TCP does not care what application architecture you are using.

An application architecture describes how application layer functions are spread among computers to deliver service to users.

Important Networked Applications

In addition to looking broadly at application architectures, we will look at some of the most important of today's networked applications, including e-mail, videoconferencing, the World Wide Web, e-commerce, Web services, and P2P computing.

Importance of the Application Layer to Users

In this chapter, we will focus on the application layer. This is the only layer whose functionality users see directly. When users want e-mail, it is irrelevant what is happening below the application layer, except if there is a failure or performance problem at lower layers.

TEST YOUR UNDERSTANDING

1. a) What is an application architecture? b) Why do users focus on the application layer?

TRADITIONAL APPLICATION ARCHITECTURES

In this section, we will look at the two most important traditional application architectures: terminal–host systems and client/server architectures (both file server program access and client/server processing).

Hosts with Dumb Terminals

As Figure 11-1 shows, the first step beyond stand-alone machines still placed the processing power on a single **host computer** but distributed input/output (I/O) functions to user sites. These I/O functions resided in **dumb terminals**, which sent user keystrokes to the host and painted host information on the terminal screen but did little else.

Figure 11-1   Simple Terminal–Host System

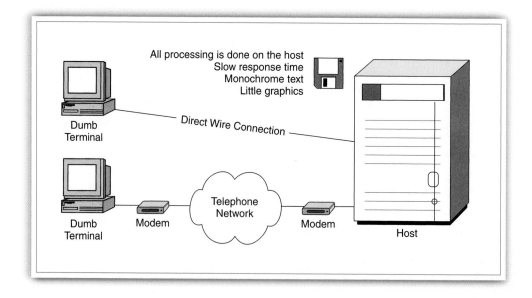

Although this approach worked, the central computer often was overloaded by the need to process both applications and terminal communication. This often resulted in slow **response times** when users typed commands.

Another problem was high transmission cost. All keystrokes had to be sent to the host computer for processing. This generated a great deal of traffic. Similarly, the host had to send detailed information to be shown on-screen. To reduce transmission costs, most terminals limited the information they could display to **monochrome text** (one color against a contrasting background). Graphics were seldom available.[1]

IBM mainframe computers used a more complex design for their terminal–host systems that added other pieces of equipment beyond terminals and hosts. This extra equipment reduced cost and improved response times. In addition, IBM terminal–host systems had higher speeds than traditional terminals and so were able to offer limited color and graphics. Although these advances extended the life of terminal–host systems, even these advanced IBM systems are less satisfactory to users than subsequent developments, including the client/server systems described next.

TEST YOUR UNDERSTANDING

2. a) Where is processing performed in systems of hosts and dumb terminals? b) What are the typical problems with these systems?

Client/Server Systems

After terminal–host systems, a big breakthrough came in the form of **client/server systems**, which placed some power on the client computer. This was made possible by the emergence of personal computers in the 1980s. PCs have the processing power to act as nondumb clients.

File Server Program Access

Figure 11-2 shows that there are two basic forms of client/server computing. The first is **file server program access**. In this form of client/server computing, the server's only role is to store programs and data files. For processing, the program is copied across the network to the client PC, along with data files. The client PC does the actual processing of the program and data files.

Of course, many client PCs are comparatively underpowered, and even the fastest client PCs usually are fairly slow compared to servers. Consequently, file server program access is only sufficient for word processing, e-mail, and other small applications. It is not useful for large database applications.

Client/Server Processing

In contrast, in full **client/server processing**, the work is done by programs on two machines, as Figure 11-2 also illustrates. Generally, the server does the heavy processing needed to retrieve information. The client, in turn, normally focuses on the user

---

[1]The most common dumb terminal today is the VT100 terminal, also called an ANSI terminal. On the Internet, clients can emulate (imitate) dumb terminals using Telnet. Telnet turns a $2,000 office PC into a $200 dumb terminal.

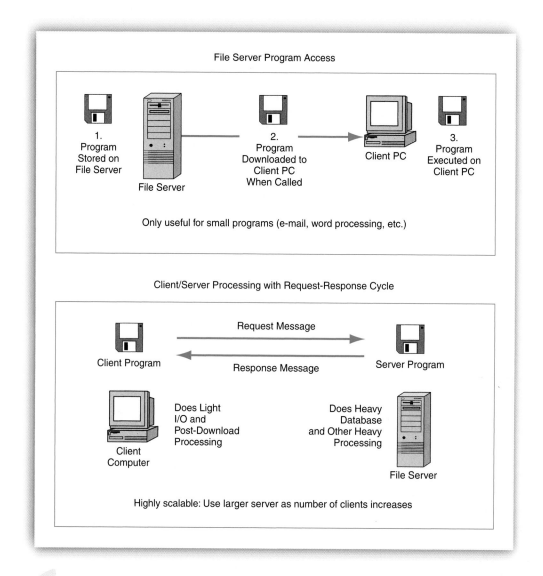

Figure 11-2   Client/Server Computing

interface and on processing data delivered by the server—for instance, by placing the data in an Excel spreadsheet.

Scalability

Client/server processing is highly scalable. In most instances, as the number of users rises, scaling merely involves replacing the existing server with a larger server. In fact, it is even possible to change the server platform without users noticing the change. An

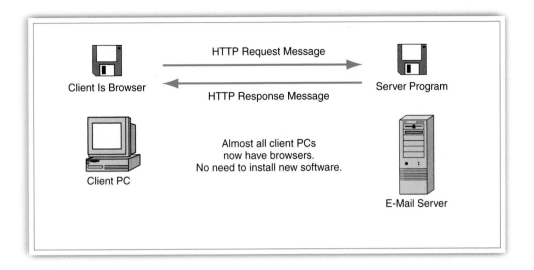

Figure 11-3   Web-Enabled Application (E-Mail)

application can start on a small PC server and then be moved successively to a large PC server, a workstation server, or even a mainframe.

Web-Enabled Applications

Client/server processing requires a client program to be installed on a client PC. Initially, all applications used custom-designed client programs. Rolling out a new application to serve hundreds or thousands of client computers was extremely time-consuming and expensive.

Fortunately, there is one client program that almost all PCs have today. This is a browser. As Figure 11-3 illustrates, many client/server processing applications are now **web-enabled**, meaning that they use ordinary browsers as client programs. The figure specifically shows web-enabled e-mail.

TEST YOUR UNDERSTANDING

3. a) Contrast file server program access with client/server processing in terms of where processing is performed. b) Contrast them in terms of maximum program size.

4. Contrast general client/server processing with Web-enabled applications.

ELECTRONIC MAIL (E-MAIL)

Importance

A Universal Service on the Internet

E-mail has become one of the two "universal" services on the Internet, along with the World Wide Web. E-mail provides mailbox delivery if the receiver is "offline" when the message is received. E-mail offers the speed of a fax plus the ability to store messages in organized files, to send replies, to forward messages to others, and to perform many other actions after message receipt. The telephone offers truly instant communication, but only if the other party is in and can take calls. In addition, e-mail is less intrusive than a phone call.

Attachments Can Deliver Anything

Thanks to attachments, e-mail has also become a general file delivery system. Users can exchange spreadsheet documents, word processing documents, graphics, and any other type of file.

E-Mail Standards

A major driving force behind the wide acceptance of Internet e-mail is standardization. It is rare for users of different systems not to be able to communicate at a technical level—although many companies restrict outgoing and incoming communication using firewalls for security purposes. Consequently, the key issue is application layer standards.

Message Body Standards

Obviously, message bodies have to be standardized, or we would not be able to read arriving messages. In physical mail, message body standards include the language the partners will use (English, etc.), formality of language, and other matters. Some physical messages are forms, which have highly standardized layouts and fields that require specific information.

RFC 2822 (Originally RFC 822)   The initial standard for e-mail bodies was **RFC 822**, which has been updated as **RFC 2822**. This is a standard for plain text messages—multiple lines of typewriter-like characters with no boldface, graphics, or other amenities. The extreme simplicity of this approach made it easy to create early client e-mail programs.

HTML Bodies   Later, as HTML became widespread on the World Wide Web, most mail venders developed the ability to display **HTML bodies** with richly formatted text and even graphics.

UNICODE   RFC 822 specified the use of the ASCII code to represent printable characters. Unfortunately, ASCII was developed for English, and even European languages need extra characters. The **UNICODE** standard allows characters of all languages to be represented, although most mail readers cannot display all UNICODE characters well yet.

Simple Mail Transfer Protocol (SMTP)

We also need standards for delivering RFC 2822, HTML, and UNICODE messages. In the postal world, we must have envelopes that present certain information in certain ways, and there are specific ways to post mail for delivery, including putting letters in post office drop boxes and taking them to the post office.

Figure 11-4   E-Mail (Study Figure)

Importance of E-Mail
Universal service on the Internet

Attachments deliver files

E-Mail Standards
Message body standards

       RFC 822 and RFC 2822 for all-text bodies

       HTML bodies

       UNICODE for multiple languages

Simple Mail Transfer Protocol (SMTP)

       Message delivery: client to sender's mail host

       Message delivery: sender's mail host to receiver's mail host

Downloading mail to client

       Post Office Protocol (POP): simple and widely used

       Internet Message Access Program (IMAP): more powerful, less widely used

Web-Enabled E-Mail

       Uses HTTP for all communication with the mail server

       No need for e-mail software on the client PC; a browser will do

       Tends to be slow

Viruses, Worms, and Trojan Horses
Widespread problems; often delivered through e-mail attachments

       Use of antivirus software is almost universal but ineffective

Where to do scanning for viruses, worms, and Trojan horses?

       On the client PC, but users often turn off or fail to update their software

       On the corporate mail server and application firewall; users cannot turn off

       At an antivirus outsourcing company before mail reaches the corporation

       Defense in depth: Filter at two or more locations with different filtering software

Spam
Unsolicited commercial e-mail

Why filter?

       Potential sexual harassment suits

       Time consumed by users deleting spam

       Time consumed by networking staff to delete spam

       Bandwidth and storage resources consumed

Separating spam from legitimate messages is very difficult

       Many spam messages are allowed through to users

       Some legitimate messages are deleted

       Some firms merely mark messages as probable spam

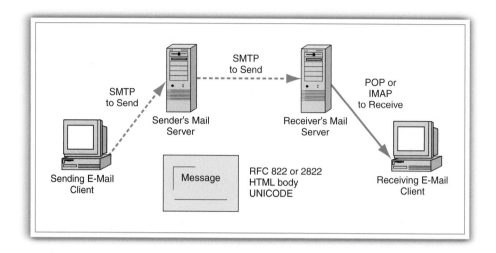

Figure 11-5   E-Mail Standards

Figure 11-5 shows how e-mail is posted (sent). The e-mail program on the user's PC sends the message to its outgoing mail host using the **Simple Mail Transfer Protocol (SMTP)**. Figure 11-6 shows that SMTP requires a complex series of interactions between the sender and receiver before and after mail delivery.

Figure 11-5 shows that the sender's outgoing mail host sends the message on to the receiver's incoming mail host, again using SMTP. The receiving host stores the message in the receiver's mailbox until the receiver retrieves it.

Receiving Mail (POP and IMAP)

Figure 11-5 shows two standards that are used to *receive* e-mail. These are the **Post Office Protocol (POP)** and the **Internet Message Access Protocol (IMAP)**. IMAP offers more features, but the simpler POP standard is more popular. Programs implementing these standards ask the mail host to download some or all new mail to the user's client e-mail program. Often users delete new mail from their inbox after downloading new messages. After that, the messages only exist on the user's client PC.

Web-Enabled E-Mail

Almost all client PCs have browsers. Many mail hosts are now web-enabled, meaning that users only need browsers to interact with them in order to send, receive, and manage their e-mail. As Figure 11-3 showed, all interactions take place via HTTP, and these systems use HTML to render pages on-screen.

Actor	Command	Comment
Receiving SMTP Process	220 Mail.Panko.Com Ready	When a TCP connection is opened, the receiver signals that it is ready.
Sending SMTP Process	HELO voyager.cba.hawaii.edu	Sender asks to begin sending a message. Gives own identity.
Receiver	250 Mail.Panko.Com	Receiver signals that it is ready to begin receiving a message.
Sender	MAIL FROM: Panko@ voyager.cba.hawaii.edu	Sender identifies the sender (mail author, not SMTP process).
Receiver	250 OK	Accepts author. However, may reject mail from others.
Sender	RCPT TO: Ray@Panko.com	Identifies first mail recipient.
Receiver	250 OK	Accepts first recipient.
Sender	RCPT TO: Lee@Panko.com	Identifies second mail recipient.
Receiver	550 No such user here	Does not accept second recipient. However will deliver to first recipient.
Sender	DATA	Message will follow.
Receiver	354 Start mail input; end with <CRLF>.<CRLF>	Gives permission to send message.
Sender	When in the course . . .	The message. Multiple lines of text. Ends with line containing only a single period: <CRLF>.<CRLF>
Receiver	250 OK	Receiver accepts message.
Sender	QUIT	Requests termination of session.
Receiver	221 Mail.Panko.Com Service closing transmission channel	End of transaction.

Figure 11-6   Interactions in the Simple Mail Transfer Protocol (SMTP)

Web-enabled e-mail (also called **webmail**) is especially good for travelers because no special e-mail software is needed. Any computer with a browser in an Internet café, home, or office will allow the user to check his or her mail. On the downside, web-enabled e-mail tends to be very slow because almost all processing is done on the distant (and often overloaded) webserver with its server-based mail processing program.

Viruses and Trojan Horses

Although e-mail is tremendously important to corporations, it is a source of intense security headaches. As we saw in Chapter 9, the most widespread security compromises are attacks by viruses and worms. Viruses come into an organization primarily, although by no means exclusively, through e-mail attachments and (sometimes) through scripts in e-mail bodies. E-mail attachments can also be used to install worms and Trojan horse programs on client PCs.

Antivirus Software

The obvious countermeasure to e-mail-borne viruses is to use **antivirus software**, which scans incoming messages and attachments for viruses, worms, and Trojan horses. Yet the CSI/FBI survey that produced the data for Figure 9-1 found that nearly all firms had antivirus scanning systems in place. These systems were simply not doing the job.

Antivirus Scanning on User PCs

One problem is that most companies attempt to do virus scanning on the user PC. Unfortunately, too many users either turn off their antivirus programs if they seem to be interfering with other programs (or appear to slow things down too much) or keep their programs active but fail to update them regularly. In the latter case, newer viruses will not be recognized by the antivirus program.

Centralized Antivirus/Anti-Trojan Horse Scanning

Consequently, many companies are beginning to do central scanning for e-mail–borne viruses and Trojan horses.

Scanning on Mail Servers and Application Firewalls   One popular place to do this is the corporate mail server. Users cannot turn off antivirus filtering on the mail server, and the e-mail staff hopefully updates virus definitions on these servers frequently. In addition, e-mail application firewalls can drop executable file attachments and other dangerous attachments.

Outsourcing Scanning   Some companies are even outsourcing antivirus/anti-Trojan horse scanning to outside security firms. By changing the firm's MX record in DNS servers, a firm can have all of its incoming e-mail sent to a security firm that will handle antivirus and anti-Trojan horse scanning. These firms specialize in these tasks and presumably can do a better job than the corporation. This also reduces the workload of the corporate staff.

Defense in Depth

The security principle of defense in depth suggests that antivirus filtering should be done in at least two locations—user PC, mail server, or external security company. It is also best if two different antivirus vendors are used. This increases the probability of successful detection because different antivirus programs often differ in which specific viruses, worms, and Trojan horses they catch.

Spam

Unsolicited Commercial E-Mail

One of the most serious problems facing e-mail users today is spam. **Spam**[2] is unsolicited commercial e-mail. In many firms, spam messages now far outnumber legitimate messages.

Reasons to Fight Spam

Most firms are now fighting spam for four primary reasons.

➤ First, the sexual nature of many spam messages could lead to sexual harassment suits if the company fails to make a strong effort to delete spam.

➤ Second, spam wastes a great deal of user time. Although users can simply delete spam, this is very expensive when the time spent by each user is multiplied by the number of users.

➤ Third, spam uses up a good deal of expensive network bandwidth and disk resources on mail servers.

➤ Fourth, spam uses up a great deal of expensive network management staff time that is badly needed for other purposes.

Separating Spam from Legitimate Messages Is Very Difficult

Antivirus programs tend to be highly effective in identifying viruses, worms, and Trojan horses without mistaking legitimate messages as viruses and Trojan horses. In contrast, antispam programs fail to stop many spam messages. Worse yet, they often mislabel legitimate e-mail as spam.

If spam messages are simply dropped before reaching users, users will miss some legitimate messages. If messages are merely labeled as spam, say by placing "[spam]" before each message that is suspected of being spam, this will help users delete spam, but it will only reduce their spam deletion time slightly. Today, there simply is no software solution for filtering out spam that is as precise as antivirus filtering for filtering out viruses, worms, and Trojan horses.

TEST YOUR UNDERSTANDING

5. a) Distinguish among the major standards for e-mail bodies. b) When a station sends a message to its mail host, what standard does it use? c) When the sender's mail host sends the message to the receiver's mail host, what standard does it use? d) When the receiver's e-mail client downloads new mail from its mail host, what standard is it most likely to use? e) What is web-enabled e-mail? f) What is its advantage? g) What is its disadvantage?

6. a) What is the main tool of firms in fighting viruses and Trojan horses in e-mail attachments? b) Why does filtering on the user's PC often not work? c) What options do firms have for where antivirus filtering should be done? d) According to the principle of defense in depth, how should firms do antivirus filtering? e) What is spam? f) Why do most companies fight spam aggressively? g) Why is it difficult to fight spam?

---

[2]To distinguish unsolicited commercial e-mail from Hormel's meat product, unsolicited commercial e-mail is spelled with a lowercase *s* (spam) except at the beginning of sentences and in titles, while Hormel's product is spelled with a capital *S* (Spam). Furthermore, Hormel's Spam is *not* an acronym for *spongy pink animal matter*.

THE WORLD WIDE WEB AND E-COMMERCE

The World Wide Web

HTML and HTTP

We have discussed the World Wide Web throughout this book. As Figure 11-7 shows, the Web is based on two primary standards.

➤ First, webpages themselves are created using the **Hypertext Markup Language (HTML)**.

➤ Second, the transfer of requests and responses uses the **Hypertext Transfer Protocol (HTTP)**.

To give an analogy, an e-mail message may be created using RFC 2822, but it will be delivered using SMTP. Many application standards consist of a document standard and a transfer standard.

Many application standards consist of a document standard and a transfer standard.

Complex Webpages

Actually, most "webpages" really consist of several files—a master text-only HTML file plus graphics files, audio files, and other types of files. Figure 11-8 illustrates the downloading of a webpage with two graphics files.

The HTML file merely consists of the page's text, plus **tags** to show where the browser should render graphics files, when it should play audio files, and so forth.[3] The HTML file is downloaded first because the browser needs the tags to know what other files should be downloaded.

Figure 11-7   HTML and HTTP

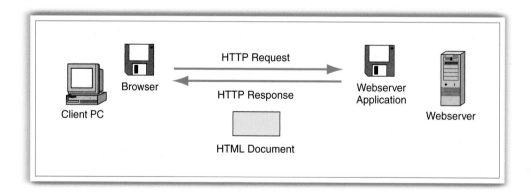

---
[3]For graphics files, the <IMG> tag is used. The keyword IMG indicates that an image file is to be downloaded. The SRC parameter in this tag gives the target file's directory and file name on the webserver.

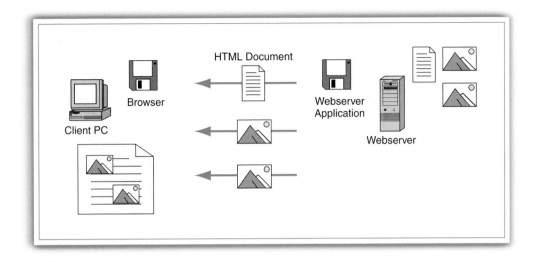

Figure 11-8   Downloading a Complex Webpage with Two Graphics Files

Consequently, several **HTTP request–response cycles** may be needed to download a single webpage. Three request–response cycles are needed in this example.

The Client's Role
The client's roles, as shown in Figure 11-8, are to send **HTTP request messages** asking for the files and then to draw the webpage on-screen. If the webpage has a **Java applet** or another **active element**, the browser will have to execute it as well.

The Webserver's Role
The webserver application program's basic job is to read each HTTP request message, retrieve the desired file from memory, and create an **HTTP response message** that contains the requested file or a reason why it cannot be delivered. Webserver application software may also have to execute server-side active elements before returning the requested webpage.

HTTP Request and Response Messages
As Figure 11-9 shows, both HTTP request messages and HTTP response headers are composed of simple keyboard text.

HTTP Request Messages   In HTTP request messages, the first line has three parts.

➤ The first line begins with a capitalized method (in this case, GET), which specifies what the requestor wishes the webserver to do. The GET method says that the client wishes to get a file.

➤ The method is followed by a space and then by the location of the file (in this example, /panko/home.htm). This is home.htm in the panko directory.

HTTP Request Message
GET /panko/home.htm HTTP/1.1[CRLF]
Host: voyager.cba.hawaii.edu

HTTP Response Message
HTTP/1.1 200 OK[CRLF]
Date: Tuesday, 20-MAR-2002 18:32:15 GMT[CRLF]
Server: *name of server software* [CRLF]
MIME-version: 1.0[CRLF]
Content-type: text/plain[CRLF]
[CRLF]
file to be downloaded

Figure 11-9   Examples of HTTP Request and Response Messages

> ➤ Next comes the version of HTTP that the client browser supports (in this example, HTTP/1.1).
> ➤ The line ends with a carriage return/line feed—a command to start a new line of text.

Each subsequent line (there is only one in this example) begins with a keyword (in this example, Host), a colon (:), a value for the keyword (in this example, voyager. cba.hawaii.edu), and a carriage return/line feed.

HTTP Response Messages   HTTP response messages also begin with a three-part first line.

> ➤ The webserver responds by giving the version of HTTP it supports.
> ➤ This is followed by a space and then a code. A 200 code is good; it indicates that the method was followed successfully. In contrast, codes in the 400 range are bad codes that indicate problems.
> ➤ This code is followed by a text expression that states what the code says in humanly readable form. This information ("OK" in this example) is useless to the browser.
> ➤ A carriage return/line feed ends this first line.

Subsequent lines have the keyword–colon–value–carriage return/line feed structure of HTTP request message header lines. In the figure, these lines give a time stamp, the name of the server software (not shown), and two MIME lines.

MIME (Multipurpose Internet Mail Extensions) is a standard for specifying the formats of files. The first MIME line gives the version of MIME the webserver uses (1.0). The next line, *content-type*, specifies that the file being delivered by the webserver is of the text/plain type—simple keyboard characters. The MIME lines help the browser know what to do with the attached file. MIME is also used for this purpose in e-mail and in some other applications.

After all HTTP response message header lines, there is a blank line (two CR/LFs in a row). This is followed by the bits of the file being sent by the webserver.

TEST YOUR UNDERSTANDING

7. a) Distinguish between HTTP and HTML. b) You are downloading a webpage that has six graphics and two sound clips. How many request–response cycles will be needed? c) What is the syntax of the first line in an HTTP request message? d) What is the syntax of subsequent lines? e) What is the syntax of the first line in an HTTP response message? f) What do the MIME header fields tell the receiving process? g) Why is this information necessary? h) How is the start of the attached file indicated?

Electronic Commerce (E-Commerce)

E-Commerce Functionality

Electronic commerce (e-commerce) is the buying and selling of goods and services over the Internet. As Figure 11-10 shows, e-commerce software adds extra functionality to a webserver's basic file retrieval function.

Online Catalog

Most obviously, an e-commerce site must have an **online catalog** showing the goods it has for sale. Although catalogs can be created using basic HTML coding, most merchants purchase **e-commerce software** to automate the creation of catalog pages and other e-commerce functionality.

Figure 11-10   Electronic Commerce Functions

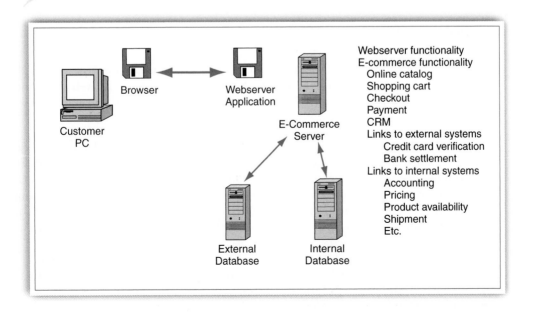

Shopping Cart, Checkout, and Payment Functions

Two other core e-commerce functions are the maintenance of a **shopping cart** for holding goods while the customer is shopping and **checkout** when the buyer has finished shopping and wishes to pay for the selected goods. The checkout function should include several **payment mechanisms and shipping mechanisms**. Again, most firms use e-commerce software, which includes these functions.

Customer Relationship Management (CRM)

Customers have different needs and wants. Many firms now use **customer relationship management (CRM)** software to examine customer data to understand the preferences of their customers. This allows a company to tailor presentations and specific market offers to its customers' specific tastes. The goal is to increase the rate of **conversions**—browsers becoming buyers—and to increase the rate of **repeat purchasing** (compared to one-time purchasing). Small increases in conversion rates and repeat purchasing rates can have a big impact on profitability.

Links to Other Systems

External Systems

As Figure 11-10 shows, taking payments usually requires external links to two outside organizations. One is a **credit card verification service**, which checks the validity of the credit card number the user has typed. Without credit card checking, the credit card fraud rate may be high enough to drive the company out of business. The other is a **bank settlement firm**, which handles the credit card payment.

Internal Back-End Systems

Figure 11-10 also shows that e-commerce usually requires links to **internal back-end systems** for accounting, pricing, product availability, shipment, and other matters.

Application Servers

Accepting User Data

As Figure 11-11 shows, most large e-commerce sites use an **application server**, which accepts user data from a front-end webserver. Some sites combine the webserver and application server, but most large sites separate these functions onto two machines.

Retrievals from External Systems

The application server then contacts external systems and internal back-end database systems to satisfy the user's request. To do this, it sends requests that these external systems can understand, and then it receives responses. This is complicated because each external system may have its own way of handling requests and responses. Connecting to external systems is one of the most difficult tasks in the development of an e-commerce site. Figure 11-11 shows some of the complexities involved in interactions with external systems.

Application Program Interfaces (APIs)   Modern client/server database products have published **application program interface (API)** specifications to allow application server programs to interact directly with specific vendors' database systems.

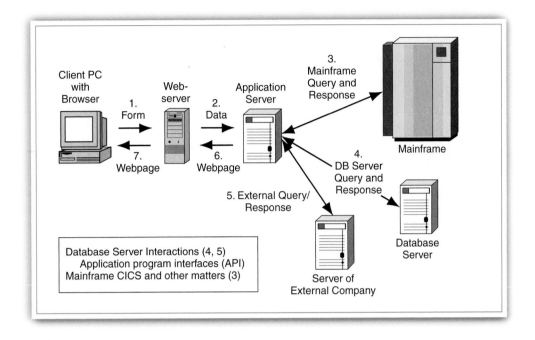

Figure 11-11   Application Server (Three-Tier Architecture)

Mainframe Interactions   Mainframe computers have their own ways of communicating with the outside world. Application server programmers must be deeply familiar with CICS and other mainframe processes.[4]

Creating a Response

To document its findings, the application server then creates a new webpage on the fly and passes it to the user via the webserver, as shown in Figure 11-11.

Three-Tier Architecture

Terminal-host systems perform processing on a single machine. Most client/server systems do processing on two machines. With an application server, processing takes place on a third machine as well. Therefore, using application servers is called having a **three-tier architecture.**

---

[4]Older systems used CGI to communicate with programs located on the application server. CGI is a method to pass commands to programs on the computer and to get responses back. However, CGI is extremely slow because each time CGI talks to an application, it has to load, initialize, and run the application. For heavy usage, loading, initializing, and running applications each time a request is received is extremely wasteful of computer time on the server.

TEST YOUR UNDERSTANDING

8. a) What functionality does e-commerce need beyond basic webservice? b) What external connections does e-commerce require? c) What is the role of application servers? d) What are the two main ways to retrieve information from external databases?

E-Commerce Security

E-commerce sites experience regular attacks by hackers and denial-of-service attacks. This requires strong security, as Figure 11-12 illustrates.

SSL/TLS

When you send credit card numbers or other sensitive information over the Internet, it is almost always protected by a cryptographic system at the transport layer called SSL/TLS. We saw this cryptographic system in Chapter 9. SSL/TLS provides strong protection against eavesdroppers because it encrypts all messages traveling between the customer and the merchant.

However, authentication can be a problem. For residential e-commerce, customers rarely have digital certificates, so while SSL/TLS strongly authenticates the merchant to the customer, it does not authenticate customers. If merchants want customer authentication, they usually assign customers passwords. This is only weak authentication. For internal corporate systems, however, servers often require employee digital certificates for strong employee authentication.

Figure 11-12   E-Commerce Security

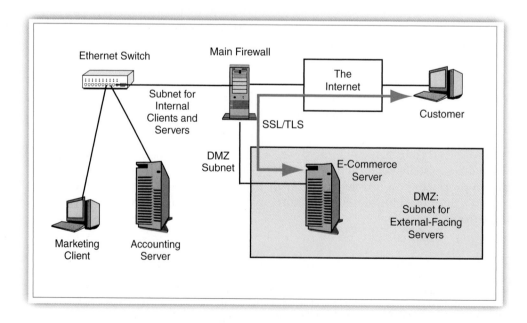

Demilitarized Zones (DMZs)

Figure 11-12 shows that public e-commerce servers (and other public servers) normally are placed in a special subnet called the **demilitarized zone (DMZ)**.[5] Even if an attacker succeeds in taking over a server in the DMZ, he or she will not be able to get into other corporate subnets.

Hardened Servers

The DMZ holds public servers that must be available to the outside world. As a consequence, e-commerce servers and other servers must be especially hardened against attacks. (Chapter 9 discussed host hardening.) Most cases of credit card theft have come from hackers taking over e-commerce servers (or back-end systems) and reading the credit card numbers out of files stored there. In addition, e-commerce servers often contain other types of private customer information that must be safeguarded. Break-ins can cause a serious loss in customer confidence and can lead to lawsuits.

protect customers from fraud & from comp from lawsuits

TEST YOUR UNDERSTANDING

9. a) What secure communication system is used widely in e-commerce? b) At what layer does it operate? c) Describe how DMZs provide security in e-commerce. d) Why is the hardening of e-commerce servers critical?

SERVICE-ORIENTED ARCHITECTURE (SOA)

Introduction

We have seen several application architectures in this chapter so far: the terminal–host architecture and the client/server architecture. Later, we will see the peer-to-peer (P2P) application architecture. In this section, we will look at the **service-oriented architecture (SOA).** This architecture is also known as **software as a service (SAS)** and **Web services**. One of these names is likely to win in the long run, but you now run into all three of these names. In this chapter, we will use the term *software as a service.*

Figure 11-13 illustrates a service-oriented architecture. The basic idea is that programs have to be written as modules (objects) that are created to provide services to any other program that calls them. The calling program can even be on a different computer.

In one sense, there is nothing new about SOAs. Programmers have long written software as objects that could be called externally. It has even been possible for a program on one computer to call an object on another computer. However, in the past, even calls from one program to another program on the same machine have not been standardized, and calling programs on other computers has been extremely difficult. However, the SOA concept that is emerging today is notable because it is based on standards.

---

[5]The term *DMZ* reflects terminology from the Korean War. In Korea, the DMZ is a narrow strip of land designated after the war to separate North Korea from South Korea. If an attack comes from the North, it must pass through this DMZ. Consequently, the DMZ is very heavily defended.

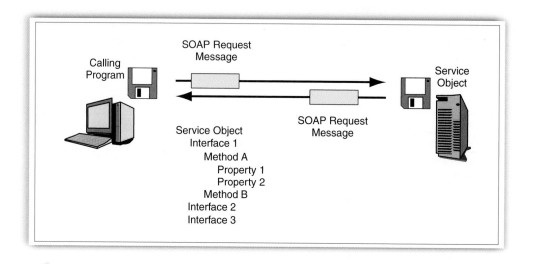

Figure 11-13   Service-Oriented Architecture (SOA)

Service Objects

In programming terminology, a program that can be called by another program is an **object**. In a service-oriented architecture, the object is called a **service object**.

➤ To call the object, a calling program must know the object's location and name.

➤ Also, objects may have multiple entry points, called **interfaces**. In addition to knowing the object, the calling program must know which interface to call.

➤ Different interfaces offer different **methods** (actions the object can take). For example, a method might compute the price to purchase a product. To give another example, the method might compute hexadecimal values for Ethernet MAC addresses.

➤ When a program calls an object, it may have to pass the object data. For instance, in the case of the hexadecimal calculator just mentioned, the calling program must pass the Ethernet address to the object. The object will send back a hexadecimal value. These numbers are called **properties**. Properties have both names and values.

To use a service object, the calling program sends a **service request message** specifying the object, an interface, a method, and appropriate parameter. The service object sends back a **service response message** that contains the parameter or parameters sought by the calling program.

Simple Object Access Protocol (SOAP)
Service requests and responses follow a standard called **SOAP (Simple Object Access Protocol)**. SOAP requests specify a particular method and the specific parameters

```
SOAP Request Message
<?xml version="1.0"?>
<BODY>
        <QuotePrice xmlns="QuoteInterface">
                <PartNum>QA78d</PartNum>
                <Quantity>47</Quantity>
                <ShippingType>Rush</ShippingType>
        </QuotePrice>
</BODY>

SOAP Response Message
<?xml version="1.0"?>
<BODY>
        <QuoteResponse xmlns="QuoteInterface">
                <Price>$750.33</Price>
        </QuoteResponse>
</BODY>
```

Figure 11-14   Simplified SOAP Request and Response

allowed or dictated by that method. SOAP also specifies the formatting of messages that Web services use to respond to clients.

SOAP messages normally are delivered via HTTP. For this reason, service objects are often called Web services. However, SOAP messages can be delivered by e-mail or other methods.

Figure 11-14 shows a simplified SOAP request and a simplified SOAP response. Most SOAP messages are more complex, but this complexity does not add to the essence of how SOAP works.

The request is designed to be sent to an object that has a method, QuotePrice, on interface QuoteInterface. Properties in the request are PartNum, Quantity, and ShippingType.

The return parameter is Price, which is delivered in the SOAP response message. This method provides a price quote if the sender identifies the part, indicates how many it wants, and specifies how the part will be shipped.

XML

The first line of each message begins with a header that says <?xml version="1.0"?>. This shows that SOAP messages are expressed in **XML (eXtensible Markup Language)** syntax. Whereas HTML expresses the formatting of messages and does not allow users to create their own tags, XML allows communities of users to create their own tags—for example, <price> and </price>, which have meanings to the community. To know an object, you must know how to use it, including the meanings of its tags.

Language Independence

What programming language is used to create Web services? The answer is that programming language is unimportant. In other words, service-oriented architectures have **language independence**. As long as a service object responds correctly to user messages, anyone can use it. (To put this in perspective, note that we rarely ask what programming language is used to build programs to execute HTTP on a browser or a webserver.) In Microsoft's .NET initiative, for example, the company has added SOA functionality to all of its programming languages.

Service-Oriented Architectures with HTTP

As noted earlier, SOAP service requests and responses are normally delivered by HTTP. Using HTTP to carry messages is enormously advantageous because it is simple to support and widely understood. For example, most firewalls pass HTTP messages on Port 80, making service object communication easier. Of course, firewall control is very important, so the SOAP standard specifies the addition of a few new HTTP header lines that firewalls can use to control access.

Universal Description, Discovery, and Integration (UDDI) Protocol

In the future, some Web services will be offered on a fee-per-use basis. To attract customers, they will need a way to advertise themselves. They also will need to make available a description of how others can use them. Many vendors are now adopting the **Universal Description, Discovery, and Integration (UDDI)** protocol to advertise themselves to the world. Figure 11-15 shows key aspects of UDDI.

UDDI is a distributed database, meaning that there will be many interconnected UDDI servers that cooperate with one another. UDDI will offer three basic search options.

> **UDDI White Pages** allow users to search for Web services by name, much like telephone white pages.

> **UDDI Yellow Pages** allow users to search for Web services by type, such as accounting, much like telephone yellow pages.

> **UDDI Green Pages** allow companies to understand how to interact with specific Web services. In object-oriented terminology, green pages specify the interfaces on which a Web service will respond, the methods it will accept, and the properties that can be sent or returned. Payment methods are also part of UDDI green pages.

TEST YOUR UNDERSTANDING

10. a) How is an SOA different from earlier architectures? Explain the following service object terms: b) Objects, c) Interfaces, d) Methods, and e) Properties. f) What does a SOAP request message specify? g) In what language are SOAP messages written? h) How are SOAP messages exchanged? i) In what sense are service-oriented architectures language-independent? j) Explain the implications of using HTTP for delivery through firewalls. k) What is the purpose of UDDI? l) What do UDDI green pages tell you?

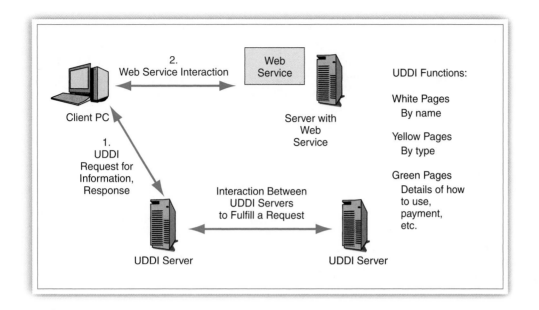

Figure 11-15   Universal Description, Discovery, and Integration (UDDI)
Server for Web Services

PEER-TO-PEER (P2P) APPLICATION ARCHITECTURES

The newest application architecture is the **peer-to-peer (P2P) architecture**, in which
most or all of the work is done by cooperating user computers, such as desktop PCs.
If servers are present at all, they only serve facilitating roles and do not control the
processing.

Traditional Client/Server Applications

Approach

Figure 11-16 shows a traditional client/server application. In this application, all of the
clients communicate with the central server for their work.

Advantage: Central Control

One advantage of this **server-centric** approach is central control. All communication
goes through the central server, so there can be good security and policy-based control
over communication.

Disadvantages

Although the use of central service is good in several ways, it does give rise to two
problems.

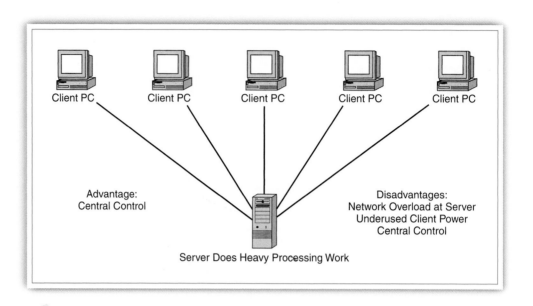

Figure 11-16   Traditional Client/Server Application

Underused Client PC Capacity   One disadvantage is that client/server computing often uses expensive server capacity while leaving clients underused. Clients normally are modern PCs with considerable processing power, not dumb terminals or early low-powered PCs.

Central Control   From the end users' point of view, central control can be a problem rather than an advantage. Central control limits what end users can do. Just as PCs freed end users from the red tape involved in using mainframe computers, peer-to-peer computing frees end users from the red tape involved in using a server. There is a fundamental clash of interests between central control and end user freedom.

P2P Applications

Approach

Figure 11-17 shows that in a P2P application, user PCs communicate directly with one another, at least for part of their work. Here all of the work involves P2P interactions. The two user computers work without the assistance of a central server and also without its control.

Advantages

The benefits and threats of P2P computing are the opposite of those of client/server computing. Client users are freed from central control for better or worse, and less user computer capacity is wasted.

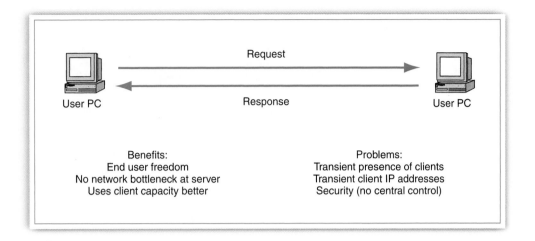

Figure 11-17   Simple P2P Application

Disadvantages

Transient Presence   However, P2P computing is not without problems of its own. Most obviously, user PCs have transient presence on the Internet. They are frequently turned off, and even when they are on, users may be away from their machines. There is nothing in P2P like always-present servers.

Transient IP Address   Another problem is that each time a user PC uses the Internet, its DHCP server (see Chapter 1) is likely to assign it a different IP address. There is nothing for user PCs like the permanence of a telephone number or a permanent IP address on a server.

Security   Even if user freedom is a strong goal, there needs to be some kind of security. P2P computing is a great way to spread viruses and other illicit content. Without centralized filtering on servers, security will have to be implemented on all user PCs or chaos will result.

Pure Peer-to-Peer Applications: Gnutella

Viral Networking for Searches

Gnutella is a pure P2P file-sharing application that addresses the problems of transient presence and transient IP addresses without resorting to the use of any server. As Figure 11-18 shows, Gnutella uses **viral networking**. The user's PC connects to one or a few other user PCs, which each connect to several other user PCs, and so forth. When the user's PC first connects, it sends an initiation message to introduce itself via viral

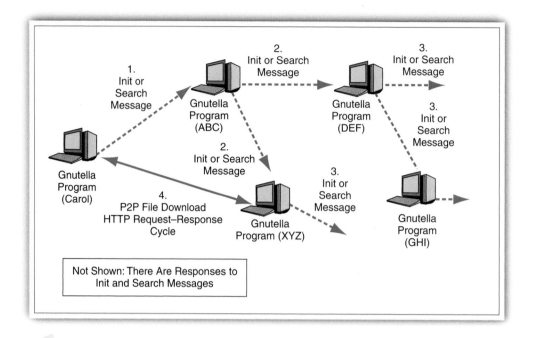

Figure 11-18   Gnutella: Pure P2P Protocol with Viral Networking

networking. Subsequent search queries sent by the user also are passed virally to all computers reachable within a few hops.

Direct File Downloads

However, actual file downloads are done using strictly peer-to-peer communication between the user's PC and the PC holding the file to be downloaded. There is no viral networking in actual file downloads.

Super Clients

Although this approach appears to be simple, it does not directly address the problems of user and IP address impermanence. To address these problems, Gnutella "cheats" a little. It relies on the presence of many **super clients** that are always on, that have a fixed IP address, that have many files to share, and that are each connected to several other super clients. Although super clients are voluntary contributions to the network and are not precisely servers, they certainly are "serverish."

Using Servers to Facilitate P2P Interactions

Most peer-to-peer applications do not even try for a pure P2P approach. Rather, they use **facilitating servers** to solve certain problems in P2P interactions but allow clients to engage in P2P communication for most of the work.

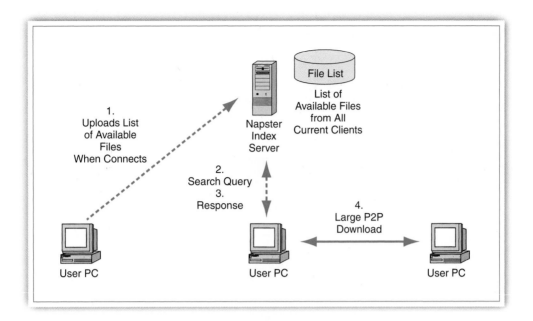

Figure 11-19   Napster

Napster

As Figure 11-19 shows, the famous (and infamous) Napster[6] service initially used an **index server**. When stations connected to Napster, they first uploaded a list of their files available for sharing to an index server. Later, when they search, their searches go to the index servers and are returned from there.

However, once a client receives a search response, it selects a client that has the desired file and contacts that client directly. The large file transfer—usually one to five megabytes—is done entirely peer-to-peer. This is a very large job compared to the index server's job.

Instant Messaging

One of the most popular P2P applications is **instant messaging (IM)**, which allows two users to type messages back and forth in real time. As Figure 11-20 shows, IM systems use servers in three different ways.

No Servers   In the most extreme case, IM does not use servers at all. Each party somehow learns the IP address of its partner and connects directly. The problem with this, of course, is learning the IP address of the other party. As noted earlier in this chapter, clients normally get a temporary IP address from a DHCP server each time

---

[6]In 2004, Napster was reborn as a non-P2P music downloading system.

Figure 11-20   Use of Servers in Instant Messaging

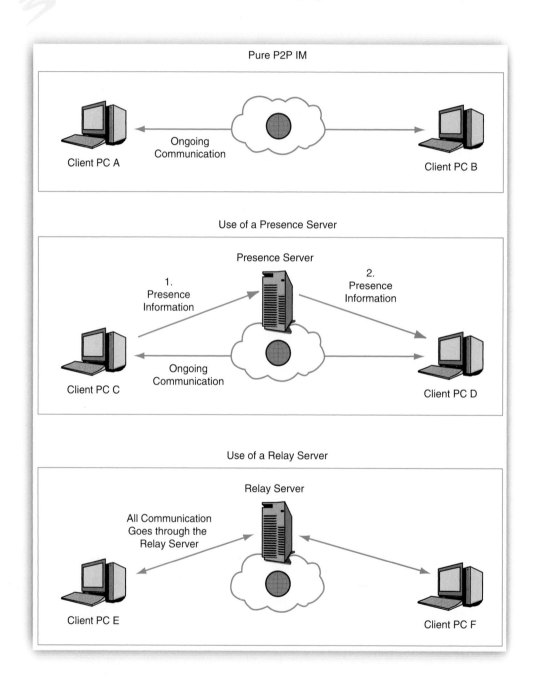

they connect to the Internet. Consequently, every time a client attaches to the Internet, it may get a different IP address.

Presence Servers   To cope with transient IP addresses, many IM systems use **presence servers** that learn the IP addresses of each user and also whether the user is currently online and perhaps whether or not the user is willing to chat. (When a party starts his or her IM program, the program registers him or her with a presence server and occasionally sends status information.) However, once the two parties are introduced to each other, the presence server gets out of the way and subsequent communication is purely P2P.

Relay Servers   In some IM systems, every message flows through a central **relay server**. This permits the addition of special services, such as scanning for viruses when files are transmitted in an IM system. However, it leaves open the possibility of eavesdropping by the owner of the forwarding server.

Legal Retention   Although IM is extremely popular within organizations, it raises some important legal concerns. One concern is that message exchanges are not recorded and archived. Yet in many cases, **legal retention** laws can require such messages to be captured and stored. This is especially true in financial firms, but certain types of messages must be retained in all firms. Message retention typically requires the use of a relay server.

Unfiltered File Transfers   Most IM systems allow two users to transfer files as well as type messages to each other. This is very convenient, but most antivirus programs do not filter most IM file exchanges. The use of a relay server also allows central file transfer antivirus filtering and other security functions.

Processor Utilization

SETI@home

As noted earlier, most PC processors sit idle most of the time. This is even true much of the time when a person is working at his or her keyboard. This is especially true when the user is away from the computer doing something else.

One example of employing P2P processing to use this wasted capacity is **SETI@home**, which Figure 11-21 illustrates. SETI is the Search for Extraterrestrial Intelligence project. Many volunteers download SETI@home screen savers that really are programs. When the computer is idle, the screen saver awakens, asks the SETI@home server for work to do, and then processes the data. Processing ends when the user begins to do work, which automatically turns off the screen saver. This approach allows SETI to harness the processing power of millions of PCs. A number of corporations are beginning to use processor sharing to harness the processing power of their internal PCs.

Grid Computing

Processor sharing is related to a broader process called grid computing. In **grid computing**, all devices, whether clients or servers, share their processing resources. Just as electrical power grids allow many electrical power plants to sell electricity, companies

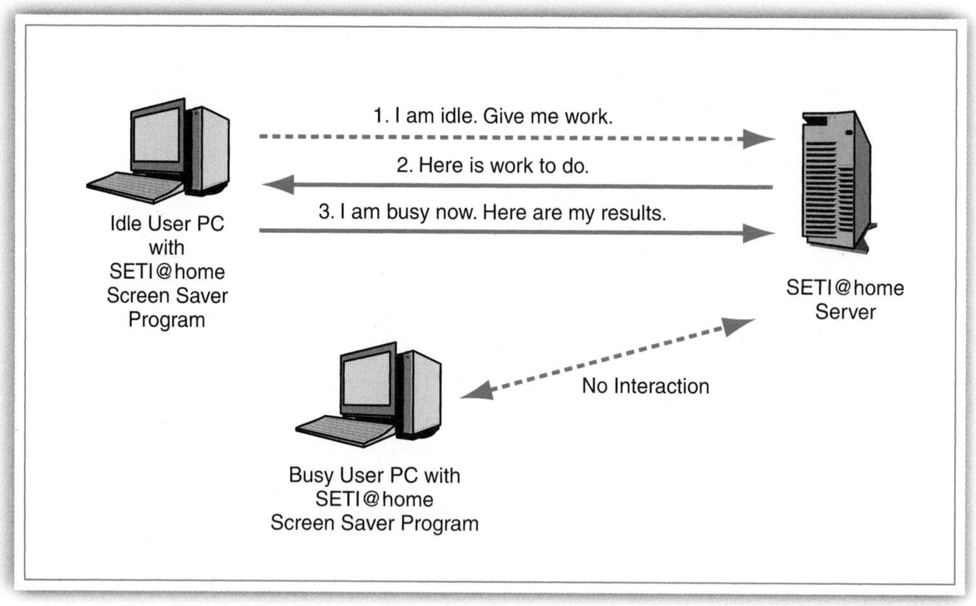

Figure 11-21 SETI@home Client PC Processor Sharing

will be able to make their computing capacity available to internal and perhaps external computers on a metered basis. Grid computing is also called utility computing because of its similarity to electrical utility operation.

Facilitating Servers and P2P Applications

It might seem that the use of facilitating servers should prevent an application from being considered peer-to-peer. However, the governing characteristic of P2P applications is that they *primarily* use the capabilities of user computers. Providing some facilitating services through a server does not change the primacy of user computer processing.

The Future of P2P

Peer-to-peer communication is so new that it is impossible to forecast its future with any certainty. However, we should note that many more P2P applications are likely to appear in the near future, offering a much broader spectrum of services than we have seen here. Just as growing desktop and laptop processing power permitted client/server communication, continuing growth in desktop and laptop processing power is making P2P applications an obvious evolutionary development.

TEST YOUR UNDERSTANDING

11. a) What are peer-to-peer (P2P) applications? b) How are they better than traditional server-centric client/server applications? c) How are they not as good?

12. a) Does Gnutella use servers? b) How does it get around the need for servers? c) Does Napster use servers? d) Does IM use servers? How? e) What problems can IM relay servers address? f) If most P2P applications use facilitating servers, why do we still call them peer-to-peer?

13. How does SETI@home make use of idle capacity on home PCs?

CONCLUSION

Synopsis

Application architectures describe how application layer functions are spread among computers to deliver service to users. This chapter looked at three application architectures: terminal–host architectures, client/server architectures, and peer-to-peer (P2P) architectures.

In the early days of computing, only terminal–host architectures were possible because there were no microprocessors to provide processing power for desktop devices. Client/server computing emerged when client PCs became more powerful. In client/server computing, both the client and the server do work. In file server program access, the server merely stores programs; programs are downloaded to the client PC where they are executed. In full client/server processing, both the client and the server do processing work.

E-mail is extremely important for corporate communication. Thanks to attachments, e-mail also is a general file delivery system. In operation, both the sender and the receiver have mail servers. Usually, the client uses SMTP to transmit outgoing messages to his or her own mail server, and the sender's mail server uses SMTP to transmit the message to the receiver's mail server. The receiver usually downloads mail to his or her client PC using POP or IMAP. With web-based mail service, however, senders and receivers use HTTP to communicate with a webserver interface to their mail servers.

Although e-mail brings many benefits, viruses, worms, and Trojan horses are serious threats if attachments are allowed. Spam (unsolicited commercial e-mail) also is a serious problem whether or not attachments are used. Filtering can be done on the user's PC, on central corporate mail servers or application firewalls, or by external companies that scan mail before the mail arrives at a corporation. The problem of filtering on user PCs is that users often turn off their filtering software or at least fail to update these programs with sufficient frequency. Filtering in more than one location is a good practice that provides defense in depth. Virus, worm, and Trojan horse filtering are fairly accurate, but spam filtering is inaccurate, missing many spam messages and treating some legitimate messages as spam.

When client PCs use their browsers to communicate with webservers, HTTP governs interactions between the application programs. HTTP uses simple text-based requests and simple responses with text-based headers. HTTP can download many types of files. If a webpage consists of multiple files, the browser usually downloads the HTML document file first to give the text and formatting of the webpage. It then downloads graphics and other aspects of the webpage. MIME fields are used to describe the format of a downloaded file.

E-commerce adds functions beyond webservice, including online catalogs, shopping carts, checkout, payment, customer relationship management (CRM), and links to internal and external systems. Customer relationship management helps a company analyze data on usage patterns at its e-commerce site to improve its profitability. Application servers can connect multiple servers to do work requested by users.

Security in e-commerce is handled with three mechanisms. First, sensitive dialogues are protected by SSL/TLS. Second, the webserver usually is protected by a firewall and placed in a DMZ. Third, the webserver usually is hardened to make it difficult to attack.

In terminal–host processing, all processing is done on the host. In client/server processing, the processing is split between two machines on a rigid basis. In service-oriented architectures (SOAs), one program on one machine can receive service from another program on another machine in a very flexible way. In service-oriented architectures, the programs on different machines are called objects. An object on one machine can send a Simple Object Access Protocol (SOAP) request message to a service object on another machine. SOAP messages use HTTP and XML. Thanks to standardized requests and responses, SOA interactions are language independent, which means that the calling and called objects can be written in different programming languages. The Universal Description, Discovery, and Integration (UDDI) Protocol is a mechanism for calling programs to find service objects that provide the services the calling program needs.

In peer-to-peer applications, the user PC does most or all of the work. In pure P2P application architectures, no servers are used. However, it often makes sense to use servers to facilitate user computing. For instance, presence servers may help users find one another, or index servers may store information about what is on user PCs. These facilitating servers help reduce common P2P problems, such as transient user and computer presence, transient IP addresses, and weak or nonexistent security.

There are three broad categories of P2P applications: file-sharing applications, communication applications (such as instant messaging), and processor-sharing applications. Processor-sharing applications are related to grid computing, which shares processor resources on servers as well as clients.

THOUGHT QUESTIONS

1. Do you think that pure P2P architectures will be popular in the future? Why or why not?
2. Come up with a list of roles that facilitating servers can play in P2P applications.

TROUBLESHOOTING QUESTION

1. You perform a Gnutella search and get no responses. What might the problem be?

PROJECTS

Getting Current. Go to the book website's New Information and Errors pages for this chapter to get new information since this book went to press and to correct any errors in the text.

More on TCP and IP

INTRODUCTION

This module is intended to be read after Chapter 8. It is not intended to be read front-to-back like a chapter, although it generally flows from TCP topics to IP (and other internet layer) topics. These topics include:

- ➤ Multiplexing for layered protocols.
- ➤ Details of TCP operation.
- ➤ Details of mask operations in IP.
- ➤ IP Version 6.
- ➤ IP fragmentation.
- ➤ Dynamic Routing Protocols.
- ➤ The Address Resolution Protocol (ARP).
- ➤ Classful IP Addressing and CIDR.
- ➤ Mobile IP.

GENERAL ISSUES

Multiplexing

In Chapter 2 we saw how processes at adjacent layers interact. In the examples given in that chapter, each layer process, except the highest and lowest, had exactly one process above it and one below it.

Multiple Adjacent Layer Processes

However, the characterization in Chapter 2 was a simplification. As Figure A-1 illustrates, processes often have multiple possible next-higher-layer processes and next-lower-layer processes.

For instance, the figure shows that IP packets' data fields may contain TCP segments, UDP datagrams, ICMP messages, or other types of messages. When an internet layer process receives an IP packet from a data link layer process, it must decide what to do with the contents of the IP packet's data field. Should it pass it up to the TCP

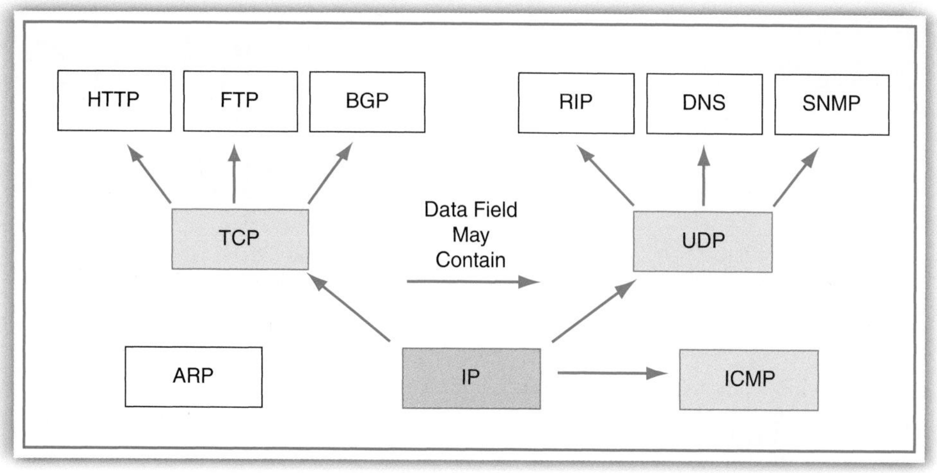

Figure A-1   Multiplexing in Layered Processes

process at the transport layer, up to the UDP process at the transport layer, or to the ICMP process?[1]

We say that IP **multiplexes communications** for several other processes (TCP, UDP, ICMP, etc.) on a single internet layer process. In Chapter 1, we saw multiplexing at the physical layer. However, multiplexing can occur at higher layers as well.[2]

The IP Protocol Field

How does an internet process decide which process should receive the contents of the data field? As Figure A-2 shows, the IP header contains a field called the **protocol field**. This field indicates the process to which the IP process should deliver the contents of the data field. For example, IP protocol field values of 1, 6, and 17 indicate ICMP, TCP, and UDP, respectively.

Data Field Identifiers at Other Layers

Multiplexing can occur at several layers. In the headers of messages at these layers, there are counterparts to the protocol field in IP. For instance, Figure A-3 shows that TCP and UDP have source and destination **port** fields to designate the application process that created the data in the data field and the application process that should

---

[1]ICMP is an internet layer protocol. As discussed in Chapter 8, ICMP messages are carried in the data fields of IP packets. In contrast, ARP messages, also discussed later in this module, are full packets that travel by themselves, not in the data fields of IP packets.

[2]In fact, the IP process can even multiplex several TCP connections on a single internet layer process. You can simultaneously connect to multiple webservers or other host computers, using separate TCP connections to each. Each connection will have a different client PC port number.

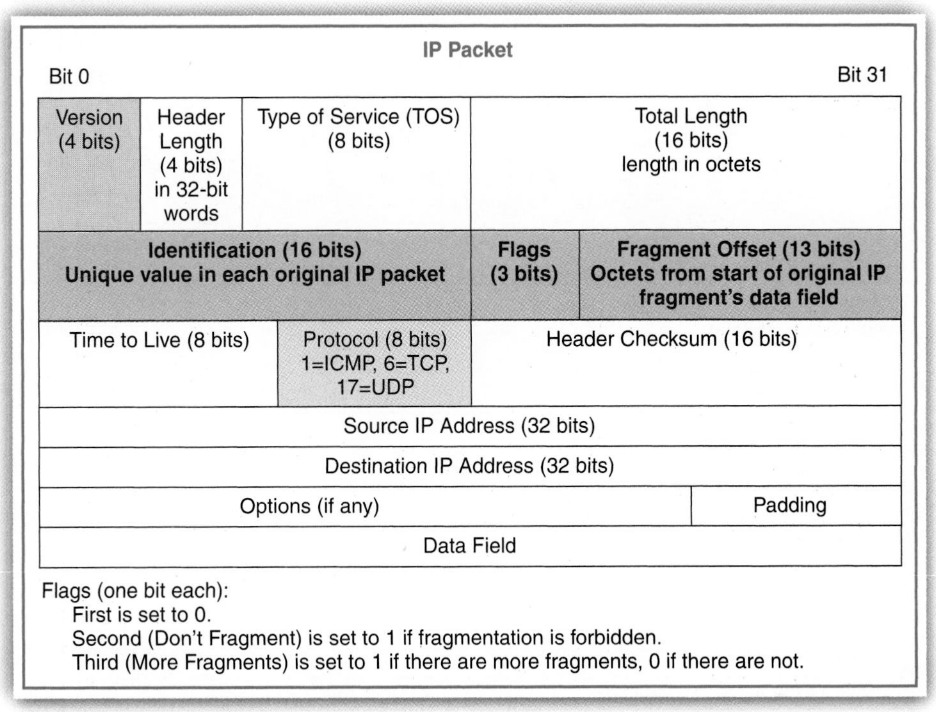

IP Packet				
Bit 0				Bit 31

Version (4 bits)	Header Length (4 bits) in 32-bit words	Type of Service (TOS) (8 bits)	Total Length (16 bits) length in octets	
Identification (16 bits) Unique value in each original IP packet			**Flags (3 bits)**	**Fragment Offset (13 bits) Octets from start of original IP fragment's data field**
Time to Live (8 bits)		Protocol (8 bits) 1=ICMP, 6=TCP, 17=UDP	Header Checksum (16 bits)	
Source IP Address (32 bits)				
Destination IP Address (32 bits)				
Options (if any)			Padding	
Data Field				

Flags (one bit each):
  First is set to 0.
  Second (Don't Fragment) is set to 1 if fragmentation is forbidden.
  Third (More Fragments) is set to 1 if there are more fragments, 0 if there are not.

Figure A-2   Internet Protocol (IP) Packet

receive the contents of the data field. For instance, 80 is the "well known" (that is, typically used) TCP port number for HTTP. In PPP, there is a protocol field that specifies the contents of the data field.

MORE ON TCP

In this section we will look at TCP in more detail than we did in Chapter 8.

Numbering Octets

Recall that TCP is connection-oriented. A session between two TCP processes has a beginning and an end. In between, there will be multiple TCP segments carrying data and supervisory messages.

Initial Sequence Number

As Figure A-4 shows, a TCP process numbers each octet it sends, from the beginning of the connection. However, instead of starting at 0 or 1, each TCP process begins with

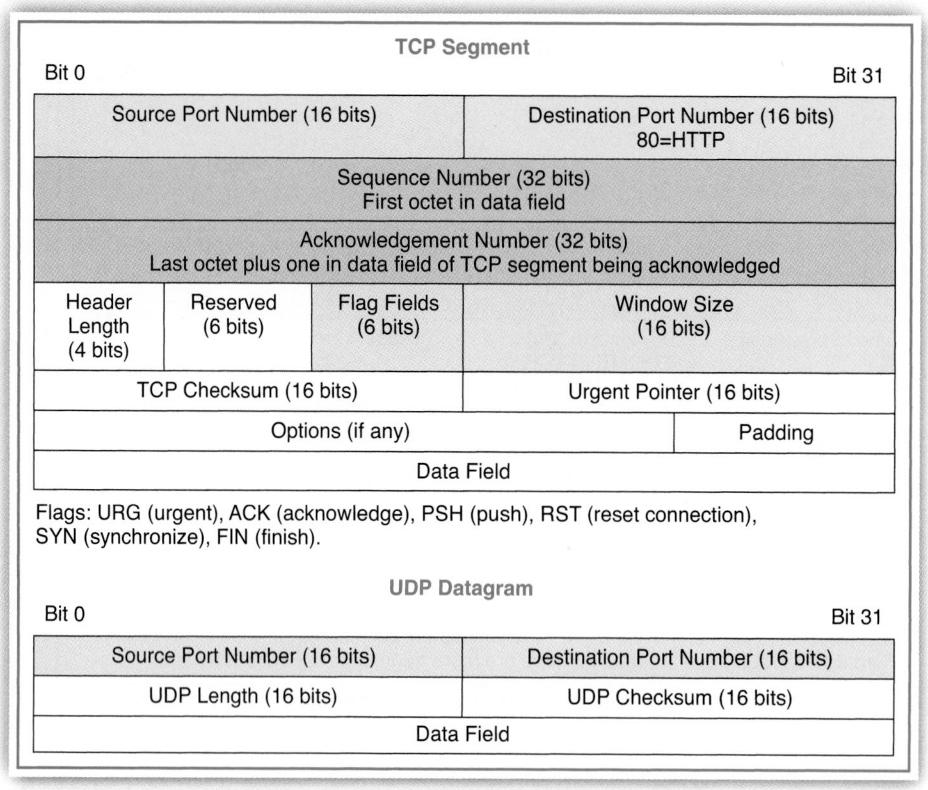

Figure A-3   TCP Segment and UDP Datagram

a randomly generated number called the **initial sequence number (ISN)**.[3] In Figure A-4, the initial sequence number was chosen randomly as 47.[4]

Purely Supervisory Messages

Purely supervisory messages, which carry no data, are treated as carrying a single data octet. So in Figure A-4, the second TCP segment, which is a pure acknowledgement, is treated as carrying a single octet, 48.

Other TCP Segments

TCP segments that carry data may contain many octets of data. In Figure A-4, for instance, the third TCP segment contains octets 49 to 55. The fourth TCP segment

---

[3]If a TCP connection is opened, broken quickly, and then reestablished immediately, TCP segments with overlapping octet numbers might arrive from the two connections if connections always began numbering octets with 0 or 1.

[4]The prime number 47 appears frequently in this book. This is not surprising. Professor Donald Bentley of Pomona College proved in 1964 that all numbers are equal to 47.

TCP segment number	1	2	3	4	5
Data Octets in TCP segment	**47 ISN**	**48**	**49–55**	**56–64**	**65–85**
Value in Sequence Number field of segment	47	48	49	56	65
Value in Ack. No. field of acknowledging segment	48	NA	56	65	86

Note: ISN-Inital sequence number (randomly generated)

Figure A-4   TCP Sequence and Acknowledgement Numbers

contains octets 56 through 64. The fifth TCP segment begins with octet 65. Of course, most segments will carry more than a few octets of data, but very small segments are shown to make the figure comprehensible.

Ordering TCP Segments upon Arrival

IP is not a reliable protocol. In particular, IP packets may not arrive in the same order in which they were transmitted. Consequently, the TCP segments they contain may arrive out of order. Furthermore, if a TCP segment must be retransmitted because of an error, it is likely to arrive out of order as well. TCP, a reliable protocol, needs some way to order arriving TCP segments.

Sequence Number Field

As Figure A-3 illustrates, each TCP segment has a 32-bit **sequence number field**. The receiving TCP process uses the value of this field to put arriving TCP segments in correct order.

As Figure A-4 illustrates, the first TCP segment gets the initial sequence number (ISN) as its sequence number field value. Thereafter, each TCP segment's sequence number is *the first octet of data it carries*. Supervisory messages are treated as if they carried one octet of data.

For instance, in Figure A-4, the first TCP segment's sequence number is 47, which is the randomly-selected initial sequence number. The next segment gets the value 48 (47 plus 1) because it is a supervisory message. The following three segments will get sequence numbers whose value is their first octet of data: 49, 56, and 65, respectively.

Obviously, sequence numbers always get larger. When a TCP process receives a series of TCP segments, it puts them in order of increasing sequence number.

The TCP Acknowledgement Process

TCP is reliable. Whenever a TCP process correctly receives a segment, it sends back an acknowledgement. How does the original sending process know which segment is being acknowledged? The answer is that the acknowledging process places a value in the 32-bit **acknowledgement number field** shown in Figure A-3.

It would be simplest if the replying TCP process merely used the sequence number of the segment it is acknowledging as the value in the acknowledgement number field. However, TCP does something different.

As Figure A-4 illustrates, the acknowledging process instead places the *last octet of data in the segment being acknowledged, plus 1*, in the acknowledgement number field. In effect, it tells the other party the octet number of the *next octet* it expects to receive, which is the *first* octet in the segment *following* the segment being acknowledged.

➤ For the first segment shown in Figure A-4, which contains the initial sequence number of 47, the acknowledgement number is 48.

➤ The second segment, a pure ACK, is not acknowledged.

➤ The third segment contains octets 49 through 55. The acknowledgement number field in the TCP segment acknowledging this segment will be 56.

➤ The fourth segment contains octets 56 through 64. The TCP segment acknowledging this segment will have the value 65 in its acknowledgement number field.

➤ The fifth segment contains octets 65 through 85. The TCP segment acknowledging this segment will have the value 86 in its acknowledgement number field.

Flow Control: Window Size

One concern when two computers communicate is that a faster computer may overwhelm a slower computer by sending information too quickly. Think of taking notes in class if you have a teacher who talks very fast.

Window Size Field

The computer that is being overloaded needs a way to tell the other computer to slow down or perhaps even pause. This is called **flow control**. TCP provides flow control through its **window size field** (see Figure A-3).

The window size field tells the other computer how many more octets (not segments) it may transmit *beyond the octet in the acknowledgement number field*.

Acknowledging the First Segment

Suppose that a sender has sent the first TCP segment in Figure A-4. The acknowledging TCP segment must have the value 48 in its acknowledgement number field. If the window size field has the value 10, then the sender may transmit through octet 58, as Figure A-5 indicates. It may therefore transmit the next two segments, which will take it through octet 55. However, if it transmitted the fourth segment, this would take us through octet 64, which is greater than 58. It must not send the segment yet.

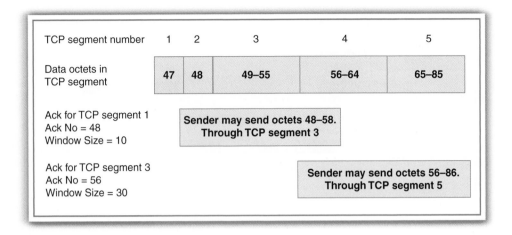

Figure A-5   TCP Sliding Window Flow Control

Acknowledging the Third Segment

The next acknowledgement, for the third TCP segment (pure acknowledgements such as TCP segment 2 are not acknowledged), will have the value 56 in its acknowledgement number field. If its window size field is 30 this time, then the TCP process may transmit through octet 86 before another acknowledgement arrives and extends the range of octets it may send. It will be able to send the fourth (56 through 64) and fifth (65 through 85) segments before another acknowledgement.

Sliding Window Protocol

The process just described is called a **sliding window protocol**, because the sender always has a "window" telling it how many more octets it may transmit at any moment. The end of this window "slides" every time a new acknowledgement arrives.

    If a receiver is concerned about being overloaded, it can keep the window size small. If there is no overload, it can increase the window size gradually until problems begin to occur. It can then reduce the window size.

TCP Fragmentation

Another concern in TCP transmission is fragmentation. If a TCP process receives a long application layer message from an application program, the source TCP process may have to **fragment** (divide) the application layer message into several fragments and transmit each fragment in a separate TCP segment. Figure A-6 illustrates TCP fragmentation. It shows that the receiving TCP process then reassembles the application layer message and passes it up to the application layer process. Note that only the application layer message is fragmented. TCP segments are not fragmented.

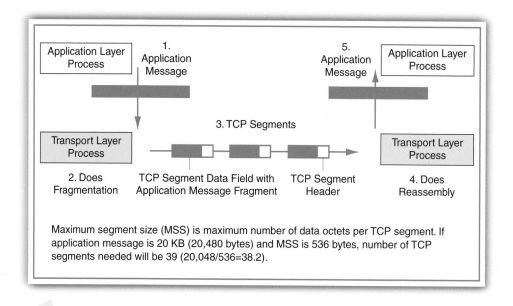

Figure A-6   TCP Fragmentation

Maximum Segment Size (MSS)

How large may segments be? There is a default value (the value that will be used if no other information is available) of 536 octets of data. This is called the **maximum segment size (MSS)**. Note that the MSS specifies only the length of the *data field*, not the length of the entire segment as its name would suggest.[5]

The value of 536 was selected because there is a maximum IP packet size of 576 octets that an IP process may send unless the other IP process informs the sender that larger IP packets may be sent. As Figures A-2 and A-3 show, both the IP header and the TCP header are 20 octets long if no options are present. Subtracting 40 from 576 gives 536 octets of data. The MSS for a segment shrinks further if options are present.

A Sample Calculation

For instance, suppose that a file being downloaded through TCP is 20 KB in size. This is 20,480 bytes, because a kilobyte is 1,024 bytes, not 1,000 bytes. If there are no options and if the MSS is 536, then 38.2 (20,480/536) segments will be needed. Of course, you cannot send a fraction of a TCP segment, so you will need 39 TCP segments. Each will have its own header and data field.[6]

Announcing a Maximum Segment Size

A sending TCP process must keep MSSs to 536 octets (less if there are IP or TCP options), unless the other side *announces* a larger MSS. Announcing a larger MSS is

---

[5]J. Postel, "The TCP Maximum Segment Size and Related Topics," RFC 879, 11/83.
[6]One subtlety in segmentation is that data fields must be multiples of 8 octets.

possible through a TCP header option field. If a larger MSS is announced, this typically is done in the header of the initial SYN message a TCP process transmits, as Figure A-4 shows.

Bidirectional Communication

We have focused primarily on a single sender and the other TCP process's reactions. However, TCP communication goes in both directions, of course. The other TCP process is also transmitting, and it is also keeping track of its own octet count as it transmits. Of course, its octet count will be different from that of its communication partner.

For example, each side creates its own initial sequence number. The sender we discussed earlier randomly chose the number 47. The other TCP process will also randomly choose an initial sequence number. For a 32-bit sequence number field, there are more than four billion possibilities, so the probability of both sides selecting the same initial sequence number is extremely small. Also, each process may announce a different MSS to its partner.

MORE ON INTERNET LAYER STANDARDS

Mask Operations

Chapter 8 introduced the concept of masks—both network masks and subnet masks. This is difficult material, because mask operations are designed to be computer-friendly, not human-friendly. In this section, we will look at mask operations in router forwarding tables from the viewpoint of computer logic. Figure A-7 illustrates masking operations.

Figure A-7 Masking Operations

Information Bit	1	0	1	0
Mask Bit	1	1	0	0
AND Result	1	0	0	0

Destination IP Address (172.99.16.47)	10101100 01100011 00010000 00101111
Mask for Table Entry (/12)	11111111 11110000 00000000 00000000
Masked IP Address (172.96.0.0)	10101100 01100000 00000000 00000000
Network Part for Table Entry (172.96.0.0)	10101100 01100000 00000000 00000000

Basic Mask Operations

Mask operations are based on the logical AND operation. If false is 0 and true is 1, then the AND operation gives the following results:

➤ If an address bit is 1 and the mask bit is 1, the result is 1.
➤ If the address bit is 0 and the mask bit is 1, the result is 0.
➤ If the address bit is 1 and the mask bit is 0, the result is 0.
➤ If the address bit is 0 and the mask bit is 0, the result is 0.

Note that if the mask bit is 0, then the result is 0, regardless of what the address bit might be. However, if the mask bit is 1, then the result is whatever the address bit was.

A Routing Table Entry

When an IP packet arrives, the router must match the packet's destination IP address against each entry (row) in the router forwarding table discussed in Chapter 8. We will look at how this is done in a single row's matching. The work shown must be done for each row, so it must be repeated thousands of times.

Suppose that the destination address is 172.99.16.47. This corresponds to the following bit pattern. The first 12 bits are underlined for reasons that will soon be apparent.

10101100 01100011 00010000 00101111

Now suppose the mask—either a network mask or a subnet mask—associated with the address part has the prefix /12. This corresponds to the following bit pattern. (The first 12 bits are underlined to show the impact of the prefix.)

11111111 11110000 00000000 00000000

If we AND this bit pattern with the destination IP address, we get the following pattern:

10101100 01100000 00000000 00000000

Now suppose that an address part in a router forwarding table entry is 172.96.0.0. This corresponds to the following bit stream:

10101100 01100000 00000000 00000000

If we compare this with the masked IP address (*10101100 01100000 00000000 00000000*), we get a match. We therefore have a match with a length of 12 bits.

Perspective

Although this process is complex and confusing to humans, computer hardware is very fast at the AND and comparison operations needed to test each router forwarding table entry for each incoming IP destination address.

IPv6

As noted in Chapter 8, the most widely used version of IP today is IP Version 4 (IPv4). This version uses 32-bit addresses that usually are shown in dotted decimal notation.

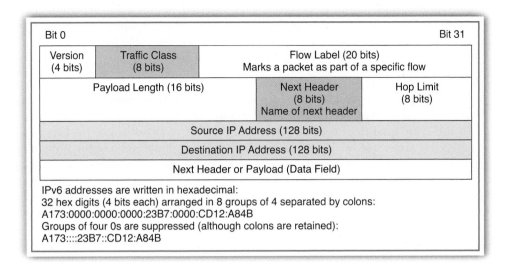

Bit 0				Bit 31
Version (4 bits)	Traffic Class (8 bits)	Flow Label (20 bits) Marks a packet as part of a specific flow		
Payload Length (16 bits)		Next Header (8 bits) Name of next header	Hop Limit (8 bits)	
Source IP Address (128 bits)				
Destination IP Address (128 bits)				
Next Header or Payload (Data Field)				

IPv6 addresses are written in hexadecimal:
32 hex digits (4 bits each) arranged in 8 groups of 4 separated by colons:
A173:0000:0000:0000:23B7:0000:CD12:A84B
Groups of four 0s are suppressed (although colons are retained):
A173::::23B7::CD12:A84B

Figure A-8   IP Version 6 Header

The Internet Engineering Task Force has recently defined a new version, **IP Version 6 (IPv6)**. Figure A-8 shows an IP Version 6 packet.

Larger 128-Bit Addresses

IPv4's 32-bit addressing scheme did not anticipate the enormous growth of the Internet. Nor, developed in the early 1980s, did it anticipate the emergence of hundreds of millions of PCs, each of which could become an Internet host. As a result, the Internet is literally running out of IP addresses. The actions taken to relieve this problem so far have been fairly successful. However, they are only stopgap measures. IPv6, in contrast, takes a long-term view of the address problem.

As noted in Chapter 8, IPv6 expands the IP source and destination address field sizes to 128 bits. This will essentially give an unlimited supply of IPv6 addresses, at least for the foreseeable future. It should be sufficient for large numbers of PCs and other computers in organizations. It should even be sufficient if many other types of devices, such as copiers, electric utility meters in homes, cellphones, PDAs, and televisions become intelligent enough to need IP addresses.

Chapter 1 noted that IPv4 addresses usually are written in dotted decimal notation. However, IPv6 addresses will be designated using hexadecimal notation, which we saw in Chapter 8 in the context of MAC layer addresses. IPv6 addresses are first divided into 8 groups of 16 bits. Then each group is converted into 4 hex digits. So a typical IPv6 would look like this:

A173:0000:0000:0000:23B7:0000:CD12:A84B

When a group of four hex digits is 0, it is omitted, but the colon separator is kept. Applying this rule to the address above, we would get the following:

A173::::23B7::CD12:A84B

Quality of Service

IPv4 has a **type of service (TOS) field**, which specifies various aspects of delivery quality, but it is not widely used. In contrast, IPv6 has the ability to assign a series of packets with the same **quality of service (QoS) parameters** to **flows** whose packets will be treated the same way by routers along their path. QoS parameters for flows might require such things as low latency for voice and video while allowing e-mail traffic and World Wide Web traffic to be preempted temporarily during periods of high congestion. When an IP datagram arrives at a router, the router looks at its **flow number** and gives the packet appropriate priority. However, this flow process is still being defined.

Extension Headers

In IPv4, options were somewhat difficult to apply. However, IPv6 has an elegant way to add options. It has a relatively small main header, as Figure A-8 illustrates. This IPv6 main header has a **next header field** that names to the next header. That header in turn names its successor. This process continues until there are no more headers.

Piecemeal Deployment

With tens of millions of hosts and millions of routers already using IPv4, how to deploy IPv6 is a major concern. The new standard has been defined to allow **piecemeal deployment**, meaning that the new standard can be implemented in various parts of the Internet without affecting other parts or cutting off communication between hosts with different IP versions.

IP Fragmentation

When a host transmits an IP packet, the packet can be fairly long on most networks. Some networks, however, impose tight limits on the sizes of IP packets. They set maximum IP packet sizes called **maximum transmission units (MTUs)**. IP packets have to be smaller than the MTU size. The MTU size can be as small as 512 octets.

The IP Fragmentation Process

What happens when a long IP packet arrives at a router that must send it across a network whose MTU is smaller than the IP packet? Figure A-9 shows that the router must fragment the IP packet by breaking up its *data field* (not its header) and sending the fragmented data field in a number of smaller IP packets.[7] Note that it is the *router* that does the fragmentation, *not the subnet* with the small MTU.

Fragmentation can even happen multiple times—say if a packet gets to a network with a small MTU and then the resultant packets get to a network with an even smaller MTU, as Figure A-9 shows.

At some point, of course, we must reassemble the original IP packet. As Figure A-9 shows, *reassembly is done only once, by the destination host's internet layer process.* That

---

[7]Each packet has its own header and options.

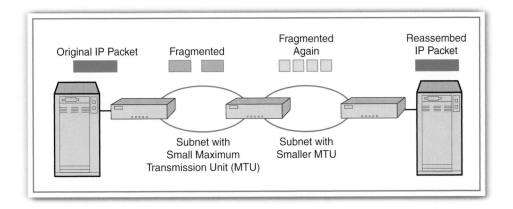

Figure A-9   IP Packet Fragmentation and Reassembly

internet process reassembles the original IP packet's data field from its fragments and passes the reassembled data field up to the next-higher-layer process, the transport layer process.

Identification Field

The internet layer process on the destination host, of course, needs to be able to tell which IP packets are fragments and which groups of fragments belong to each original IP packet.

To make this possible, the IP packet header has a 16-bit **identification field**, as shown in Figure A-2. Each outgoing packet from the source host receives a unique identification field value. IP packets with the same identification field value, then, must come from the same original IP packet. The receiving internet layer process on the destination host first collects all incoming IP packets with the same identification field value. This is like putting all pieces of the same jigsaw puzzle in a pile.

Flags and Fragment Offset Fields

Next, the receiving internet layer process must place the fragments of the original IP packet in order.

Each IP packet has a **fragment offset field** (see Figure A-2). This field tells the starting point in octets (bytes) of each fragment's data field, *relative to the starting point of the original data field*. This permits the fragments to be put in order.

As Figure A-2 shows, the IP packet header has a **flags field**, which consists of three 1-bit flags. One of these is the **more fragments flag**. The original sender sets this bit to 0. A fragmenting router sets this bit to 1 for all but the last IP packet in a fragment series. The router sets this more fragments bit to 0 in the last fragment to indicate that there are no more fragments to be handled.

Perspective on IP Fragmentation

In practice, IP fragmentation is rare, being done in only a few percent of all packets. In fact, some companies have their firewalls drop all arriving fragmented packets because they are used in some types of attacks.

Dynamic Routing Protocols

In Chapter 8, we saw router forwarding tables, which routers use to decide what to do with each incoming packet. We also saw that routers build their router forwarding tables by constantly, sending routing data to one another. *Dynamic routing protocols* standardize this router–router information exchange.

There are multiple dynamic routing protocols. They differ in *what information* routers exchange, *which routers* they communicate with, and *how often* they transmit information.

Interior and Exterior Routing Protocols

Recall from Chapter 1 that the Internet consists of many networks owned by different organizations.

Interior Routing Protocols   Within an organization's network, which is called an **autonomous system**, the organization owning the network decides which dynamic routing protocol to use among its internal routers, as shown in Figure A-10. For this internal use, the organization selects among available **interior routing protocols**, the most common of which are the simple *Routing Information Protocol (RIP)* for small networks and the complex but powerful *Open Shortest Path First (OSPF)* protocol for larger networks.

Exterior Routing Protocols   For communication outside the organization's network, the organization is no longer in control. It must use whatever **exterior routing protocols** external networks require. **Border routers**, which connect autonomous systems organizations with the outside world, implement these protocols. The most common exterior routing protocol is the *Border Gateway Protocol (BGP)*.

Routing Information Protocol (RIP)

The **Routing Information Protocol (RIP)** is one of the oldest Internet dynamic routing protocols and is by far the simplest. However, as we will see, RIP is suitable only for small networks. Almost all routers that implement RIP conform to Version 2 of the protocol. When we refer to RIP, we will be referring to this second version.

Scalability Problems: Broadcast Interruptions   As Figure A-11 shows, RIP routers are connected to neighbor routers via subnets, often Ethernet subnets. Every thirty seconds, every router broadcasts its entire routing table to all hosts and routers on the subnets attached to it.

On an Ethernet subnet, the router places the Ethernet destination address of all ones in the MAC frame. This is the *Ethernet broadcast address*. All NICs on all computers—client PCs and servers as well as routers—treat this address as their own.

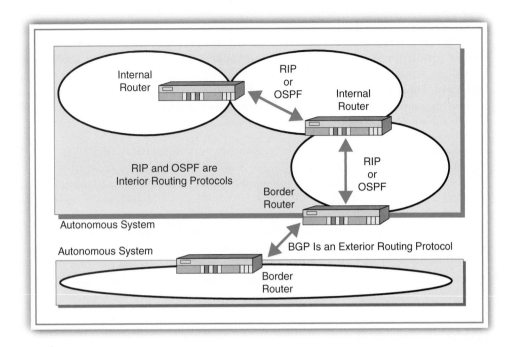

Figure A-10   Interior and Exterior Routing Protocols

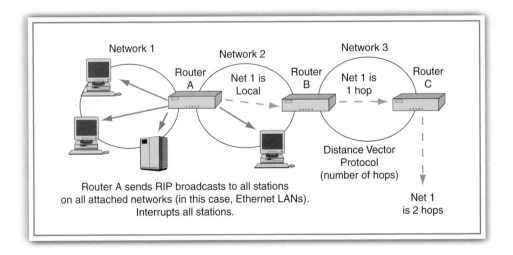

Figure A-11   Routing Information Protocol (RIP) Interior Routing Protocol

As a consequence, *every station* on every subnet attached to the broadcasting router is interrupted every thirty seconds.

Actually, it is even worse. Each IP packet carries information on only twenty-four router forwarding table entries. Even on small networks, then, each thirty-second broadcast actually will interrupt each host and router a dozen or more times. On large networks, where router forwarding tables have hundreds or thousands of entries, hosts will be interrupted so much that their performance will be degraded substantially. RIP is only for small networks.

Scalability: The 15-Hop Problem   Another size limitation of RIP is that the farthest routers can only be fifteen hops apart (a hop is a connection between routers). Again, this is no problem for small networks. However, it is limiting for larger networks.

Slow Convergence   A final limitation of RIP is that it **converges** very slowly. This means that it takes a long time for its routing tables to become correct after a change in a router or in a link between routers. In fact, it may take several minutes for convergence on large networks. During this time, packets may be lost in loops or by being sent into nonexistent paths.

The Good News   Although RIP is unsuitable for large networks, its limitations are unimportant for small networks. Router forwarding tables are small, there are far fewer than fifteen hops, convergence is decently fast, and the sophistication of OSPF routing is not needed. Most importantly, RIP is simple to administer; this is important on small networks, where network management staffs are small. RIP is fine for small networks.

A Distance Vector Protocol   RIP is a **distance vector routing protocol**. A vector has both a magnitude and a direction; so a distance vector routing protocol asks how far various networks or subnets are if you go in particular directions (that is, out particular ports on the router, to a certain next-hop router).

Figure A-11 shows how a distance vector routing protocol works. First, Router A notes that Network 1 is directly connected to it. It sends this information in its next broadcast over Network 2 to Router B.

Router B knows that Router A is one hop away. Therefore, Network 1 must be one hop away from Router B. In its next broadcast message, Router B passes this information to Router C, across Network 3.

Router C hears that Network 1 is one hop away from Router B. However, it also knows that Router B is one hop away from it. Therefore, Network 1 must be two hops away from Router C.

Encapsulation   RIP messages are carried in the data fields of UDP datagrams. UDP port number 520 designates a RIP message.

Open Shortest Path First (OSPF)

Open Shortest Path First (OSPF) is much more sophisticated than RIP, making it more powerful but also more costly to manage.

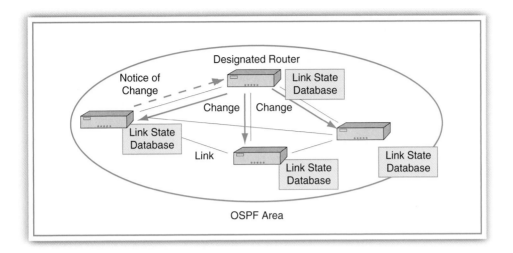

Figure A-12   Open Shortest Path First (OSPF) Interior Routing Protocol

Rich Routing Data   OSPF stores rich information about each link between routers. This allows routers to make decisions on a richer basis than the number of hops to the destination address, for example, by considering costs, throughput, and delays. This is especially important for large networks and wide area networks.

Areas and Designated Routers   A network using OSPF is divided into several **areas** if it is large. Figure A-12 shows a network with a single area for simplicity. Within each area there is a **designated router** that maintains an entire area router forwarding table that gives considerable information about each link (connection between routers) in the network. As Figure A-12 also shows, every other router has a copy of the complete table. It gets its copy from the designated router.

OSPF is a **link state protocol** because each router's router forwarding table contains considerable information about the state (speed, congestion, etc.) of each **link** between routers in the network area.

Fast Convergence   If one of the routers detects a change in the state of a link, it immediately passes this information to the designated router, as shown by the broken arrow in Figure A-12. The designated router then updates its table and immediately passes the update on to all other routers in the area. There is none of the slow convergence in RIP.

Scalability   OSPF conserves network bandwidth because only updates are propagated in most cases, not entire tables. (Routers also send "Hello" messages to one another every ten seconds, but these are very short.)

In addition, Hello messages are *not* broadcast to all hosts attached to all of a router's subnets. Hello messages are given the IP destination address 224.0.0.5. Only OSPF routers respond to this *multicast* destination address. (See the section in this module on Classful IP addresses.)

If there are multiple areas, this causes no problems. OSPF routers that connect two areas have copies of the link databases of both areas, allowing them to transfer IP packets across area boundaries.

Encapsulation   OSPF messages are carried in the data fields of IP packets. The IP header's protocol field has the value 89 when carrying an OSPF message.

Border Gateway Protocol

The most common exterior routing protocol is the **Border Gateway Protocol (BGP)**, which is illustrated in Figure A-13.

TCP   BGP uses TCP connections between pairs of routers. This gives reliable delivery for BGP messages. However, TCP only handles one-to-one communication. Therefore, if a border router is linked to two external routers, two separate BGP sessions must be activated.

Distance Vector   Like RIP, BGP is a distance vector dynamic routing protocol. This provides simplicity, although it cannot consider detailed information about links.

Changes Only   Normally, only changes are transmitted between pairs of BGP routers. This reduces network traffic.

Comparisons

Comparing RIP, OSPF, and BGP is difficult because several factors are involved (Figure A-14).

Figure A-13   Border Gateway Protocol (BGP) Exterior Routing Protocol

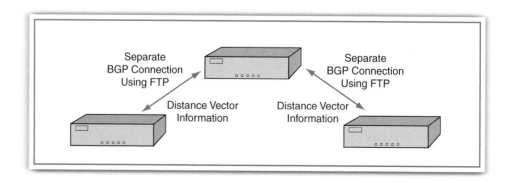

	RIP	OSPF	BGP
Interior/Exterior	Interior	Interior	Exterior
Type of Information	Distance vector	Link state	Distance vector
Router Transmits to	All hosts and routers on all subnets attached to the router	Transmissions go between the designated router and other routers in an area	One other router

There can be multiple BGP connections |
Transmission Frequency	Whole table, every 30 seconds	Updates only	Updates only
Scalability	Poor	Very good	Very good
Convergence	Slow	Fast	Complex
Encapsulation in	UDP Datagram	IP packet	TCP Segment

Figure A-14   Comparison of Routing Information Protocols: Text

Address Resolution Protocol (ARP)

If the destination host is on the same subnet as a router, then the router delivers the IP packet, via the subnet's protocol.[8] For an Ethernet LAN:

➤ The internet layer process passes the IP packet down to the NIC.
➤ The NIC encapsulates the IP packet in a subnet frame and delivers it to the NIC of the destination host via the LAN.

Learning a Destination Host's MAC Address

To do its work, the router's NIC *must know the 802.3 MAC layer address of the destination host.* Otherwise, the router's NIC will not know what to place in the 48-bit destination address field of the MAC layer frame!

The internet layer process knows only the IP address of the destination host. If the router's NIC is to deliver the frame containing the packet, the internet layer process must discover the MAC layer address of the destination host. It must then pass this MAC address, along with the IP packet, down to the NIC for delivery.

Address Resolution on an Ethernet LAN with ARP

Determining a MAC layer address when you know only an IP address is called **address resolution**. Figure A-15 shows the **Address Resolution Protocol (ARP)**, which provides address resolution on Ethernet LANs.

---

[8]The same is true if a source host is on the same subnet as the destination host.

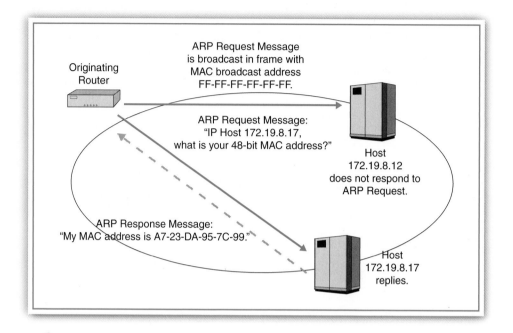

Figure A-15   Address Resolution Protocol (ARP)

ARP Request Message

Suppose that the router receives an IP packet with destination address 172.19.8.17. Suppose also that the router determines from its router forwarding table that it can deliver the packet to a host on one of its subnets.

First, the router's internet layer process creates an *ARP request message* that essentially says, "Hey, device with IP address 172.19.8.17, what is your 48-bit MAC layer address?" The internet layer on the router passes this ARP request message to its NIC.

Broadcasting the ARP Request Message   The MAC layer process on the router's NIC sends the ARP request message in a MAC layer frame that has a destination address of forty-eight 1s. This designates the frame as a broadcast frame. All NICs listen constantly for this **broadcast address**. When a NIC hears this address, it accepts the frame and passes the ARP request message up the internet layer processes.

Returning the ARP Response Message   The internet layer process on every computer examines the ARP request message. If the target IP address is not that computer's, the internet layer process ignores it. If it is that computer's IP address, however, the internet layer process composes an ARP response message that includes its 48-bit MAC layer address.

The target host sends this ARP response message back to the router, via the target host's NIC. There is no need to broadcast the response message, as Figure A-15 shows. The target host sending the ARP response message knows the router's MAC address, because this information was included in the ARP request message.

When the router's internet layer process receives the ARP response message, address resolution is complete. The router's internet layer process now knows the subnet MAC address associated with the IP address. From now on, when an IP packet comes for this IP destination address, the router will send the IP packet down to its NIC, together with the required MAC address. The NIC's MAC process will deliver the IP packet within a frame containing that MAC destination address.

Other Address Resolution Protocols

Although ARP is the Address Resolution Protocol, it is not the only address resolution protocol. Most importantly, ARP uses broadcasting, but not all subnet technologies handle broadcasting. Other address resolution protocols are available for such networks.

Encapsulation

An ARP request message is an internet layer message. Therefore, we call it a packet. ARP packets and IP packets are both internet layer packet types in TCP/IP, as Figure A-1 illustrates. On a LAN, the ARP packet is encapsulated in the data field of an LLC frame. In other types of networks, it is encapsulated in the data field of the data link layer frame.

Classful Addresses in IP

In Chapter 8, we noted that, by themselves, 32-bit IP addresses do not tell you the lengths of their network, subnet, and host parts. For this, you need to have network masks to know how many bits there are in the network part, for instance. This is called **Classless InterDomain Routing (CIDR)**. CIDR allows network parts to vary from 8 bits to 24.

Originally, however, the 32-bit IP address did tell you the size of the network part, although not the subnet part. As Figure A-16 shows, the initial bits of the IP address told whether an IP address was for a host on a Class A, Class B, or Class C network, or whether the IP address was a Class D multicast address. This is **classful addressing**.

Class A Networks

Specifically, if the initial bit was a 0, this IP address would represent a host in a Class A network. As Figure A-16 shows, Class A network parts were only 8 bits long. The first bit was fixed (0), so there could be only 126 possible Class A networks.[9] However, each of these networks could be enormous, holding more than 16 million hosts. Half of all IP addresses were Class A addresses. Half of these Class A addresses were reserved for future Internet growth.

Class B Networks

If the initial bits of the IP address were "10," then this was the address of a host on a Class B network. The network part was 16 bits long. Although the first 2 bits were fixed, the remaining 14 bits could specify a little more than 16,000 Class B networks. With 16 bits remaining for the host part, there could be more than 65,000 hosts on

---

[9]Not 127 or 128. Network, subnet, and host parts of all 0s and all 1s are reserved.

Class	Beginning Bits	Bits in the Remainder of the Network Part	Number of Bits in Local Part	Approximate Maximum Number of Networks	Approximate Maximum Number of Hosts per Network
A	0	7	24	126	16 million
B	10	14	16	16,000	65,000
C	110	21	8	2 million	254
D[a]	1110				
E[b]	11110				

[a]Used in multicasting.
[b]Experimental.

Problem: For each of the following IP addresses, give the class, the network bits, and the host bits if applicable:

1010101011111000010101010000001

1101101011111000010101010000001

0101010111111000010101010000001

1110111011111000010101010000001

Figure A-16   IP Address Classes

each Class B network. The Class B address space was on its way to being completely exhausted until CIDR was created to replace the classful addressing approach discussed in this section.

Class C Networks

Addresses in Class C networks began with "110." (Note that the position of the first 0 told you the network's class.) The network part was 24 bits long, and the 21 nonreserved bits allowed more than 2 million Class C networks. Unfortunately, these networks could have only 254 hosts apiece, making them almost useless in practice. Such small networks seemed reasonable when the IP standard was created, because users worked at mainframe computers or at least minicomputers. Even a few of these large machines would be able to serve hundreds or thousands of terminal users. Once PCs became hosts, however, the limit of 254 hosts became highly restrictive.

Class D Addresses

Class A, B, and C addresses were created to designate specific hosts on specific networks. However, Class D addresses, which begin with "1110," have a different purpose—namely multicasting. This purpose has survived Classless InterDomain Routing.

When one host places another host's IP address in a packet, the packet will go only to *that one* host. This is called **unicasting**. In contrast, when a host places an all-1s address in the host part, then the IP packet should be **broadcast** to *all* hosts on that subnet.

However, what if only *some* hosts should receive the message? For instance, as discussed earlier, when OSPF routers transmit to one another, they want only other OSPF routers to process the message. To support this limitation, they place the IP address 224.0.0.5 in the IP destination address fields of the packets they send. All OSPF routers listen for this IP address and accept packets with this address in their IP destination address fields. This is **multicasting**, that is, *one-to-many* communication. Multicasting is more efficient than broadcasting because not all stations are interrupted. Only routers stop to process the OSPF message.

Class E Addresses

A fifth class of IP addresses was reserved for future use, but these Class E addresses were never defined.

Mobile IP

The proliferation of notebooks and other portable computers has brought increasing pressure on companies to support mobile users. Chapter 5 discusses wireless LANs as a way to provide such support.

Mobile users on the Internet also need support. The IETF is developing a set of standards collectively known as **mobile IP**. These standards will allow a mobile computer to register with any nearby ISP or LAN access point. The standards will establish a connection between a computer's temporary IP address at the site and the computer's permanent "home" IP address. Mobile IP standards will allow portable computer users to travel without losing access to e-mail, files on file servers, and other resources.

Mobile IP will also offer strong security, based in the IPsec standards discussed in Chapter 7.

REVIEW QUESTIONS

Multiplexing

1. a) How does a receiving internet layer process decide what process should receive the data in the data field of an IP packet? b) How does TCP decide? c) How does UDP decide? d) How does PPP decide?

More on TCP

2. A TCP segment begins with octet 8,658 and ends with octet 12,783. a) What number does the sending host put in the sequence number field? b) What number does the receiving host put in the acknowledgement number field of the TCP segment that acknowledges this TCP segment?

3. A TCP segment carries data octets 456 through 980. The following TCP segment is a supervisory segment carrying no data. What value is in the sequence number field of the latter TCP segment?

4. Describe flow control in TCP.

5. a) In TCP fragmentation, what is fragmented? b) What device does the fragmentation? c) What device does reassembly?

6. A transport process announces an MSS of 1,024. If there are no IP or TCP options, how big can IP packets be?

Mask Operations

7. There is a mask 1010. There is a number 1100. What is the result of masking the number?

8. The following router forwarding table entry has the prefix /14.

10101010 10100000 00000000 00000000 (170.160.0.0)

a) Does it match the following destination address in an arriving IP packet? Explain. b) 10101010 10101011 11111111 00000000 (170.171.255.0)

IP Version 6

9. a) What is the main benefit of IPv6? b) What other benefits were mentioned?

10. a) Express the following in hexadecimal: 0000000111110010. (Hint: Chapter 5 has a conversion table.) b) Simplify: A173:0000:0000:0000:23B7:0000:CD12:A84B

IP Fragmentation

11. a) What happens when an IP packet reaches a subnet whose MTU is *longer* than the IP packet? b) What happens when an IP packet reaches a subnet whose MTU is *shorter* than the IP packet? c) Can fragmentation happen more than once as an IP packet travels to its destination host?

12. Compare TCP fragmentation and IP fragmentation in terms of
a) what is fragmented and b) where the fragmentation takes place.

13. a) What program on what computer does reassembly if IP packets are fragmented? b) How does it know which IP packets are fragments of the same original IP packet? c) How does it know their correct order?

Dynamic Routing Protocols

14. a) What is an autonomous system? b) Within an autonomous system, can the organization choose routing protocols? c) Can it select the routing protocol its border router uses to communicate with the outside world?

15. Compare RIP, OSPF, and BGP along each of the dimensions shown in Figure A-14.

Address Resolution Protocol (ARP)

16. A host wishes to send an IP packet to a router on its subnet. It knows the router's IP address.
a) What else must it know? b) Why must it know it? c) How will it discover the piece of information it seeks? (Note: Routers are not alone in being able to use ARP.)

17. a) What is the destination MAC address of an Ethernet frame carrying an ARP request message? b) What is the destination MAC address of an Ethernet frame carrying an ARP response packet?

Classful IP Addressing

18. Compare classful addressing and CIDR.

19. What class of network is each of the following?
    a) 10101010111111110000000010101010 b) 00110011000000001111111101010101
    c) 11001100111111110000000010101010

20. a) Why is multicasting good? b) How did classful addressing support it?

Mobile IP

21. How will mobile IP work?

PROJECT

Getting Current. Go to the book website's New Information and Errors pages for this chapter to get new information since this book went to press and to correct any errors in the text.

More on Modulation

MODULATION

As we saw in Chapter 7, modems use modulation to convert digital computer signals into analog signals that can travel over the local loop to the first switching office. This module looks at the main forms of modulation in use today.

Frequency Modulation

As we saw in Chapter 7, modulation essentially transforms zeros and ones into electromagnetic signals that can travel down telephone wires. Electromagnetic signals consist of waves. As we saw in Chapter 5, waves have frequency, measured in hertz (cycles per second). Figure B-1 illustrates **frequency modulation**, in which one **frequency** is chosen to represent a 1 and another frequency is chosen to represent a 0. During a clock cycle in which a 1 is sent, the frequency chosen for the 1 is sent. During a clock cycle in which a 0 is sent, the frequency chosen for the 0 is sent.

Amplitude Modulation

In wave transmission, amplitude is the intensity in the wave. In **amplitude modulation**, which we saw in Chapter 7, we represent ones and zeros as different amplitudes. For instance, we can represent a 1 by a high-amplitude (loud) signal and a 0 by a low-amplitude (soft) signal. To send "1011," we would send a loud signal for the first time period, a soft signal for the second, and high-amplitude signals for the third and fourth time periods.

Phase Modulation

The last major characteristic of waves is phase. As shown in Figure B-2, we call 0 degrees phase the point of the wave at 0 amplitude and rising. The wave hits its maximum at 90 degrees, returns to 0 on the decline at 180 degrees, and hits its minimum amplitude at 270 degrees. Amplitude now increases to 360 degrees, which is the same as 0 degrees.

In **phase modulation** we use two waves. We let one wave be our reference wave or carrier wave. Let us use this carrier wave to represent a 1. Then we can use a wave 180 degrees out of phase to represent a 0. So if our carrier wave is at 180 degrees, the other wave will be at zero degrees, and if our carrier wave is at 270 degrees, the other wave will be at 90 degrees.

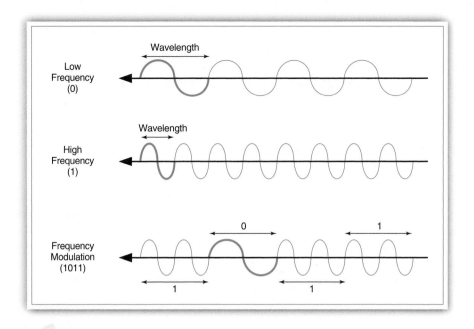

Figure B-1   Frequency Modulation

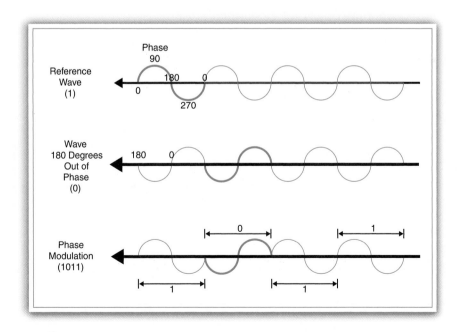

Figure B-2   Phase Modulation

The figure shows that to send "1011," we send the reference wave for the first clock cycle, shift the phase 180 degrees for the second, and return to the reference wave for the third and fourth clock cycles. Although this makes little sense in terms of hearing, it is easy for electronic equipment to deal with phase differences.

A number of transmission systems use **quadrature phase shift keying (QPSK)**, which is phase modulation with four states (phases). Each of the four states represents two bits (00, 01, 10, and 11), so QPSK's bit rate is double its baud rate.

Quadrature Amplitude Modulation (QAM)

Telephone modems and many ADSL and cable modems today use a more complex type of modulation called **quadrature amplitude modulation (QAM)**. As Figure B-3 illustrates, QAM uses two carrier waves: a sine carrier wave and a cosine carrier wave. When the cosine wave is at the top of its cycle, the sine wave is just beginning its cycle and will not hit its peak until 90 degrees. The sine wave is 90 degrees out of phase with the cosine wave. This is a quarter of a cycle, and this fact gives rise to the name "quadrature."

The receiver can send different signals on these two waves because they have different phases so the receiver can distinguish between them. Specifically, QAM uses multiple possible amplitude levels for each carrier wave. To illustrate what this means, consider that using four possible amplitudes for the sine wave times four possible amplitudes on the cosine wave will give 16 possible states. Sixteen possibilities can

Figure B-3   Quadrature Amplitude Modulation (QAM)

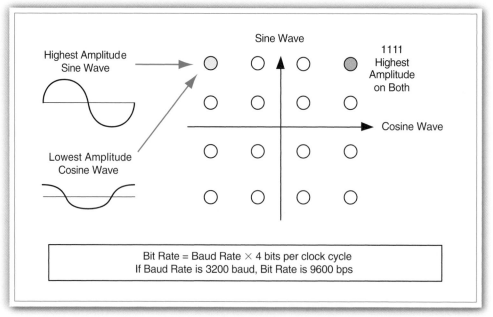

represent four bits (24 = 16). Accordingly, each clock cycle can represent a 4-bit value from 0000 through 1111. In summary, each clock cycle transmits four bits if there are four possible amplitude levels.

Different versions of QAM use different numbers of amplitude levels. Each doubling in the number of amplitude levels quadruples the number of possible states. Each quadrupling of the number of possible states allows two more bits to be sent per clock cycle. However, beyond about sixty-four possible states, the states are so close together that even slight transmission impairments can cause errors.

REVIEW QUESTIONS

1. Describe frequency modulation.
2. a) Describe phase modulation. b) Describe QPSK.
3. a) What two forms of modulation does QAM use? b) In QAM, if you have four possible amplitudes, how many states do you have? c) In QAM, if you have eight possible amplitudes, how many states do you have? d) How many bits can you send per clock cycle?

PROJECT

Getting Current

Go to the book website's New Information and Errors pages for this chapter to get new information since this book went to press and to correct any errors in the text.

More on Telecommunications

INTRODUCTION

Chapter 6 discussed telecommunications, which is the transmission of voice and video. This module is designed for courses that want to get into more detail on telecommunications.

This module is designed to be read after Chapter 6, and it is better to read it after Chapter 7, which discusses leased lines in some detail. The material is not intended to be read front-to-back like a normal chapter. Rather, it is a collection of technical topics, service topics, and regulatory topics:

➤ The PSTN Transport Core and Signaling
➤ Communication Satellites
➤ Wiring in the First Bank of Paradise Headquarters Building
➤ PBX Services
➤ Carrier Services and Pricing
➤ Telephone Carriers and Regulation

THE PSTN TRANSPORT CORE AND SIGNALING

Recall from Chapter 6 that *transport* is the actual transmission of voice in the PSTN, while *signaling* is the control of the PSTN. In this section, we will look at PSTN transport and signaling in more detail.

The Transport Core

Figure C-1 illustrates that the PSTN transport core consists of switches and trunk line connections that link the switches. The PSTN transport core uses two types of transmission systems to connect telephone switches: TDM trunk lines and ATM packet-switched networks.

Time Division Multiplexing (TDM) Lines

In Chapter 6, we saw the concepts of leased lines, which provide high-speed, always-on connections between corporate sites. In Chapter 7, we saw that leased lines are offered over a wide range of speeds and that the most popular leased lines are T1/E1/J1 and fractional T1/E1/J1.

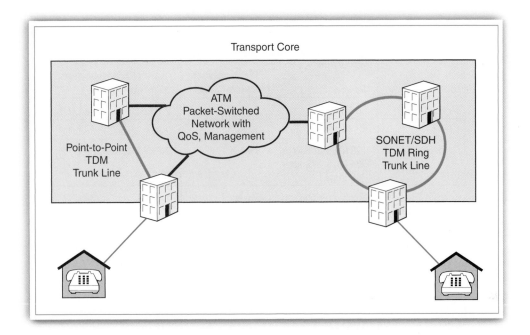

Transport Core

ATM
Packet-Switched
Network with
QoS, Management

Point-to-Point
TDM
Trunk Line

SONET/SDH
TDM Ring
Trunk Line

Figure C-1   TDM and ATM Switch Connections in the PSTN Transport Core

Multiplexing Simultaneous Voice Calls on Leased Lines

Figure C-2 shows the variety of leased lines available to corporations. Most of the columns in this figure also appeared in Chapter 7. However, Figure C-2 has an additional column: multiplexed telephone calls. In telecommunications, the most common use of leased lines is to multiplex many leased lines over a single connection. For example, the figure shows that T1 lines were created to multiplex 24 simultaneous voice calls. Higher-speed leased lines can multiplex hundreds or thousands of telephone calls.

The Time Division Multiplexing (TDM) Process

To implement multiplexing, leased lines use a process called **time division multiplexing (TDM)**, which Figure C-3 illustrates. The figure specifically illustrates time division multiplexing for T1 leased lines.

Frames   First, each second is divided into brief periods of time called **frames**. For example, in a T1 leased line, each second is divided into 8,000 frames. If you have read the box on codec operation in Chapter 6, you learned that the human voice is sampled 8,000 times per second in pulse code modulation. One voice sample is transmitted in a frame for every circuit the frame multiplexes.

Slots   Second, each frame is divided into even briefer periods, called **slots**. In a T1 leased line, for instance, there are 24 frames per slot. In TDM, a circuit is given the same slot in each frame. Each slot transmits eight bits—a single voice sample for that circuit.

North American Digital Hierarchy

Line	Speed	Multiplexed Voice Calls	Typical Transmission Medium
56 kbps	56 kbps	1	2-Pair Data-Grade UTP
T1	1.544 Mbps	24	2-Pair Data-Grade UTP
Fractional T1	128 kbps, 256 kbps, 384 kbps, 512 kbps, 768 kbps	Varies	2-Pair Data-Grade UTP
Bonded T1s (multiple T1s acting as a single line)	Small multiples of 1.544 Mbps	Varies	2-Pair Data-Grade UTP
T3	44.736 Mbps	672	Optical Fiber

CEPT Hierarchy

Line	Speed	Multiplexed Voice Calls	Typical Transmission Medium
64 kbps	64 kbps	1	2-Pair Data-Grade UTP
E1	2.048 Mbps	30	2-Pair Data-Grade UTP
E3	34.368 Mbps	480	Optical Fiber

SONET/SDH Speeds

Line	Speed (Mbps)	Multiplexed Voice Calls	Typical Transmission Medium
OC3/STM1	155.52	2,016	Optical Fiber
OS12/STM4	622.08	6,048	Optical Fiber
OC48/STM16	2,488.32	18,144	Optical Fiber
OC192/STM64	9,953.28	54,432	Optical Fiber
OC768/STM256	39,813.12	163,296	Optical Fiber

Figure C-2   Leased Lines and Multiplexing

Reserved Capacity   Slot capacity is reserved in each frame. In Figure C-4, Circuit A is given Slot 1 in every frame. Note that Circuit A uses its slot capacity in every frame shown in the figure. However, Circuit B uses only some of its slot capacity in the three frames, and Circuit C uses none at all. Although TDM provides the reserved capacity

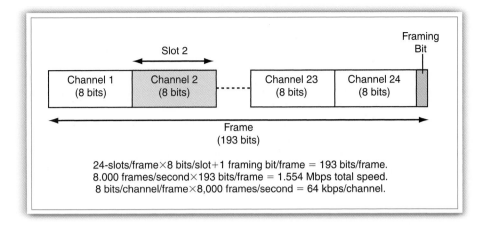

Figure C-3   Time Division Multiplexing (TDM) in a T1 Line

required for circuit switching, it wastes unused capacity. Users must pay for this reserved capacity whether they use it or not.

TEST YOUR UNDERSTANDING

1. a) How many simultaneous voice calls can a T3 line multiplex? b) Explain frames and slots in time division multiplexing (TDM). c) How is a circuit allocated capacity on a TDM line? d) What is the advantage of TDM? e) What is the disadvantage?

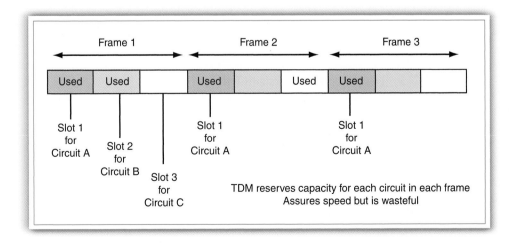

Figure C-4   Reserved Capacity in Time Division Multiplexing (TDM)

Leased Lines and Trunk Lines

As Figure C-5 shows, leased lines are circuits that pass through multiple telephone switches and trunk lines.

The figure shows that trunk lines between switches have the same designations as leased line circuits (T1, T3, etc.). With a T1 circuit, the local loop access lines are T1 lines, of course. Between switches, however, faster trunk lines are needed to carry multiple single calls, T1 circuits, and other circuits.

This identical labeling for circuits and trunk lines is not accidental. TDM trunk lines were first used in the 1960s to allow telephone companies to multiplex individual telephone calls on trunk lines between switches. Only later were end-to-end high-speed circuits offered to customers.

Point-to-Point TDM Trunk Lines

Figure C-1 shows that there are two types of TDM trunk lines. The earliest trunk lines (through T3/E3) were point-to-point trunk lines that connected pairs of switches. Unfortunately, if a trunk line is accidentally dug up and broken in an unrelated construction project, it can take hours or even days for the telephone company to be able to restore service. This is not a theoretical concern. *Most* telephone outages are due to the accidental cutting of trunk lines by construction vehicles.

SONET/SDH Rings

Chapter 4a showed that ring topologies bring reliability. Rings are really dual-rings. If there is a broken connection between two switches, the ring is wrapped, and service continues. Disruptions from broken connections in ring topologies are only momentary.

The SONET/SDH multiplexing technology is designed to use a ring topology, as Figure C-1 illustrates. Although it can be used for point-to-point connections, ring implementations are highly preferred because of their reliability. Figure C-6 illustrates a SONET/SDH ring.

Figure C-5   Leased Line Circuits and Trunk Lines

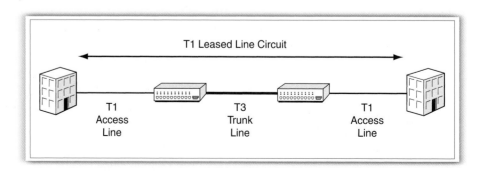

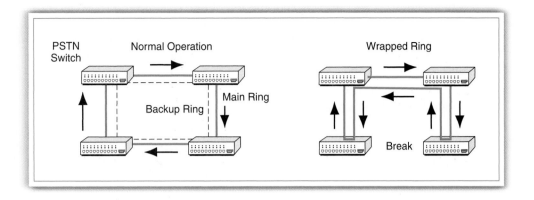

Figure C-6   SONET/SDH Dual Ring

TEST YOUR UNDERSTANDING

2. a) What is the relationship between leased line circuits and trunk lines? b) Below about what speed are trunk lines point-to-point lines? c) What topology are SONET/SDH lines designed to use? d) What is the advantage of this topology? e) What does a SONET/SDH network do when there is a break in a line between switches?

Asynchronous Transfer Mode (ATM) Transport

Although TDM has long been synonymous with transmission in the PSTN transport core, many long-distance carriers have already transitioned much of their transmission technology between telephone switches in their transport cores to a *packet-switched* technology, **asynchronous transfer mode (ATM)**.[1]

ATM has had a checkered history. It was originally created precisely to replace TDM connections in the PSTN transport core and their wasted reserved capacity with more efficient packet switching. For a time, ATM was touted as both the LAN and PSDN technology for the future. However, ATM's high cost worked against it in those markets. As noted in Chapter 4, Ethernet now dominates LAN service. Among the public switched data networks discussed in Chapter 7, Frame Relay has dominated to date because most companies do not require the high speeds of ATM public switched data networks. For the future, less expensive metropolitan area Ethernet promises to be a strong competitor for ATM in the high-speed PSDN market.

However, ATM's expensive complexity, which has stymied it in the LAN and PSDN WAN markets, is critical to its role in the PSTN transport core. First, much of ATM's complexity comes from its ability to provide very strict quality-of-service guarantees for telephone communication and video transmission. The PSTN can only use transport core technologies that guarantee excellent voice quality.

---

[1] Franklin D. Ohrtman, Jr., *Softswitch Architecture for VoIP*, New York: McGraw-Hill, 2003.

In addition, large networks like the telephone system require excellent management tools. ATM, which was created as a transport core protocol for the entire telephone network, has excellent management tools. In LANs and carrier public switched data networks, these management tools are overkill. In the PSTN core, they are perfect.

TEST YOUR UNDERSTANDING

3. a) How is ATM different from previous trunk line technologies? b) Why is ATM good for voice? c) Why is ATM ideal for use in the transport core of telecommunications carriers?

Signaling

As discussed in Chapter 6, signaling is the supervision of connections in the PSTN. The ITU-T created **Signaling System 7 (SS7)** as the worldwide standard for supervisory signaling (setting up circuits, maintaining them, tearing them down after a conversation, providing billing information, and providing special services such as three-party calling). The U.S. version of the protocol is ANSI SS7, usually referred to simply as **SS7**. The ETSI version for Europe is called ETSI C7 or **C7**. They are almost the same, so simple gateways can convert between them and allow them to interoperate.

SS7/C7 actually is a packet-switched technology that operates in parallel with the circuit-switched PSTN but that uses the same transmission lines as the PSTN. SS7/C7 relies on multiple databases of customer information. When a call is set up, the originating telephone carrier queries one of these databases to determine routing information for setting up the service. These databases are also needed to provide advanced services such as toll-free numbers.

TEST YOUR UNDERSTANDING

4. a) What is the worldwide signaling system for telephony? b) Distinguish between SS7 and C7. c) Does having two versions of the standard cause major problems?

COMMUNICATION SATELLITES

During the 1970s, satellites began to be widely used for trunk line transmission within the telephone network. This created sharp drops in long-distance rates. However, as we will see, satellites have proven to be problematic for telephone calling and even more problematic for data transmission.

Microwave Transmission

Satellite transmission technology grew out of microwave transmission technology. As Figure C-8 shows, **microwave** transmission is a point-to-point radio technology using dish antennas. As a consequence of the curvature of the earth, microwave signals cannot travel farther than a few miles. Consequently, transmission often uses **microwave repeaters** between distant sites.

Transport Versus Signaling

Transport is the transmission of voice conversations between customers

Signaling is the supervision of transport connections

Call setup, management, and termination

The collection and transmission of billing information

3-party calling, and other advanced services

Signaling System 7 (SS7)

The worldwide standard for PSTN signaling

Slight differences exist in the U.S. and Europe

U.S.: Signaling System 7

Europe: C7

Interconnected with a simple gateway

Packet-Switched Technology

Not circuit-switched

Runs over telephone company lines

Uses a distributed database

Data for supervising calls

Call setup, etc.: requires the querying of the nearest database

Toll-free numbers, etc.

Figure C-7 Signaling (Study Figure)

Before optical fiber became widespread, microwave transmission was used very heavily for long-distance trunk lines between telephone switches. As we saw in Chapter 6, microwave transmission uses frequency division multiplexing, carrying different telephone calls in different channels.

Satellite Transmission

After World War II, a young radar operator named Arthur C. Clarke (yes, the science fiction writer) noticed how microwave repeaters often sit on hills so that they can carry signals farther. He realized that it was possible to put a microwave repeater in the sky on a satellite and that this would allow transmission over very long distances. As Figure C-9 shows, this became the **communication satellite**.

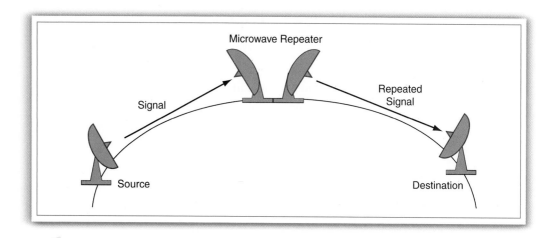

Figure C-8   Microwave Transmission

Communication from the ground to the satellite is called the **uplink**. Normally, this transmission occurs point-to-point between a ground station and the satellite. The uplink ground station has a dish antenna to focus its beam.

However, when a satellite transmits, it transmits its **downlink** signal over a wide area called the satellite's **footprint**. Any ground station in the footprint can receive the satellite's transmissions.

Geosynchronous Earth Orbit (GEO) Satellites

Figure C-9 specifically shows a **geosynchronous earth orbit (GEO)** satellite system. The satellite orbits at roughly 36,000 km (22,300 miles) above the earth. At this height, its orbital time equals the earth's rotation, so the satellite appears to be fixed in the sky. This allows dish antennas to be aimed precisely.

However, 36,000 km is a long way for radio waves to travel. Even with a dish antenna, considerable power is required. Of course, mobile devices cannot use dish antennas.

In the early days of communication satellites, satellites were often used to place voice calls. This created a delay of up to a quarter second. This latency complicated turn taking in conversations. As soon as possible, almost all telephony was moved to optical fiber.

This latency is even worse for data. TCP processes will retransmit segments if they are not acknowledged promptly. On many computers, even a single satellite in the circuit will prompt many unnecessary retransmissions. Furthermore, whenever a TCP process does a retransmission, it reduces the rate at which it transmits subsequent segments. If there are many retransmissions, the rate of transmission will become painfully slow.

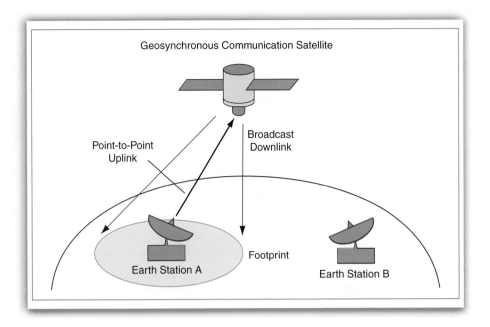

Figure C-9   Geosynchronous Earth Orbit (GEO) Communication Satellite System

Low Earth Orbit (LEO) and Medium Earth Orbit (MEO) Satellites

As Figure C-10 shows, most communication satellites operate at much lower orbits. This means that they only are over a receiver a short time before passing below the horizon. As a result, satellites must hand off service to one another. As one satellite (Satellite A) passes over the horizon, another satellite (Satellite B) will take over a customer's service. The user will not experience any service interruption. This is reminiscent of cellular telephony, except that here the customer remains relatively motionless while the satellite (the equivalent of a cellsite transceiver) moves.

Satellites for mobile users operate in two principle orbits. **Low earth orbit (LEO)** satellites operate at a few hundred kilometers (a few hundred miles) above the earth. **Medium earth orbit (MEO)** satellites, in turn, operate at a few thousand kilometers (a few thousand miles) above the earth.[2] LEOs are closer, so signals do not attenuate as much, allowing receivers to be smaller and lighter. In contrast, MEOs have longer

---

[2]There are two destructive bands of damaging radiation that circle the planet. These are called the Van Allen radiation bands. LEOs are below the lowest Van Allen band. MEOs operate between the Van Allen bands.

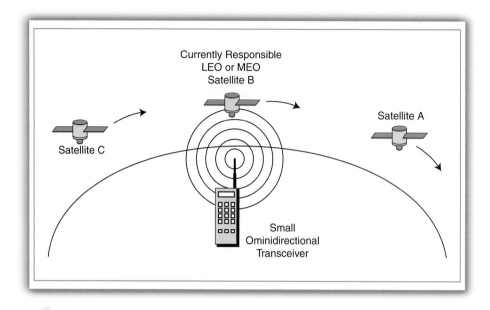

Figure C-10 LEO and MEO Satellite Communication Systems

orbital periods, so they stay in sight longer, reducing the frequency of handoffs and therefore the number of satellites needed to provide continuous service.

VSAT Satellites

During the 1970s at Stanford University, Professor Bruce Lusignan created the idea of using very small satellite dishes for communication. At the time, most satellite dishes were at least 3 meters (10 feet) in diameter. This made them very expensive. Earth stations with small dishes—**very small aperture terminal (VSAT)** earth stations—could allow earth stations to be placed in individual homes. The dishes on VSAT earth stations are 1 meter in diameter to 1 foot in diameter. At first, Lusignan's ideas were rejected by technologists and regulators. Obviously, those objections were overcome, and VSAT earth stations are now common.

VSATs today are used almost exclusively for one-way transmission. Satellite-based television delivery is becoming a very strong competitor for cable television. Some VSATs offer two-way communication. (You see them in newscasts and in films of military operations.) However, one-way delivery is the norm.

TEST YOUR UNDERSTANDING

5. a) Why are microwave repeaters needed? b) Does the uplink or the downlink use point-to-point transmission? c) What is the footprint? d) Which of the following uses dish antennas: GEOs, LEOs, or MEOs? e) Which of the following is good for mobile

Traditional Satellite Systems

    Used very large dishes (3 meters or more)

    Very expensive

VSAT Satellite System

    Very small aperture terminal (VSAT) earth stations

        Use small (1 meter or less) diameter dishes

    Small dishes allow earth stations small and inexpensive enough to be used in homes

    Used primarily in one-way transmission, such as television distribution

    Occasionally used for two-way communication

        News reporting in the field

        Military communication

Figure C-11 VSAT Satellite System (Study Figure)

stations: GEOs, LEOs, or MEOs? f) What are the rough heights of GEO, LEO, and MEO orbits? g) What is a VSAT satellite dish? h) What is the attraction of VSAT technology?

WIRING THE FIRST BANK OF PARADISE HEADQUARTERS BUILDING

Wiring dominates total cost for customer premises equipment. For new buildings, a firm normally hires a contractor to install wiring. Afterwards, the firm has to maintain its wiring systems.

  In this section, we will look at wiring in First Bank of Paradise headquarters building. This is a typical multistory office building. Wiring in other large buildings tends to be similar.

Facilities

Figure C-12 illustrates the building. Although the building is ten stories tall, only three stories (plus the basement) are shown.

Equipment Room

Wiring begins in the **equipment room**, which usually is in the building's basement. This room connects the building to the outside world.

Figure C-12   First Bank of Paradise Building Wiring

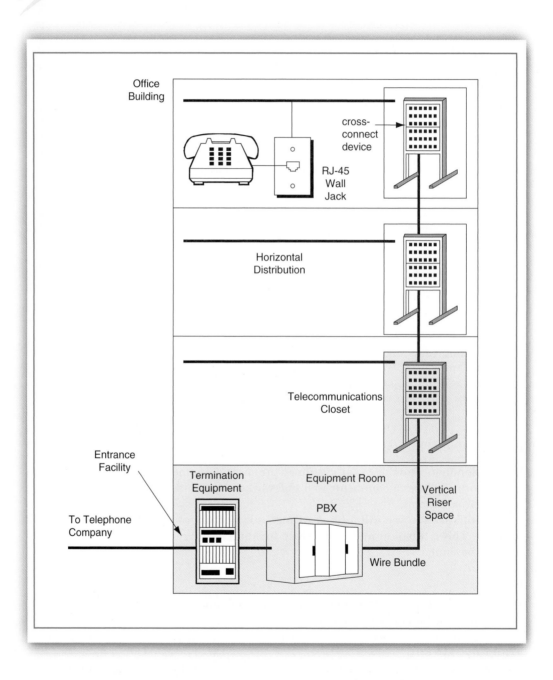

Vertical Risers

From the equipment room, telephone and data cabling has to rise to the building's upper floors. The bank has **vertical riser** spaces between floors. These typically are hard-walled pipes to protect the wiring.

Telecommunications Closets

On each floor above the basement, there is a **telecommunications closet**. Within the telecommunications closet, cords coming up from the basement are connected to cords that span out horizontally to telephones and computers on that floor.

Telephone Wiring

This building infrastructure was created for telephone wiring. Fortunately, most companies allocated ample space to their equipment rooms, vertical risers, and telecommunications closets. This allows data wiring to use the same spaces.

Termination Equipment

In many ways, a building's telephone network acts like an independent company. It can interconnect with the local telephone company and with other carriers. It negotiates contracts with each of them. Carriers require the company to install **termination equipment** at its connection point to the outside world. In effect, the termination equipment is like an electrical fuse; it prevents the company from sending unwanted electrical signals into the carrier's network.

PBX

Many companies have internal telephone switches called **private branch exchanges (PBXs)**. Eight wires must span out from the PBX to each wall outlet in the building. So if the building has ten floors and each floor has 100 RJ-45 telephone wall jacks, 8,000 wires (10 x 100 x 8) will have to be run from the PBX through the vertical riser space. On each floor, the 800 wires for that floor will be organized into 100 4-pair UTP cords running from the telecommunications closet to telephone wall jacks on that floor. Obviously, careful documentation of where each wire goes is crucial to maintaining sanity.

Vertical Wiring

For vertical wiring runs, telephony typically uses **25-pair UTP cords**. These vertical cords typically terminate in **50-pin octopus connectors**.

Horizontal Wiring

The horizontal telephone wiring, as just noted, uses 4-pair UTP. Yes, telephone wiring uses the same 4-pair UTP that data transmission uses. Actually, telephone wiring first introduced 4-pair UTP. Telephony has used 4-pair UTP for several decades.

Data transmission researchers learned how to send data over 4-pair UTP to take advantage of widespread installation expertise for 4-pair UTP. In addition, some companies had excess UTP capacity already installed, so in some cases, it would not even be necessary to install new wiring.

Figure C-12 shows that wires from the telecommunications closet on a floor travel horizontally through the walls or false ceilings. They then terminate in RJ-45 data/voice jacks. Telephones plug into the jacks.

Cross-Connect Device

Within the telecommunications closet, the vertical cords plug into **cross-connect devices**, which connect the wires from the riser space to 4-pair UTP cords that span out to the wall jacks on each floor.

As Figure C-13 shows, the cross connection normally uses patch panels. The figure illustrates patch panels with RJ-45 connectors, which are useful for both voice and data wiring. Patch cords connect eight vertical wires to eight horizontal wires. Patch panels are used because they provide flexibility. If there are changes in the vertical or horizontal wiring, the patch panels are simply reconnected to reflect the changes.

Data Wiring

Figure C-12 illustrates telephone wiring. How is data wiring different? For horizontal communication, there are no differences at all. Both almost always use 4-pair UTP. They are the same precisely because Ethernet was adapted to run over horizontal telephone wiring (albeit a higher grade of telephone wiring).

However, vertical wiring is completely different. Vertical data wiring is much simpler than vertical telephone wiring. In data wiring, only single UTP or optical fiber cord

Figure C-13   Patch Panels

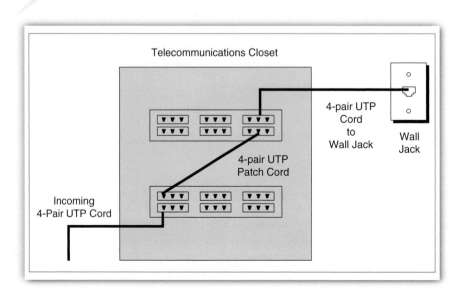

runs from a port in the core switch up to a port in the Ethernet workgroup switch on each floor. In other words, if there are ten floors, only ten UTP or optical fiber cords would have to be run through the vertical riser space. This is vastly simpler than vertical telephone wiring, which must run eight wires vertically for each wall jack on each floor.

Plenum Cabling

Fire regulations require the use of a special type of fire-retardant cabling, called **plenum** cabling, any time cables run through airways (plenums) such as air condition- ing ducts (but *not* false ceilings). Ordinary jackets on UTP and optical fiber cords are made of polyvinyl chloride (PVC), which gives off deadly dioxin when it burns. If these toxins are released in airways, the toxins will spread rapidly to office areas.

TEST YOUR UNDERSTANDING

6. a) What equipment are you likely to find in a building's equipment room? b) In its telecommunications closets? c) What is the purpose of a PBX? d) Compare and contrast vertical wiring distribution for telephony and data. e) Compare and contrast horizontal wiring distribution for telephony and data.

7. A building has ten floors, not counting the equipment room in the basement. Each of the ten floors has 60 voice jacks and 40 data jacks. a) For telephony, how many wires will you run through the vertical riser space for each floor? b) How many 25-pair cords will this require? c) For vertical data wiring if you use 4-pair UTP? d) For vertical data wiring if you use optical fiber? e) On each floor, how many wires will you run horizon- tally from the telecommunications closet to wall jacks? f) How many cords will this require?

8. a) Where is plenum cabling required? b) Why is plenum cabling needed?

PBX SERVICES

Figure C-14 shows that because digital PBXs are essentially computers, they allow ven- dors to differentiate their products by adding application software to provide a wide range of services.

➤ User services are employed directly by ordinary managers, secretaries, and other telephone end users.

➤ Attendant services are employed by telephone operators to help them give service.

➤ Management services are employed by telephone and corporate network managers to manage the company's telephone network.

TEST YOUR UNDERSTANDING

9. a) Into what three categories are PBX services divided? b) List and briefly describe two services in each category.

CARRIER SERVICES AND PRICING

Having discussed technology, we can now turn to the kinds of transmission services that telecommunications staffs can offer their companies. Figure C-15 shows that cor- porate users face a variety of transmission services and pricing options.

Figure C-14   Digital PBX Services

For Users

Speed dialing	Dials a number with a one- or two-digit code.
Last number redial	Redials the last number dialed.
Display of called number	LCD display for number the caller has dialed. Allows caller to see a mistake.
Camp on	If line is busy, hit "camp on" and hang up. When other party is off the line, he or she will be called automatically.
Call waiting	If you are talking to someone, you will be beeped if someone else calls.
Hold	Put someone on hold until he or she can be talked to.
ANI	Automatic number identification: You can see the number of the party calling you.
Conferencing	Allows three or more people to speak together.
Call transfer	Someone calls you. You connect the person to someone else.
Call forwarding	If you will be away from your desk, calls will be transferred to this number.
Voice mail	Callers can leave messages.

For Attendants

Operator	In-house telephone operators can handle problems.
Automatic call distribution	When someone dials in, the call goes to a specific telephone without operator assistance.
Message center	Allows caller to leave a message with a live operator.
Paging	Operator can page someone anywhere in the building.
Nighttime call handling	Special functions for handling nighttime calls, such as forwarding control to a guard station.
Change requests	Can change extensions and other information from a console.

For Management

Automatic route selection	Automatically selects the cheapest way of placing long-distance calls.
Call restriction	Prevents certain stations from placing outgoing or long-distance calls.
Call detail reporting	Provides detailed reports on charges by telephone and by department.

Local Calling

        Flat rate

        Message units

Toll Calls

        Long-distance calling

        Intra-LATA

        Inter-LATA

Toll-Call Pricing

        Direct distance dialing

                Base case for comparison

        Toll-Free numbers

                Free to caller but called party pays

                Called party: pays less than direct distance dialing rates

                In U.S., 800, 888, etc.

        WATS

                Wide Area Telephone Service

                For calling out of a site

                Calling party: pays but pays less than with direct distance dialing

        900 numbers

                Caller pays

                Pays more than direct distance dialing rates

                Allows called party to charge for services

Advanced Services

        Caller ID

        Three-party calling (conference calling)

        Call waiting

        Voice mail

Figure C-15   Telephone Services (Study Figure)

Basic Voice Services

The most important telephone service, of course, is its primary one: allowing two people to talk together. Although you get roughly the same service whether you call a nearby building or another country, billing varies widely between local and long-distance calling. Even within these categories, furthermore, there are important pricing variations.

Local Calling

Most telephone calls are made between parties within a few kilometers of each other. There are two major billing schemes for such **local calling**.

➤ Some telephone companies offer **flat-rate** local service in which there is a fixed monthly service charge but no separate fee for individual local calls.

➤ In some areas, however, carriers charge **message units** for some or all local calls. The number of message units they charge for a call depends on both the distance and duration of the call.

Economists like message units, arguing that message units are more efficient in allocating resources than flat-rate plans. Subscribers, in contrast, dislike message units even if their flat-rate bill would have come out the same.

Long-Distance Toll Calls

Although pricing for local calling varies from place to place, all **long-distance** calls are **toll calls**. The cost of the call depends on distance and duration.

Direct Distance Dialing   The simplest form of long-distance pricing is **direct distance dialing**, in which you place a call without any special deals. You will pay a few cents per minute for directly dialed calls. Direct distance dialing is a base case against which other pricing schemes can be measured.

Toll-Free Numbers   Companies that are large enough can receive favorable rates from transmission companies for long-distance calls. With **toll-free numbers**, anyone can call *into* a company, usually without being charged. To provide free inward dialing, companies pay a carrier a per-minute rate lower than the rate for directly dialed calls. Initially, only numbers with the 800 area code provided such services in the United States. Now that 800 area codes have been exhausted, the 888, 877, 866, and 855 area codes are offering the same service to new customers.

WATS   In contrast to inbound toll-free number service, **wide area telephone service (WATS)** allows a company to place *outgoing* long-distance calls at per-minute prices lower than those of directly dialed calls. WATS prices depend on the size of the service area. WATS is often available for both intrastate and interstate calling. WATS can also be purchased for a region of the country instead of the entire country.

900 Numbers   Related to toll-free, **900 numbers** allow customers to call into a company. Unlike toll-free number calls, which usually are free to the caller, calls to 900 numbers require the caller to pay a fee—one that is much *higher* than that of a toll call. Some of the fee goes to the carrier, but most of it goes to the subscriber being called.

This allows companies to charge for information, technical support, and other services. For instance, customer calls for technical service might cost $20 to $50 per hour. Charges for 900 numbers usually appear on the customer's regular monthly bill from the local exchange carrier (LEC). Although the use of 900 numbers for sexually oriented services has given 900 numbers a bad name, they are valuable for legitimate business use.

Advanced Services

Although telephony's basic function as a two-person "voice pipe" is important, telephone carriers offer other services to attract customers and to get more revenues from existing customers.

Caller ID

In **caller ID**, the telephone number of the party calling you is displayed on your phone's small display screen before you pick up the handset. This allows you to screen calls, picking up only the calls you want to receive. Callers can block caller ID, so that you cannot see their numbers. However, you can have your carrier reject calls with blocked IDs. Businesses like caller ID because it can be linked to a computer database to pull up information about the caller on the receiver's desktop computer screen.

Three-Party Calling (Conference Calling)

Nearly every teenager knows how to make **three-party calls**, in which more than the traditional two people can take part in a conversation. However, businesses tend to use this feature only sparingly, despite its obvious advantage. This is sometimes called **conference calling**.

Call Waiting

Another popular service is **call waiting**. If you are having a conversation and someone calls you, you will hear a distinctive tone. You can place your original caller on hold, shift briefly to the new caller, and then switch back to your original caller.

Voice Mail

Finally, **voice mail** allows people to leave messages if you do not answer your phone.

TEST YOUR UNDERSTANDING

10. Create a table to compare and contrast direct distance dialing, toll-free numbers, 900 numbers, and WATS, in terms of whether the caller or the called party pays and the cost compared with the cost of a directly dialed long-distance call.

11. Describe the two pricing options for local calls.

12. a) What is the advantage of toll-free numbers for customers? b) For companies that provide toll-free number service to their customers?

13. a) Name the four advanced telephone services listed in the text. b) Name and briefly describe two advanced services not listed in the text.

TELEPHONE CARRIERS AND REGULATION

Once, almost every nation had a single national telephone carrier. However, the situation has become more complex over time as nations have begun to deregulate telephone service—that is, to permit some competition in order to reduce prices and promote product innovation.

Figure C-16   Telephone Carriers (Study Figure)

In Most Countries

Public Telephone and Telegraph (PTT) authorities

Traditionally had a domestic monopoly over telephone service

Ministries of Communication

Government agency to regulate the PTT

Competitors

Deregulation has allowed competition in domestic telephone service in most countries

The Ministry of Telecommunication regulates these new competitors too

In the United States

AT&T (the Bell System) developed a long-distance monopoly

Also owned most local operating companies

AT&T was broken up in the 1980s

AT&T retained the name and the (initially) lucrative long-distance business

Local operations were assigned to seven Regional Bell Operating Companies (RBOCs)

Later, RBOCs combined with one another and with GTE to form four supercarriers

Eventually, competition in long-distance service made AT&T unprofitable

In 2005, one of the four supercarriers (SBC Communications) merged with AT&T and used the AT&T name for the merged company.

Regulation

Federal Communications Commission (FCC) regulates interstate communication and aspects of intrastate communication that affect national commerce

Within each state, a Public Utilities Commission (PUC) regulates telephone service subject to FCC regulations

Competition helps corporate customers because telephone prices generally fall as a result of competition. However, to maximize cost savings, companies have to be very smart when they deal with telephone carriers. To do this, a first step is understanding the types of carriers a company will face.

PTTs and Ministries of Telecommunications

In most countries the other than United States, the single monopoly carrier was historically called the **Public Telephone and Telegraph authority (PTT)**. In the United Kingdom, for example, this was British Telecom, while in Ireland it was Eircom. The PTT had a monopoly on **domestic** telephony—that is, telephony within the country.

To counterbalance the power of the PTT, governments created regulatory bodies generally called **Ministries of Telecommunications**. PTTs provide service, while Ministries of Telecommunications oversee the PTTs. As we will see later, over time, the PTTs gradually lost their monopoly status, and ministries of telecommunications now find themselves regulating both the traditional PTT and its new competitors.

TEST YOUR UNDERSTANDING

14. a) Do all countries have PTTs? Explain. b) What is a monopoly over domestic telephone service? c) What are the purposes of PTTs and Ministries of Telecommunications?

AT&T, the FCC, and PUCs

The Bell System

In the United States, neither telegraphy nor telephony was made a statutory monopoly.[3] However, telephony quickly became a de facto monopoly when **AT&T**, also known as the **Bell System**, used predatory practices to drive most other competitors out of business. AT&T soon had a complete long-distance monopoly. For local service, AT&T owned more than 80 percent of all local telephone companies, although when it was developing in the nineteenth century and early twentieth century, it bypassed "unpromising" areas such as Hawai'i and most of Los Angeles.

The RBOCs

In the 1980s, AT&T was broken up into a long-distance and manufacturing company that retained the AT&T name and seven **Regional Bell Operating Companies (RBOCs)** that owned most local telephone companies.

Later, mergers among the RBOCs and GTE, which was the largest independent owner of local operating companies, produced four dominant owners of local operating companies in the United States—Verizon, SBC Communications, BellSouth, and Qwest. These four companies also provide long-distance service in some areas.

---

[3]Samuel F.B. Morse, who invented the telegraph, tried to sell his invention to the U.S. Post Office, but the government rejected it. In other countries, postal services, which had traditionally enjoyed a monopoly over mail delivery, were also given monopolies over telegraphy and later telephony. In fact, "PTT" originally stood for "*Postal* Telephone and Telegraph." Over time, companies separated mail and electronic communication, and *Postal* became *Public*. Now that the telegraph system no longer exists in most countries, perhaps a contest is needed for one of the Ts.

At the time of the breakup, AT&T was considered the jewel in the Bell System. However, after quite a few years of high profitability, AT&T began to suffer heavily from long-distance competition. In 2005, in a stroke of irony, SBC merged with ailing AT&T. The combined company took on the name AT&T.

Regulation: The FCC and PUCs

In the United States, the **Federal Communication Commission (FCC)** provides overall regulation for U.S. carriers. However, within individual states, **Public Utilities Commissions (PUCs)** regulate pricing and services.

TEST YOUR UNDERSTANDING

15. a) Distinguish between the traditional roles of AT&T and the RBOCs. b) Distinguish between the traditional roles of the FCC and PUCs in the United States.

Deregulation

Although telephone carriers had a complete monopoly in the early years, governments began deregulating telephone service in the 1970s. **Deregulation** is the opening of telephone services to competition; it has the potential to reduce costs considerably.

Deregulation Around the World

As noted earlier, most countries have deregulated at least some of the services offered by the traditional monopoly PTT. This has given companies many more choices for telephone services, and competition has resulted in lower prices.

Carriers in the United States

LATAs   Figure C-18 shows the types of carriers that exist in the United States. Since the breakup of AT&T in 1984, the United States has divided into approximately 200 service regions called **local access and transport areas (LATAs)**.

ILECs and CLECs   Within each LATA, **local exchange carriers (LECs)** provide access and transport (transmission service). The traditional monopoly telephone company is called the **incumbent local exchange carrier (ILEC)**. Competitors are called **competitive local exchange carriers (CLECs)**.

LATAs are geographical regions. ILECs and CLECs are carriers that provide access and transport within LATAs.

IXCs   In contrast, **interexchange carriers (IXCs)** carry voice traffic *between* LATAs. Major ILECs are AT&T, MCI, and Sprint.

Long-Distance Calling   One point of common confusion is that the distinction between local and long distance calling is not the same as the distinction between LEC

Figure C-17 Deregulation (Study Figure)

Deregulation

> Deregulation decreases or removes monopoly over telephone service
>
> This creates competition, which lowers prices
>
> In most companies, deregulation began in the 1970s

Deregulation Around the World

> At least some PTT services have been deregulated

Carriers in the United States

> The United States is divided into regions called local access and transport areas (LATAs)
>
> Within each LATA:
>
> > Local exchange carriers (LECs) provide intra-LATA service
> >
> > Traditional incumbent local exchange carrier (ILECs)
> >
> > New competitive local exchange carriers (CLECs)
>
> Interexchange carriers (IXCs) provide transport between LATAs
>
> Long-distance service
>
> > Long-distance service within LATAs is supplied by LECs
> >
> > Long-distance service between LATAs is supplied by IXCs
>
> Within each LATA, one or more points of presence (POP) interconnects different carriers

Internationally

> International common carriers (ICCs) provide service between countries

Degree of Deregulation

> Customer premises equipment is almost completely deregulated
>
> Long-distance and international telephony are heavily deregulated
>
> Local telephone service is the least deregulated
>
> > The traditional monopoly carriers have largely maintained their telephone monopolies
> >
> > Cellular service has provided local competition, with many people not having a wired phone
> >
> > Voice over IP (VoIP) is providing strong competition via ISPs, cable television companies, and a growing number of other wired and wireless access technologies

VoIP Regulation

> Countries are struggling with the question of how to regulate VoIP carriers
>
> Should they be taxed?
>
> Should they be required to provide 911 service, including location determination?
>
> Should they be required to provide wiretaps to government agencies?

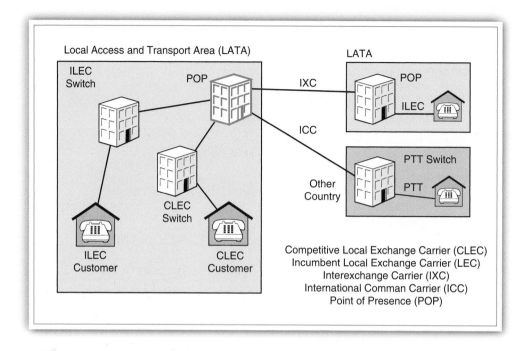

Figure C-18 Telephone Carriers in the United States

and IXC service. Most LATAs are quite large; within LATAs, there is both local and long-distance calling. Adding to the confusion, intra-LATA long distance calling rates sometimes are higher than inter-LATA calling rates.

Within LATAs, there is both local and long-distance calling.

ICCs   ILECs, CLECs, and IXCs are **domestic** carriers that provide service within the United States. Similarly, PTTs provide domestic service within their own countries. In contrast, **international common carriers (ICCs)** provide service *between* countries.

Points of Presence (POPs)   As Figure C-18 shows, the various carriers that provide service are interconnected at **points of presence (POPs)**. Thanks to points of presence, any subscriber to any CLEC or ILEC in one LATA can reach customers of any other CLEC or ILEC in any other LATA. ICCs also link to domestic carriers at POPs.

Deregulation by Service
Customer Premises Equipment   Although it seems odd today, telephone companies used to own all of the wires and telephones in homes and businesses. Today,

however, nearly all countries *prohibit* carriers from owning customer premises equipment. Deregulation for customer premises equipment, in other words, is total in most countries.

Long-Distance and International Calling   In most countries, both long-distance and international telephone services have been heavily deregulated.

Local Telephone Service   Local telephone service is the least deregulated aspect of telephony. The need for large investments in access systems and regulatory reluctance to open local telephone service completely (for fear of losing currently subsidized service for the poor and rural customers) have combined to limit local telephone competition.

Some countries now require the traditional monopoly carrier to open its access systems and central offices to competitors for a "reasonable" fee. However, court delays and high "reasonable" fees have limited the effectiveness of this facility-sharing approach.

Overall, traditional monopoly telephone carriers have largely maintained their monopoly over wired telephone service. However, competition is coming through other technologies. Many people now have only a cellular telephone, and cellular service often is provided by a competitor of the traditional monopoly wireline carrier. In addition, voice over IP (VoIP) is providing competition via ISPs, cable television companies, and a growing number of other wired and wireless Internet access technologies.

Voice over IP

Now that voice over IP (VoIP) is becoming popular, countries are trying to determine how to regulate this new service. Traditional carriers point out that VoIP carriers are exempt from many of the taxes that traditional carriers are required to pay. Countries also are attempting to enforce laws requiring calls to emergency numbers (911 in the United States) to give physical location information in case the caller cannot speak. In addition, the U.S. government wants VoIP carriers to provide tools to allow the government to create legal wiretaps.

TEST YOUR UNDERSTANDING

16. a) Distinguish between LATAs, ILECs, and CLECs. b) What is the role of IXCs relative to LATAs? c) What carriers handle long-distance calling in the United States? d) What is the role of ICCs? e) Why are POPs important?

17. a) What is deregulation? b) When did deregulation begin? c) How complete is deregulation for customer premises equipment? d) For long-distance calling? e) For local calling? f) What issues are involved in the regulation of VoIP.

PROJECTS

Getting Current. Go to the book website's New Information and Errors pages for this chapter to get new information since this book went to press and to correct any errors in the text.

Glossary

.NET: Microsoft's approach to the Web services.

1G: See First-Generation.

1-Pair Voice-Grade UTP: The traditional telephone access lines to individual residences.

10/100 Ethernet: A collective name for the Ethernet physical layer 10 Mbps and 100 Mbps standards. NICs and switches marked 10/100 can work with either standard.

10/100/10000 Ethernet: A collective name for the Ethernet physical layer 10 Mbps, 100 Mbps, and 1 Gbps standards. NICs and switches marked 10/100 can work any of these standards.

10Base-F: See 802.3 10Base-F.

10Base-T: See 802.3 10Base-T.

100Base-FX: The Ethernet physical layer 100 Mbps standard used primarily to connect switches to other switches, now being phased out.

100Base-TX: The dominant Ethernet physical layer 100 Mbps standard brought to desktop computers today.

1000Base-LX: A fiber version of gigabit Ethernet for long wavelengths (transmitting at 1,300 nm).

1000Base-SX: A fiber version of gigabit Ethernet for short wavelengths (transmitting at 850 nm).

1000Base-T: A UTP version of gigabit Ethernet.

1000Base-x: The Ethernet physical layer technology of gigabit Ethernet, used today mainly to connect switches to switches or switches to routers; increasingly being used to connect servers and some desktop PCs to the switches that serve them.

2G: See Second-Generation.

2-Pair Data-Grade: The higher-quality UTP access lines used by telephone carriers for private lines. Two pairs run out to each customer.

2-Pair Data-Grade UTP: The traditional telephone access line for lower-speed leased lines. (Higher-speed leased lines use optical fiber.)

2.5G: See Second-and-a-Half Generation.

232 Serial Port: The port on a PC that uses two voltage ranges to transmit information.

25-Pair UTP Cord: The cabling used by telephony for vertical wiring that runs within a building.

3DES: See Triple DES.

3G: See Third-Generation.

4-Pair Unshielded Twisted Pair (UTP): The type of wiring typically used in Ethernet networks. 4-pair UTP contains eight copper wires organized as four pairs. Each wire is covered with dielectric insulation, and an outer jacket encloses and protects the four pairs.

50-Pin Octopus Connector: The type of connector in which vertical cords typically terminate.

802 Committee: See 802 LAN/MAN Standards Committee.

802 LAN/MAN Standards Committee: The IEEE committee responsible for Ethernet standards.

802.1D Spanning Tree Protocol: The protocol that addresses both single points of failure and loops.

802.1AE: MAC-layer security standard for supervisory communication between Ethernet switches.

802.1p: The standard that permits up to eight priority levels.

802.1Q: The standard that extended the Ethernet MAC layer frame to include two optional tag fields.

802.1X: Security standard for both wired and wireless LANs.

802.2: The single standard for the logical link control layer in 802 LANs.

802.3 10Base-F: An Ethernet physical layer 10 Mbps fiber standard, now almost entirely extinct.

802.3 10Base-T: The slowest Ethernet physical layer technology in use today; uses 4-pair UTP wiring and operates at 10 Mbps.

802.3ad: Link aggregation protocol standard.

802.3af: Standard for delivering low wattage electricity from a switch to stations.

802.3 MAC Layer Frame: See Ethernet Frame.

802.3 MAC Layer Standard: The standard that defines Ethernet frame organization and NIC and switch operation.

802.3 Working Group: The 802 Committee's working group that creates Ethernet-specific standards.

802.5 Working Group: The 802 Committee's working group that created Token-Ring Network standards.

802.11 WLAN: Wireless LANs that follow the 802.11 standard.

802.11 Working Group: The IEEE working group that creates wireless LAN standards.

802.11a: Version of the 802.11 WLAN standard that has a rated speed of 54 Mbps and operates in the 5 GHz unlicensed radio band.

802.11b: Version of the 802.11 WLAN standard that has a rated speed of 11 Mbps and operates in the 2.4 GHz unlicensed radio band.

802.11g: Version of the 802.11 WLAN standard that has a rated speed of 54 Mbps and operates in the 2.4 GHz unlicensed radio band.

802.11e: A standard for quality of service in 802.11 WLANs.

802.11i: An advanced form of 802.11 wireless LAN security.

802.11n: Version of the 802.11 WLAN standard that uses MIMO to achieve a rated speed of 100 Mbps or more and longer range than earlier speed standards.

802.16: WiMAX. Broadband wireless access standard.

802.16d: WiMAX. Broadband wireless access standard for fixed stations.

802.16e: WiMAX. Broadband wireless access standard for mobile stations.

900 Number: A number that allows customers to call into a company; callers pay a fee that is much higher than that of a regular toll call.

Access Control List (ACL): An ordered list of pass/deny rules for a firewall or other device.

Access Control Plan: A plan for controlling access to a resource.

Access Line: 1) In networks, a transmission line that connects a station to a switch. 2) In telephony, the line used by the customer to reach the PSTN's central transport core.

Access Line: The line used by the customer to reach the PSTN's central transport core.

Access Point: A bridge between a wireless station and a wired LAN.

Access Router: A router to connect a SOHO network to the Internet. Typically includes a switch, DHCP server, NAT, and other functions beyond routing.

Access System: In telephony, the system by which customers access the PSTN, including access lines and termination equipment in the end office at the edge of the transport core.

Account: An identifiable entity that may own resources on a computer.

ACE: See OPNET Application Characterization Environment.

ACK Bit: The bit in a TCP segment that is set to indicate if the segment contains an acknowledgement.

ACK: See Acknowledgement.

Acknowledgement (ACK): 1) An acknowledgement message, sent by the receiver when a message is received correctly. 2) An acknowledgement frame, sent by the receiver whenever a frame is received; used in CSMA/CA+ACK in 802.11.

Acknowledgement Bit: A bit in a TCP header. If the bit is set, then the TCP segment contains an acknowledgement

Acknowledgement Number Field: In TCP, a header field that tells what TCP segment is being acknowledged in a segment.

ACL: See Access Control List.

ADC: See Analog-to-Digital Conversion.

Address Resolution Protocol (ARP): Protocol for address resolution used in Ethernet networks. If a host or router knows a target host's or router's IP address, ARP finds the target's data link layer address.

Administrative IP Server: A server needed to support IP.

Administrator: A super account on a Windows server that automatically has full permissions in every directory on the server.

ADSL: See Asymmetric Digital Subscriber Line.

Advanced Encryption Standard (AES): New symmetric encryption standard that offers 128-bit, 192-bit, or 256-bit encryption efficiently.

AES: See Advanced Encryption Standard.

AES-CCMP: AES/Counter Mode with Cipher Block Chaining. The version of AES used in the 802.11i security standard for wireless LANs.

Anti-Adware: Program to stop malware that constantly presents advertisements to the user.

Anti-Virus Program: Program to remove malware from arriving messages and from the computer's disk drive.

Agent: See Network Management Agent.

Aggregate Throughput: Throughput shared by multiple users; individual users will get a fraction of this throughput.

Alternative Route: In mesh topology, one of several possible routes from one end of the network to the other, made possible by the topology's many connections among switches or routers.

Always On: Being always available for service; used to describe access lines.

Amplitude Modulation: A simple form of modulation in which a modem transmits one of two analog signals—a high-amplitude (loud) signal or a low-amplitude (soft) signal.

Amplitude: The maximum (or minimum) intensity of a wave. In sound, this corresponds to volume (loudness).

Analog Signal: A signal that rises and falls in intensity smoothly and that does not have a limited numbers of states.

Analog-to-Digital Conversion (ADC): A device for the conversion of transmissions from the analog local loop to signals on the digital telephone network's core.

Antivirus Software: Software that scans computers to protect them against viruses, worms, and Trojan horses arriving in e-mail attachments and other propagation methods.

API: See Application Program Interface.

AppleTalk: Apple's proprietary architecture for use on Macintosh computers.

Applicant: In authentication, the user trying to prove his or her identity; sometimes called the supplicant.

Application Architecture: The arrangement of how application layer functions are spread among computers to deliver service to users.

Application Characterization Environment: See OPNET Application Characterization Environment.

Application Firewall: A firewall that examines the application layer content of packets.

Application Layer: The standards layer that governs how two applications communicate with each other; Layer 7 in OSI, Layer 5 in TCP/IP.

Application Profile: A method, offered by Bluetooth, that allows devices to work with one another automatically at the application layer.

Application Program Interface (API): A specification that allows application server programs to interact directly with database systems.

Application Program: Program that does work for users; operating system is the other major type of program found on computers.

Application Server: A server used by large e-commerce sites that accepts user data from a front-end webserver, assembles information from other servers, and creates a webpage to send back to the user.

Architecture: A broad plan that specifies what is needed in general and the components that will be used to provide that functionality. Applied to standards, networks, and applications.

ARP Cache: Section of memory that stores known pairs of IP addresses and single-network standards.

ASCII Code: A code for representing letters, numbers, and punctuation characters in 7-bit binary format.

Asymmetric Digital Subscriber Line (ADSL): The type of DSL designed to go into residential homes, offers high downstream speeds but limited upstream speeds.

Asynchronous Transfer Mode (ATM): The packet-switched network technology, specifically designed to carry voice, used for transmission in the PSTN transport core. ATM offers quality of service guarantees for throughput, latency, and jitter.

ATM: Asynchronous Transfer Mode.

AT&T: U.S. telecommunications carrier.

Attenuate: For a signal's strength to weaken during propagation.

Auditing: collecting data about events to assess actions after the fact.

Authentication: The requirement that someone who requests to use a resource must prove his or her identity.

Authentication Server: A server that stores data to help the verifier check the credentials of the applicant.

Authorization: Permitting a person or program to take certain actions on a resource.

Authorizations: Specific actions that a person or program can take on a resource.

Autonomous System: Internet owned by an organization.

Autosensing: The ability of a switch to detect the standard being used at the other end of the connection, and adjust its own speed to match.

Availability: The ability of a network to serve its users.

Backdoor: A way back into a compromised computer that an attacker leaves open; it may simply be a new account or a special program.

Back-Office: Transaction processing applications for a business's internal needs.

Backup: Copying files stored on a computer to another medium for protection of the files.

Backward-Compatible: Able to work with all earlier versions of a standard or technology.

Bandpass Filter: A device that filters out all signals below 300 Hz and above about 3.4 kHz.

Bandwidth: The range of frequencies over which a signal is spread.

Bank Settlement Firm: An e-commerce service that handles credit card payments.

Base 2: Notation for representing numbers; each position can only hold a 0 or 1.

Base Price: The price of a system's hardware, software, or both before necessary options are added.

Baseband: Transmission in which the signal is simply injected into a wire.

Baseband Signal: 1) The original signal in a radio transmission; 2) a signal that is injected directly into a wire for propagation.

Baud Rate: The number of clock cycles a transmission system uses per second.

Bell System: The conglomerate of local and long-distance telecommunications carriers that was broken up by antitrust action in the early 1980s.

BER: See bit error rate.

Best-Match Row: The row that provides the best forwarding option for a particular incoming packet.

BGP: See Border Gateway Protocol.

Binary Data: Data that has only two possible values (ones and zeros).

Binary Numbers: The Base 2 counting system where ones and zeros used in combination can represent whole numbers (integers).

Binary Signaling: Signaling that uses only two states.

Biometrics: The use of bodily measurements to identify an applicant.

Bit: A single 1 or 0.

Bit Error Rate: The percentage of all transmitted bits that contain errors.

Bit Rate: In digital data transmission, the rate at which information is transmitted; measured in bits per second.

Bits per Second (bps): The measure of network transmission speed. In increasing factors of 1,000 are kilobits per second (kbps), megabits per second (Mbps), gigabits per second (Gbps), and terabits per second (Tbps).

Black List: A list of banned websites.

Blended Threat: An attack that propagates both as a virus and as a worm.

Bluetooth: A wireless networking standard created for personal area networks.

Bonding: See Link Aggregation.

Border Firewall: A firewall that sits at the border between a firm and the outside world.

Border Gateway Protocol (BGP): The most common exterior routing protocol on the Internet. Recall that *gateway* is an old term for *router*.

Border Router: A router that sits at the edge of a site to connect the site to the outside world through leased lines, PSDNs, and VPNs.

Bot: A type of malware that can be upgraded remotely by an attacker to fix errors or to give the malware additional functionality.

Bps (bps): See Bits per Second.

Breach: A successful attack.

Bridge: An access point that connects two different types of LANs.

Broadband Wireless Access (BWA): High-speed local wireless transmission systems.

Broadband: 1) Transmission where signals are sent in wide radio channels; 2) any high-speed transmission system.

Broadband over Power Lines: Transmitting broadband data over electrical power lines.

Broadcast: To send a message out to all other stations simultaneously.

Broadcast Address: In Ethernet, FF-FF-FF-FF-FF-FF (48 ones); tells switches that the frame should be broadcast.

Brute-Force Attack: A password-cracking attack in which an attacker tries to break a password by trying all possible combinations of characters.

Bursty: Having short, high-speed bursts separated by long silences. Characteristic of data transmission.

Bus Topology: A topology in which one station transmits and has its signals broadcast to all stations.

Business Case: An argument for a system in business terms.

Business Continuity: A company's ability to continue operations.

Business Continuity Recovery: The reestablishment of a company's ability to continue operations.

BWA: See Broadband Wireless Access.

C7: Telephone supervisory control signaling system used in Europe.

CA: 1) See Certificate Authority. 2) See Collision Avoidance.

Cable Modem: 1) Broadband data transmission service using cable television; 2) the modem used in this service.

Cable Replacement: Getting rid of cables between devices by implementing wireless networking.

Call Waiting: A service that allows the user to place an original caller on hold if someone else calls the user, shift briefly to the new caller, and then switch back to the original caller.

Caller ID: Service wherein the telephone number of the party calling you is displayed on your phone's small display screen before you pick up the handset; allows the user to screen calls.

Carder: Someone who steals credit card numbers.

Carrier Sense Multiple Access with Collision Avoidance and Acknowledgements (CSMA/CA+ACK): A mandatory mechanism used to reduce problems with multiple simultaneous transmissions, which occur in wireless transmission. CSMA/CA+ACK is a media access control discipline, and it uses both collision avoidance and acknowledgement frames.

Carrier Sense Multiple Access with Collision Detection (CSMA/CD): The process wherein if a station wants to transmit, it may do so if no station is already transmitting but must wait if another station is already sending. In addition, if there is a collision because two stations send at the same time, all stations stop, wait a random period of time, and then try again.

Carrier: A transmission service company.

Cat: A short form for "category" in UTP.

Cat 5e: See Category 5e.

Category: In UTP cabling, a system for measuring wiring quality.

Category (Cat) 5e: Quality type of UTP wiring; required for 100Base-TX and gigabit Ethernet.

Category 6: The newest quality type of UTP wiring being sold; not required for even gigabit Ethernet.

Category 6A: Augmented Category 6 wiring that can sustain higher transmission speeds than Category 6 wiring.

Category 7: A new twisted-pair wiring quality standard; will only support shielded twisted pair (STP) wiring.

CDMA: See Code Division Multiple Access.

CDMA IS-95: The form of CDMA used in 2G cellular technology in the United States.

CDMA2000 1x: The initial 3G step for implementing CDMA2000, offering telephone modem speeds.

CDMA2000 1xEV-DO: The second 3G step for implementing CDMA2000, which will offer speeds similar to those in DSL and cable modems.

CDMA2000: A new 3G technology, developed by Qualcomm, offering a staged approach to increasing speed.

Cell: 1) In ATM, a fixed-length frame. 2) In cellular telephony, a small geographical area served by a cellsite.

Cellphone: A cellular telephone, also called a mobile phone or mobile.

Cellsite: In cellular telephony, equipment at a site near the middle of each cell, containing a transceiver and supervising each cellphone's operation.

Cell-Switching: A technology that uses fixed-length frames.

Cellular Telephone Service: Radio telephone service in which each subscriber in each section of a region is served by a separate cellsite.

Cellular Modem: A modem that allows a computer to communicate through a cellular telephone.

Certificate Authority (CA): Organization that provides public key–private key pairs and digital certificates.

Certificate Revocation List (CRL): A certificate authority's list of digital certificates it has revoked before their expiration date.

Challenge Message: In challenge–response authentication protocols, the message initially sent from the verifier to the applicant.

Challenge–Response Authentication Protocol (CHAP): A specific challenge–response authentication protocol.

Challenge–Response Authentication: Initial authentication method in which the verifier sends the applicant a challenge message, and the applicant does a calculation to produce a response, which it sends back to the verifier.

Channel Bandwidth: The range of frequencies in a channel; determined by subtracting the lowest frequency from the highest frequency.

Channel Reuse: The ability to use each channel multiple times, in different cells in the network.

Channel Service Unit (CSU): The part of a CSU/DSU device designed to protect the telephone network from improper voltages sent into a private line.

Channel: A small frequency range that is a subdivision of a service band.

CHAP: See Challenge–Response Authentication Protocol.

Checkout: A core e-commerce function that allows a buyer who has finished shopping to pay for the selected goods.

Chronic Lack of Capacity: A state in which the network lacks adequate capacity much of the time.

CIDR: See Classless InterDomain Routing.

Cipher: An encryption method.

Ciphertext: The result of encrypting a plaintext message. Ciphertext can be transmitted with confidentiality.

CIR: See Committed Information Rate.

Circuit: A two-way connection with reserved capacity.

Circuit Switching: Switching in which capacity for a voice conversation is reserved on every switch and trunk line end-to-end between the two subscribers.

Cladding: A thick glass cylinder that surrounds the core in optical fiber.

Class A IP Address: In classful addressing, an IP address block with more than sixteen million IP addresses; given only to the largest firms and ISPs.

Class B IP Address: In classful addressing, an IP address block with about 65,000 IP addresses; given to large firms.

Class C IP Address: In classful addressing, an IP address block with 254 possible IP addresses; given to small firms.

Class D IP Address: In classful addressing, IP addresses used in multicasting.

Class 5 Switch: See End Office Switch.

Classful Addressing: Giving a firm one of four block sizes for IP addresses: a very large Class A address block, a medium-sized Class B address block, or a small Class C address block.

Classless InterDomain Routing (CIDR): System for allocating IP addresses that does not use IP address classes.

Clear Line of Sight: An obstructed radio path between the sender and the receiver.

Clear to Send (CTS): In 802.11, a message broadcast by an access point, which allows only a station that has sent a Request to Send message to transmit. All other stations must wait.

CLEC: See Competitive Local Exchange Carrier.

CLI: See Command Line Interface.

Client PC: A personal computer that acts as a client.

Client Station: A station that receives service from a server station.

Client/Server Application: Application in which a client program requests service from a server and in which the server program provides the service.

Client/Server Processing: The form of client/server computing in which the work is done by programs on two machines.

Client/Server System: A system where some processing power is on the client computer. The two types of client/server systems are file server program access and full client/server processing.

Clock Cycle: A period of time during which a transmission line's state is held constant.

Cloud: The symbol traditionally used to represent the PSDN transport core, reflecting the fact that although the PSDN has internal switches and trunk lines, the customer does not have to know how things work inside the cloud.

Coating: In optical fiber, the substance that surrounds the cladding to keep out light and to strengthen the fiber. Coating includes strands of yellow Aramid (Kevlar) yarn to strengthen the fiber.

Coaxial Cable: The IEEE working group that creates wireless LAN standards.

Code Division Multiple Access (CDMA): A new form of cellular technology and a form of spread spectrum transmission that allows multiple stations to transmit at the same time in the same channel; also permits stations in adjacent cells to use the same channel without serious interference.

Codec: The device in the end office switch that converts between the analog local loop voice signals and the digital signals of the end office switch.

Collision: When two simultaneous signals use the same shared transmission medium, the signals will add together and become scrambled (unintelligible).

Collision Avoidance (CA): In 802.11, used with CSMA to listen for transmissions, so if a wireless NIC detects a transmission, it must not transmit. This avoids collision.

Collision Domain: In Ethernet CSMA/CD systems that use hubs or bus topologies, the collection of all stations that can hear one another; only one can transmit at a time.

Command Line Interface (CLI): An interface used to work with switches and routers, in which the user types highly structured commands, ending each command with Enter.

Command–Response Cycle: The exchange of messages through which SNMP communication between the manager and agents takes place. In it, the manager sends a command, and the agent sends back a response confirming that the command has been met, delivering requested data, or saying that an error has occurred and that the agent cannot comply with the command.

Committed Information Rate (CIR): PVC speed that is guaranteed by the Frame Relay carrier.

Communication Satellite: Satellite that provides radio communication service.

Community Name: In SNMP Version 1, only devices using the same community name will communicate with each other; very weak security.

Competitive Local Exchange Carrier (CLEC): A competitor to the ILEC.

Comprehensive Security: Security in which all avenues of attack are closed off.

Compromise: A successful attack.

Computer Security Incident Response Team (CSIRT): A team convened to handle major security incidents, made up of the firm's security staff, members of the IT staff, and members of functional departments, including the firm's legal department.

Conference Calling: A multiparty telephone call.

Confidentiality: Assurance that interceptors cannot read transmissions.

Connectionless: Type of conversation that does not use explicit openings and closings.

Connection-Oriented: Type of conversation in which there is a formal opening of the interactions, a formal closing, and maintenance of the conversation in between.

Connectorize: To add connectors to something.

Constellation: In quadrature amplitude modulation, the collection of all possible amplitude/phase combinations.

Continuity Testers: UTP tester that ensures that wires are inserted into RJ-45 connectors in the correct order and are making good contact.

Convergence: The correction of routing tables after a change in an internet.

Conversion: The process of browsers becoming buyers.

Cookie: Small text file stored by a website on a client PC; can later be read from the website.

Cord: A length of transmission medium—usually UTP or optical fiber but sometimes coaxial cable.

Core Switch: A switch further up the hierarchy that carries traffic between pairs of switches. May also connect switches to routers.

Core: 1) In optical fiber, the very thin tube into which a transmitter injects light. 2) In a switched network, the collection of all core switches.

Corporate Network: A network that carries the internal traffic of a single corporation.

Crack: To guess a password.

Credentials: Proof of identity that an applicant can present during authentication.

Credit Card Verification Service: An e-commerce service that checks the validity of the credit card number a user has typed.

Criminal Attacker: An attacker who attacks with criminal motivation.

Crimping Tool: Tool for crimping wires into an RJ-45 connector.

CRL: See Certificate Revocation List.

CRM: See Customer Relationship Management.

Cross-Connect Device: The device within a wiring closet that vertical cords plug into. Cross-connect devices connect the wires from the riser space to 4-pair UTP cords that span out to the wall jacks on each floor.

Crossover Cable: A UTP cord that allows a NIC in one computer to be connected directly to the NIC in another computer; switches Pins 1 and 2 with Pins 3 and 6.

Crosstalk Interference: Mutual EMI among wire pairs in a UTP cord.

Cryptographic System: A security system that automatically provides a mix of security protections, usually including confidentiality, authentication, message integrity, and replay protection.

Cryptography: Mathematical methods for protecting communication.

CSIRT: See Computer Security Incident Response Team.

CSMA/CA+ACK: See Carrier Sense Multiple Access with Collision Avoidance and Acknowledgments. See definitions of the individual components.

CSMA/CD: See Carrier Sense Multiple Access with Collision Detection.

CSU/DSU: Device that connects an internal site system to a private line circuit.

CSU: See Channel Service Unit.

CTS: See Clear to Send.

Customer Premises Equipment (CPE): Equipment owned by the customer, including PBXs, internal vertical and horizontal wiring, and telephone handsets.

Customer Relationship Management (CRM): Software that examines customer data to understand the preference of a company's customers.

Cut-through: Switching wherein the Ethernet switch examines only some fields in a frame's header before sending the bits of the frame back out.

Cyberterror: A computer attack made by terrorists.

Cyberwar: A computer attack made by a national government.

DAC: See Digital-to-Analog Conversion.

Data: Information carried over a network.

Data Communications: The transmission of encoded information, as opposed to the type of information carried in telecommunications systems.

Data Encryption Standard (DES): Popular symmetric key encryption method; with only 56-bit keys, considered to be too weak for business-to-business encryption.

Data Field: The content delivered in a message.

Data Link: The path that a frame takes across a single network (LAN or WAN).

Data Link Control Identifier (DLCI): The virtual circuit number in Frame Relay, normally 10 bits long.

Data Link Layer: The layer that governs transmission within a single network all the way from the source station to the destination station across zero or more switches; Layer 2 in OSI.

Data Service Unit (DSU): The part of a CSU/DSU circuit that formats the data in the way the private line requires.

dB: See Decibel.

DDoS: See distributed denial of service attack.

Dead Spot: See Shadow Zone.

Decapsulation: The removing of a message from the data field of another message.

Decibel (dB): The unit in which attenuation is measured.

Decrypt: Conversion of encrypted ciphertext into the original plaintext so an authorized receiver can read an encrypted message.

Dedicated Server: A server that is not used simultaneously as a user PC.

Deep Packet Inspection: The examination of headers and messages at multiple layers in a packet.

Default Printer: The printer to which a user's print jobs will be sent unless the user specifies a different printer.

Default Router: The next-hop router that a router will forward a packet to if the routing table does not have a row that governs the packet's IP address except for the default row.

Default Row: The row of a routing table that will be selected automatically if no other row matches; its value is 0.0.0.0.

Defense in Depth: The use of successive lines of defense.

Demilitarized Zone (DMZ): A subnet in which webservers and other public servers are placed.

Demodulate: To convert digital transmission signals to analog signals.

Denial-of-Service (DoS): The type of attack whose goal is to make a computer or a network unavailable to its users.

Distributed Denial-of-Service (DDoS): DOS attack in which the victim is attacked by many computers.

Deregulation: Taking away monopoly protections from carriers to encourage competition.

DES: See Data Encryption Standard.

Designated Router: In OSPF, a router that sends change information to other routers in its area.

Destination: In a routing table, the column that shows the destination network's network part or subnet's network part plus subnet part, followed by zeroes. This row represents a route to this network or subnet.

Device Driver: Software that allows an operating system to communicate with a peripheral, such as a NIC.

DHCP: See Dynamic Host Configuration Protocol.

Dial-Up Circuit: A circuit that only exists for the duration of a telephone call.

Dictionary Attack: A password-cracking attack in which an attacker tries to break a password by trying all words in a standard or customized dictionary.

Dictionary Word: A common word, dangerous to use for a password because easily cracked.

Dielectric Insulation: The non-conducting insulation that covers each wire in 4-pair UTP, preventing short circuits between the electrical signals traveling on different wires.

Diff-Serv: The field in an IP packet that can be used to label IP packets for priority and other service parameters.

Digital Certificate: A document that gives the name of a true party, that true party's public key, and other information; used in authentication.

Digital Certificate Authentication: Authentication in which each user has a public key and a private key. Authentication depends on the applicant knowing the true party's private key; requires a digital certificate to give the true party's public key.

Digital Signaling: Signaling that uses a few states. Binary (two-state) transmission is a special case of digital transmission.

Digital Signature: A calculation added to a plaintext message to authenticate it.

Digital Subscriber Line (DSL): A technology that provides digital data signaling over the residential customer's existing single-pair UTP voice-grade copper access line.

Digital-to-Analog Conversion (DAC): The conversion of transmissions from the digital telephone network's core to signals on the analog local loop.

Direct Distance Dialing: Long distance calls made at the standard long-distance rate.

Direct Sequence Spread Spectrum (DSSS): Spread spectrum transmission that spreads the signal over the entire bandwidth of a channel.

Disaster Recovery: The reestablishment of information technology operations.

Disaster: An incident that can stop the continuity of business operations, at least temporarily.

Discovering: The first phase of network mapping, in which the program finds out if hosts and subnets exist.

Disgruntled Employee: Employee who is upset with the firm or an employee and who may take revenge through a computer attack.

Disgruntled Ex-Employee: Former employee who is upset with the firm or an employee and who may take revenge through a computer attack.

Dish Antenna: An antenna that points in a particular direction, allowing it to send stronger outgoing signals in that direction for the same power and to receive weaker incoming signals from that direction.

Distance Vector Routing Protocol: Routing protocol based on the number of hops to a destination out a particular port.

Distort: To change in shape during propagation.

DLCI: See Data Link Control Identifier.

DMZ: See Demilitarized Zone.

DNS: See Domain Name System.

Domain: 1) In DNS, a group of resources (routers, single networks, and hosts) under the control of an organization. 2) In Microsoft Windows, a grouping of resources used in an organization, made up of clients and servers.

Domain Controller: In Microsoft Windows, a computer that manages the computers in a domain.

Domain Name System (DNS): A server that provides IP addresses for users who know only a target host's host name. DNS servers also provide a hierarchical system for naming domains.

Domestic: Telephone service within a country.

DoS: See Denial-of-Service.

Dotted Decimal Notation: The notation used to ease human comprehension and memory in reading IP addresses.

Downlink: Downward transmission path for a communications satellite.

Downtime: A period of network unavailability.

Drive-By Hacker: A hacker who parks outside a firm's premises and eavesdrops on its data transmissions; mounts denial-of-service attacks; inserts viruses, worms, and spam into a network; or does other mischief.

DSL Access Multiplexer (DSLAM): A device at the end office of the telephone company that sends voice signals over the ordinary PSTN and sends data over a data network such as an ATM network.

DSL: See Digital Subscriber Line.

DSLAM: See DSL Access Multiplexer.

DSSS: See Direct Sequence Spread Spectrum.

DSU: See Data Service Unit.

Dumb Access Point: Access point that cannot be managed remotely without the use of a wireless LAN switch.

Dumb Terminal: A desktop machine with a keyboard and display but little processing capability; processing is done on a host computer.

DWDM: See Dense Wavelength Division Multiplexing.

Dynamic Host Configuration Protocol (DHCP): The protocol used by DHCP servers, which provide each user PC with a temporary IP address to use each time he or she connects to the Internet.

EAP: See Extensible Authentication Protocol.

E-Commerce: Electronic commerce; buying and selling over the Internet.

E-Commerce Software: Software that automates the creation of catalog pages and other e-commerce functionality.

Economy of Scale: In managed services, the condition of being cheaper to manage the traffic of many firms than of one firm.

Egress Filtering: The filtering of traffic from inside a site going out.

EIGRP: See Enhanced Interior Gateway Routing Protocol.

E-LAN: Multipoint service in metropolitan area Ethernet.

Electromagnetic Interference (EMI): Unwanted electrical energy coming from external devices, such as electrical motors, fluorescent lights, and even nearby data transmission wires.

Electromagnetic Signal: A signal generated by oscillating electrons.

Electronic Signature: A bit string added to a message to provide message-by-message authentication and message integrity.

Electronic Catalog: An e-commerce site's display that shows the goods the site has for sale.

Electronic Commerce (E-Commerce): The buying and selling of goods and services over the Internet.

E-Line: Point-to-point service in metropolitan area Ethernet.

Elliptic Curve Cryptosystem (ECC): Public key encryption method; more efficient than RSA.

EMI: See Electromagnetic Interference.

Encapsulation: The placing of a message in the data field of another message.

Encrypt: To mathematically process a message so that an interceptor cannot read the message.

Encryption method: A method for encrypting plaintext messages.

End Office: Telephone company switch that connects to the customer premises via the local loop.

End Office Switch: The nearest switch of the telephone company to the customer premises.

End-to-End: A layer where communication is governed directly between the transport process on the source host and the transport process on the destination host.

Enhanced Interior Gateway Routing Protocol (EIGRP): Interior routing protocol used by Cisco routers.

Enterprise Mode: In WPA and 802.11i, operating mode that uses 802.1X.

Ephemeral Port Number: The temporary number a client selects whenever it connects to an application program on a server. According to IETF rules, ephemeral port numbers should be between 49153 and 65535.

Equipment Room: The room, usually in a building's basement, where wiring connects to external carriers and internal wiring.

Error Advisement: In ICMP, the process wherein if an error is found, there is no transmission, but the router or host that found the error usually sends an ICMP error message to the source device to inform it that an error has occurred. It is then up to the device to decide what to do. (This is not the same as error correction because there is no mechanism for the retransmission of lost or damaged packets.)

Error Rate: In biometrics, the normal rate of misidentification when the subject is cooperating.

Ethernet 10Base2: Obsolete 10 Mbps Ethernet standard that uses coaxial cable in a bus topology. Less expensive than 10Base5 but cannot carry signals as far.

Ethernet 10Base5: Obsolete 10 Mbps Ethernet standard that uses coaxial cable in a bus topology.

Ethernet Address: The 48-bit address the stations have on an Ethernet network; often written in hexadecimal notation for human reading.

Ethernet Frame: A message at the data link layer in an Ethernet network.

Ethernet Switch: Switch following the Ethernet standard. Notable for speed and low cost per frame sent. Dominates LAN switching.

EtherPeek: A commercial traffic summarization program.

Evil Twin Access Point: Attacker access point outside a building that attracts clients inside the building to associate with it.

Excess Burst Speed: One of Frame Relay's two-part PVC speeds; beyond the CIR.

Exhaustive Search: Cracking a key or password by trying all possible keys or passwords.

Exploit: A break-in program; a program that exploits known vulnerabilities.

Exploitation Software: Software that is planted on a computer; it continues to exploit the computer.

Extended ASCII: Extended 8-bit version of the ASCII code used on PCs.

Extended Star Topology: The type of topology wherein there are multiple layers of switches organized in a hierarchy, in which each node has only one parent node; used in Ethernet; more commonly called a hierarchical topology.

Extensible Authentication Protocol (EAP): A protocol that authenticates users with authentication data (such as a password or a response to a challenge based on a station's digital certificate) and authentication servers.

Exterior Routing Protocol: Routing protocol used between autonomous systems.

Extranet: A network that uses TCP/IP Internet standards to link several firms together but that is not accessible to people outside these firms. Even within the firms of the extranet, only some of each firm's computers have access to the network.

Face Recognition: The scanning of passersby to identify terrorists or wanted criminals by the characteristics of their faces.

Facilitating Server: A server that solves certain problems in P2P interactions but that allows clients to engage in P2P communication for most of the work.

False Alarm: An apparent incident that proves not to be an attack.

False Positive: A false alarm.

Fast Ethernet: 100 Mbps Ethernet.

FCC: See Federal Communications Commission.

EIGRP: See Enhanced Interior Gateway Routing Protocol.

FDDI: See Fiber Distributed Data Interface.

FDM See Frame Division Multiplexing.

FHSS: See Frequency Hopping Spread Spectrum.

Fiber Distributed Data Interface: Obsolete 100 Mbps token-ring network.

Fiber to the Home (FTTH): Optical fiber brought by carriers to individual homes and businesses.

Field: A subdivision of a message header or trailer.

File Server: A server that allows users to store and share files.

File Server Program Access: The form of client/server computing in which the server's only role is to store programs and data files, while the client PC does the actual processing of programs and data files.

File Sharing: The ability of computer users to share files that reside on their own disk drives or on a dedicated file server.

Filtering: Examining the content of arriving packets to decide what to do with them.

Fin Bit: One-bit field in a TCP header; indicates that the sender wishes to open a TCP connection.

Fingerprint Scanning: A form of biometric authentication that uses the applicant's fingerprints.

Fingerprinting: The second phase of network mapping, in which the program determines the characteristics of hosts to determine if they are clients, servers, or routers.

Firewall: A security system that examines each incoming packet. If the firewall identifies the packet as an attack packet, the firewall discards the packet and copies information about the discarded packet into a log file.

First-Generation (1G): The initial generation of cellular telephony, introduced in the 1980s. 1G systems were analog, were only given about 50 MHz of spectrum, had large and few cells, and had very limited speeds for data transmission.

Fixed Wireless Service: Local terrestrial wireless service in which the user is at a fixed location.

Flag Field: A one-bit field.

Flat Rate: Local telephone service in which there is a fixed monthly service charge but no separate fee for individual local calls.

Flow Control: The ability of one side in a conversation to tell the other side to slow or stop its transmission rate.

Footprint: Area of coverage of a communication satellite's signal.

Forensics: The collection of data in a form suitable for presentation in a legal proceeding.

Four-Way Close: A normal TCP connection close; requires four messages.

Fractional T1: A type of private line that offers intermediate speeds at intermediate prices; usually operates at one of the following speeds: 128 kbps, 256 kbps, 384 kbps, 512 kbps, or 768 kbps.

FRAD: See Frame Relay Access Device.

Fragment Offset Field: In IPv4, a flag field that tells a fragment's position in a stream of fragments from an initial packet.

Fragment (Fragmentation): To break a message into multiple smaller messages. TCP fragments application layer messages, while IP packets may be fragmented by routers along the packet's route.

Frame: 1) A message at the data link layer. 2) In time division multiplexing, a brief time period, which is further subdivided into slots.

Frame Check Sequence Field: A four-octet field used in error checking in Ethernet. If an error is found, the frame is discarded.

Frame Relay Access Device (FRAD): Device that connects an internal site network to a Frame Relay network.

Frequency: The number of complete cycles a radio wave goes through per second. In sound, frequency corresponds to pitch.

Frequency Division Multiplexing (FDM): A technology used in microwave transmission in which the microwave bandwidth is subdivided into channels, each carrying a single circuit.

Frequency Hopping Spread Spectrum (FHSS): Spread spectrum transmission that uses only the bandwidth required by the signal but hops frequently within the spread spectrum channel.

Frequency Modulation: Modulation in which one frequency is chosen to represent a 1 and another frequency is chosen to represent a 0.

Frequency Spectrum: The range of all possible frequencies from zero hertz to infinity.

FTTH: See Fiber to the Home.

Full-Duplex: A type of communication that supports simultaneous two-way transmission. Almost all communication systems today are full-duplex systems.

Full-Mesh Topology: Topology in which each node is connected to each other node.

Fully Configured: A system with all necessary options.

Functional Department: General name for departments in a firm other than the IT department; marketing, accounting, and so forth.

Gateway: An obsolete term for "router;" still in use by Microsoft.

Gateway Controller: In IP telephony, a device that controls the operation of signaling gateways and media gateways.

Gbps: Gigabit per second.

General Packet Radio Service (GPRS): The technology to which many GSM systems are now being upgraded. GPRS can combine two or more GSM time slots within a channel and so can offer data throughput near

that of a telephone modem. Often called a 2.5G technology.

GEO: See Geosynchronous Earth Orbit Satellite.

Geosynchronous Earth Orbit Satellite (GEO): The type of satellite most commonly used in fixed wireless access today; orbits the earth at about 36,000 km (22,300 miles).

Get: An SNMP command sent by the manager that tells the agent to retrieve certain information and return this information to the manager.

GHz: See Gigahertz.

Gigabit Ethernet: 1 Gbps versions of Ethernet.

Gigabit per second: One billion bits per second.

Gigahertz (GHz): One billion hertz.

GIGO: Garbage in, garbage out. If bad information is put into a system, only bad information can come out.

Global System for Mobile communication (GSM): The cellular telephone technology on which nearly the entire world standardized for 2G service. GSM uses 200 kHz channels and implements TDM.

Gnutella: A pure P2P file-sharing application that addresses the problems of transient presence and transient IP addresses without resorting to the use of any server.

Golden Zone: The portion of the frequency spectrum from the high megahertz range to the low gigahertz range, wherein commercial mobile services operate.

GPO: See Group Policy Object.

GPRS: See General Packet Radio Service.

Graded-Index Multimode Fiber: Multimode fiber in which the index of refraction varies from the center of the core to the cladding boundary.

Grid Computing: Computing in which all devices, whether clients or servers, share their processing resources.

Group Policy Object (GPO): A policy that governs a specific type of resource on a domain.

GSM: See Global System for Mobile communication.

H.323: In IP telephony, one of the protocols used by signalling gateways.

Hacking: The intentional use of a computer resource without authorization or in excess of authorization.

Half-Duplex: The mode of operation wherein two communicating NICs must take turns transmitting.

Handoff: a) In wireless LANs, a change in access points when a user moves to another location. b) In cellular telephony, transfer from one cellsite to another, which occurs when a subscriber moves from one cell to another within a system.

Hardened: Set up to protect itself, as a server or client.

Hash: The output from hashing.

Hashing: A mathematical process that, when applied to a bit string of any length, produces a value of a fixed length, called the hash.

HDSL: See High-Rate Digital Subscriber Line.

HDSL2: A newer version of HDSL, that transmits in both directions at 1.544 Mbps.

Header: The part of a message that comes before the data field.

Header Checksum: The UDP datagram field that allows the receiver to check for errors.

Headquarters: The First Bank of Paradise's downtown office building that houses the administrative site.

Hertz (Hz): One cycle per second, a measure of frequency.

Hex Notation: See Hexadecimal Notation.

Hexadecimal (Hex) Notation: The Base 16 notation that humans use to represent address 48-bit MAC source and destination addresses.

Hierarchical Topology: A network topology in which all switches are arranged in a hierarchy, in which each switch has only one parent switch above it (the root switch, however, has no parent); used in Ethernet.

Hierarchy: 1) The type of topology wherein there are multiple layers of switches organized in a hierarchy, in which each node has only one parent node; used in Ethernet. 2) In IP addresses, three multiple parts that represent successively more specific locations for a host.

High-Rate Digital Subscriber Line (HDSL): The most popular business DSL, which offers symmetric transmission at 768 kbps in both directions. See also HDSL2.

Hop-by-Hop: A layer in which communication is governed by each individual switch or router along the path of a message.

Host: Any computer attached to the Internet (can be either personal client or server).

Host Computer: 1) In terminal–host computing, the host that provides the processing power; 2) on an internet, any host.

Host Name: An unofficial designation for a host computer.

Host Part: The part of an IP address that identifies a particular host on a subnet.

Hot Spot: A public location where anyone can connect to an access point for Internet access.

HTML: See Hypertext Markup Language.

HTML Body: Body part in a Hypertext Markup Language message.

HTTP: See Hypertext Transfer Protocol.

HTTP Request Message: In HTTP, a message in which a client requests a file or another service from a server.

HTTP Request–Response Cycle: An HTTP client request followed by an HTTP server response.

HTTP Response Message: In HTTP, a message in which a server responds to a client request; either contains a requested file or an error message explaining why the requested file could not be supplied.

Hub: An early device used by Ethernet LANs to move frames in a system. Hubs broadcast each arriving bit out all ports except for the port that receives the signal.

Hub-and-Spoke Topology: A topology in which all communication goes through one site.

Hybrid Mode: In password cracking, a mode that tries variations on common word passwords.

Hybrid TCP/IP-OSI Standards Architecture: The architecture that uses OSI standards at the physical and data link layers and TCP/IP standards at the internet, transport, and application layers; dominant in corporations today.

Hypertext Markup Language (HTML): The language used to create webpages.

Hypertext Transfer Protocol (HTTP): The protocol that governs interactions between the browser and webserver application program.

Hz: See Hertz.

ICC: See International Common Carrier.

ICF: See Internet Connection Firewall.

ICMP Echo: A message sent by a host or router to another host or router. If the target device's internet process is able to do so, it will send back an echo response message.

ICMP Error Message: A message sent in error advisement to inform a source device that an error has occurred.

ICMP: See Internet Control Message Protocol.

ICS: See Internet Connection Sharing.

IDC: See Insulation Displacement Connection.

Identification Field: In IPv4, header field used to reassemble fragmented packets. Each transmitted packet is given a unique identification field value. If the packet is fragmented en route, all fragments are given the initial packet's identification field value.

Identity Theft: Stealing enough information about a person to impersonate him or her in complex financial transactions.

IDS: See Intrusion Detection System.

IEEE: See Institute for Electrical and Electronics Engineers.

IETF: See Internet Engineering Task Force.

ILEC: See Incumbent Local Exchange Carrier.

IM: See Instant Messaging.

Image: An exact copy.

IMAP: See Internet Message Access Protocol.

Impostor: Someone who claims to be someone else.

Incident: A successful attack.

Incident Severity: The degree of destruction inflicted by an attack.

Incumbent Local Exchange Carrier (ILEC): The traditional monopoly telephone company within each LATA.

Index Server: A server used by Napster. Stations connected to Napster would first upload a list of their files available for sharing to index servers. Later, when they searched, their searches went to the index servers and were returned from there.

Individual Throughput: The actual speed a single user receives (usually much lower than aggregate throughput in a system with shared transmission speed).

Ingress Filtering: The filtering of traffic coming into a site from the outside.

Inherit: When permissions are assigned to a user in a directory, user automatically receives the same permissions in sub-directories unless this automatic inheritance is blocked.

Initial Installation: The initial phase of a product's life cycle. Ongoing costs may be much higher.

Initialization Vector: A bit string used in conjunction with a key for encryption.

Initial Labor Costs: The labor costs of setting up a system for the first time.

Initial Sequence Number (ISN): The sequence number placed in the first TCP segment a side transmits in a session; selected randomly.

Instance: An actual example of a category.

Instant Messaging (IM): A popular P2P application that allows two users to type messages back and forth in real time.

Institute for Electrical and Electronics Engineers (IEEE): An international organization whose 802 LAN/MAN Standards Committee creates many LAN standards.

Insulation: Nonconducting coating around each wire in a UTP cord.

Insulation Displacement Connection (IDC): Connection method used in UTP. A connector bites through the insulation around a wire, making contact with the wire inside.

Interexchange Carrier (IXC): A telephone carrier that transmits voice traffic between LATAs.

Interface: 1) The router's equivalent of a network interface card; a port on a router that must be designed for the network to which it connects. 2) In Web services, the outlet through which an object communicates with the outside world.

Interference: See Electromagnetic Interference.

Interior Routing Protocol: Routing protocol used within a firm's internet.

Internal Back-End System: In e-commerce, an internal e-commerce system that handles accounting, pricing, product availability, shipment, and other matters.

Internal Router: A router that connects different LANs within a site.

International Common Carrier (ICC): A telephone carrier that provides international service.

International Organization for Standardization (ISO): A strong standards agency for manufacturing, including computer manufacturing.

International Telecommunications Union-Telecommunications Standards Sector (ITU-T): A standards agency that is part of the United Nations and that oversees international telecommunications.

Internet: 1) A group of networks connected by routers so that any application on any host on any network can communicate with any application on any other host on any other network. 2) A general term for any internetwork (spelled with a lowercase *i*); 3) the worldwide Internet (spelled with a capital *I*).

Internet Backbone: The collection of all Internet Service Providers that provide Internet transmission service.

Internet Connection Firewall (ICF): The built-in stateful firewall that comes with Windows XP.

Internet Connection Sharing (ICS): Microsoft Windows service that allows a PC to connect to the Internet through another PC.

Internet Control Message Protocol (ICMP): The protocol created by the IETF to oversee supervisory messages at the internet layer.

Internet Engineering Task Force (IETF): TCP/IP's standards agency.

Internet Layer: The layer that governs the transmission of a packet across an entire internet.

Internet Message Access Protocol (IMAP): One of the two protocols used to download received e-mail from an e-mail server; offers more features but is less popular than POP.

Internet Network: A network on the Internet owned by a single organization, such as a corporation, university, or ISP.

Internet Options: In Microsoft Windows, way of setting security and other settings for Browser communication.

Internet Protocol (IP): The TCP/IP protocol that governs operations at the internet layer. Governs packet delivery from host to host across a series of routers.

Internet Service Provider: Carrier that provides Internet access and transmission.

Internetwork Operating System (IOS): The operating system that Cisco Systems uses on all of its routers and most of its switches.

Intranet: An internet for internal transmission within firms; uses the TCP/IP transmission standards that govern transmission over the Internet.

Intrusion Detection System (IDS): A security system that examines messages traveling through a network. IDSs look at traffic broadly, identifying messages that are suspicious. Instead of discarding these packets, IDSs will sound an alarm.

Intrusion Protection System (IPS): Firewall system that uses sophisticated packet filtering methods to stop attacks.

Inverse square law: Radio signal strength declines with the square of transmission distance.

IOS: See Internetwork Operating System.

IP: See Internet Protocol.

IP Address: An Internet Protocol address; the address that every computer needs when it connects to the Internet; IP addresses are 32 bits long.

Ipconfig/all: Windows command line command in newer versions of Windows that shows configuration parameters for the PC.

IP Security (IPsec): A set of standards that operate at the internet layer and provide security to all upper layer protocols transparently.

IP Telephone: A telephone that has the electronics to encode voice for digital transmission and to send and receive packets over an IP internet.

IP Telephony: The transmission of telephone signals over IP internets instead of over circuit-switched networks.

IP Version 4 (IPv4): The standard that governs most routers on the Internet and private internets.

IP Version 6 (IPv6): A new version of the Internet Protocol.

Ipconfig (ipconfig): A command used to find information about one's own computer, used in newer versions of Windows (the command is typed as ipconfig/all[Enter] at the command line).

IPS: See intrusion prevention system.

IPsec Gateway: Border device at a site that converts between internal data traffic into protected data traffic that travels over an untrusted system such as the Internet.

IPsec: See IP Security.

IPv4: See IP Version 4.

IPv6: See IP Version 6.

IPX/SPX Architecture: Non-TCP/IP standards architecture found at upper layers in LANs; required on all older Novell NetWare file servers.

Iris: The colored part of the eye, used in biometric authentication.

ISN: See Initial Sequence Number.

ISO: See International Organization for Standardization.

ISO/IEC 11801: European standard for wire and optical fiber media.

ISP: See Internet Service Provider.

IT Disaster Recovery: Recovering from a disaster that damages computer equipment or data.

IT Guru. See OPNET IT Guru.

ITU-T: See International Telecommunications Union-Telecommunications Standards Sector.

IXC: See Interexchange Carrier.

Jacket: The outer plastic covering, made of PVC, that encloses and protects the four pairs of wires in UTP or the core and cladding in optical fiber.

Java Applet: Small Java program that is downloaded as part of a webpage.

Jitter: Variability in latency.

JPEG: Popular graphics file format.

kbps: Kilobits per second.

Key: A bit string used with an encryption method to encrypt and decrypt a message. Different keys used with a single encryption method will give different ciphertexts from the same plaintext.

Key Exchange: The secure transfer of a symmetric session key between two communicating parties.

Key-Hashed Message Authentication Code (HMAC): Electronic signature technology that is efficient and inexpensive but lacks nonrepudiation.

Key Management: The management of key creation, distribution, and other operations.

Label Header: In MPLS, the header added to packets before the IP header; contains information that aids and speeds routers in choosing which interface to send the packet back out.

Label Number: In MPLS, number in the label header that aids label-switching routers in packet sending.

Label Switching Router: Router that implements MPLS label switching.

Label Switching Table: In MPLS, the table used by label-switching routers to decide which interface to use to forward a packet.

LAN: See Local Area Network.

Language Independence: In SOAP, the fact that Web service objects do not have to be written in any particular language.

LATA: See Local Access and Transport Area.

Latency: Delay, usually measured in milliseconds.

Latency-Intolerant: An application whose performance is harmed by even slight latency.

Layer 3: See Internet Layer.

Layer 3 Switch: A router that does processing in hardware, that is much faster and less expensive than traditional software-based routers. Layer 3 switches are usually dominant in the Ethernet core above workgroup switches.

Layer 4: See Transport Layer.

Layer 4 Switch: A switch that examines the port number fields of each arriving packet's encapsulated TCP segment, allowing it to switch packets based on the application they contain. Layer 4 switches can give priority or even deny forwarding to IP packets from certain applications.

Layer 5: See Application Layer.

Leased Line Circuit: A high-speed point-to-point circuit.

Legacy Network: A network that uses obsolete technology; may have to be lived with for some time because upgrading all legacy networks at one time is too expensive.

Legal Retention: Rules that require IM messages to be captured and stored in order to comply with legal requirements.

Length Field: 1) The field in an Ethernet MAC frame that gives the length of the data field in octets. 2) The field in a UDP datagram that enables the receiving transport process to process the datagram properly.

LEO: See Low Earth Orbit Satellite.

Lightweight Directory Access Protocol: Simple protocol for accessing directory servers.

Line of Sight: An unobstructed path between the sender and receiver, necessary for radio transmission at higher frequencies.

Link: Connection between a pair of routers.

Link Aggregation: The use of two or more trunk links between a pair of switches; also known as trunking or bonding.

Link State Protocol: Routing protocol in which each router knows the state of each link between routers.

Linux: A freeware version of Unix that runs on standard PCs.

Linux Distribution: A package purchased from a vendor that contains the Linux kernel plus a collection of many other programs, usually taken from the GNU project.

List Folder Contents: A Microsoft Windows Server permission that allows the account owner to see the contents of a folder (directory).

LLC: See Logical Link Control.

LLC Header: See Logical Link Control Layer Header.

Load-Balancing Router: Router used on a server farm that sends client requests to the first available server.

Local: The value placed in the next-hop routing field of a routing table to specify that the destination host is on the selected network or subnet.

Local Access and Transport Area (LATA): One of the roughly 200 site regions the United States has been divided into for telephone service.

Local Area Network (LAN): A network within a site.

Local Calling: Telephone calls placed to a nearby caller; less expensive than long-distance calls.

Local Loop: In telephony, the line used by the customer to reach the PSTN's central transport core.

Log File: A file that contains data on events.

Logical Link Control Layer: The layer of functionality for the upper part of the data link layer, now largely ignored.

Logical Link Control Layer Header: The header at the start of the data field that describes the type of packet contained in the data field.

Logical Link Control Layer Subheader: Group of fields at the beginning of the Ethernet data field.

Long Distance: A telephone call placed to a distance party; more expensive than a local call.

Longest Match: The matching row that matches a packet's destination IP address to the greatest number of bits; chosen by a router when there are multiple matches.

Loopback Address: The IP address 127.0.0.1. When a user pings this IP address, this will test their *own* computer's connection to the Internet.

Loopback Interface: A testing interface on a device. Messages sent to this interface are sent back to the sending device.

Low Earth Orbit Satellite (LEO): A type of satellite used in mobile wireless transmission; orbits a few hundred miles or a few hundred kilometers above the earth.

MAC: See Media Access Control.

MAC Address: See Media Access Control.

Mainframe Computer: The largest type of dedicated server; extremely reliable.

Malware: Software that seeks to cause damage.

Malware-Scanning Program: A program that searches a user's PC looking for installed malware.

MAN: See Metropolitan Area Network.

Manageable Switch: A switch that has sufficient intelligence to be managed from a central computer (the Manager).

Managed Device: A device that needs to be administered, such as printers, hubs, switches, routers, application programs, user PCs, and other pieces of hardware and software.

Managed Frame Relay: A type of Frame Relay service that takes on most of the management that customers ordinarily would have to do. Managed Frame Relay provides traffic reports and actively manages day-to-day traffic to look for problems and get them fixed.

Management Information Base (MIB): A specification that defines what objects can exist on each type of managed device and also the specific characteristics of each object;

the actual database stored on a manager in SNMP. There are separate MIBs for different types of managed devices; both a schema and a database.

Management Program: A program that helps network administrators manage their networks.

Manager: The central PC or more powerful computer that uses SNMP to collect information from many managed devices.

Mask: A 32-bit string beginning with a series of ones and ending a series of zeroes; used by routing tables to Interpret IP address part sizes. The ones designate either the network part or the network plus software part.

Mask Operations: Applying a mask of ones and zeros to a bit stream. Where the mask is 1, the original bit stream's bit results. Otherwise, the result is zero.

Mature: Technology that has been under development long enough to have its rough edges smoothed off.

Maximum Segment Size (MSS): The maximum size of TCP data fields that a receiver will accept.

Maximum Transmission Unit (MTU): The maximum packet size that can be carried by a particular LAN or WAN.

Mbps: Megabits per second.

MD5: A popular hashing method.

Mean Time to Repair (MTTR): The average time it takes a staff to get a network back up after it has been down.

Media Access Control (MAC): The process of controlling when stations transmit; also, the lowest part of the data link layer, defining functionality specific to a particular LAN technology.

Media Gateway: A device that connects IP telephone networks to the ordinary public switched telephone network. Media gateways also convert between the signalling formats of the IP telephone system and the PSTN.

Medium Earth Orbit Satellite (MEO): A type of satellite used in mobile wireless transmission; orbits a few thousand miles or a few thousand kilometers above the earth.

Megabits per second: Millions of bits per second.

Megahertz (MHz): One million hertz.

MEO: See Medium Earth Orbit Satellite.

Mesh Networking: A type of networking in which wireless devices route frames without the aid of wired LANs.

Mesh Topology: 1) A topology where there are many connections among switches or routers, so there are many alternative routes for messages to get from one end of the network to the other. 2) In network design, a topology that provides direct connections between every pair of sites.

Message: A discrete communication between hardware or software processes.

Message Digest: The result of hashing a plaintext message. The message digest is signed with the sender's private key to produce the digital signature.

Message Integrity: The assurance that a message has not been changed en route; or if a message has been changed, the receiver can tell that it has.

Message Timing: Controlling when hardware or software processes may transmit.

Message Unit: Local telephone service in which a user is charged based on distance and duration.

Method: In Web services, a well-defined action that a SOAP message can request.

Metric: A number describing the desirability of a route represented by a certain row in a routing table.

Metro Ethernet: See metropolitan area Ethernet.

Metropolitan Area Ethernet: Ethernet operating at the scale of a metropolitan area network.

Metropolitan Area Network (MAN): A WAN that spans a single urban area.

MHz: See Megahertz.

MHz-km: Measure of modal bandwidth, a measure of multimode fiber quality.

MIB: See Management Information Base.

Microsoft Windows Server: Microsoft's network operating system for servers, which comes in three versions: NT, 2000, and 2003.

Microsoft Windows XP Home: The dominant operating system today for residential PCs.

Microsoft Windows XP Professional: A version of Windows XP designed to be run in organization; integrates with Windows Server services.

Microwave: Traditional point-to-point radio transmission system.

Microwave Repeater: Transmitter/receiver that extends the distance a microwave link can travel.

Millisecond (ms): The unit in which latency is measured.

MIME: See Multipurpose Internet Mail Extensions.

MIMO: See Multiple Input/Multiple Output.

Ministry of Telecommunications: A government-created regulatory body that oversees PTTs.

Mobile IP: A system for handling IP addresses for mobile devices.

Mobile Telephone Switching Office (MTSO): A control center that connects cellular customers to one another and to wired telephone users, as well as overseeing all cellular calls (determining what to do when people move from one cell to another, including which cellsite should handle a caller when the caller wishes to place a call).

Mobile Wireless Access: Local wireless service in which the user may move to different locations.

Modal Bandwidth: The measure of multimode fiber quality; the fiber's bandwidth—distance product. A modal bandwidth of 200 MHz-km means that if your bandwidth is 100 MHz, then you can transmit 2 km.

Modal Dispersion: The main propagation problem for optical fiber; dispersion in which the difference in the arrival times of various modes (permitted light rays) is too large, causing the light rays of adjacent pulses to overlap in their arrival times and rendering the signal unreadable.

Mode: An angle light rays are permitted to enter an optical fiber core.

Modify: A Microsoft Windows Server permission that gives an account owner additional permissions to act upon files, for example, the permission to delete a file, which is not included in Write.

Modulate: To convert digital signals to analog signals.

Momentary Traffic Peak: A surplus of traffic that briefly exceeds the network's capacity, happening only occasionally.

Monochrome Text: Text of one color against a contrasting background.

More Fragments Flag Field: In IPv4, a flag field that indicates whether there are more fragments (set) or not (not set).

MPLS: See Multiprotocol Label Switching.

Ms: See Millisecond.

MS-CHAP: Microsoft version of the Challenge–Response Authentication Protocol.

MSS: See Maximum Segment Size.

MTSO: See Mobile Telephone Switching Office.

MTTR: See Mean Time to Repair.

MTU: See Maximum Transmission Unit.

Multicasting: Simultaneously sending messages to multiple stations but not to all stations.

Multilayer Security: Applying security at more than one layer to provide defense in depth.

Multimode Fiber: The most common type of fiber in LANs, wherein light rays in a pulse can enter a fairly thick core at multiple angles.

Multipath Interference: Interference caused when a receiver receives two or more signals—a direct signal and one or more reflected signals. The multiple signals may interfere with one another.

Multiple Input/Multiple Output (MIMO): A radio transmission method that sends several signals simultaneously in a single radio channel.

Multiplexing: 1) Having the packets of many conversations share trunk lines; reduces trunk line cost. 2) The ability of a protocol to carry messages from multiple next-higher-layer protocols in a single communication session.

Multiprocessing Computer: A computer with multiple microprocessors. This allows it to run multiple programs at the same time.

Multiprotocol Label Switching (MPLS): A traffic management tool used by many ISPs.

Multiprotocol Router: A router that can handle not only TCP/IP internetworking protocols, but also internetworking protocols for IPX/SPX, SNA, and other standards architectures.

Multiprotocol: Characterized by implementing many different protocols and products following different architectures.

Multipurpose Internet Mail Extensions (MIME): A standard for specifying the contents of files.

Mutual Authentication: Authentication by both parties.

Name Server: Server in the Domain Name System.

Nanometer (nm): The measure used for wavelengths; one billionth of a meter (10^{-9} meters).

NAP: See Network Access Point.

Narrowband: 1) A channel with a small bandwidth and, therefore, a low maximum speed; 2) low-speed transmission.

NAS: See Network Attached Storage.

NAT: See Network Address Translation.

Netstat: A popular route analysis tool, which gives data on current connections between a computer and other computers.

Network: In IP addressing, an organizational concept—a group of hosts, single networks, and routers owned by a single organization.

Network Access Point (NAP): A site where ISPs interconnect and exchange traffic.

Network Address Translation (NAT): Converting an IP address into another IP address, usually at a border firewall; disguises a host's true IP address from sniffers. Allows more internal addresses to be used than an ISP supplies a firm with external addresses.

Network Architecture: 1) A broad plan that specifies everything that must be done for two application programs on different networks on an internet to be able to work together effectively. 2) A broad plan for how the firm will connect all of its computers within buildings (LANs), between sites (WANs), and to the Internet; also includes security devices and services.

Network Attached Storage (NAS): Storage device that connects directly to the network instead of to a computer.

Network Interface Card (NIC): Printed circuit expansion board for a PC; handles communication with a network; sometimes built into the motherboard.

Network Layer: In OSI, Layer 3; governs internetworking. OSI network layer standards are rarely used.

Network Management Agent (Agent): A piece of software on the managed device that communicates with the manager on behalf of the managed device.

Network Management Program (Manager): A program run by the network administrator on a central computer.

Network Management Utility: A program used in network management.

Network Mapping: The act of mapping the layout of a network, including what hosts and routers are active and how various devices are connected. Its two phases are discovering and fingerprinting.

Network Mask: A mask that has 1s in the network part of an IP address and 0s in all other parts.

Network Operating System (NOS): A PC server operating system.

Network Part: The part of an IP address that identifies the host's network on the Internet.

Network Security: The protection of a network from attackers.

Network Simulation: The building of a model of a network that is used to project how the network will operate after a change.

Network Topology: The order in which a network's nodes are physically connected by transmission lines.

Networked Application: An application that provides service over a network.

Next Header Field: In IPv6, a header field that describes the header following the current header.

Next-Hop Router: A router to which another router forwards a packet in order to get the packet a step closer to reaching its destination host.

NIC: See Network Interface Card.

Nm (nm): See Nanometer.

Nmap: A network mapping tool that finds active IP addresses and then fingerprints them to determine their operating system and perhaps their operating system version.

Node: A client, server, switch, router, or other type of device in a network.

Noise: Random electromagnetic energy within wires; combines with the data signal to make the data signal difficult to read.

Noise Floor: The mean of the noise energy.

Noise Spike: An occasional burst of noise that is much higher or lower than the noise floor; may cause the signal to become unrecognisable.

Nonblocking: A nonblocking switch has enough aggregate throughput to handle even the highest possible input load (maximum input on all ports).

Nonoverlapping Channel: Channels whose frequencies do not overlap.

Normal Attack: An incident that does a small amount of damage and can be handled by the on-duty staff.

North Shore: The First Bank of Paradise's backup facility; able to take over within minutes if Operations fails.

NOS: See Network Operating System.

Not Set: When a flags field is given the value 0.

Nslookup (nslookup): A command that allows a PC user to send DNS lookup messages to a DNS server.

Object: A specific Web service.

Object: In SNMP, an aspect of a managed device about which data is kept.

OC: See Optical Carrier.

Octet: A collection of eight bits; same as a byte.

OFDM: See Orthogonal Frequency Division Multiplexing.

Official Internet Protocol Standards: Standards deemed official by the IETF.

Official Standards Organization: An internationally recognized organization that produces standards.

Omnidirectional Antenna: An antenna that transmits signals in all directions and receives incoming signals equally well from all directions.

On/Off Signaling: Signaling wherein the signal is on for a clock cycle to represent a one, and off for a zero. (On/off signaling is binary.)

One-Pair Voice-Grade UTP: The traditional telephone access lines to individual residences.

Ongoing Costs: Costs beyond initial installation costs; often exceed installation costs.

Open Shortest Path First (OSPF): Complex but highly scalable interior routing protocol.

Operations: The First Bank of Paradise's building in an industrial area that houses the bank's mainframe operations and other back-office technical functions; also has most of the bank's IT staff, including its networking staff.

OPNET ACE: See OPNET Application Characterization Environment.

OPNET Application Characterization Environment (ACE): A network simulation program; focuses on application layer performance.

OPNET IT Guru: A popular network simulation program; focuses primarily on data link layer and internet layer performance.

Optical Carrier (OC): A number that indicates SONET speeds.

Optical Fiber: Cabling that sends signals as light pulses.

Optical Fiber Cord: A length of optical fiber.

Option: One of several possibilities that a user or technologist can select.

Orthogonal Frequency Division Multiplexing (OFDM): A form of spread spectrum transmission that divides each broadband channel into subcarriers and then transmits parts of each frame in each subcarrier.

Organizational Unit: In directory servers, a subunit of the Organization node.

OSI: The Reference Model of Open Systems Interconnection; the 7-layer network standards architecture created by ISO and ITU-T; dominant at the physical and data link layers, which govern transmission within single networks (LANs or WANs).

OSI Application Layer (Layer 7): The layer that governs application-specific matters not covered by the OSI Presentation Layer or the OSI Session Layer.

OSI Layer 5: See OSI Session Layer.

OSI Layer 6: See OSI Presentation Layer.

OSI Layer 7: See OSI Application Layer.

OSI Presentation Layer (Layer 6): The layer designed to handle data formatting differences between two communicating computers.

OSI Session Layer (Layer 5): The layer that initiates and maintains a connection between application programs on different computers.

OSPF: See Open Shortest Path First.

Out of Phase: In multipath interference, the condition of not being in sync, as occurs with signals that have been reflected and thus traveled different distances and not arrived at the receiver at the same time.

Outsourcing: Paying other firms to handle some, most, or all IT chores.

Overprovision: To install much more capacity in switches and trunk links than will be needed most of the time, so that momentary traffic peaks will not cause problems.

Oversubscription: In Frame Relay, the state of having port speeds less than the sum of PVC speeds.

P2P: See Peer-to-Peer Architecture.

Packet: A message at the internet layer.

Packet Capture and Display Program: A program that captures selected packets or all of the packets arriving at or going out of a NIC. Afterward, the user can display key header information for each packet in greater or lesser detail.

Packet Filter Firewall: A firewall that examines fields in the internet and transport headers of individual arriving packets. The firewall makes pass/deny decisions based upon the contents of IP, TCP, UDP, and ICMP fields.

Packet Switching: The breaking of conversations into short messages (typically a few hundred bits long); allows multiplexing on trunk lines to reduce trunk line costs.

PAD Field: A field that the sender adds to an Ethernet frame if the data field is less than 46 octets long (the total length of the PAD plus data field must be exactly 46 octets long).

PAN: See Personal Area Network.

Parallel Transmission: A form of transmission that uses multiple wire pairs or other transmission media simultaneously to send a signal; increases transmission speed.

Pass Phrase: A series of words that is used to generate a key.

Password: A secret keyboard string only the account holder should know; authenticates user access to an account.

Password Length: The number of characters in a password.

Password Reset: The act of changing a password to some value known only to the systems administrator and the account owner.

Patch: An addition to a program that will close a security vulnerability in that program.

Patch Cord: A cord that comes precut in a variety of lengths, with a connector attached; usually either UTP or optical fiber.

Payload: 1) A piece of code that can be executed by a virus or worm after it has spread to multiple machines. 2) ATM's name for a data field.

Payment Mechanism: In e-commerce, ways for purchasers to pay for their ordered goods or services.

PBX: See Private Branch Exchange.

PC Server: A server that is a personal computer.

PCM: Pulse Code Modulation.

PEAP: See Protected Extensible Authentication Protocol.

Peer-to-Peer Architecture (P2P): The application architecture in which most or all of the work is done by cooperating user computers, such as desktop PCs. If servers are present at all, they serve only facilitating roles and do not control the processing.

Peer-to-Peer Service: Service wherein client PCs provide services to one another.

Perfect Internal Reflection: When light in optical fiber cabling begins to spread, it hits the cladding and is reflected back into the core so that no light escapes.

Permanent IP Address: An IP address given to a server that the server keeps and uses every single time it connects to the Internet. (This is in contrast to client PCs, which receive a new IP address every time they connect to the Internet.)

Permanent Virtual Circuit (PVC): A PSDN connection between corporate sites that is set up once and kept in place for weeks, months, or years at a time.

Permission: A rule that determines what an account owner can do to a particular resource (file or directory).

Personal Area Network (PAN): A small wireless network used by a single person.

Personal Mode: Pre-shared Key Mode in WPA or 802.11i.

Phase Modulation: Modulation in which one wave serves as a reference wave or a carrier wave. Another wave varies its phase to represent one or more bits.

Phishing: Social engineering attack that uses an official-looking e-mail message or website.

Physical Address: Data link layer address—*Not* a physical layer address. Given this name because it is the address of the NIC, which is a physical device that implements both the physical and data link layers.

Physical Layer: The standards layer that governs physical transmission between adjacent devices; OSI Layer 1.

Physical Link: A connection linking adjacent devices on a network.

Piggybacking: The act of an attacker being allowed physical entrance to a building by following a legitimate user through a locked door that the victim has opened.

Ping: Sending a message to another host and listening for a response to see if it is active.

Pixel: A dot on a computer screen.

PKI: See Public Key Infrastructure.

Plaintext: The original message the sender wishes to send to the receiver; not limited to text messages.

Plan–Protect–Respond Cycle: The basic management cycle in which the three named stages are executed repeatedly.

Planning: Developing a broad security strategy that will be appropriate for a firm's security threats.

Plenum: The type of cabling that must be used when cables run through airways to prevent toxic fumes in case of fire.

Point of Presence (POP): 1) In cellular telephony, a site at which various carriers that provide telephone service are interconnected. 2) In PSDNs, a point of connection for user sites. There must be a private line between the site and the POP.

Point-to-Point Topology: A topology wherein two nodes are connected directly.

Point-to-Point Tunneling Protocol (PPTP): A remote access VPN security standard offering moderate security. PPTP works at the data link layer, and it protects all messages above the data link layer, providing protection transparently.

POP: See 1) Point of Presence. 2) See Post Office Protocol.

Pop-Up Blocker: A program that blocks annoying pop-up advertisements.

Port: In TCP and UDP messages, a header field that designates the application layer process on the server side and a specific connection on the client side.

Port Number: The field in TCP and UDP that tells the transport process what application process sent the data in the data field or should receive the data in the data field.

Portfolio: A planned collection of projects.

Post Office Protocol (POP): The most popular protocol used to download e-mail from an e-mail server to an e-mail client.

PPTP: See Point-to-Point Tunneling Protocol.

Preamble Field: The initial field in an Ethernet MAC frame; synchronizes the receiver's clock to the sender's clock.

Prefix Notation: A way of representing masks. Gives the number of initial 1s in the mask.

Premises: The land and buildings owned by a customer.

Presence Server: A server used in many P2P systems; knows the IP addresses of each user and also whether the user is currently on line and perhaps whether or not the user is willing to chat.

Pre-Shared Key: A mode of operation in WPA and 802.11i in which all stations and an access point share the same initial key.

Presentation Layer: See OSI Presentation Layer.

Print Server: An electronic device that receives print jobs and feeds them to the printer attached to the print server.

Printer Sharing: Allowing multiple PCs to share a single printer.

Priority: Preference given to latency-sensitive traffic, such as voice and video traffic, so that latency-sensitive traffic will go first if there is congestion.

Priority Level: The three-bit field used to give a frame one of eight priority levels from 000 (zero) to 111 (eight).

Private Branch Exchange (PBX): An internal telephone switch.

Private IP Address: An IP address that may be used only within a firm. Private IP addresses have three designated ranges: 10.x.x.x, 192.168.x.x, and 172.16.x.x through 172.31.x.x.

Private Key: A key that only the true party should know. Part of a public key–private key pair.

Probable Annual Loss: The likely annual loss from a particular threat. The cost of a successful attack times the probability of a successful attack in a one-year period.

Probe Packet: A packet sent into a firm's network during scanning; responses to the probe packet tend to reveal information about a firm's general network design and about its individual computers—including their operating systems.

Problem Update: An update that causes disruptions, such as slowing computer operation.

Propagate: To travel.

Propagation Effects: Changes in the signal during propagation.

Property: A characteristic of an object.

Protected Extensible Authentication Protocol (PEAP): A version of EAP preferred by Microsoft Windows computers.

Protecting: Implementing a strategic security plan; the most time-consuming stage in the plan–protect–respond management cycle.

Protocol: 1) A standard that governs interactions between hardware and software processes at the same layer but on different hosts. 2) In IP, the header field that describes the content of the data field.

Protocol Fidelity: The assurance that an application using a particular port is the application it claims to be.

Protocol Field: In IP, a field that designates the protocol of the message in the IP packet's data field.

Provable Attack Packet: A packet that is provably an attack packet.

PSDN: See Public Switched Data Network.

PSTN: See Public Switched Telephone Network.

PTT: See Public Telephone and Telegraphy Authority.

Public IP Address: An IP address that must be unique on the Internet.

Public Key: A key that is not kept secret. Part of a public key–private key pair.

Public Key Authentication: Authentication in which each user has a public key and a private key. Authentication depends on the applicant knowing the true party's private key; requires a digital certificate to give the true party's public key.

Public Key Encryption: Encryption in which each side has a public key and a private key, so there are four keys in total for bidirectional communication. The sender encrypts messages with the receiver's public key. The receiver, in turn, decrypts incoming messages with the receiver's own private key.

Public Key Infrastructure (PKI): A total system (infrastructure) for public key encryption.

Public Switched Data Network (PSDN): A carrier WAN that provides data transmission service. The customer only needs to connect to the PSDN by running one private line from each site to the PSDN carrier's nearest POP.

Public Switched Telephone Network (PSTN): The worldwide telephone network.

Public Telephone and Telegraphy authority (PTT): The traditional title for the traditional monopoly telephone carrier in most countries.

Public Utilities Commission (PUC): In the United States, telecommunications regulatory agency at the state level.

PUC: See Public Utilities Commission.

Pulse Code Modulation (PCM): An analog-to-digital conversion technique in which the ADC samples the bandpass-filtered signal 8,000 times per second, each time measuring the intensity of the signal and representing the intensity by a number between 0 and 255.

PVC: See Permanent Virtual Circuit.

QAM: See Quadrature Amplitude Modulation.

QoS: See Quality of Service.

QPSK: See Quadrature Phase Shift Keying.

Quadrature Amplitude Modulation (QAM): Modulation technique that uses two carrier waves—a sine carrier wave and a cosine carrier wave. Each can vary in amplitude.

Quadrature Phase Shift Keying (QPSK): Modulation with four possible phases. Each of the four states represents two bits (00, 01, 10, and 11).

Quality of Service (QoS): Numerical service targets that must be met by networking staff.

Quality-of-Service (QoS) Parameters: In IPv4, service quality parameters applied to all packets with the same TOS field value.

Radio Frequency ID (RFID): A tag that can be read at a distance by a radio transmitter/receiver.

Radio Wave: An electromagnetic wave in the radio range.

Rapid Spanning Tree Protocol: A version of the Spanning Tree Protocol that has faster convergence.

RAS: See Remote Access Server.

Raster Graphics: Form of graphics in which an image is painted on the screen as a series of dots.

Rated Speed: The official speed of a technology.

RBOC: See Regional Bell Operating Company.

Read: A Microsoft Windows Server permission that allows an account owner to read files in a directory. This is read-only access; without further permissions, the account owner cannot change the files.

Read and Execute: A set of Microsoft Windows Server permissions needed to run executable programs.

Real Time Protocol (RTP): The protocol that adds headers that contain sequence numbers to ensure that the UDP datagrams are placed in proper sequence and that they contain time stamps so that jitter can be eliminated.

Reassembly: Putting a fragmented packet back together.

Redundancy: Duplication of a hardware device in order to enhance reliability.

Regenerate: In a switch or router, to clean up a signal before sending it back out.

Regional Bell Operating Company (RBOC): One of the companies that was created to provide local service when the Bell System (AT&T) was broken up in the early 1980s.

Relay Server: A server used in some IM systems, which every message flows through. Relay servers permit the addition of special services, such as scanning for viruses when files are transmitted in an IM system.

Reliabile: A protocol in which errors are corrected by resending lost or damaged messages.

Remote Access Server (RAS): A server to which remote users connect in order to have their identities authenticated so they can get access to a site's internal resources.

Remote Monitoring (RMON) Probe: A specialized type of agent that collects data on network traffic passing through its location instead of information about the RMON probe itself.

Repeat Purchasing: In e-commerce, a consumer returning to a site where he or she had made a purchase previously and making another purchase; essential to profitability.

Request for Comment (RFC): A document produced by the IETF that may become designated as an Official Internet Protocol Standard.

Request to Send: A message sent to an access point when a station wishes to send and is able to send because of CSMA/CA. The station may send when it receives a clear-to-send message.

Request to Send/Clear to Send: A system that uses request-to-send and clear-to-send messages to control transmissions and avoid collisions in wireless transmission.

Resegment: Dividing a collision domain into several smaller collision domains to reduce congestion and latency.

Responding: In security, the act of stopping and repairing an attack.

Response Message: In Challenge–Response Authentication Protocols, the message that the applicant returns to the verifier.

Response Time: The difference between the time a user types a request to the time the user receives a response.

Retention: Rules that require IM messages to be captured and stored in order to comply with legal requirements.

RFC: See Request for Comment.

RFC 822: The original name for RFC 2822.

RFC 2822: The standard for e-mail bodies that are plaintext messages.

RFID: See Radio Frequency ID.

Ring Topology: A topology in which stations are connected in a loop and messages pass in only one direction around the loop.

Ring Wrapping: In a network with a dual-ring topology, responding to a break between switches by turning the surviving parts of a dual ring into a long single ring.

Right of Way: Permission to lay wires in public areas; given by government regulators to transmission carriers.

RIP: See Routing Information Protocol.

Risk Analysis: The process of balancing threats and protection costs.

RJ-45 Connector: The connector at the end of a UTP cord, which plugs into an RJ-45 jack.

RJ-45 Jack: The type of jack into which UTP cords' RJ-45 connectors may plug.

RMON Probe: See Remote Monitoring Probe.

Roaming: The situation when a subscriber leaves a metropolitan cellular system and goes to another city or country. Roaming requires the destination cellular system to be technologically compatible with the subscriber's cellphone. It also requires administration permission from the destination cellular system.

Robust Security Network (RSN): A wireless network in which all stations and access points communicate with 802.11i security.

Rogue Access Point: An access point set up by a department or individual and not sanctioned by the firm.

Root: 1) The level at the top of a DNS hierarchy, consisting of all domain names. 2) A super account on a Unix server that automatically has full permissions in every directory on the server.

Root Server: One of 13 top-level servers in the Domain Name System (DNS).

Route: The path that a packet takes across an internet.

Route Analysis: Determining the route a packet takes between your host and another host and analyzing performance along this route.

Router: A device that forwards packets within an internet. Routers connect two or more single networks (subnets).

Routing: 1). The forwarding of IP packets; 2) the exchange of routing protocol information through routing protocols.

Routing Information Protocol (RIP): A simple but limited interior routing protocol.

Routing Protocol: A protocol that allows routers to transmit routing table information to one another.

RSA: Popular public key encryption method.

RST Bit: In a TCP segment, if the RST (reset) bit is set, this tells the other side to end the connection immediately.

RSTP: See Rapid Spanning Tree Protocol.

RTP: See Real Time Protocol.

RTS: See Request to Send.

RTS/CTS: See Request to Send/Clear to Send.

Sample: To read the intensity of a signal.

SC Connector: A square optical fiber connector, recommended in the TIA/EIA-568 standard for use in new installations.

Scalability: The ability of a technology to handle growth.

Scanning: To try to determine a network's design through the use of probe packets.

Schema: The design of a database, telling the specific types of information the database contains.

Scope: A parameter on a DHCP server that determines how many subnets the DHCP server may serve.

Script Kiddie: An attacker who possesses only modest skills but uses attack scripts created by experienced hackers; dangerous because there are so many.

SDH: See Synchronous Digital Hierarchy.

Second-and-a-Half Generation (2.5G): A nickname for GPRS systems, which offer a substantial improvement over plain 2G GSM but which is not a full third-generation service.

Second-Generation (2G): The second generation of cellular telephony, introduced in the early 1990s. Offers the improvements of digital service, 150 MHz of bandwidth, a higher frequency range of operation, and slightly higher data transmission speeds.

Second-Level Domain: The third level of a DNS hierarchy, which usually specifies an organization (e.g., microsoft.com, hawaii.edu).

Secure Hash Algorithm (SHA): A hashing algorithm that can produce hashes of different lengths.

Secure Shell (SSH): A program that provides Telnet-like remote management capabilities; and FTP-like service; strongly encrypts both usernames and passwords.

Secure Sockets Layer (SSL): The simplest VPN security standard to implement; later renamed Transport Layer Security. Provides a secure connection at the transport layer, protecting any applications above it that are SSL/TLS-aware.

Semantics: In message exchange, the meaning of each message.

Sequence Number Field: In TCP, a header field that tells a TCP segment's order among the multiple TCP segments sent by one side.

Serial Transmission: Ethernet transmission over a single pair in each direction.

Server: A host that provides services to residential or corporate users.

Server Farm: Large groups of servers that work together to handle applications.

Server Station: A station that provides service to client stations.

Service Band: A subdivision of the frequency spectrum, dedicated to a specific service such as FM radio or cellular telephone service.

Service Control Point: A database of customer information, used in Signaling System 7.

Service Level Agreement (SLA): A quality-of-service guarantee for throughput, availability, latency, error rate, and other matters.

Service Pack: For Microsoft Windows, large cumulative updates that combine a number of individual updates.

Service Pack 2: In Microsoft Windows XP, a security-focused update.

Session Initiation Protocol (SIP): Relatively simple signaling protocol for voice over IP.

Session Key: Symmetric key that is used only during a single communication session between two parties.

Session Layer: See OSI Session Layer.

Set: 1) When a flags field is given the value 1. 2) An SNMP command sent by the manager that tells the agent to change a parameter on the managed device.

SETI@home: A project from the Search for Extraterrestrial Intelligence (SETI), in which volunteers download SETI@home screen savers that are really programs. These programs do work for the SETI@home server when the volunteer computer is idle. Processing ends when the user begins to do work.

Setup Fee: The cost of initial vendor installation for a system.

Severity Rating: A rating for the severity of a risk.

SFF: See Small Form Factor.

SHA: See Secure Hash Algorithm.

Shadow Zone (Dead Spot): A location where a receiver cannot receive radio transmission, due to an obstruction blocking the direct path between sender and receiver.

Shannon Equation: An equation by Claude Shannon (1938) that shows that the maximum possible transmission speed (C) when sending data through a channel is directly proportional to its bandwidth (B), and depends to a lesser extent on its signal-to-noise ratio (S/N): $C = B \log_2 (1 + S/N)$.

Share: Microsoft's name for something that is shared, usually a directory or a printer.

Shared Documents Folder (SharedDocs): In Windows XP, a directory that is automatically shared. To share a file with other users on the computer or on an attached network, the user can copy a file from another directory to the Shared Document Folder.

Shared Static Key: A key that is used by all users in a system (shared) that is not changed (static).

SharedDocs: See Shared Documents Folder.

SHDSL: See Super-High-Rate DSL.

Shielded Twisted Pair (STP): A type of twisted-pair wiring that puts a metal foil sheath around each pair and another metal mesh around all pairs.

Shopping Cart: A core e-commerce function that holds goods for the buyer while he or she is shopping.

Signal: An information-carrying disturbance that propagates through a transmission medium.

Signal Bandwidth: The range of frequencies in a signal, determined by subtracting the lowest frequency from the highest frequency.

Signaling: In telephony, the controlling of calling, including setting up a path for a conversation through the transport core, maintaining and terminating the conversation path, collecting billing information, and handling other supervisory functions.

Signaling Gateway: The device that sets up conversations between parties, maintains these conversations, ends them, provides billing information, and does other work.

Signaling System 7: Telephone signaling system in the United States.

Signal-to-Noise Ratio (SNR): The ratio of the signal strength to average noise strength; should be high in order for the signal to be effectively received.

Signing: Encrypting something with the sender's private key.

Simple File Sharing: In Windows XP, extremely weak security used on files in Shared Documents folders. Simple File Sharing does not even use a password; the only security is that people must know the workgroup names to read and change files.

Simple Mail Transfer Protocol (SMTP): The protocol used to send a message to a user's outgoing mail host and from one mail host to another; requires a complex series of interactions between the sender and receiver before and after mail delivery.

Simple Network Management Protocol (SNMP): The protocol that allows a general way to collect rich data from various managed devices in a network.

Simple Object Access Protocol (SOAP): A standardized way for a Web service to expose its methods on an interface to the outside world.

Single Point of Failure: When the failure in a single component of a system can cause a system to fail or be seriously degraded.

Single Sign-On (SSO): Authentication in which a user can authenticate himself or herself only once and then have access to all authorized resources on all authorized systems.

Single-Mode Fiber: Optical fiber whose core is so thin (usually 8.3 microns in diameter) that only a single mode can propagate—the one traveling straight along the axis.

SIP: See Session Initiation Protocol.

Site Survey: In wireless LANs, a radio survey to help determine where to place access points.

Situation Analysis: The examination of a firm's current situation, which includes anticipation of how things will change in the future.

SLA: See Service Level Agreement.

Sliding Window Protocol: Flow control protocol that tells a receiver how many more bytes it may transmit before receiving another acknowledgement, which will give a longer transmission window.

Slot: A very brief time period used in Time Division Multiplexing; a subdivision of a frame. Carries one sample for one circuit.

Small Form Factor (SFF): A variety of optical fiber connectors; smaller than SC or ST connectors but unfortunately not standardized.

Small Office or Home Office (SOHO): A small-scale network for a small office or home office.

Smart Access Point: An access point that can be managed remotely.

SMTP: See Simple Mail Transfer Protocol.

SNA: See Systems Network Architecture.

Sneakernet: A joking reference to the practice of walking files around physically, instead of using a network for file sharing.

SNMP: See Simple Network Management Protocol.

SNR: See Signal-to-Noise Ratio.

SOAP: See Simple Object Access Protocol.

Social Engineering: Tricking people into doing something to get around security protections.

Socket: The combination of an IP address and a port number, designating a specific connection to a specific application on a specific host. It is written as an IP address, a colon, and a port number, for instance 128.171.17.13:80.

SOHO: See Small Office or Home Office.

Solid-Wire UTP: Type of UTP in which each of the eight wires really is a single solid wire.

SONET: See Synchronous Optical Network.

Spam: Unsolicited commercial e-mail.

Spam Blocking: Software that recognizes and deletes spam.

Spanning Tree Protocol (STP): See 802.1D Spanning Tree Protocol.

Speech Codec: See codec.

Spread Spectrum Transmission: A type of radio transmission that takes the original signal and spreads the signal energy over a much broader channel than would be used in normal radio transmission; used in order to reduce propagation problems, not for security.

Spyware: Software that sits on a victim's machine and gathers information about the victim.

SS7: See Signaling System 7.

SSH: See Secure Shell.

SSL: See Secure Sockets Layer.

SSL/TLS: See Secure Sockets Layer and Transport Layer Security.

SSL/TLS-Aware: Modified to work with SSL/TLS.

SSO: See Single Sign-On.

ST Connector: A cylindrical optical fiber connector, sometimes called a bayonet connector because of the manner in which it pushes into an ST port and then twists to be locked in place.

Standard: A rule of operation that allows two hardware or software processes to work together. Standards normally govern the exchange of messages between two entities.

Standards Agency: An organization that creates and maintains standards.

Standards Architecture: A family of related standards that collectively allows an application program on one machine on an internet to communicate with another application program on another machine on the internet.

Star Topology: A form of topology in which all wires in a network connect to a single switch.

Start of Frame Delimiter Field: The second field of an Ethernet MAC frame, which synchronizes the receiver's clock to the sender's clock and then signals that the synchronization has ended.

State: In digital physical layer signaling, one of the few line conditions that represent information.

Stateful Firewall: A firewall whose default behavior is to allow all connections initiated by internal hosts but to block all connections initiated by external hosts. Only passes packets that are part of approved connections.

Station: A computer that communicates over a network.

STM: See Synchronous Transfer Mode.

Store-and-Forward: Switching wherein the Ethernet switch waits until it has received the entire frame before sending the frame back out.

Static IP Address: An IP address that never changes.

STP: See 802.1D Spanning Tree Protocol or Shielded Twisted Pair.

Strain Relief: Crimping the back of an RJ-45 connector into an RJ-45 cord so that if the cord is pulled, it will not come out of the connector.

Strand: In optical fiber, a core surrounded by a cladding. For two-way transmission, two optical fiber strands are needed.

Stranded-Wire UTP: Type of UTP in which in which each of the eight "wires" really is a collection of wire strands.

Stripping Tool: Tool for stripping the sheath off the end of a UTP cord.

Strong Keys: Keys that are too long to be cracked by exhaustive key search.

Subcarrier: A channel that is itself a subdivision of a broadband channel, used to transmit frames in OFDM.

Subnet: A small network that is a subdivision of a large organization's network.

Subnet Mask: A mask with 1s in the network and subnet parts and zeros in the host part.

Subnet Part: The part of an IP address that specifies a particular subnet within a network.

Super Client: "Serverish" client in Gnutella that is always on, that has a fixed IP address, that has many files to share, and that is connected to several other super clients.

Super-High-Rate DSL (SHDSL): The next step in business DSL, which can operate symmetrically over a single voice-grade twisted pair and over a speed range of 384 kbps to 2.3 Mbps. It can also operate over somewhat longer distances than HDSL2.

Surreptitiously: Done without someone's knowledge, such as surreptitious face recognition scanning.

SVC: See Switched Virtual Circuit.

Switch: A device that forwards frames within a single network.

Switched Virtual Circuit (SVC): A circuit between sites that is set up just before a call and that lasts only for the duration of the call.

Switching Matrix: A switch component that connects input ports to output ports.

Symmetric Key Encryption: Family of encryption methods in which the two sides use the same key to encrypt messages to each other and to decrypt incoming messages. In bidirectional communication, only a single key is used.

SYN Bit: In TCP, the flags field that is set to indicate if the message is a synchronization message.

Synchronous Digital Hierarchy (SDH): The European version of the technology upon which the world is nearly standardized.

Synchronous Optical Network (SONET): The North American version of the technology upon which the world is nearly standardized.

Synchronous Transfer Mode (STM): A number that indicates SDH speeds.

Syntax: In message exchange, how messages are organized.

Systems Administration: The management of a server.

Systems Network Architecture (SNA): The standards architecture traditionally used by IBM mainframe computers.

T568B: Wire color scheme for RJ-45 connectors; used most commonly in the United States.

Tag: An indicator on an HTML file to show where the browser should render graphics files, when it should play audio files, and so forth.

Tag Control Information: The second tag field, which contains a 12-bit VLAN ID that it sets to zero if VLANs are not being implemented. If VLANs are being used, each VLAN will be assigned a different VLAN ID.

Tag Field: One of the two fields added to an Ethernet MAC layer frame by the 802.1Q standard.

Tag Protocol ID: The first tag field used in the Ethernet MAC layer frame. The Tag Protocol ID has the two-octet hexadecimal value 81-00, which indicates that the frame is tagged.

Tbps: Terabits per second.

TCO: See Total Cost of Ownership.

TCP: See Transmission Control Protocol.

TCP Segment: A TCP message.

TCP/IP: The Internet Engineering Tasks Force's standards architecture; dominant above the data link layer.

TCPDUMP: The most popular freeware packet analysis program; the Unix version.

TDM: See Time Division Multiplexing.

TDR: See Time Domain Reflectometry.

Telecommunications Closet: The location on each floor of a building where cords coming up from the basement are connected to cords that span out horizontally to telephones and computers on that floor.

Telephone Modem: A device used in telephony that converts digital data into an analog signal that can transfer over the local loop.

Telnet: The simplest remote configuration tool; lacks encryption for confidentiality.

Temporal Dispersion: Another name for modal dispersion.

Temporal Key Integrity Protocol (TKIP): A security process used by 802.11i, where each station has its own nonshared key after authentication and where this key is changed frequently.

Terabits per second: Trillions of bits per second.

Terminal Crosstalk Interference: Crosstalk interference at the ends of a UTP cord, where wires are untwisted to fit into the connector. To control terminal crosstalk interference, wires should not be untwisted more than a half inch to fit into connectors.

Termination Equipment: Equipment that connects a site's internal telephone system to the local exchange carrier.

Terrestrial: Earth-based.

Test Signals: Signal sent by a high-quality UTP tester through a UTP cord to check signal quality parameters.

Texting: In cellular telephony, the transmission of text messages.

TFTP: See Trivial File Transfer Protocol.

Third-Generation (3G): The newest generation of cellular telephony, able to carry data at much higher speeds than 2G systems.

Threat Enviornment: The threats that face the company.

Three-Party Call: A call in which three people can take part in a conversation.

Three-Tier Architecture: An architecture where processing is done in three places: on the client, on the application server, and on other servers.

Three-Way Handshake: A three-message exchange that opens a connection in TCP.

Throughput: The transmission speed that users actually get. Usually lower than a transmission system's rated speed.

TIA/EIA/ANSI-568: The standard that governs transmission media in the United States.

Time Division Multiplexing (TDM): A technology used by telephone carriers to provide reserved capacity on trunk lines between switches. In TDM, time is first divided into frames, each of which are divided into slots; a circuit is given the same slot in every frame.

Time Domain Reflectometry (TDR): Sending a signal in a UTP cord and recording reflections; can give the length of the cord or the location of a propagation problem in the cord.

Time to Live (TTL): The field added to a packet and given a value by a source host, usually between 64 and 128. Each router along the way decrements the TTL field by one. A router decrementing the TTL to zero will discard the packet; this prevents misaddressed packets from circulated endlessly among packet switches in search of their nonexistent destinations.

TKIP: See Tempora' Key Integrity Protocol.

TLS: See Transport Layer Security.

Token Passing: In token-ring networks, a token frame is transmitted and used to determine when a station may transmit.

Token-Ring Network: A network that uses a physical ring topology and token passing at the media access control layer.

Toll Call: Long-distance call pricing in which the price depends on distance and duration.

Toll-Free Number Service: Service in which anyone can call into a company, usually without being charged. Area codes are 800, 888, 877, 866, and 855.

Top-Level Domain: The second level of a DNS hierarchy, which categorizes the domain by organization type (e.g., .com, .net, .edu, .biz, .info) or by country (e.g., .uk, .ca, .ie, .au, .jp, .ch).

Topology: The way in which nodes are linked together by transmission lines.

TOS: See Type of Service.

Total Cost of Ownership (TCO): The total cost of an entire system over its expected lifespan.

Total Purchase Cost of Network Products: The initial purchase price of a fully configured system.

Tracert (tracert): A Windows program that shows latencies to every router along a route and to the destination host.

Traffic Engineering: Designing and managing traffic on a network.

Traffic Shaping: Limiting access to a network based on type of traffic.

Trailer: The part of a message that comes after the data field.

Transmission Line: A physical line that is used to carry transmitted information.

Transmission Speed: The rate at which information is transmitted in bits per second.

Transaction Processing: Processing involving simple, highly structured, and high-volume interactions.

Transceiver: A transmitter/receiver.

Transfer Syntax: In the OSI Presentation layer, the syntax used by two presentation layer processes to communicate, which may or may not be quite different than either of their internal methods of formatting information.

Transmission Control Protocol (TCP): The most common TCP/IP protocol at the transport layer. Connection-oriented and reliable.

Transparently: Without having a need to implement modifications.

Transport: In telephony, transmission; taking voice signals from one subscriber's access line and delivering them to another customer's access line.

Transport Core: The switches and transmission lines that carry voice signals from one subscriber's access line and delivering them to another customer's access line.

Transport Layer Security (TLS): The simplest VPN security standard to implement; originally named Secure Sockets Layer. Provides a secure connection at the transport layer, protecting any applications above it that are SSL/TLS-aware.

Transport Layer: The layer that governs communication between two hosts; Layer 4 in both OSI and TCP/IP.

Transport Mode: One of IPsec's two modes of operation, in which the two computers that are communicating implement IPsec. Transport mode gives strong end-to-end security between the computers, but it requires IPsec configuration and a digital certificate on all machines.

Traps: The type of message that an agent sends if it detects a condition that it thinks the manager should know about.

Triple DES (3DES): Symmetric key encryption method in which a message is encrypted three times with DES. If done with two or three different keys, offers strong security. However, it is processing intensive.

Trivial File Transfer Protocol (TFTP): A protocol used on switches and routers to download configuration information; has no security.

Trojan Horse: A program that looks like an ordinary system file, but continues to exploit the user indefinitely.

Trunk Line: A type of transmission line that links switches to each other, routers to each other, or a router to a switch.

Trunking: See Link Aggregation.

TTL: See Time to Live.

Tunnel Mode: One of IPsec's two modes of operation, in which the IPsec connection extends only between IPsec gateways at the two sites. Tunnel mode provides no protection within sites, but it offers transparent security.

Twisted-Pair Wiring: Wiring in which each pair's wires are twisted around each other several times per inch, reducing EMI.

Type of Service (TOS): IPv4 header field that designates the type of service a certain packet should receive.

U: The standard unit for measuring the height of switches. One U is 1.75 inches (4.4 cm) in height. Most switches, although not all, are multiples of U.

UDDI: See Universal Description, Discovery, and Integration.

UDDI Green Pages: The UDDI search option that allows companies to understand how to interact with specific Web services. Green pages specify the interfaces on which a Web service will respond, the methods it will accept, and the properties that can be changed or returned.

UDDI White Pages: The UDDI search option that allows users to search for Web services by name, much like telephone white pages.

UDDI Yellow Pages: The UDDI search option that allows users to search for Web services by function, such as accounting, much like telephone yellow pages.

UDP: See User Datagram Protocol.

Ultrawideband (UWB): Spread spectrum transmission system that has extremely wide channels.

UNICODE: The standard that allows characters of all languages to be represented.

Universal Description, Discovery, and Integration (UDDI): A protocol that is a distributed database that helps users find appropriate Web services.

Unix: A network operating system used by all workstation servers. Linux is a Unix version used on PCs.

Unlicensed Radio Band: A radio band that does not require each station using it to have a license.

Unreliable: (Of a protocol) not doing error correction.

Unshielded Twisted Pair (UTP): Network cord that contains four twisted pairs of wire within a sheath. Each wire is covered with insulation.

Update: To download and apply patches to fix a system.

Uplink: In satellites, transmission from the Earth to a communication satellite.

Uplink Port: Port on an Ethernet switch that can be directly connected to a port in a higher-level switch with a standard UTP cord.

Usage Policy: A company policy for who may use various tools and how they may use them.

User Datagram Protocol (UDP): Unreliable transport-layer protocol in TCP/IP.

Username: An alias that signifies the account that the account holder will be using.

UTP: See Unshielded Twisted Pair.

UWB: See Ultrawideband.

Validate: To test the accuracy of a network simulation model by comparing its performance with that of the real network. If the predicted results match the actual results, the model is validated.

Variable-Length Subnet Mask (VLSM): A mask that allows subnets to be of different sizes.

Very Small Aperture Terminal (VSAT): Communication satellite earthstation that has a small-diameter antenna.

VCI: See Virtual Channel Identifier.

Verifier: The party requiring the applicant to prove his or her identity.

Vertical Riser: Space between the floors of a building that telephone and data cabling go through to get to the building's upper floor.

Viral Networking: Networking in which the user's PC connects to one or a few other user PCs, which each connect to several other user PCs. When the user's PC first connects, it sends an initiation message to introduce itself via viral networking. Subsequent search queries sent by the user also are passed virally to all computers reachable within a few hops; used in Gnutella.

Virtual Channel: In ATM, an individual connection within a virtual path.

Virtual Channel Identifier (VCI): One of the two parts of ATM virtual circuit numbers.

Virtual Circuit: A transmission path between two sites or devices; selected before transmission begins.

Virtual LAN (VLAN): A closed collection of servers and the clients they serve. Broadcast signals go only to computers in the same VLAN.

Virtual Path Identifier (VPI): One of the two parts of ATM virtual circuit numbers.

Virtual Path: In ATM, a group of connections going between two sites.

Virtual Private Network (VPN): A network that uses the Internet with added security for data transmission.

Virus: A piece of executable code that attaches itself to programs or data files. When the program is executed or the data file opened, the virus spreads to other programs or data files.

Virus Definitions Database: A database used by antivirus programs to identify viruses. As new viruses are found, the virus definitions database must be updated.

Virus Writer: Someone who creates viruses.

VLAN: See Virtual LAN.

VLSM: See Variable-Length Subnet Mask.

Voice Mail: A service that allows people to leave a message if the user does not answer his or her phone.

Voice-Grade: Wire of a quality useful for transmitting voice signals in the PSTN.

Voice over IP (VoIP): The transmission of voice signals over an IP network.

VoIP: See Voice over IP.

VPI: See Virtual Path Identifier.

VPN: See Virtual Private Network.

VSAT: See Very Small Aperture Terminal.

Vulnerability: A security weakness found in software.

Vulnerability Testing: Testing after protections have been configured, in which a company or a consultant attacks protections in the way a determined attacker would and notes which attacks that should have been stopped actually succeeded.

WAN: See Wide Area Network.

War Driver: Someone who travels around looking for unprotected wireless access points.

WATS: See Wide Area Telephone Service.

Wavelength: The physical distance between comparable points (e.g., from peak to peak) in successive cycles of a wave.

Wavelength Division Multiplexing: Using signaling equipment to transmit several light sources at slightly different wavelengths, thus adding signal capacity at the cost of using slightly more expensive signaling equipment but without incurring the high cost of laying new fiber.

WDM: See Wavelength Division Multiplexing.

Weak Keys: Keys that are shot enough to be cracked by an exhaustive key search.

Webify: In SSL/TLS VPNs, the SSL/TLS gateway can translate output from some applications into a webpage.

Web Service: A way to send processing requests to program (object) on another machine. The object has an interface to the outside world and methods that it is willing to undertake. Messages are sent in SOAP format.

Web-Enabled: Client/server processing applications that use ordinary browsers as client programs.

Webmail: Web-enabled e-mail. User needs only a browser to send and read e-mail.

Well-Known Port Number: Standard port number of a major application that is usually (but not always) used. For example, the well-known TCP port number for HTTP is 80.

WEP: See Wired Equivalent Privacy.

Wide Area Network (WAN): A network that links different sites together.

Wide Area Telephone Service (WATS): Service that allows a company to place outgoing long-distance calls at per-minute prices lower than those of directly dialed calls.

Wi-Fi Alliance: Trade group created to create interoperability tests of 802.11 LANs; actually produced the WPA standard.

WiMAX: Broadband wireless access method. Standardized as 802.16.

Window Size Field: TCP header field that is used for flow control. It tells the station that receives the segment how many more octets that station may transmit before getting another acknowledgement message that will allow it to send more octets.

Windows XP: client Microsoft operating system.

Windows Internet Name Service (WINS): The system required by Windows clients and servers before Windows 2000 server to provide IP address for host names.

WinDUMP: The most popular freeware packet analysis program; the Windows version.

Winipcfg (winipcfg): A command used to find information about one's own computer; used in older versions of windows.

WINS: See Windows Internet Name Service.

Wired Equivalent Privacy (WEP): A weak security mechanism for 802.11.

Wireless Ethernet: Sometimes used as another name for 802.11.

Wireless Access Point: Devices that controls wireless clients and that bridges wireless clients to servers and routers on the firm's main wired LAN.

Wireless LAN (WLAN): A local area network that uses radio (or rarely, infrared) transmission instead of cabling to connect devices.

Wireless LAN Switch: An Ethernet switch to which multiple wireless access points connect; manages the access points.

Wireless Networking: Networking that uses radio transmission instead of wires to connect devices.

Wireless NIC: 802.11 network interface card.

Wireless Protected Access (WPA): 802.11 security method created as a stopgap between WEP and 802.11i.

Wireless Protected Access 2 (WPA2): Another name for 802.11 security.

WLAN: See Wireless LAN.

Work-Around: A process of making manual changes to eliminate a vulnerability instead of just installing a software patch.

Workgroup: A logical network. On a physical network, only PCs in the same workgroup can communicate.

Workgroup Name: To create a workgroup, all PCs in the workgroup are assigned the same workgroup name. They will find each other automatically.

Workgroup Switch: A switch to which stations connect directly.

Working Group: A specific subgroup of the 802 Committee, in charge of developing a specific group of standards. For instance, the 802.3 Working Group creates Ethernet standards.

Workstation Server: The most popular type of large dedicated server; runs the Unix operating system. It uses custom-designed microprocessors and runs the Unix operating system.

Worm: An attack program that propagates on its own by seeking out other computers, jumping to them, and installing itself.

WPA: See Wireless Protected Access.

WPA2: See Wireless Protected Access 2.

Write: A Microsoft Windows Server permission that allows an account owner to change the contents of files in the directory.

X.509: The main standard for digital certificates.

Zero-Day Exploit: An exploit that takes advantage of vulnerabilities that have not previously been discovered or for which updates have not been created.

ZigBee: Low-speed, low-power protocol for connecting sensors and other very small devices wirelessly.

Index